Tell us what you think about SHONEN JUMP manga!

Our survey is now available online.
Go to: www.*SHONENJUMP*.com/mangasurvey

Help us make our product offering better!

THE REAL ACTION
STARTS IN...

www.shonenjump.com

ADVANCED

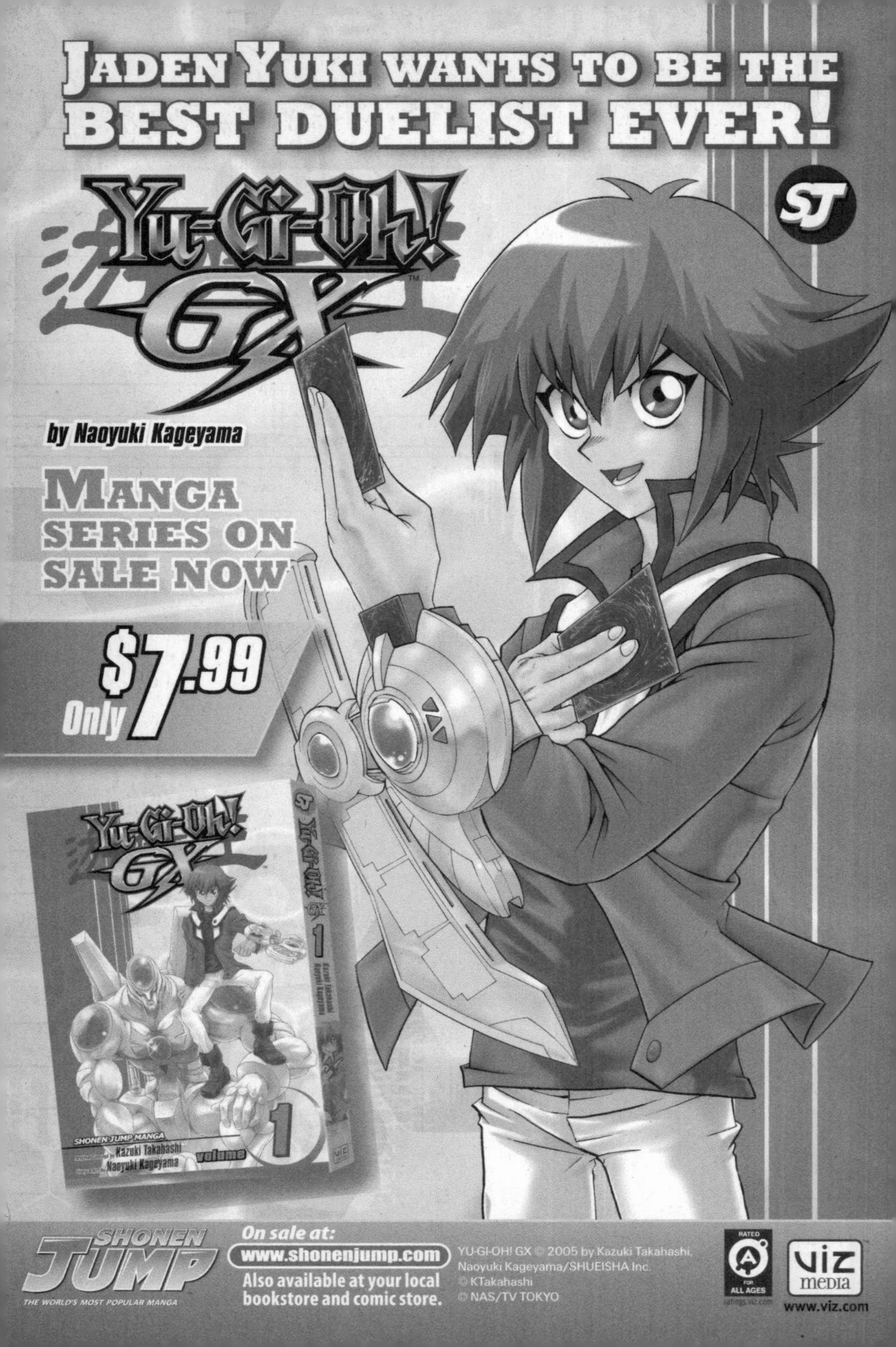

JADEN YUKI WANTS TO BE THE BEST DUELIST EVER!
SJ
YU-GI-OH! GX™
by Naoyuki Kageyama
MANGA SERIES ON SALE NOW
Only $7.99
YU-GI-OH! GX
1
SHONEN JUMP MANGA
Kazuki Takahashi
Naoyuki Kageyama
volume 1
SHONEN JUMP
THE WORLD'S MOST POPULAR MANGA
On sale at:
www.shonenjump.com
Also available at your local bookstore and comic store.
YU-GI-OH! GX © 2005 by Kazuki Takahashi, Naoyuki Kageyama/SHUEISHA Inc. © KTakahashi © NAS/TV TOKYO
RATED A FOR ALL AGES
ratings.viz.com
VIZ media
www.viz.com

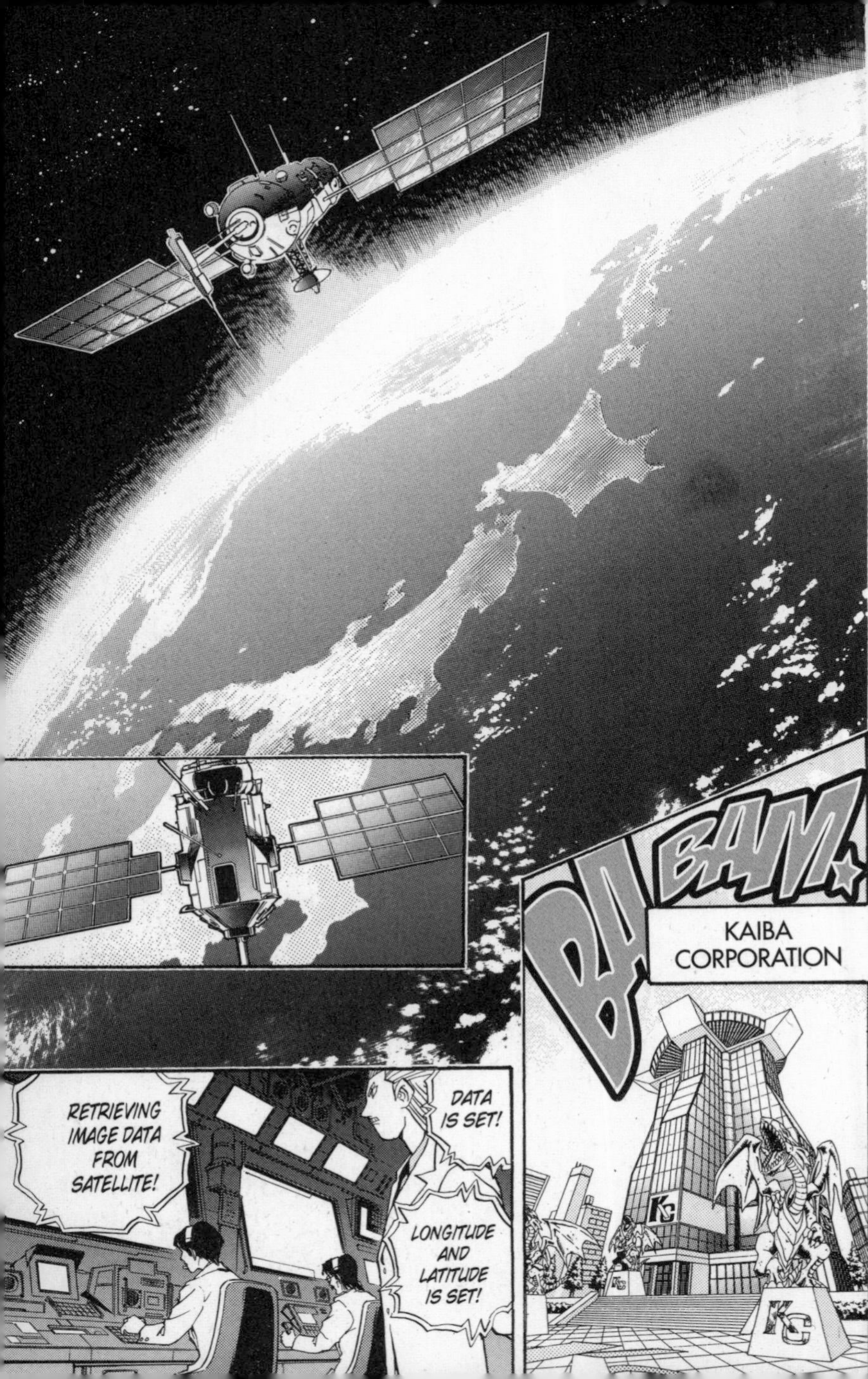
BA BAM
KAIBA CORPORATION
DATA IS SET!
RETRIEVING IMAGE DATA FROM SATELLITE!
LONGITUDE AND LATITUDE IS SET!

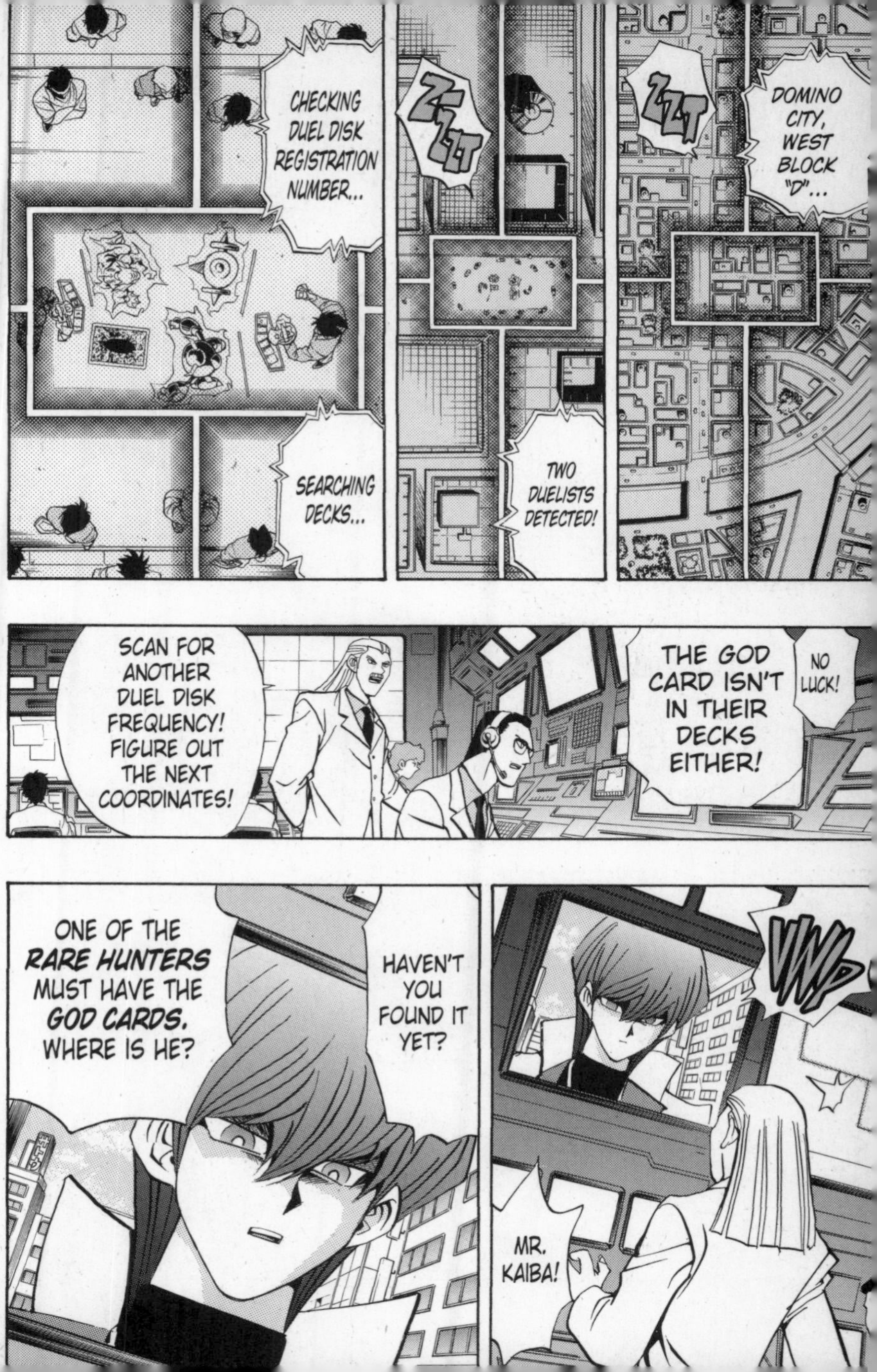
ZZZT
DOMINO CITY, WEST BLOCK "D"...
ZZZT
TWO DUELISTS DETECTED!
CHECKING DUEL DISK REGISTRATION NUMBER...
SEARCHING DECKS...
NO LUCK!
THE GOD CARD ISN'T IN THEIR DECKS EITHER!
SCAN FOR ANOTHER DUEL DISK FREQUENCY! FIGURE OUT THE NEXT COORDINATES!
MR. KAIBA!
HAVEN'T YOU FOUND IT YET?
ONE OF THE *RARE HUNTERS* MUST HAVE THE *GOD CARDS.* WHERE IS HE?

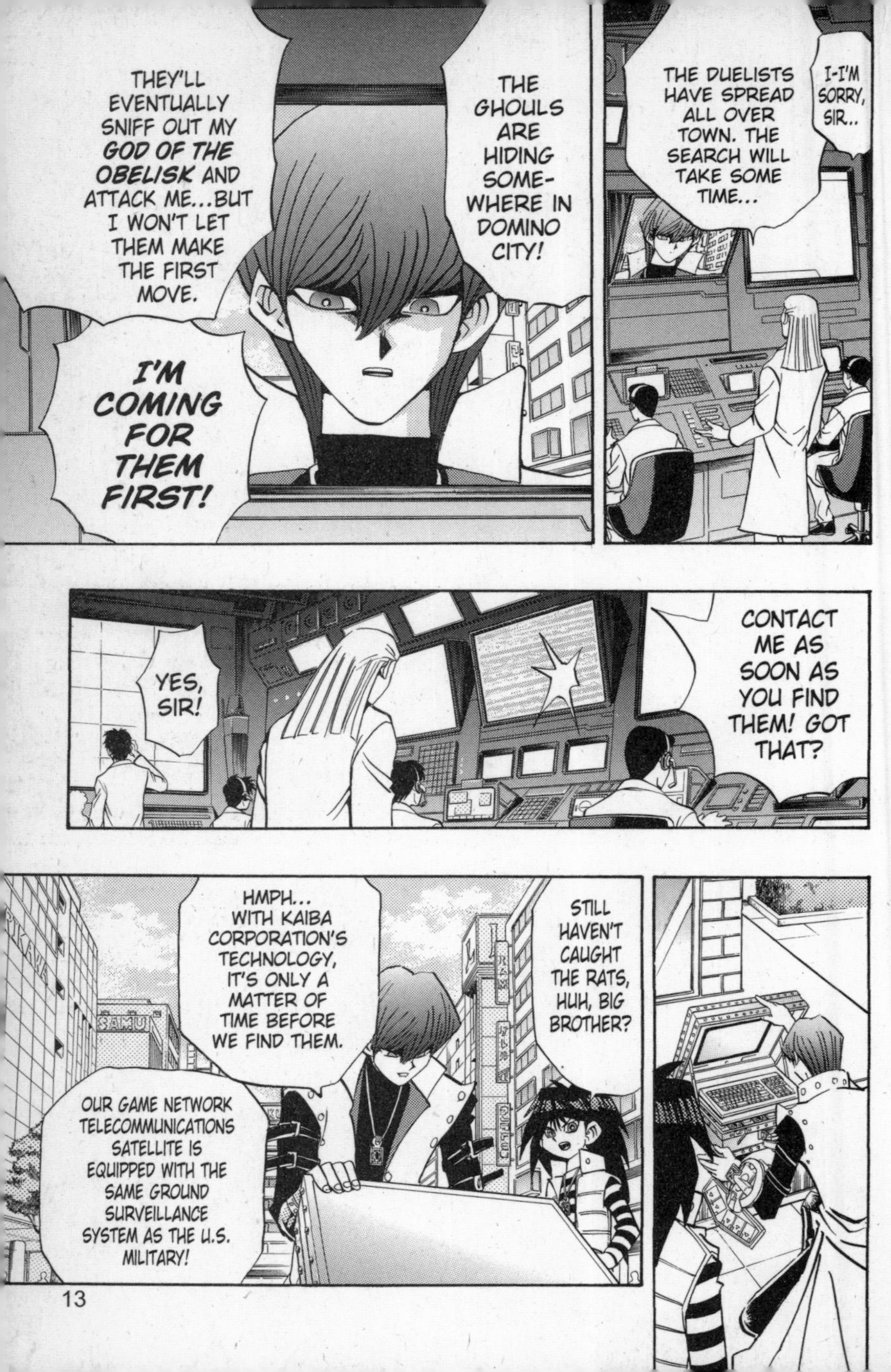
I-I'M SORRY, SIR...
THE DUELISTS HAVE SPREAD ALL OVER TOWN. THE SEARCH WILL TAKE SOME TIME...
THE GHOULS ARE HIDING SOME-WHERE IN DOMINO CITY!
THEY'LL EVENTUALLY SNIFF OUT MY *GOD OF THE OBELISK* AND ATTACK ME...BUT I WON'T LET THEM MAKE THE FIRST MOVE.
I'M COMING FOR THEM FIRST!
CONTACT ME AS SOON AS YOU FIND THEM! GOT THAT?
YES, SIR!
STILL HAVEN'T CAUGHT THE RATS, HUH, BIG BROTHER?
HMPH... WITH KAIBA CORPORATION'S TECHNOLOGY, IT'S ONLY A MATTER OF TIME BEFORE WE FIND THEM.
OUR GAME NETWORK TELECOMMUNICATIONS SATELLITE IS EQUIPPED WITH THE SAME GROUND SURVEILLANCE SYSTEM AS THE U.S. MILITARY!

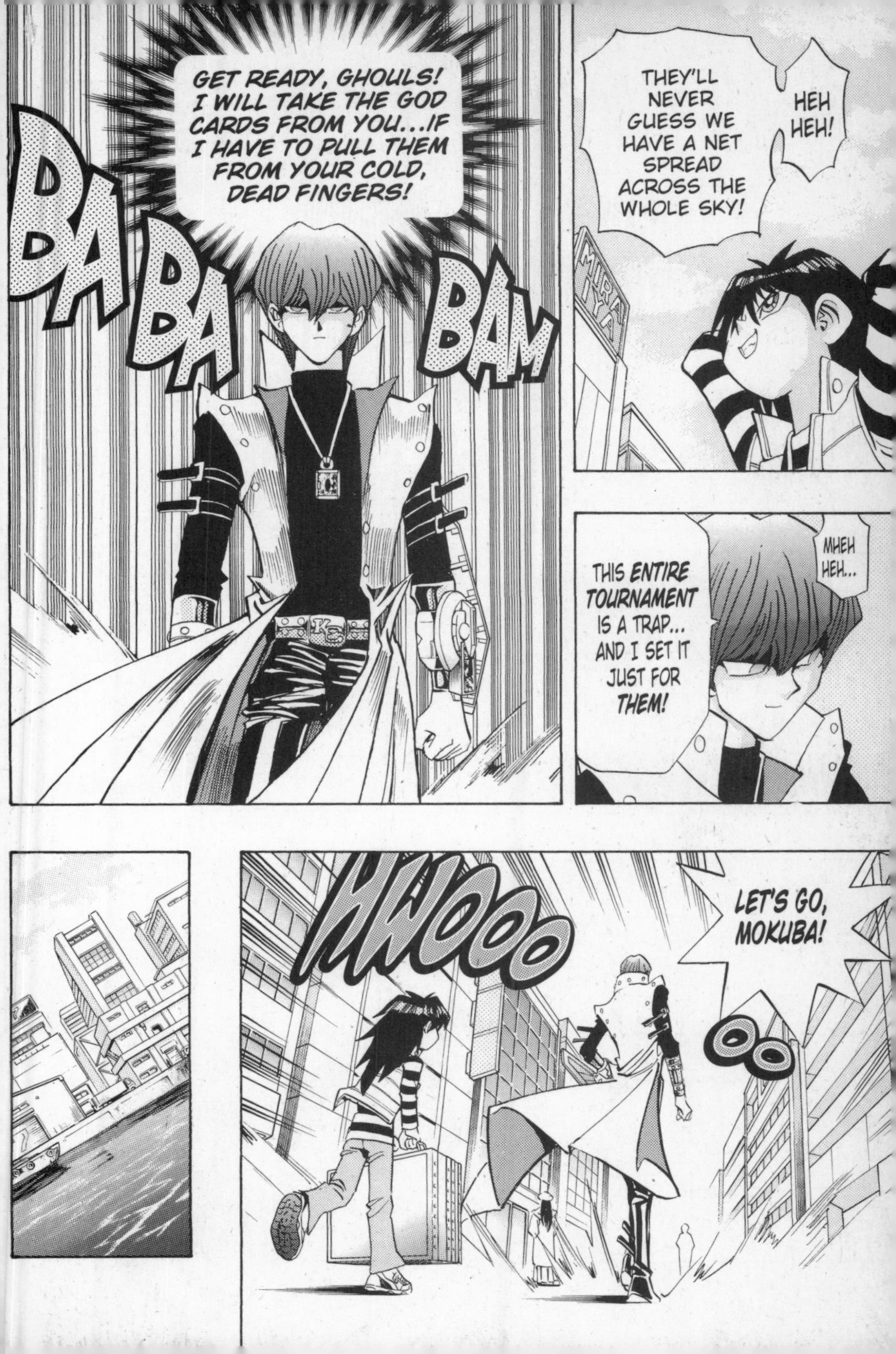
THEY'LL NEVER GUESS WE HAVE A NET SPREAD ACROSS THE WHOLE SKY!
HEH HEH!
MHEH HEH...
THIS ENTIRE TOURNAMENT IS A TRAP... AND I SET IT JUST FOR THEM!
GET READY, GHOULS! I WILL TAKE THE GOD CARDS FROM YOU...IF I HAVE TO PULL THEM FROM YOUR COLD, DEAD FINGERS!
BA BA BA BAM
HWOOOO
LET'S GO, MOKUBA!
OO

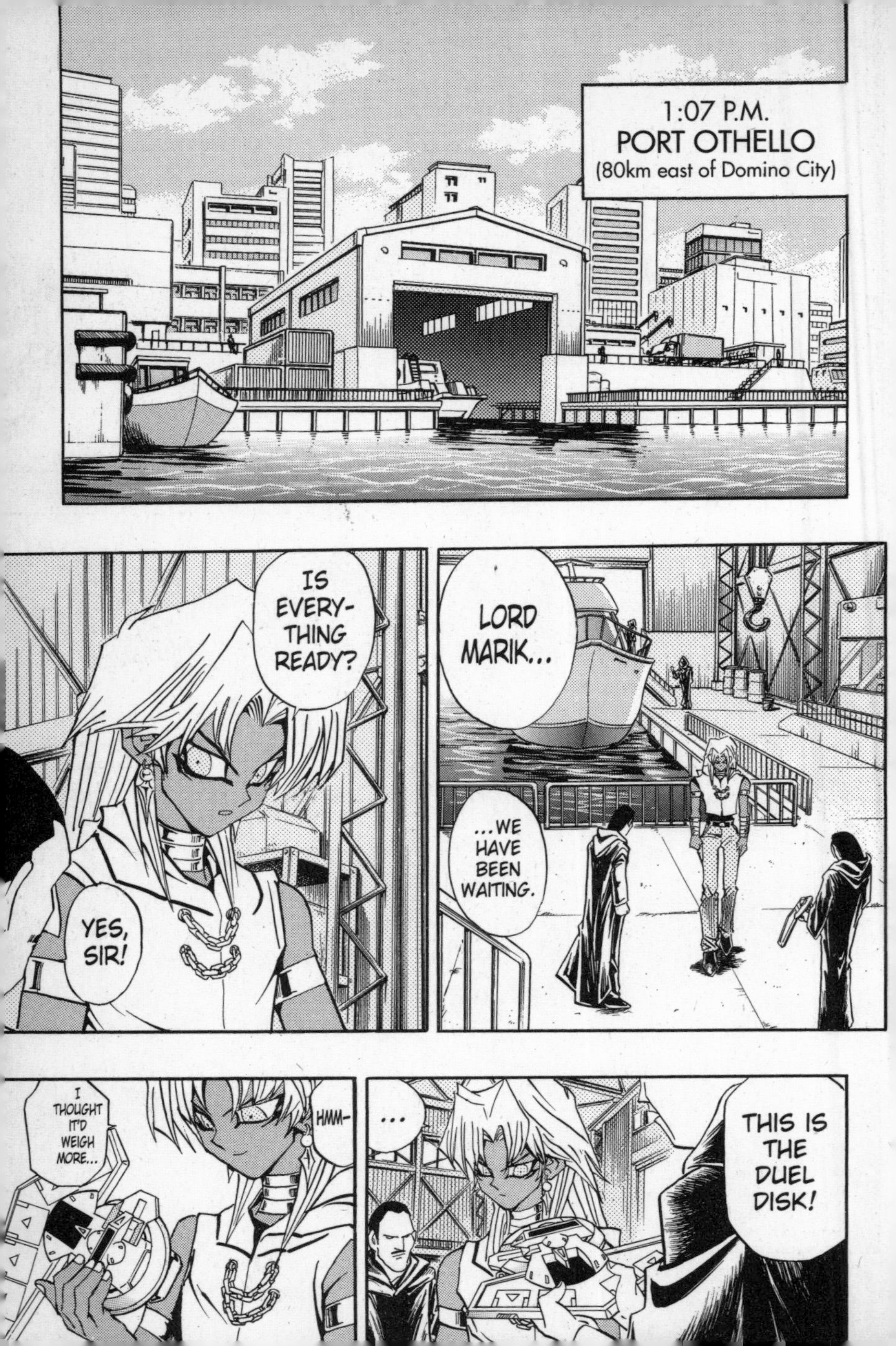
1:07 P.M.
PORT OTHELLO
(80km east of Domino City)
LORD MARIK...
...WE HAVE BEEN WAITING.
IS EVERY-THING READY?
YES, SIR!
THIS IS THE DUEL DISK!
...
HMM-
I THOUGHT IT'D WEIGH MORE...

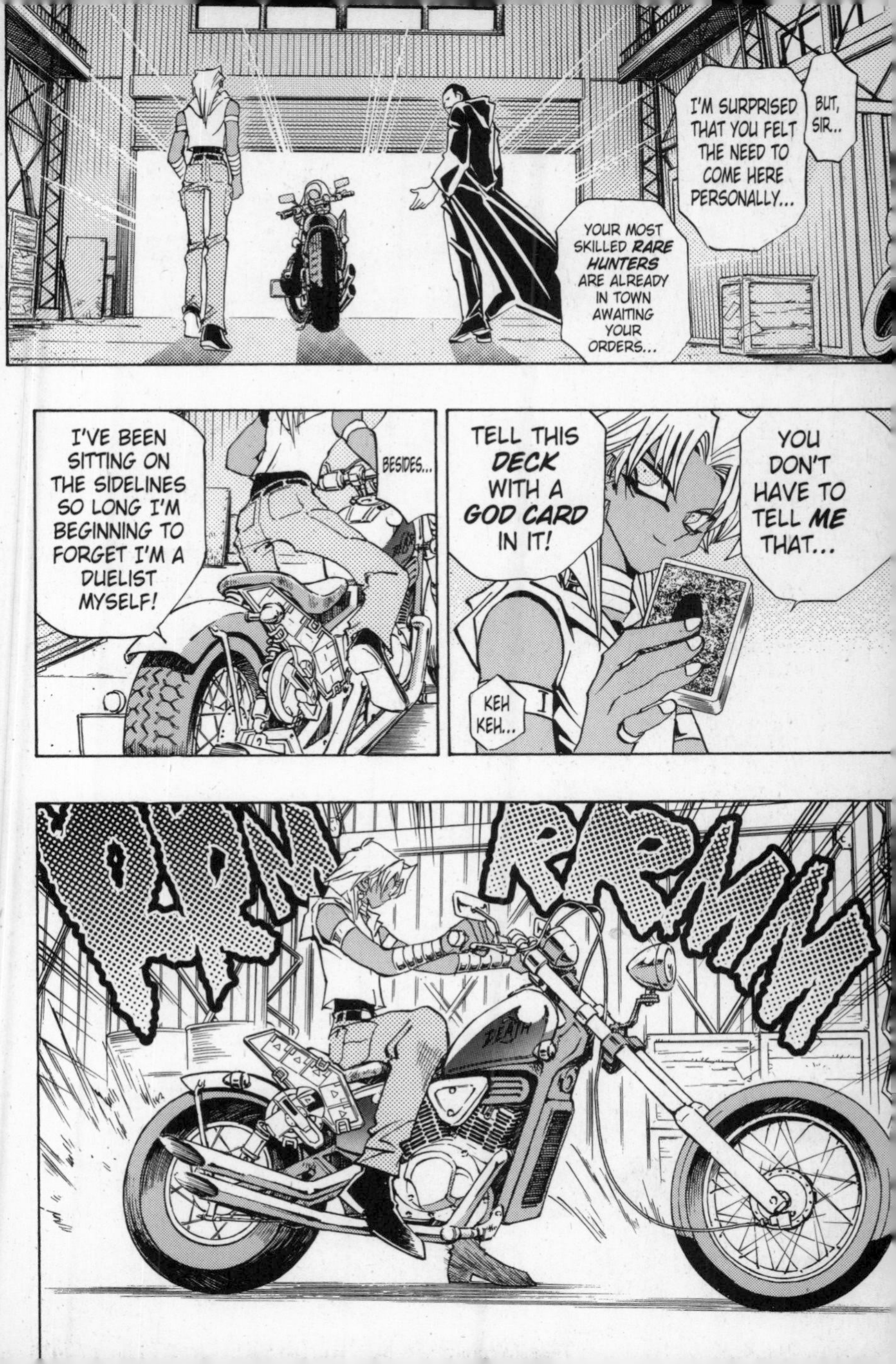
BUT, SIR...
I'M SURPRISED THAT YOU FELT THE NEED TO COME HERE PERSONALLY...
YOUR MOST SKILLED RARE HUNTERS ARE ALREADY IN TOWN AWAITING YOUR ORDERS...
YOU DON'T HAVE TO TELL ME THAT...
TELL THIS DECK WITH A GOD CARD IN IT!
KEH KEH...
BESIDES...
I'VE BEEN SITTING ON THE SIDELINES SO LONG I'M BEGINNING TO FORGET I'M A DUELIST MYSELF!

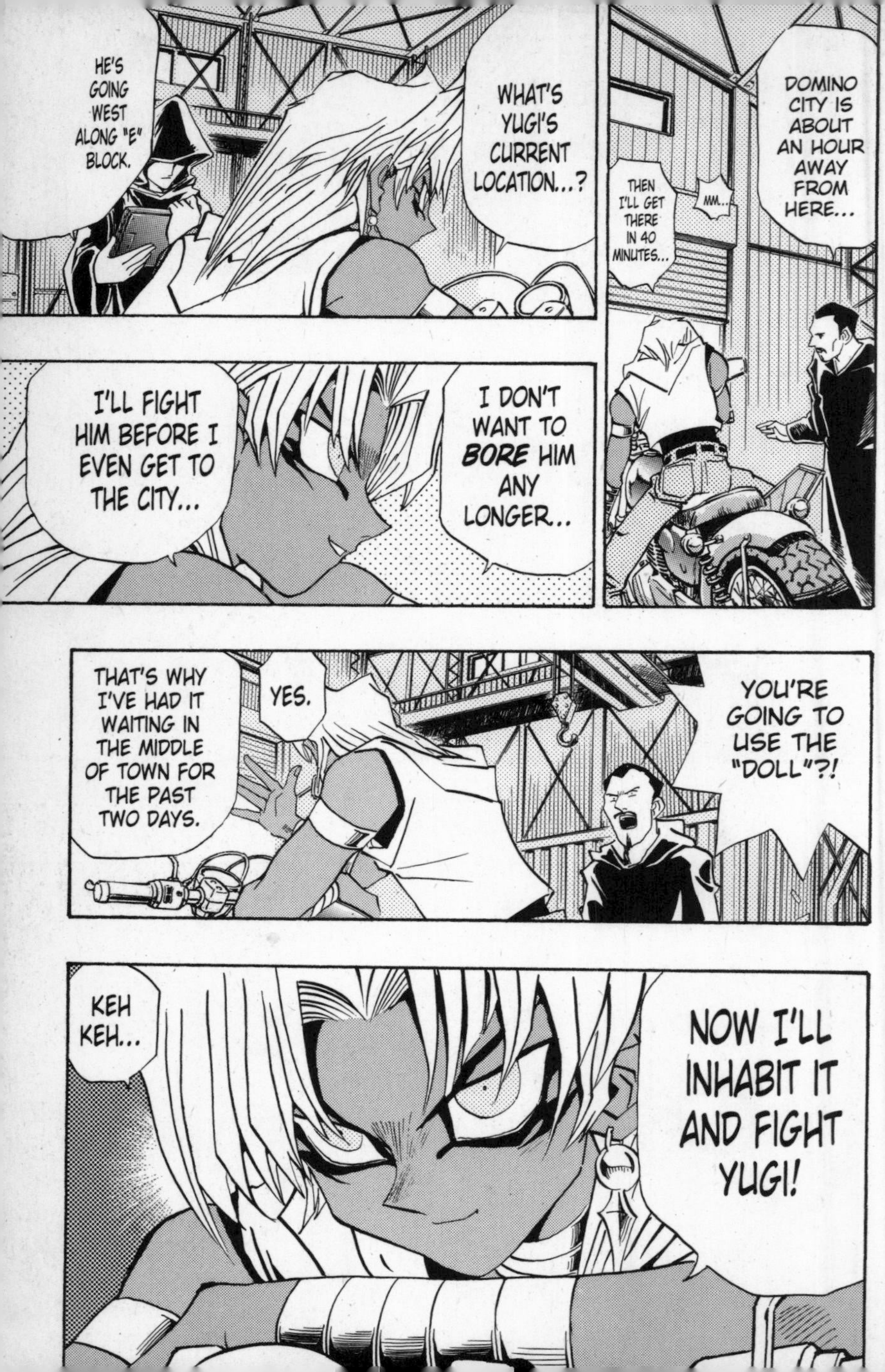
WHAT'S YUGI'S CURRENT LOCATION...?
HE'S GOING WEST ALONG "E" BLOCK.
DOMINO CITY IS ABOUT AN HOUR AWAY FROM HERE...
MM...
THEN I'LL GET THERE IN 40 MINUTES...
I DON'T WANT TO BORE HIM ANY LONGER...
I'LL FIGHT HIM BEFORE I EVEN GET TO THE CITY...
YOU'RE GOING TO USE THE "DOLL"?!
YES.
THAT'S WHY I'VE HAD IT WAITING IN THE MIDDLE OF TOWN FOR THE PAST TWO DAYS.
KEH KEH...
NOW I'LL INHABIT IT AND FIGHT YUGI!

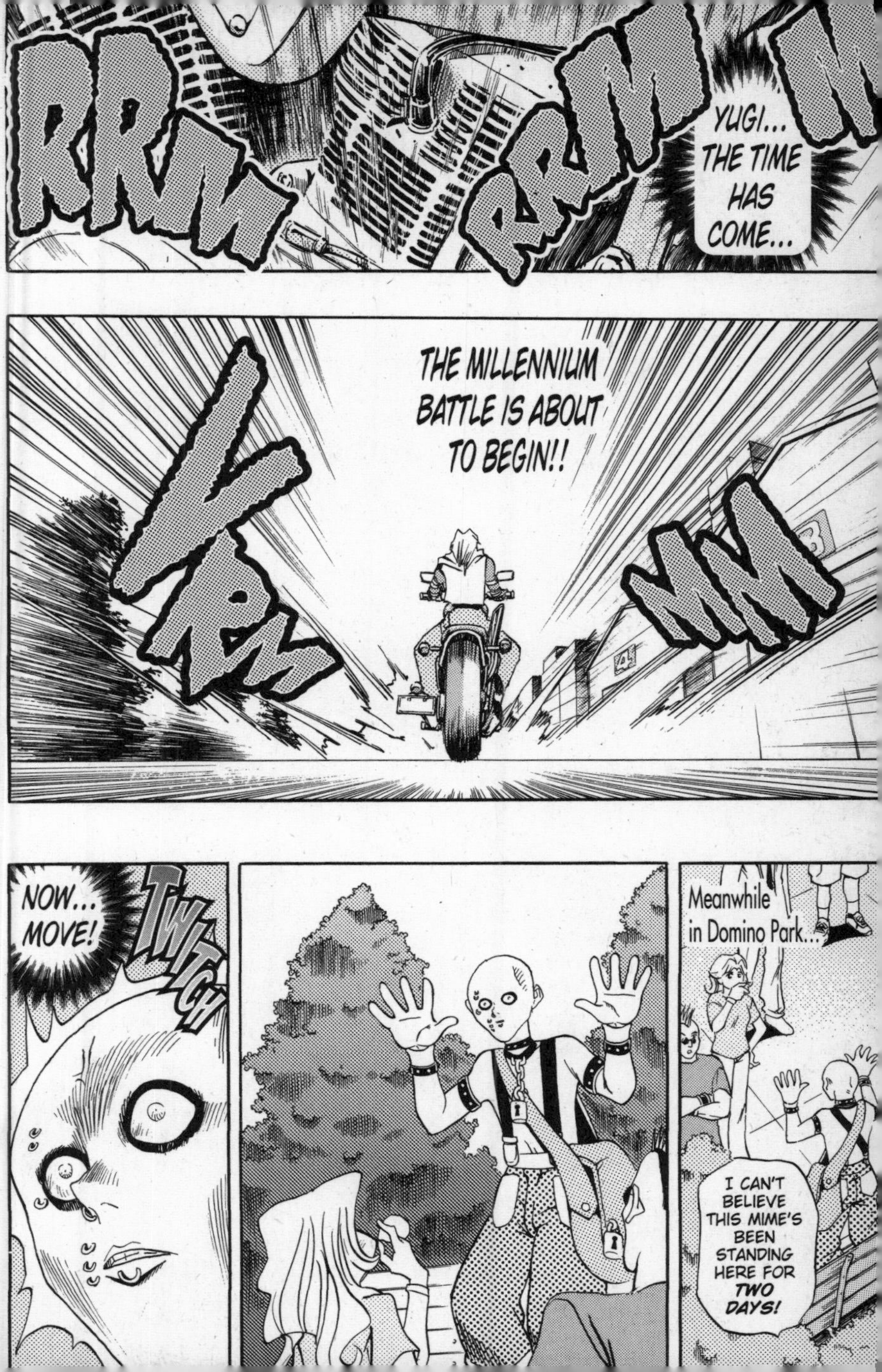
YUGI... THE TIME HAS COME...
THE MILLENNIUM BATTLE IS ABOUT TO BEGIN!!
Meanwhile in Domino Park...
I CAN'T BELIEVE THIS MIME'S BEEN STANDING HERE FOR TWO DAYS!
NOW... MOVE!
TWITCH

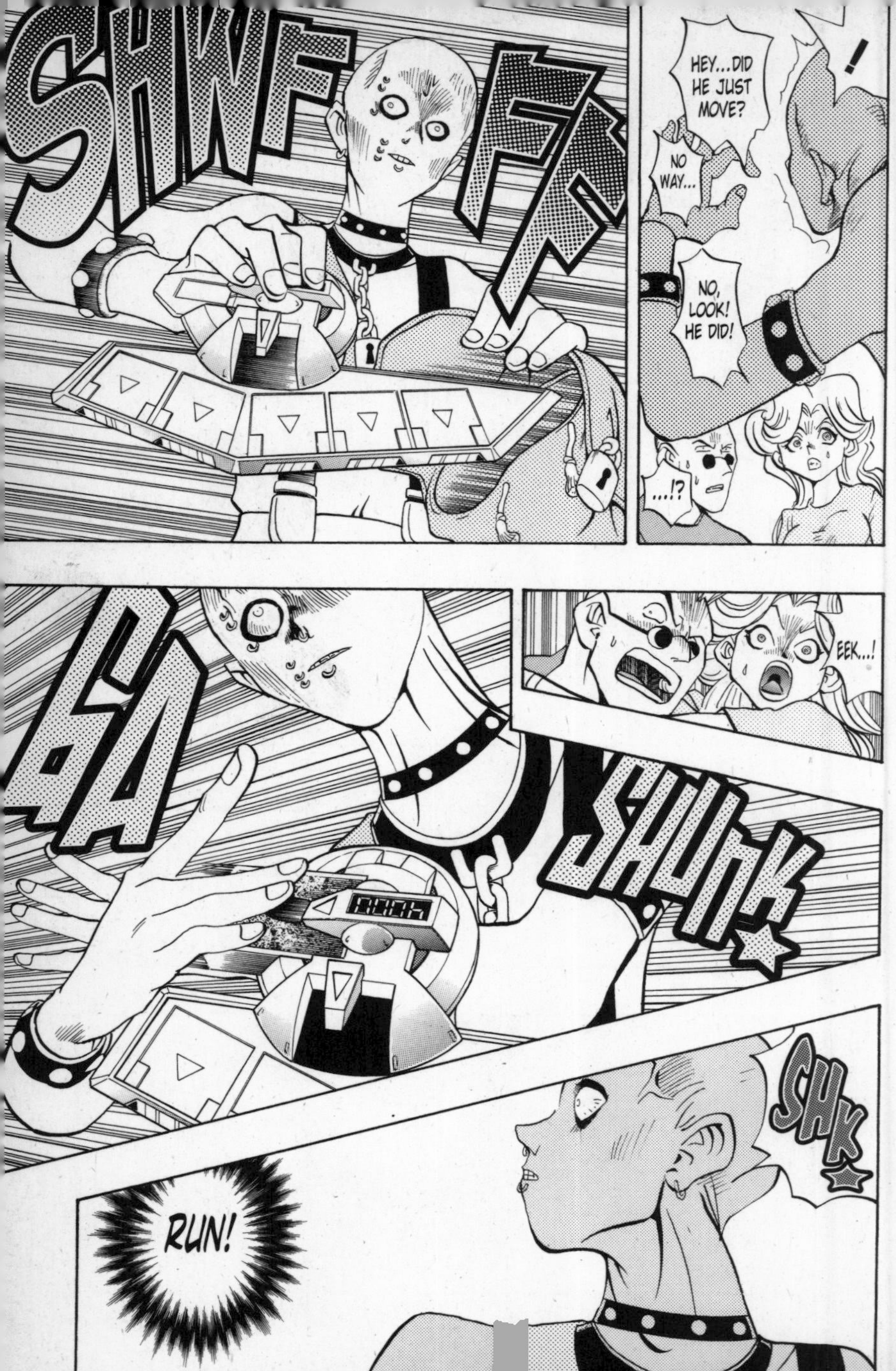
HEY...DID HE JUST MOVE?
!
NO WAY...
NO, LOOK! HE DID!
...!?
SHWF
EEK...!
GA
SHUNK
SHK
RUN!

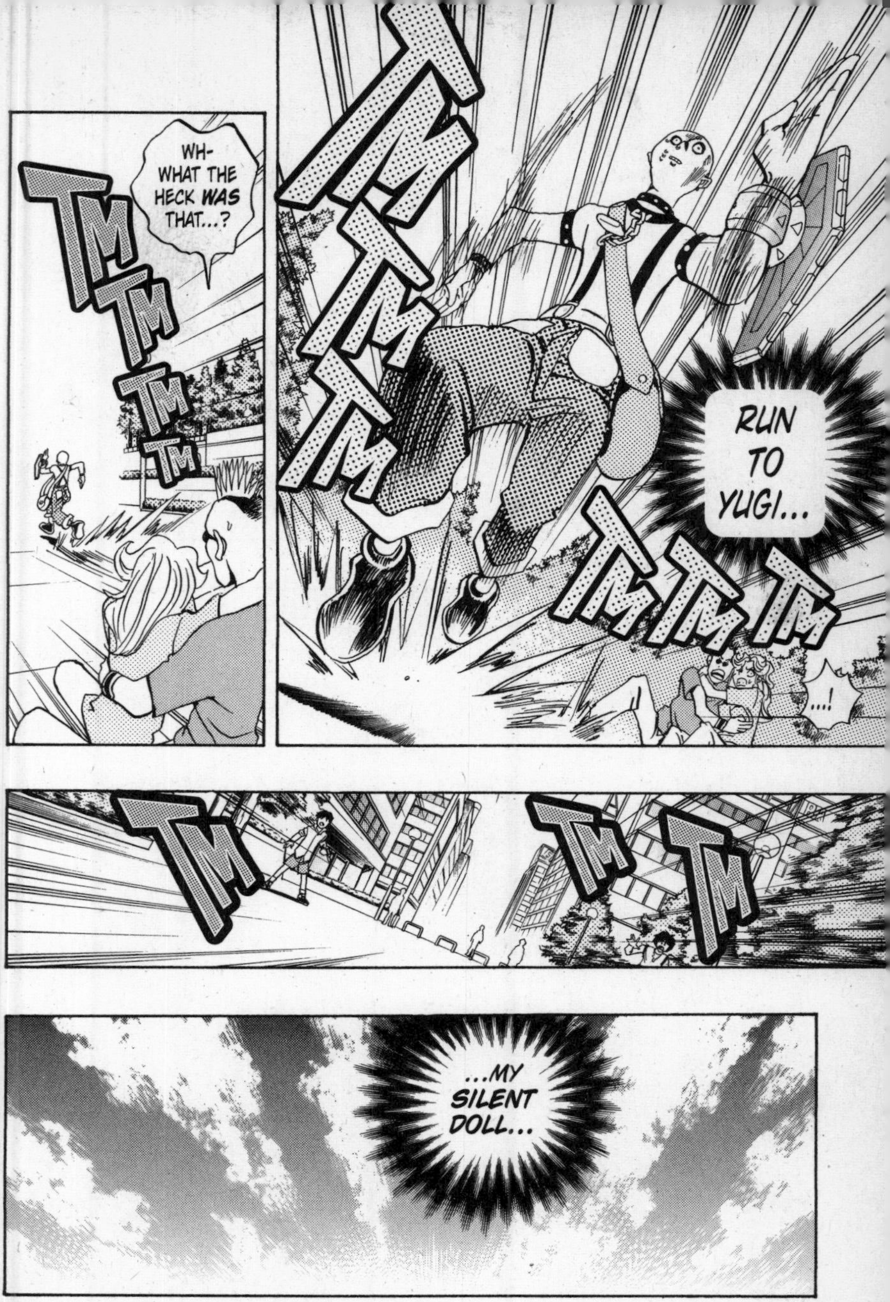
TM TM TM TM
RUN TO YUGI...
TM TM TM TM
...!
WH- WHAT THE HECK WAS THAT...?
TM TM TM TM
TM TM TM
...MY SILENT DOLL...

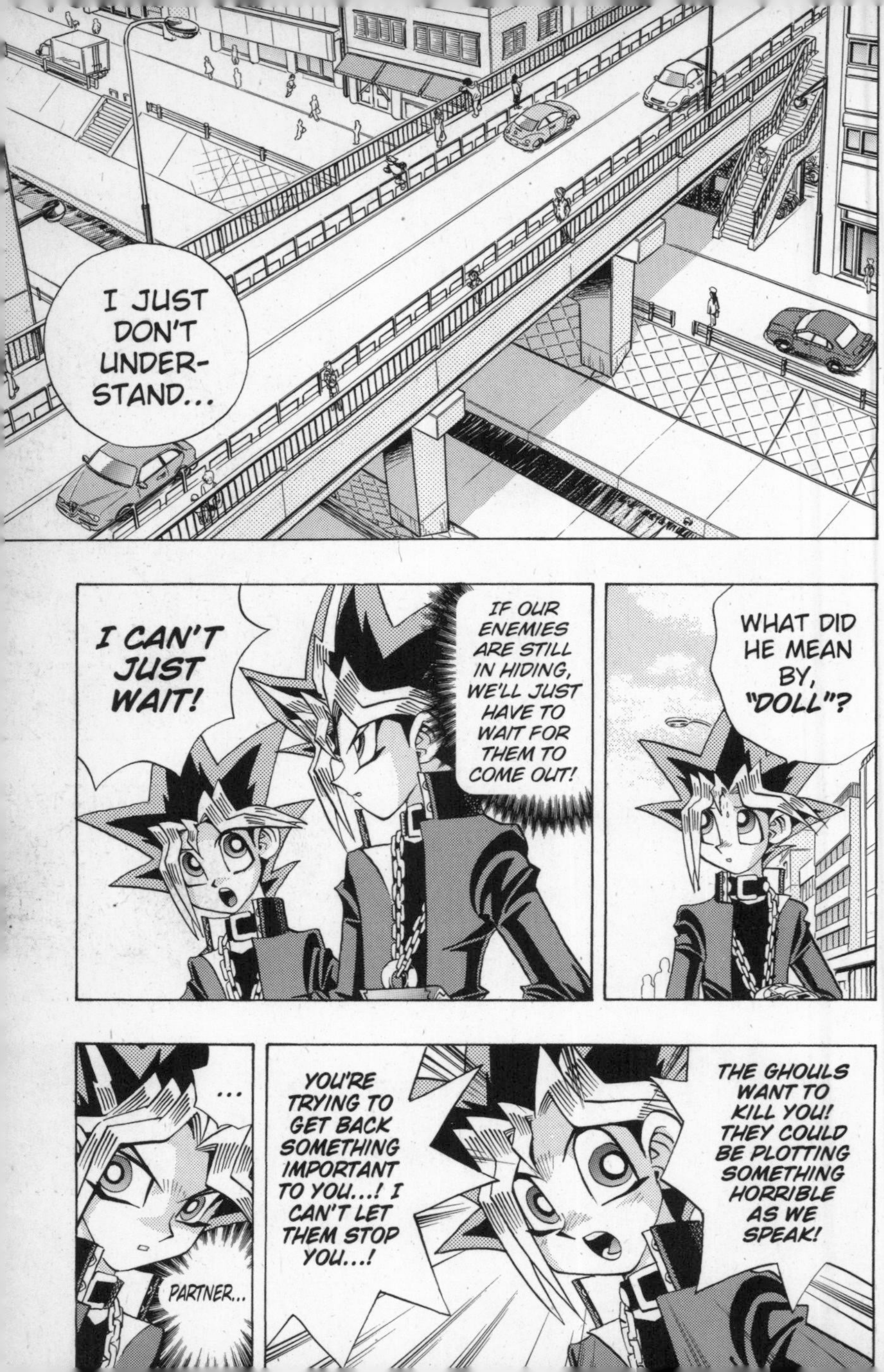
I JUST DON'T UNDER-STAND...
WHAT DID HE MEAN BY, "DOLL"?
IF OUR ENEMIES ARE STILL IN HIDING, WE'LL JUST HAVE TO WAIT FOR THEM TO COME OUT!
I CAN'T JUST WAIT!
THE GHOULS WANT TO KILL YOU! THEY COULD BE PLOTTING SOMETHING HORRIBLE AS WE SPEAK!
YOU'RE TRYING TO GET BACK SOMETHING IMPORTANT TO YOU...! I CAN'T LET THEM STOP YOU...!
...
PARTNER...

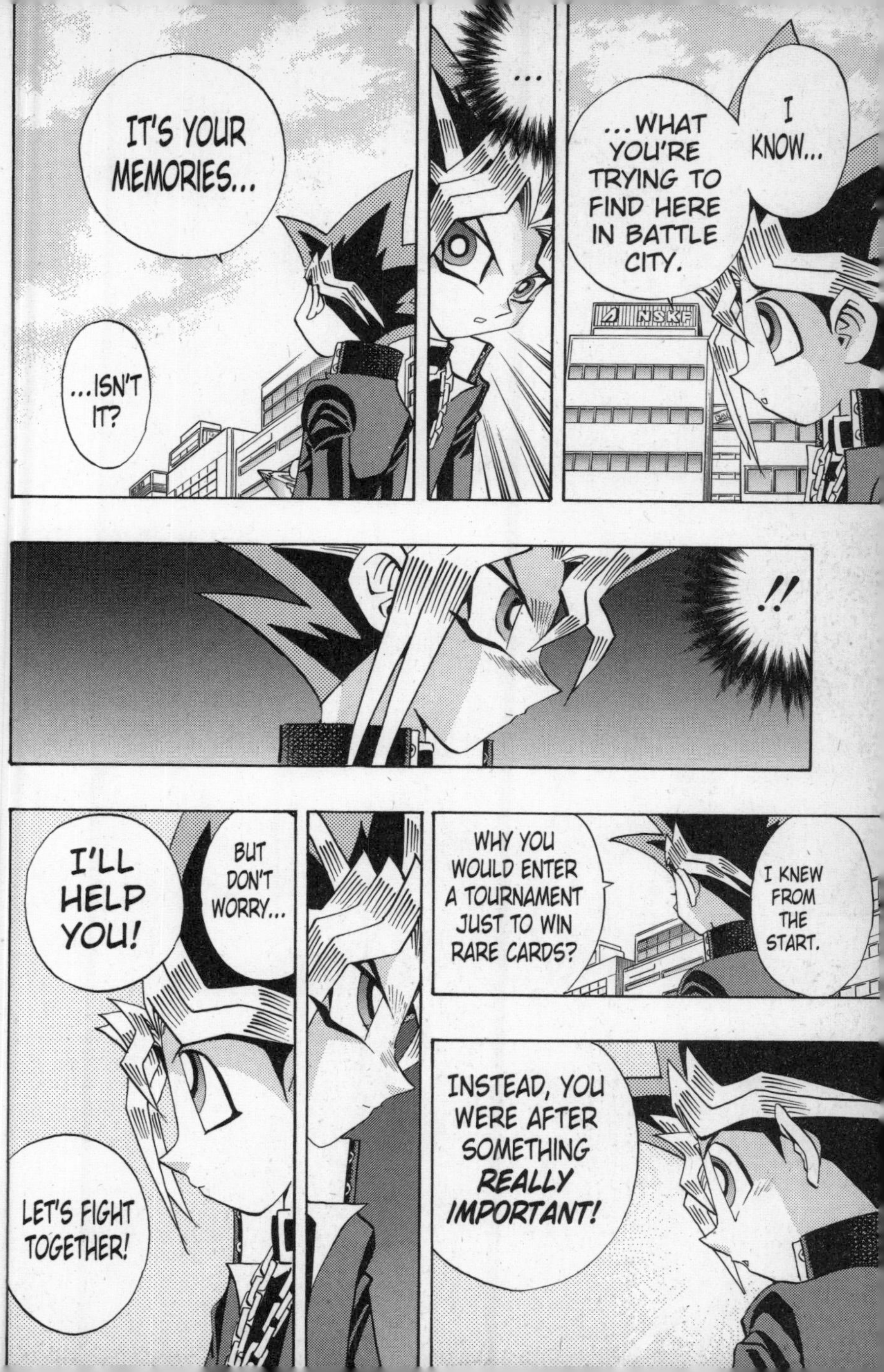
I KNOW...
...WHAT YOU'RE TRYING TO FIND HERE IN BATTLE CITY.
NSKF
...
IT'S YOUR MEMORIES...
...ISN'T IT?
!!
I KNEW FROM THE START.
WHY YOU WOULD ENTER A TOURNAMENT JUST TO WIN RARE CARDS?
INSTEAD, YOU WERE AFTER SOMETHING *REALLY IMPORTANT!*
BUT DON'T WORRY...
I'LL HELP YOU!
LET'S FIGHT TOGETHER!

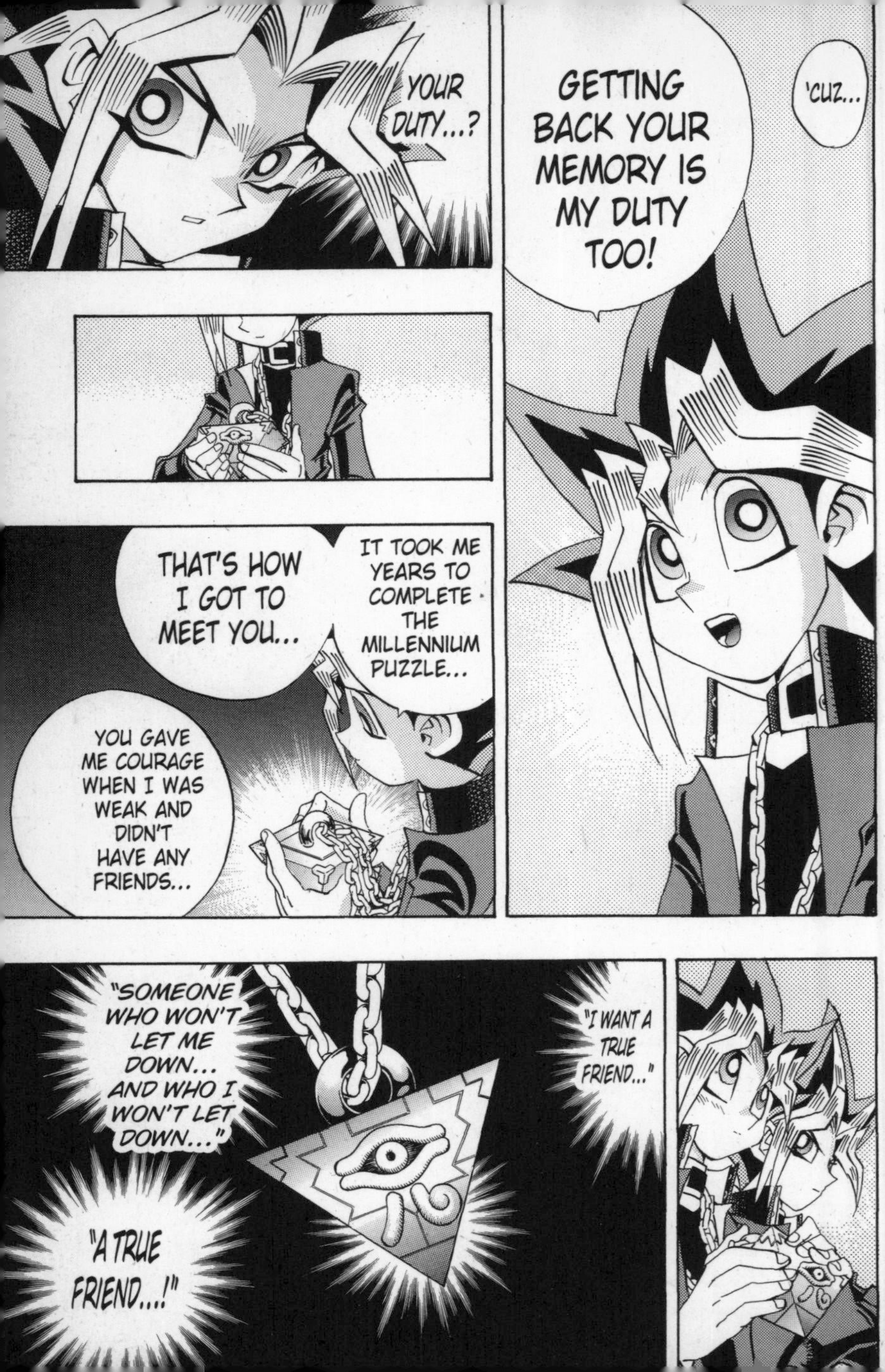
'CUZ...
GETTING BACK YOUR MEMORY IS MY DUTY TOO!
YOUR DUTY...?
IT TOOK ME YEARS TO COMPLETE THE MILLENNIUM PUZZLE...
THAT'S HOW I GOT TO MEET YOU...
YOU GAVE ME COURAGE WHEN I WAS WEAK AND DIDN'T HAVE ANY FRIENDS...
"I WANT A TRUE FRIEND..."
"SOMEONE WHO WON'T LET ME DOWN... AND WHO I WON'T LET DOWN..."
"A TRUE FRIEND...!"

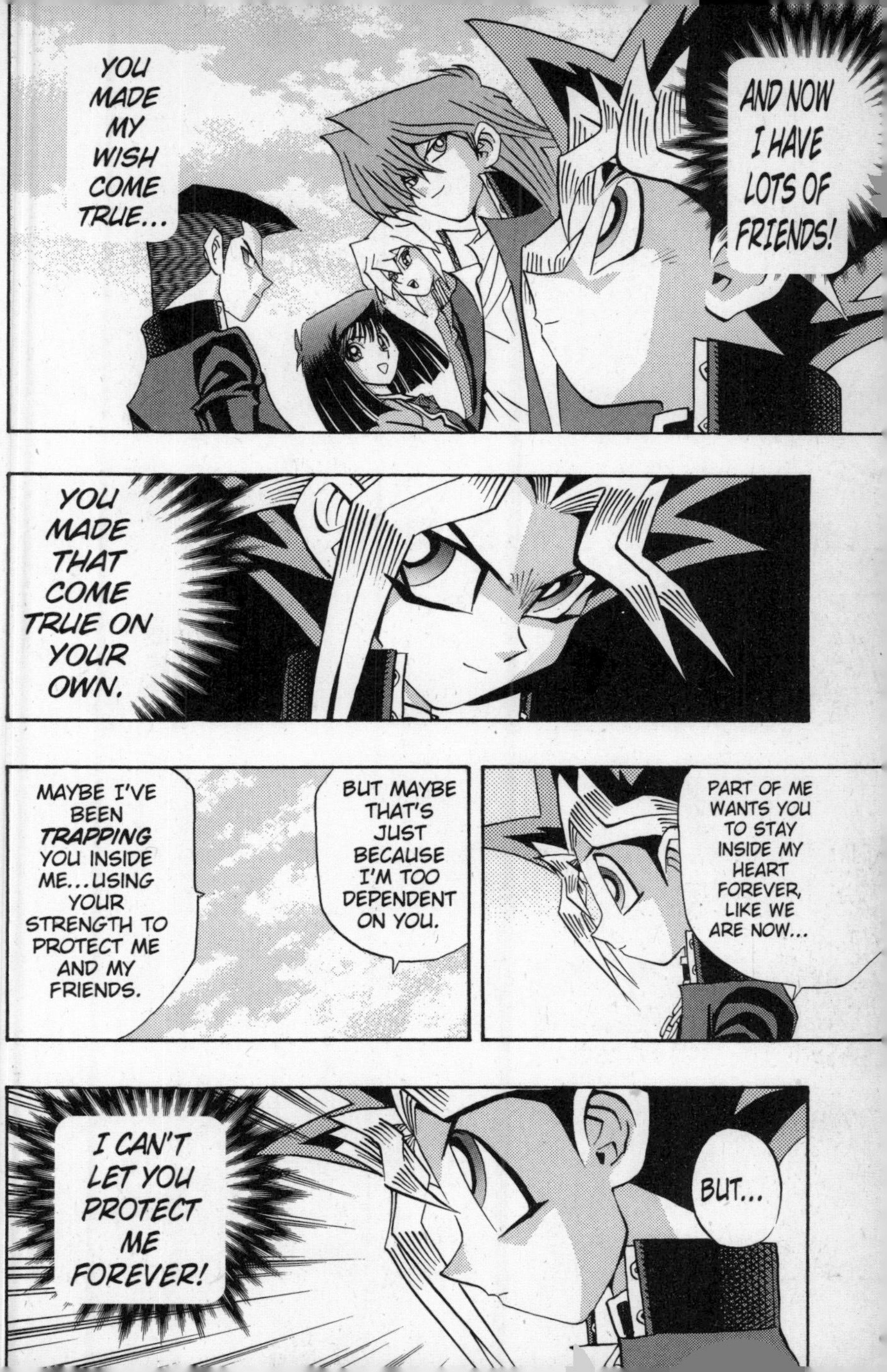
AND NOW I HAVE LOTS OF FRIENDS!
YOU MADE MY WISH COME TRUE...
YOU MADE THAT COME TRUE ON YOUR OWN.
PART OF ME WANTS YOU TO STAY INSIDE MY HEART FOREVER, LIKE WE ARE NOW...
BUT MAYBE THAT'S JUST BECAUSE I'M TOO DEPENDENT ON YOU.
MAYBE I'VE BEEN TRAPPING YOU INSIDE ME...USING YOUR STRENGTH TO PROTECT ME AND MY FRIENDS.
BUT...
I CAN'T LET YOU PROTECT ME FOREVER!

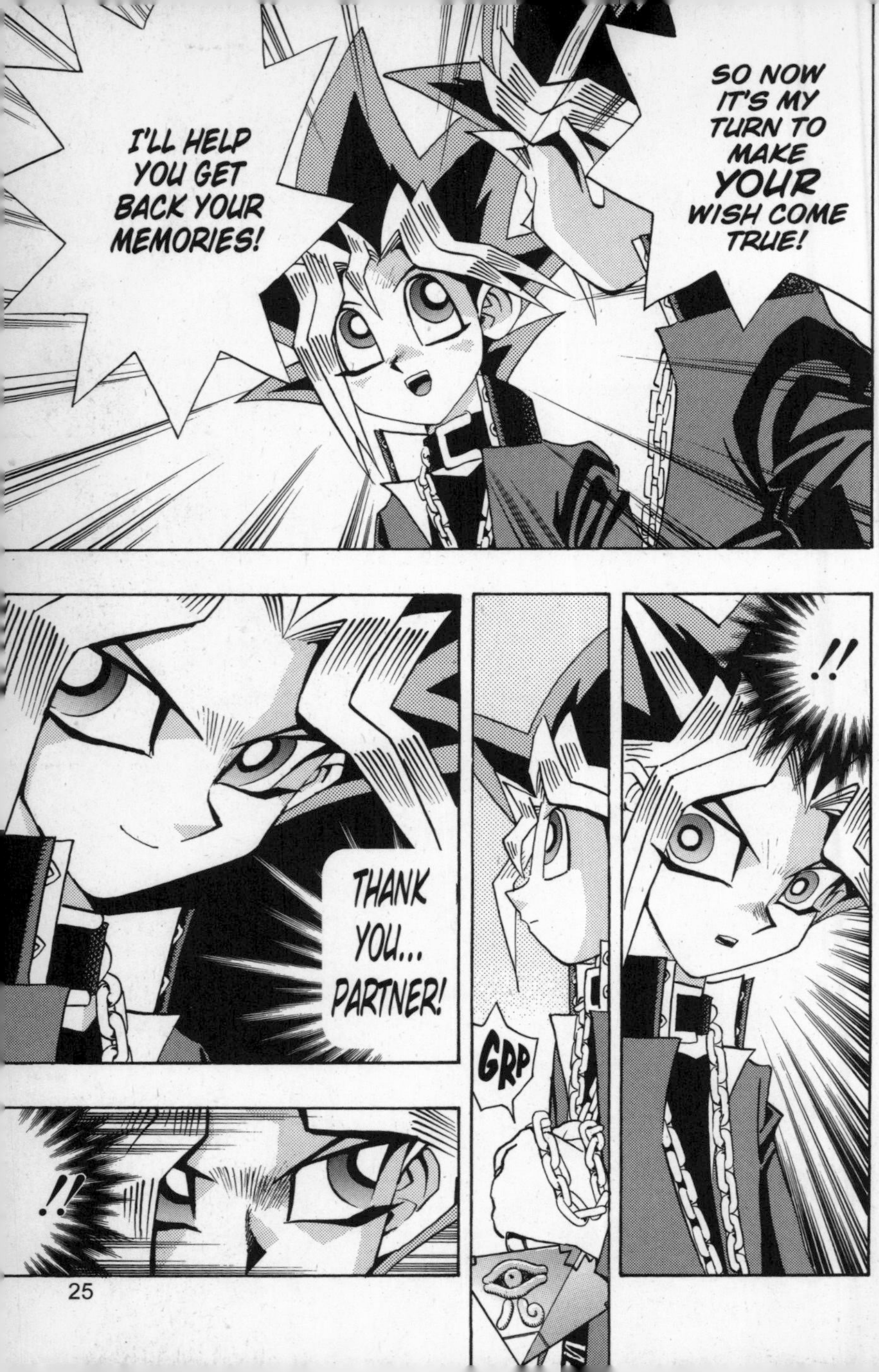
SO NOW IT'S MY TURN TO MAKE YOUR WISH COME TRUE!
I'LL HELP YOU GET BACK YOUR MEMORIES!
!!
GRP
THANK YOU... PARTNER!
!!

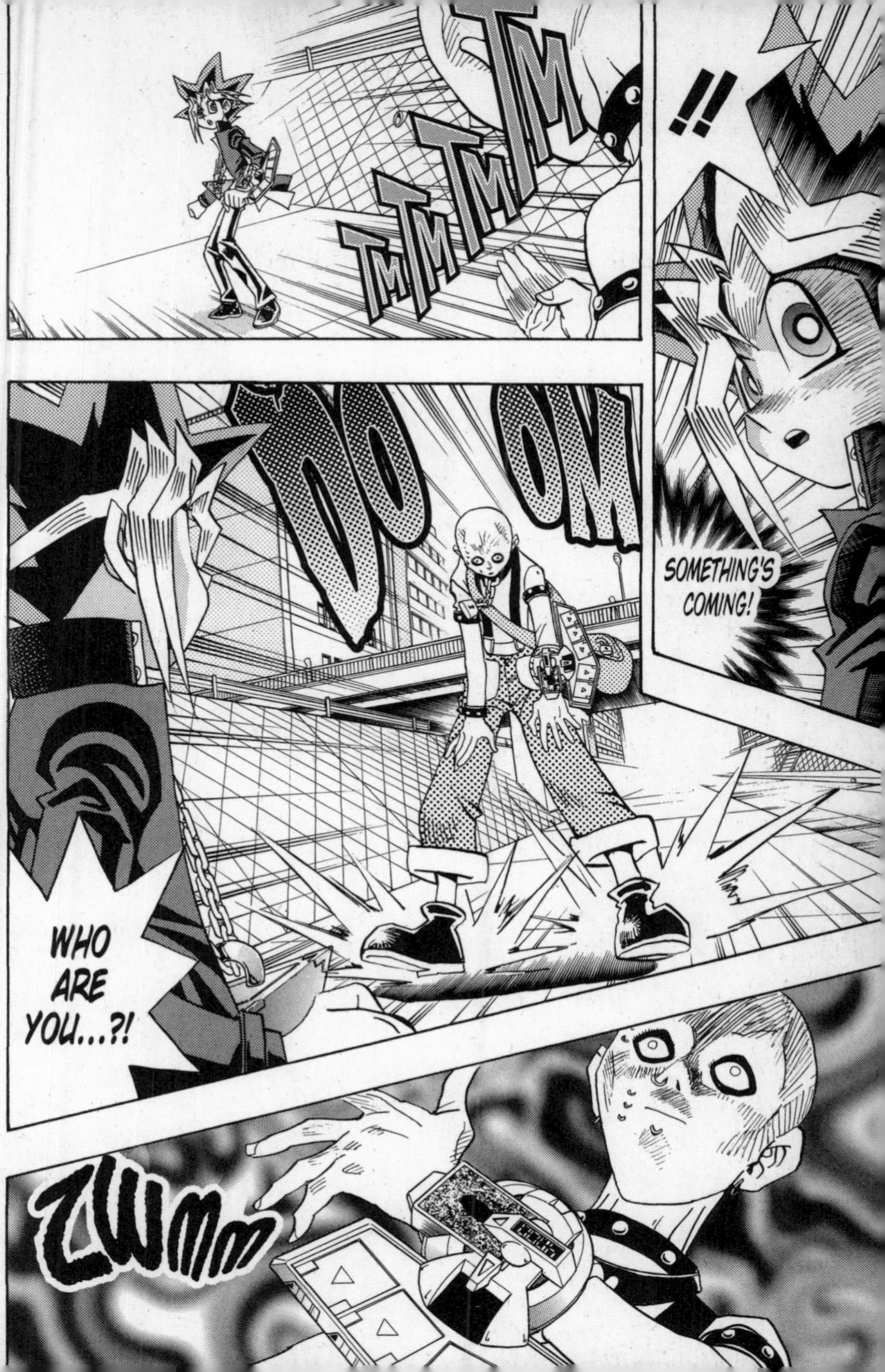
!!
SOMETHING'S COMING!
TMTMTMTM
DOOM
WHO ARE YOU...?!
ZUMm

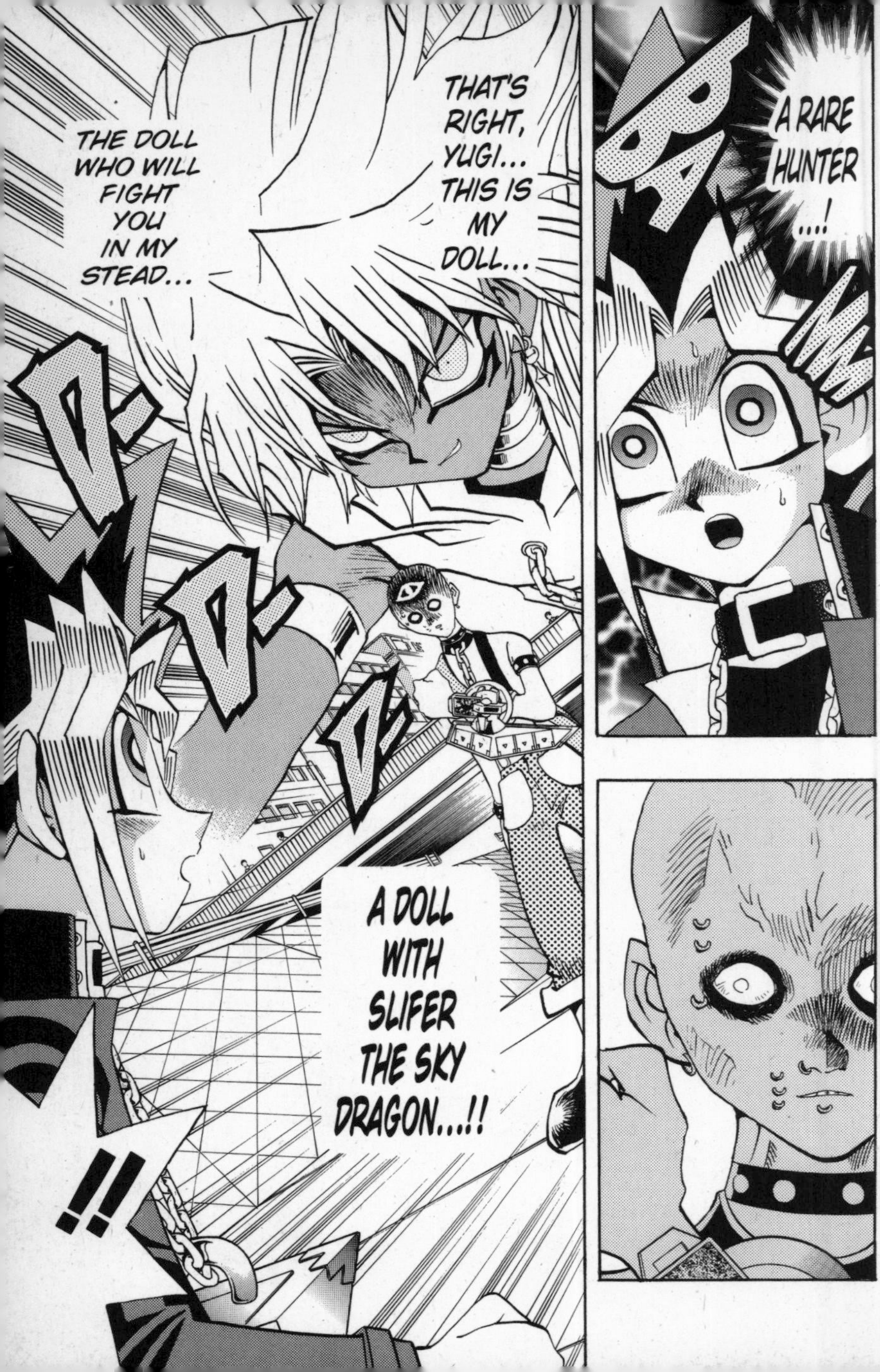

A RARE HUNTER ...!
THAT'S RIGHT, YUGI... THIS IS MY DOLL...
THE DOLL WHO WILL FIGHT YOU IN MY STEAD...
A DOLL WITH SLIFER THE SKY DRAGON...!!
!!

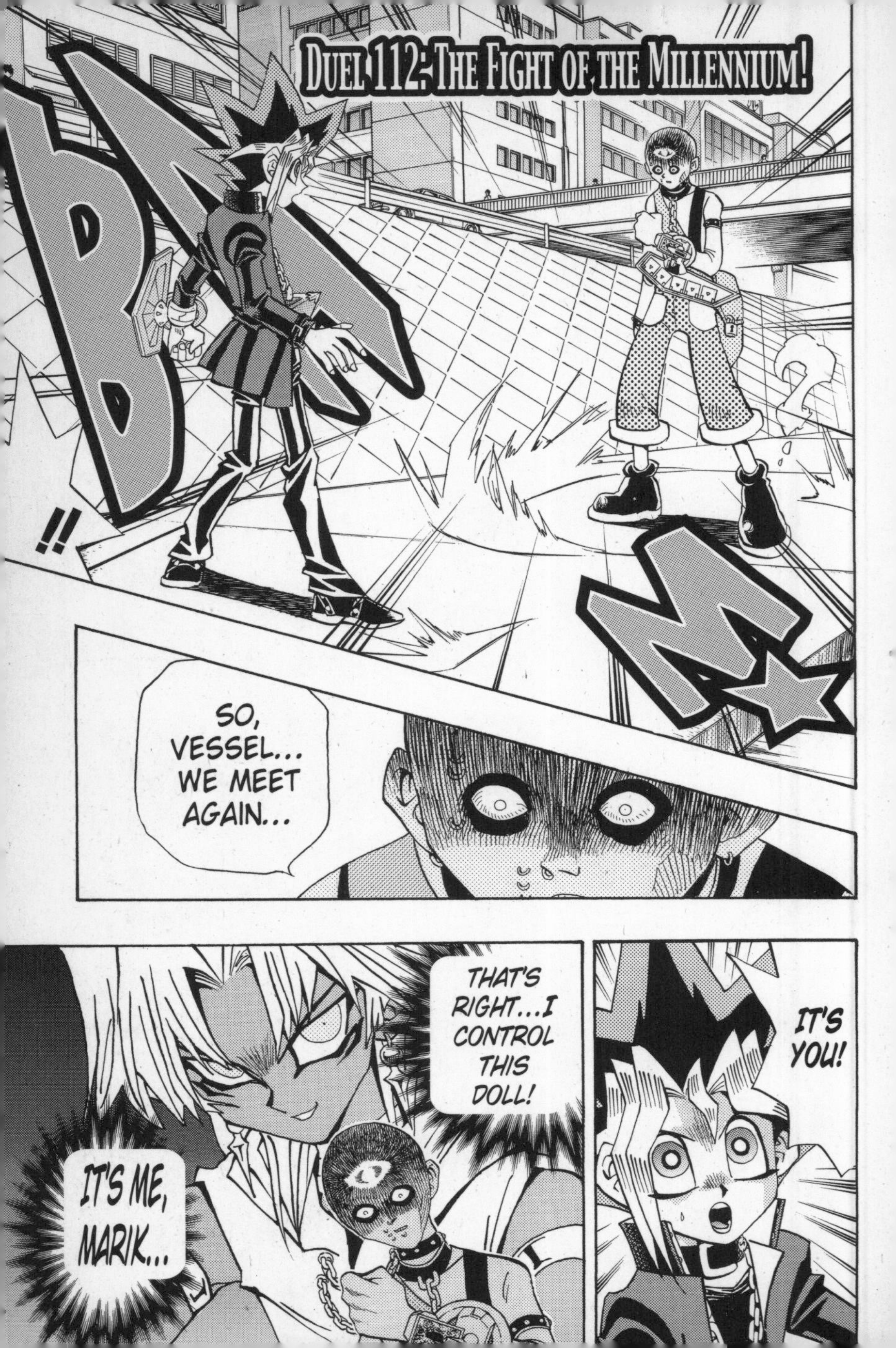
Duel 112: The Fight of the Millennium!
!!
SO, VESSEL... WE MEET AGAIN...
IT'S YOU!
THAT'S RIGHT...I CONTROL THIS DOLL!
IT'S ME, MARIK...

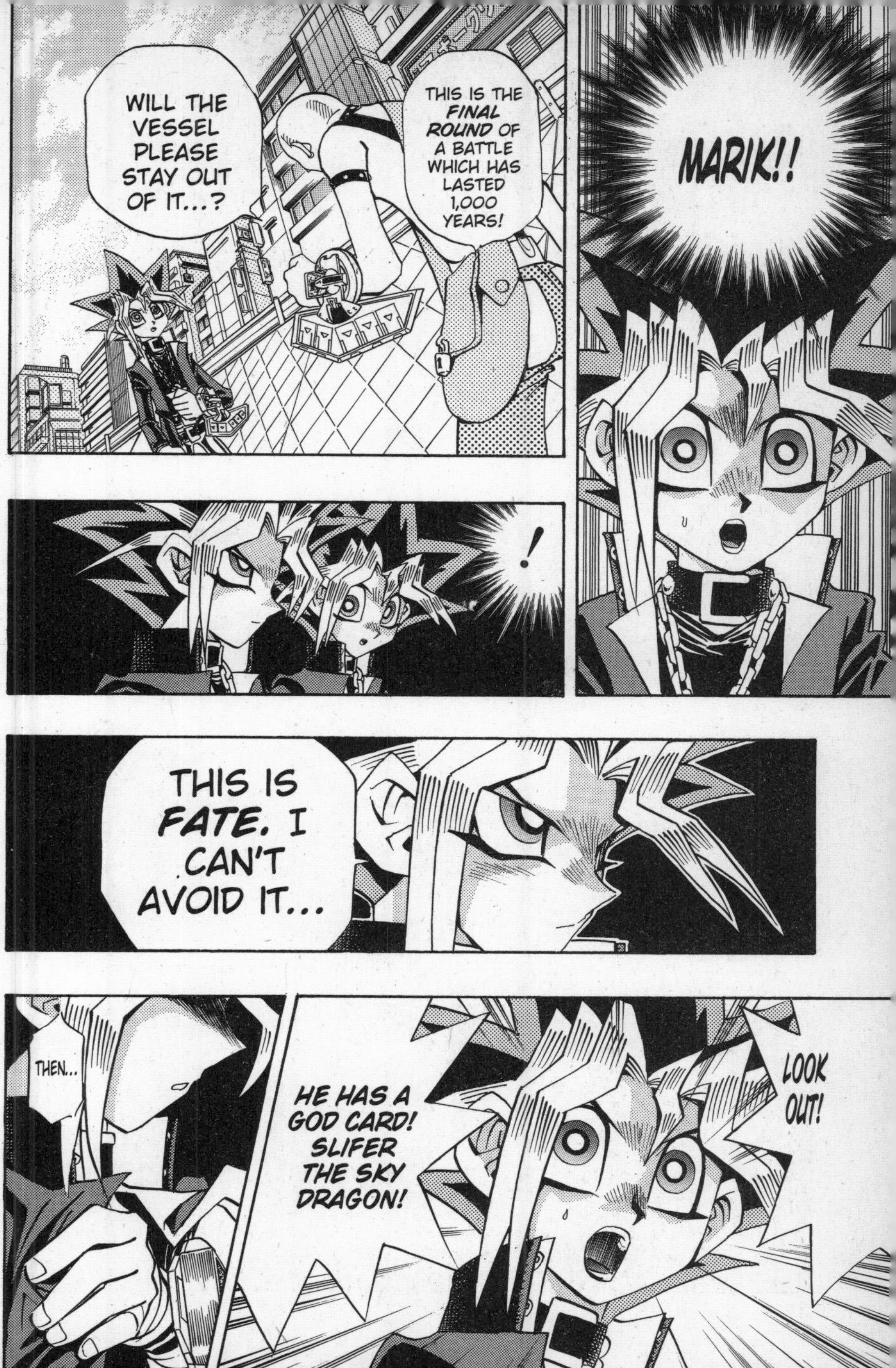
MARIK!!
THIS IS THE FINAL ROUND OF A BATTLE WHICH HAS LASTED 1,000 YEARS!
WILL THE VESSEL PLEASE STAY OUT OF IT...?
!
THIS IS FATE. I CAN'T AVOID IT...
LOOK OUT!
HE HAS A GOD CARD! SLIFER THE SKY DRAGON!
THEN...

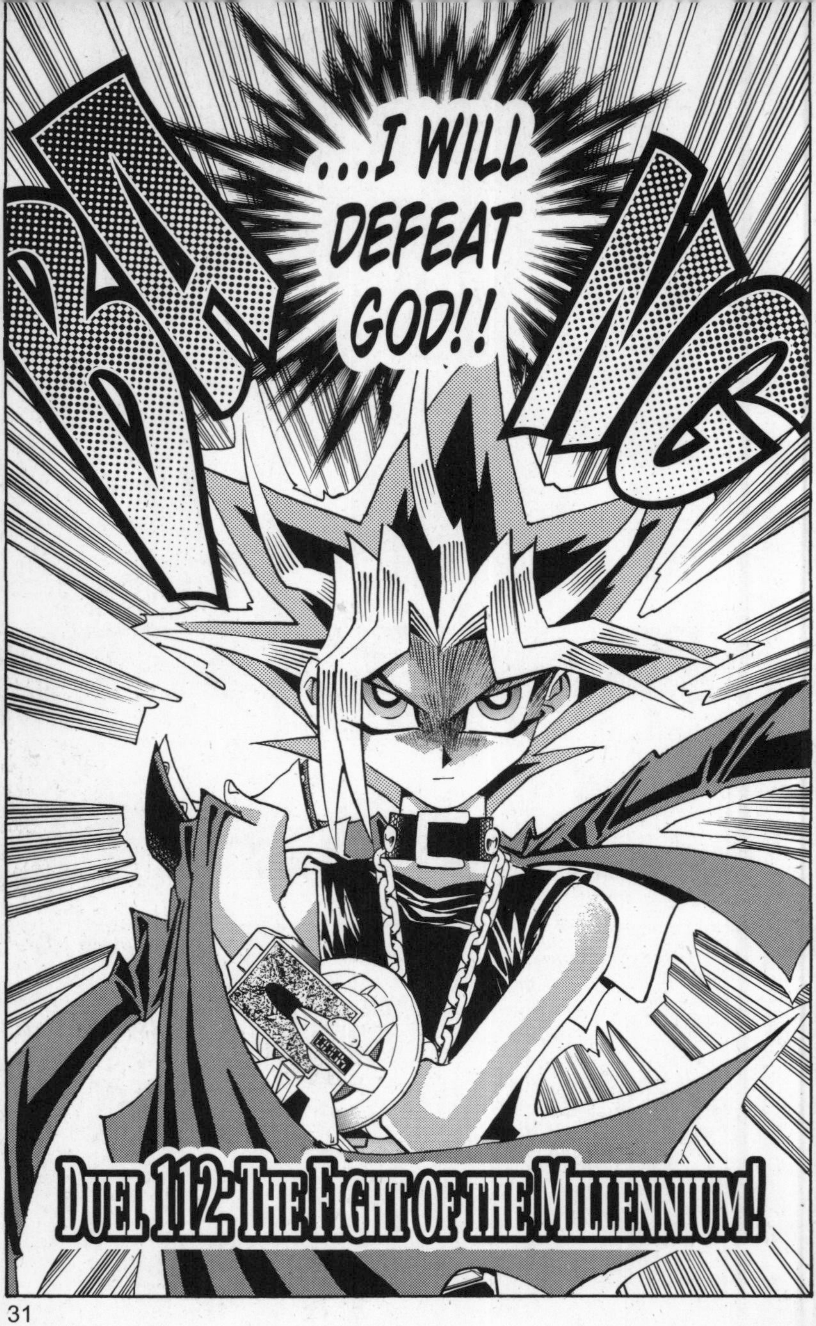
...I WILL DEFEAT GOD!!
DUEL 112: THE FIGHT OF THE MILLENNIUM!

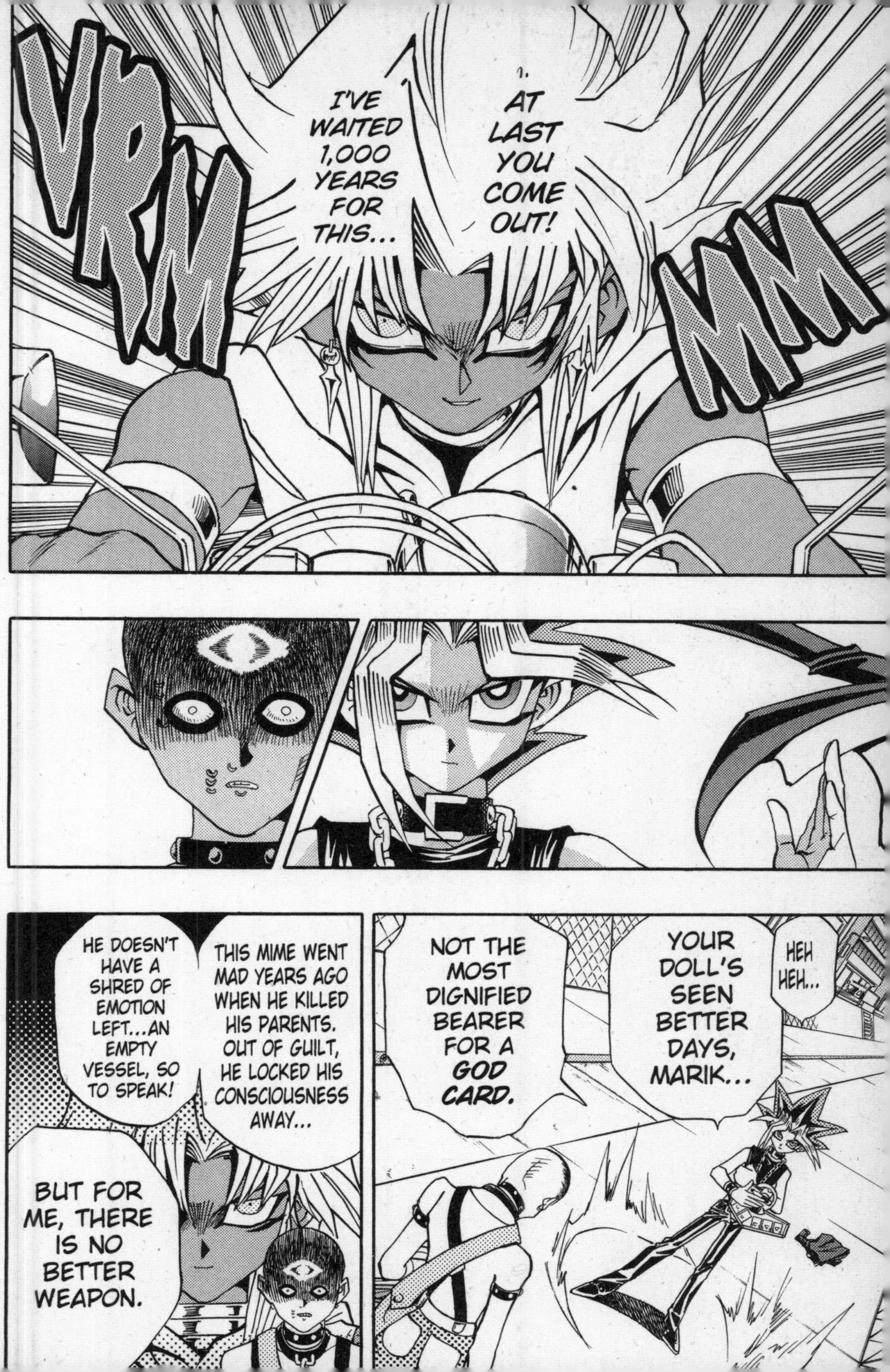
VRM
MM
AT LAST YOU COME OUT!
I'VE WAITED 1,000 YEARS FOR THIS...
HEH HEH...
YOUR DOLL'S SEEN BETTER DAYS, MARIK...
NOT THE MOST DIGNIFIED BEARER FOR A GOD CARD.
THIS MIME WENT MAD YEARS AGO WHEN HE KILLED HIS PARENTS. OUT OF GUILT, HE LOCKED HIS CONSCIOUSNESS AWAY...
HE DOESN'T HAVE A SHRED OF EMOTION LEFT...AN EMPTY VESSEL, SO TO SPEAK!
BUT FOR ME, THERE IS NO BETTER WEAPON.

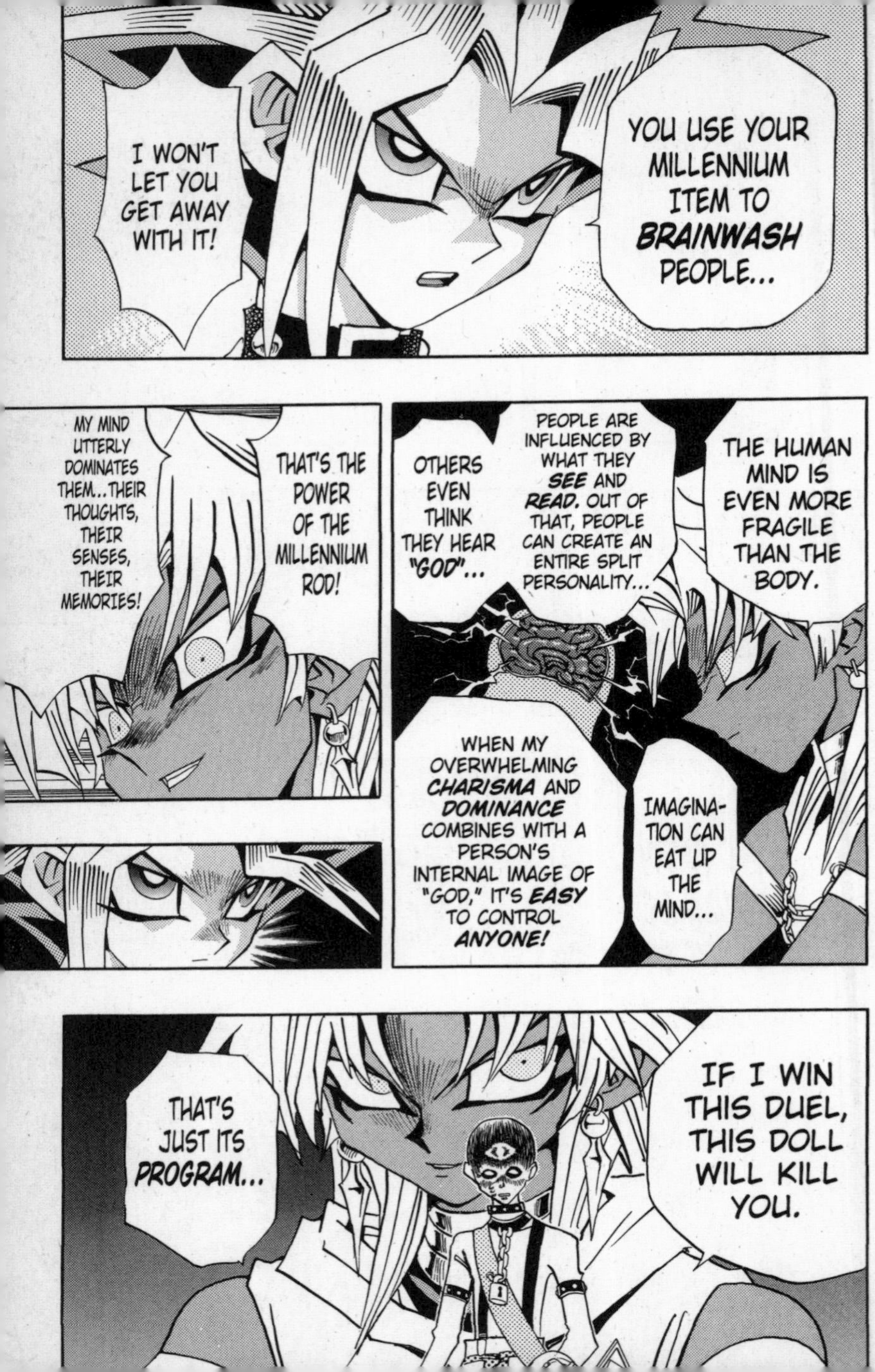
YOU USE YOUR MILLENNIUM ITEM TO BRAINWASH PEOPLE...
I WON'T LET YOU GET AWAY WITH IT!
THE HUMAN MIND IS EVEN MORE FRAGILE THAN THE BODY.
PEOPLE ARE INFLUENCED BY WHAT THEY SEE AND READ. OUT OF THAT, PEOPLE CAN CREATE AN ENTIRE SPLIT PERSONALITY...
OTHERS EVEN THINK THEY HEAR "GOD"...
IMAGINA-TION CAN EAT UP THE MIND...
WHEN MY OVERWHELMING CHARISMA AND DOMINANCE COMBINES WITH A PERSON'S INTERNAL IMAGE OF "GOD," IT'S EASY TO CONTROL ANYONE!
THAT'S THE POWER OF THE MILLENNIUM ROD!
MY MIND UTTERLY DOMINATES THEM...THEIR THOUGHTS, THEIR SENSES, THEIR MEMORIES!
IF I WIN THIS DUEL, THIS DOLL WILL KILL YOU.
THAT'S JUST ITS PROGRAM...

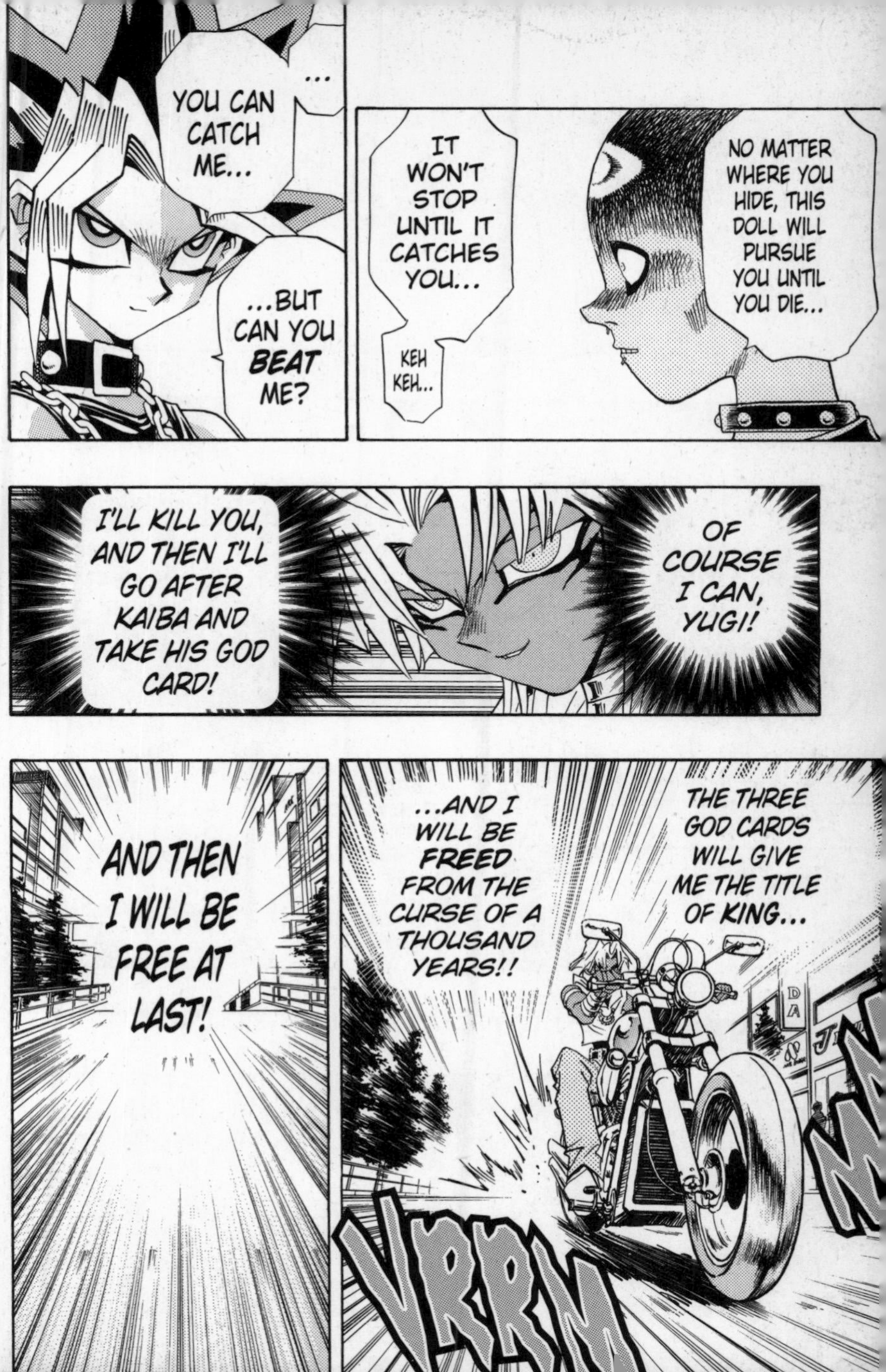
NO MATTER WHERE YOU HIDE, THIS DOLL WILL PURSUE YOU UNTIL YOU DIE...
IT WON'T STOP UNTIL IT CATCHES YOU...
KEH KEH...
...
YOU CAN CATCH ME...
...BUT CAN YOU BEAT ME?
OF COURSE I CAN, YUGI!
I'LL KILL YOU, AND THEN I'LL GO AFTER KAIBA AND TAKE HIS GOD CARD!
THE THREE GOD CARDS WILL GIVE ME THE TITLE OF KING...
...AND I WILL BE FREED FROM THE CURSE OF A THOUSAND YEARS!!
VRRM
AND THEN I WILL BE FREE AT LAST!

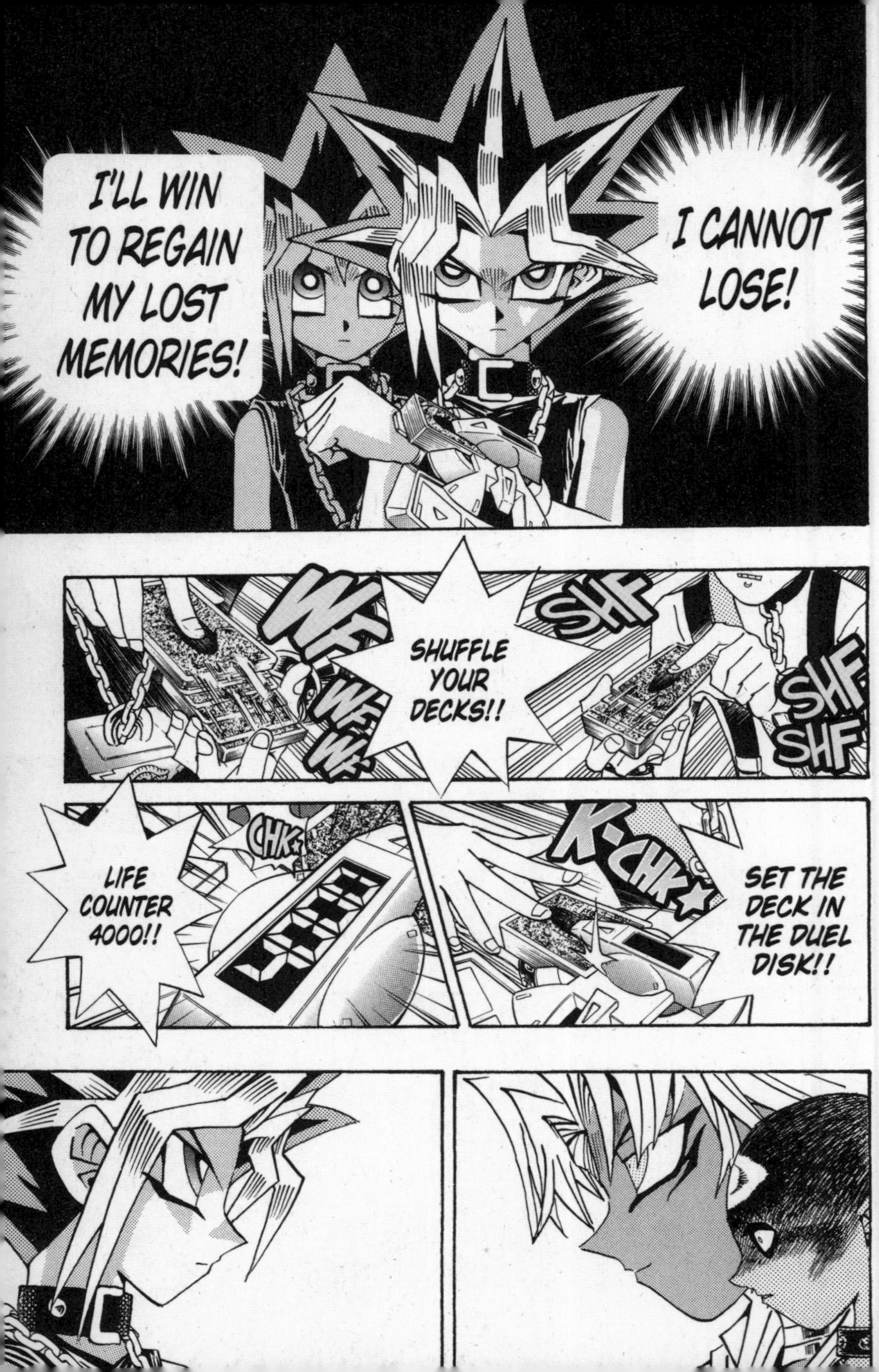
I CANNOT LOSE!
I'LL WIN TO REGAIN MY LOST MEMORIES!
SHF
SHF
SHF
SHUFFLE YOUR DECKS!!
WF
WF
WF
K-CHK
SET THE DECK IN THE DUEL DISK!!
CHK
LIFE COUNTER 4000!!

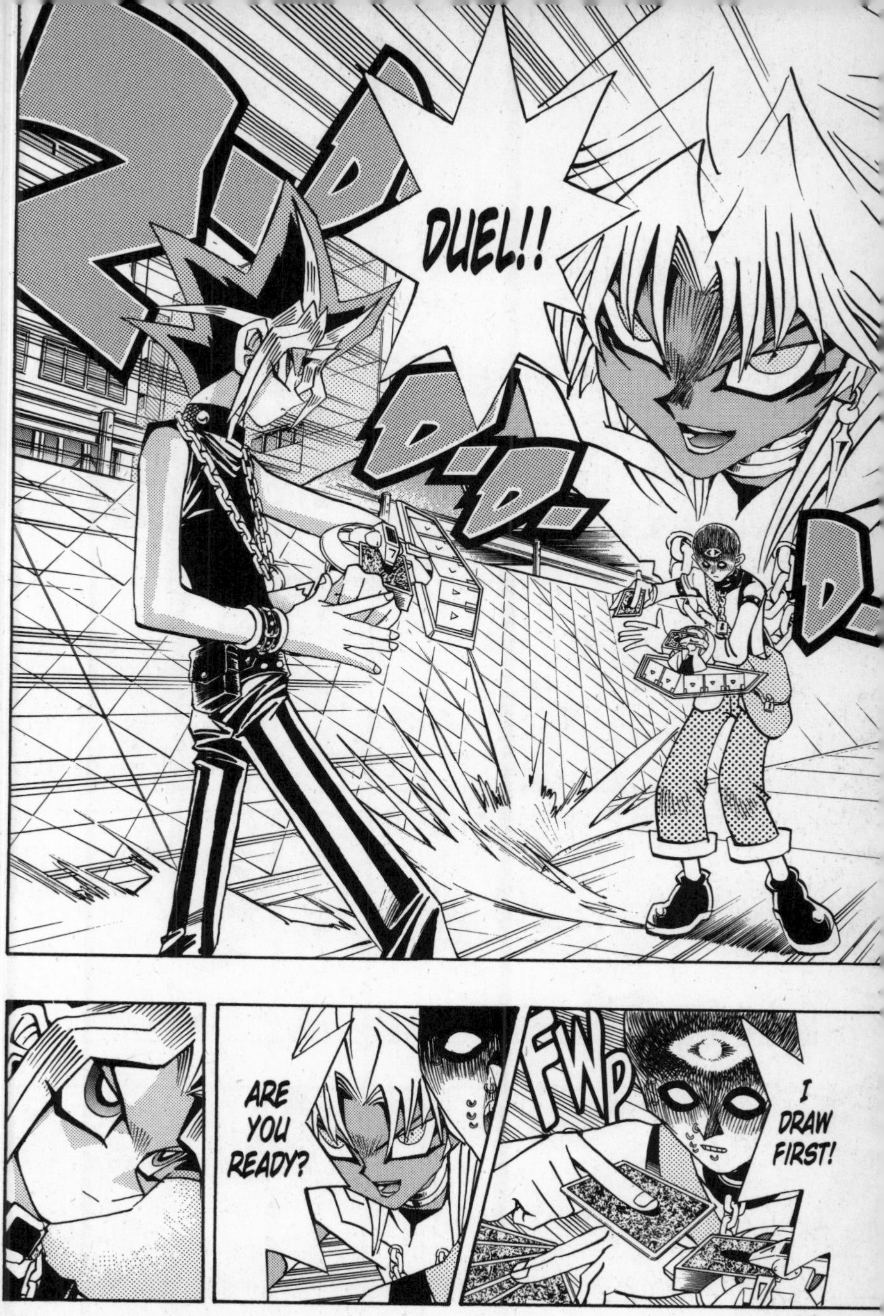
DUEL!!
FWP
I DRAW FIRST!
ARE YOU READY?

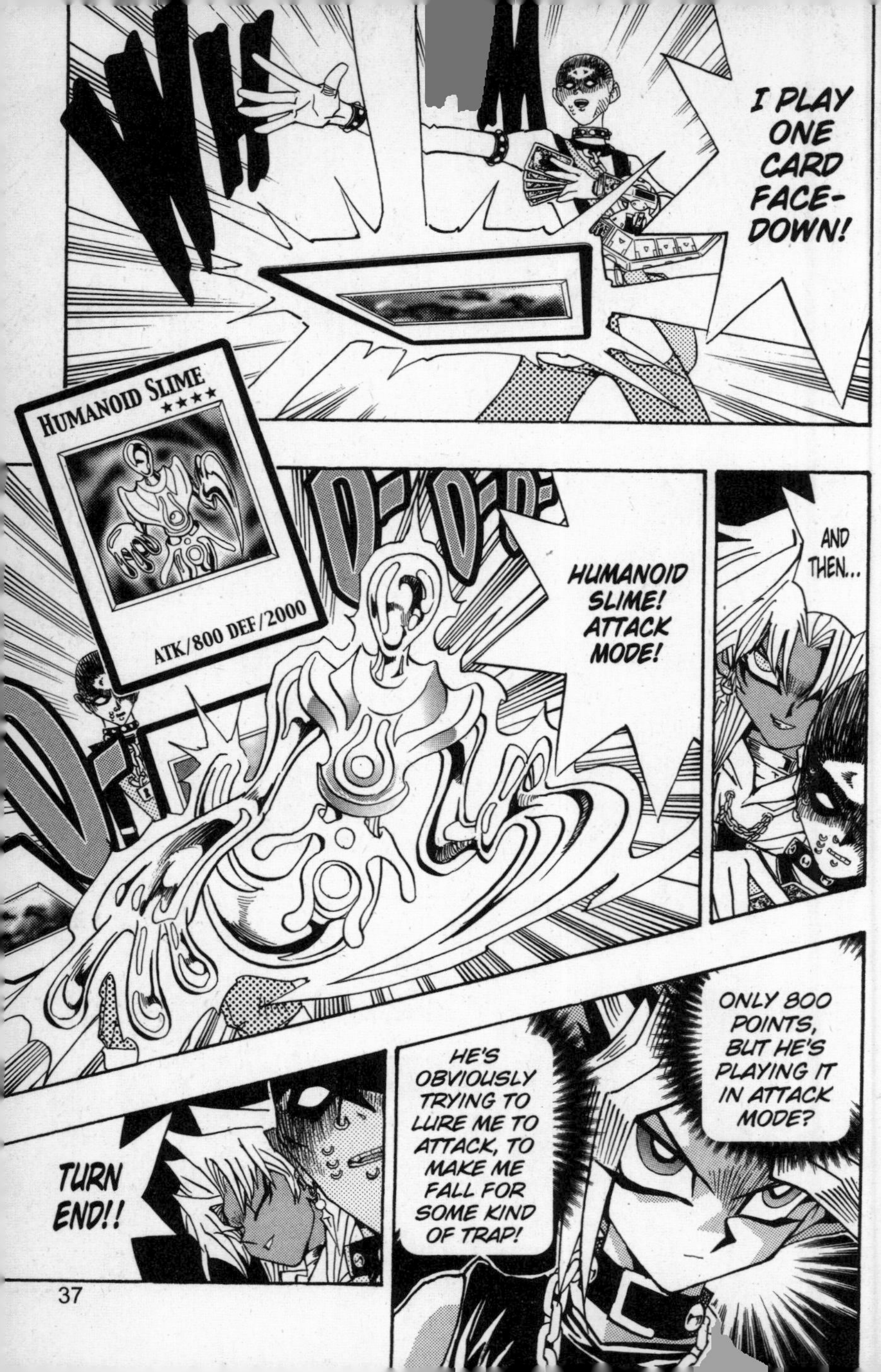
I PLAY ONE CARD FACE-DOWN!
HUMANOID SLIME
ATK/800 DEF/2000
AND THEN...
HUMANOID SLIME! ATTACK MODE!
ONLY 800 POINTS, BUT HE'S PLAYING IT IN ATTACK MODE?
HE'S OBVIOUSLY TRYING TO LURE ME TO ATTACK, TO MAKE ME FALL FOR SOME KIND OF TRAP!
TURN END!!

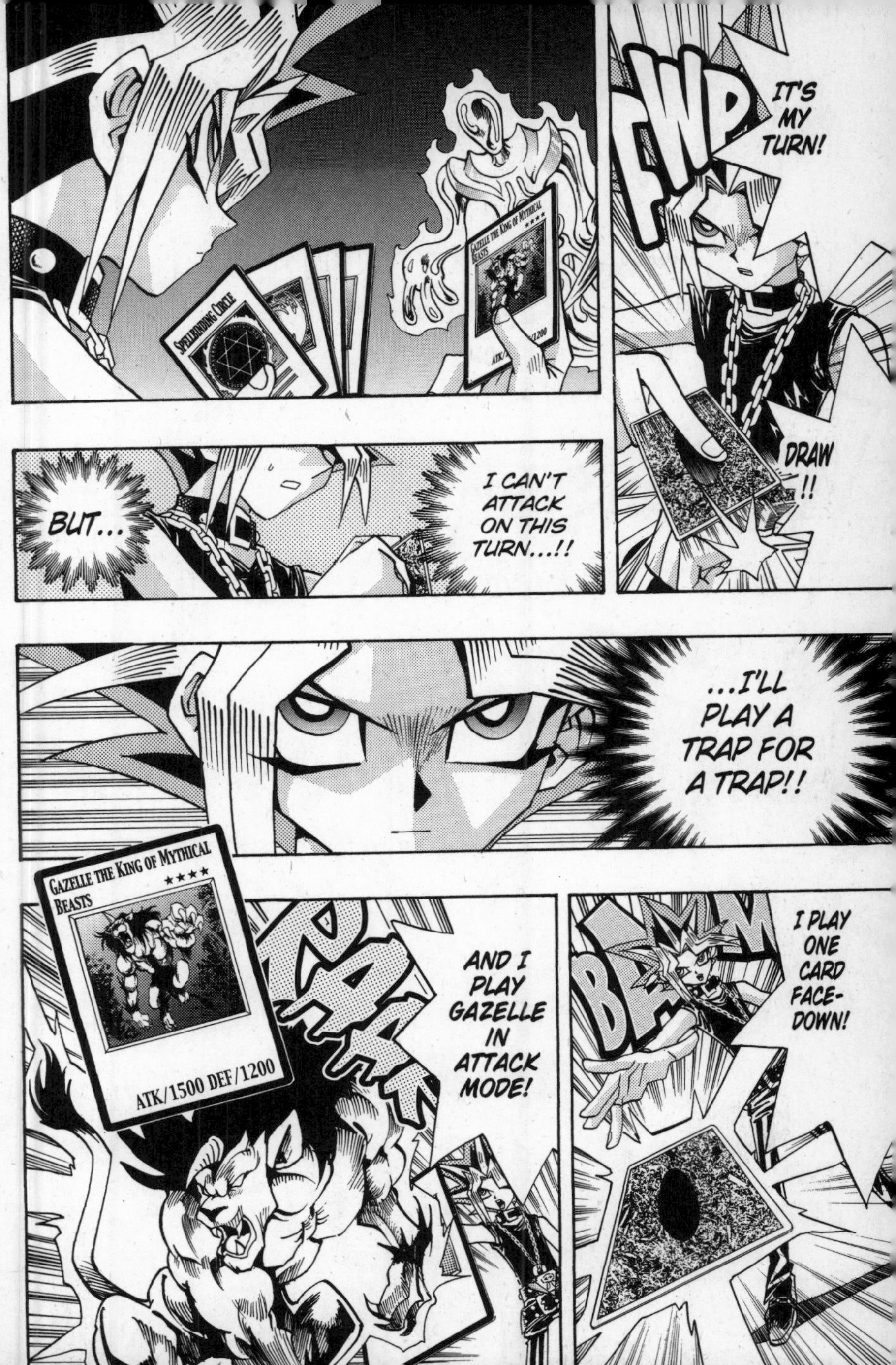
IT'S MY TURN!
DRAW!!
SPELLBINDING CIRCLE
GAZELLE THE KING OF MYTHICAL BEASTS
I CAN'T ATTACK ON THIS TURN...!!
BUT...
...I'LL PLAY A TRAP FOR A TRAP!!
I PLAY ONE CARD FACE-DOWN!
AND I PLAY GAZELLE IN ATTACK MODE!
GAZELLE THE KING OF MYTHICAL BEASTS
ATK/1500 DEF/1200

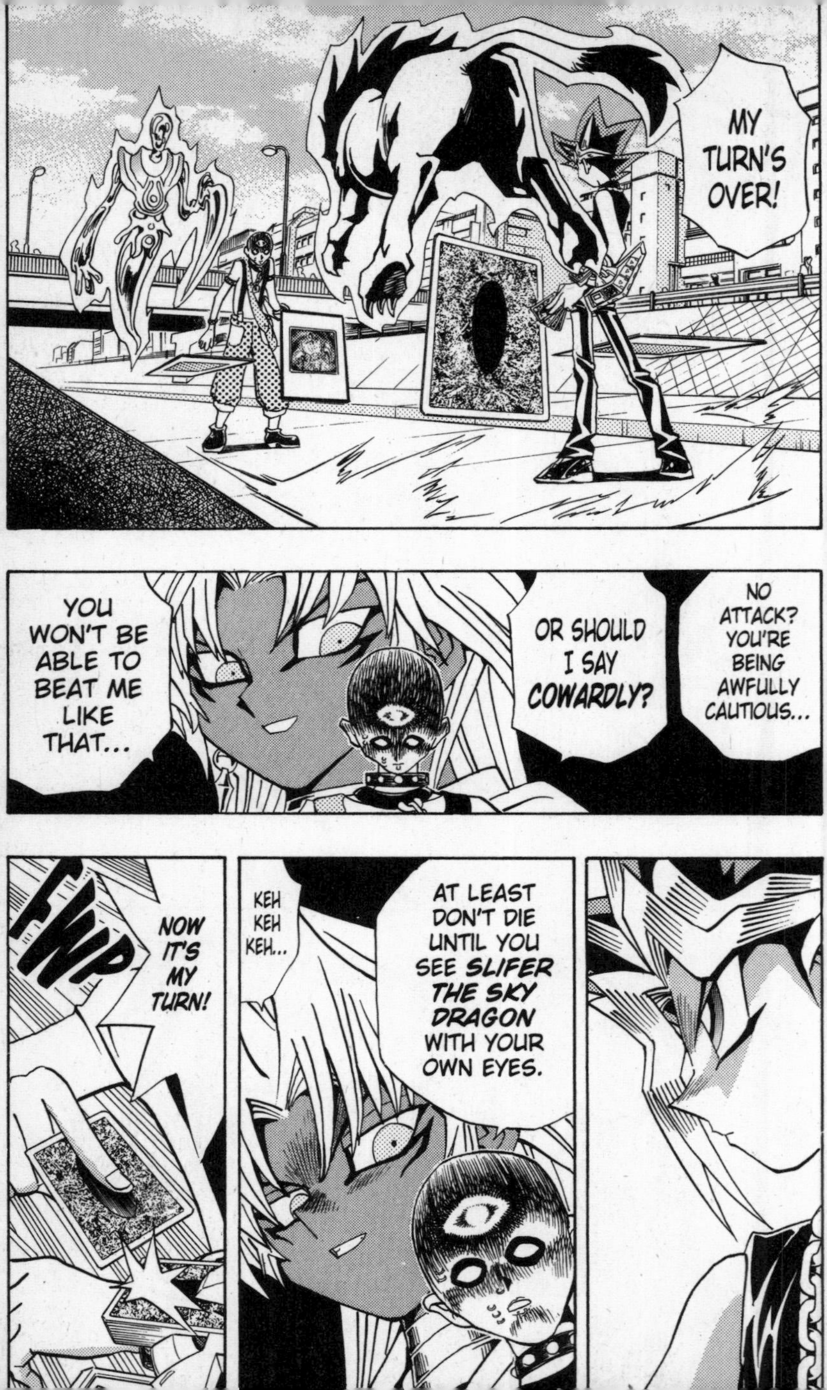
MY TURN'S OVER!
NO ATTACK? YOU'RE BEING AWFULLY CAUTIOUS...
OR SHOULD I SAY COWARDLY?
YOU WON'T BE ABLE TO BEAT ME LIKE THAT...
AT LEAST DON'T DIE UNTIL YOU SEE SLIFER THE SKY DRAGON WITH YOUR OWN EYES.
KEH KEH KEH...
NOW IT'S MY TURN!
FWIP

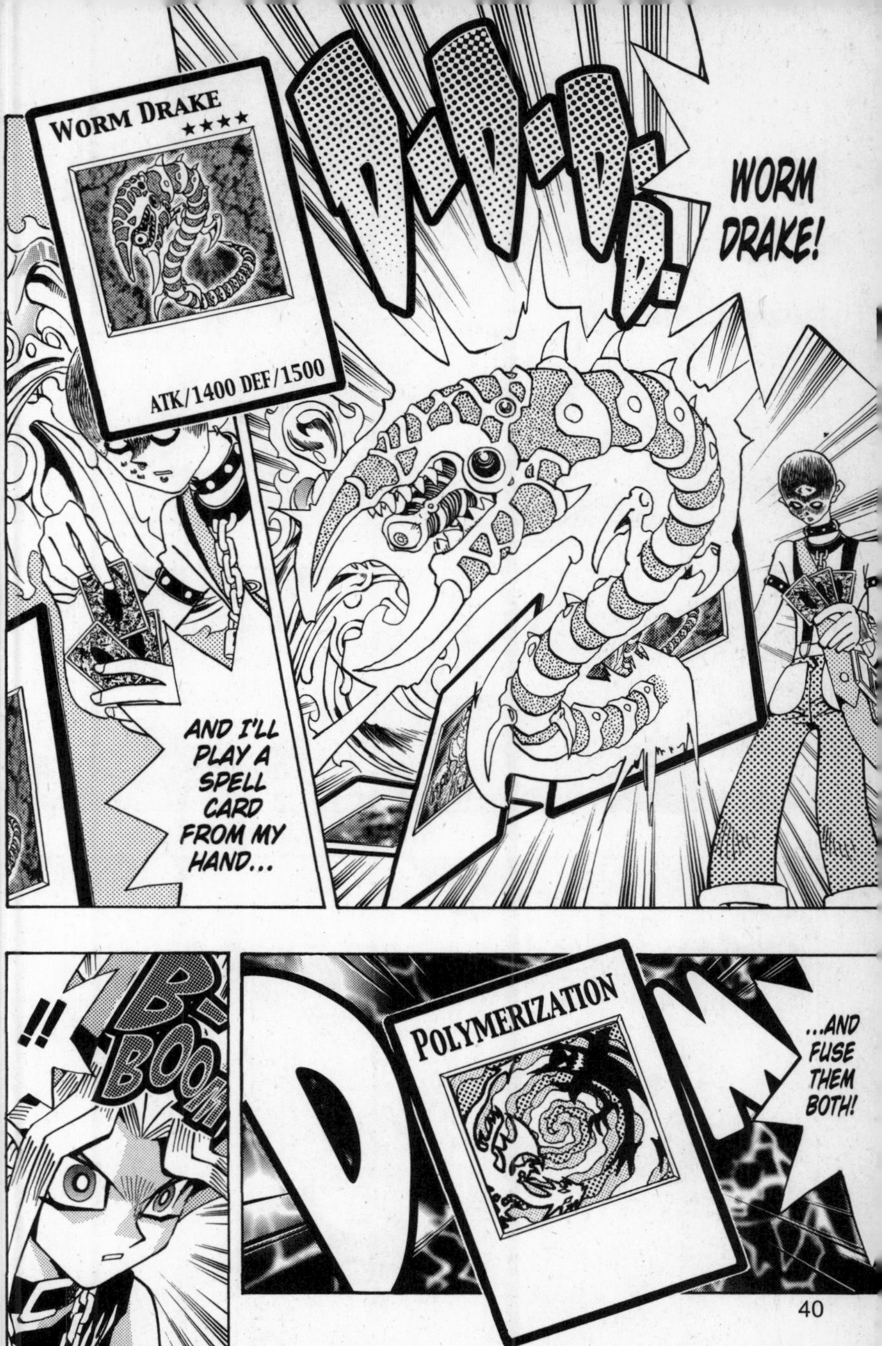
WORM DRAKE!
WORM DRAKE ★★★★
ATK/1400 DEF/1500
AND I'LL PLAY A SPELL CARD FROM MY HAND...
...AND FUSE THEM BOTH!
POLYMERIZATION
!!
B-BOOM

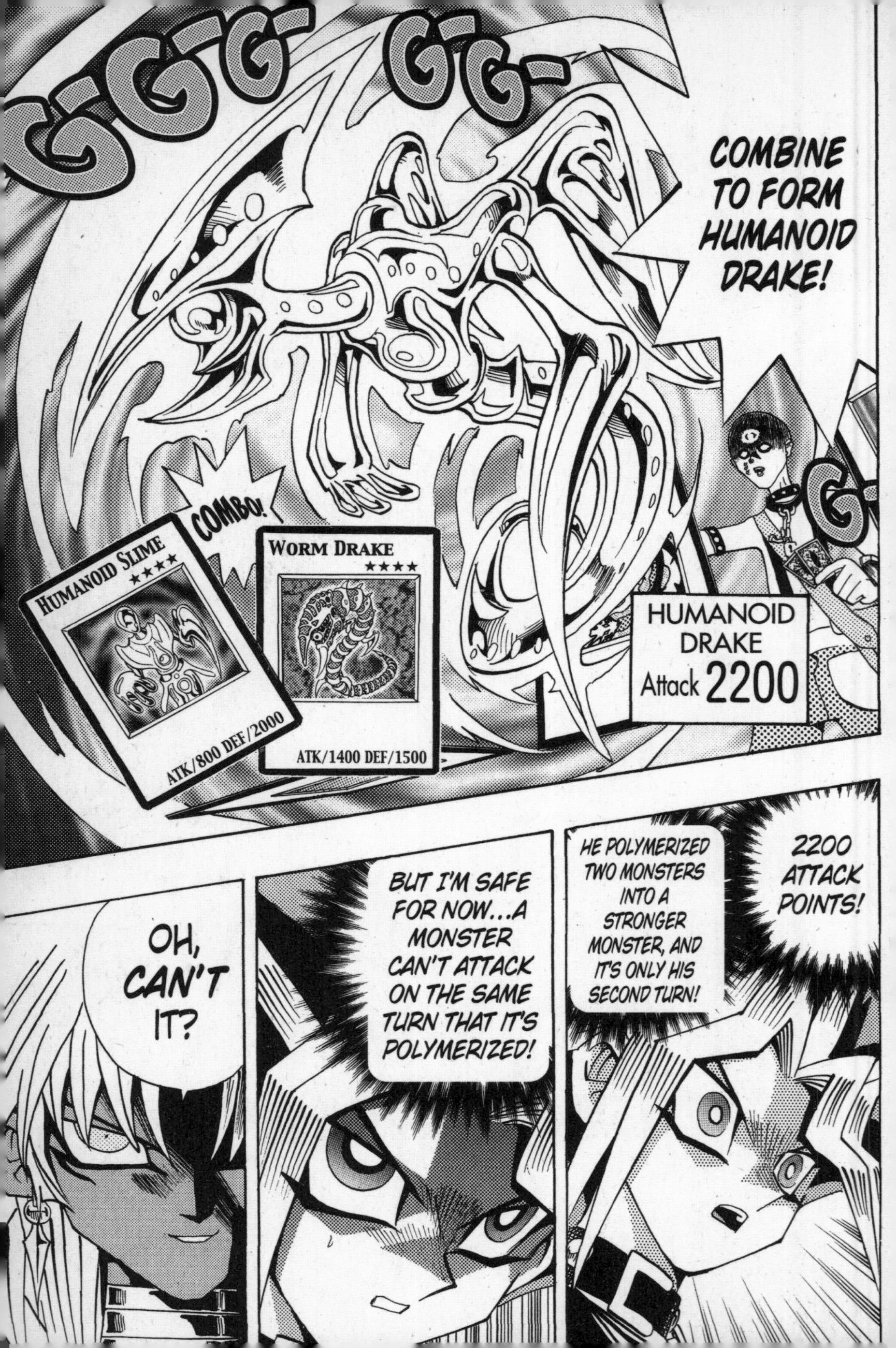
G-G-G- G-G-
COMBINE TO FORM HUMANOID DRAKE!
G-G
COMBO!
WORM DRAKE ★★★★ ATK/1400 DEF/1500
HUMANOID SLIME ★★★★ ATK/800 DEF/2000
HUMANOID DRAKE Attack 2200
2200 ATTACK POINTS!
HE POLYMERIZED TWO MONSTERS INTO A STRONGER MONSTER, AND IT'S ONLY HIS SECOND TURN!
BUT I'M SAFE FOR NOW...A MONSTER CAN'T ATTACK ON THE SAME TURN THAT IT'S POLYMERIZED!
OH, CAN'T IT?

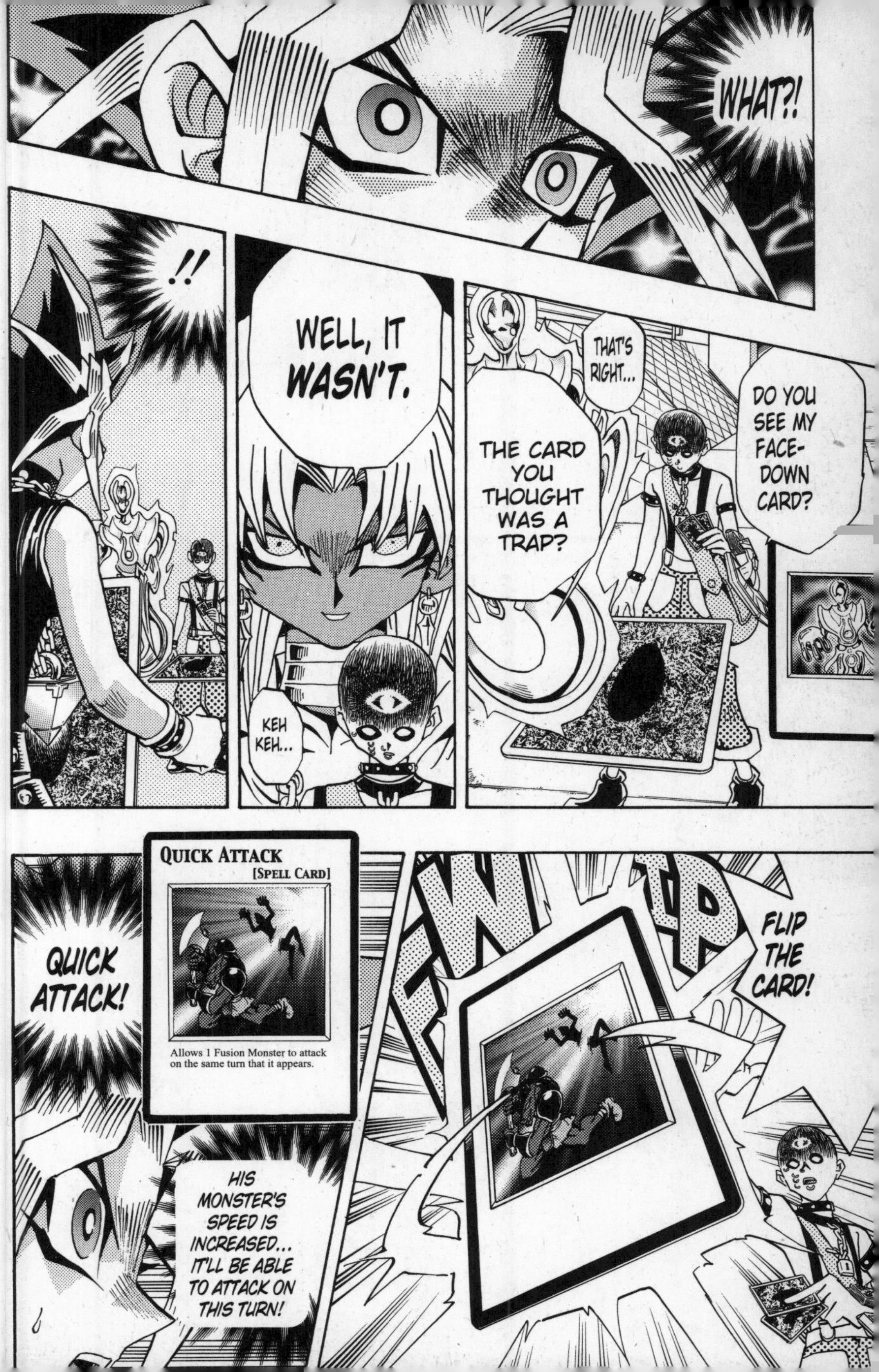
WHAT?!
DO YOU SEE MY FACE-DOWN CARD?
THAT'S RIGHT...
THE CARD YOU THOUGHT WAS A TRAP?
WELL, IT WASN'T.
KEH KEH...
!!
FLIP THE CARD!
QUICK ATTACK
[SPELL CARD]
Allows 1 Fusion Monster to attack on the same turn that it appears.
QUICK ATTACK!
HIS MONSTER'S SPEED IS INCREASED... IT'LL BE ABLE TO ATTACK ON THIS TURN!

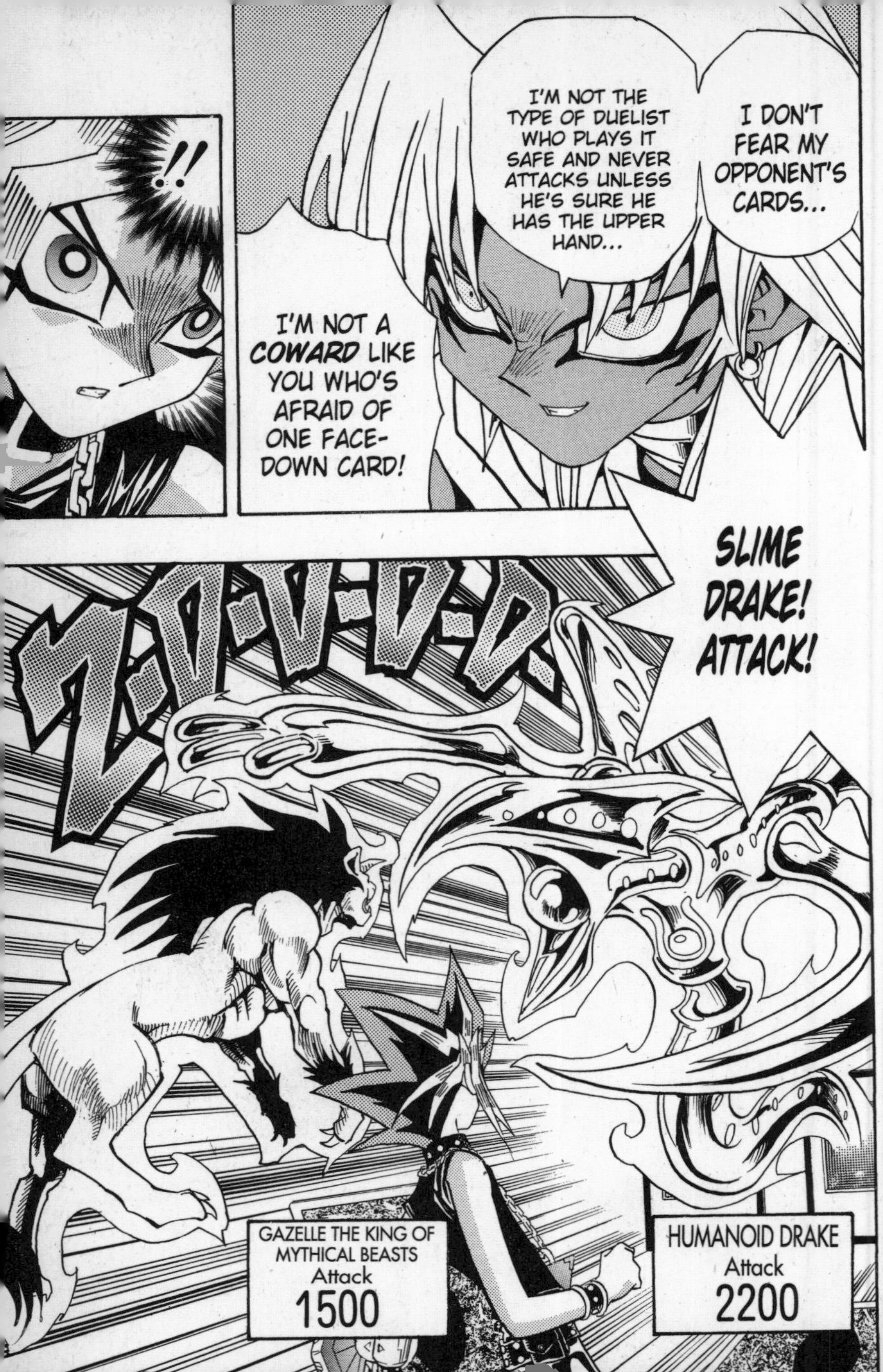
I DON'T FEAR MY OPPONENT'S CARDS...
I'M NOT THE TYPE OF DUELIST WHO PLAYS IT SAFE AND NEVER ATTACKS UNLESS HE'S SURE HE HAS THE UPPER HAND...
I'M NOT A COWARD LIKE YOU WHO'S AFRAID OF ONE FACE-DOWN CARD!
!!
SLIME DRAKE! ATTACK!
HUMANOID DRAKE Attack 2200
GAZELLE THE KING OF MYTHICAL BEASTS Attack 1500

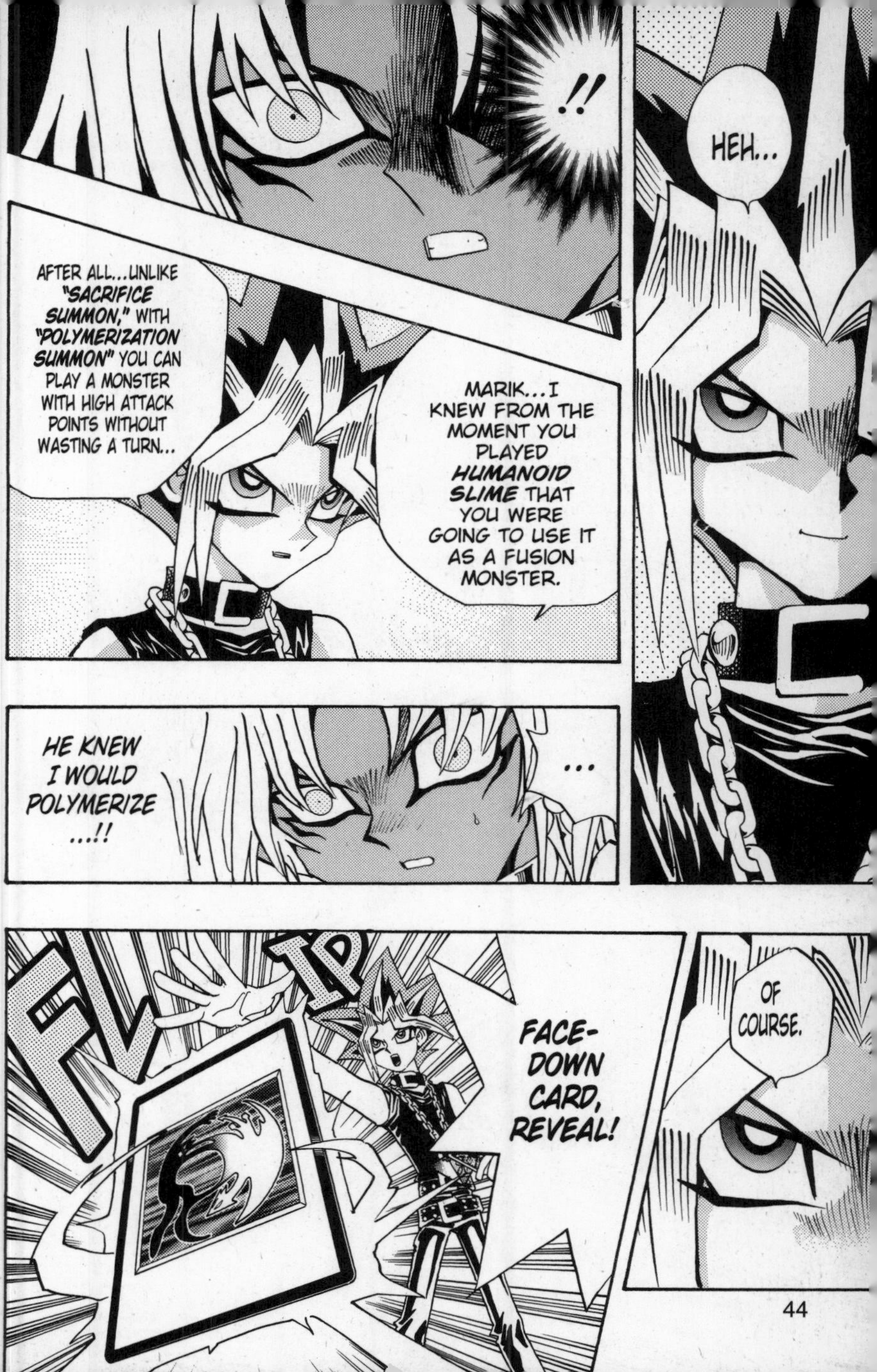
HEH...
!!
MARIK...I KNEW FROM THE MOMENT YOU PLAYED HUMANOID SLIME THAT YOU WERE GOING TO USE IT AS A FUSION MONSTER.
AFTER ALL...UNLIKE "SACRIFICE SUMMON," WITH "POLYMERIZATION SUMMON" YOU CAN PLAY A MONSTER WITH HIGH ATTACK POINTS WITHOUT WASTING A TURN...
...
HE KNEW I WOULD POLYMERIZE ...!!
OF COURSE.
FACE-DOWN CARD, REVEAL!
FLIP

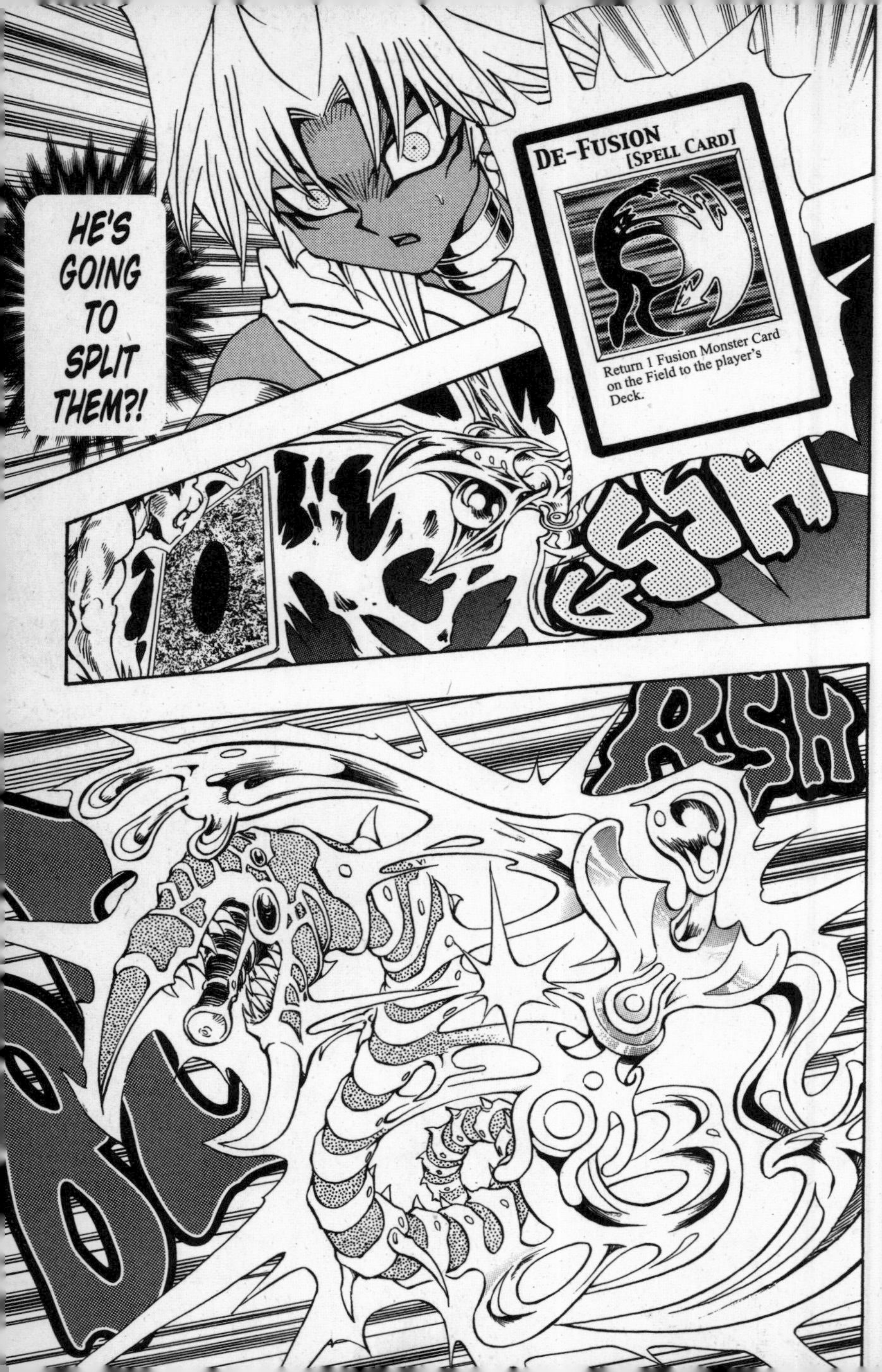
DE-FUSION
[SPELL CARD]
Return 1 Fusion Monster Card on the Field to the player's Deck.
HE'S GOING TO SPLIT THEM?!
GSSH
RSH

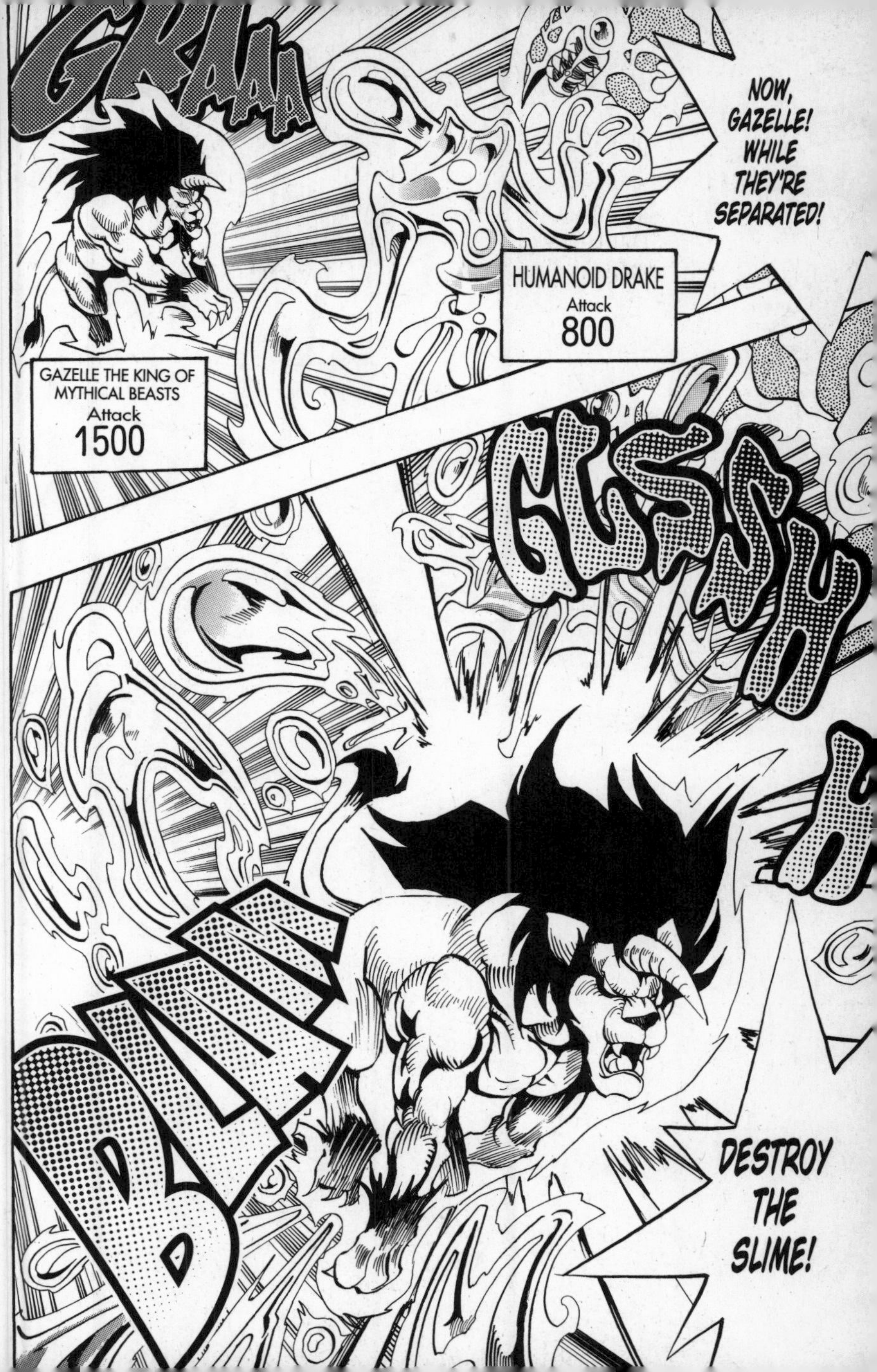
NOW, GAZELLE! WHILE THEY'RE SEPARATED!
HUMANOID DRAKE
Attack
800
GAZELLE THE KING OF MYTHICAL BEASTS
Attack
1500
GRAAA
DESTROY THE SLIME!

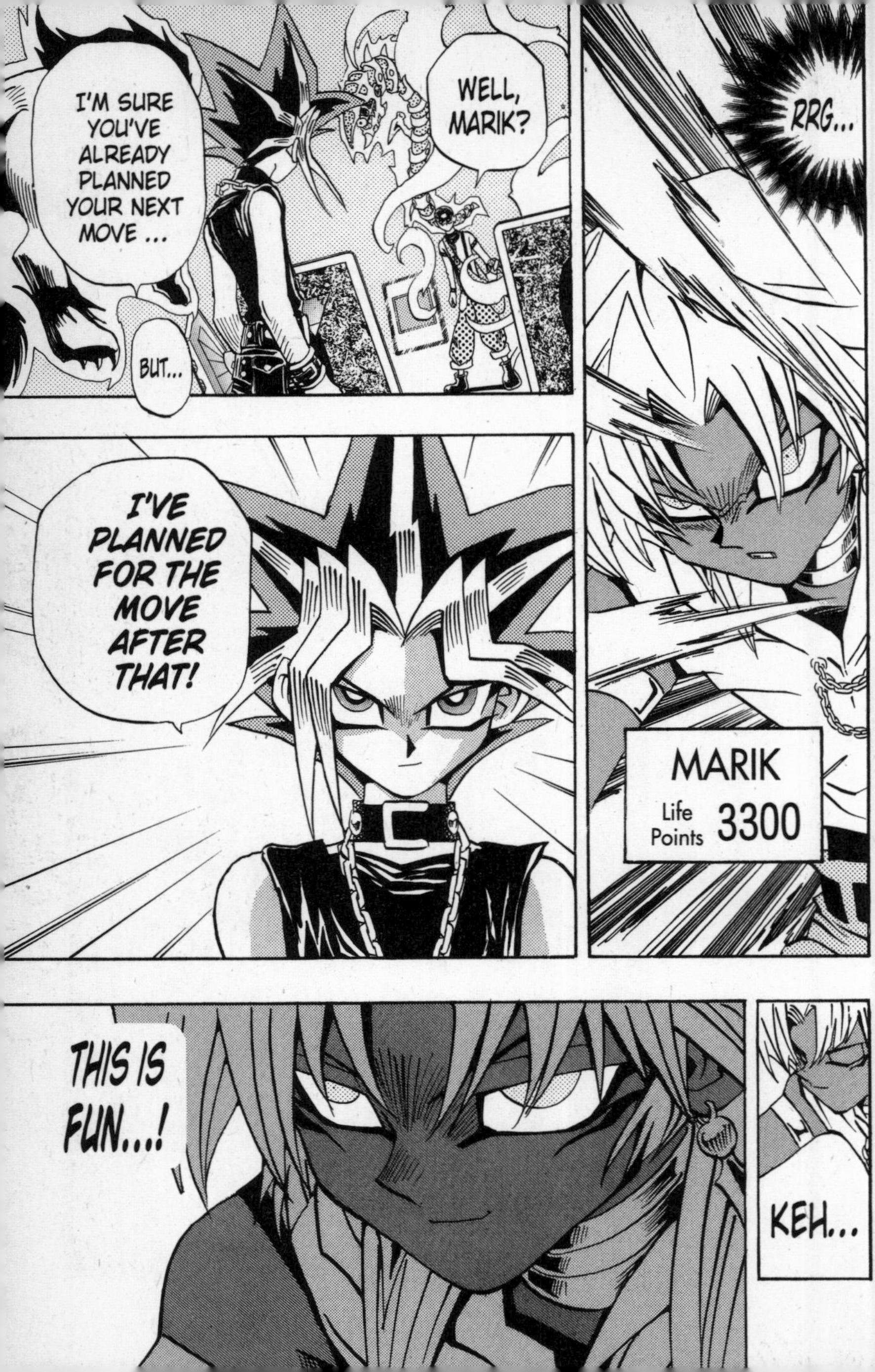
RRG...
MARIK
Life Points 3300
WELL, MARIK?
I'M SURE YOU'VE ALREADY PLANNED YOUR NEXT MOVE ...
BUT...
I'VE PLANNED FOR THE MOVE AFTER THAT!
KEH...
THIS IS FUN...!

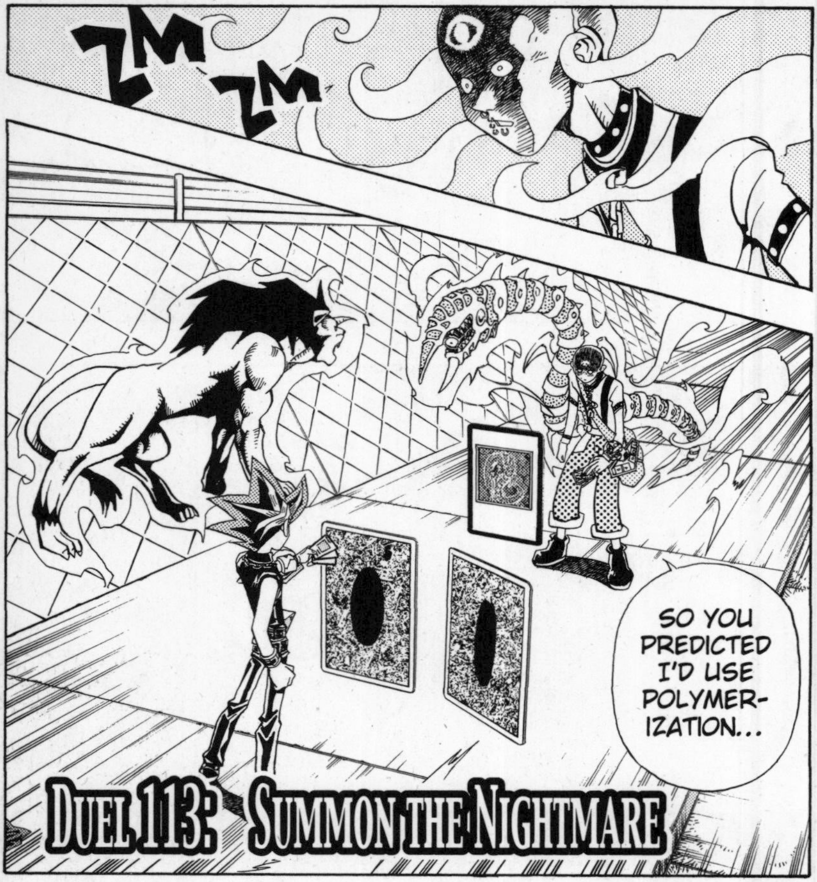
ZM ZM
SO YOU PREDICTED I'D USE POLYMER-IZATION...
DUEL 113: SUMMON THE NIGHTMARE

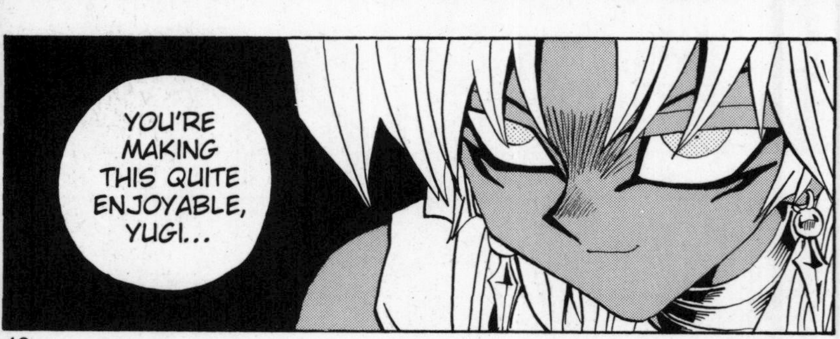
YOU'RE MAKING THIS QUITE ENJOYABLE, YUGI...

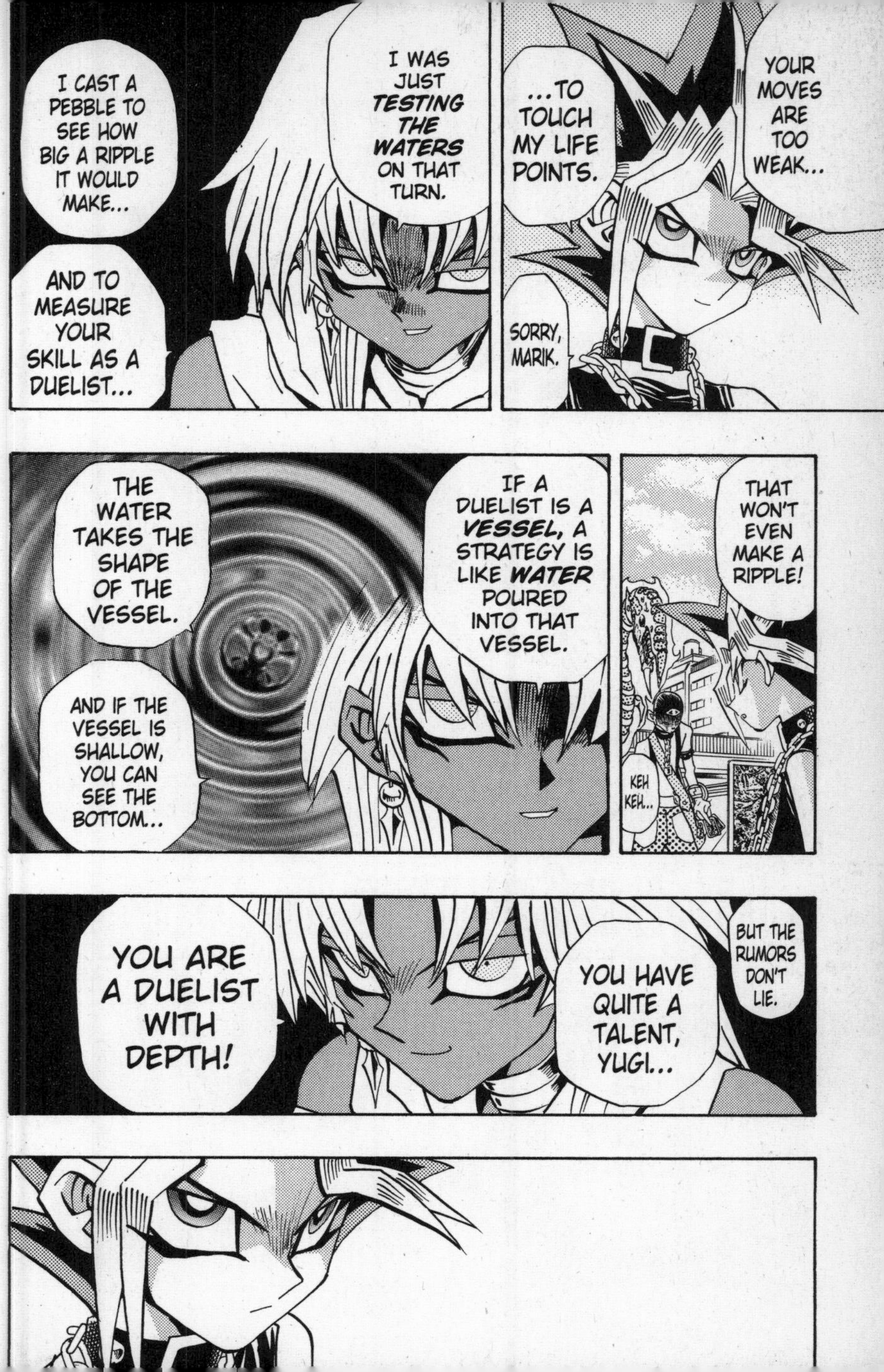
YOUR MOVES ARE TOO WEAK...
...TO TOUCH MY LIFE POINTS.
SORRY, MARIK.
I WAS JUST ***TESTING THE WATERS*** ON THAT TURN.
I CAST A PEBBLE TO SEE HOW BIG A RIPPLE IT WOULD MAKE...
AND TO MEASURE YOUR SKILL AS A DUELIST...
THAT WON'T EVEN MAKE A RIPPLE!
KEH KEH...
IF A DUELIST IS A ***VESSEL,*** A STRATEGY IS LIKE ***WATER*** POURED INTO THAT VESSEL.
THE WATER TAKES THE SHAPE OF THE VESSEL.
AND IF THE VESSEL IS SHALLOW, YOU CAN SEE THE BOTTOM...
BUT THE RUMORS DON'T LIE.
YOU HAVE QUITE A TALENT, YUGI...
YOU ARE A DUELIST WITH DEPTH!

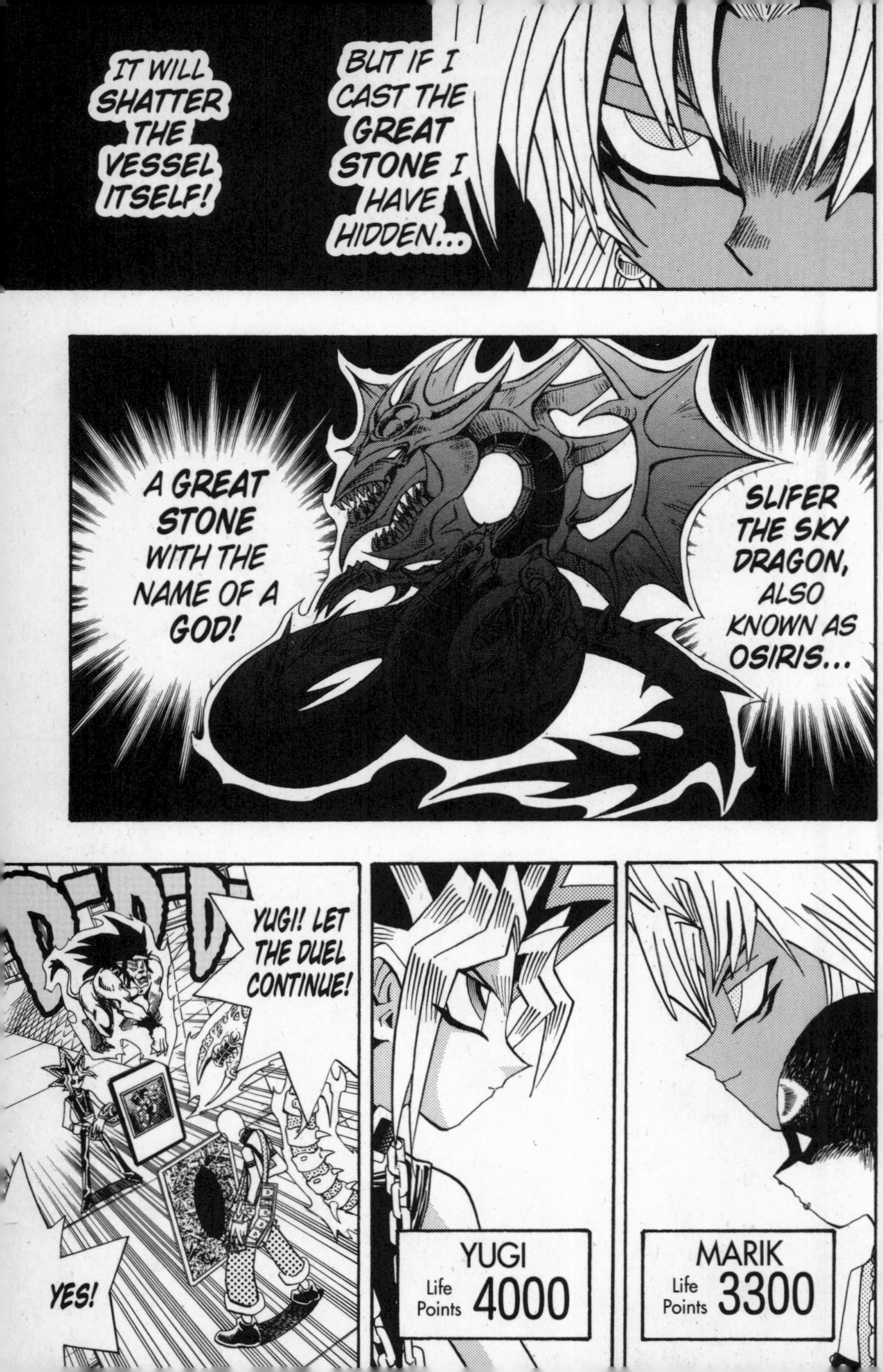
BUT IF I CAST THE GREAT STONE I HAVE HIDDEN...
IT WILL SHATTER THE VESSEL ITSELF!
SLIFER THE SKY DRAGON, ALSO KNOWN AS OSIRIS...
A GREAT STONE WITH THE NAME OF A GOD!
MARIK Life Points 3300
YUGI Life Points 4000
YUGI! LET THE DUEL CONTINUE!
YES!

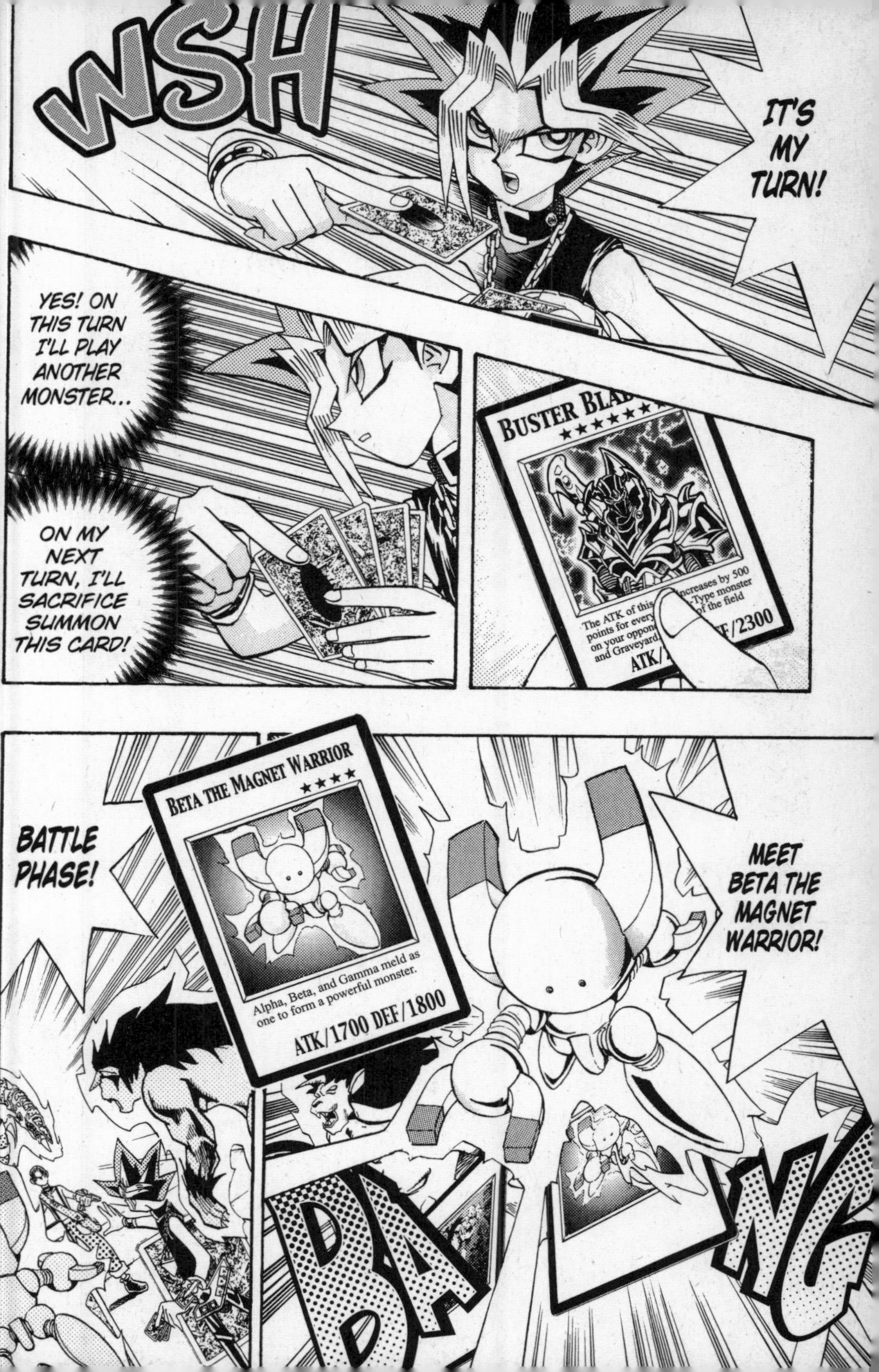
WSH
IT'S MY TURN!
YES! ON THIS TURN I'LL PLAY ANOTHER MONSTER...
ON MY NEXT TURN, I'LL SACRIFICE SUMMON THIS CARD!
MEET BETA THE MAGNET WARRIOR!
BETA THE MAGNET WARRIOR
Alpha, Beta, and Gamma meld as one to form a powerful monster.
ATK/1700 DEF/1800
BATTLE PHASE!
BANG

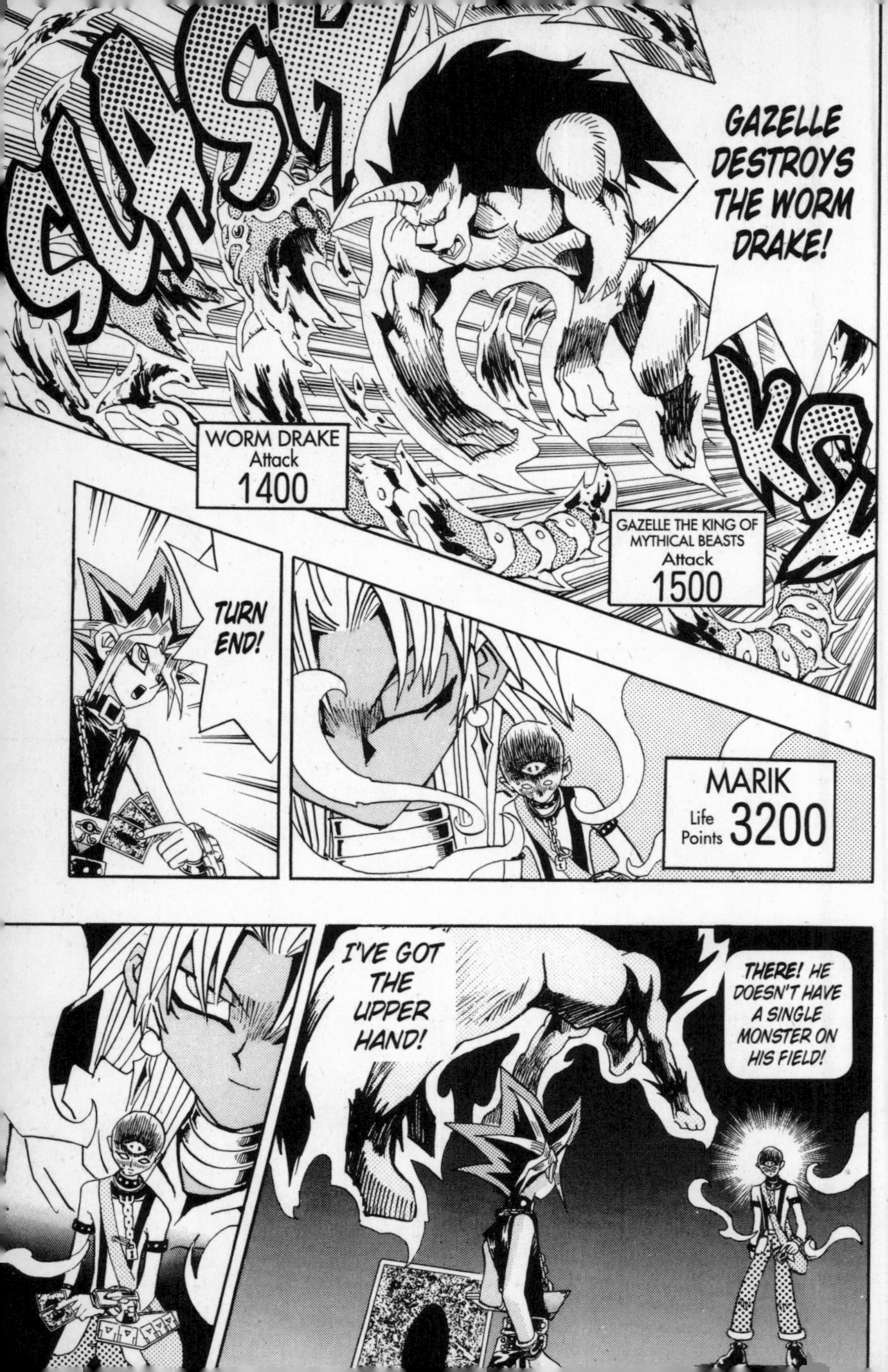
GAZELLE DESTROYS THE WORM DRAKE!
WORM DRAKE Attack 1400
GAZELLE THE KING OF MYTHICAL BEASTS Attack 1500
MARIK Life Points 3200
TURN END!
THERE! HE DOESN'T HAVE A SINGLE MONSTER ON HIS FIELD!
I'VE GOT THE UPPER HAND!

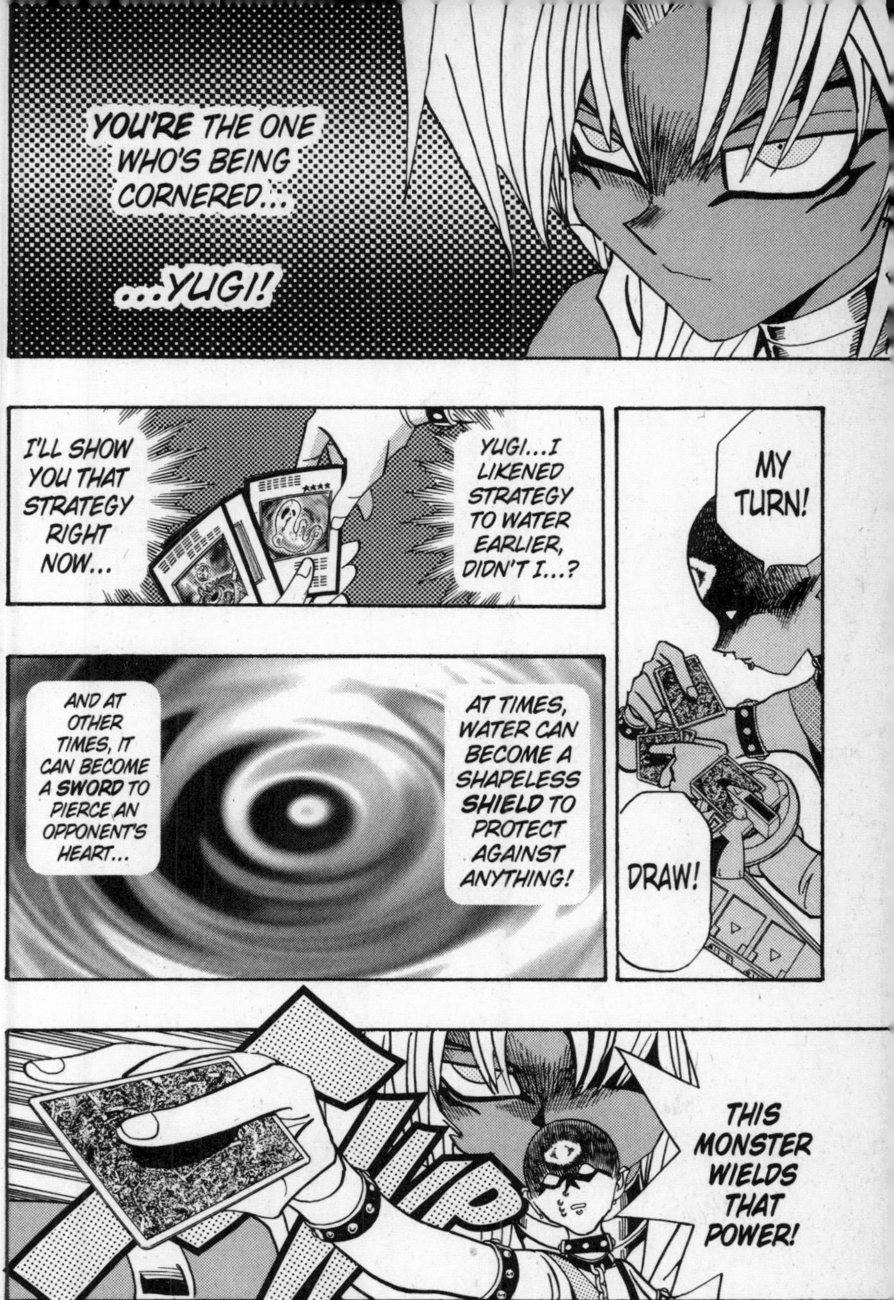
YOU'RE THE ONE WHO'S BEING CORNERED...
...YUGI!
MY TURN!
DRAW!
YUGI...I LIKENED STRATEGY TO WATER EARLIER, DIDN'T I...?
I'LL SHOW YOU THAT STRATEGY RIGHT NOW...
AT TIMES, WATER CAN BECOME A SHAPELESS SHIELD TO PROTECT AGAINST ANYTHING!
AND AT OTHER TIMES, IT CAN BECOME A SWORD TO PIERCE AN OPPONENT'S HEART...
THIS MONSTER WIELDS THAT POWER!

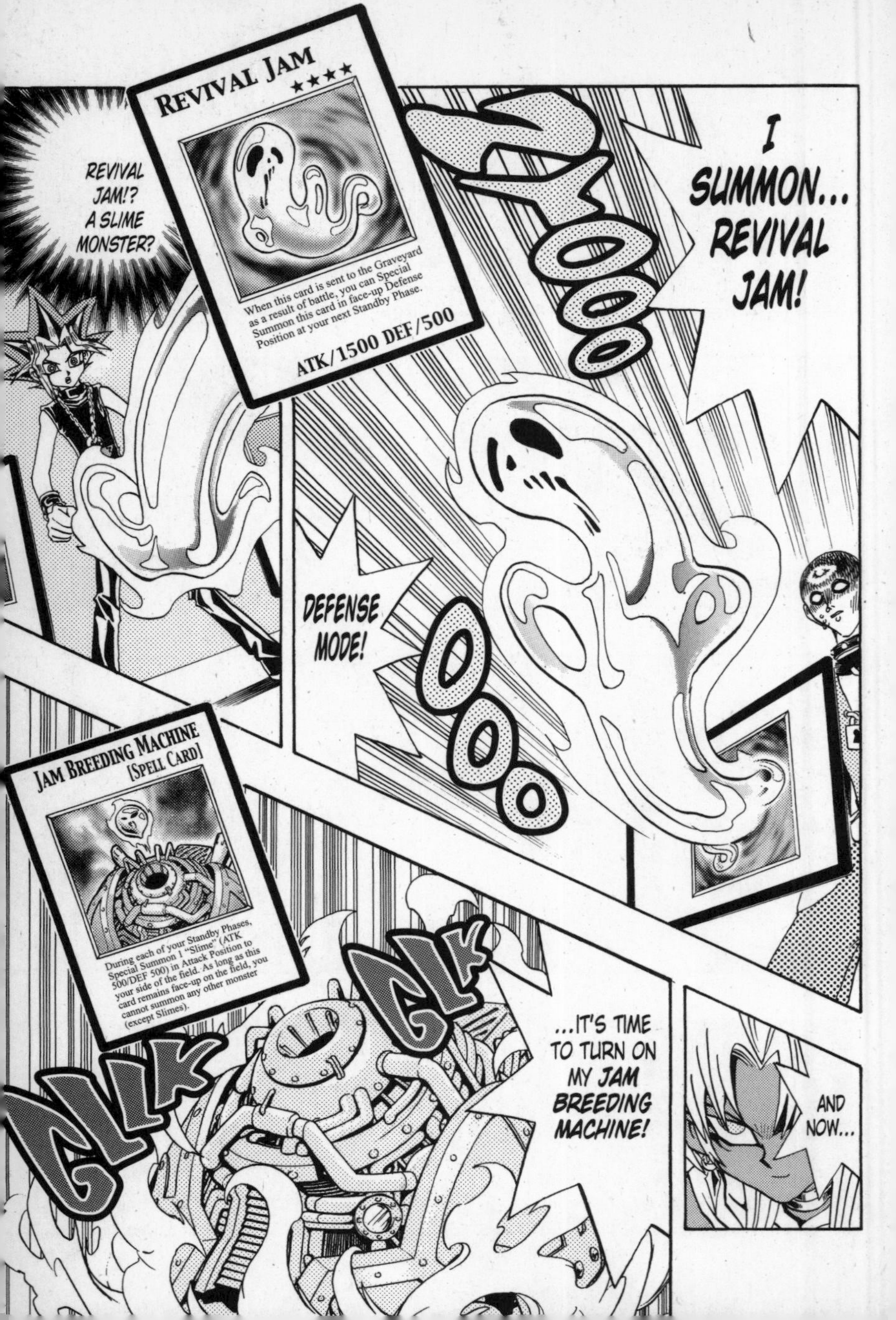
I SUMMON... REVIVAL JAM!
ZOOOO
REVIVAL JAM ★★★★
When this card is sent to the Graveyard as a result of battle, you can Special Summon this card in face-up Defense Position at your next Standby Phase.
ATK/1500 DEF/500
REVIVAL JAM!? A SLIME MONSTER?
OOOOO
DEFENSE MODE!
AND NOW...
...IT'S TIME TO TURN ON MY JAM BREEDING MACHINE!
JAM BREEDING MACHINE
[SPELL CARD]
During each of your Standby Phases, Special Summon 1 "Slime" (ATK 500/DEF 500) in Attack Position to your side of the field. As long as this card remains face-up on the field, you cannot summon any other monster (except Slimes).
CLIK
CLIK

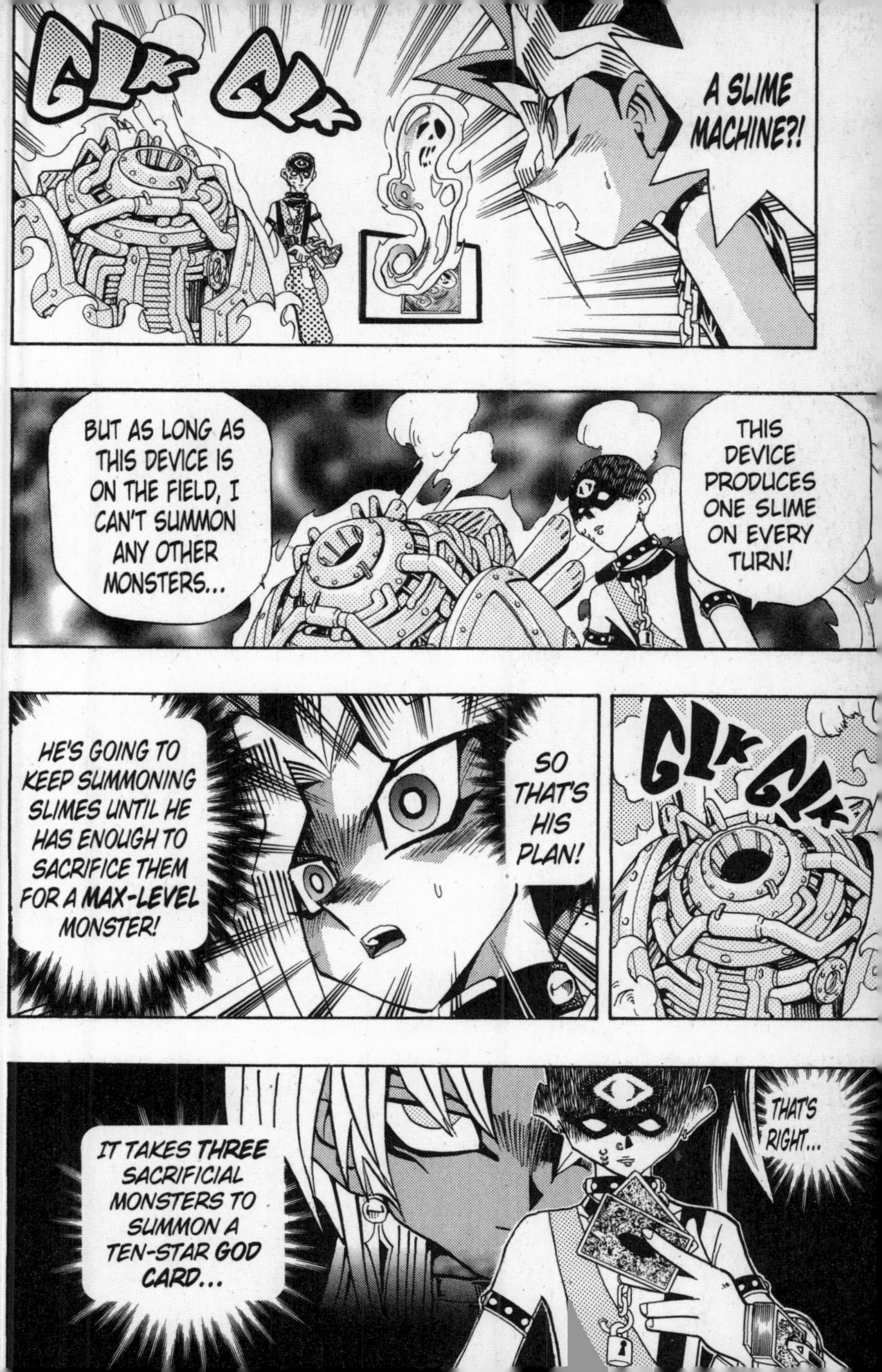
A SLIME MACHINE?!
GLK GLK
THIS DEVICE PRODUCES ONE SLIME ON EVERY TURN!
BUT AS LONG AS THIS DEVICE IS ON THE FIELD, I CAN'T SUMMON ANY OTHER MONSTERS...
GLK GLK
SO THAT'S HIS PLAN!
HE'S GOING TO KEEP SUMMONING SLIMES UNTIL HE HAS ENOUGH TO SACRIFICE THEM FOR A MAX-LEVEL MONSTER!
THAT'S RIGHT...
IT TAKES THREE SACRIFICIAL MONSTERS TO SUMMON A TEN-STAR GOD CARD...

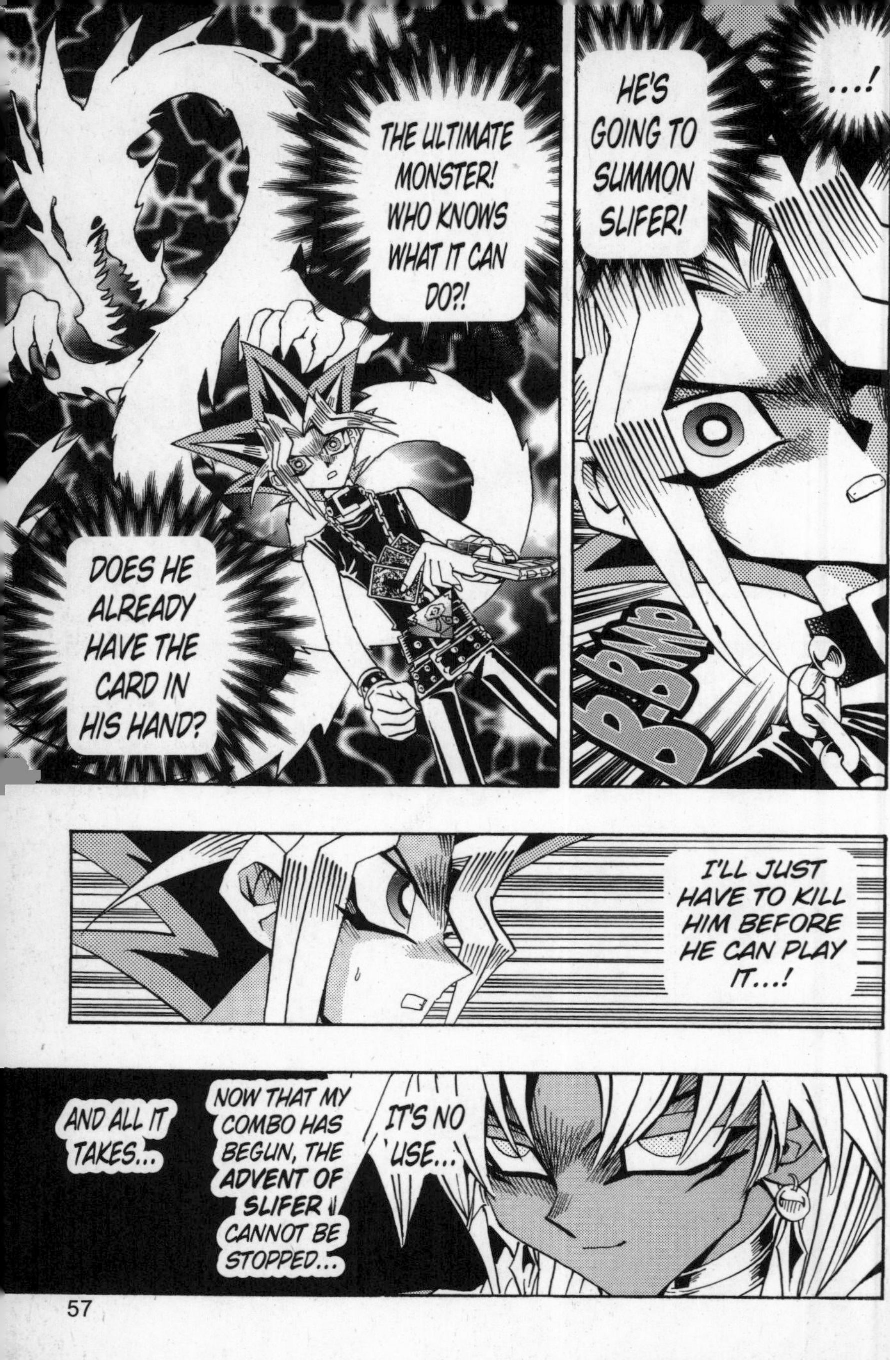
...!
HE'S GOING TO SUMMON SLIFER!
B-BMP
THE ULTIMATE MONSTER! WHO KNOWS WHAT IT CAN DO?!
DOES HE ALREADY HAVE THE CARD IN HIS HAND?
I'LL JUST HAVE TO KILL HIM BEFORE HE CAN PLAY IT...!
IT'S NO USE...
NOW THAT MY COMBO HAS BEGUN, THE ADVENT OF SLIFER CANNOT BE STOPPED...
AND ALL IT TAKES...

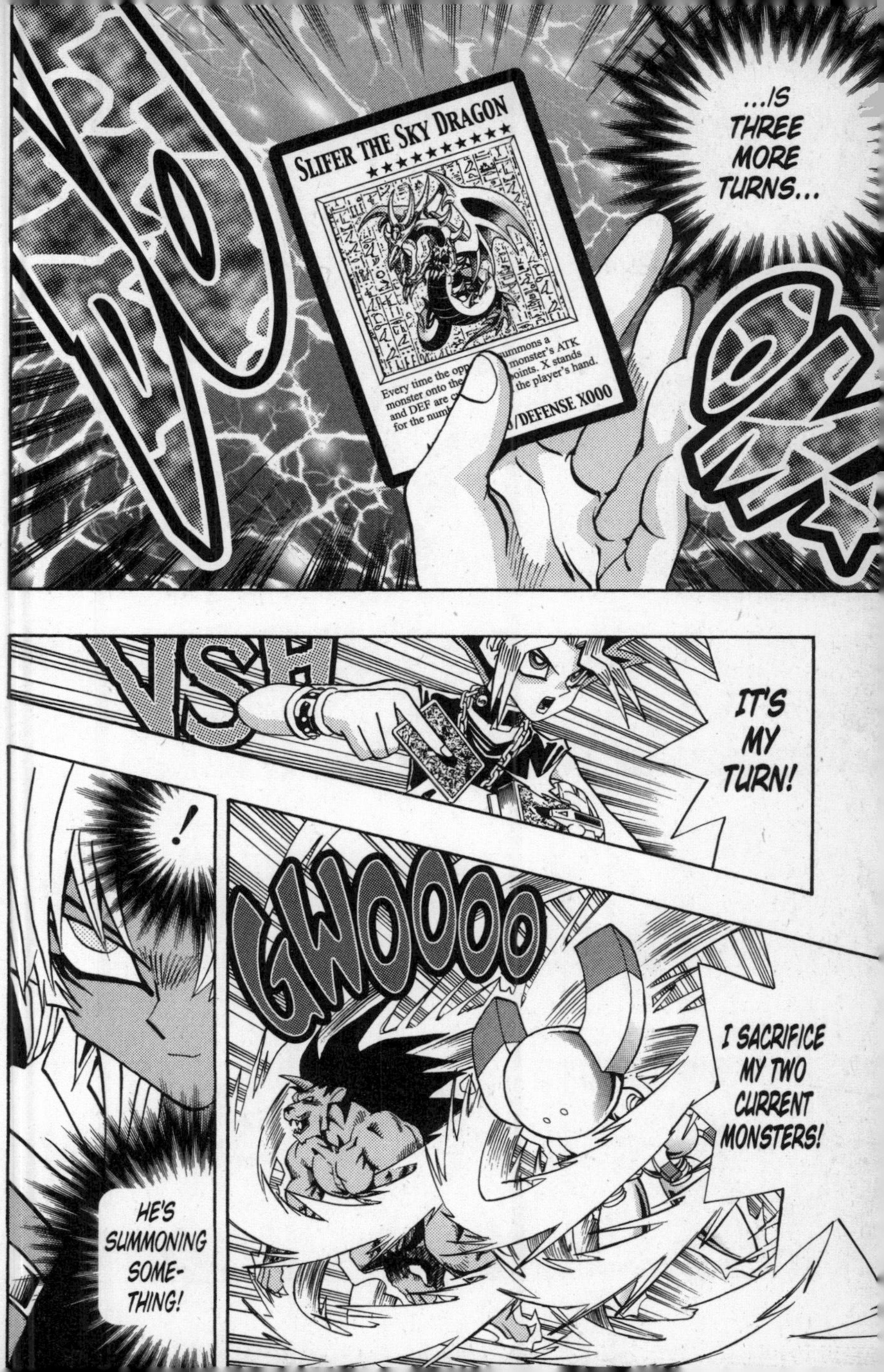
...IS THREE MORE TURNS...
SLIFER THE SKY DRAGON
IT'S MY TURN!
I SACRIFICE MY TWO CURRENT MONSTERS!
GWOOOO
!
HE'S SUMMONING SOME-THING!

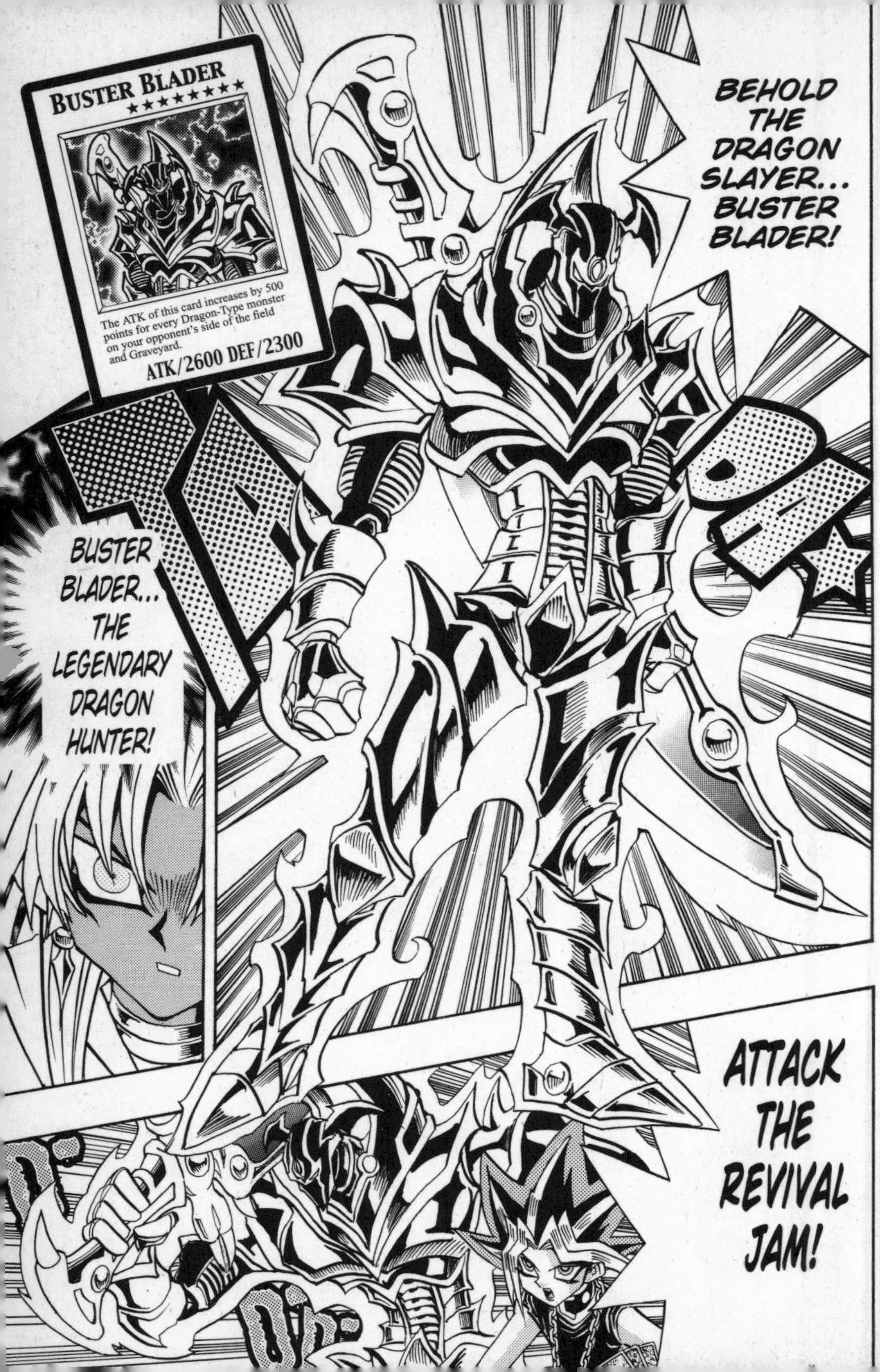
BEHOLD THE DRAGON SLAYER... BUSTER BLADER!
BUSTER BLADER
The ATK of this card increases by 500 points for every Dragon-Type monster on your opponent's side of the field and Graveyard.
ATK/2600 DEF/2300
BUSTER BLADER... THE LEGENDARY DRAGON HUNTER!
ATTACK THE REVIVAL JAM!

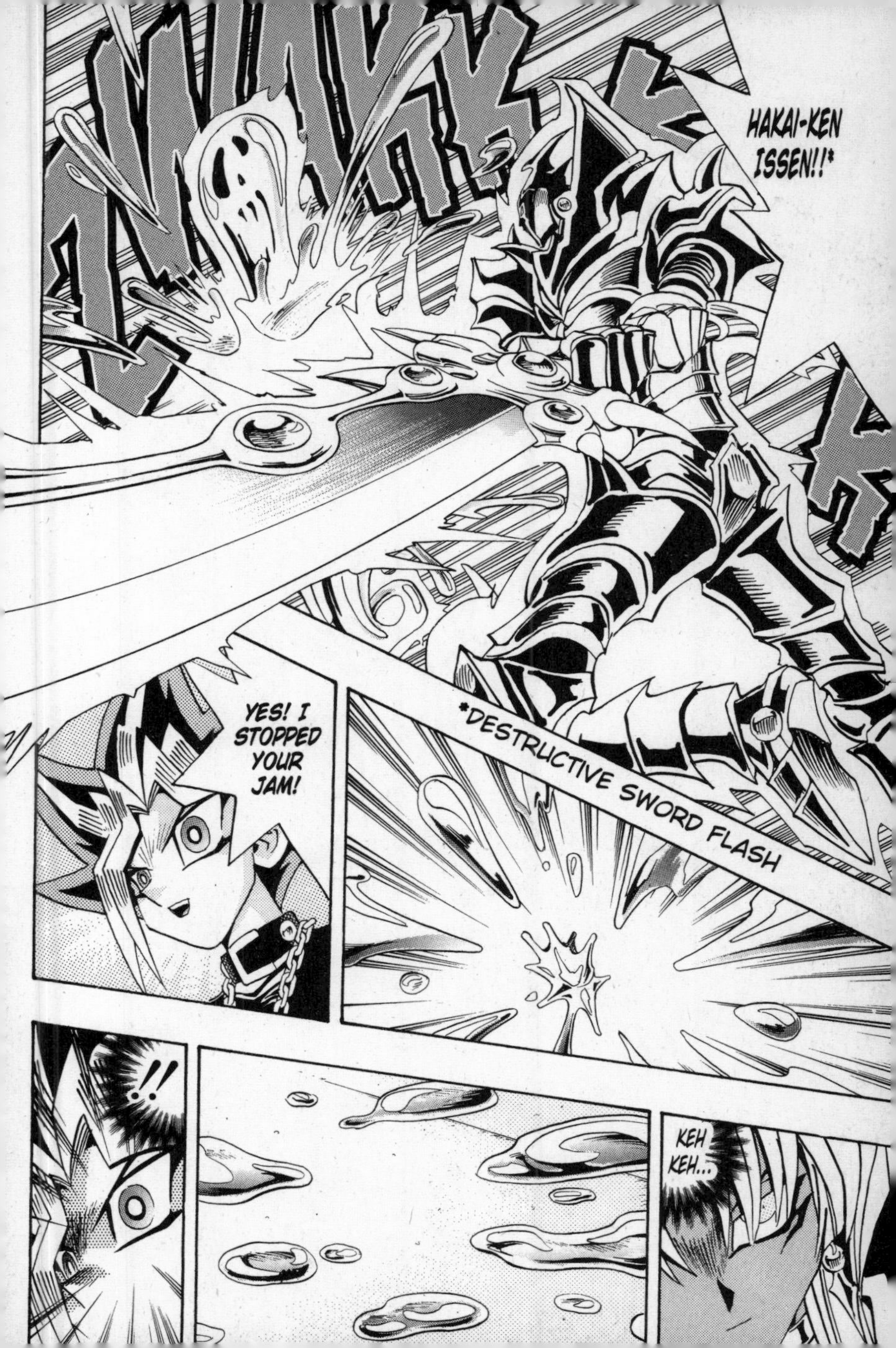
HAKAI-KEN ISSEN!!*
*DESTRUCTIVE SWORD FLASH
YES! I STOPPED YOUR JAM!
KEH KEH...
!!

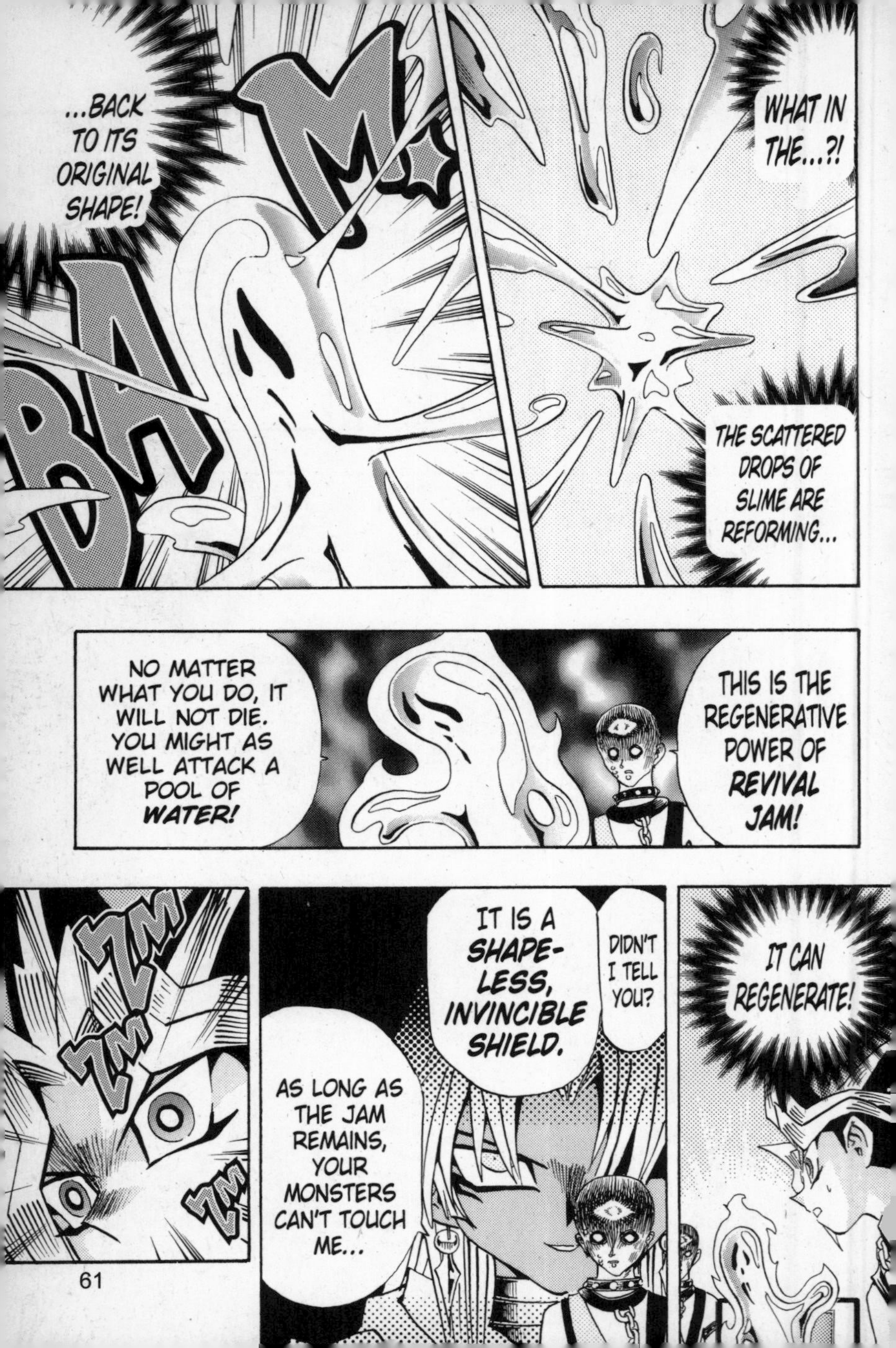
WHAT IN THE...?!
THE SCATTERED DROPS OF SLIME ARE REFORMING...
...BACK TO ITS ORIGINAL SHAPE!
THIS IS THE REGENERATIVE POWER OF REVIVAL JAM!
NO MATTER WHAT YOU DO, IT WILL NOT DIE. YOU MIGHT AS WELL ATTACK A POOL OF WATER!
IT CAN REGENERATE!
DIDN'T I TELL YOU?
IT IS A SHAPE-LESS, INVINCIBLE SHIELD.
AS LONG AS THE JAM REMAINS, YOUR MONSTERS CAN'T TOUCH ME...
ZM ZM
ZM
ZM

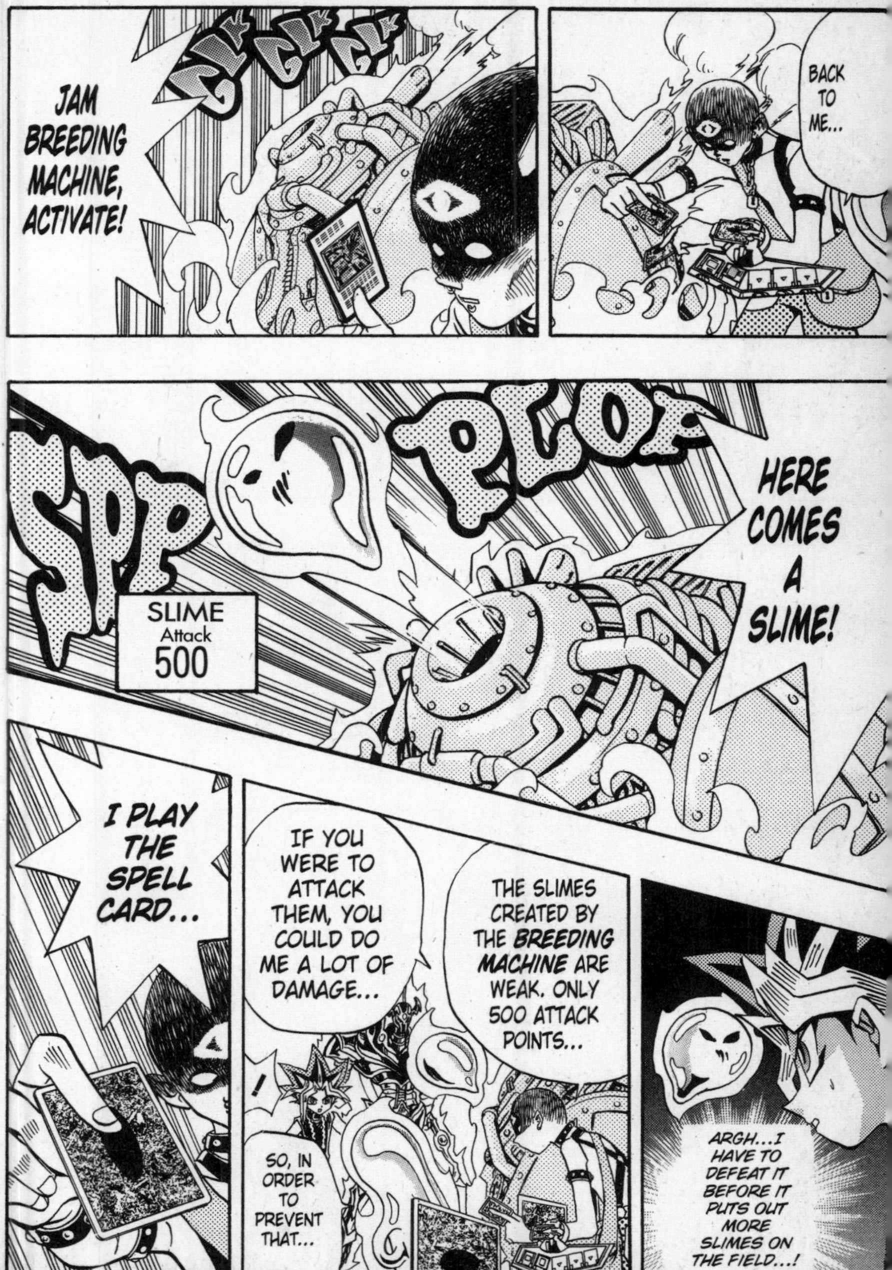
BACK TO ME...
GIK GIK
JAM BREEDING MACHINE, ACTIVATE!
HERE COMES A SLIME!
PLOP
SPP
SLIME Attack 500
ARGH...I HAVE TO DEFEAT IT BEFORE IT PUTS OUT MORE SLIMES ON THE FIELD...!
THE SLIMES CREATED BY THE BREEDING MACHINE ARE WEAK. ONLY 500 ATTACK POINTS...
IF YOU WERE TO ATTACK THEM, YOU COULD DO ME A LOT OF DAMAGE...
!
SO, IN ORDER TO PREVENT THAT...
I PLAY THE SPELL CARD...

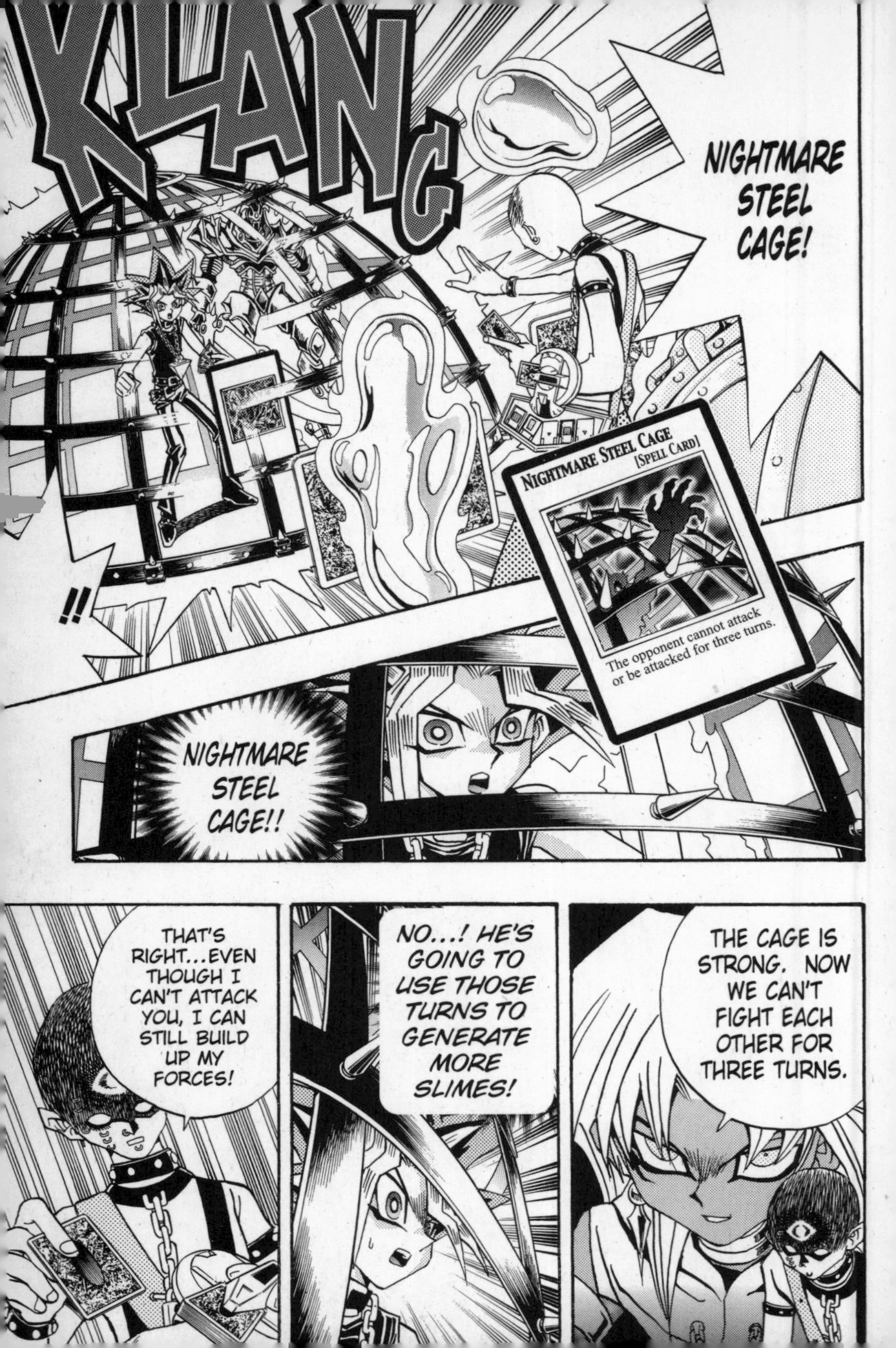

NIGHTMARE STEEL CAGE!
KLANG
NIGHTMARE STEEL CAGE [SPELL CARD]
The opponent cannot attack or be attacked for three turns.
!!
NIGHTMARE STEEL CAGE!!
THE CAGE IS STRONG. NOW WE CAN'T FIGHT EACH OTHER FOR THREE TURNS.
NO...! HE'S GOING TO USE THOSE TURNS TO GENERATE MORE SLIMES!
THAT'S RIGHT...EVEN THOUGH I CAN'T ATTACK YOU, I CAN STILL BUILD UP MY FORCES!

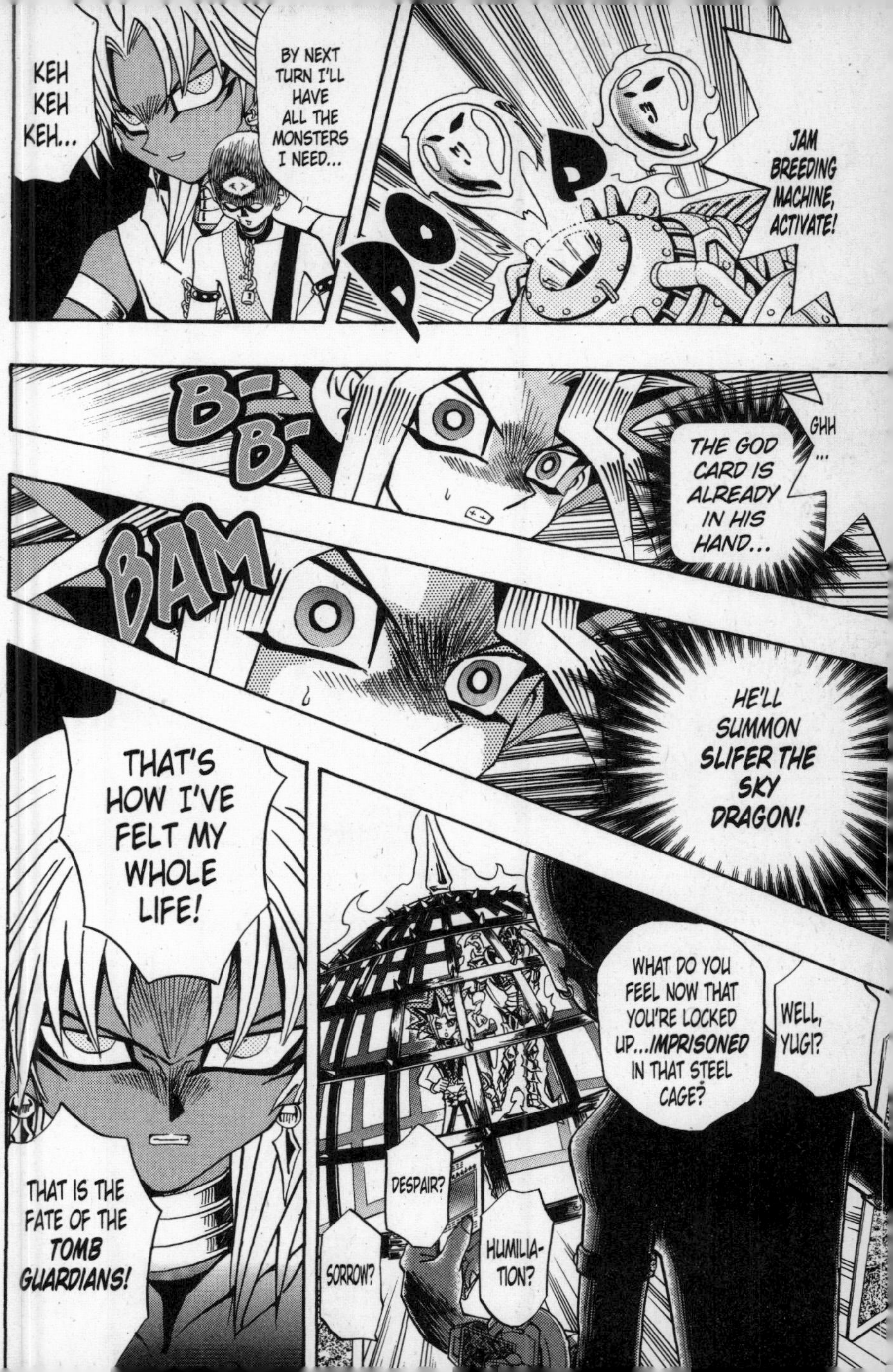
JAM BREEDING MACHINE, ACTIVATE!
BY NEXT TURN I'LL HAVE ALL THE MONSTERS I NEED...
KEH KEH KEH...
GHH...
THE GOD CARD IS ALREADY IN HIS HAND...
B- B-
BAM
HE'LL SUMMON SLIFER THE SKY DRAGON!
WELL, YUGI?
WHAT DO YOU FEEL NOW THAT YOU'RE LOCKED UP...IMPRISONED IN THAT STEEL CAGE?
DESPAIR?
HUMILIATION?
SORROW?
THAT'S HOW I'VE FELT MY WHOLE LIFE!
THAT IS THE FATE OF THE TOMB GUARDIANS!

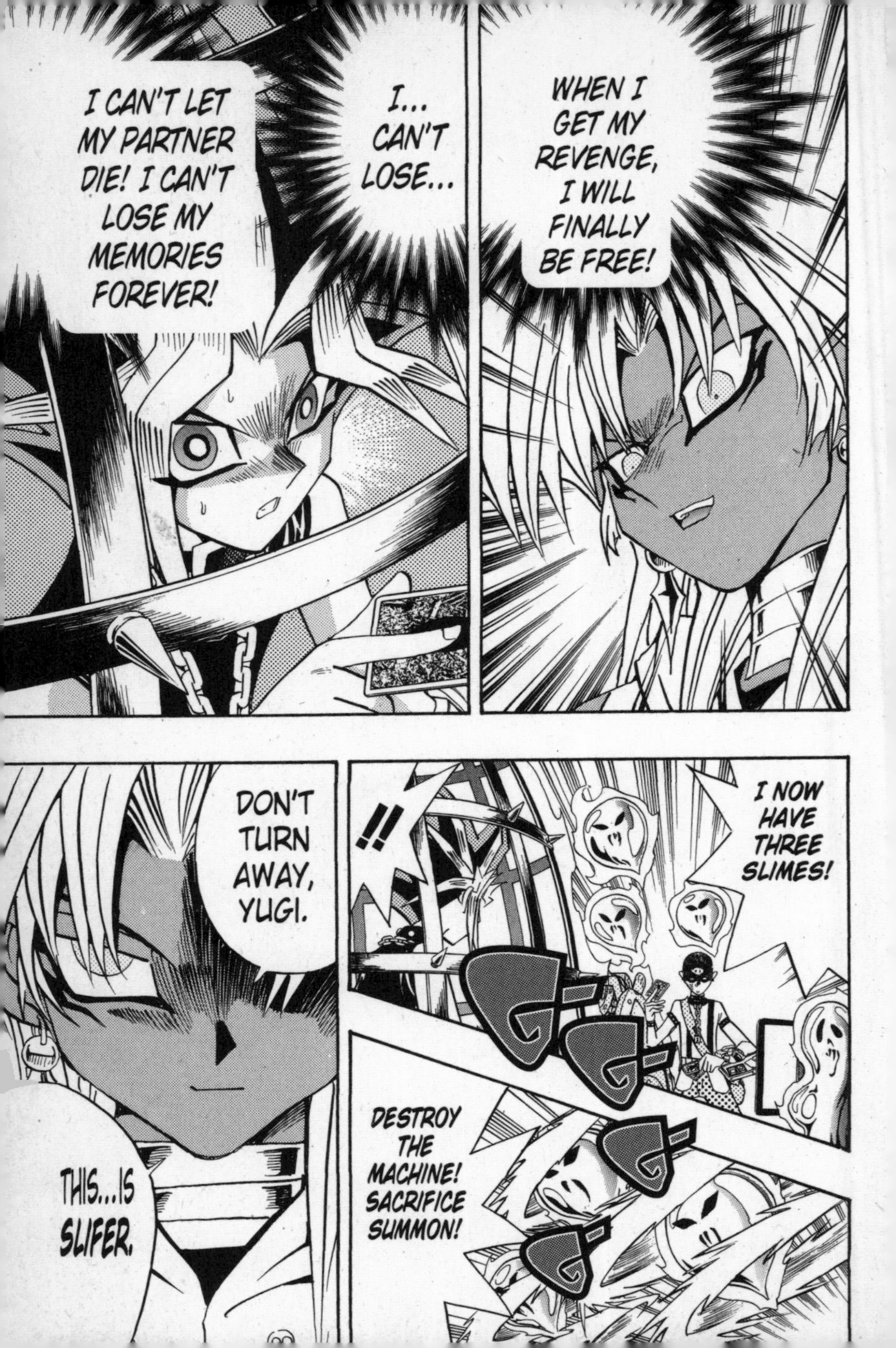
WHEN I GET MY REVENGE, I WILL FINALLY BE FREE!
I... CAN'T LOSE...
I CAN'T LET MY PARTNER DIE! I CAN'T LOSE MY MEMORIES FOREVER!
I NOW HAVE THREE SLIMES!
!!
DESTROY THE MACHINE! SACRIFICE SUMMON!
DON'T TURN AWAY, YUGI.
THIS...IS SLIFER.

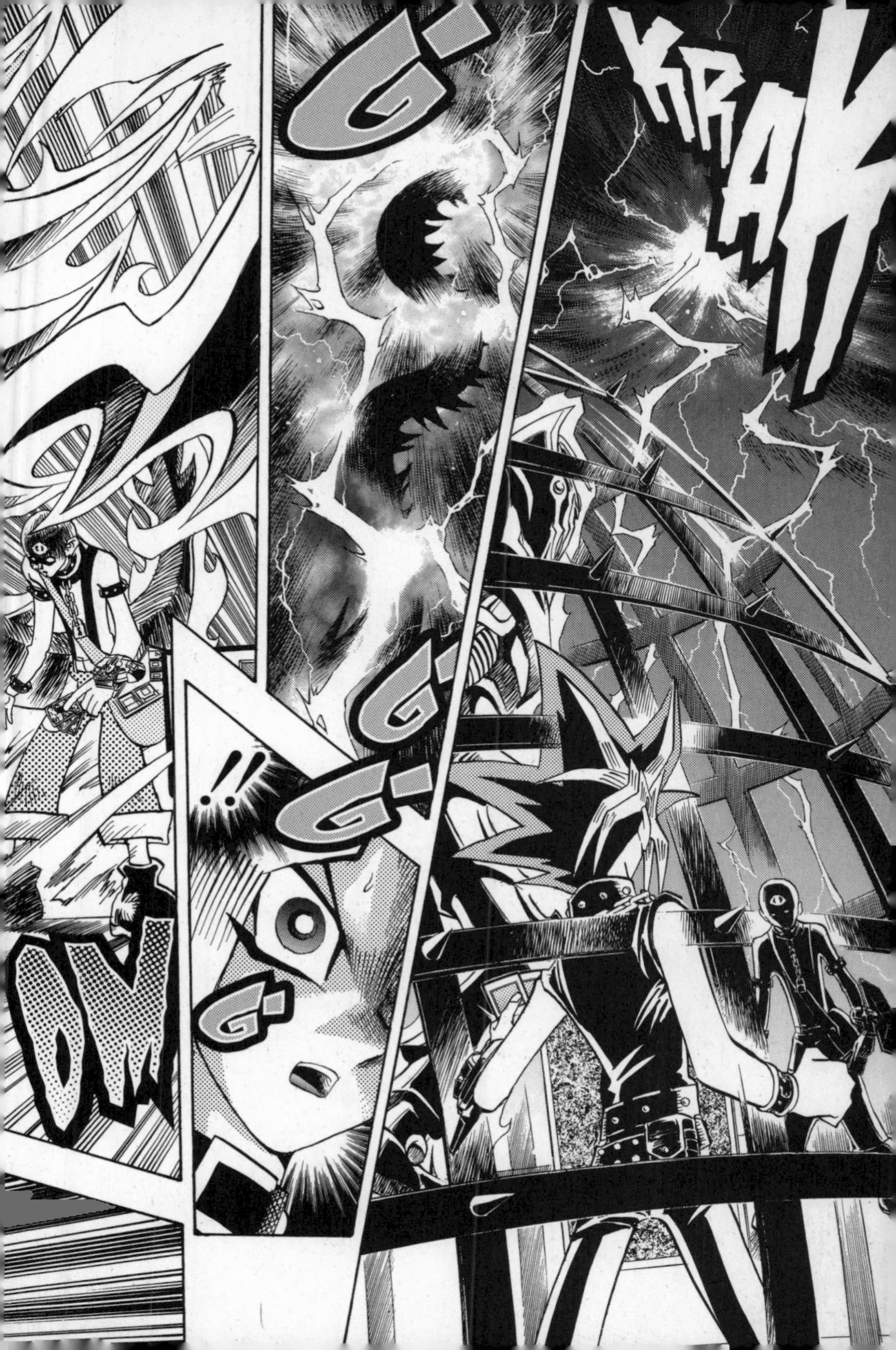

KRAK
G
G
G
!!
G
OM

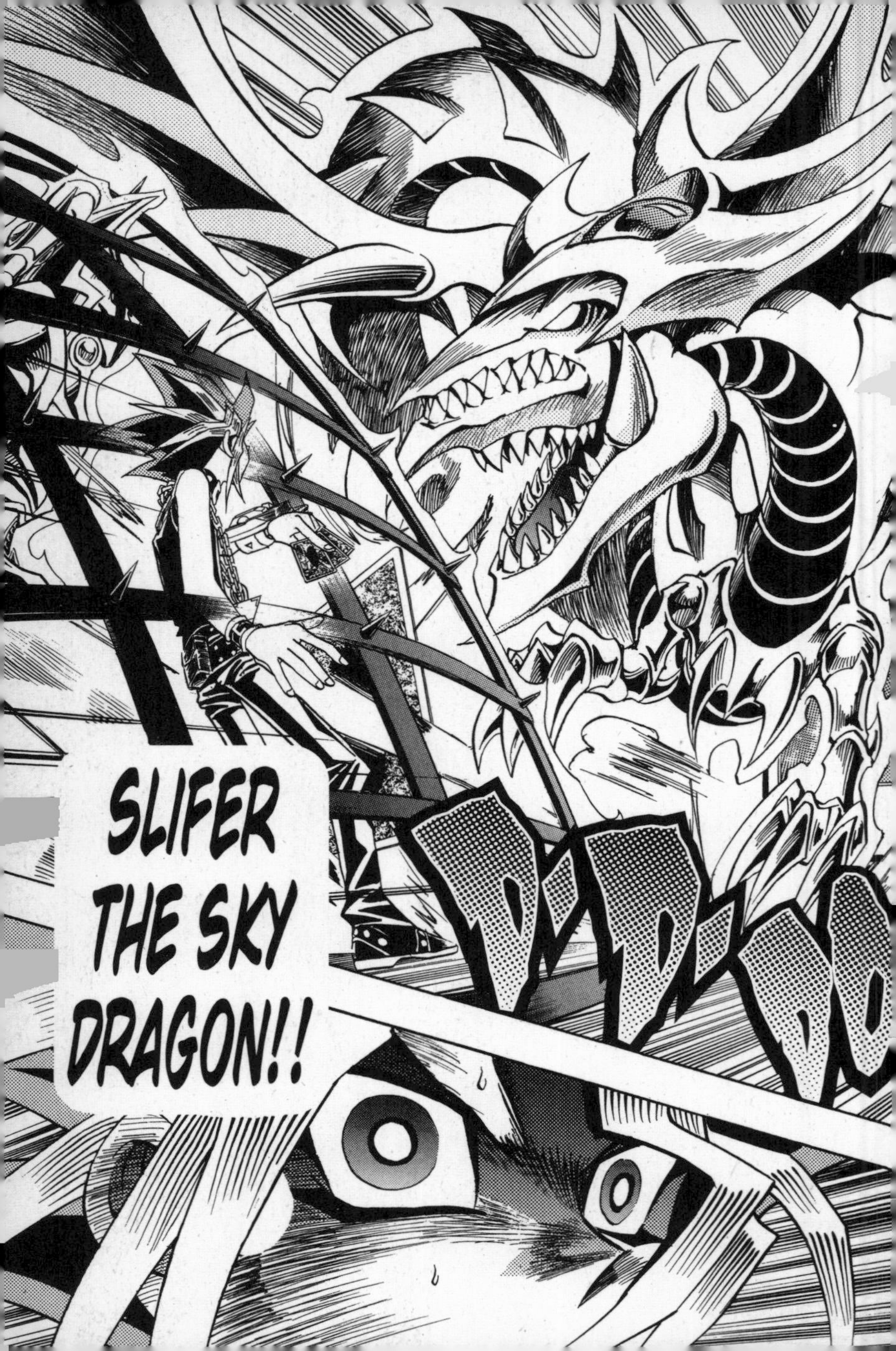
SLIFER THE SKY DRAGON!!

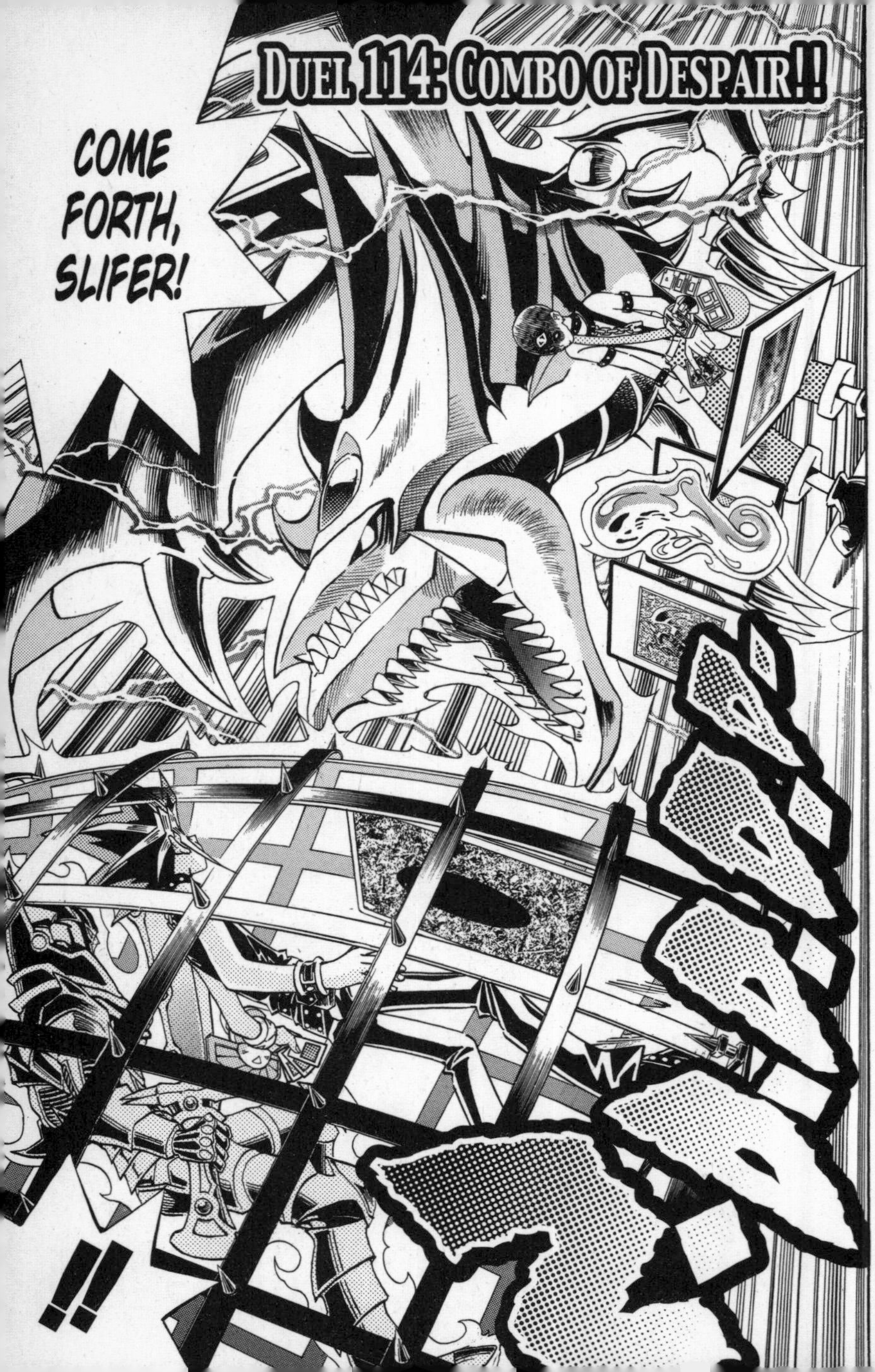
DUEL 114: COMBO OF DESPAIR!!
COME FORTH, SLIFER!
!!

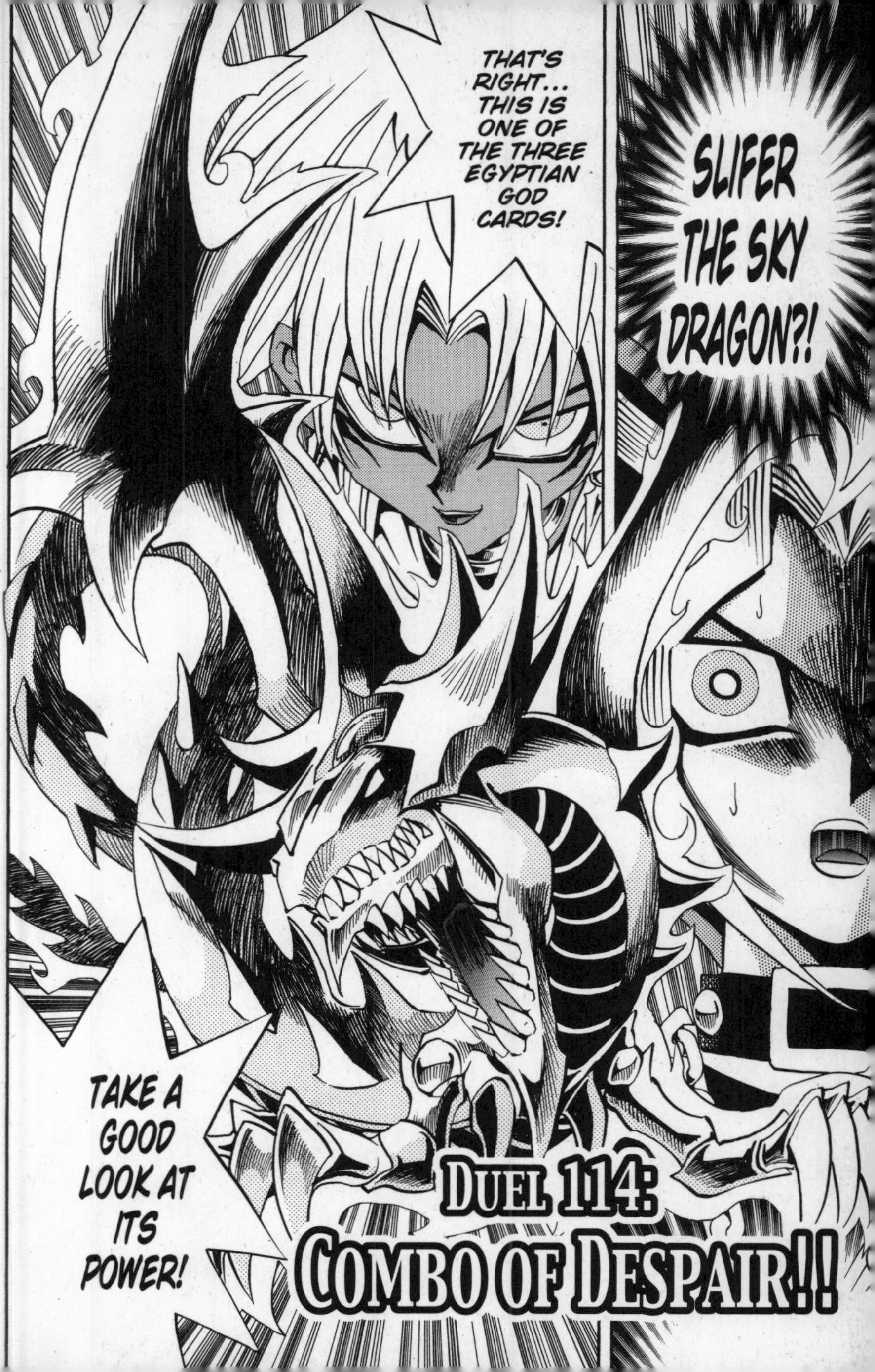
SLIFER THE SKY DRAGON?!
THAT'S RIGHT... THIS IS ONE OF THE THREE EGYPTIAN GOD CARDS!
TAKE A GOOD LOOK AT ITS POWER!
DUEL 114: COMBO OF DESPAIR!!

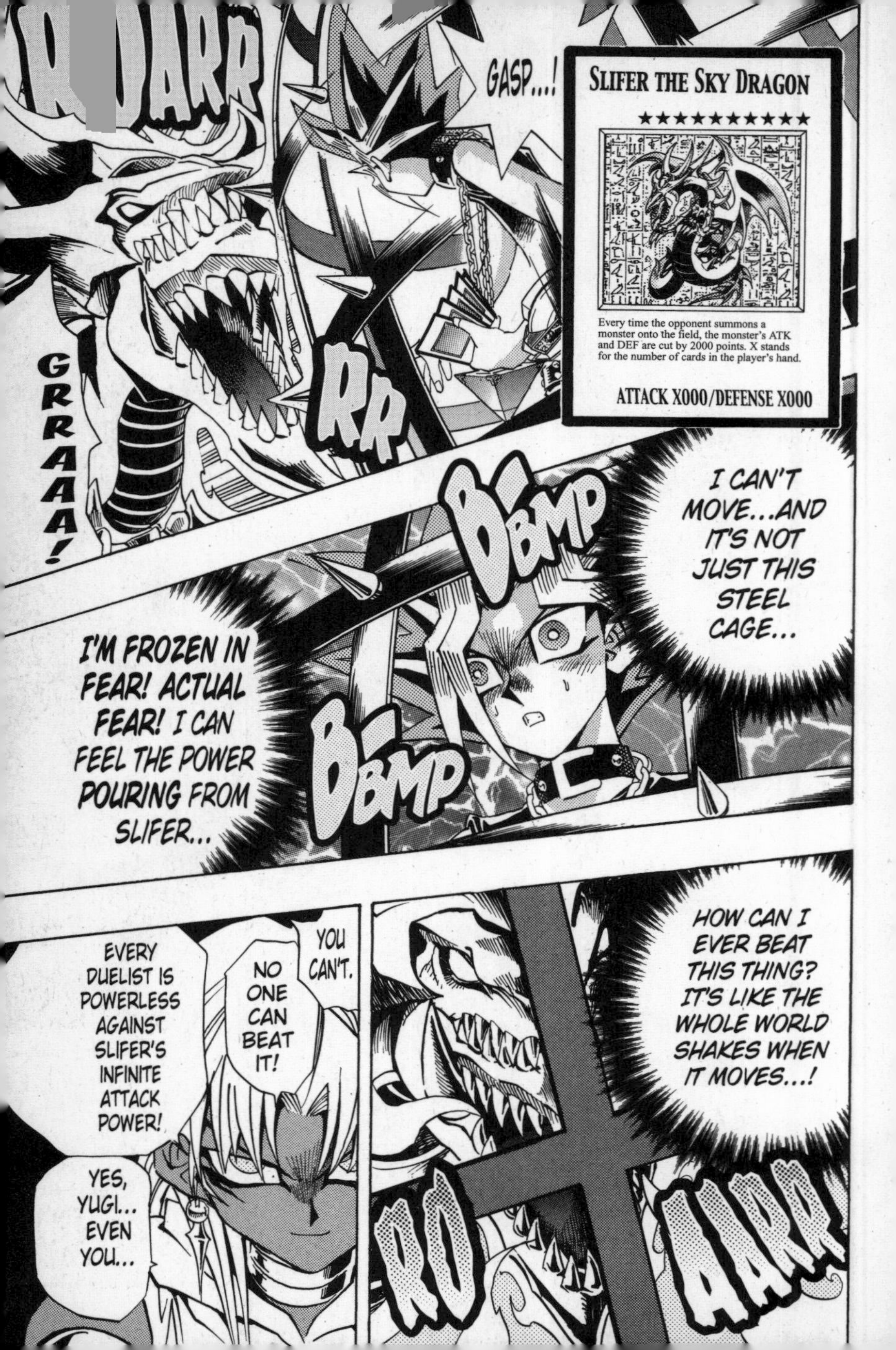
SLIFER THE SKY DRAGON
★★★★★★★★★★★★
Every time the opponent summons a monster onto the field, the monster's ATK and DEF are cut by 2000 points. X stands for the number of cards in the player's hand.
ATTACK X000/DEFENSE X000
GASP...!
RR
GRRAAAA!
I CAN'T MOVE...AND IT'S NOT JUST THIS STEEL CAGE...
B-BMP
B-BMP
I'M FROZEN IN FEAR! ACTUAL FEAR! I CAN FEEL THE POWER POURING FROM SLIFER...
HOW CAN I EVER BEAT THIS THING? IT'S LIKE THE WHOLE WORLD SHAKES WHEN IT MOVES...!
ROARR!
YOU CAN'T.
NO ONE CAN BEAT IT!
EVERY DUELIST IS POWERLESS AGAINST SLIFER'S INFINITE ATTACK POWER!
YES, YUGI... EVEN YOU...

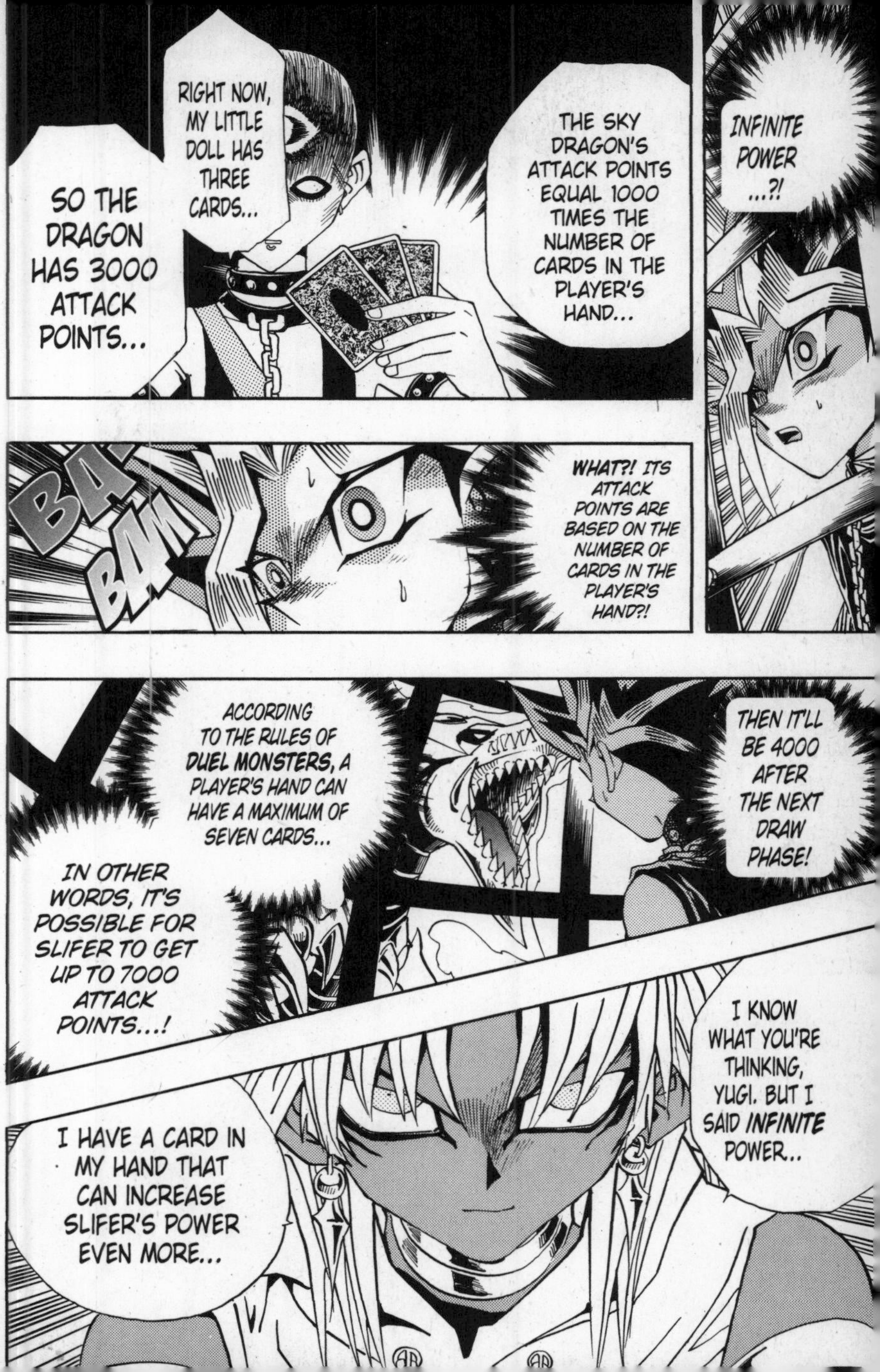
INFINITE POWER ...?!
THE SKY DRAGON'S ATTACK POINTS EQUAL 1000 TIMES THE NUMBER OF CARDS IN THE PLAYER'S HAND...
RIGHT NOW, MY LITTLE DOLL HAS THREE CARDS...
SO THE DRAGON HAS 3000 ATTACK POINTS...
WHAT?! ITS ATTACK POINTS ARE BASED ON THE NUMBER OF CARDS IN THE PLAYER'S HAND?!
BAM
BAM
THEN IT'LL BE 4000 AFTER THE NEXT DRAW PHASE!
ACCORDING TO THE RULES OF **DUEL MONSTERS**, A PLAYER'S HAND CAN HAVE A MAXIMUM OF SEVEN CARDS...
IN OTHER WORDS, IT'S POSSIBLE FOR SLIFER TO GET UP TO 7000 ATTACK POINTS...!
I KNOW WHAT YOU'RE THINKING, YUGI. BUT I SAID *INFINITE* POWER...
I HAVE A CARD IN MY HAND THAT CAN INCREASE SLIFER'S POWER EVEN MORE...

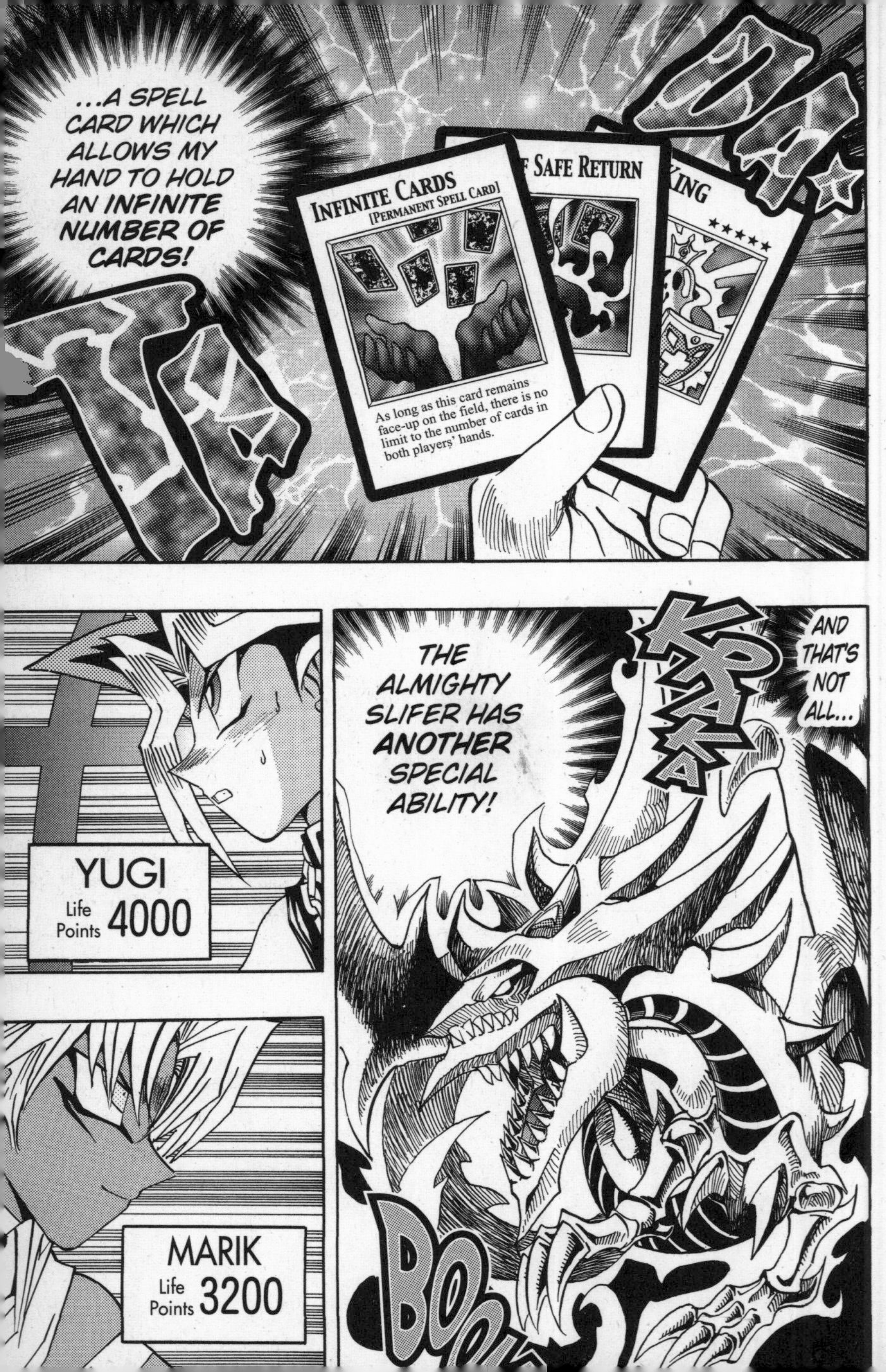

KING
F SAFE RETURN
INFINITE CARDS
[PERMANENT SPELL CARD]
As long as this card remains face-up on the field, there is no limit to the number of cards in both players' hands.
...A SPELL CARD WHICH ALLOWS MY HAND TO HOLD AN INFINITE NUMBER OF CARDS!
AND THAT'S NOT ALL...
KRAKA
THE ALMIGHTY SLIFER HAS ANOTHER SPECIAL ABILITY!
YUGI
Life Points 4000
MARIK
Life Points 3200

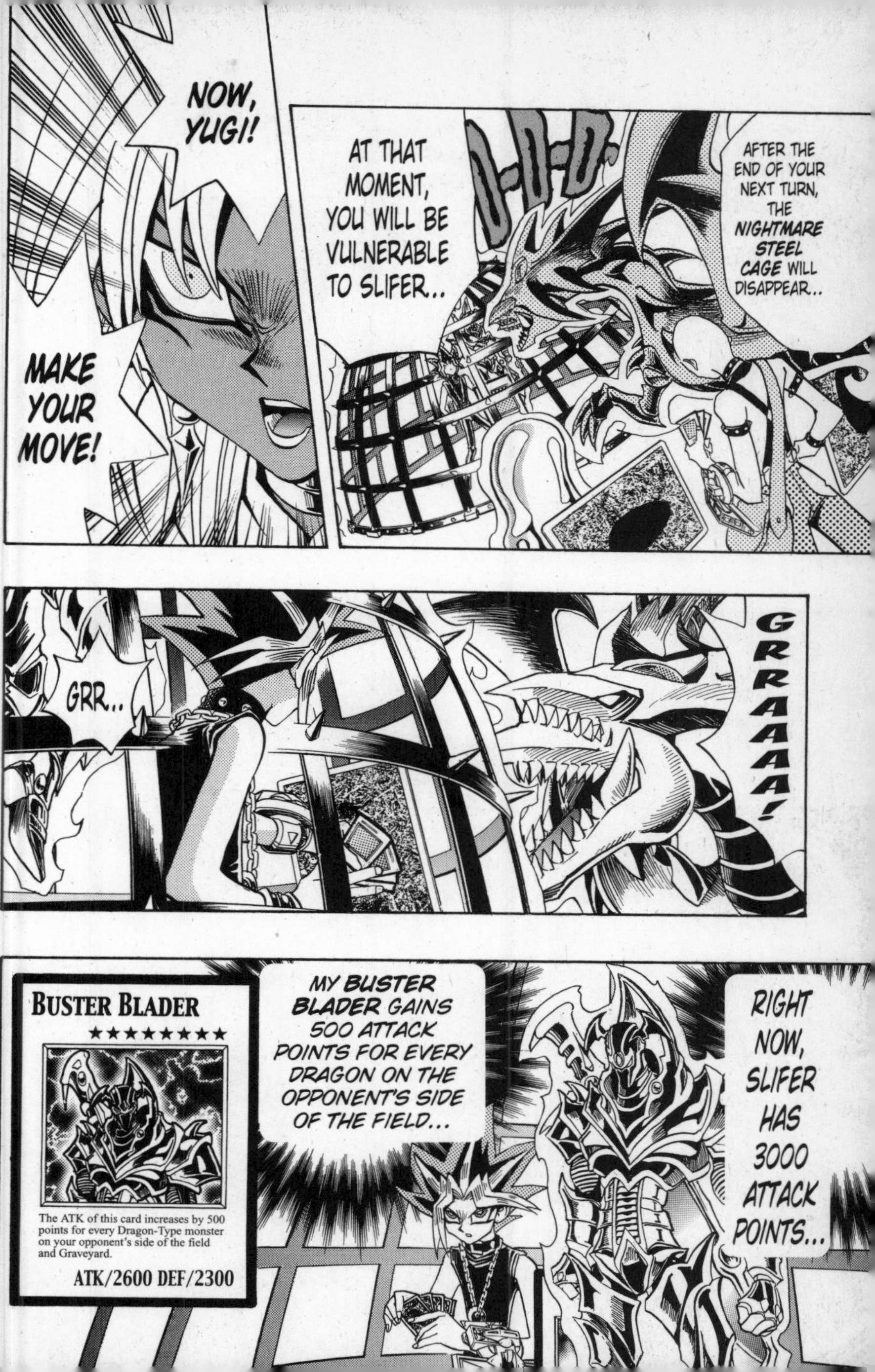
AFTER THE END OF YOUR NEXT TURN, THE NIGHTMARE STEEL CAGE WILL DISAPPEAR...
D-D-D-
AT THAT MOMENT, YOU WILL BE VULNERABLE TO SLIFER...
NOW, YUGI!
MAKE YOUR MOVE!
GRRAAAAA!
GRR...
RIGHT NOW, SLIFER HAS 3000 ATTACK POINTS...
MY BUSTER BLADER GAINS 500 ATTACK POINTS FOR EVERY DRAGON ON THE OPPONENT'S SIDE OF THE FIELD...
BUSTER BLADER
★★★★★★★★
The ATK of this card increases by 500 points for every Dragon-Type monster on your opponent's side of the field and Graveyard.
ATK/2600 DEF/2300

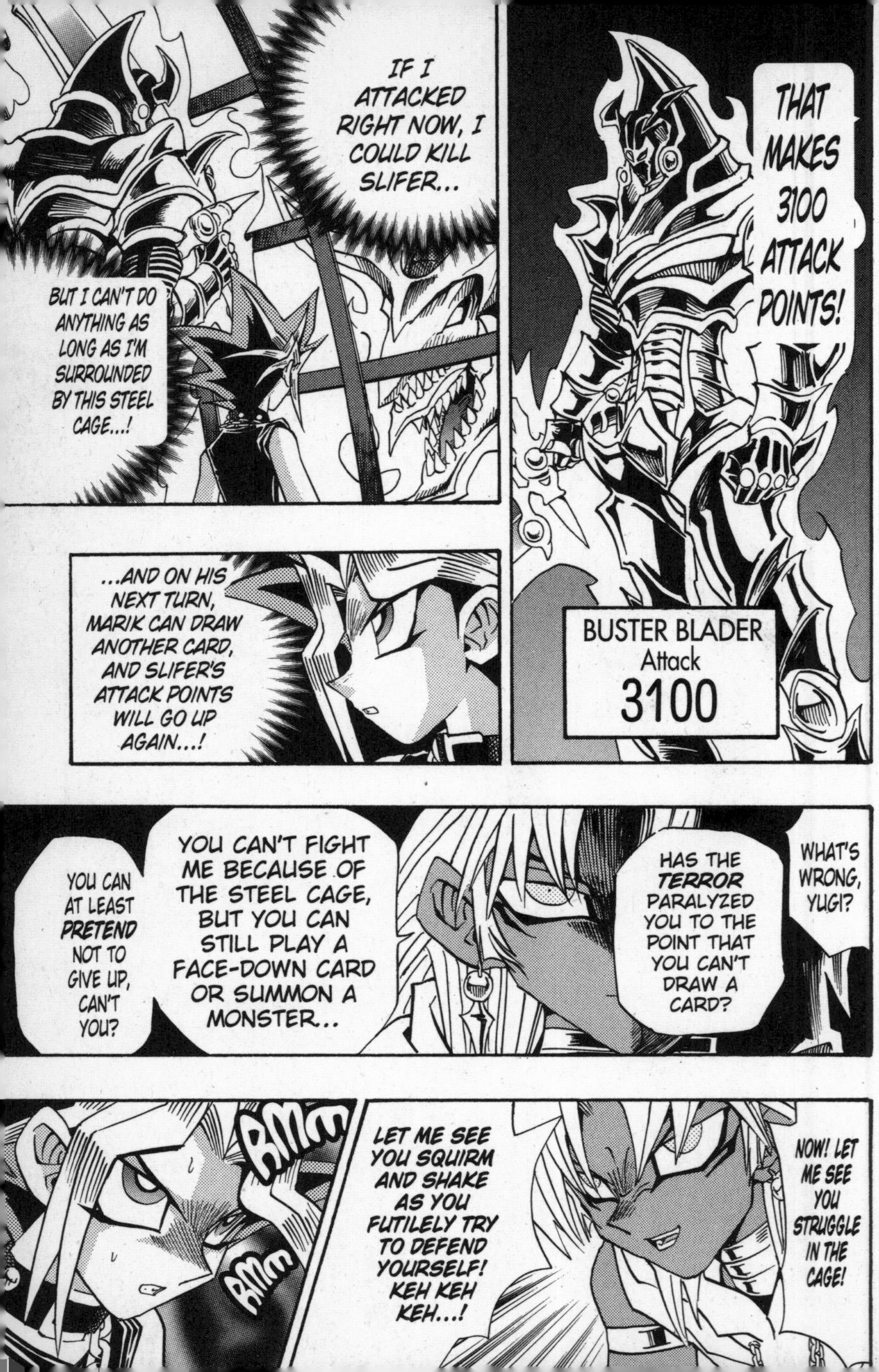
THAT MAKES 3100 ATTACK POINTS!
BUSTER BLADER Attack 3100
IF I ATTACKED RIGHT NOW, I COULD KILL SLIFER...
BUT I CAN'T DO ANYTHING AS LONG AS I'M SURROUNDED BY THIS STEEL CAGE...!
...AND ON HIS NEXT TURN, MARIK CAN DRAW ANOTHER CARD, AND SLIFER'S ATTACK POINTS WILL GO UP AGAIN...!
WHAT'S WRONG, YUGI?
HAS THE TERROR PARALYZED YOU TO THE POINT THAT YOU CAN'T DRAW A CARD?
YOU CAN'T FIGHT ME BECAUSE OF THE STEEL CAGE, BUT YOU CAN STILL PLAY A FACE-DOWN CARD OR SUMMON A MONSTER...
YOU CAN AT LEAST PRETEND NOT TO GIVE UP, CAN'T YOU?
NOW! LET ME SEE YOU STRUGGLE IN THE CAGE!
LET ME SEE YOU SQUIRM AND SHAKE AS YOU FUTILELY TRY TO DEFEND YOURSELF! KEH KEH KEH...!
BMM
BMM

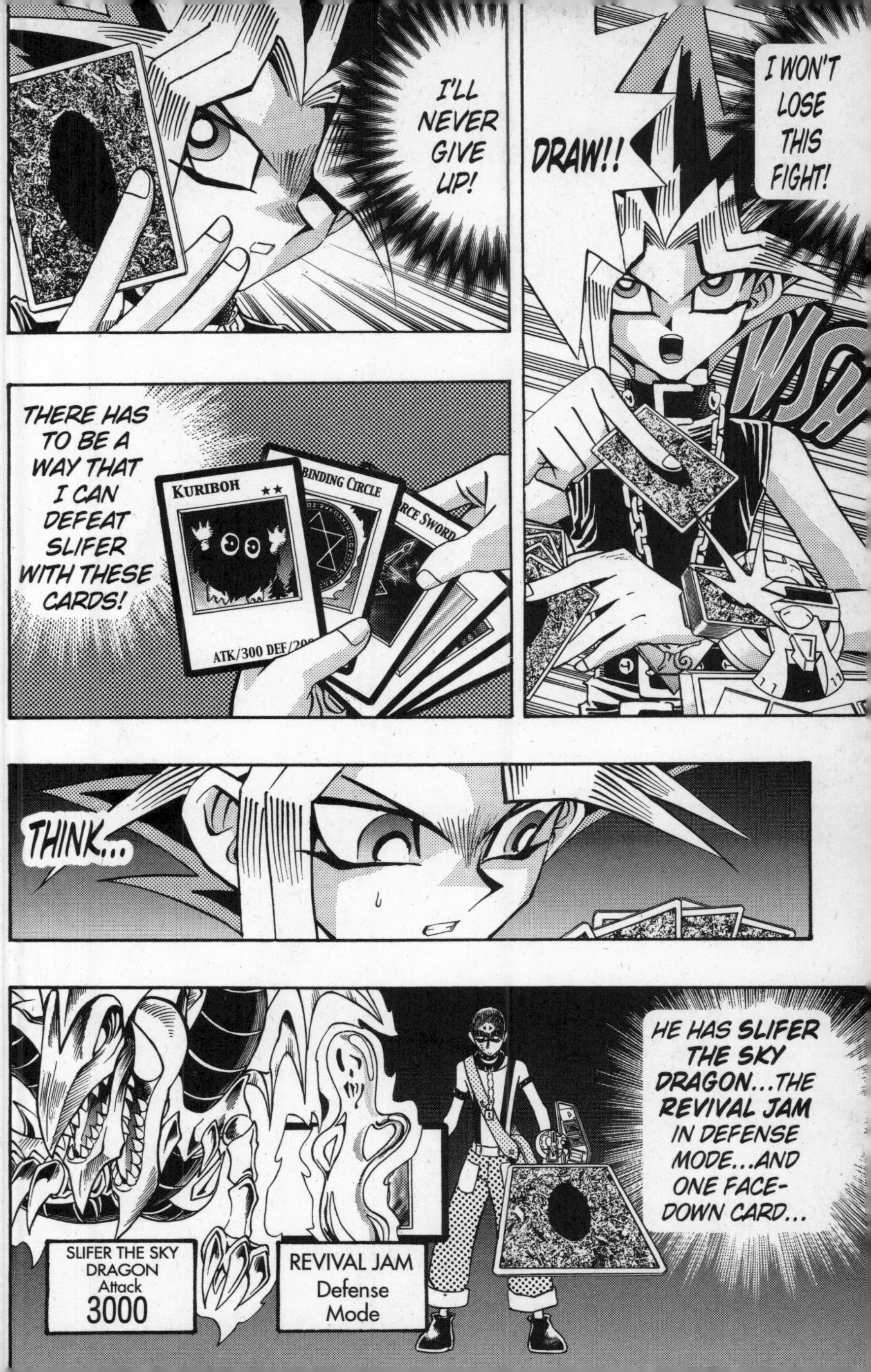
I WON'T LOSE THIS FIGHT!
DRAW!!
WSH
I'LL NEVER GIVE UP!
THERE HAS TO BE A WAY THAT I CAN DEFEAT SLIFER WITH THESE CARDS!
KURIBOH
BINDING CIRCLE
THINK...
HE HAS SLIFER THE SKY DRAGON...THE REVIVAL JAM IN DEFENSE MODE...AND ONE FACE-DOWN CARD...
SLIFER THE SKY DRAGON
Attack
3000
REVIVAL JAM
Defense
Mode

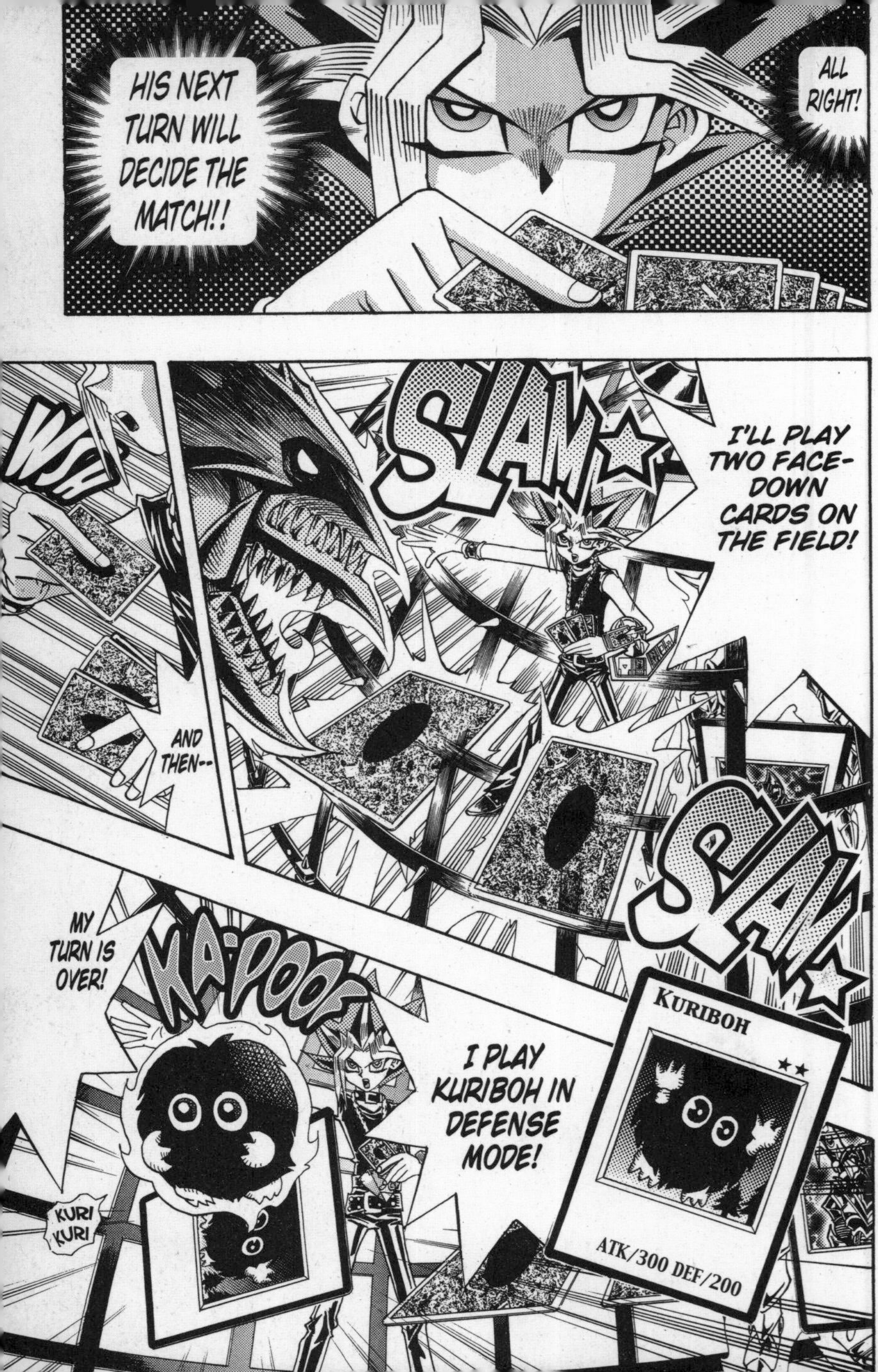
ALL RIGHT!
HIS NEXT TURN WILL DECIDE THE MATCH!!
SLAM
I'LL PLAY TWO FACE-DOWN CARDS ON THE FIELD!
SLAM
WSH
AND THEN--
KURIBOH
ATK/300 DEF/200
I PLAY KURIBOH IN DEFENSE MODE!
KA-POOF
MY TURN IS OVER!
KURI KURI

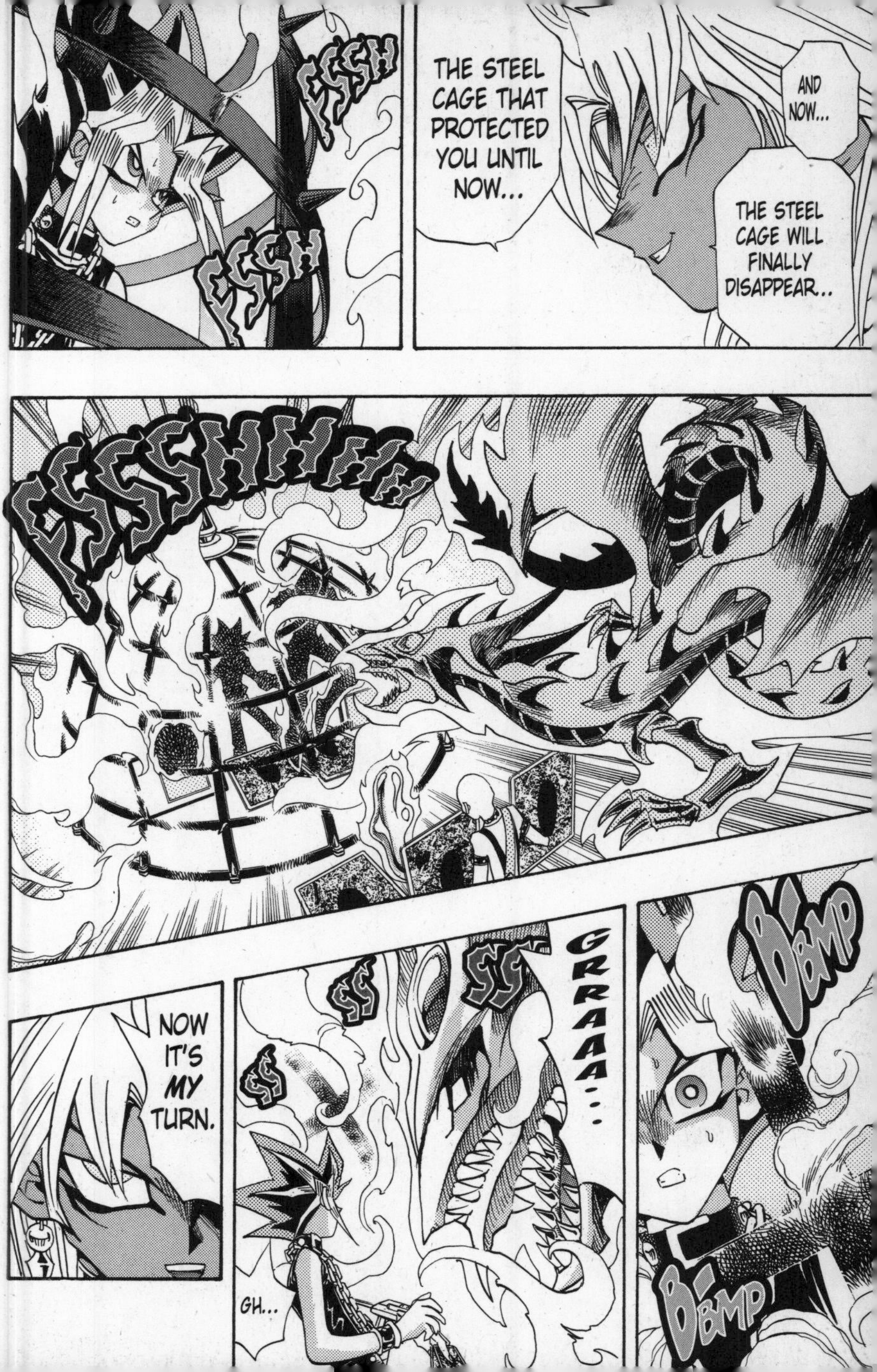
THE STEEL CAGE THAT PROTECTED YOU UNTIL NOW...
AND NOW...
THE STEEL CAGE WILL FINALLY DISAPPEAR...
FSSH
FSSH
FSSHHHH
GRRAAA...
GH...
NOW IT'S MY TURN.

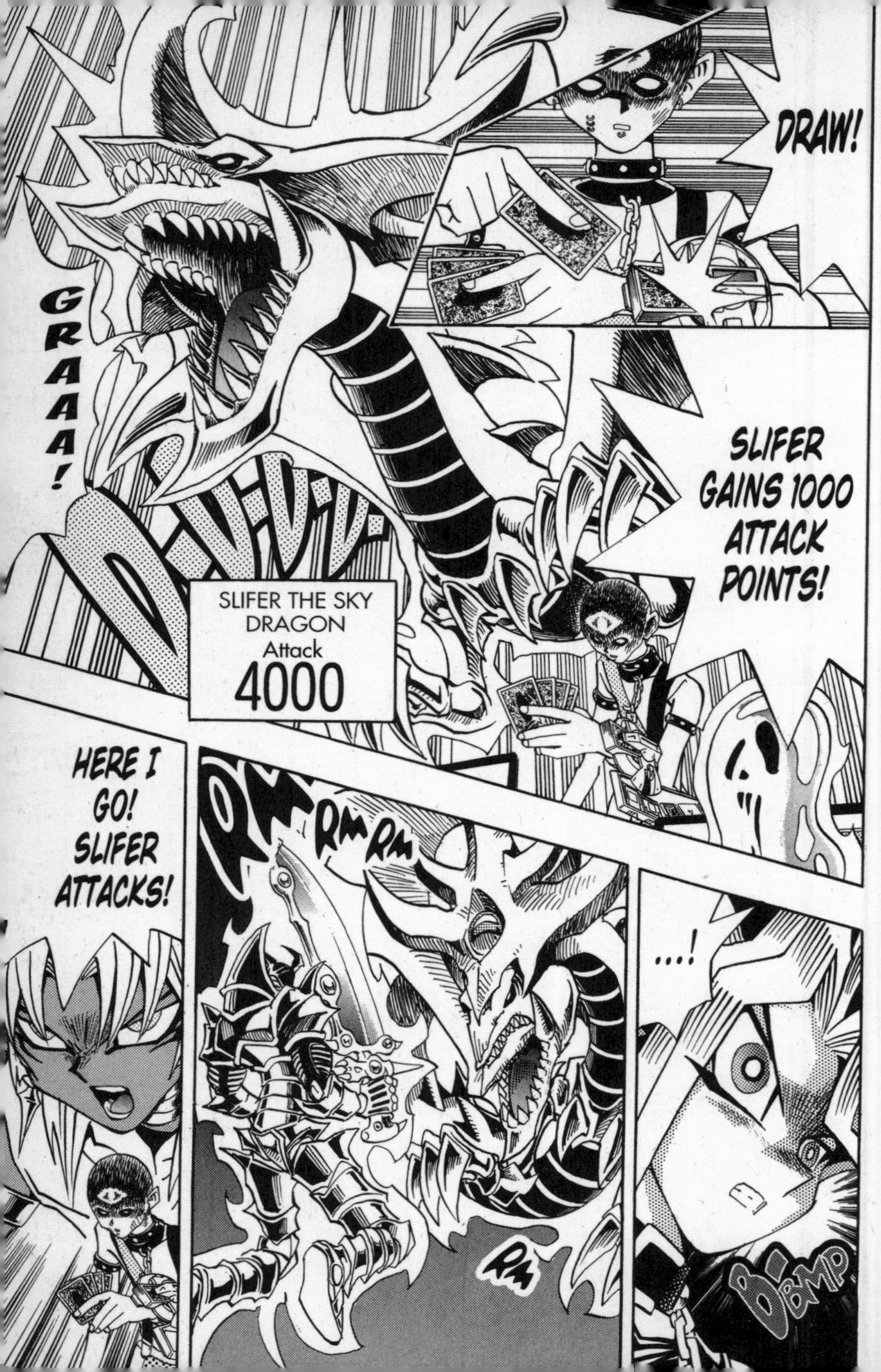
DRAW!
GRAAAA!
SLIFER GAINS 1000 ATTACK POINTS!
SLIFER THE SKY DRAGON Attack 4000
...!
HERE I GO! SLIFER ATTACKS!

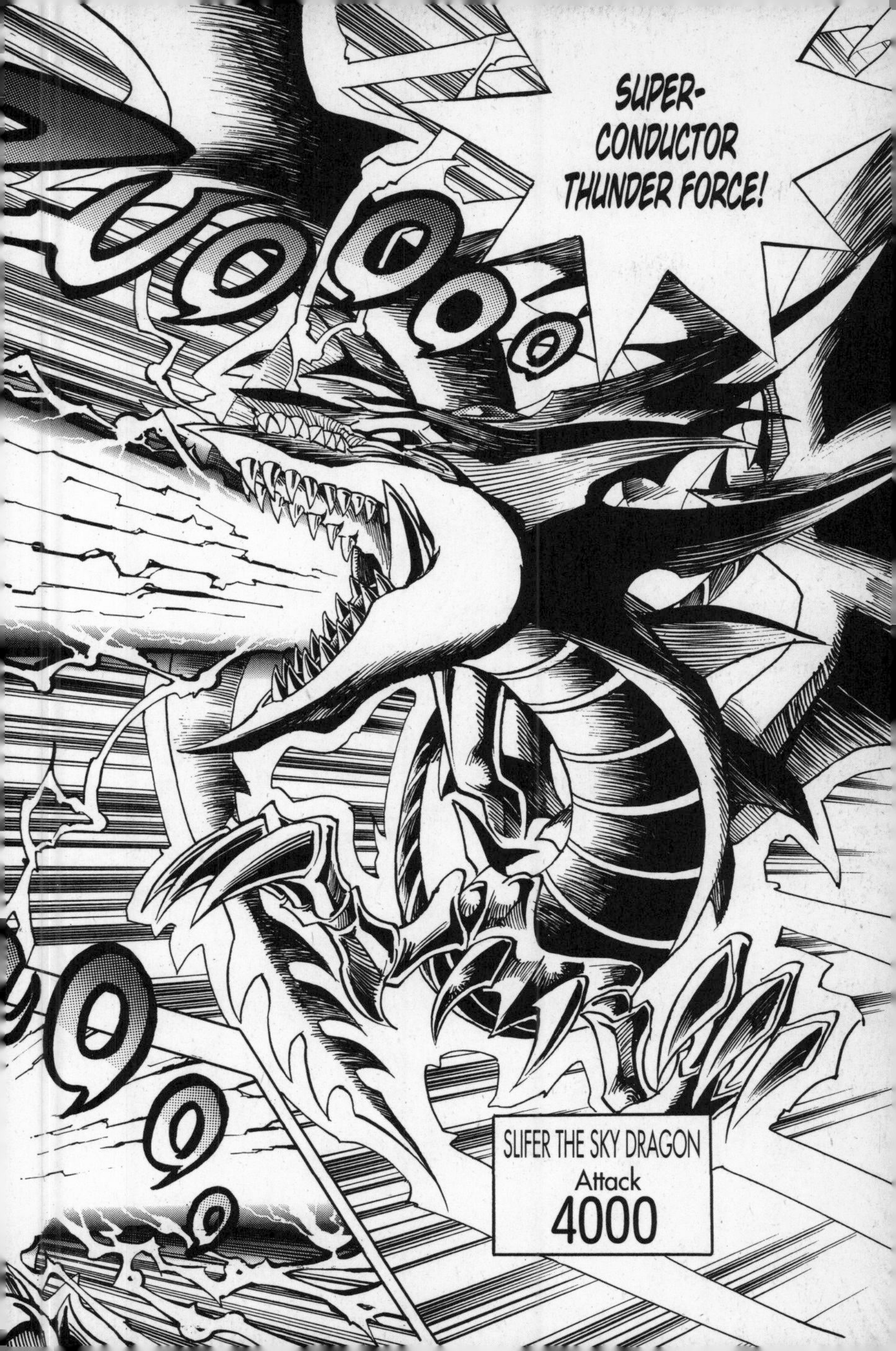
SUPER-CONDUCTOR THUNDER FORCE!
SLIFER THE SKY DRAGON
Attack
4000

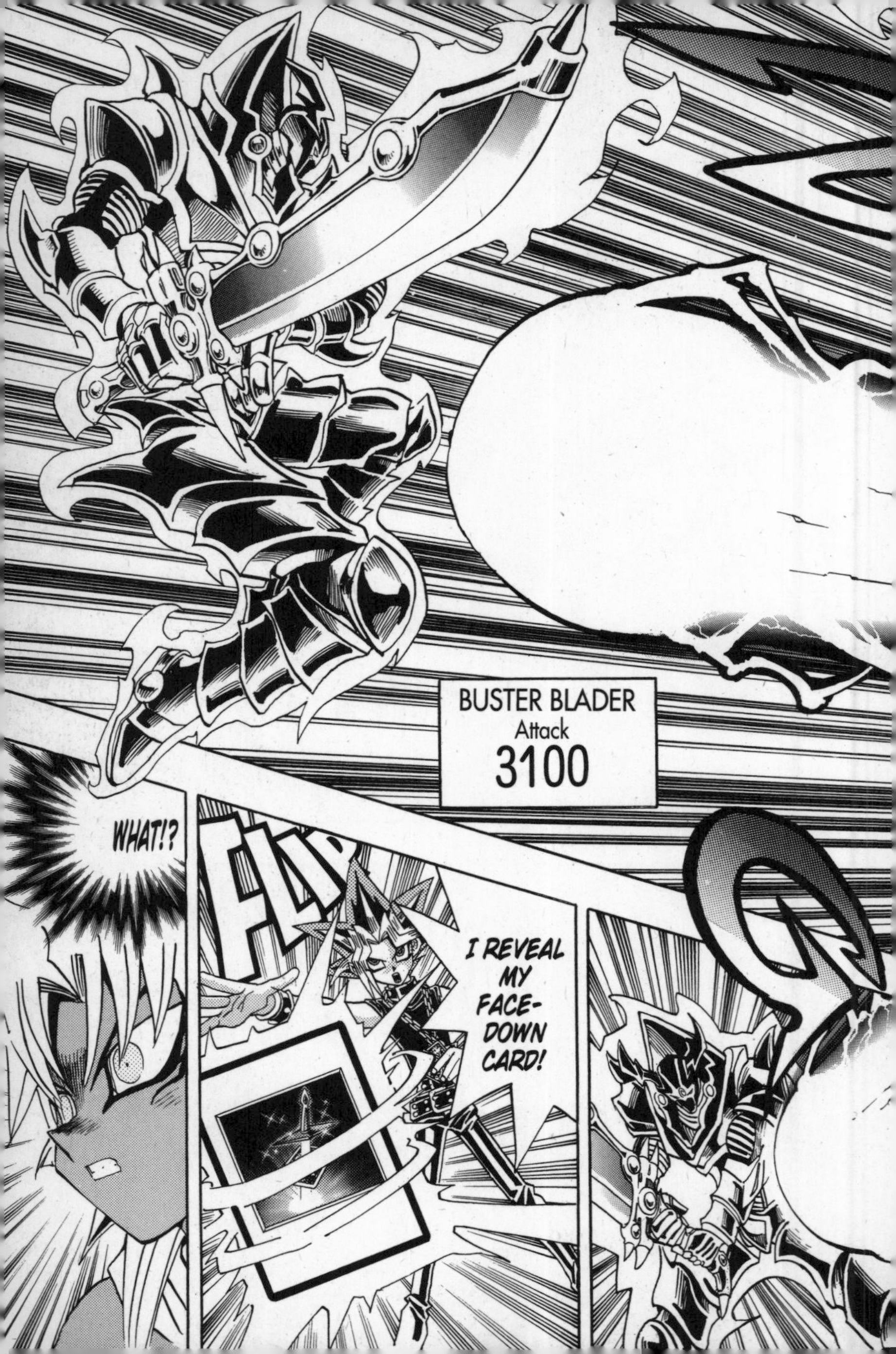
BUSTER BLADER
Attack
3100
WHAT!?
I REVEAL MY FACE-DOWN CARD!

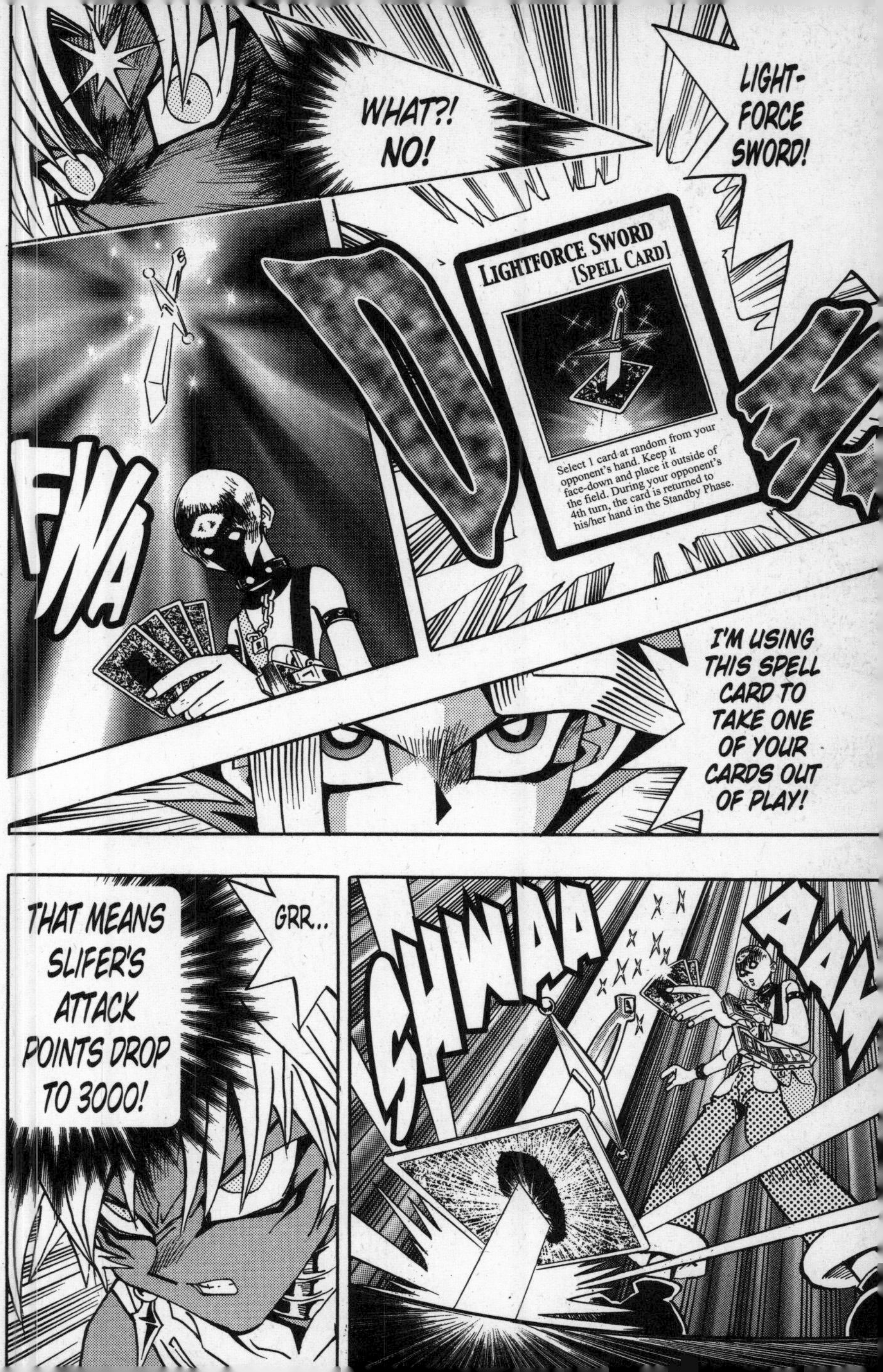
LIGHT-FORCE SWORD!
WHAT?! NO!
LIGHTFORCE SWORD
[SPELL CARD]
Select 1 card at random from your opponent's hand. Keep it face-down and place it outside of the field. During your opponent's 4th turn, the card is returned to his/her hand in the Standby Phase.
I'M USING THIS SPELL CARD TO TAKE ONE OF YOUR CARDS OUT OF PLAY!
GRR...
THAT MEANS SLIFER'S ATTACK POINTS DROP TO 3000!

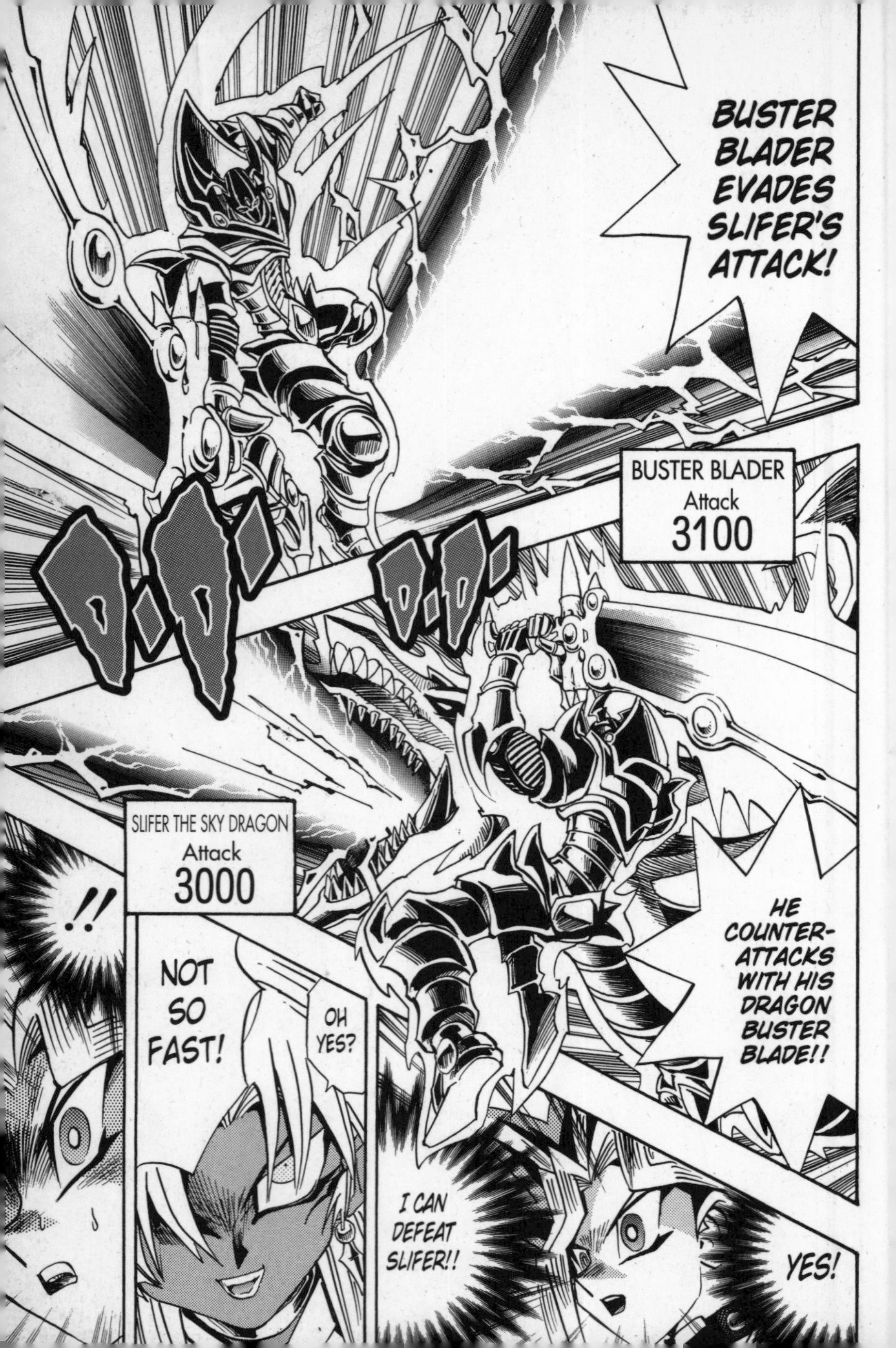
BUSTER BLADER EVADES SLIFER'S ATTACK!
BUSTER BLADER
Attack
3100
HE COUNTER-ATTACKS WITH HIS DRAGON BUSTER BLADE!!
SLIFER THE SKY DRAGON
Attack
3000
YES!
I CAN DEFEAT SLIFER!!
OH YES?
NOT SO FAST!
!!

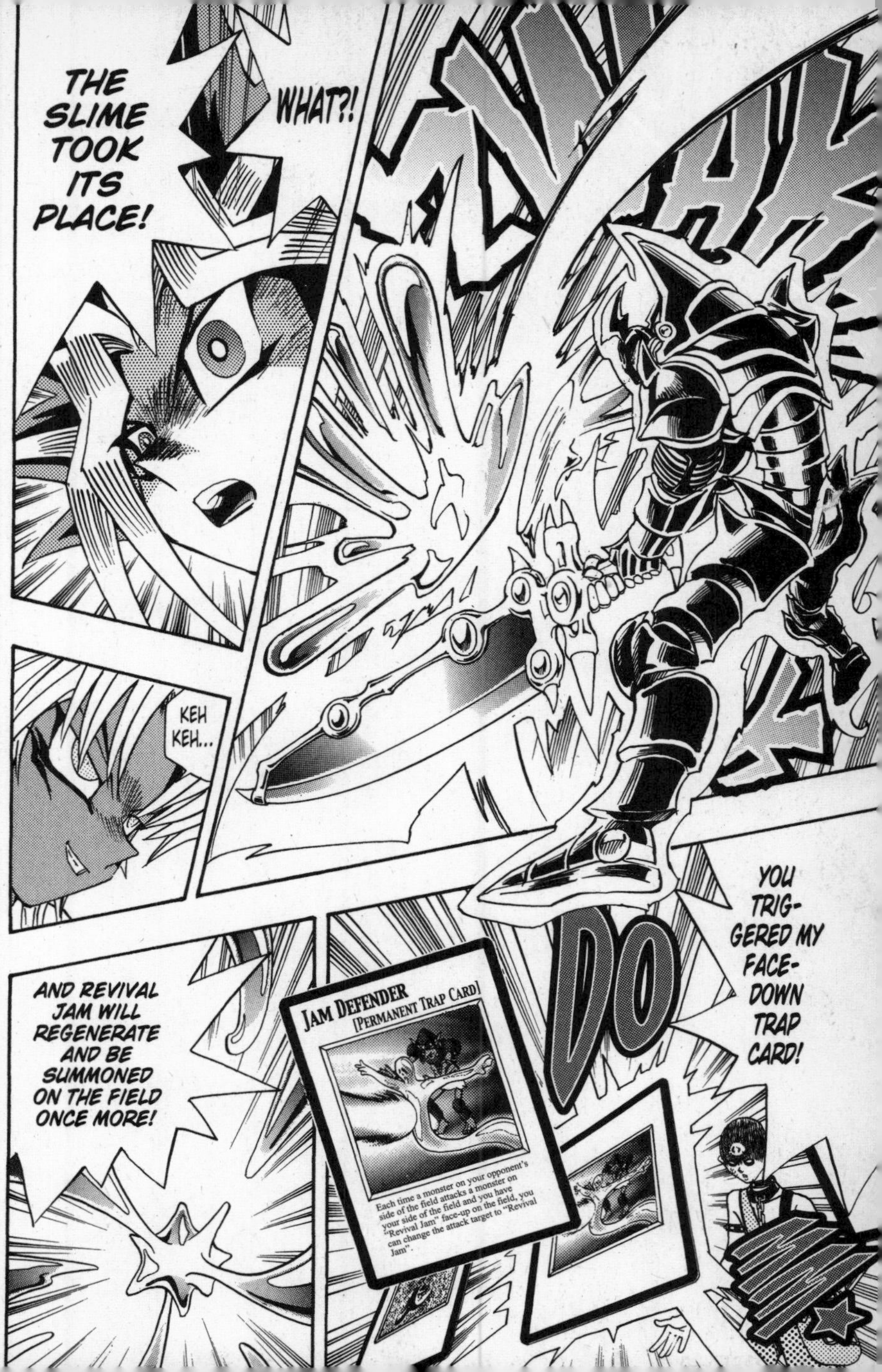
THE SLIME TOOK ITS PLACE!
WHAT?!
KEH KEH...
YOU TRIG-GERED MY FACE-DOWN TRAP CARD!
DO
JAM DEFENDER
[PERMANENT TRAP CARD]
Each time a monster on your opponent's side of the field attacks a monster on your side of the field and you have "Revival Jam" face-up on the field, you can change the attack target to "Revival Jam".
AND REVIVAL JAM WILL REGENERATE AND BE SUMMONED ON THE FIELD ONCE MORE!

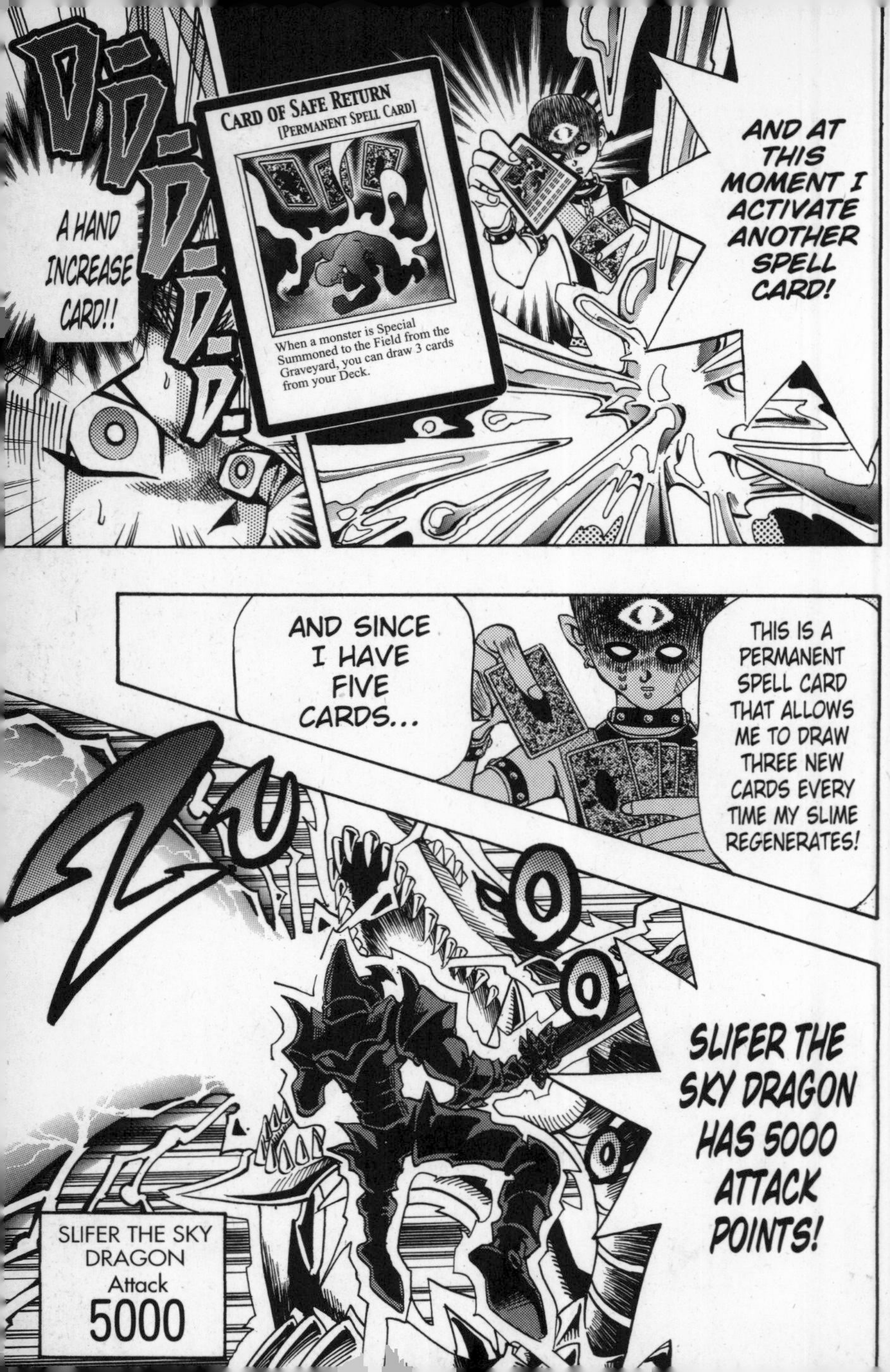
AND AT THIS MOMENT I ACTIVATE ANOTHER SPELL CARD!
CARD OF SAFE RETURN
[PERMANENT SPELL CARD]
When a monster is Special Summoned to the Field from the Graveyard, you can draw 3 cards from your Deck.
A HAND INCREASE CARD!!
THIS IS A PERMANENT SPELL CARD THAT ALLOWS ME TO DRAW THREE NEW CARDS EVERY TIME MY SLIME REGENERATES!
AND SINCE I HAVE FIVE CARDS...
SLIFER THE SKY DRAGON HAS 5000 ATTACK POINTS!
SLIFER THE SKY DRAGON
Attack
5000

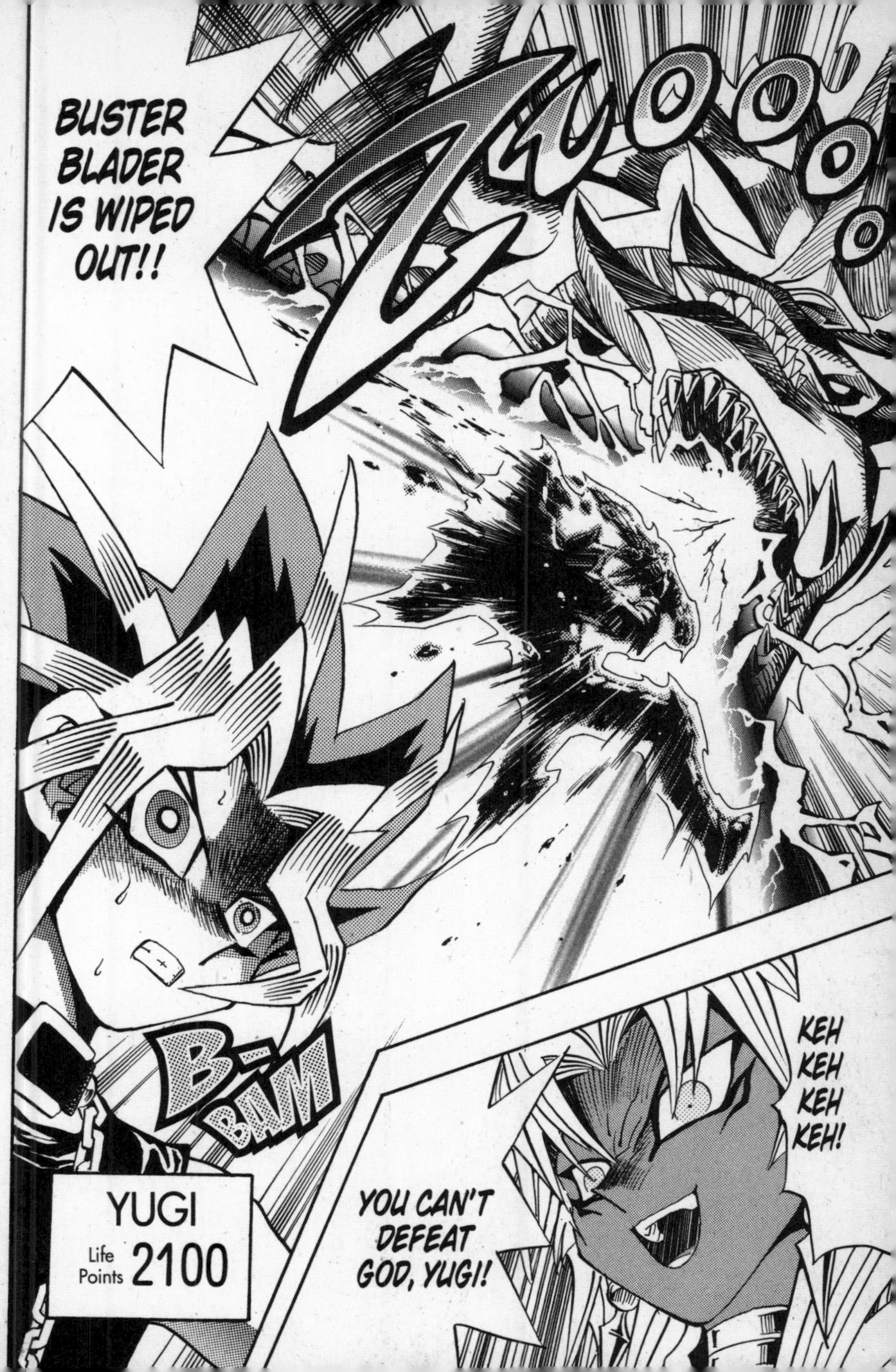
BUSTER BLADER IS WIPED OUT!!
B-BAM
YUGI
Life Points 2100
KEH KEH KEH KEH!
YOU CAN'T DEFEAT GOD, YUGI!

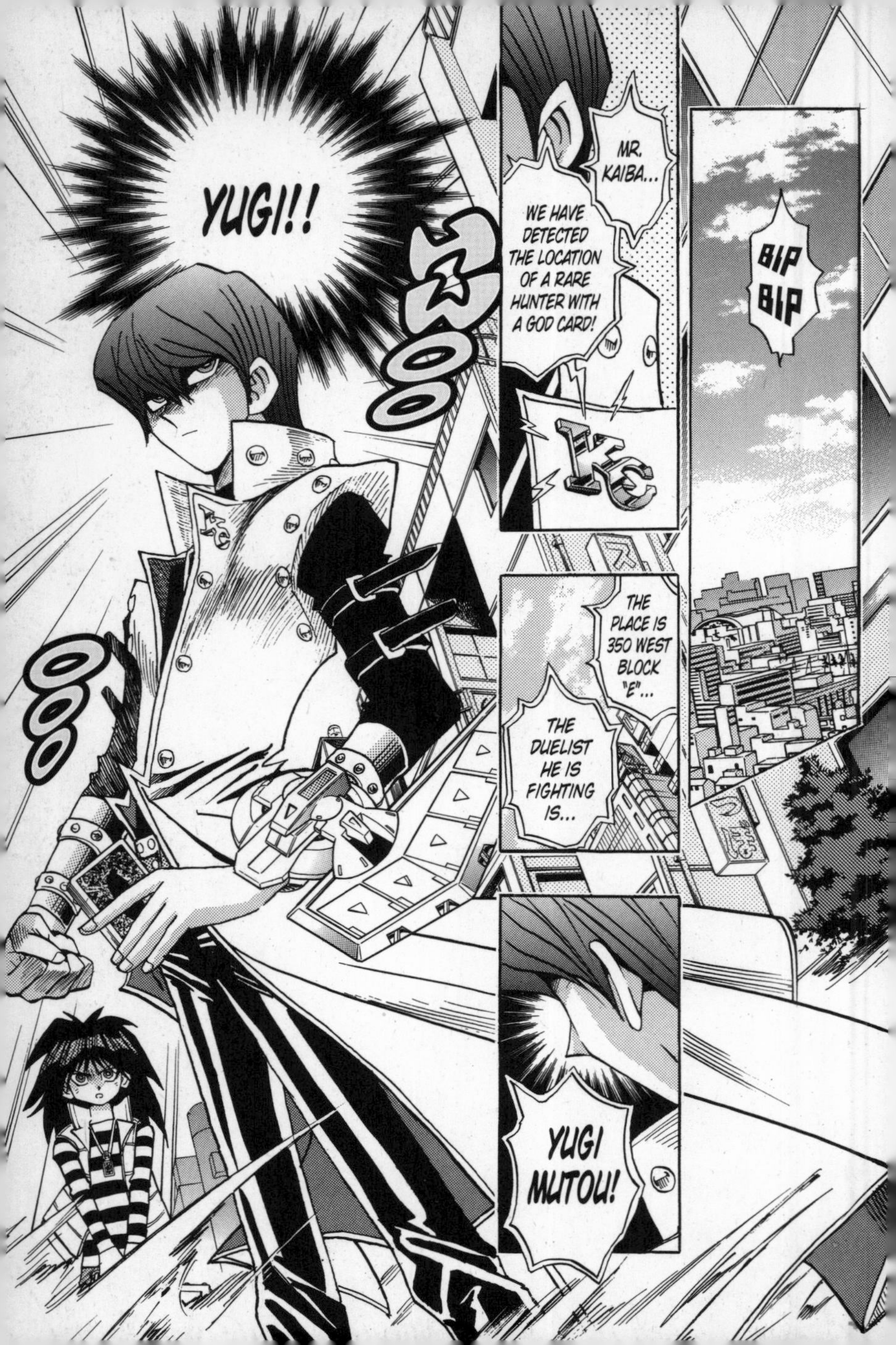
BIP BIP
MR. KAIBA...
WE HAVE DETECTED THE LOCATION OF A RARE HUNTER WITH A GOD CARD!
THE PLACE IS 350 WEST BLOCK "E"...
THE DUELIST HE IS FIGHTING IS...
YUGI MUTOU!
YUGI!!
WOOOO
OOOO

DUEL 115: THE COMBO OF GOD!!

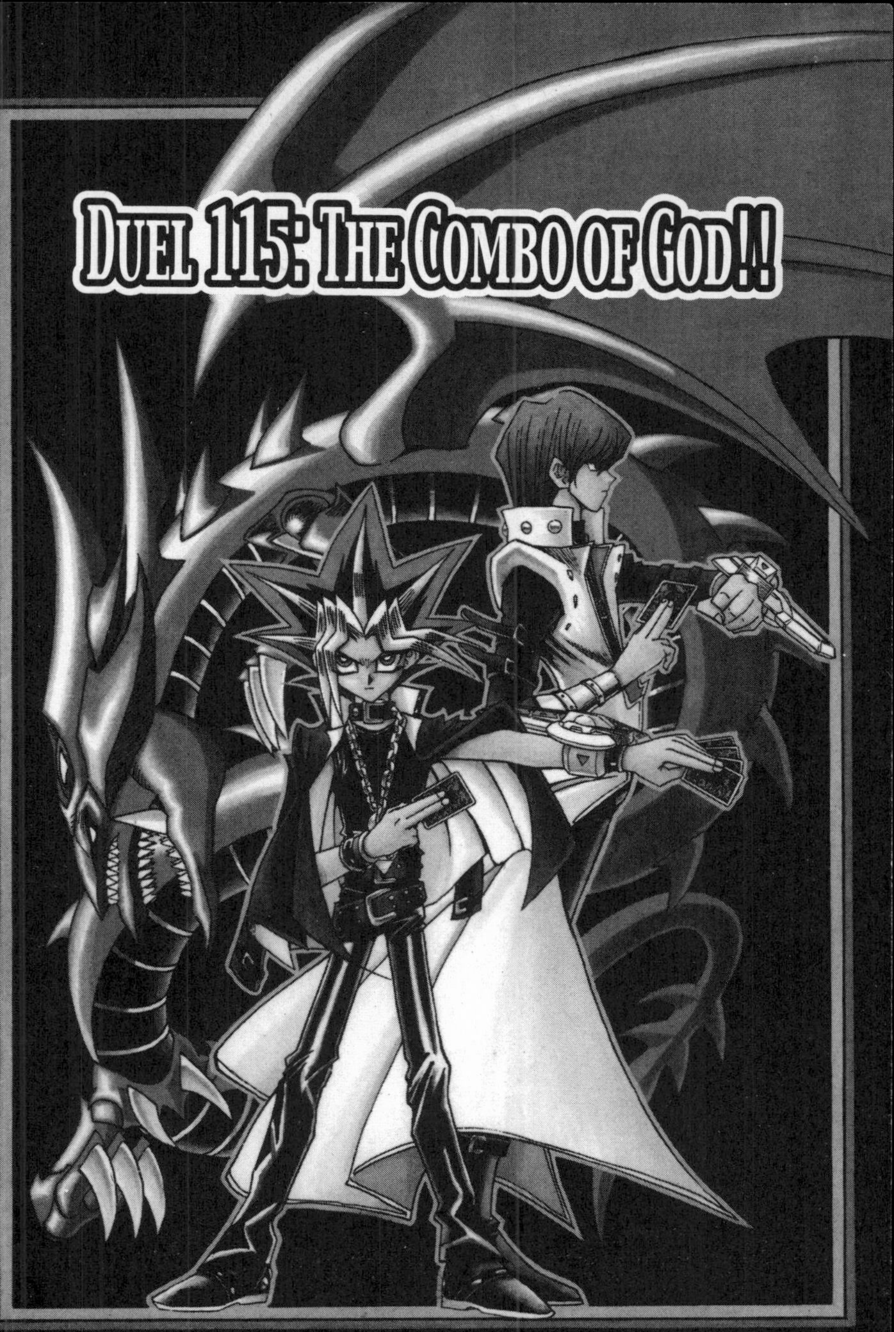

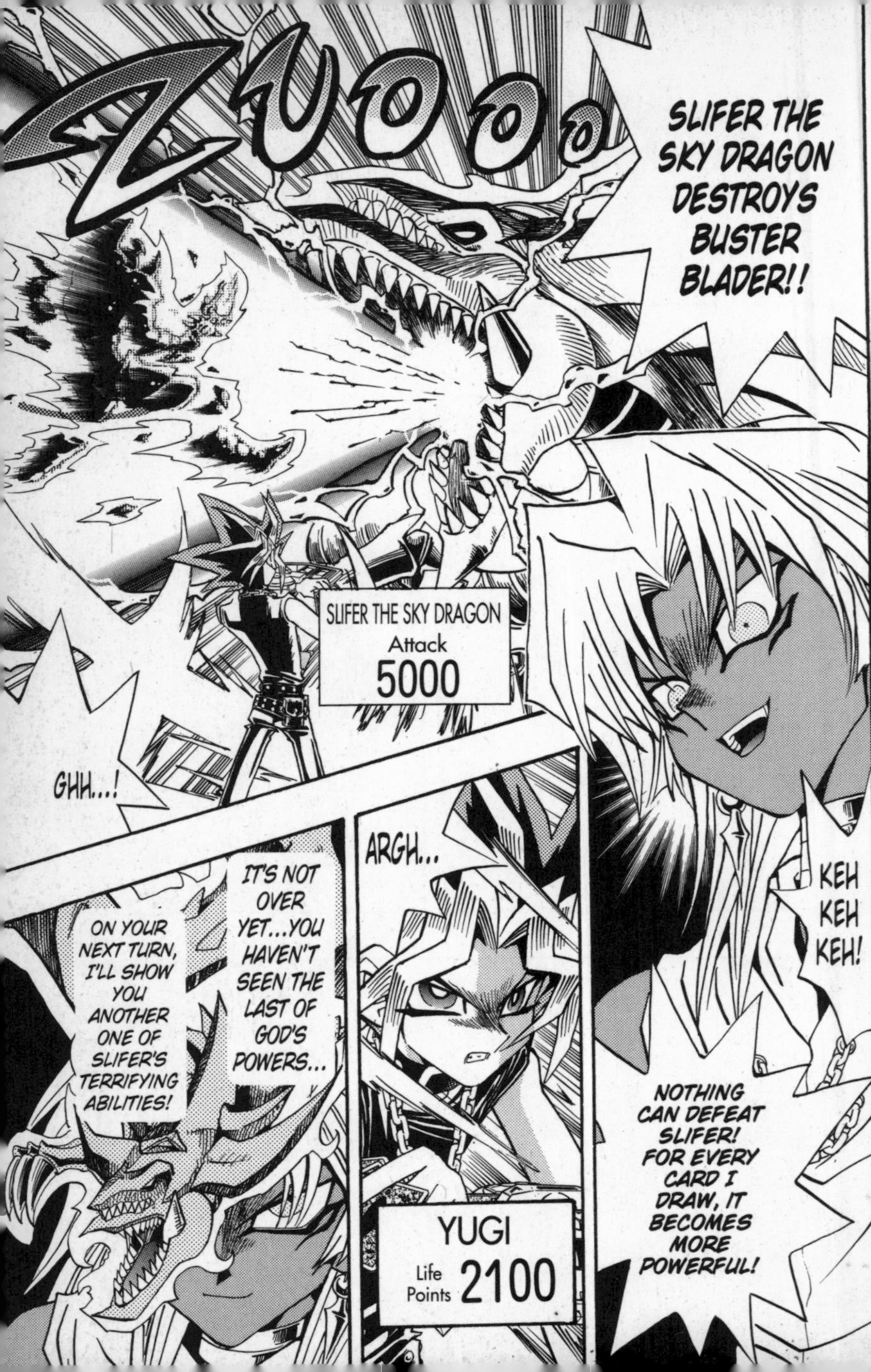
ZUOOOO
SLIFER THE SKY DRAGON DESTROYS BUSTER BLADER!!
SLIFER THE SKY DRAGON Attack 5000
GHH...!
KEH KEH KEH!
NOTHING CAN DEFEAT SLIFER! FOR EVERY CARD I DRAW, IT BECOMES MORE POWERFUL!
ARGH...
IT'S NOT OVER YET...YOU HAVEN'T SEEN THE LAST OF GOD'S POWERS...
YUGI Life Points 2100
ON YOUR NEXT TURN, I'LL SHOW YOU ANOTHER ONE OF SLIFER'S TERRIFYING ABILITIES!

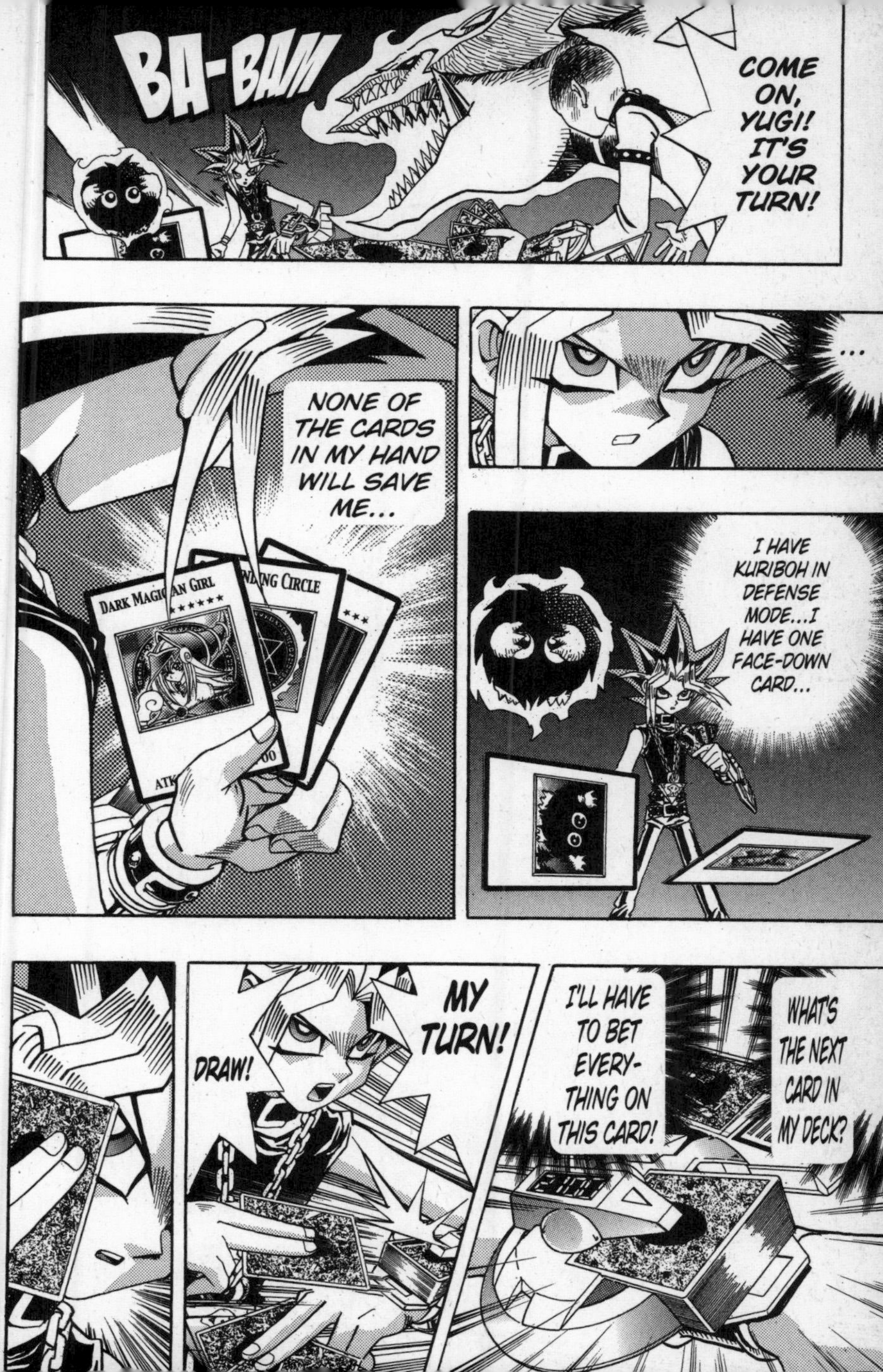
BA-BAM
COME ON, YUGI! IT'S YOUR TURN!
...
I HAVE KURIBOH IN DEFENSE MODE...I HAVE ONE FACE-DOWN CARD...
NONE OF THE CARDS IN MY HAND WILL SAVE ME...
WHAT'S THE NEXT CARD IN MY DECK?
I'LL HAVE TO BET EVERYTHING ON THIS CARD!
MY TURN!
DRAW!

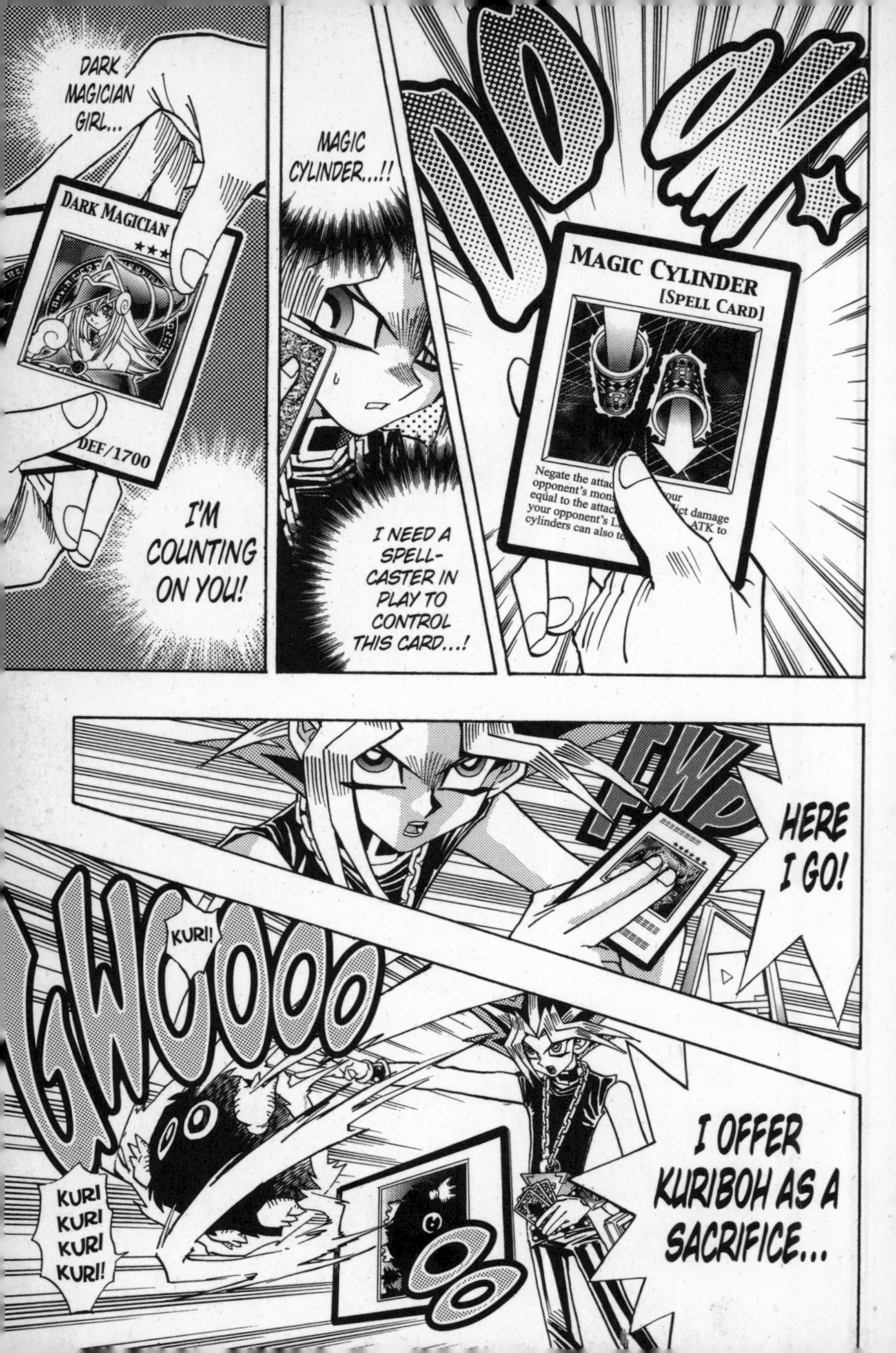
MAGIC CYLINDER
[SPELL CARD]
MAGIC CYLINDER...!!
I NEED A SPELL-CASTER IN PLAY TO CONTROL THIS CARD...!
DARK MAGICIAN GIRL...
DARK MAGICIAN
DEF/1700
I'M COUNTING ON YOU!
HERE I GO!
I OFFER KURIBOH AS A SACRIFICE...
KURI!
SHWOOOO
KURI KURI KURI KURI!

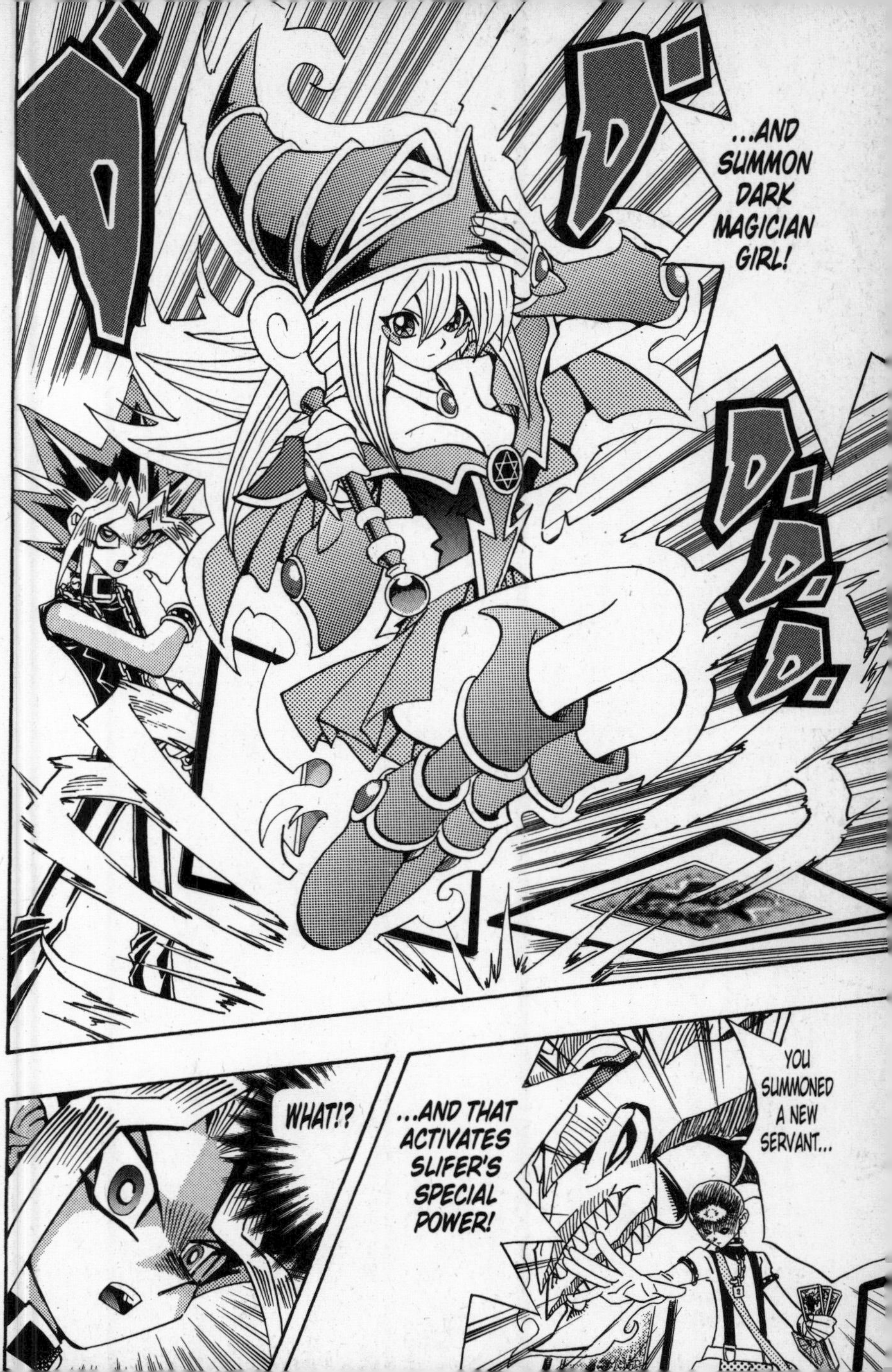
...AND SUMMON DARK MAGICIAN GIRL!
YOU SUMMONED A NEW SERVANT...
...AND THAT ACTIVATES SLIFER'S SPECIAL POWER!
WHAT!?

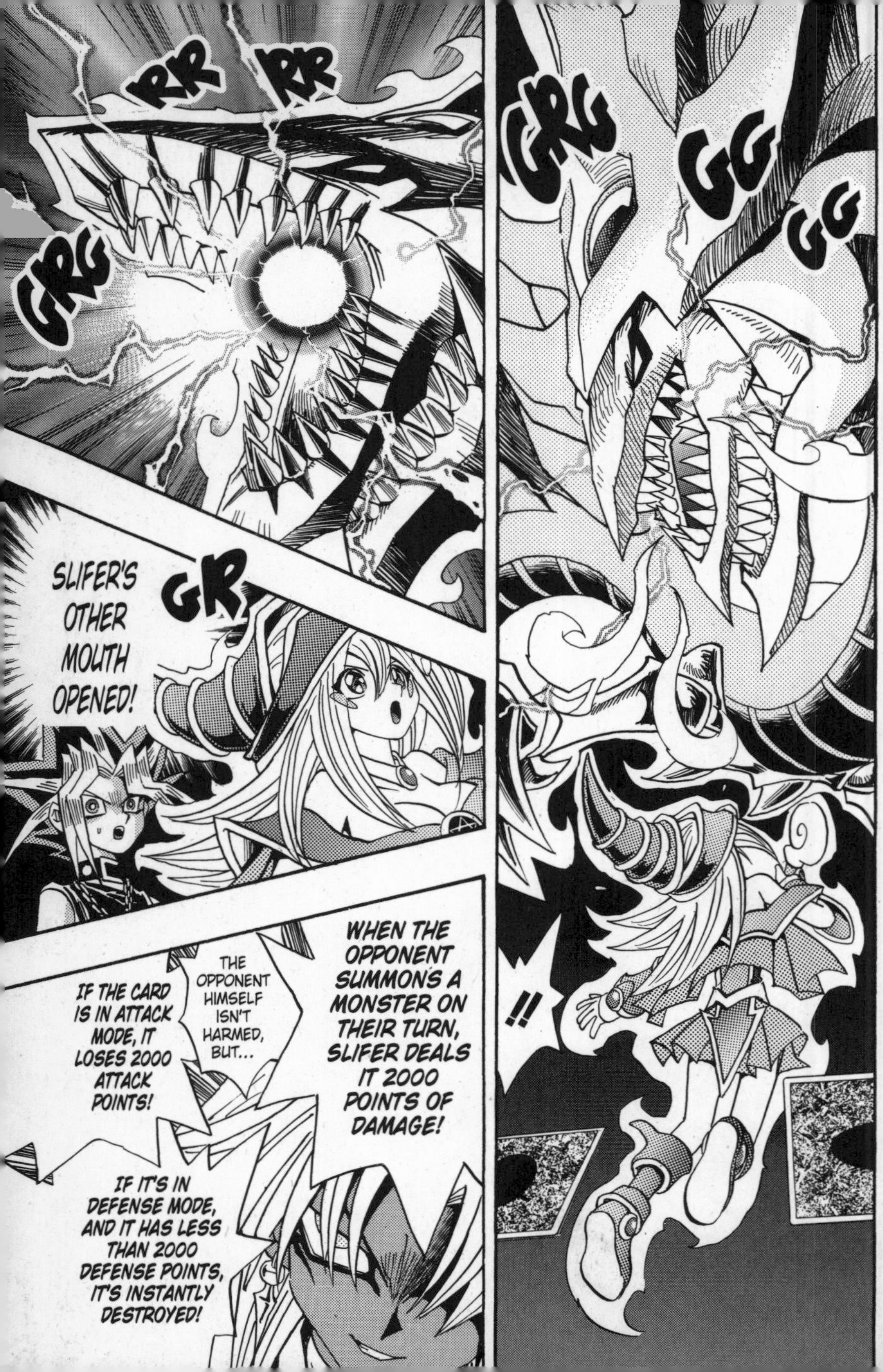
GRRG
GG
GG
!!
RR RR
GRG
GR
SLIFER'S OTHER MOUTH OPENED!
WHEN THE OPPONENT SUMMON'S A MONSTER ON THEIR TURN, SLIFER DEALS IT 2000 POINTS OF DAMAGE!
THE OPPONENT HIMSELF ISN'T HARMED, BUT...
IF THE CARD IS IN ATTACK MODE, IT LOSES 2000 ATTACK POINTS!
IF IT'S IN DEFENSE MODE, AND IT HAS LESS THAN 2000 DEFENSE POINTS, IT'S INSTANTLY DESTROYED!

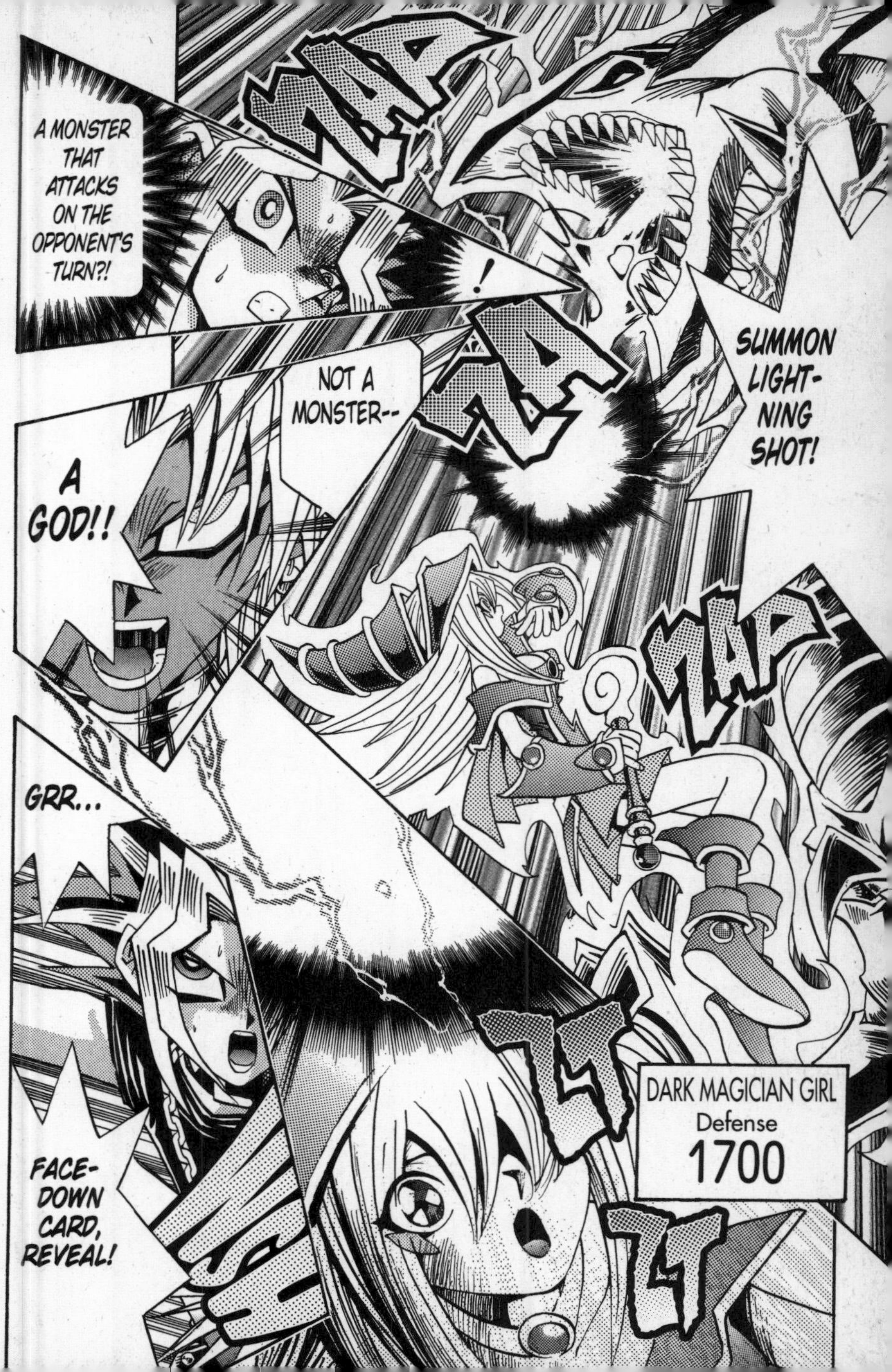
SUMMON LIGHTNING SHOT!
A MONSTER THAT ATTACKS ON THE OPPONENT'S TURN?!
!
NOT A MONSTER--
A GOD!!
ZAP
DARK MAGICIAN GIRL
Defense
1700
GRR...
FACE-DOWN CARD, REVEAL!

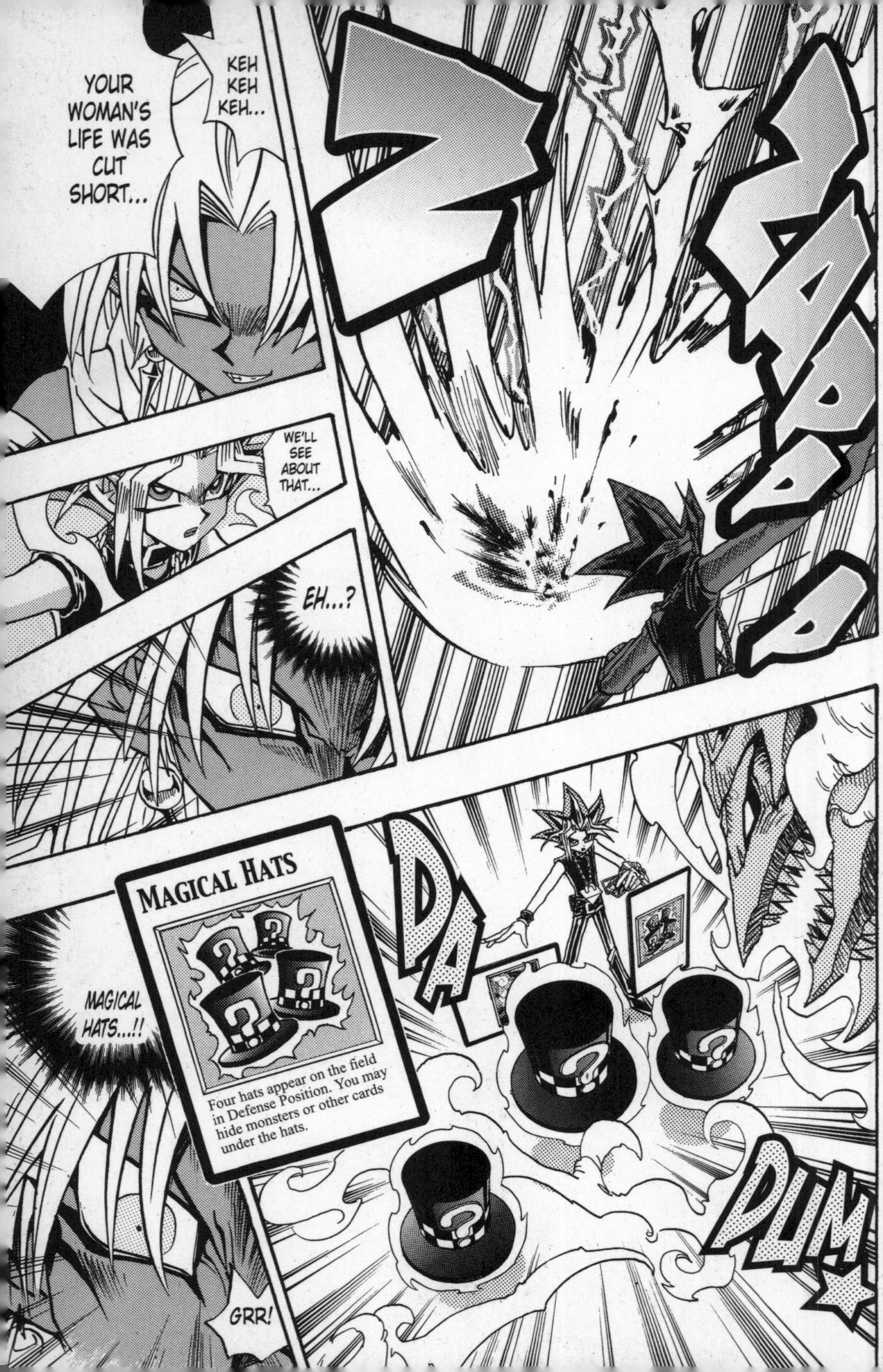
ZAP
KEH KEH KEH...
YOUR WOMAN'S LIFE WAS CUT SHORT...
WE'LL SEE ABOUT THAT...
EH...?
DUM
DA
MAGICAL HATS
Four hats appear on the field in Defense Position. You may hide monsters or other cards under the hats.
MAGICAL HATS...!!
GRR!

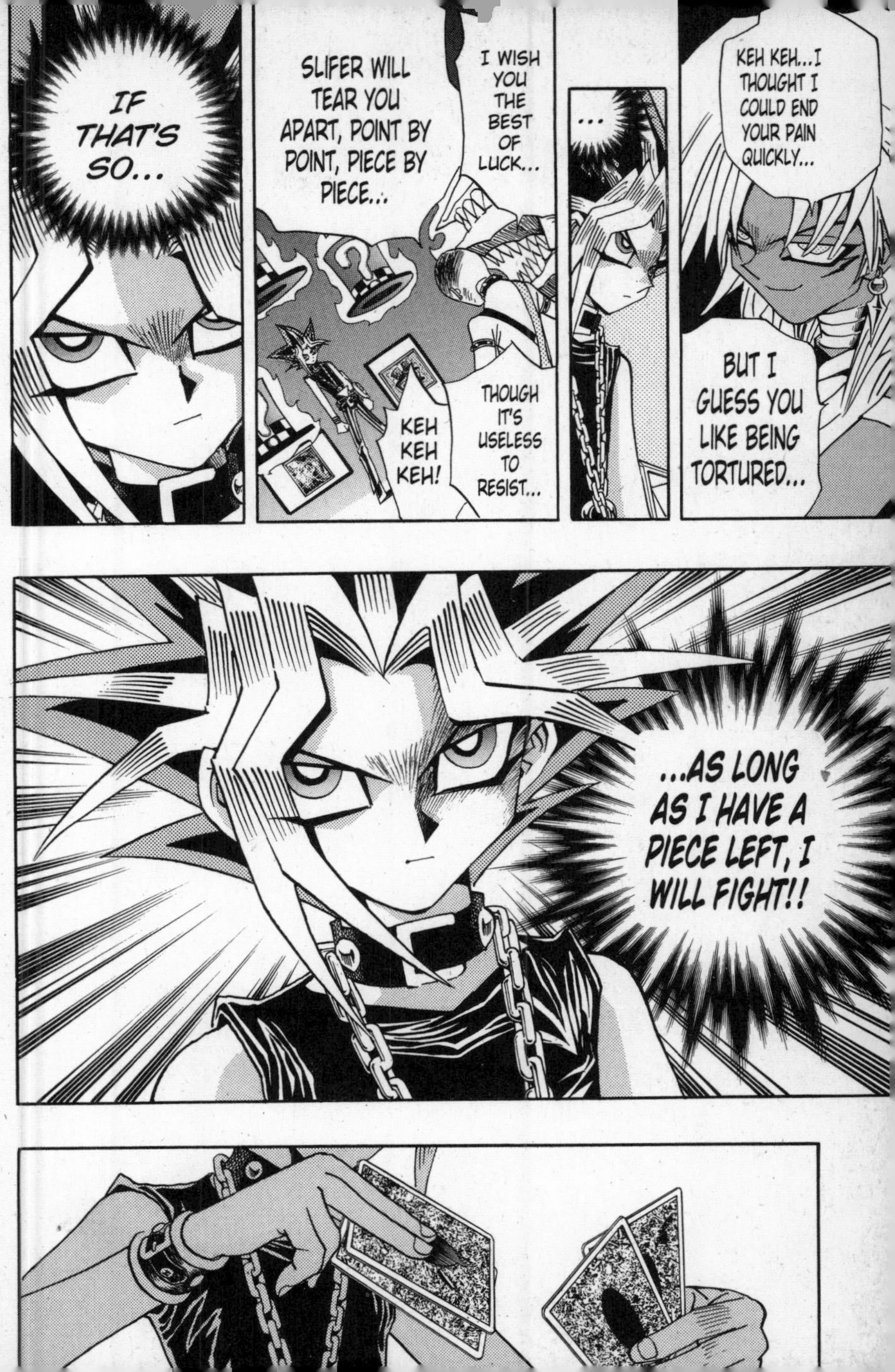

KEH KEH...I THOUGHT I COULD END YOUR PAIN QUICKLY...
BUT I GUESS YOU LIKE BEING TORTURED...
...
I WISH YOU THE BEST OF LUCK...
SLIFER WILL TEAR YOU APART, POINT BY POINT, PIECE BY PIECE...
THOUGH IT'S USELESS TO RESIST...
KEH KEH KEH!
IF THAT'S SO...
...AS LONG AS I HAVE A PIECE LEFT, I WILL FIGHT!!

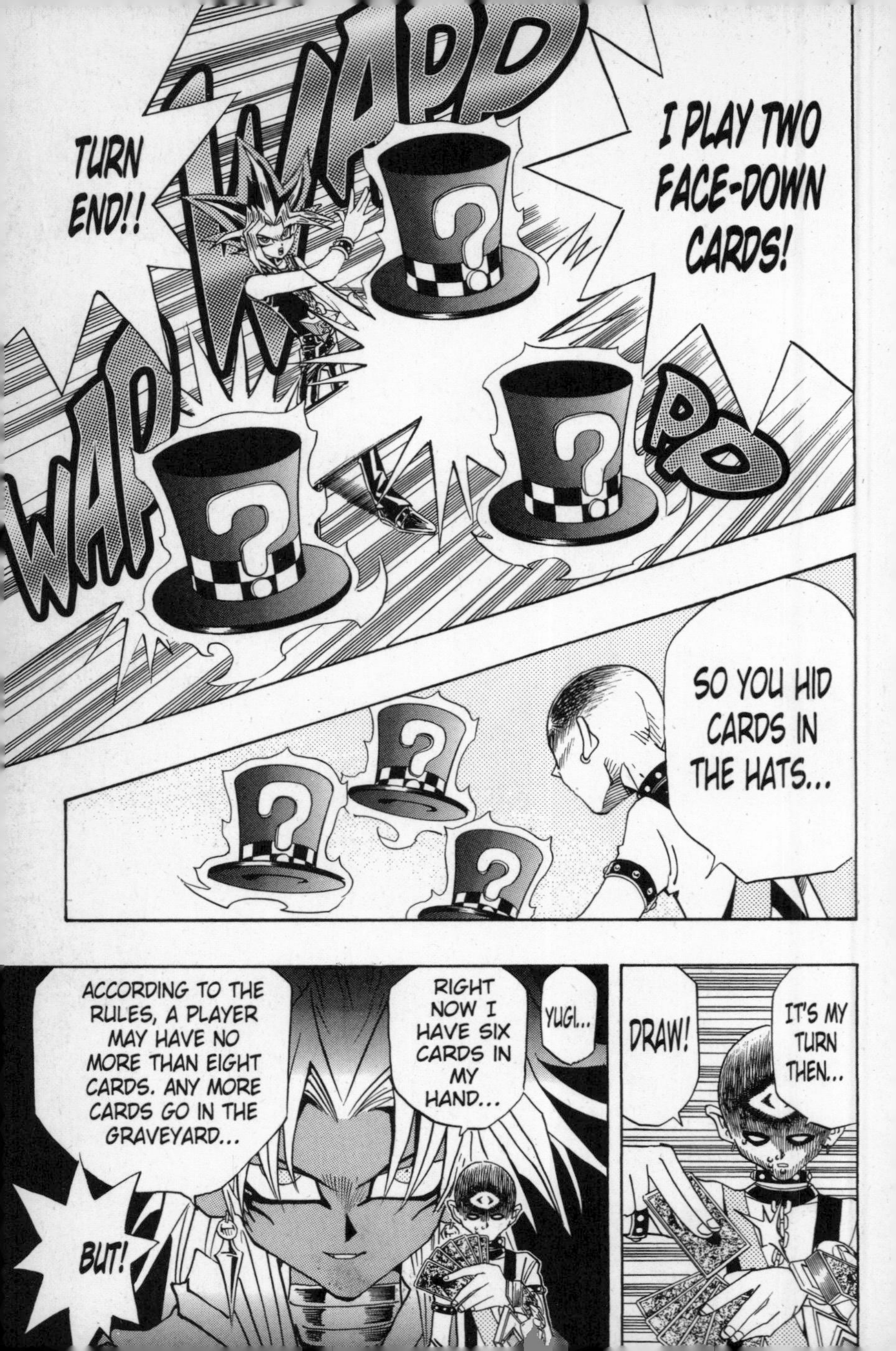
I PLAY TWO FACE-DOWN CARDS!
TURN END!!
SO YOU HID CARDS IN THE HATS...
IT'S MY TURN THEN...
DRAW!
YUGI...
RIGHT NOW I HAVE SIX CARDS IN MY HAND...
ACCORDING TO THE RULES, A PLAYER MAY HAVE NO MORE THAN EIGHT CARDS. ANY MORE CARDS GO IN THE GRAVEYARD...
BUT!

INFINITE CARDS!?

IF I PLAY *THIS* CARD, I CAN HAVE *AS MANY CARDS AS I WANT!*

INFINITE CARDS
[PERMANENT SPELL CARD]

As ... as this card remains ... field, there is no ... number of cards in ... hands.

YOU KNOW WHAT THIS MEANS, DON'T YOU...?

KEH KEH...

SLIFER WILL INCREASE ITS ATTACK POINTS INFINITELY!!

PERMANENT MAGIC! INFINITE CARDS!!

THAT'S RIGHT.

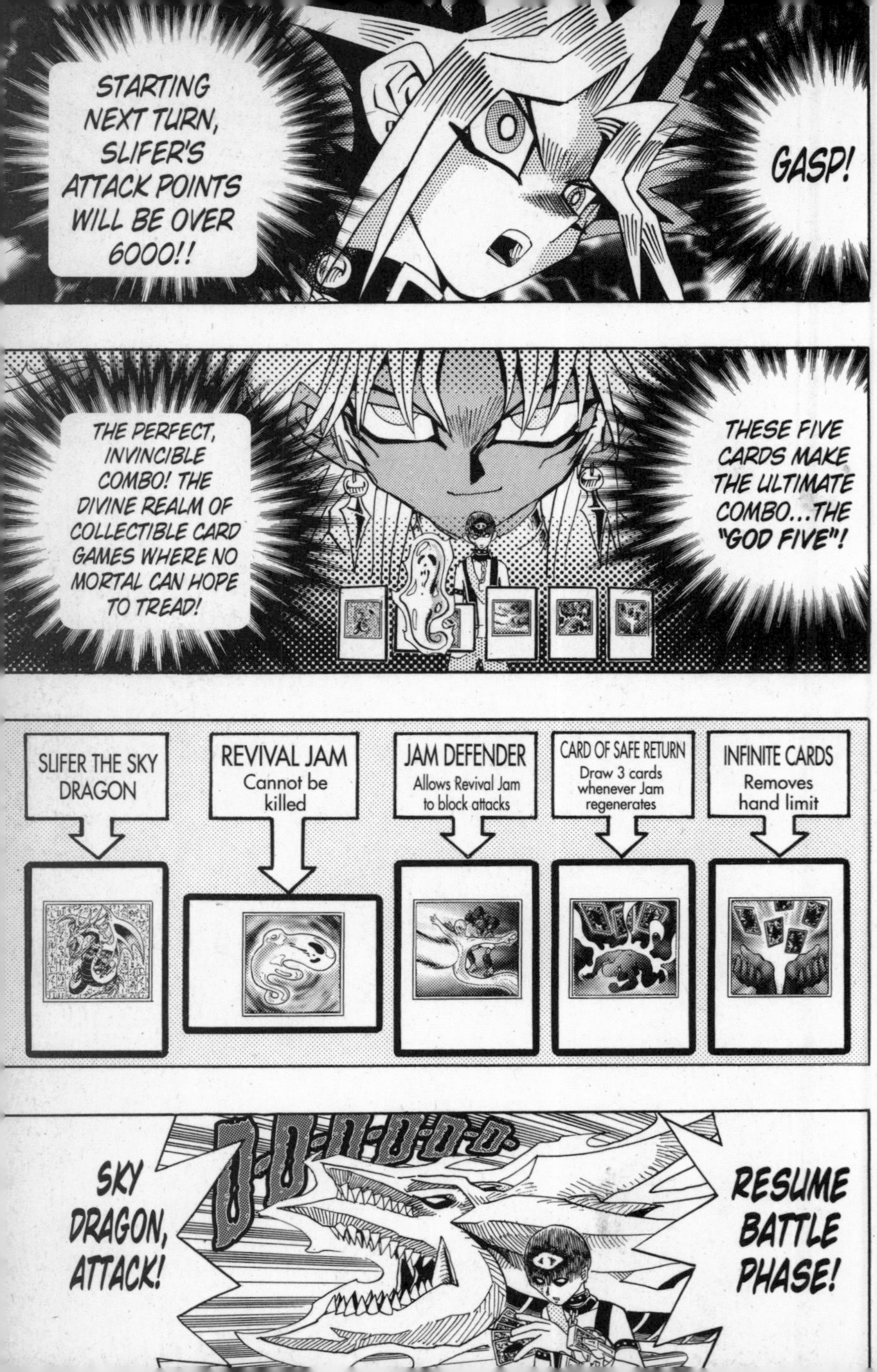
STARTING NEXT TURN, SLIFER'S ATTACK POINTS WILL BE OVER 6000!!
GASP!
THESE FIVE CARDS MAKE THE ULTIMATE COMBO...THE "GOD FIVE"!
THE PERFECT, INVINCIBLE COMBO! THE DIVINE REALM OF COLLECTIBLE CARD GAMES WHERE NO MORTAL CAN HOPE TO TREAD!
SLIFER THE SKY DRAGON
REVIVAL JAM
Cannot be killed
JAM DEFENDER
Allows Revival Jam to block attacks
CARD OF SAFE RETURN
Draw 3 cards whenever Jam regenerates
INFINITE CARDS
Removes hand limit
RESUME BATTLE PHASE!
SKY DRAGON, ATTACK!

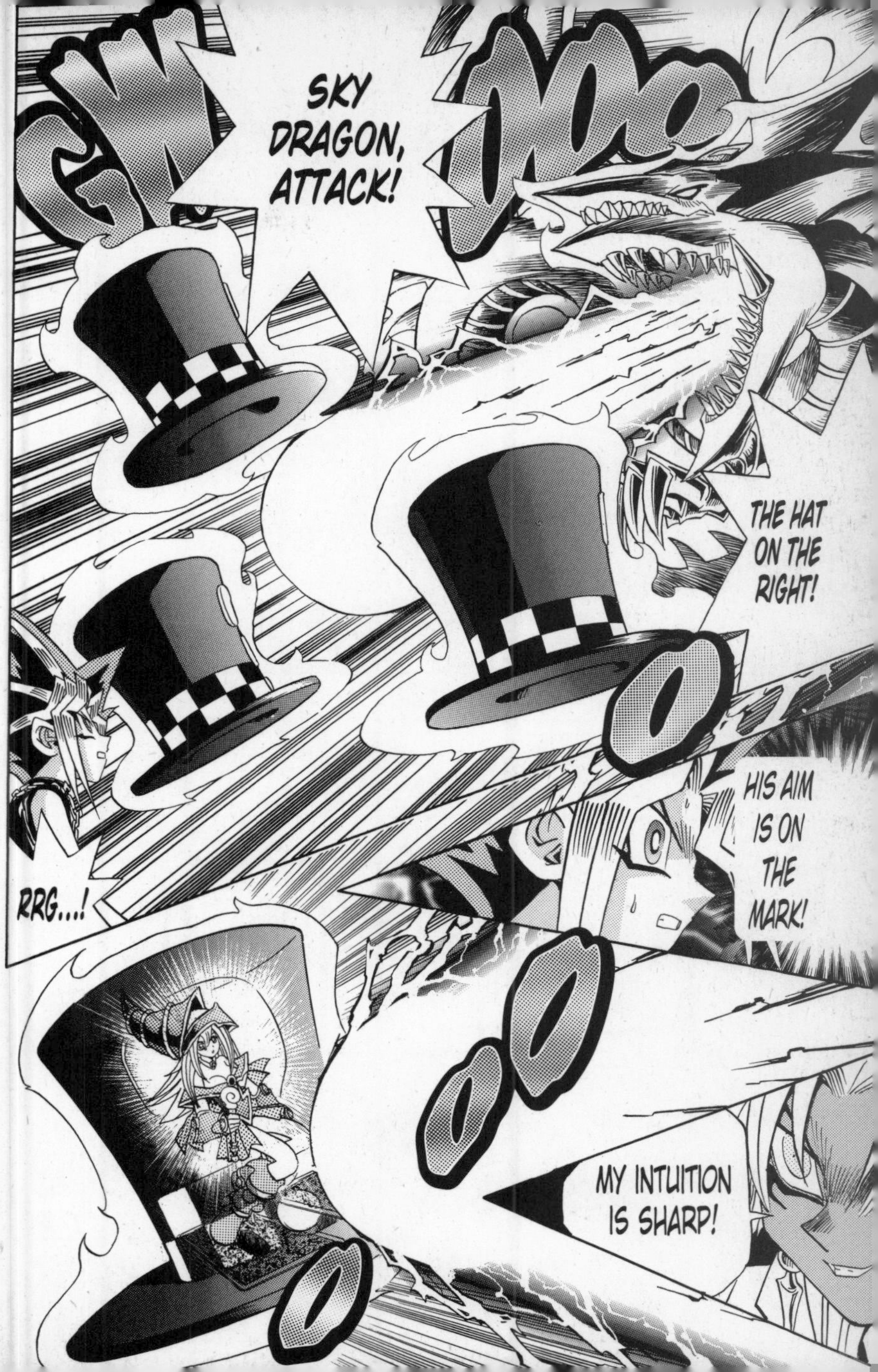
SKY DRAGON, ATTACK!
THE HAT ON THE RIGHT!
HIS AIM IS ON THE MARK!
RRG...!
MY INTUITION IS SHARP!

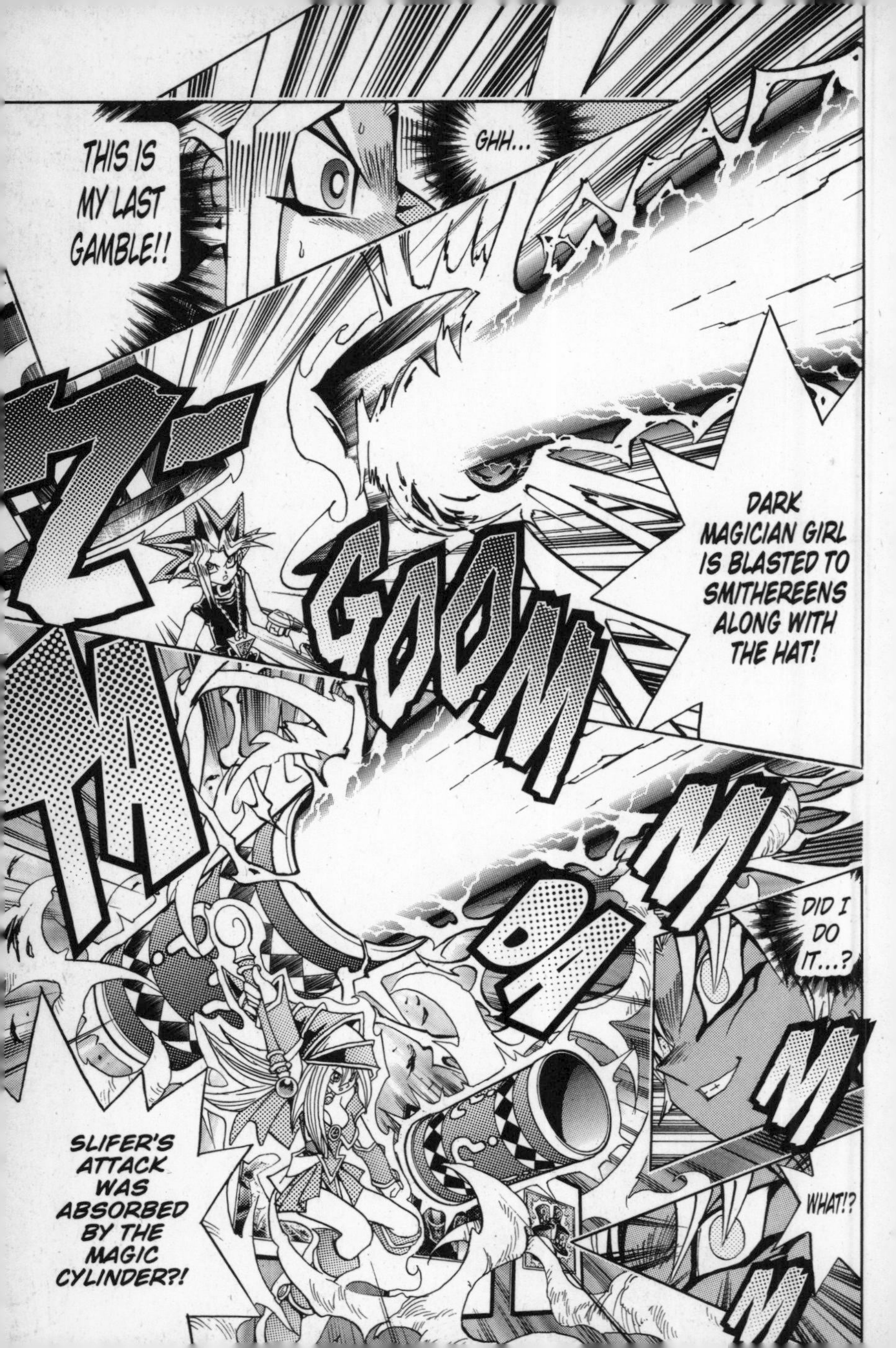
GHH...
THIS IS MY LAST GAMBLE!!
DARK MAGICIAN GIRL IS BLASTED TO SMITHEREENS ALONG WITH THE HAT!
GOOM
DID I DO IT...?
WHAT!?
SLIFER'S ATTACK WAS ABSORBED BY THE MAGIC CYLINDER?!

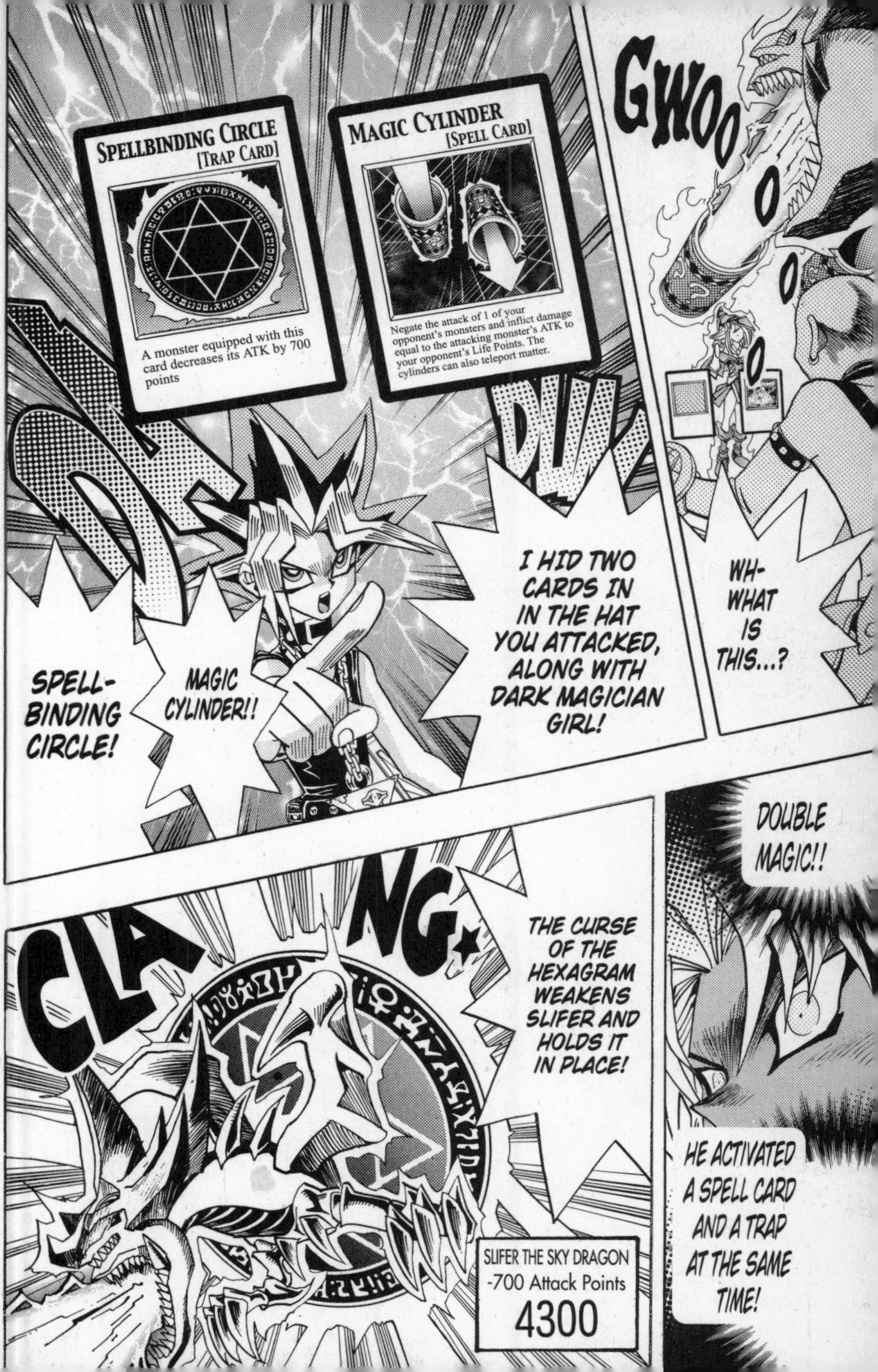
GWOOOOOO
WH-WHAT IS THIS...?
SPELLBINDING CIRCLE
[TRAP CARD]
A monster equipped with this card decreases its ATK by 700 points
MAGIC CYLINDER
[SPELL CARD]
Negate the attack of 1 of your opponent's monsters and inflict damage equal to the attacking monster's ATK to the your opponent's Life Points. The cylinders can also teleport matter.
DU
I HID TWO CARDS IN IN THE HAT YOU ATTACKED, ALONG WITH DARK MAGICIAN GIRL!
MAGIC CYLINDER!!
SPELL-BINDING CIRCLE!
DOUBLE MAGIC!!
HE ACTIVATED A SPELL CARD AND A TRAP AT THE SAME TIME!
CLA NG
THE CURSE OF THE HEXAGRAM WEAKENS SLIFER AND HOLDS IT IN PLACE!
SLIFER THE SKY DRAGON
-700 Attack Points
4300

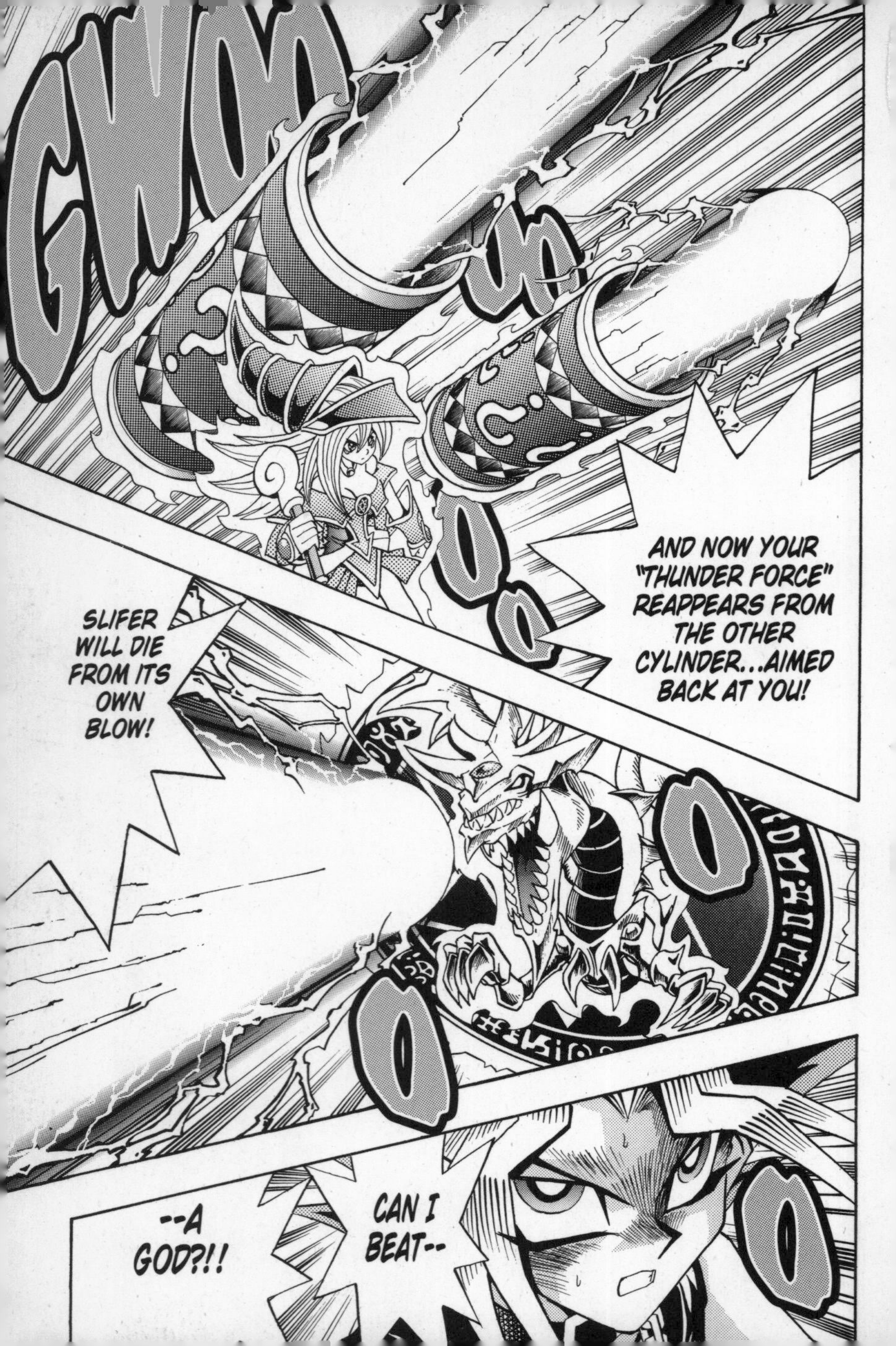
GWOO
AND NOW YOUR "THUNDER FORCE" REAPPEARS FROM THE OTHER CYLINDER...AIMED BACK AT YOU!
SLIFER WILL DIE FROM ITS OWN BLOW!
CAN I BEAT--
--A GOD?!!

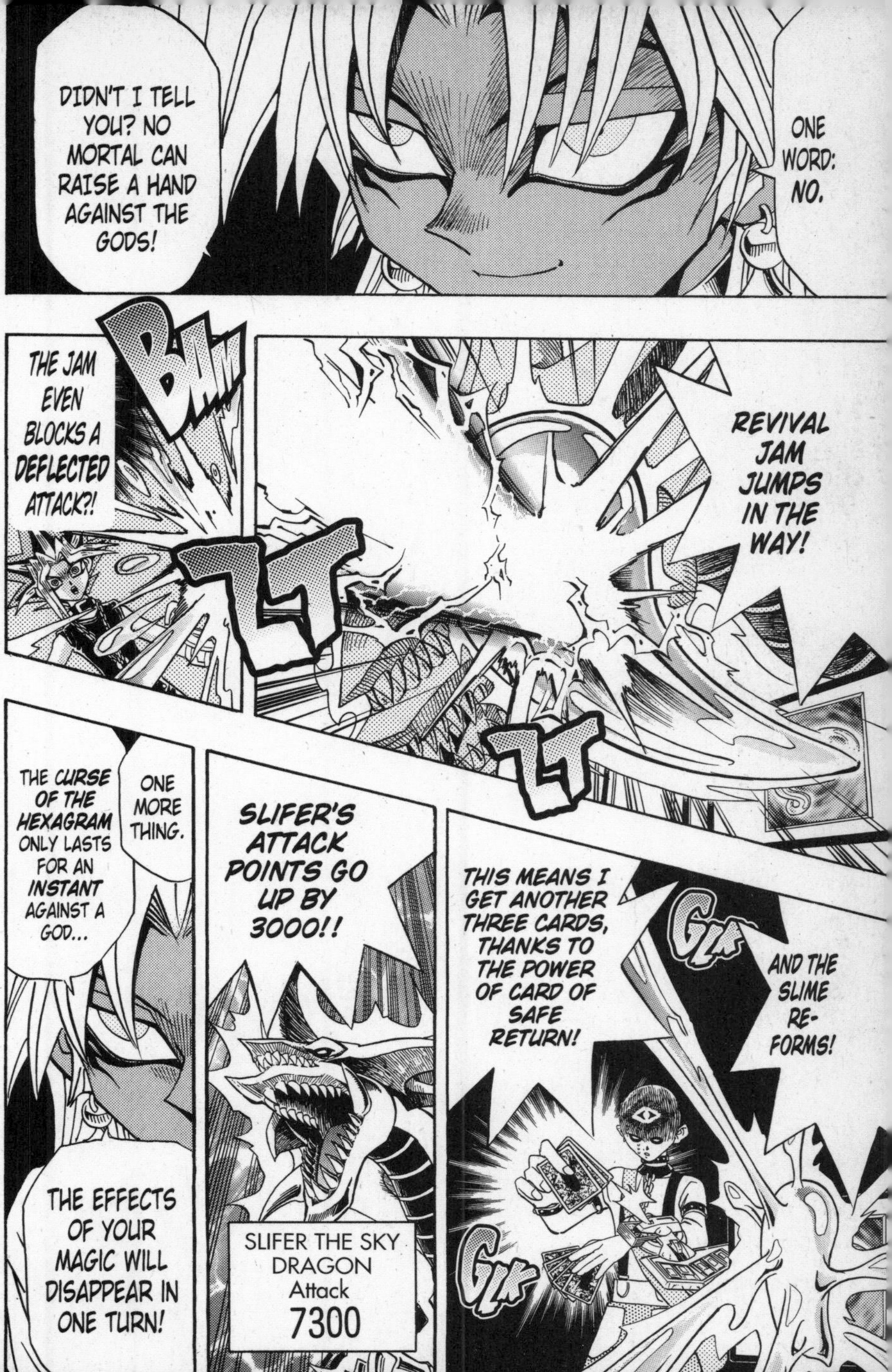
ONE WORD: NO.
DIDN'T I TELL YOU? NO MORTAL CAN RAISE A HAND AGAINST THE GODS!
REVIVAL JAM JUMPS IN THE WAY!
THE JAM EVEN BLOCKS A DEFLECTED ATTACK?!
AND THE SLIME RE-FORMS!
THIS MEANS I GET ANOTHER THREE CARDS, THANKS TO THE POWER OF CARD OF SAFE RETURN!
SLIFER'S ATTACK POINTS GO UP BY 3000!!
SLIFER THE SKY DRAGON Attack 7300
ONE MORE THING.
THE CURSE OF THE HEXAGRAM ONLY LASTS FOR AN INSTANT AGAINST A GOD...
THE EFFECTS OF YOUR MAGIC WILL DISAPPEAR IN ONE TURN!

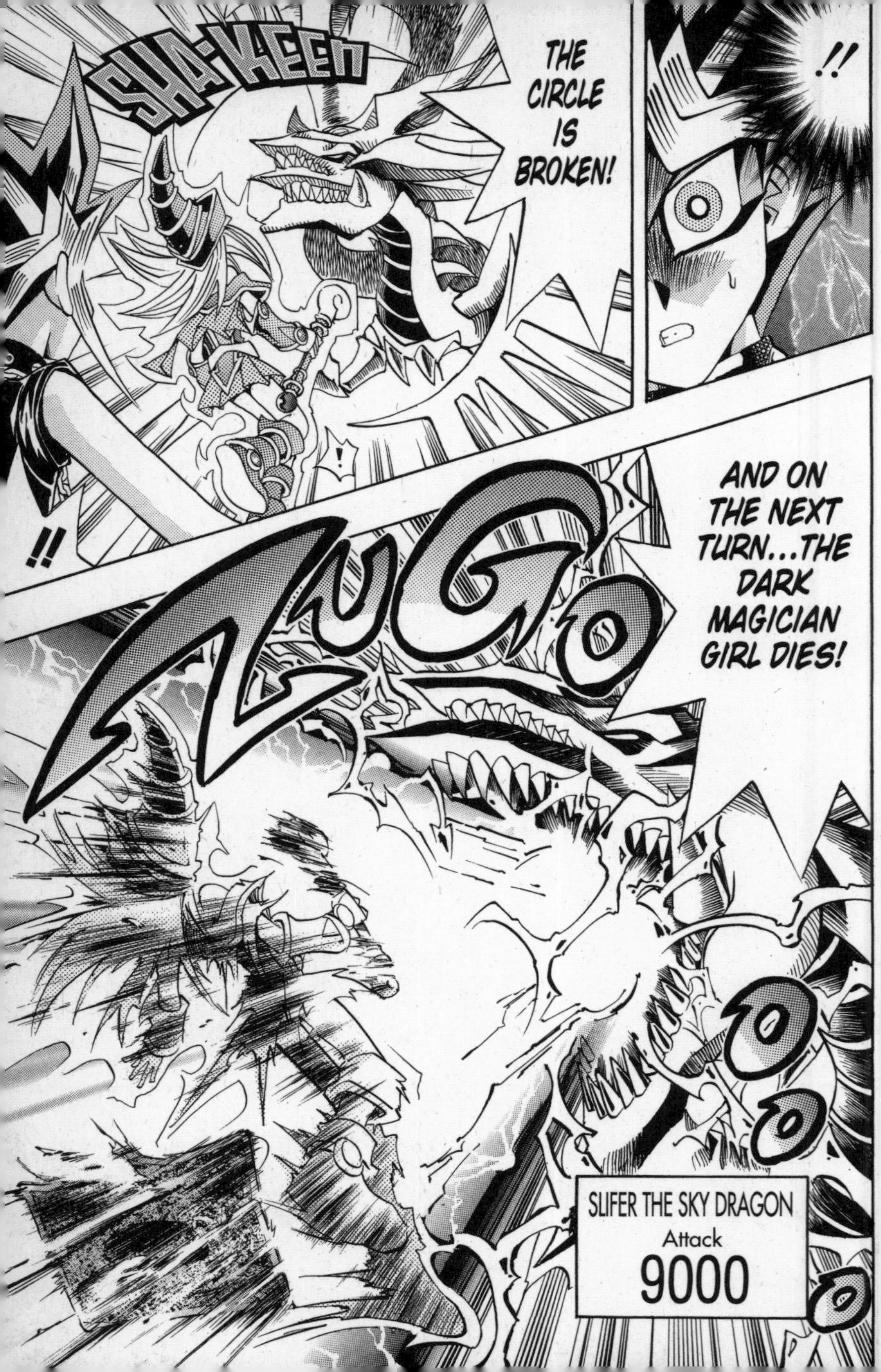
!!
THE CIRCLE IS BROKEN!
SHA-KEEN
!
!!
AND ON THE NEXT TURN...THE DARK MAGICIAN GIRL DIES!
ZUGO
SLIFER THE SKY DRAGON
Attack
9000

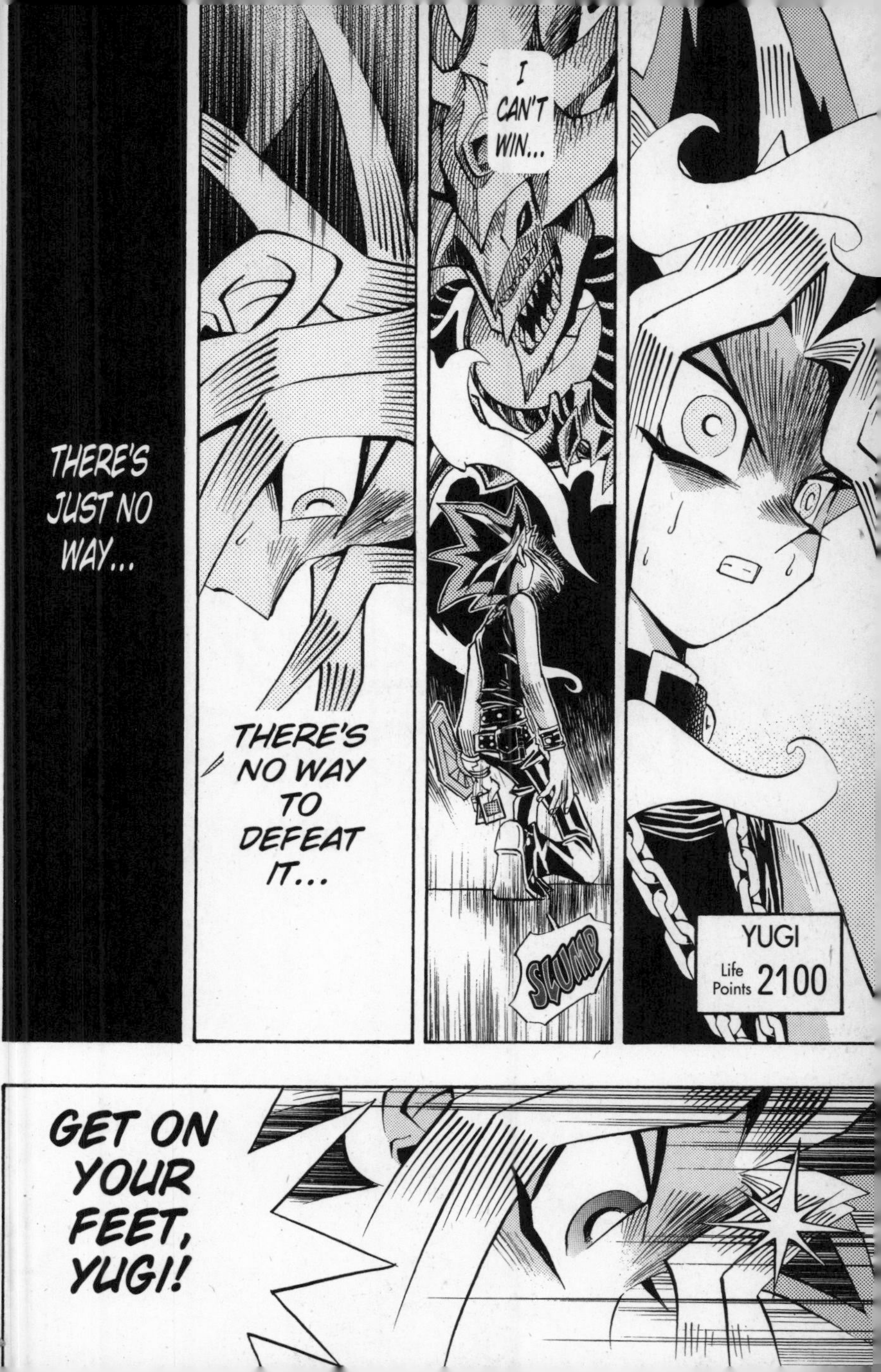
YUGI
Life Points 2100
I CAN'T WIN...
SLUMP
THERE'S NO WAY TO DEFEAT IT...
THERE'S JUST NO WAY...
GET ON YOUR FEET, YUGI!

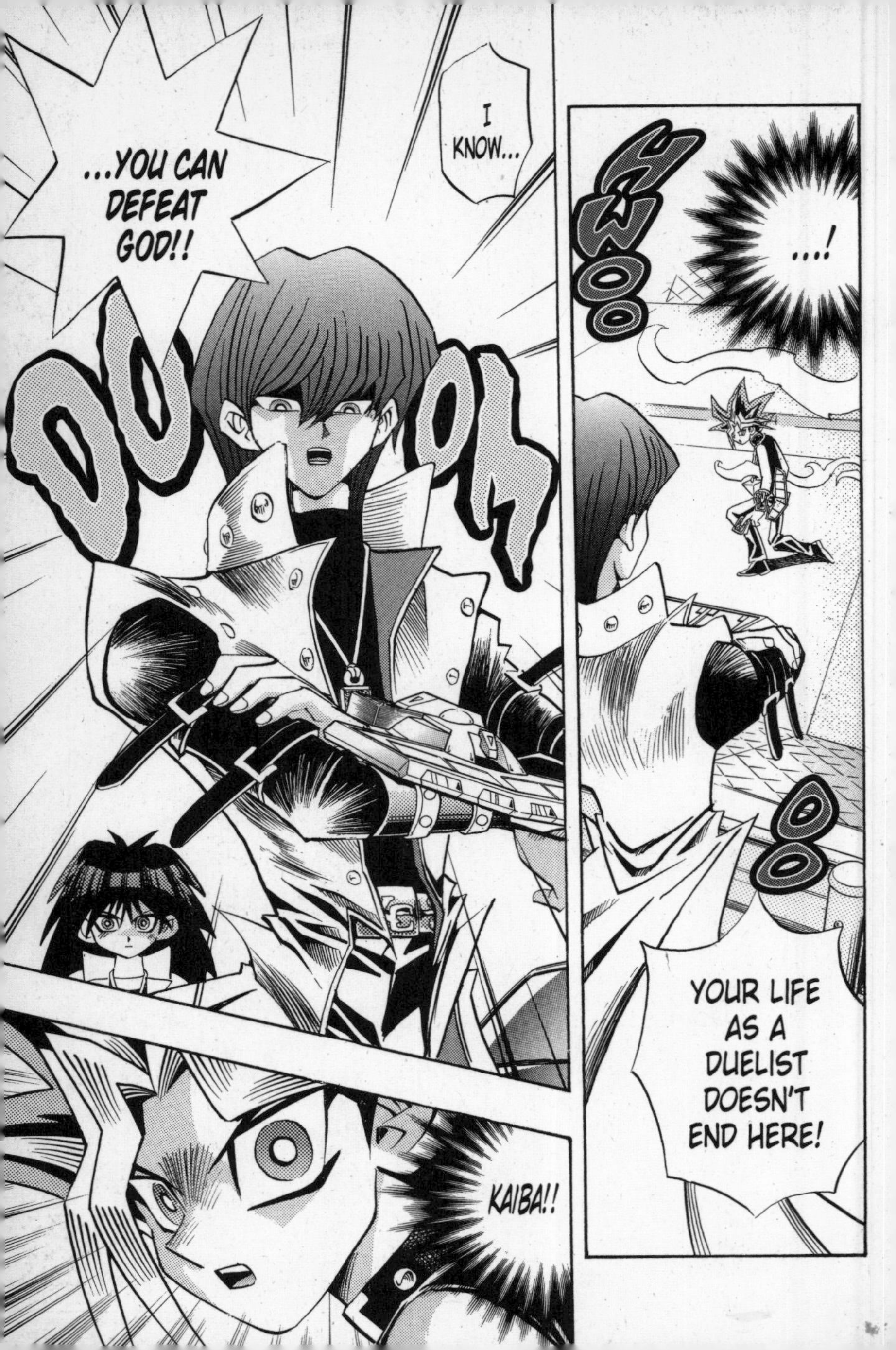
...!
YOUR LIFE AS A DUELIST DOESN'T END HERE!
I KNOW...
...YOU CAN DEFEAT GOD!!
KAIBA!!

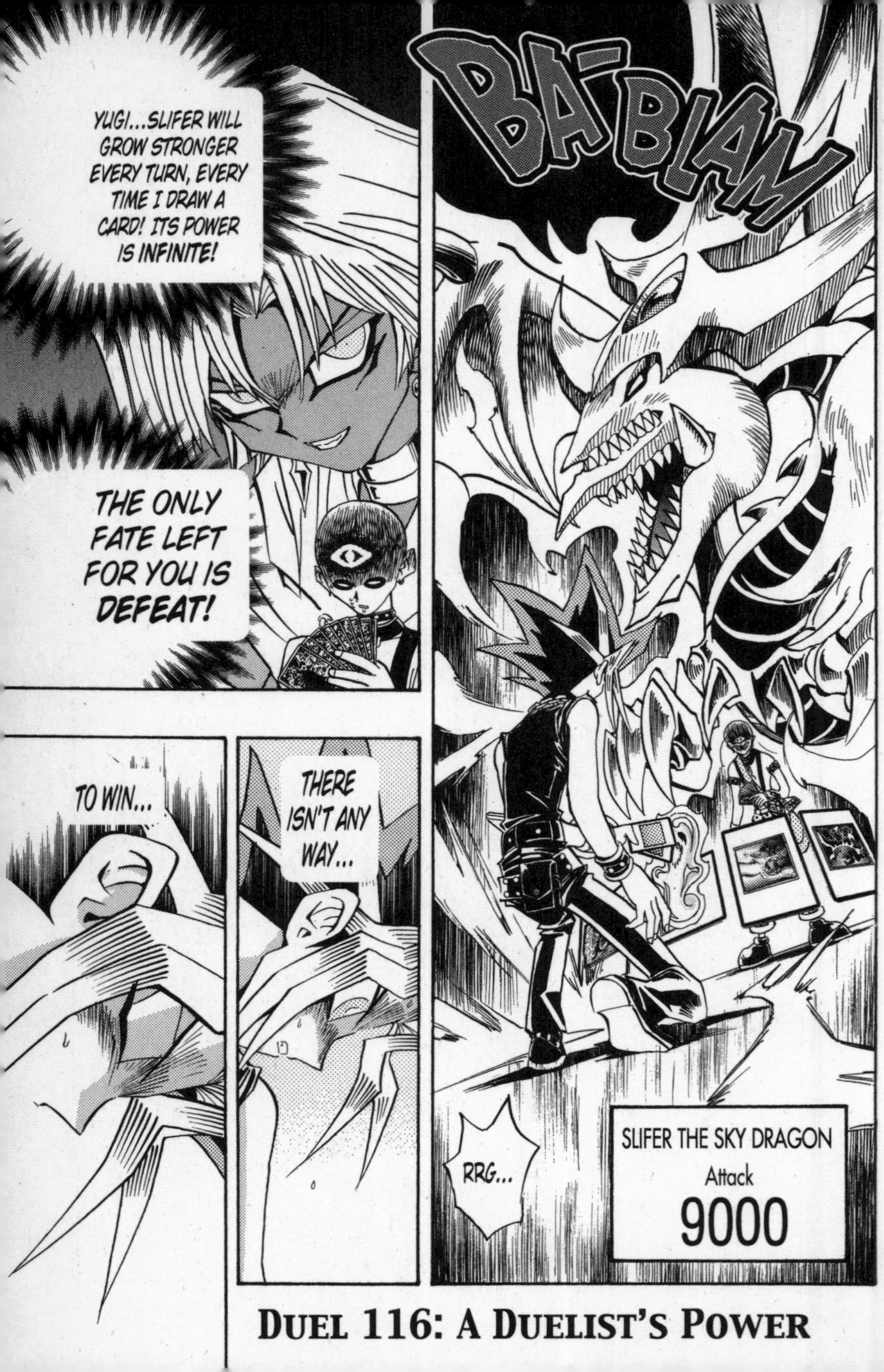
BA-BLAM
RRG...
SLIFER THE SKY DRAGON
Attack
9000
YUGI...SLIFER WILL GROW STRONGER EVERY TURN, EVERY TIME I DRAW A CARD! ITS POWER IS INFINITE!
THE ONLY FATE LEFT FOR YOU IS DEFEAT!
THERE ISN'T ANY WAY...
TO WIN...

Duel 116: A Duelist's Power

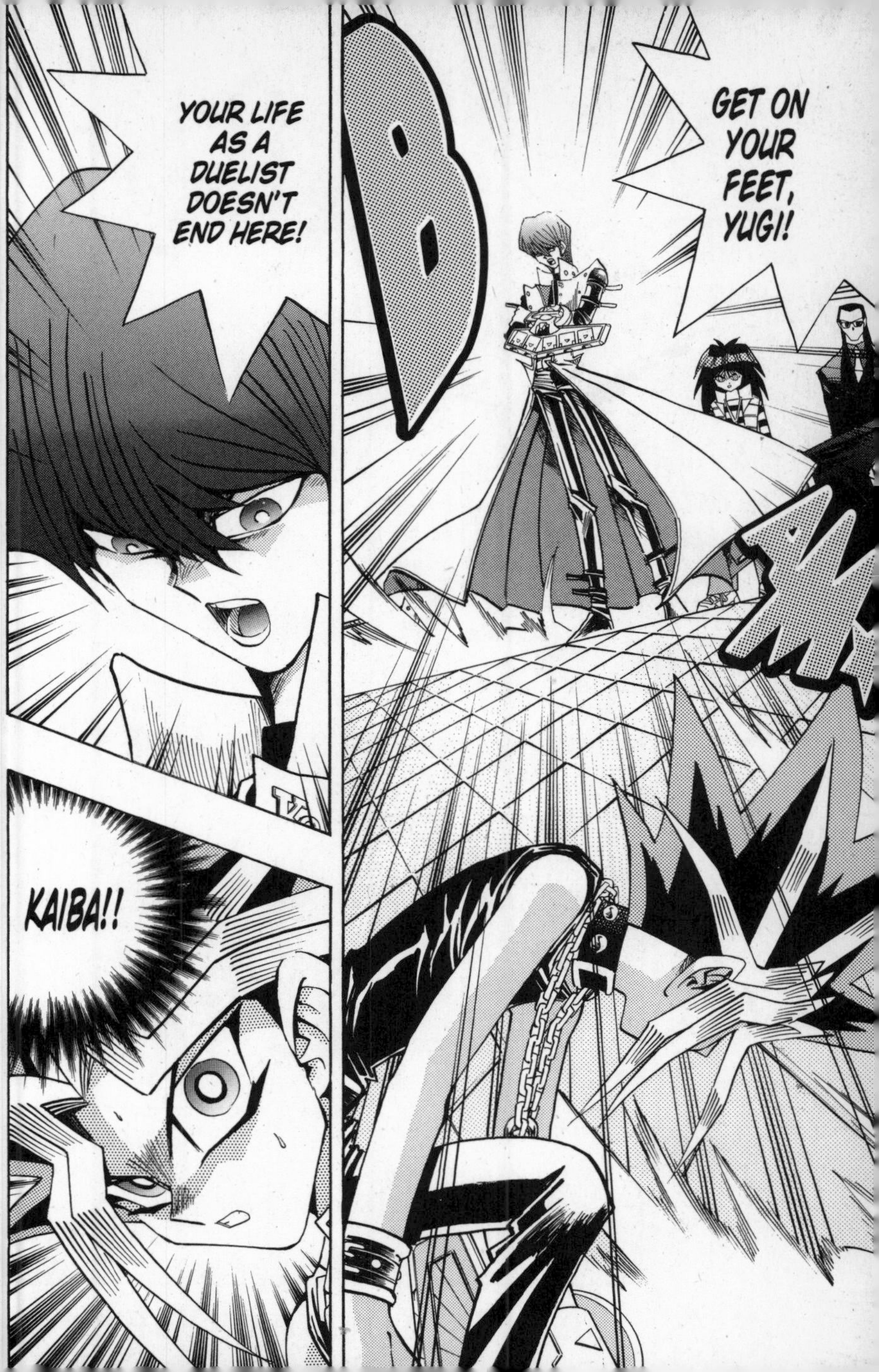
GET ON YOUR FEET, YUGI!
YOUR LIFE AS A DUELIST DOESN'T END HERE!
KAIBA!!

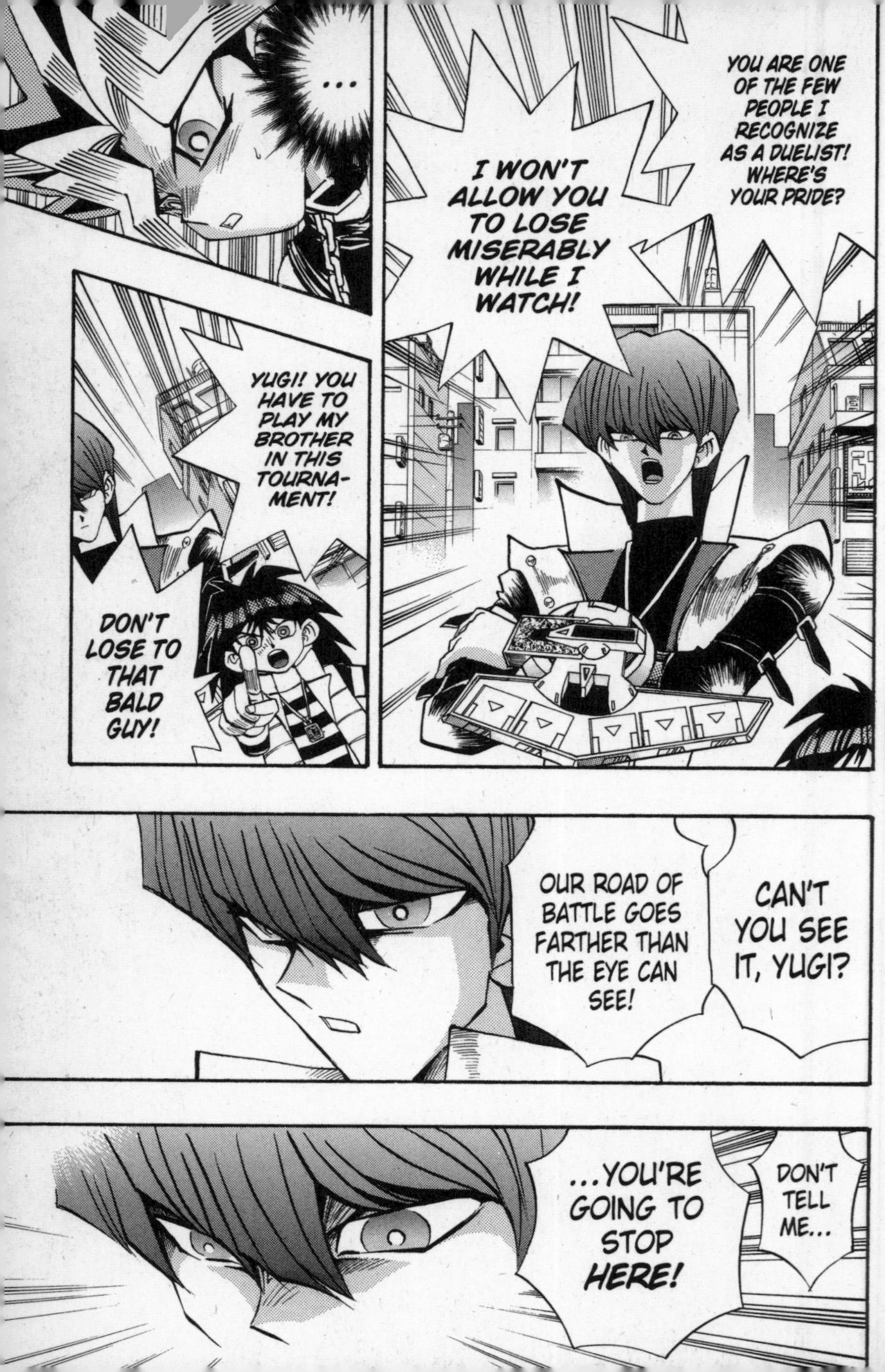
YOU ARE ONE OF THE FEW PEOPLE I RECOGNIZE AS A DUELIST! WHERE'S YOUR PRIDE?
I WON'T ALLOW YOU TO LOSE MISERABLY WHILE I WATCH!
...
YUGI! YOU HAVE TO PLAY MY BROTHER IN THIS TOURNA-MENT!
DON'T LOSE TO THAT BALD GUY!
CAN'T YOU SEE IT, YUGI?
OUR ROAD OF BATTLE GOES FARTHER THAN THE EYE CAN SEE!
DON'T TELL ME...
...YOU'RE GOING TO STOP HERE!

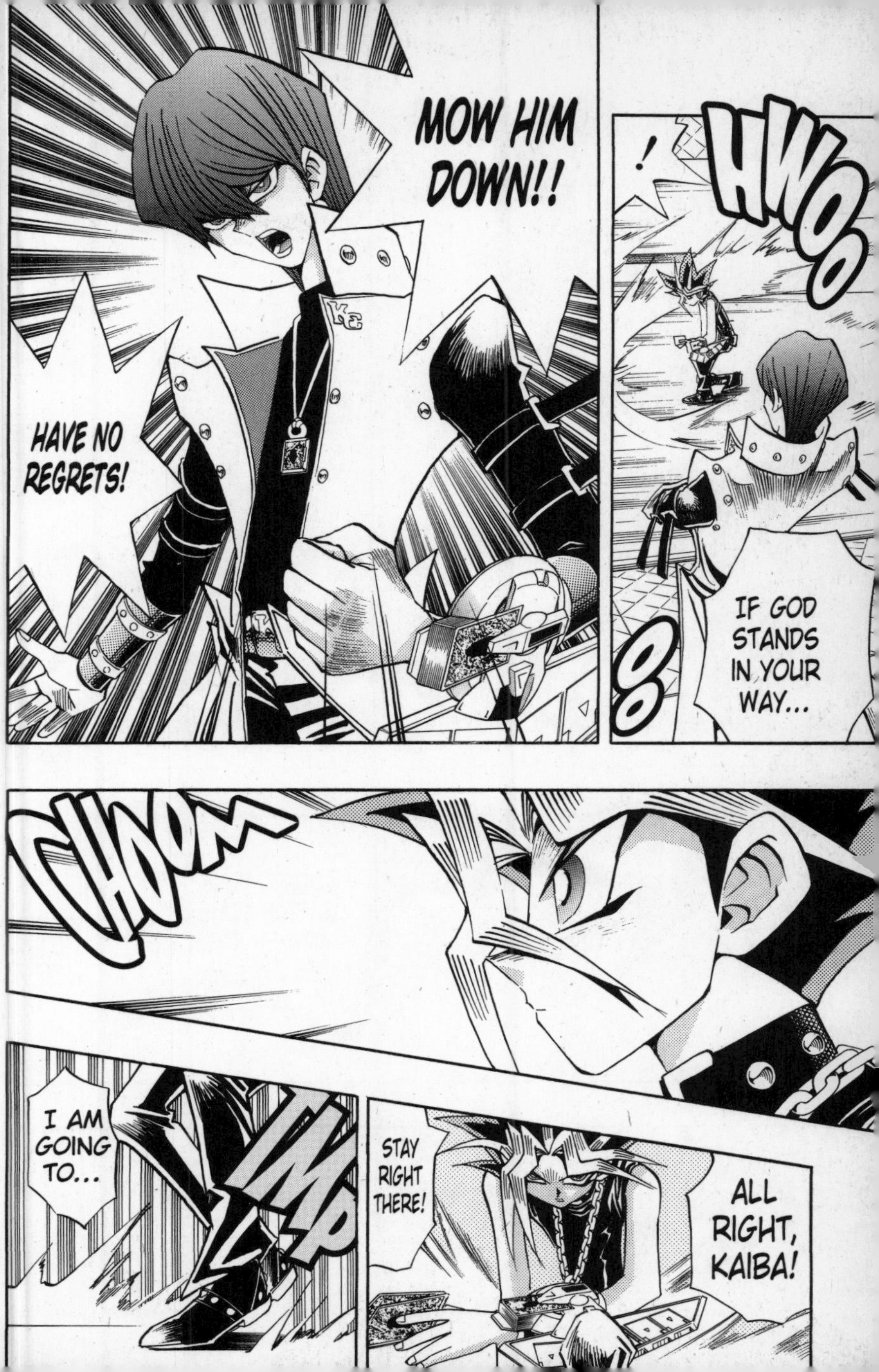
HWOO
!
IF GOD STANDS IN YOUR WAY...
MOW HIM DOWN!!
HAVE NO REGRETS!
CHOOM
ALL RIGHT, KAIBA!
STAY RIGHT THERE!
TMP
I AM GOING TO...

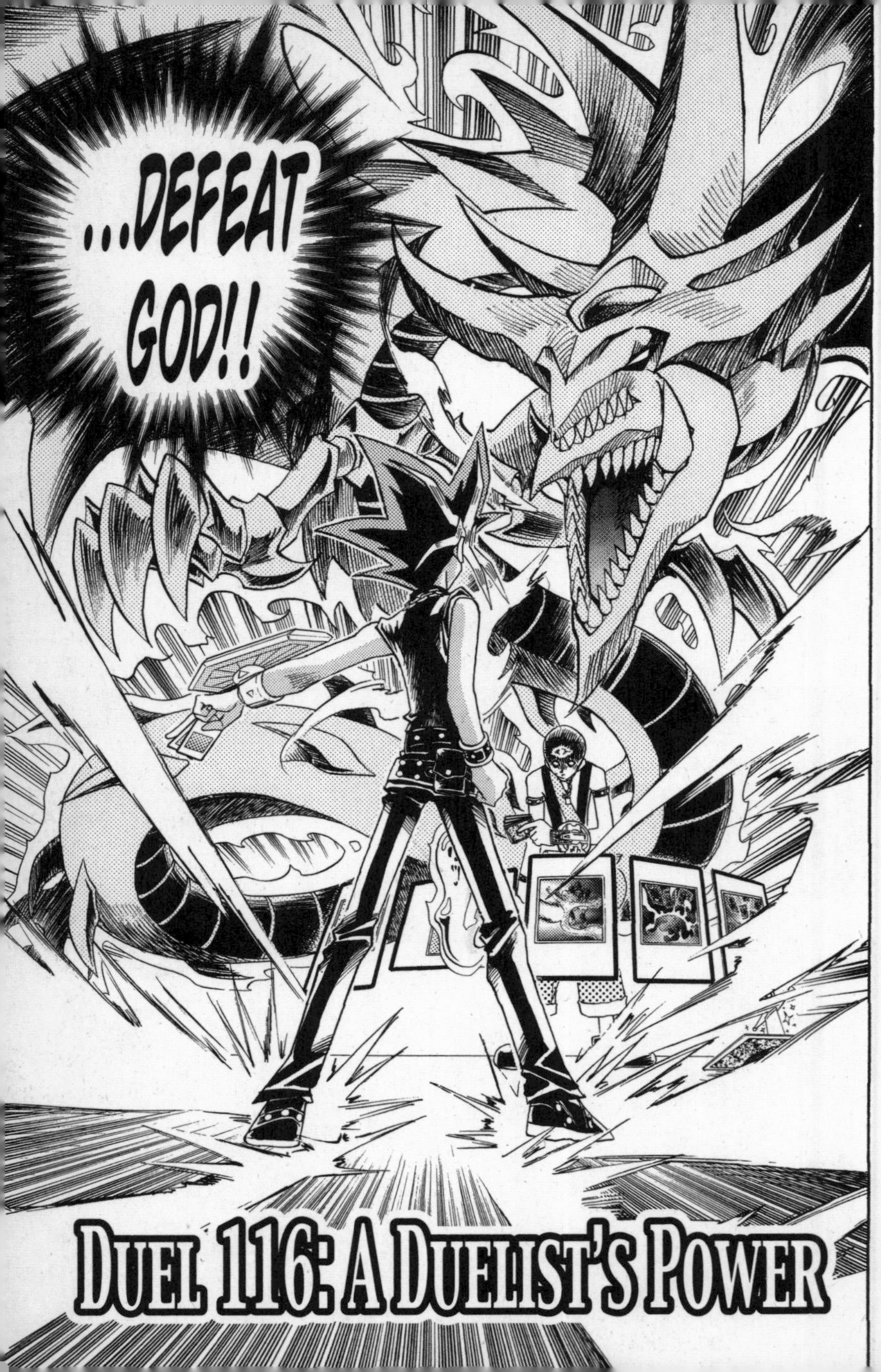
...DEFEAT GOD!!
DUEL 116: A DUELIST'S POWER

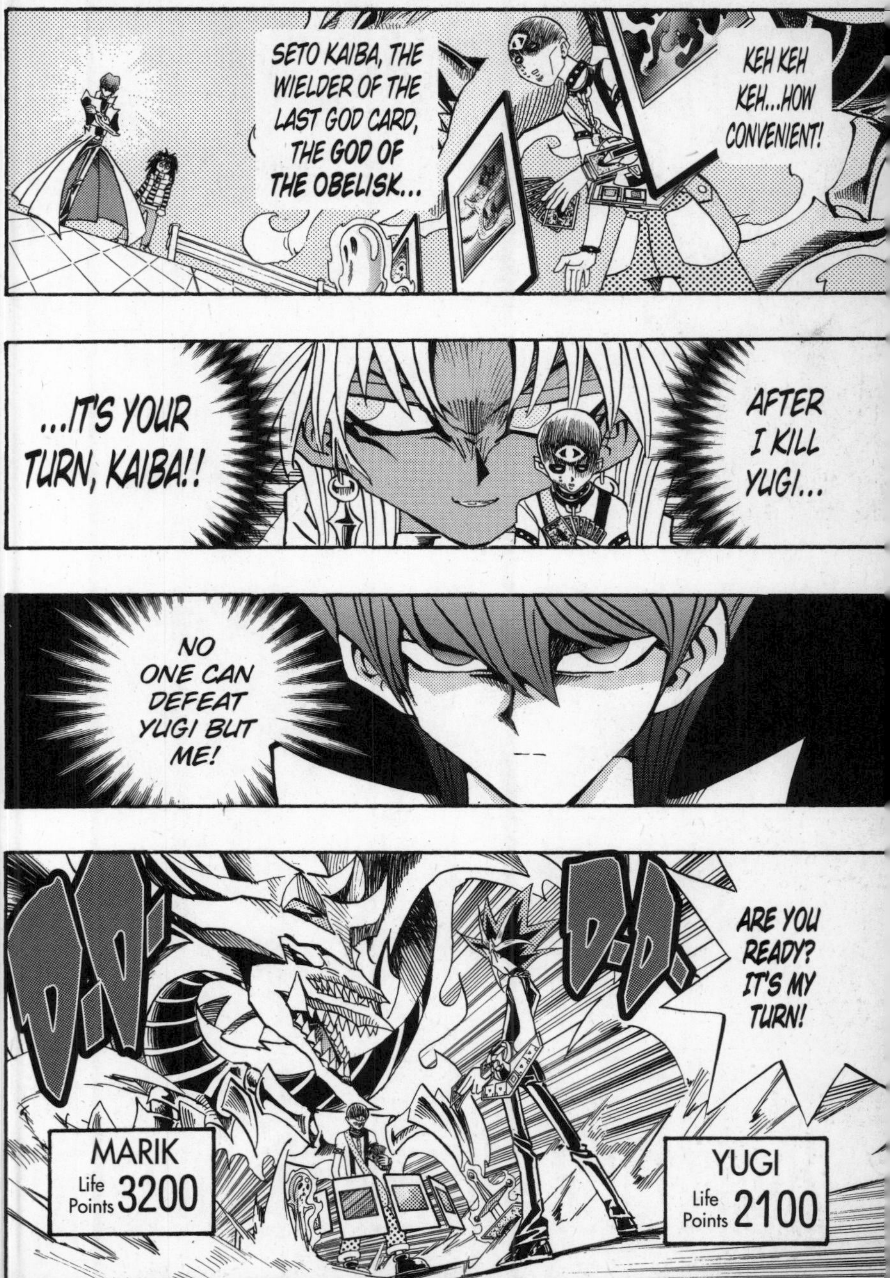
KEH KEH KEH...HOW CONVENIENT!
SETO KAIBA, THE WIELDER OF THE LAST GOD CARD, THE GOD OF THE OBELISK...
AFTER I KILL YUGI...
...IT'S YOUR TURN, KAIBA!!
NO ONE CAN DEFEAT YUGI BUT ME!
ARE YOU READY? IT'S MY TURN!
D.D.
D.D.
YUGI Life Points 2100
MARIK Life Points 3200

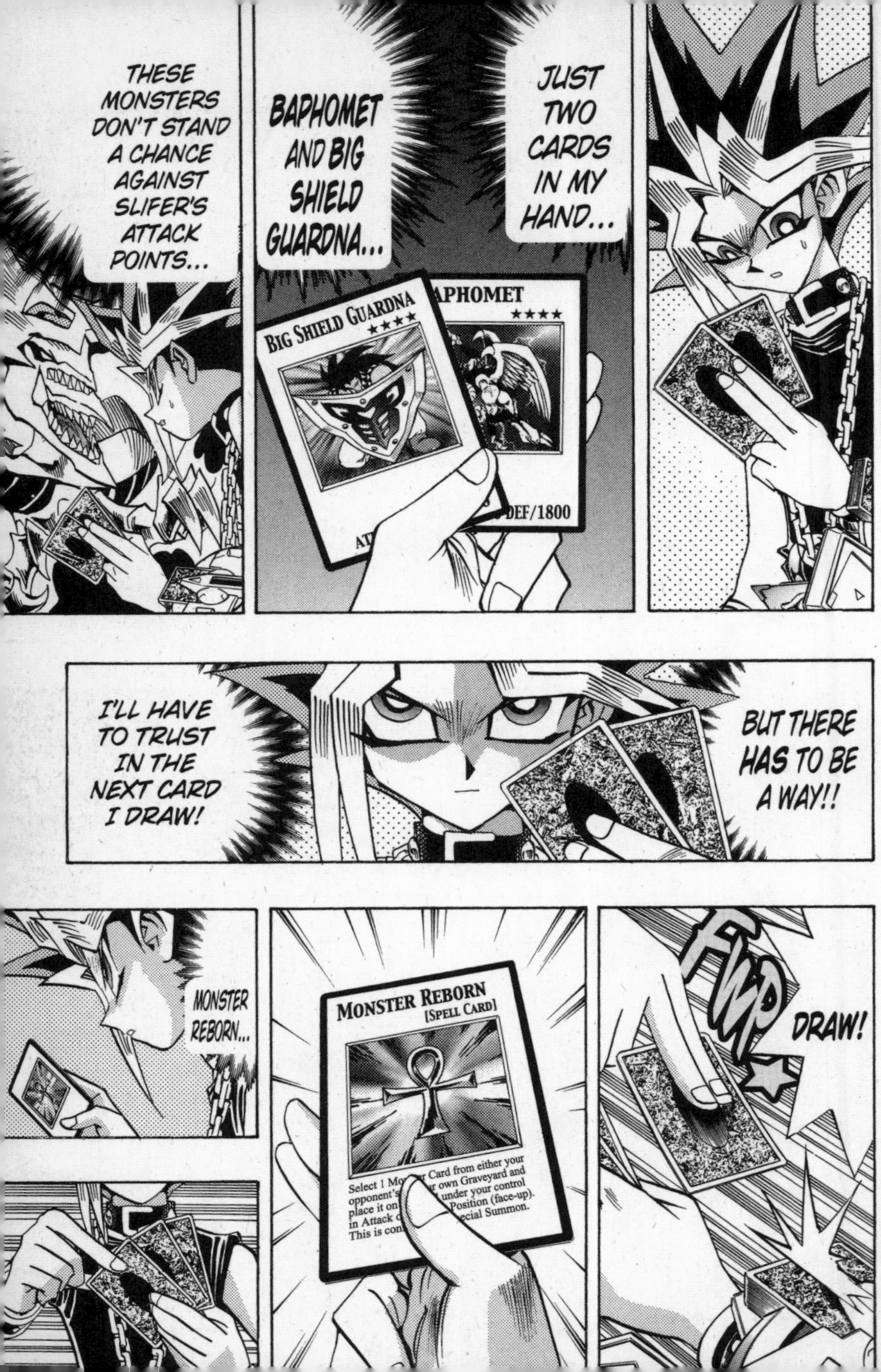
JUST TWO CARDS IN MY HAND...
BAPHOMET AND BIG SHIELD GUARDNA...
BIG SHIELD GUARDNA
THESE MONSTERS DON'T STAND A CHANCE AGAINST SLIFER'S ATTACK POINTS...
BUT THERE HAS TO BE A WAY!!
I'LL HAVE TO TRUST IN THE NEXT CARD I DRAW!
FWP
DRAW!
MONSTER REBORN
[SPELL CARD]
MONSTER REBORN...

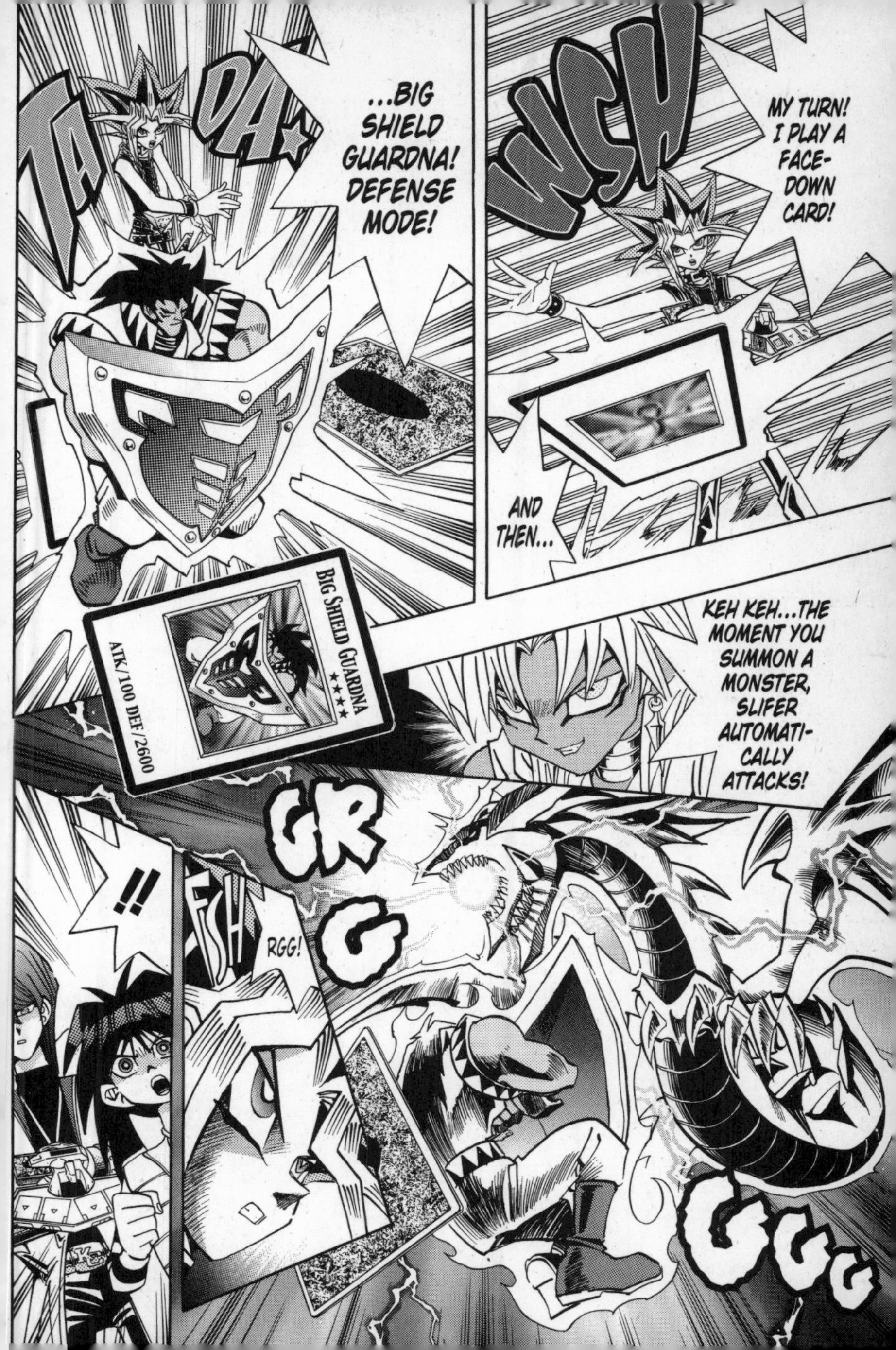
WUSH
MY TURN! I PLAY A FACE-DOWN CARD!
AND THEN...
TA DA
...BIG SHIELD GUARDNA! DEFENSE MODE!
BIG SHIELD GUARDNA
★★★★
ATK/100 DEF/2600
KEH KEH...THE MOMENT YOU SUMMON A MONSTER, SLIFER AUTOMATICALLY ATTACKS!
GR
G
GGG
RGG!
FSH
!!

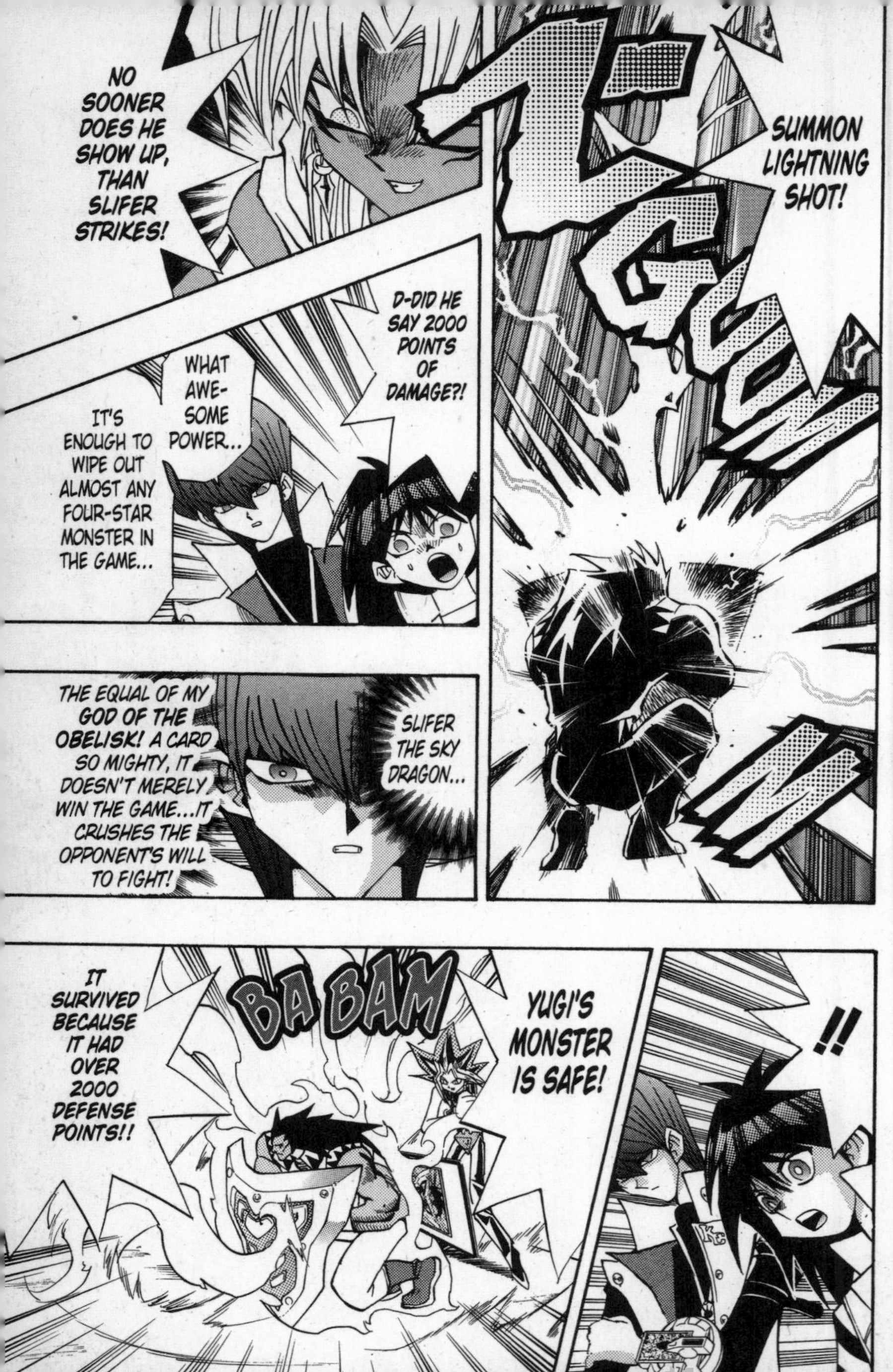
SUMMON LIGHTNING SHOT!
NO SOONER DOES HE SHOW UP, THAN SLIFER STRIKES!
D-DID HE SAY 2000 POINTS OF DAMAGE?!
WHAT AWE-SOME POWER...
IT'S ENOUGH TO WIPE OUT ALMOST ANY FOUR-STAR MONSTER IN THE GAME...
SLIFER THE SKY DRAGON...
THE EQUAL OF MY GOD OF THE OBELISK! A CARD SO MIGHTY, IT DOESN'T MERELY WIN THE GAME...IT CRUSHES THE OPPONENT'S WILL TO FIGHT!
!!
YUGI'S MONSTER IS SAFE!
BA BAM
IT SURVIVED BECAUSE IT HAD OVER 2000 DEFENSE POINTS!!

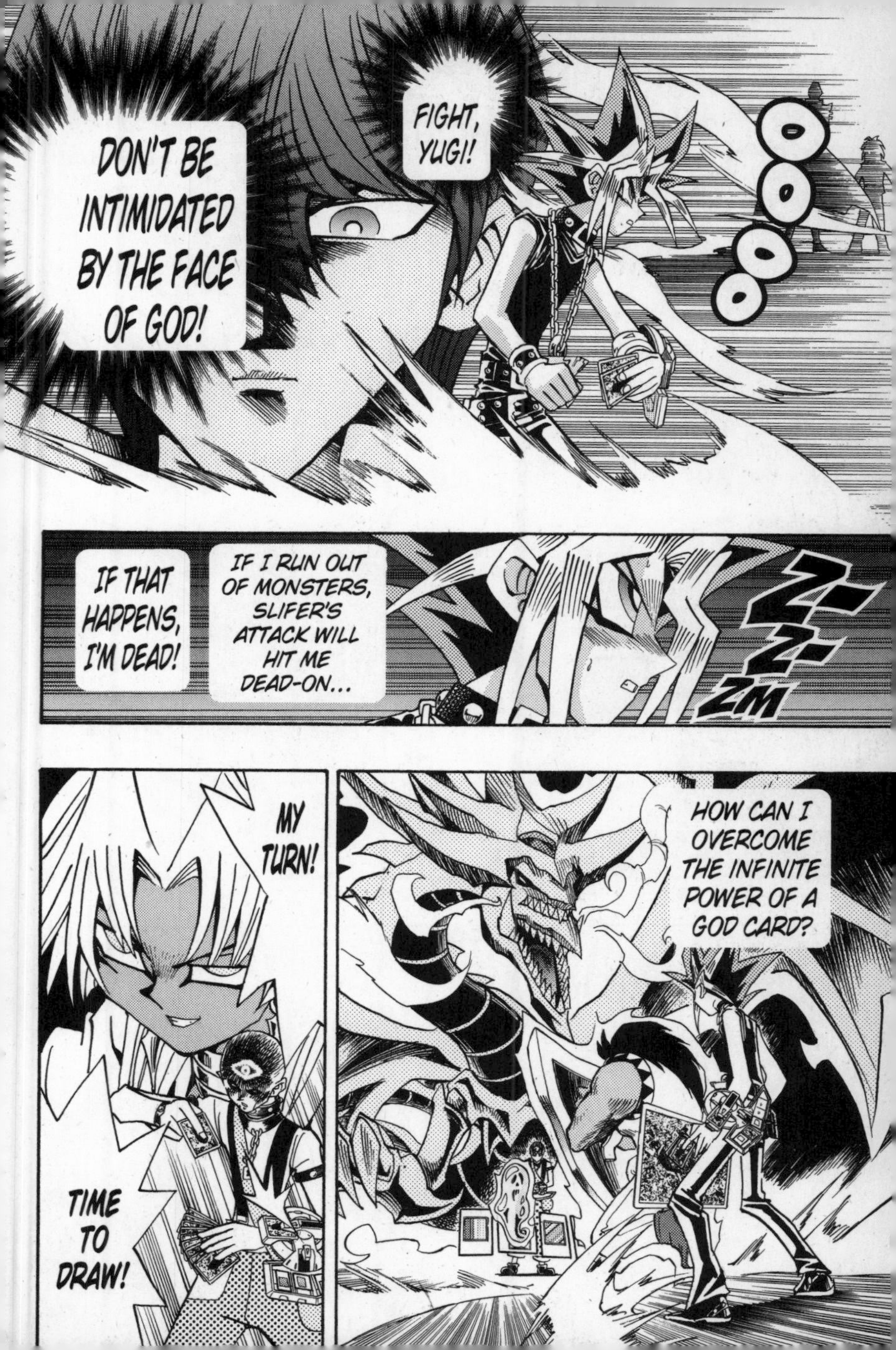
OOOO
FIGHT, YUGI!
DON'T BE INTIMIDATED BY THE FACE OF GOD!
Z-Z-Z-ZM
IF I RUN OUT OF MONSTERS, SLIFER'S ATTACK WILL HIT ME DEAD-ON...
IF THAT HAPPENS, I'M DEAD!
HOW CAN I OVERCOME THE INFINITE POWER OF A GOD CARD?
MY TURN!
TIME TO DRAW!

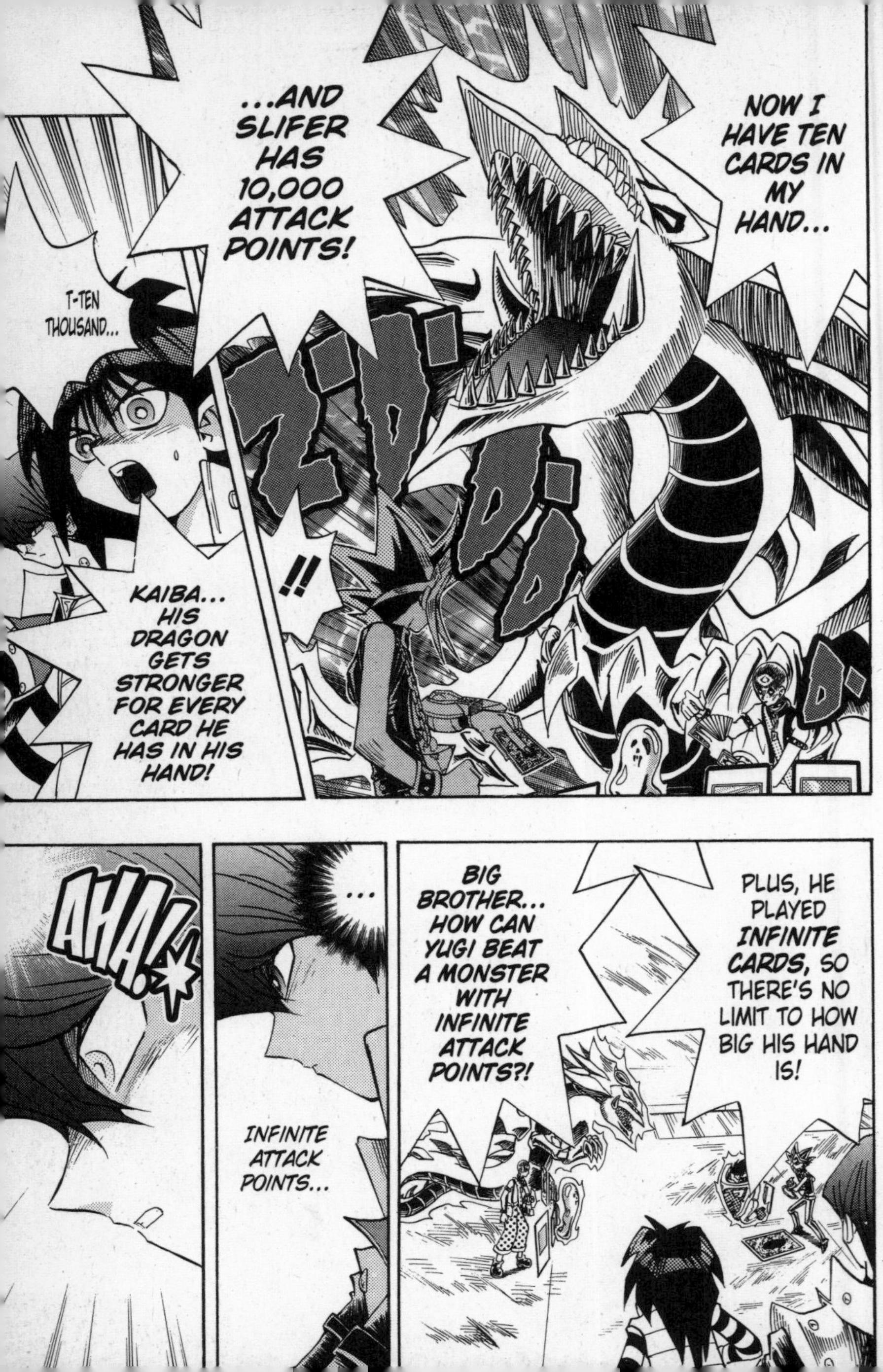
NOW I HAVE TEN CARDS IN MY HAND...
...AND SLIFER HAS 10,000 ATTACK POINTS!
T-TEN THOUSAND...
!!
KAIBA... HIS DRAGON GETS STRONGER FOR EVERY CARD HE HAS IN HIS HAND!
PLUS, HE PLAYED INFINITE CARDS, SO THERE'S NO LIMIT TO HOW BIG HIS HAND IS!
BIG BROTHER... HOW CAN YUGI BEAT A MONSTER WITH INFINITE ATTACK POINTS?!
...
INFINITE ATTACK POINTS...
AHA!

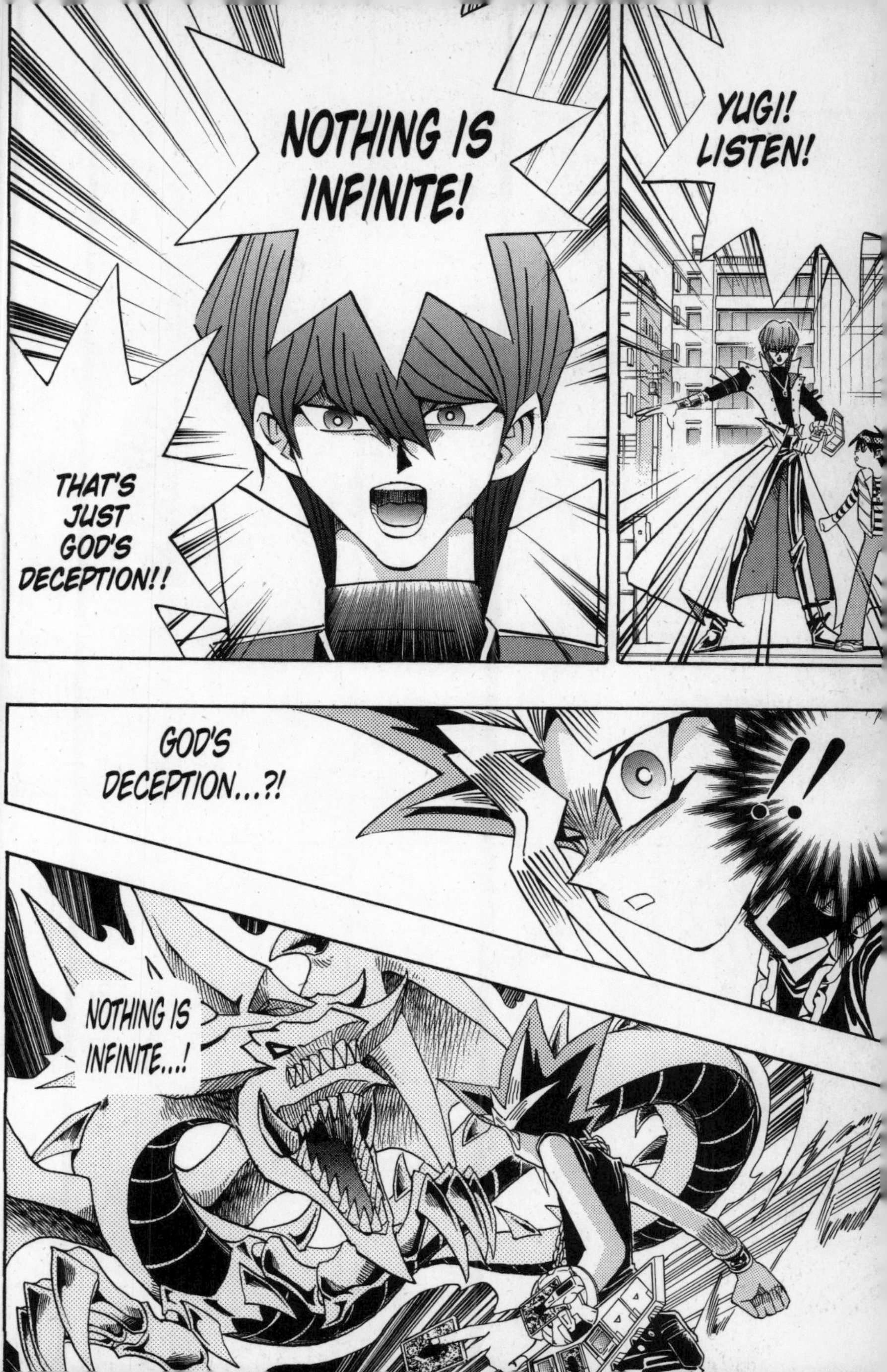
YUGI! LISTEN!
NOTHING IS INFINITE!
THAT'S JUST GOD'S DECEPTION!!
GOD'S DECEPTION...?!
!!
NOTHING IS INFINITE...!

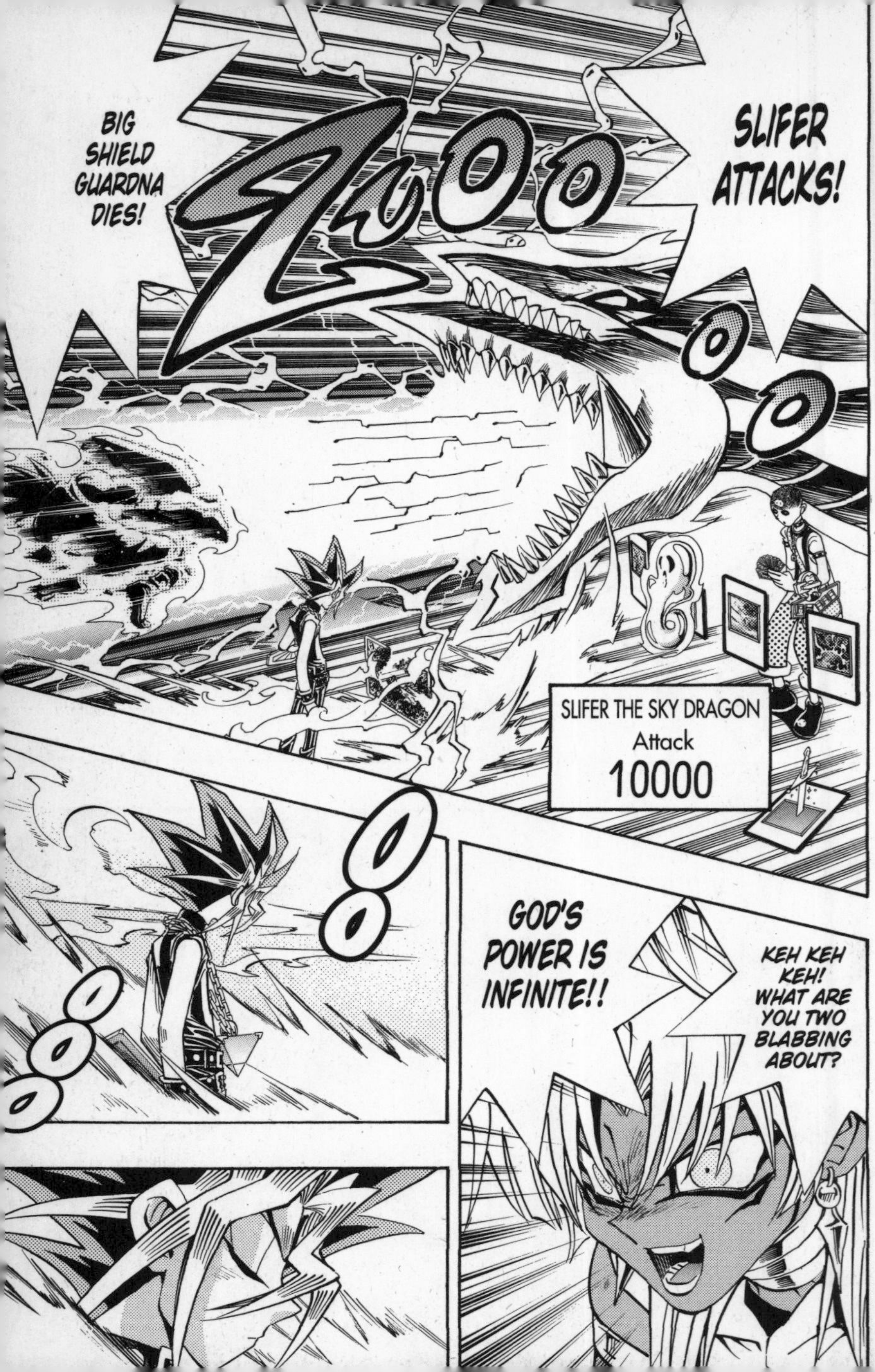
SLIFER ATTACKS!
BIG SHIELD GUARDNA DIES!
SLIFER THE SKY DRAGON
Attack
10000
KEH KEH KEH! WHAT ARE YOU TWO BLABBING ABOUT?
GOD'S POWER IS INFINITE!!

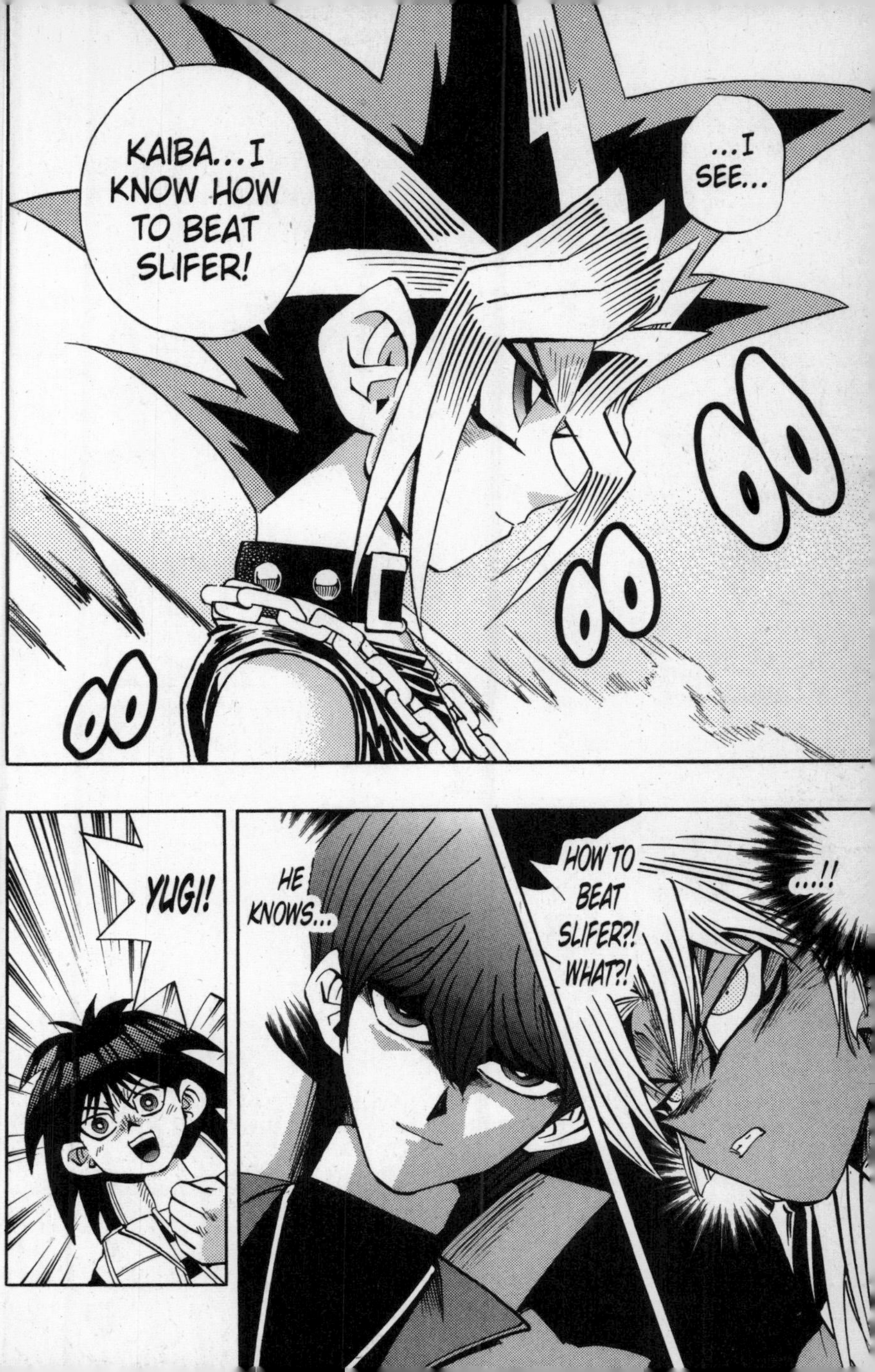
KAIBA...I KNOW HOW TO BEAT SLIFER!
...I SEE...
...!!
HOW TO BEAT SLIFER?! WHAT?!
HE KNOWS...
YUGI!

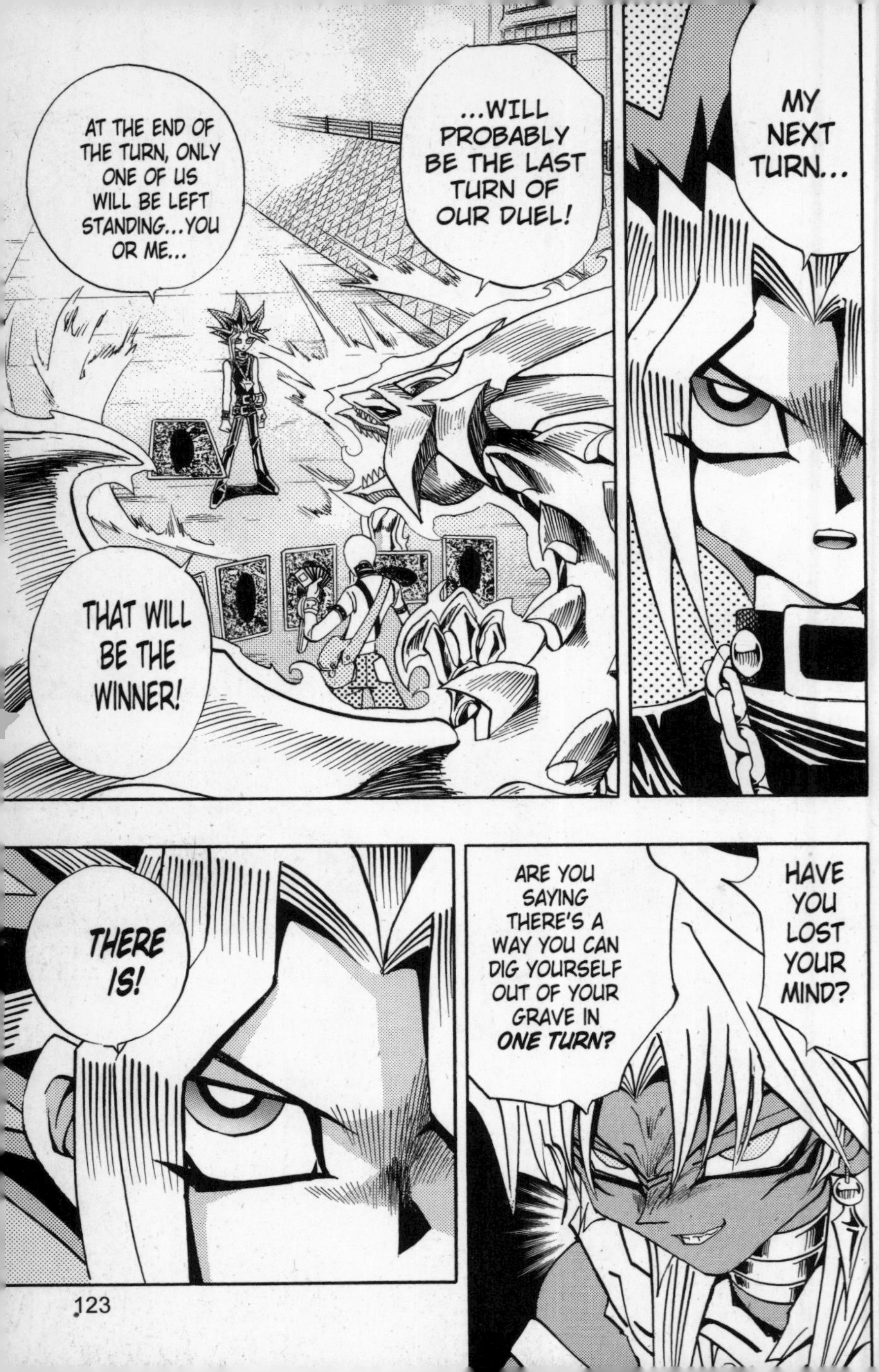
MY NEXT TURN...
...WILL PROBABLY BE THE LAST TURN OF OUR DUEL!
AT THE END OF THE TURN, ONLY ONE OF US WILL BE LEFT STANDING...YOU OR ME...
THAT WILL BE THE WINNER!
HAVE YOU LOST YOUR MIND?
ARE YOU SAYING THERE'S A WAY YOU CAN DIG YOURSELF OUT OF YOUR GRAVE IN ONE TURN?
THERE IS!

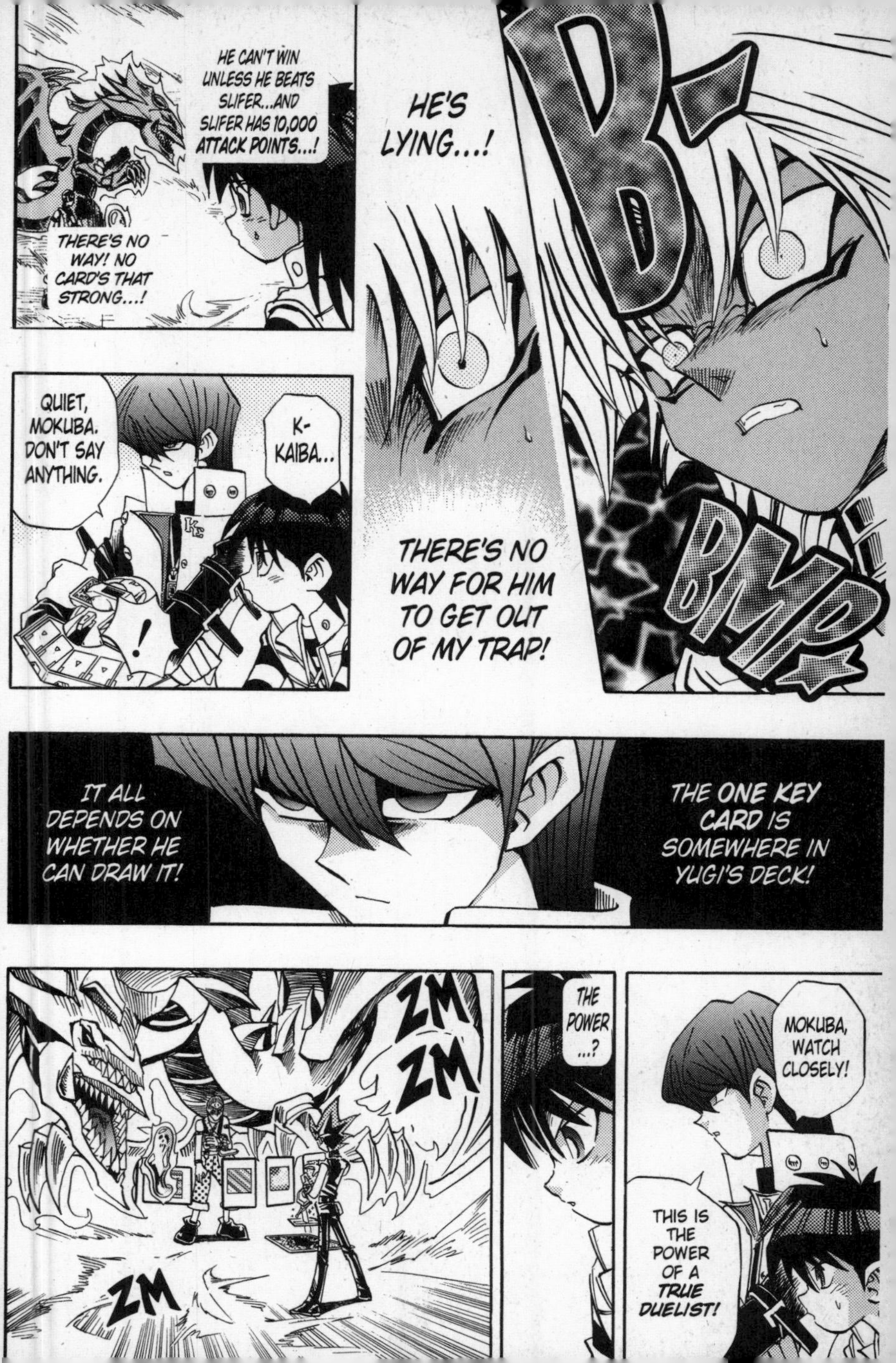
B-
HE'S LYING...!
THERE'S NO WAY FOR HIM TO GET OUT OF MY TRAP!
BMP
HE CAN'T WIN UNLESS HE BEATS SLIFER...AND SLIFER HAS 10,000 ATTACK POINTS...!
THERE'S NO WAY! NO CARD'S THAT STRONG...!
K-KAIBA...
QUIET, MOKUBA. DON'T SAY ANYTHING.
!
THE ONE KEY CARD IS SOMEWHERE IN YUGI'S DECK!
IT ALL DEPENDS ON WHETHER HE CAN DRAW IT!
MOKUBA, WATCH CLOSELY!
THIS IS THE POWER OF A TRUE DUELIST!
THE POWER...?
ZM
ZM
ZM

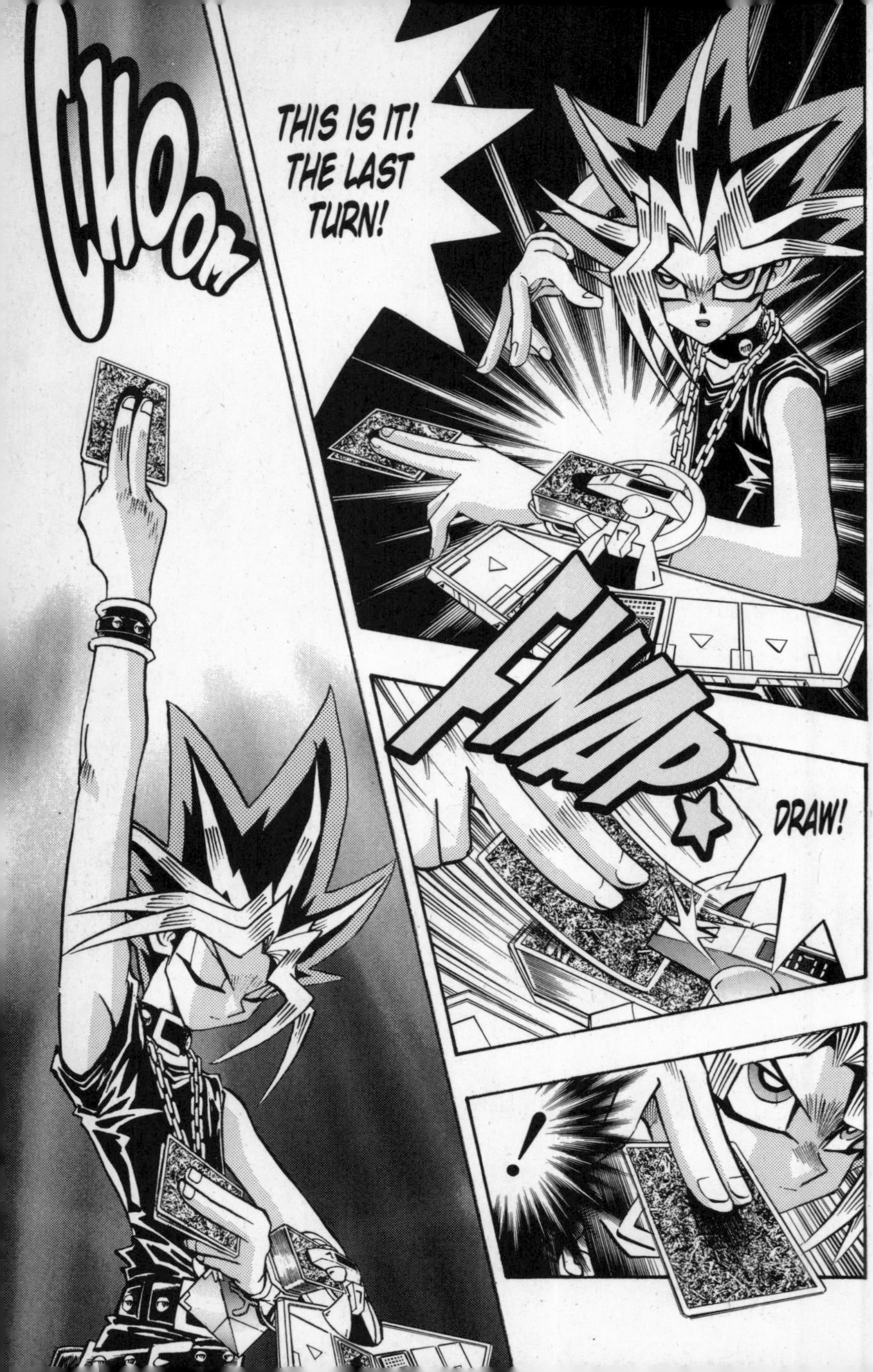
THIS IS IT! THE LAST TURN!
FWAP
DRAW!
!
CHOOM

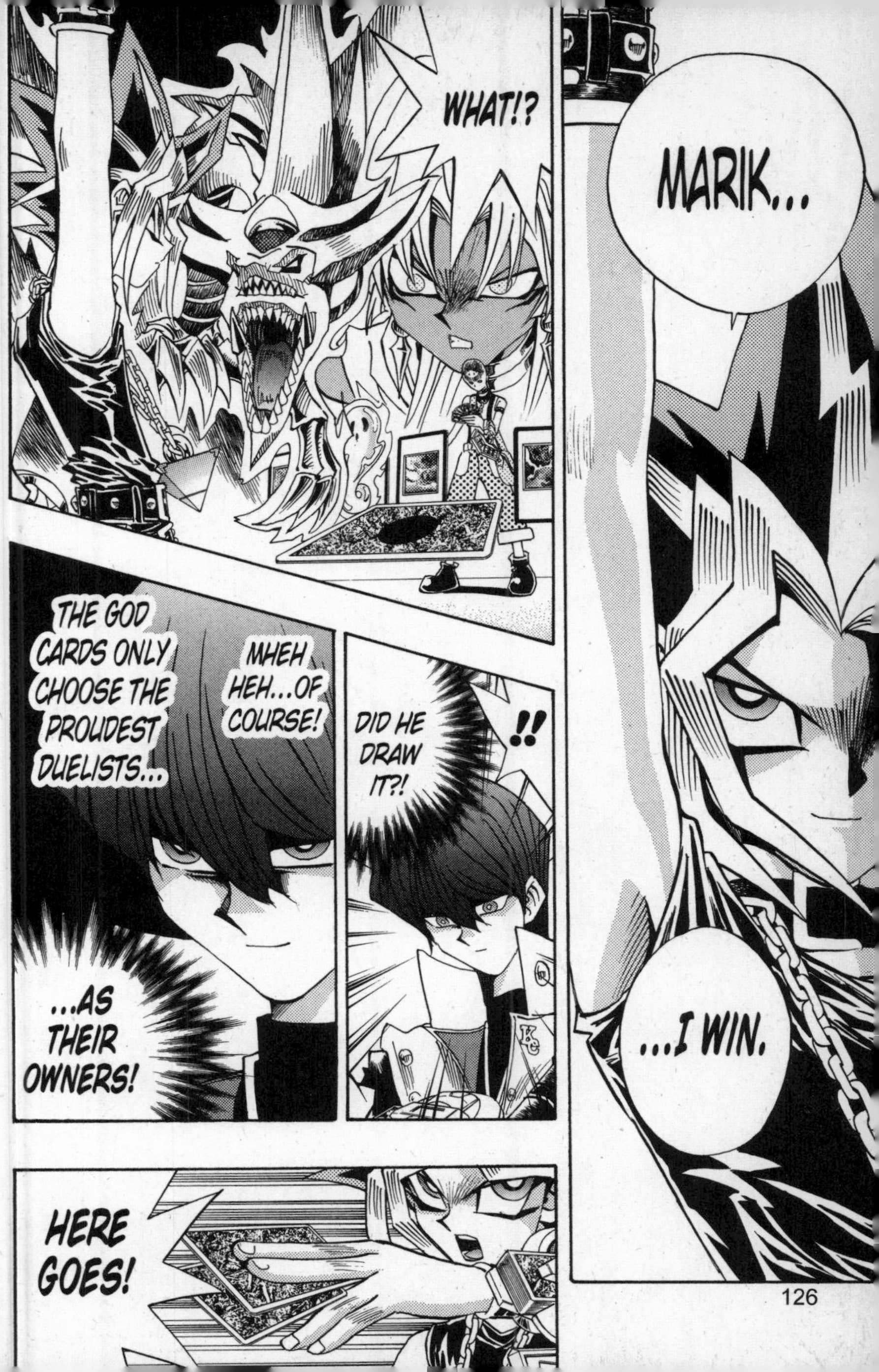
MARIK...
...I WIN.
WHAT!?
DID HE DRAW IT?!
!!
MHEH HEH...OF COURSE!
THE GOD CARDS ONLY CHOOSE THE PROUDEST DUELISTS...
...AS THEIR OWNERS!
HERE GOES!

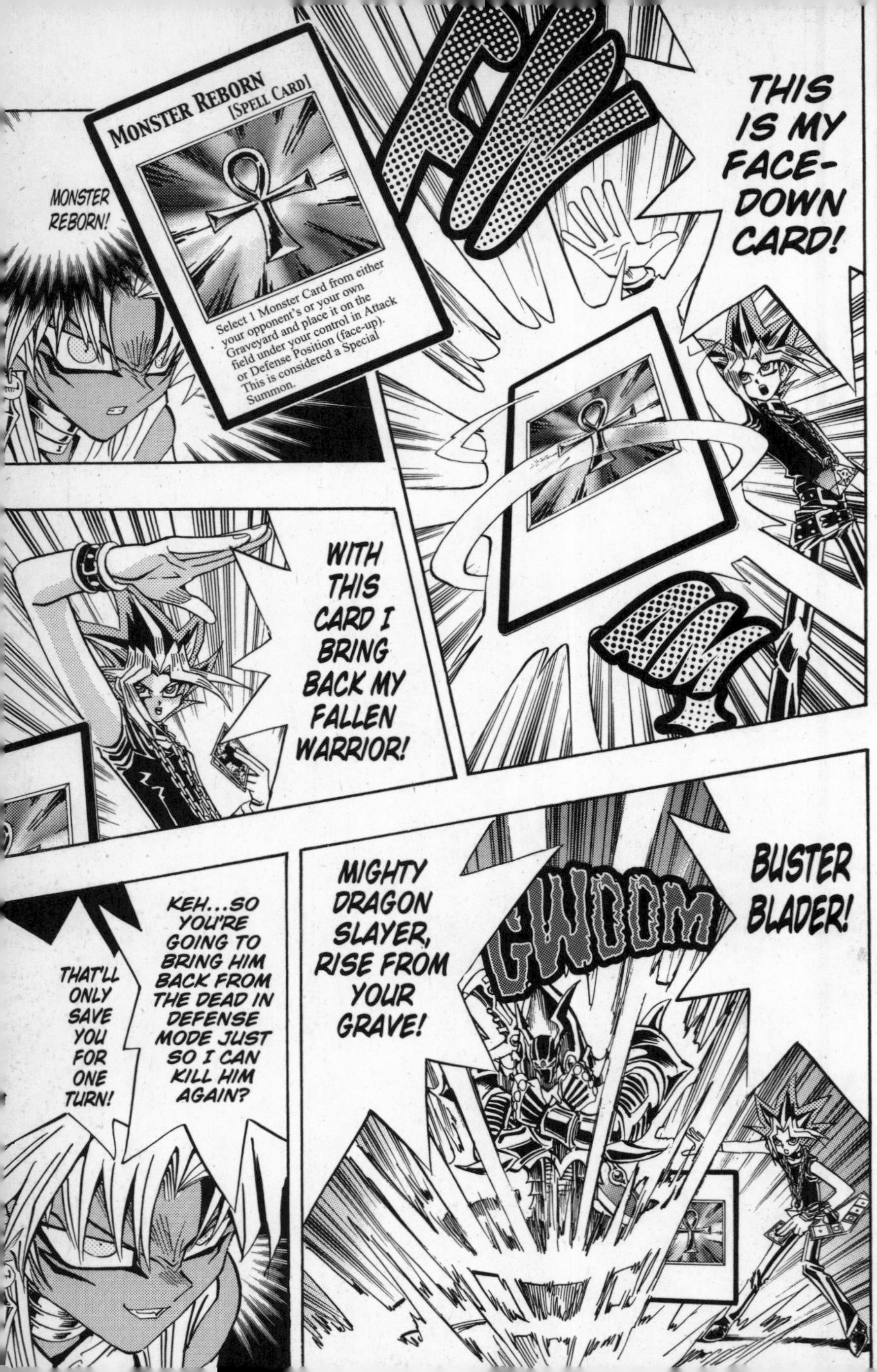
THIS IS MY FACE-DOWN CARD!
MONSTER REBORN!
MONSTER REBORN
[SPELL CARD]
Select 1 Monster Card from either your opponent's or your own Graveyard and place it on the field under your control in Attack or Defense Position (face-up). This is considered a Special Summon.
WITH THIS CARD I BRING BACK MY FALLEN WARRIOR!
BUSTER BLADER!
MIGHTY DRAGON SLAYER, RISE FROM YOUR GRAVE!
GWOOM
KEH...SO YOU'RE GOING TO BRING HIM BACK FROM THE DEAD IN DEFENSE MODE JUST SO I CAN KILL HIM AGAIN?
THAT'LL ONLY SAVE YOU FOR ONE TURN!

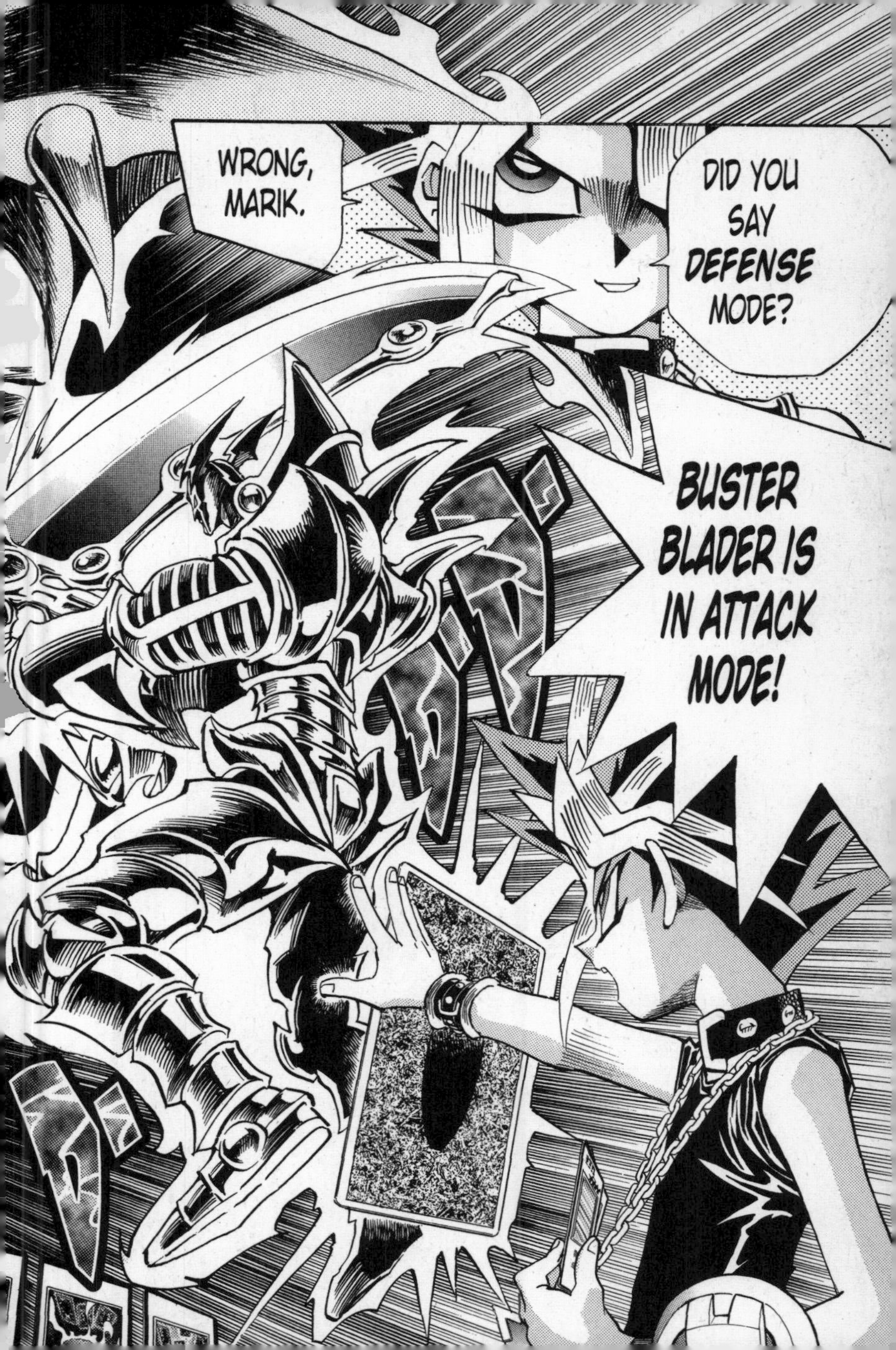
DID YOU SAY DEFENSE MODE?
WRONG, MARIK.
BUSTER BLADER IS IN ATTACK MODE!

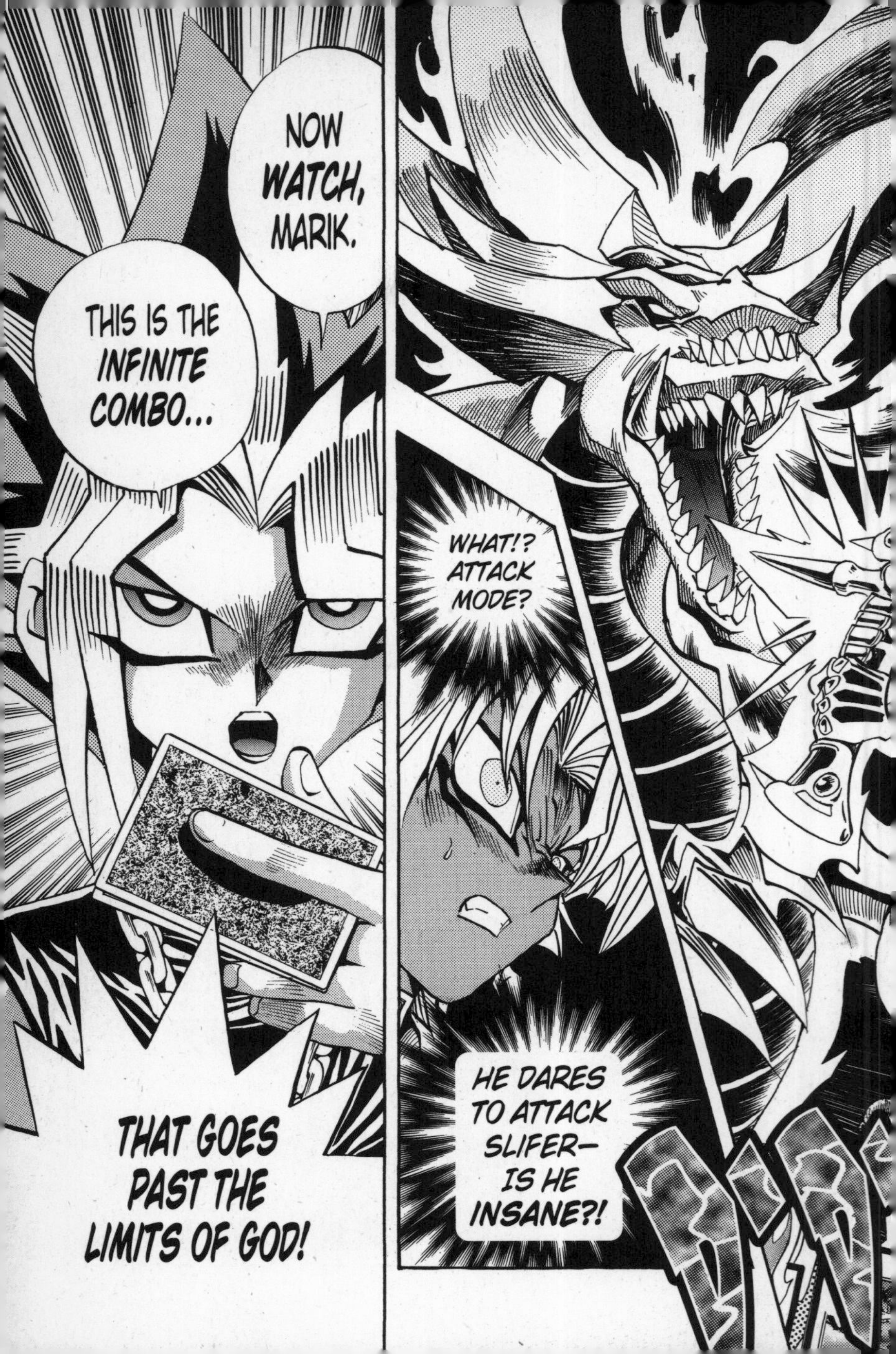
WHAT!? ATTACK MODE?
HE DARES TO ATTACK SLIFER— IS HE INSANE?!
NOW WATCH, MARIK.
THIS IS THE INFINITE COMBO...
THAT GOES PAST THE LIMITS OF GOD!

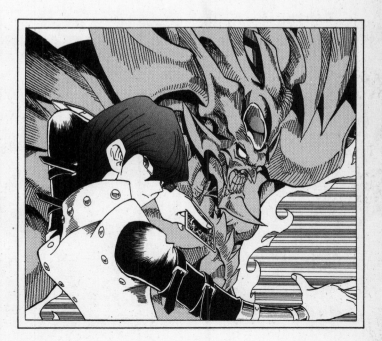

Duel 117: God Falls!?

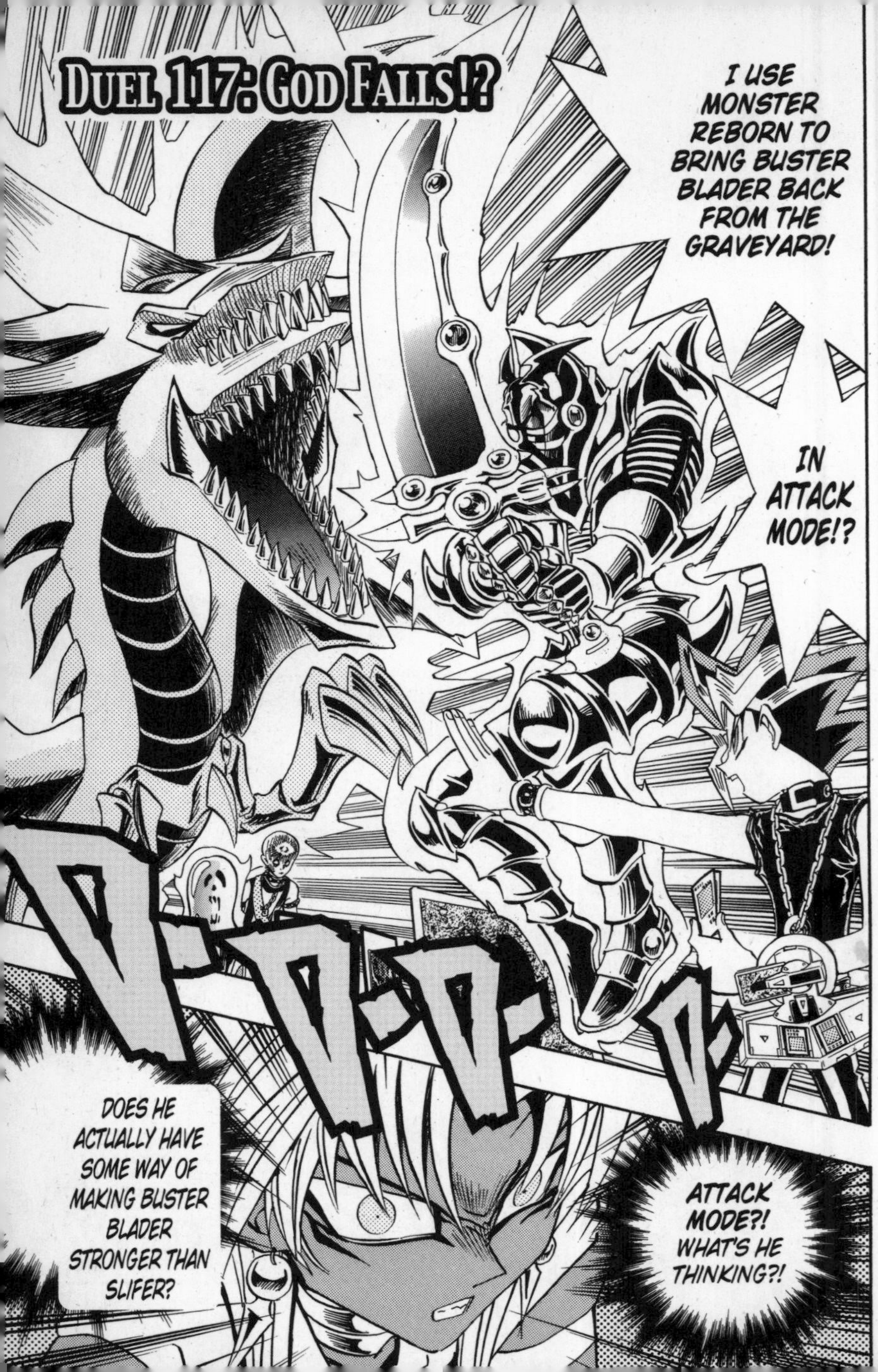
I USE MONSTER REBORN TO BRING BUSTER BLADER BACK FROM THE GRAVEYARD!
IN ATTACK MODE!?
ATTACK MODE?! WHAT'S HE THINKING?!
DOES HE ACTUALLY HAVE SOME WAY OF MAKING BUSTER BLADER STRONGER THAN SLIFER?

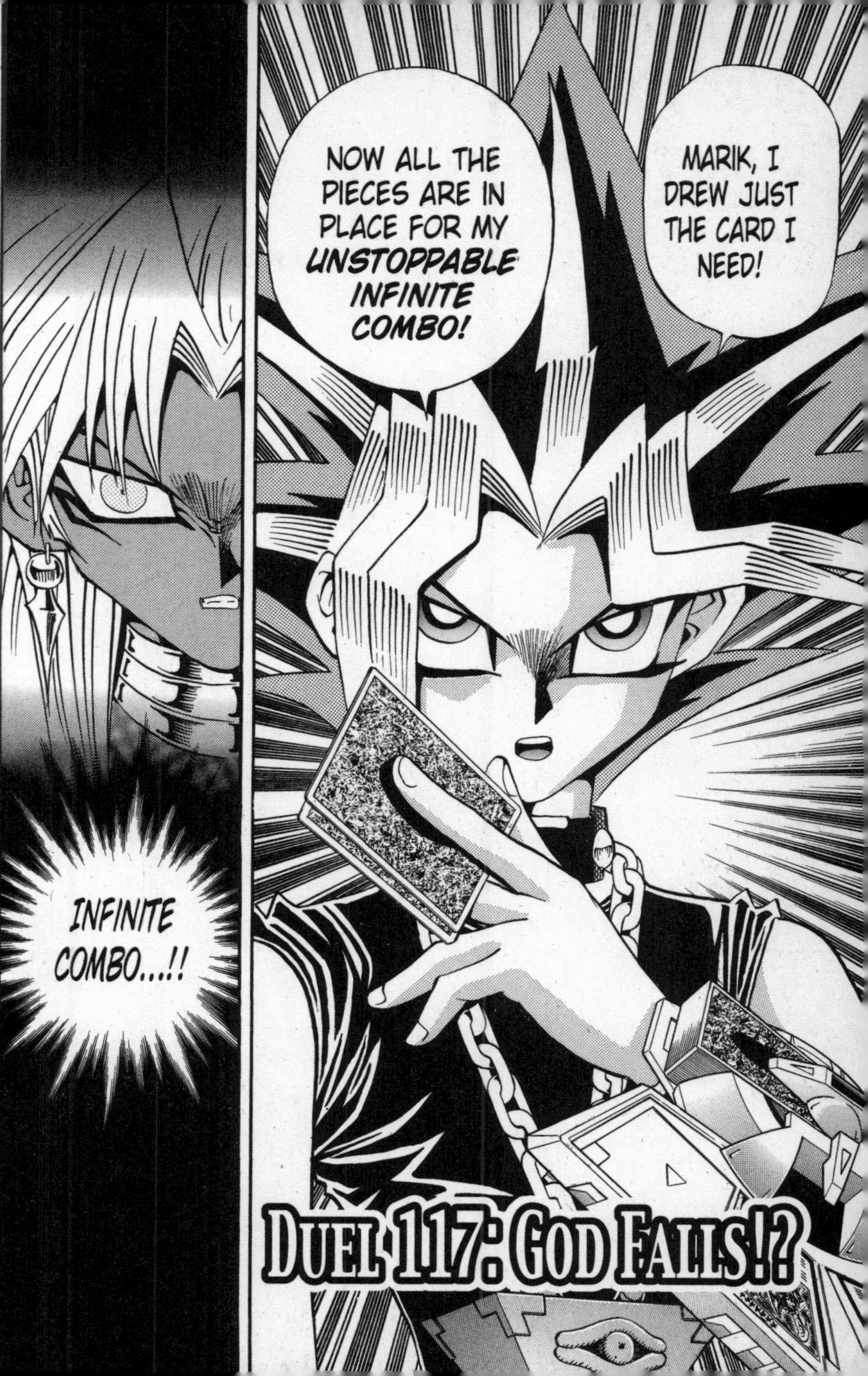
MARIK, I DREW JUST THE CARD I NEED!
NOW ALL THE PIECES ARE IN PLACE FOR MY UNSTOPPABLE INFINITE COMBO!
DUEL 117: GOD FALLS!?
INFINITE COMBO...!!

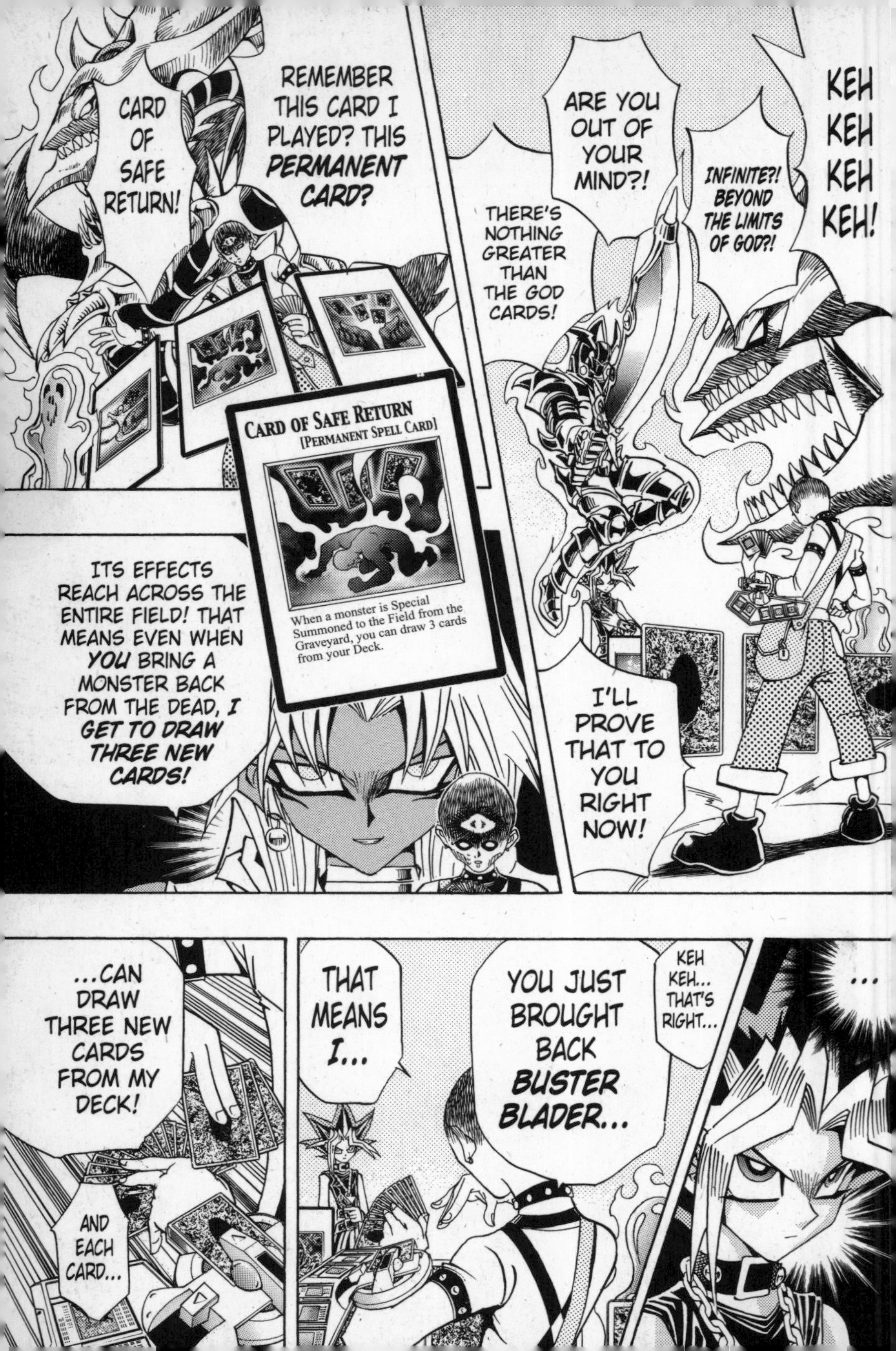
ARE YOU OUT OF YOUR MIND?!
THERE'S NOTHING GREATER THAN THE GOD CARDS!
INFINITE?! BEYOND THE LIMITS OF GOD?!
KEH KEH KEH KEH!
I'LL PROVE THAT TO YOU RIGHT NOW!
CARD OF SAFE RETURN!
REMEMBER THIS CARD I PLAYED? THIS PERMANENT CARD?
CARD OF SAFE RETURN
[PERMANENT SPELL CARD]
When a monster is Special Summoned to the Field from the Graveyard, you can draw 3 cards from your Deck.
ITS EFFECTS REACH ACROSS THE ENTIRE FIELD! THAT MEANS EVEN WHEN YOU BRING A MONSTER BACK FROM THE DEAD, I GET TO DRAW THREE NEW CARDS!
...
KEH KEH... THAT'S RIGHT...
YOU JUST BROUGHT BACK BUSTER BLADER...
THAT MEANS I...
...CAN DRAW THREE NEW CARDS FROM MY DECK!
AND EACH CARD...

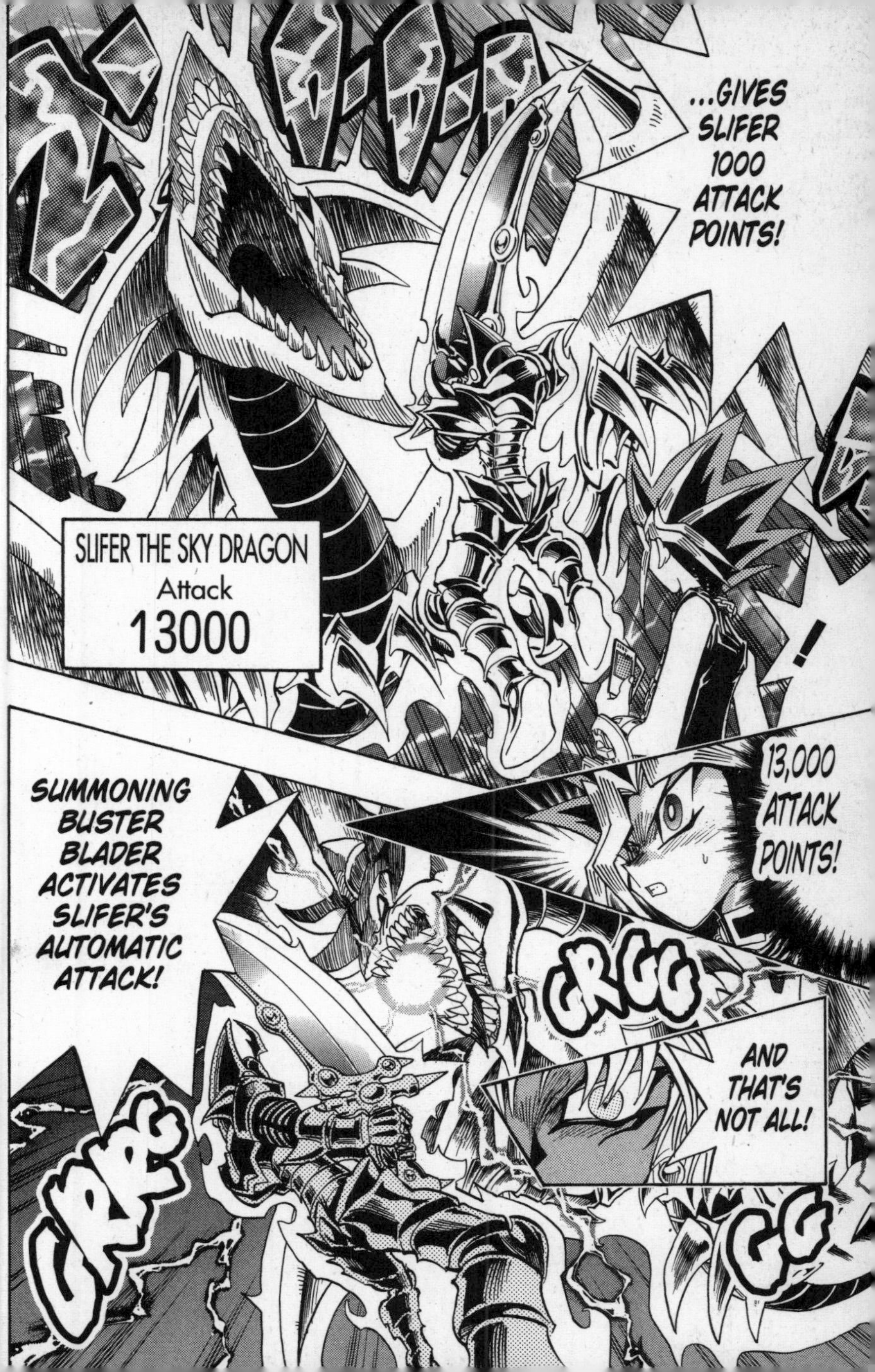
...GIVES SLIFER 1000 ATTACK POINTS!
SLIFER THE SKY DRAGON
Attack
13000
!
13,000 ATTACK POINTS!
GRGG
AND THAT'S NOT ALL!
GG
SUMMONING BUSTER BLADER ACTIVATES SLIFER'S AUTOMATIC ATTACK!

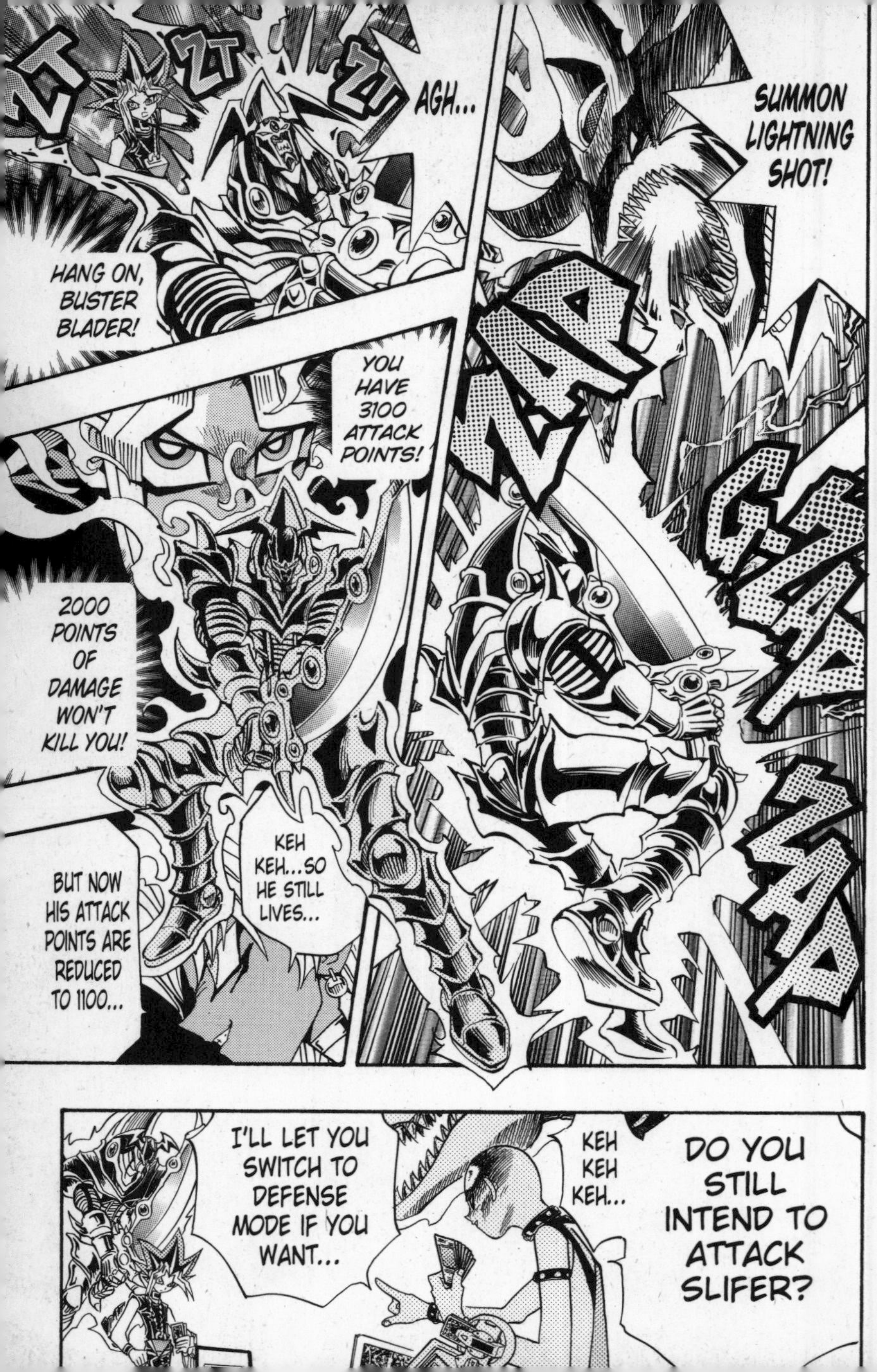
SUMMON LIGHTNING SHOT!
ZT
ZT
ZT
AGH...
HANG ON, BUSTER BLADER!
YOU HAVE 3100 ATTACK POINTS!
2000 POINTS OF DAMAGE WON'T KILL YOU!
KEH KEH...SO HE STILL LIVES...
BUT NOW HIS ATTACK POINTS ARE REDUCED TO 1100...
DO YOU STILL INTEND TO ATTACK SLIFER?
KEH KEH KEH...
I'LL LET YOU SWITCH TO DEFENSE MODE IF YOU WANT...

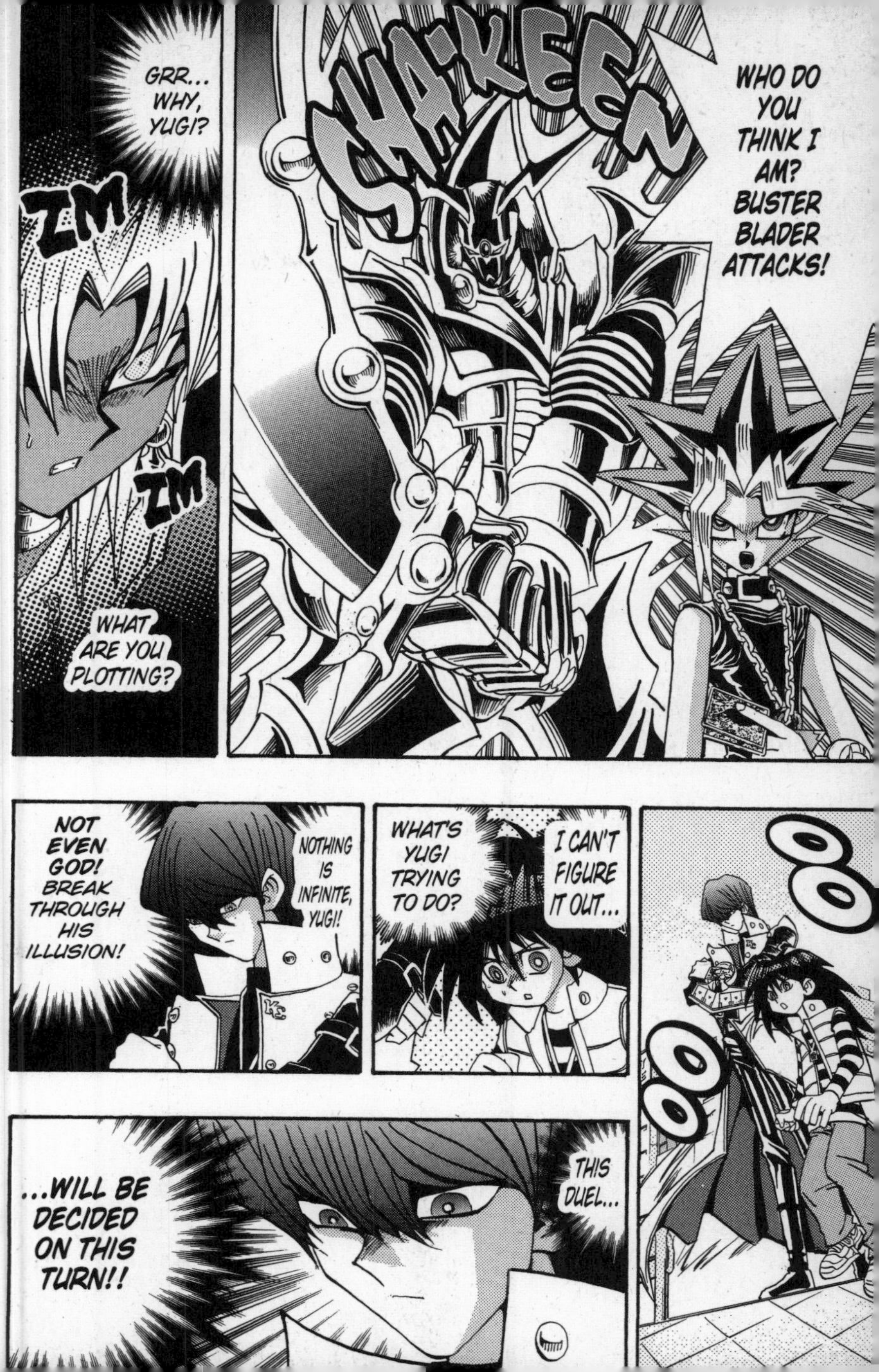
CHAKEEN
WHO DO YOU THINK I AM? BUSTER BLADER ATTACKS!
GRR... WHY, YUGI?
ZM
ZM
WHAT ARE YOU PLOTTING?
I CAN'T FIGURE IT OUT...
WHAT'S YUGI TRYING TO DO?
NOTHING IS INFINITE, YUGI!
NOT EVEN GOD! BREAK THROUGH HIS ILLUSION!
THIS DUEL...
...WILL BE DECIDED ON THIS TURN!!

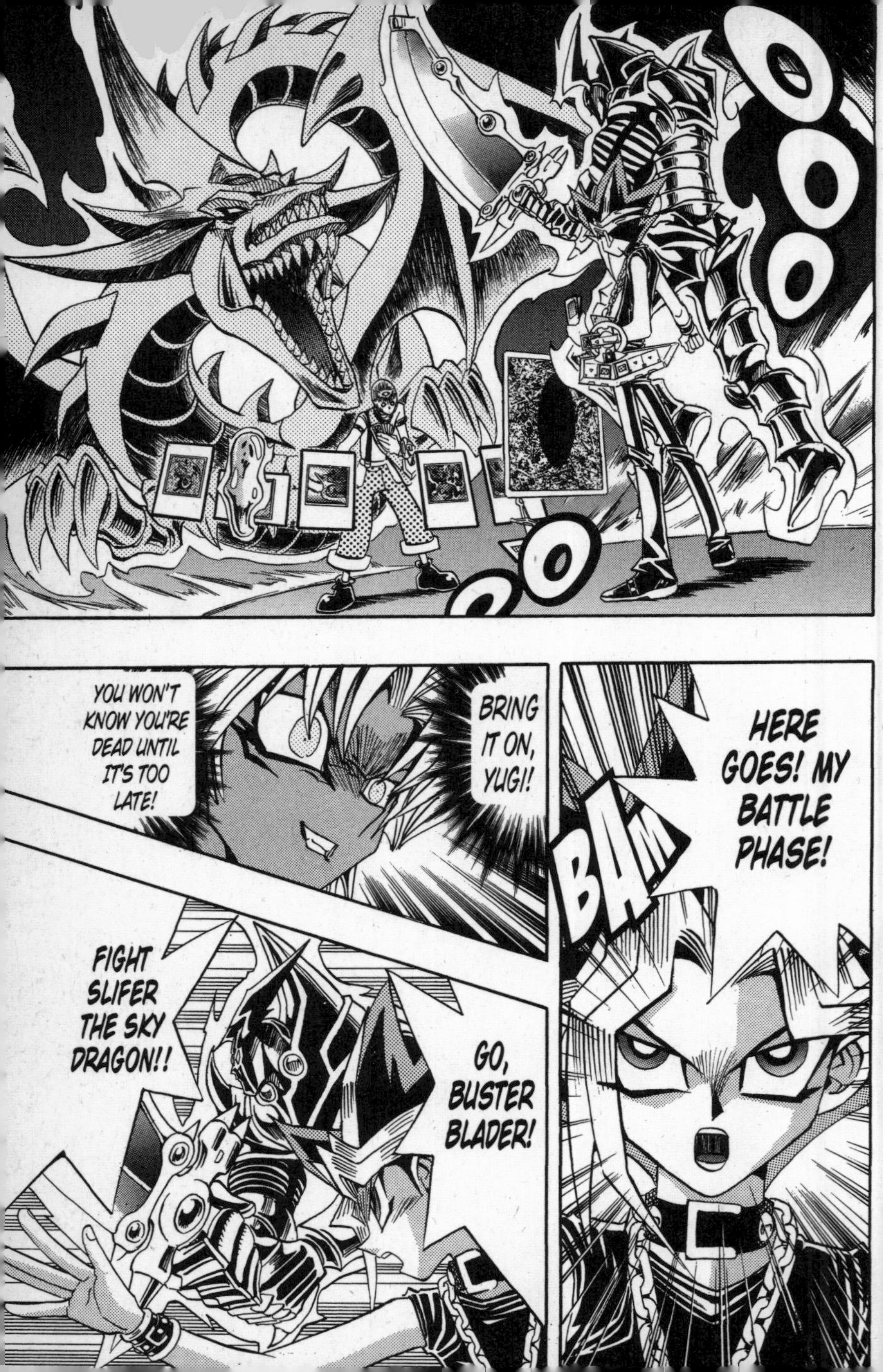
HERE GOES! MY BATTLE PHASE!
BAM
BRING IT ON, YUGI!
YOU WON'T KNOW YOU'RE DEAD UNTIL IT'S TOO LATE!
GO, BUSTER BLADER!
FIGHT SLIFER THE SKY DRAGON!!

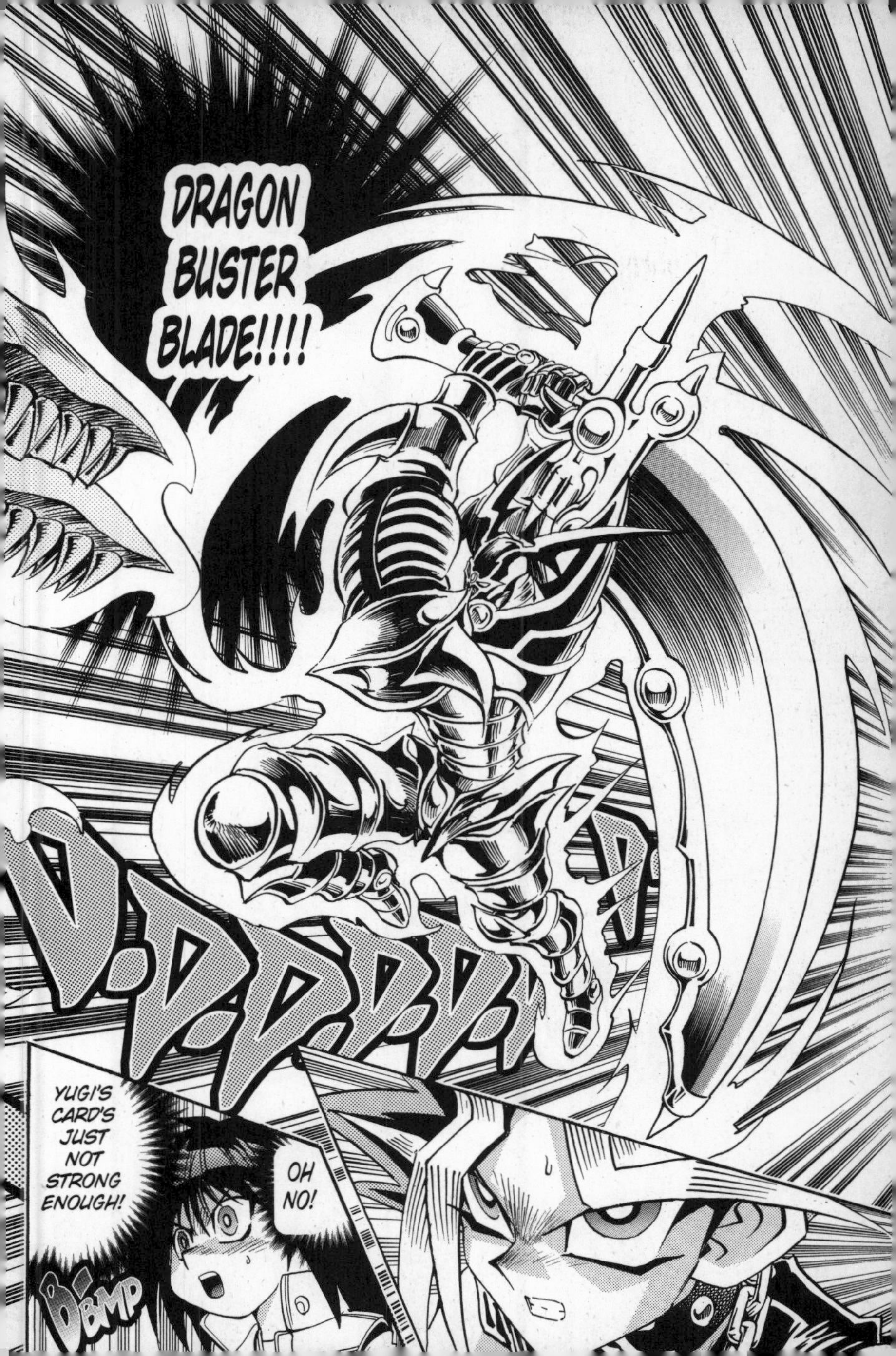
DRAGON BUSTER BLADE!!!!
OH NO!
YUGI'S CARD'S JUST NOT STRONG ENOUGH!
B'BMP

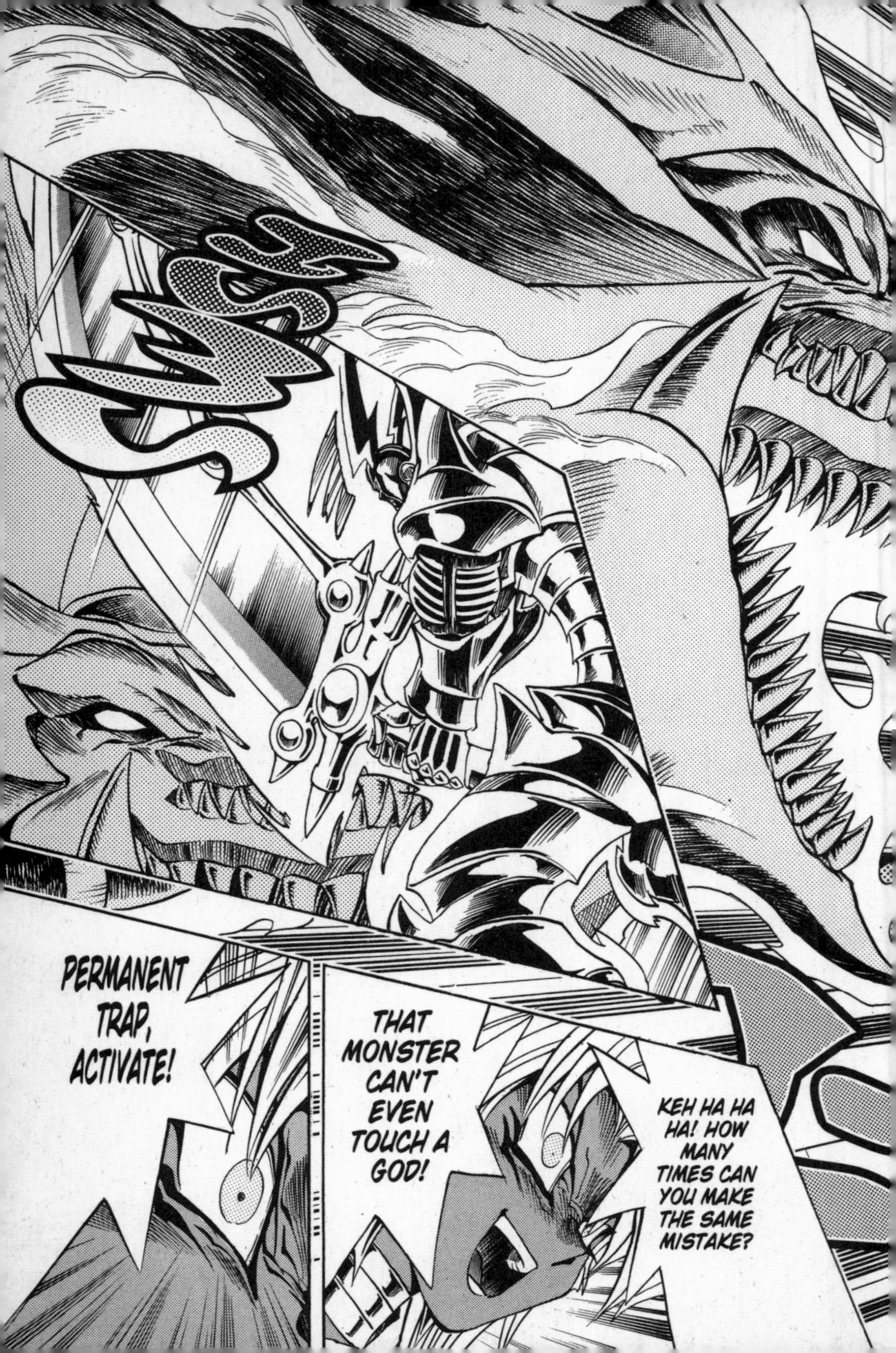
KEH HA HA HA! HOW MANY TIMES CAN YOU MAKE THE SAME MISTAKE?
THAT MONSTER CAN'T EVEN TOUCH A GOD!
PERMANENT TRAP, ACTIVATE!

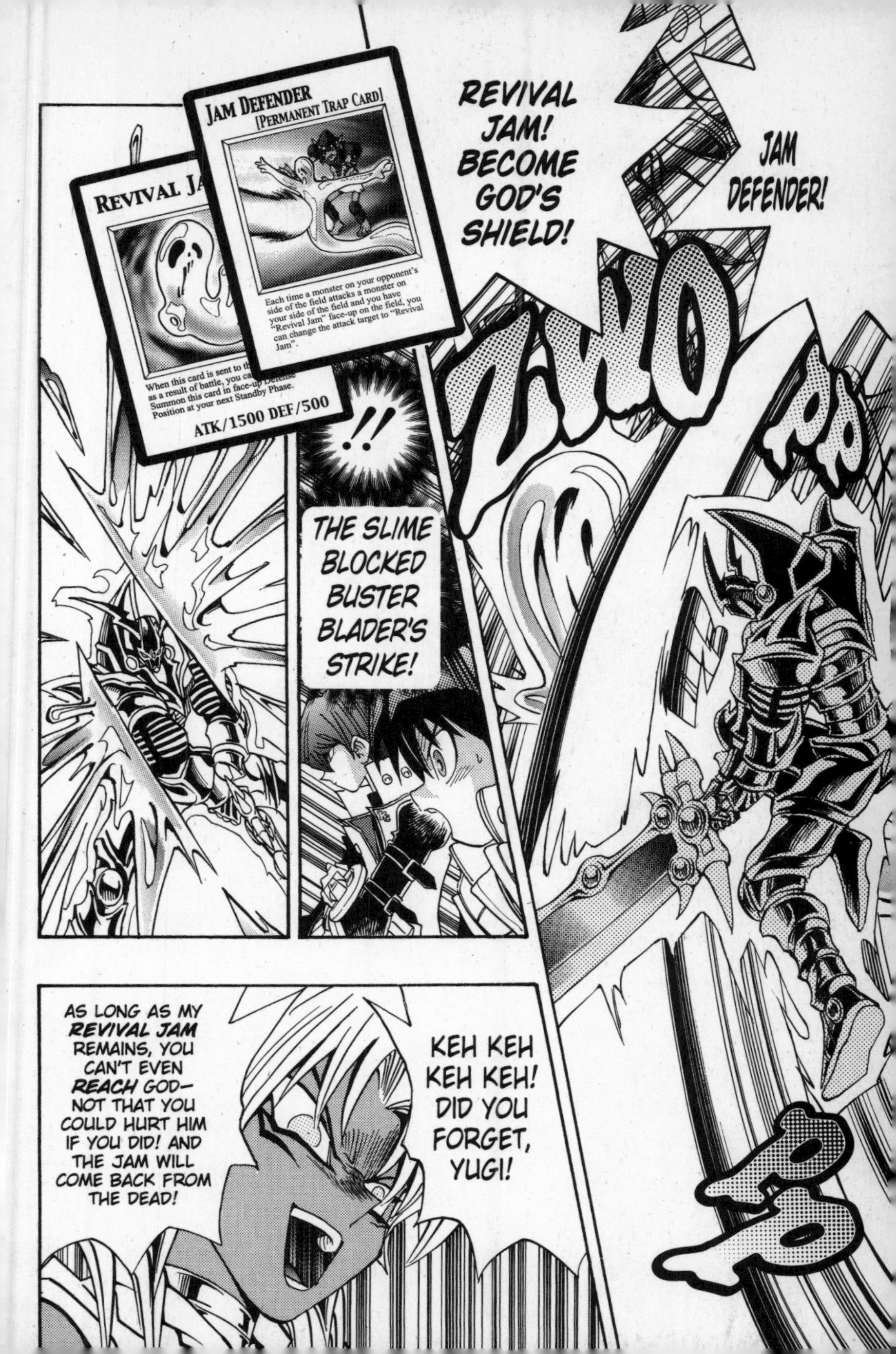
JAM DEFENDER!
REVIVAL JAM! BECOME GOD'S SHIELD!
!!
THE SLIME BLOCKED BUSTER BLADER'S STRIKE!
JAM DEFENDER [PERMANENT TRAP CARD]
Each time a monster on your opponent's side of the field attacks a monster on your side of the field and you have "Revival Jam" face-up on the field, you can change the attack target to "Revival Jam".
ATK/1500 DEF/500
KEH KEH KEH KEH! DID YOU FORGET, YUGI!
AS LONG AS MY REVIVAL JAM REMAINS, YOU CAN'T EVEN REACH GOD— NOT THAT YOU COULD HURT HIM IF YOU DID! AND THE JAM WILL COME BACK FROM THE DEAD!

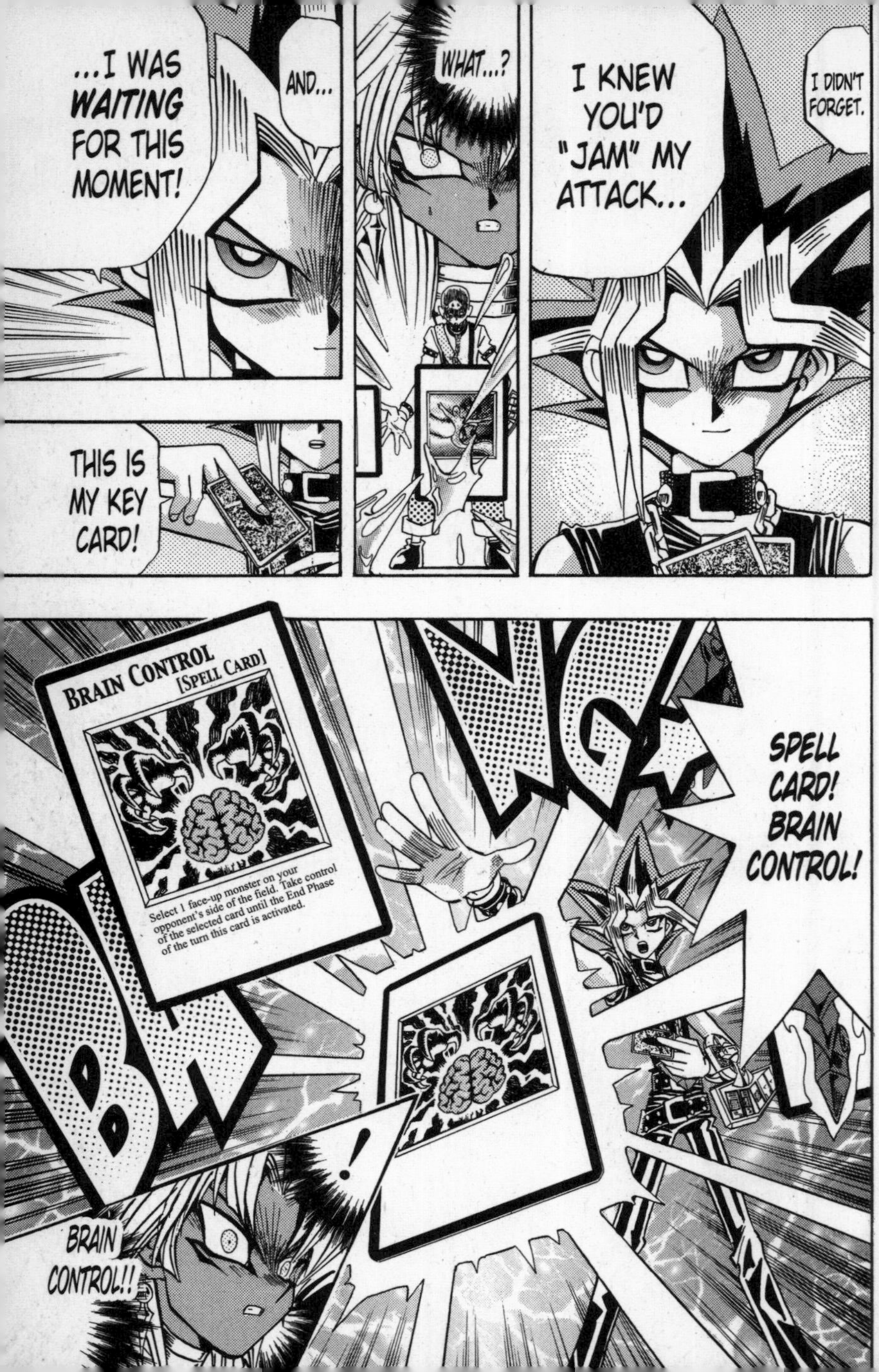
I DIDN'T FORGET.
I KNEW YOU'D "JAM" MY ATTACK...
WHAT...?
AND...
...I WAS WAITING FOR THIS MOMENT!
THIS IS MY KEY CARD!
SPELL CARD! BRAIN CONTROL!
BRAIN CONTROL
[SPELL CARD]
Select 1 face-up monster on your opponent's side of the field. Take control of the selected card until the End Phase of the turn this card is activated.
!
BRAIN CONTROL!!

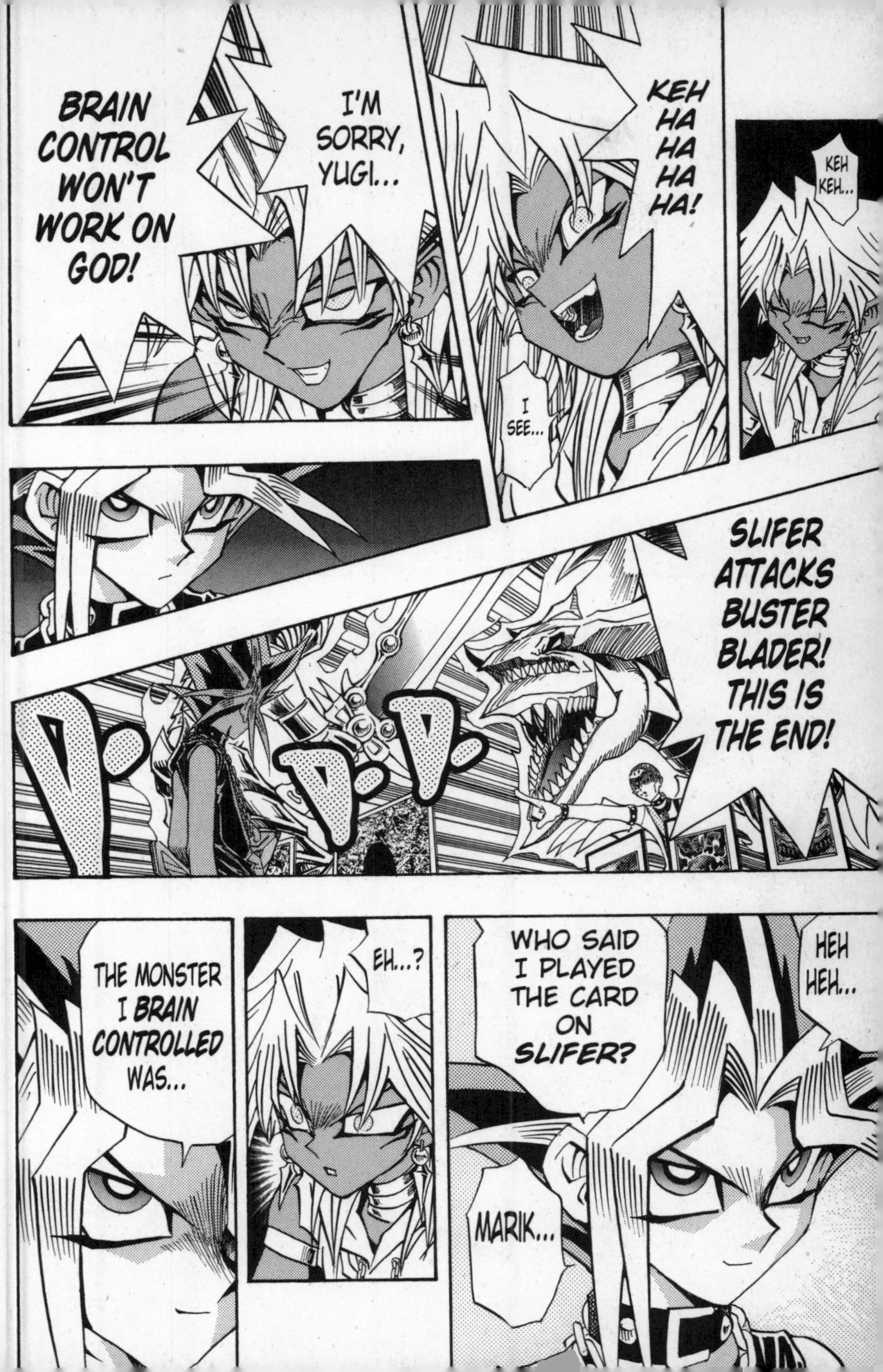
KEH KEH...
KEH HA HA HA HA!
I SEE...
I'M SORRY, YUGI...
BRAIN CONTROL WON'T WORK ON GOD!
SLIFER ATTACKS BUSTER BLADER! THIS IS THE END!
HEH HEH...
WHO SAID I PLAYED THE CARD ON SLIFER?
MARIK...
EH...?
THE MONSTER I BRAIN CONTROLLED WAS...

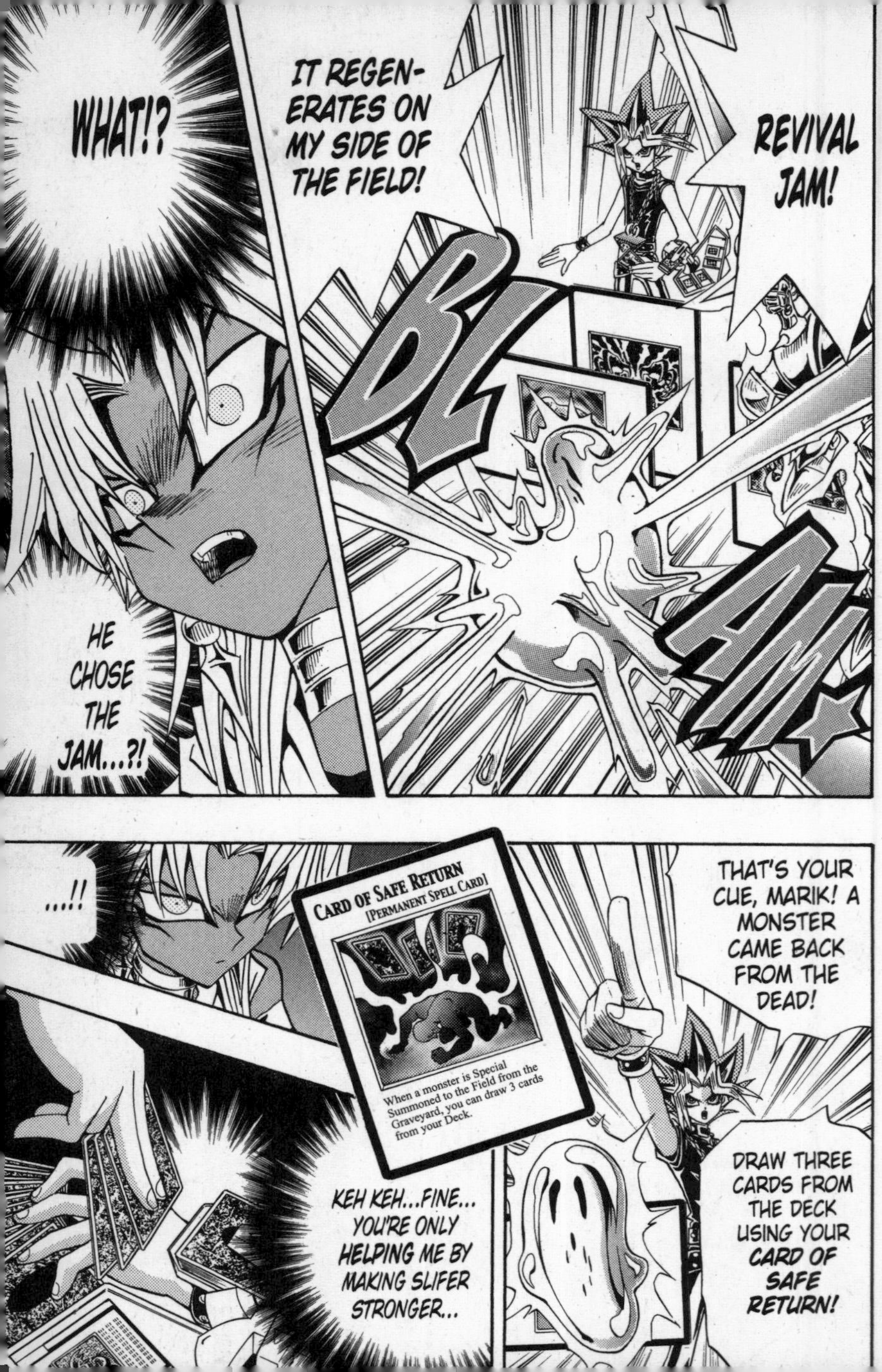
REVIVAL JAM!
IT REGENERATES ON MY SIDE OF THE FIELD!
BLAM
WHAT!?
HE CHOSE THE JAM...?!
THAT'S YOUR CUE, MARIK! A MONSTER CAME BACK FROM THE DEAD!
DRAW THREE CARDS FROM THE DECK USING YOUR CARD OF SAFE RETURN!
CARD OF SAFE RETURN
[PERMANENT SPELL CARD]
When a monster is Special Summoned to the Field from the Graveyard, you can draw 3 cards from your Deck.
...!!
KEH KEH...FINE... YOU'RE ONLY HELPING ME BY MAKING SLIFER STRONGER...

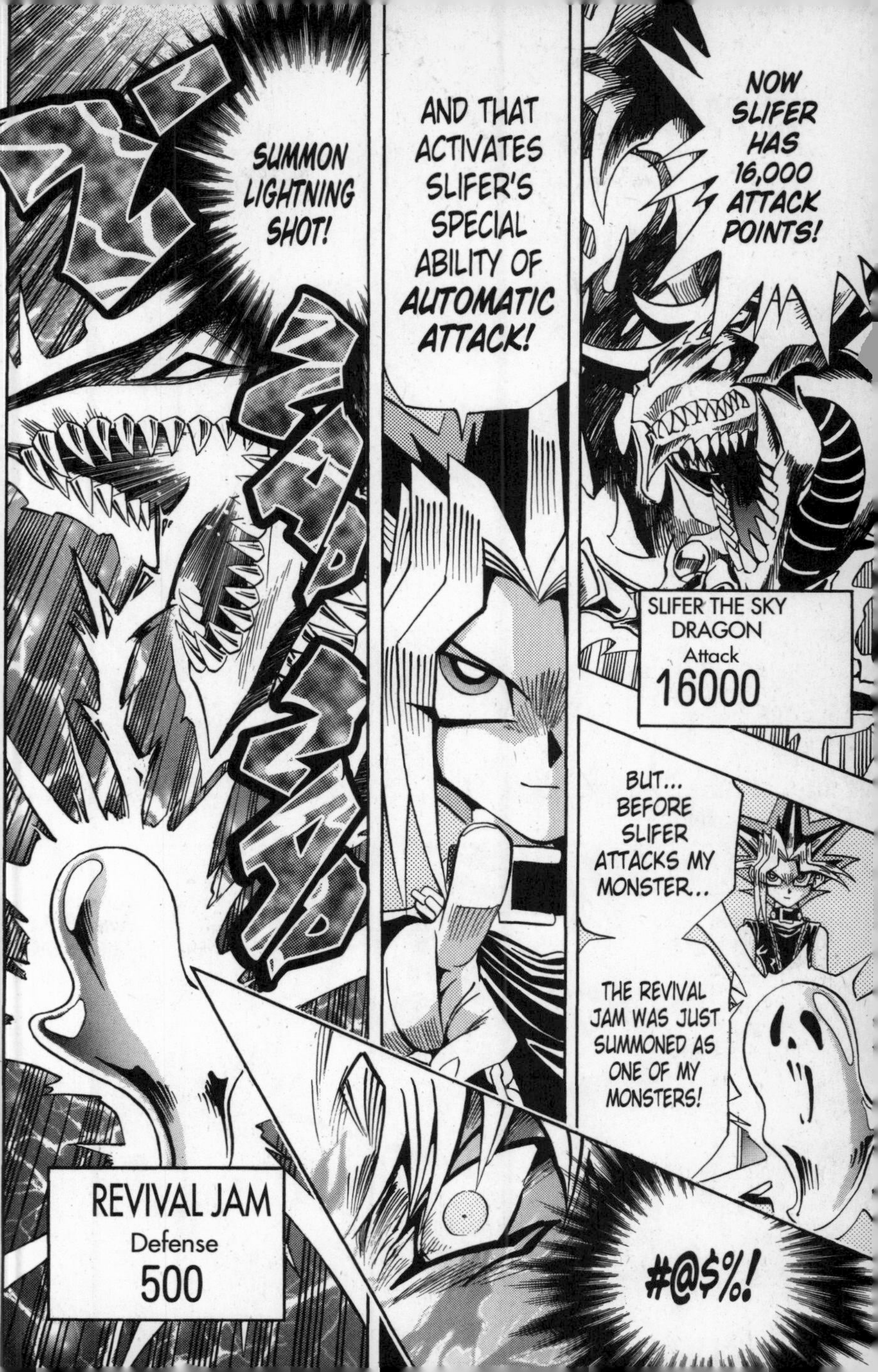
SUMMON LIGHTNING SHOT!
REVIVAL JAM
Defense
500
AND THAT ACTIVATES SLIFER'S SPECIAL ABILITY OF AUTOMATIC ATTACK!
NOW SLIFER HAS 16,000 ATTACK POINTS!
SLIFER THE SKY DRAGON
Attack
16000
BUT... BEFORE SLIFER ATTACKS MY MONSTER...
THE REVIVAL JAM WAS JUST SUMMONED AS ONE OF MY MONSTERS!
#@$%!

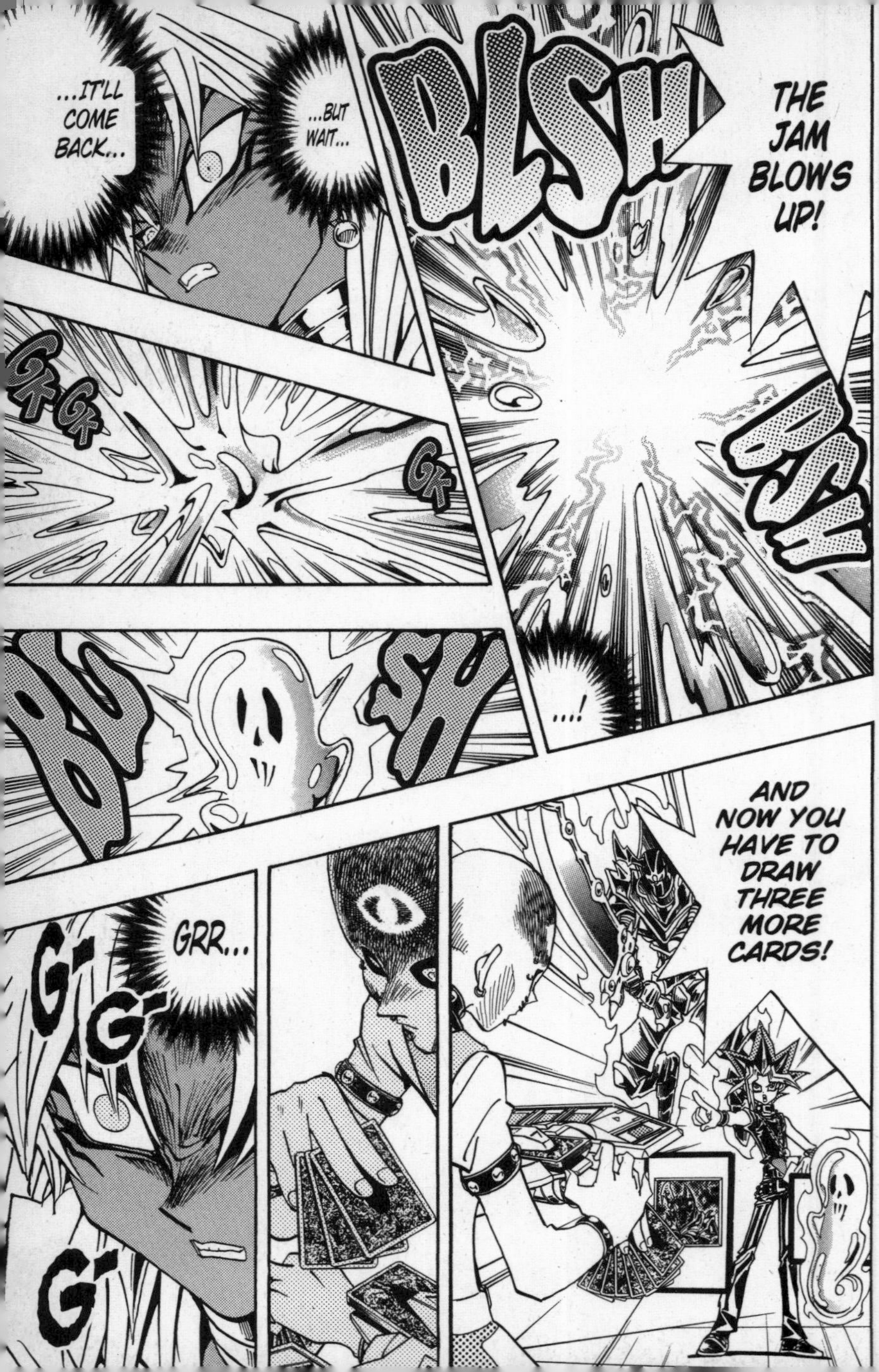
BLSH
THE JAM BLOWS UP!
...!
...BUT WAIT...
...IT'LL COME BACK...
GK GK GK
GK
AND NOW YOU HAVE TO DRAW THREE MORE CARDS!
GRR...
G-G-
G-

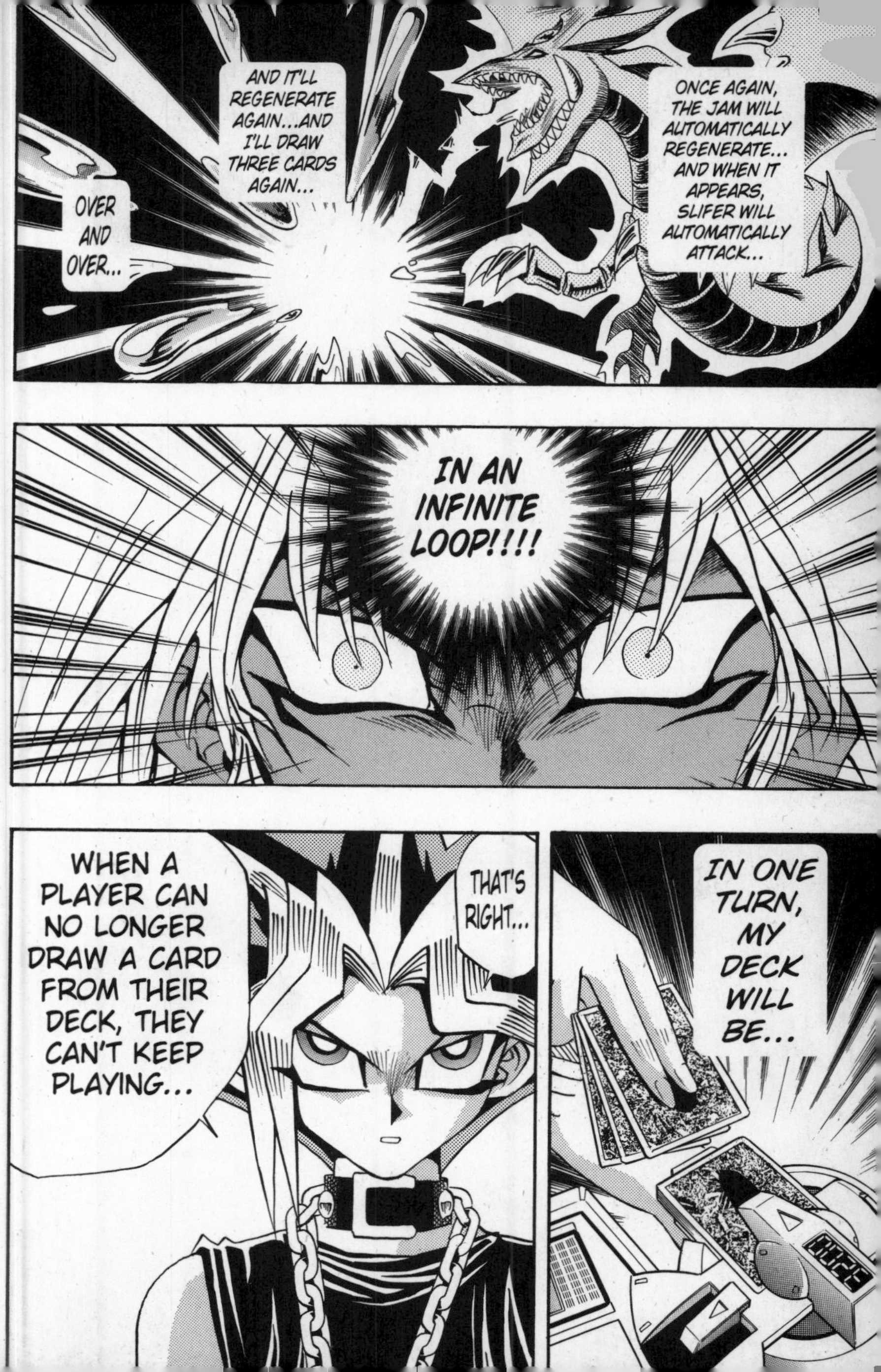
ONCE AGAIN, THE JAM WILL AUTOMATICALLY REGENERATE... AND WHEN IT APPEARS, SLIFER WILL AUTOMATICALLY ATTACK...
AND IT'LL REGENERATE AGAIN...AND I'LL DRAW THREE CARDS AGAIN...
OVER AND OVER...
IN AN INFINITE LOOP!!!!
IN ONE TURN, MY DECK WILL BE...
THAT'S RIGHT...
WHEN A PLAYER CAN NO LONGER DRAW A CARD FROM THEIR DECK, THEY CAN'T KEEP PLAYING...

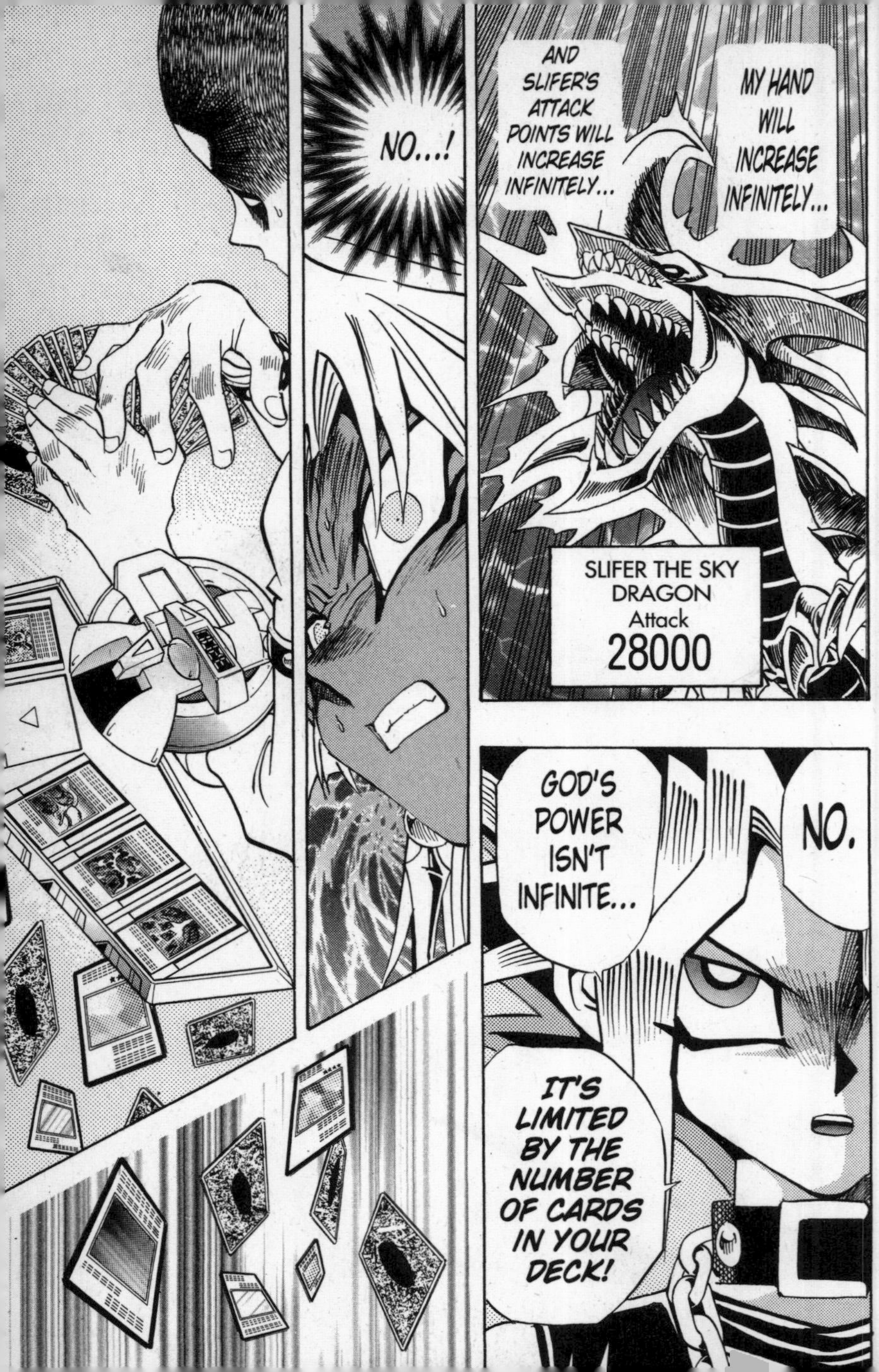
MY HAND WILL INCREASE INFINITELY...
AND SLIFER'S ATTACK POINTS WILL INCREASE INFINITELY...
SLIFER THE SKY DRAGON Attack 28000
NO.
GOD'S POWER ISN'T INFINITE...
IT'S LIMITED BY THE NUMBER OF CARDS IN YOUR DECK!
NO...!

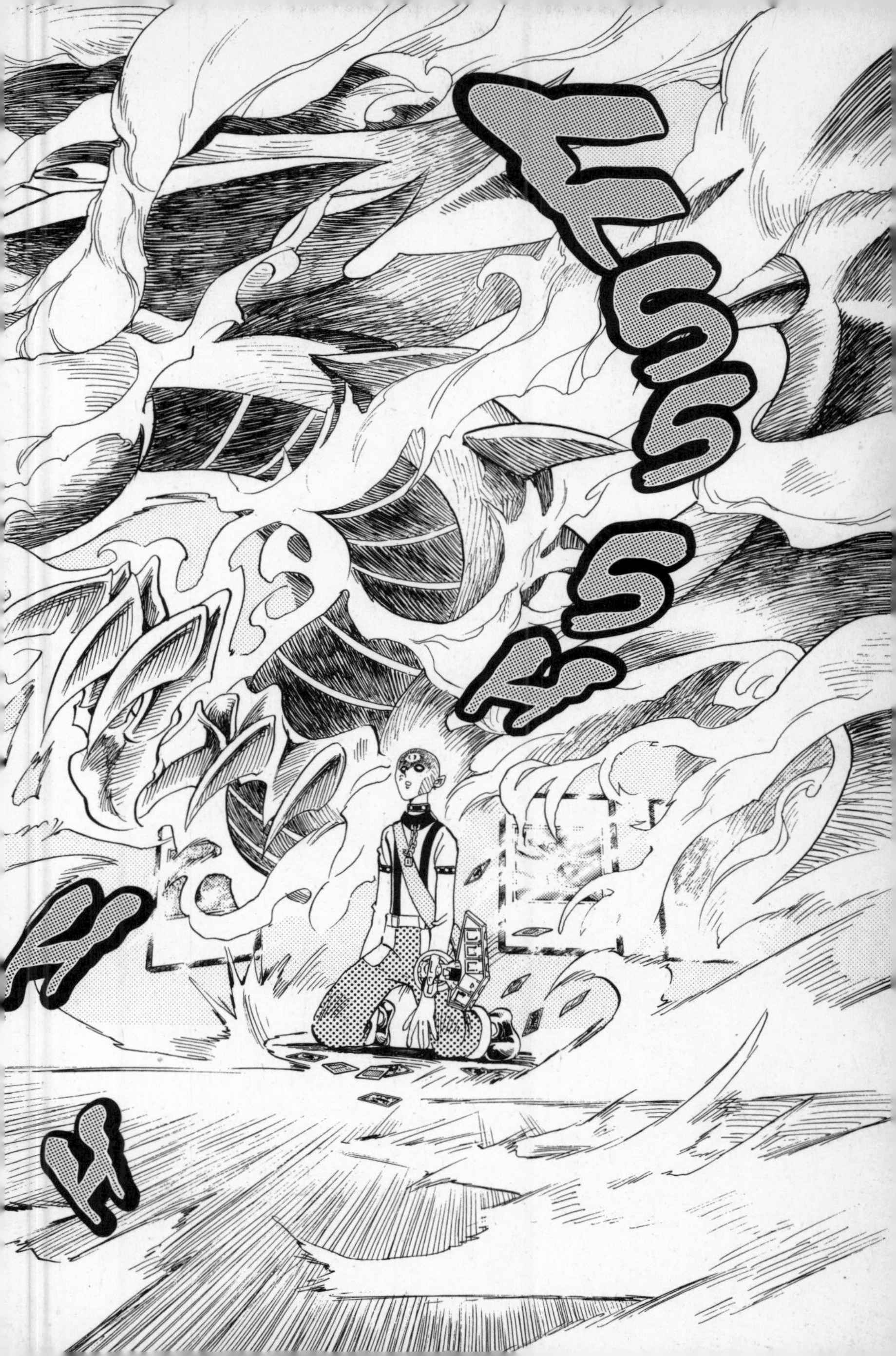

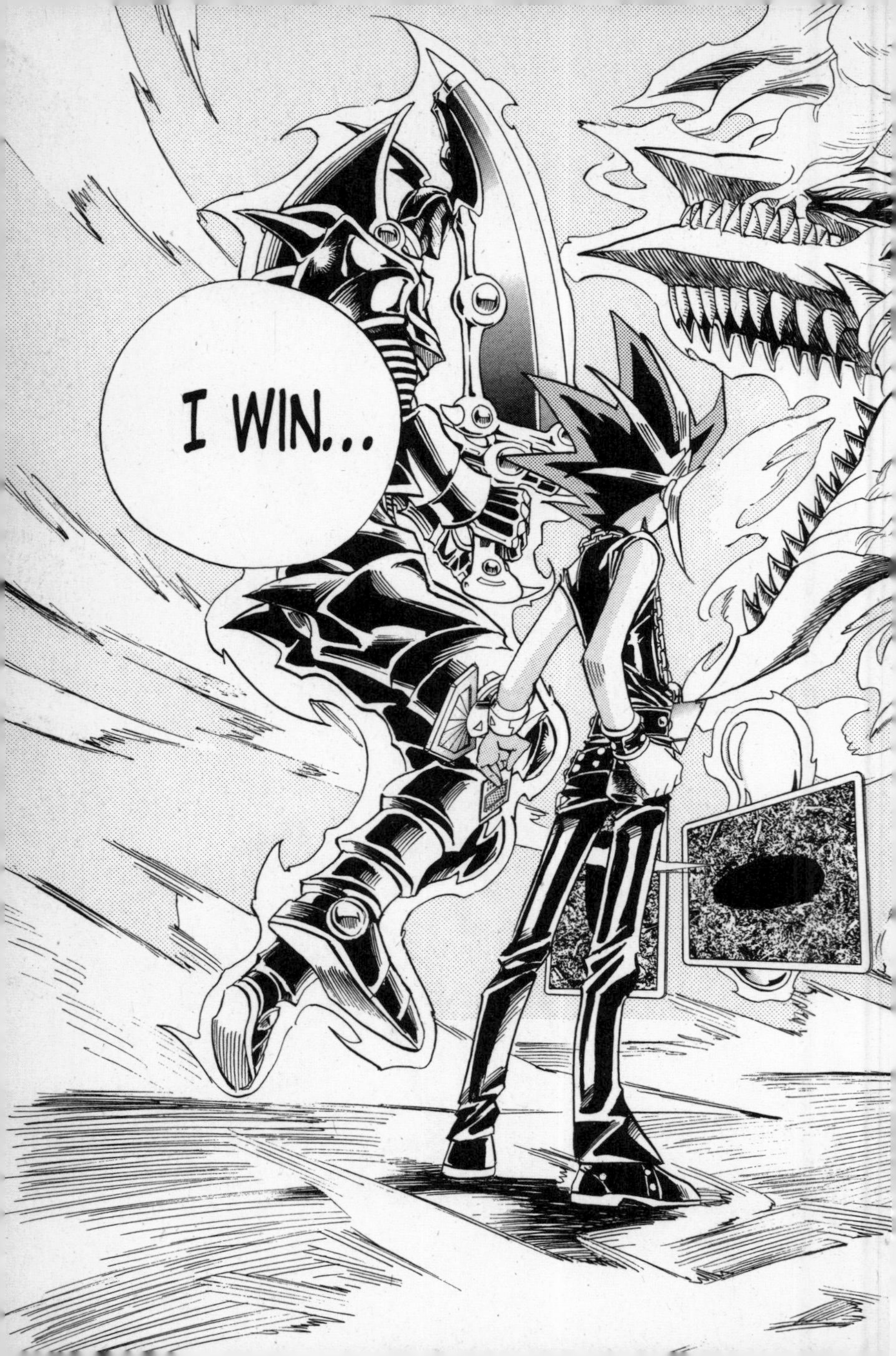
I WIN...

REVIVAL JA[M]

When this card is sent to t[he]
as a result of battle, you ca[n]
Summon this card in face-up [Defense]
Position at your next Standby Phase.

ATK/1500 DEF/500

JAM DEFENDER
[PERMANENT TRAP CARD]

Each time a monster on your opponent's
side of the field attacks a monster on
your side of the field and you have
"Revival Jam" face-up on the field, you
can change the attack target to "Revival
Jam".

Duel 118: Targets!

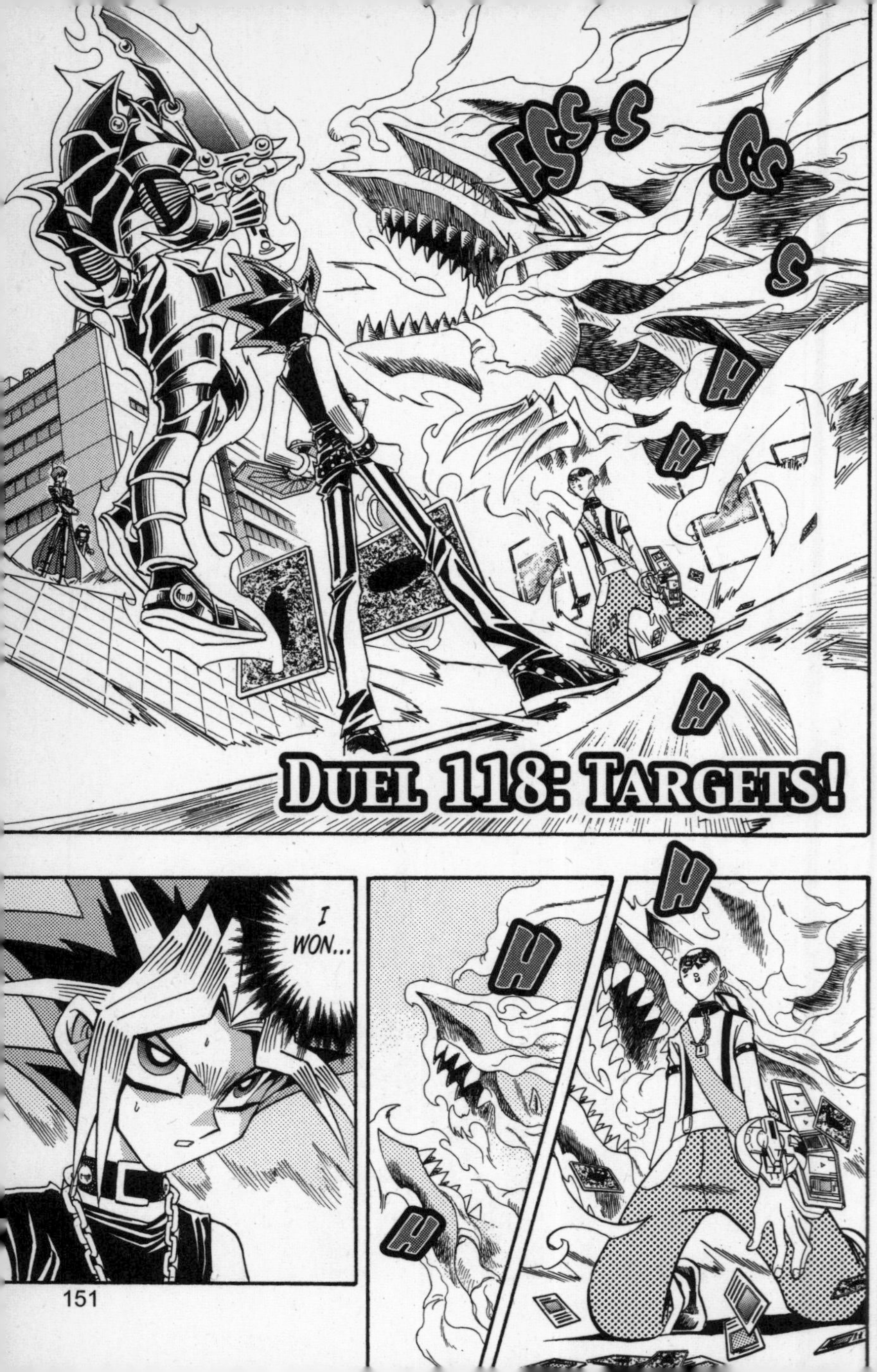
FSSS
SSS
S
H
H
H
H
H
H
I WON...

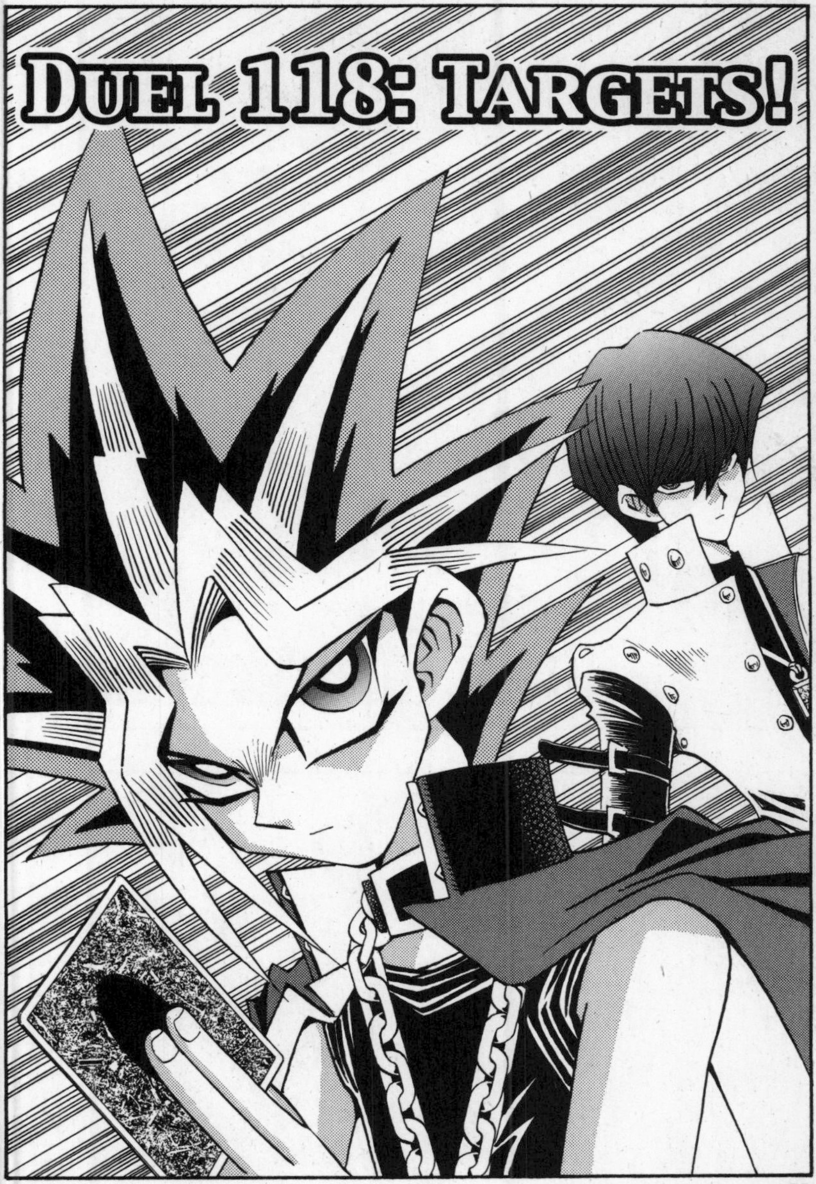
DUEL 118: TARGETS!

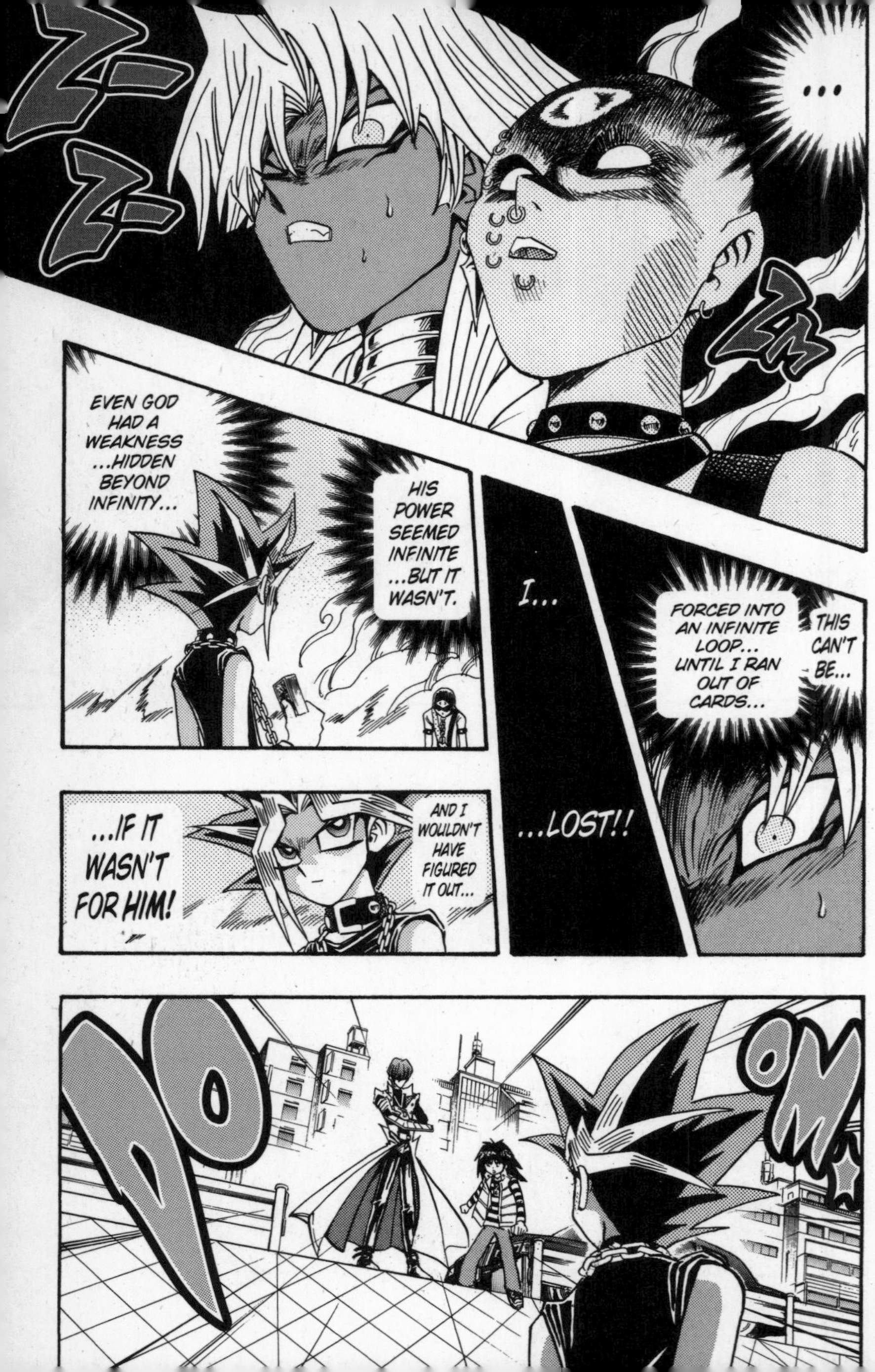
...
ZAM
Z- Z-
THIS CAN'T BE...
FORCED INTO AN INFINITE LOOP... UNTIL I RAN OUT OF CARDS...
I...
...LOST!!
HIS POWER SEEMED INFINITE ...BUT IT WASN'T.
EVEN GOD HAD A WEAKNESS ...HIDDEN BEYOND INFINITY...
AND I WOULDN'T HAVE FIGURED IT OUT...
...IF IT WASN'T FOR HIM!
DOOM!

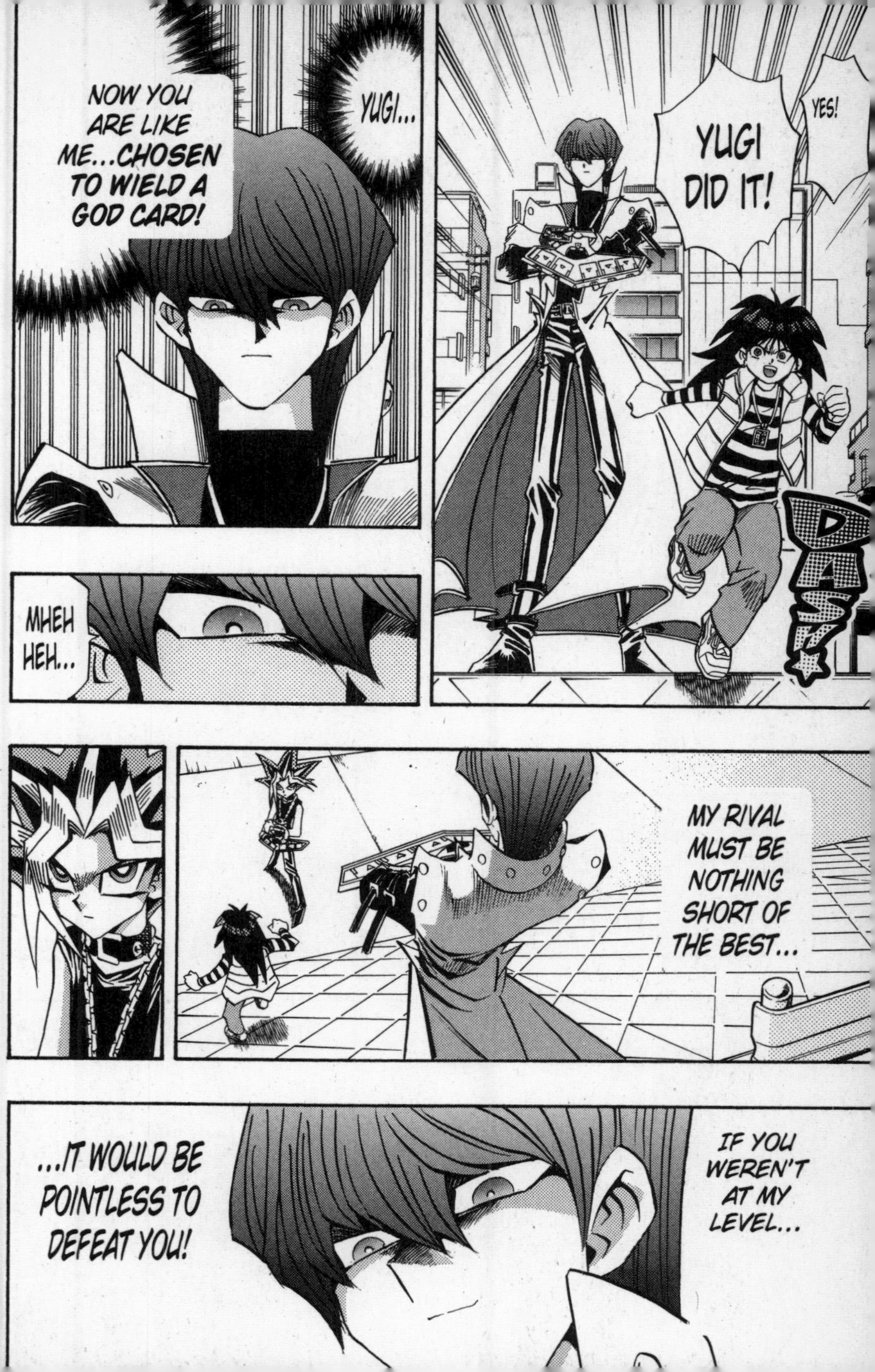
YES!
YUGI DID IT!
DASH
YUGI...
NOW YOU ARE LIKE ME...CHOSEN TO WIELD A GOD CARD!
MHEH HEH...
MY RIVAL MUST BE NOTHING SHORT OF THE BEST...
IF YOU WEREN'T AT MY LEVEL...
...IT WOULD BE POINTLESS TO DEFEAT YOU!

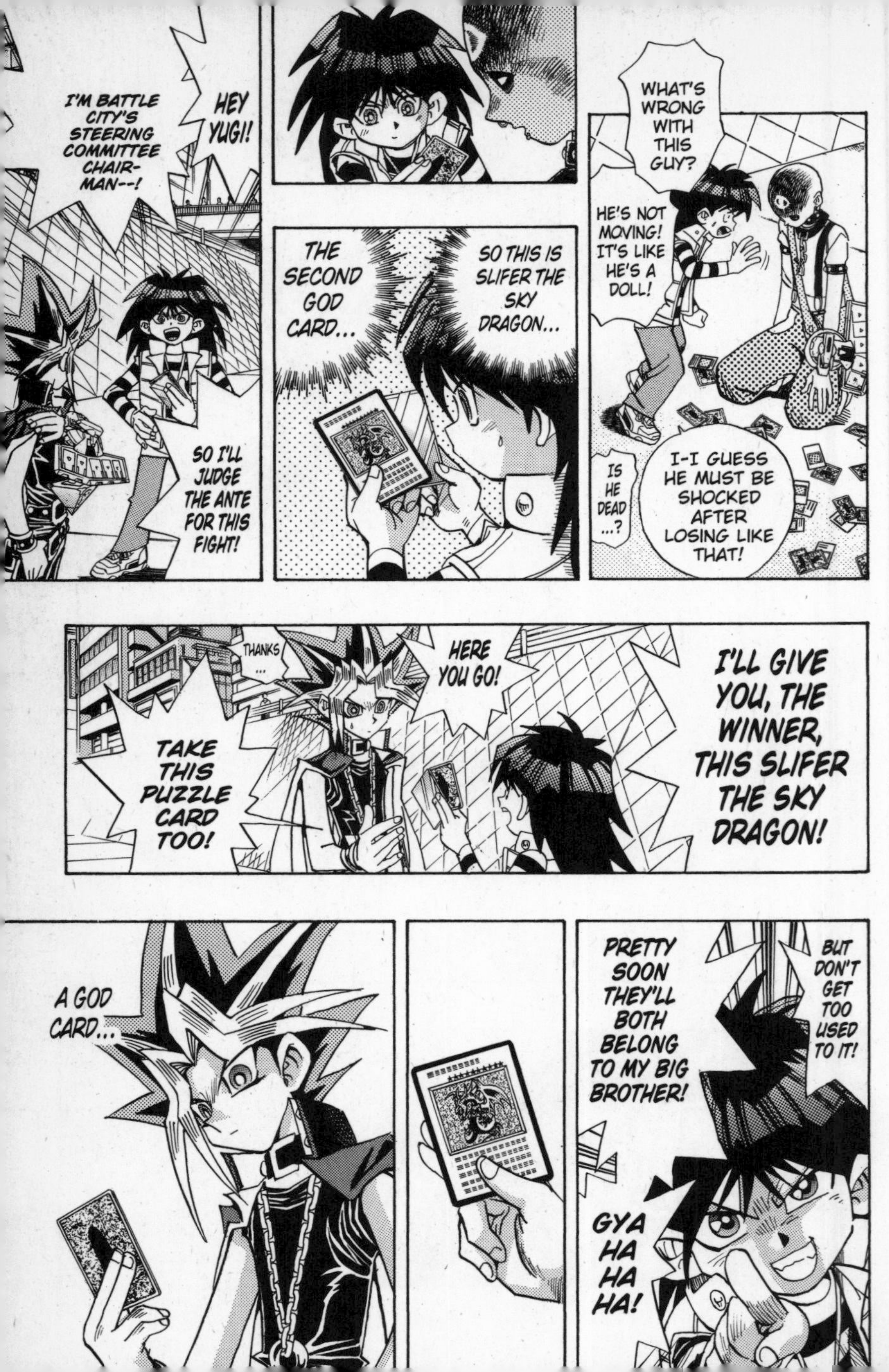
WHAT'S WRONG WITH THIS GUY?
HE'S NOT MOVING! IT'S LIKE HE'S A DOLL!
I-I GUESS HE MUST BE SHOCKED AFTER LOSING LIKE THAT!
IS HE DEAD ...?
SO THIS IS SLIFER THE SKY DRAGON...
THE SECOND GOD CARD...
HEY YUGI!
I'M BATTLE CITY'S STEERING COMMITTEE CHAIRMAN--!
SO I'LL JUDGE THE ANTE FOR THIS FIGHT!
I'LL GIVE YOU, THE WINNER, THIS SLIFER THE SKY DRAGON!
HERE YOU GO!
THANKS ...
TAKE THIS PUZZLE CARD TOO!
BUT DON'T GET TOO USED TO IT!
PRETTY SOON THEY'LL BOTH BELONG TO MY BIG BROTHER!
GYA HA HA HA!
A GOD CARD...

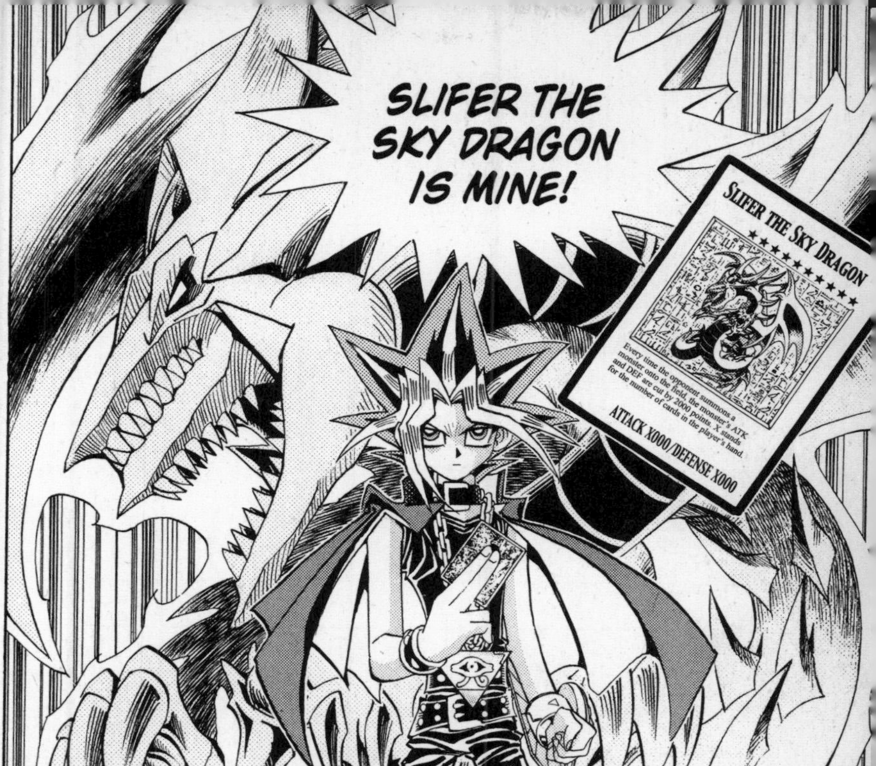
SLIFER THE SKY DRAGON IS MINE!
SLIFER THE SKY DRAGON
Every time the opponent summons a monster onto the field, the monster's ATK and DEF are cut by 2000 points. X stands for the number of cards in the player's hand.
ATTACK X000/DEFENSE X000
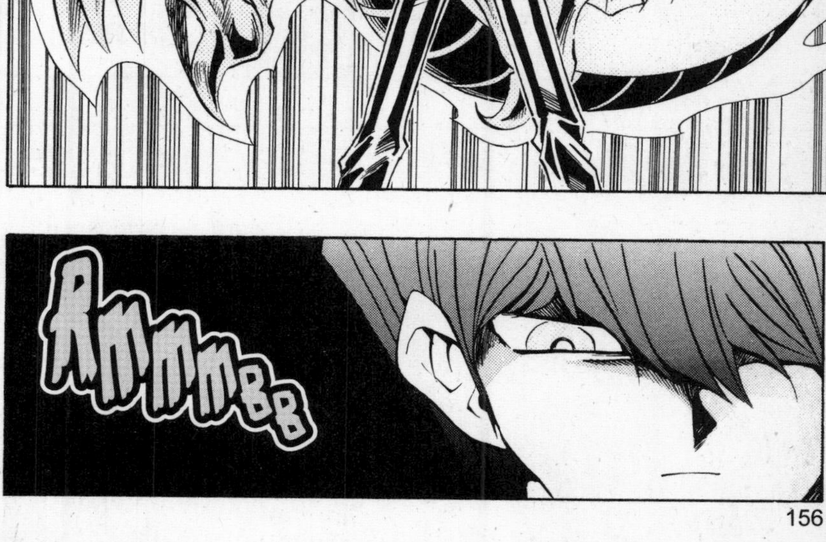
RMMMBB

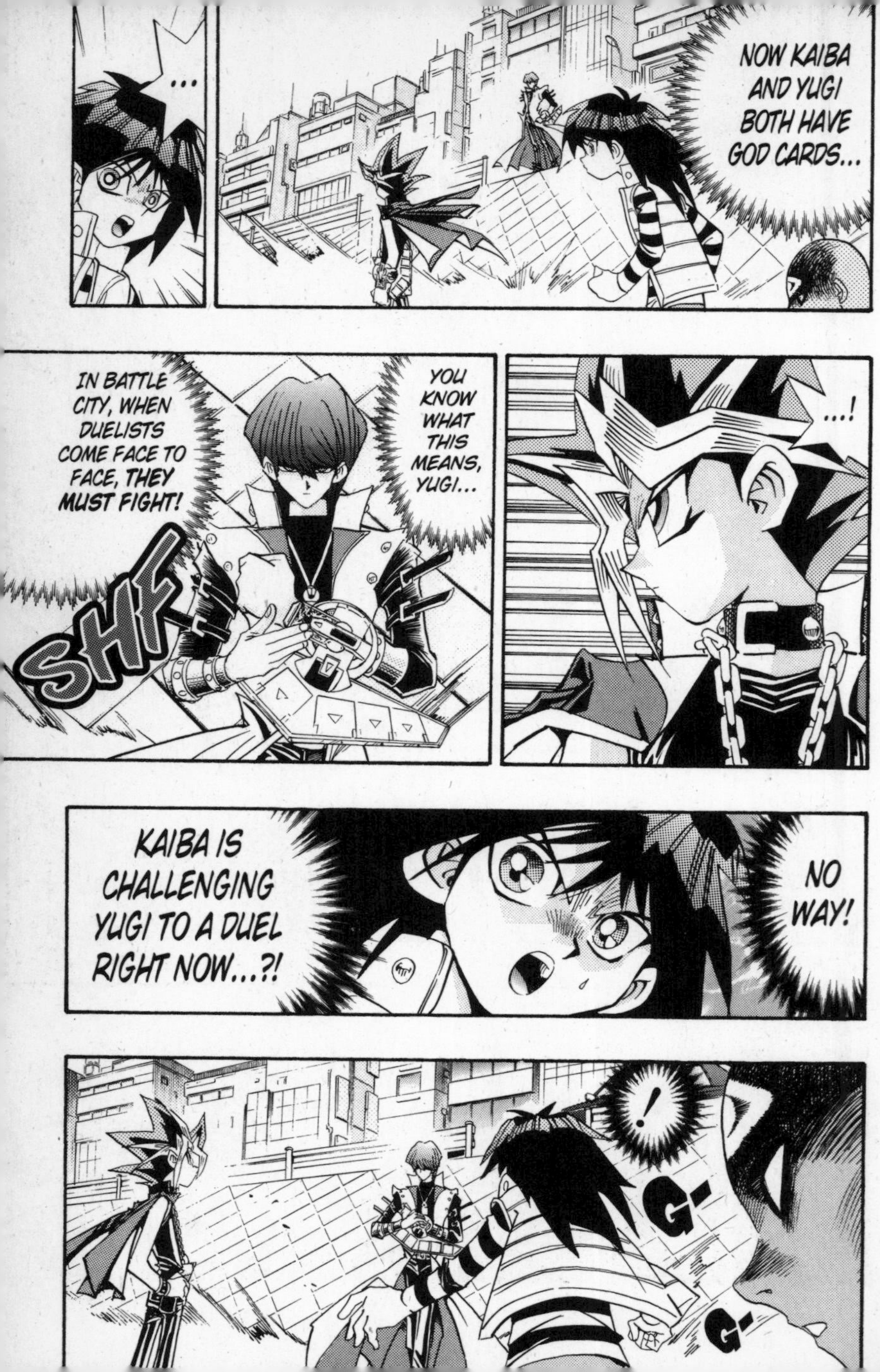
NOW KAIBA AND YUGI BOTH HAVE GOD CARDS...
...
...!
YOU KNOW WHAT THIS MEANS, YUGI...
IN BATTLE CITY, WHEN DUELISTS COME FACE TO FACE, THEY MUST FIGHT!
SHF
NO WAY!
KAIBA IS CHALLENGING YUGI TO A DUEL RIGHT NOW...?!
!
G-
G-

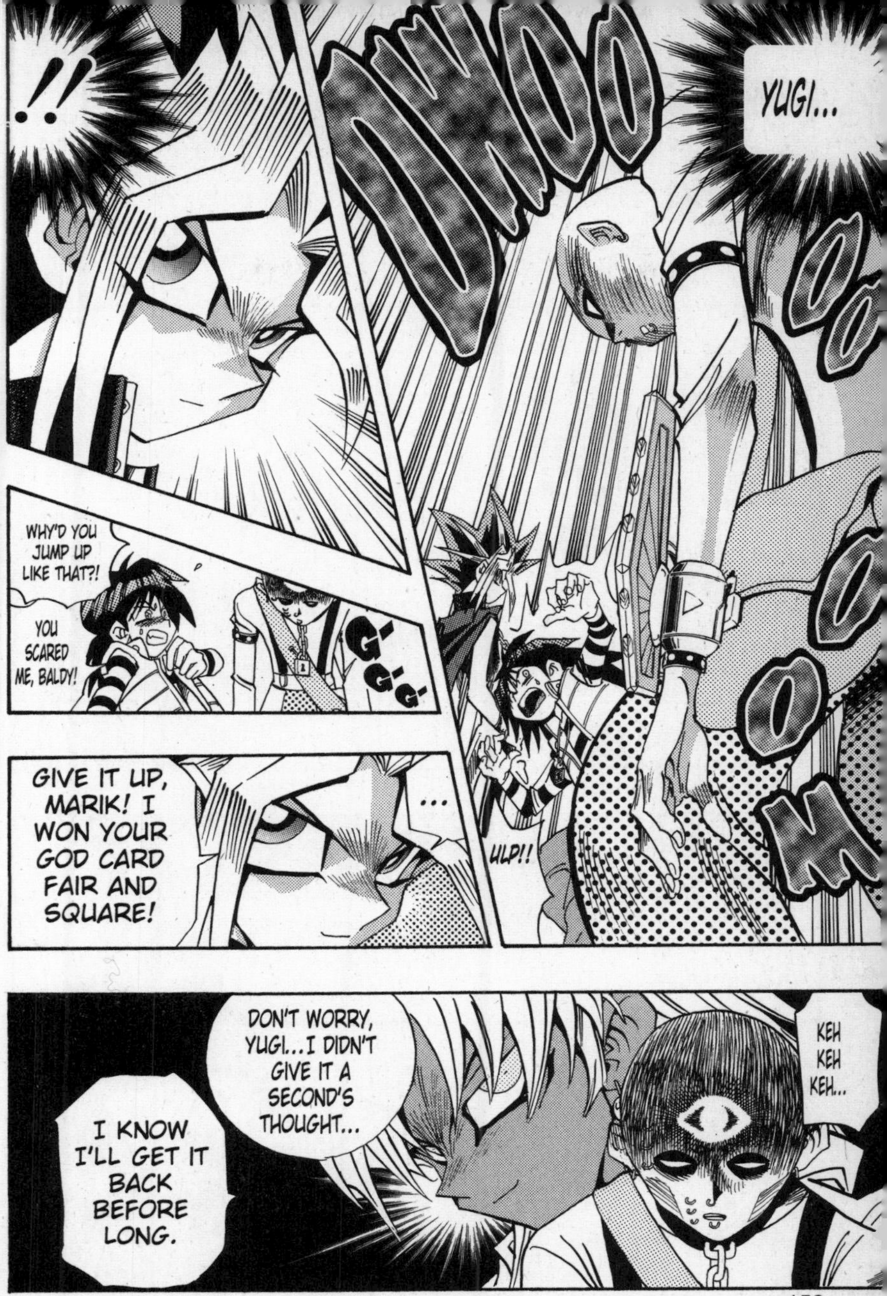
YUGI...
ULP!!
!!
WHY'D YOU JUMP UP LIKE THAT?!
YOU SCARED ME, BALDY!
G-G-G-
...
GIVE IT UP, MARIK! I WON YOUR GOD CARD FAIR AND SQUARE!
KEH KEH KEH...
DON'T WORRY, YUGI...I DIDN'T GIVE IT A SECOND'S THOUGHT...
I KNOW I'LL GET IT BACK BEFORE LONG.

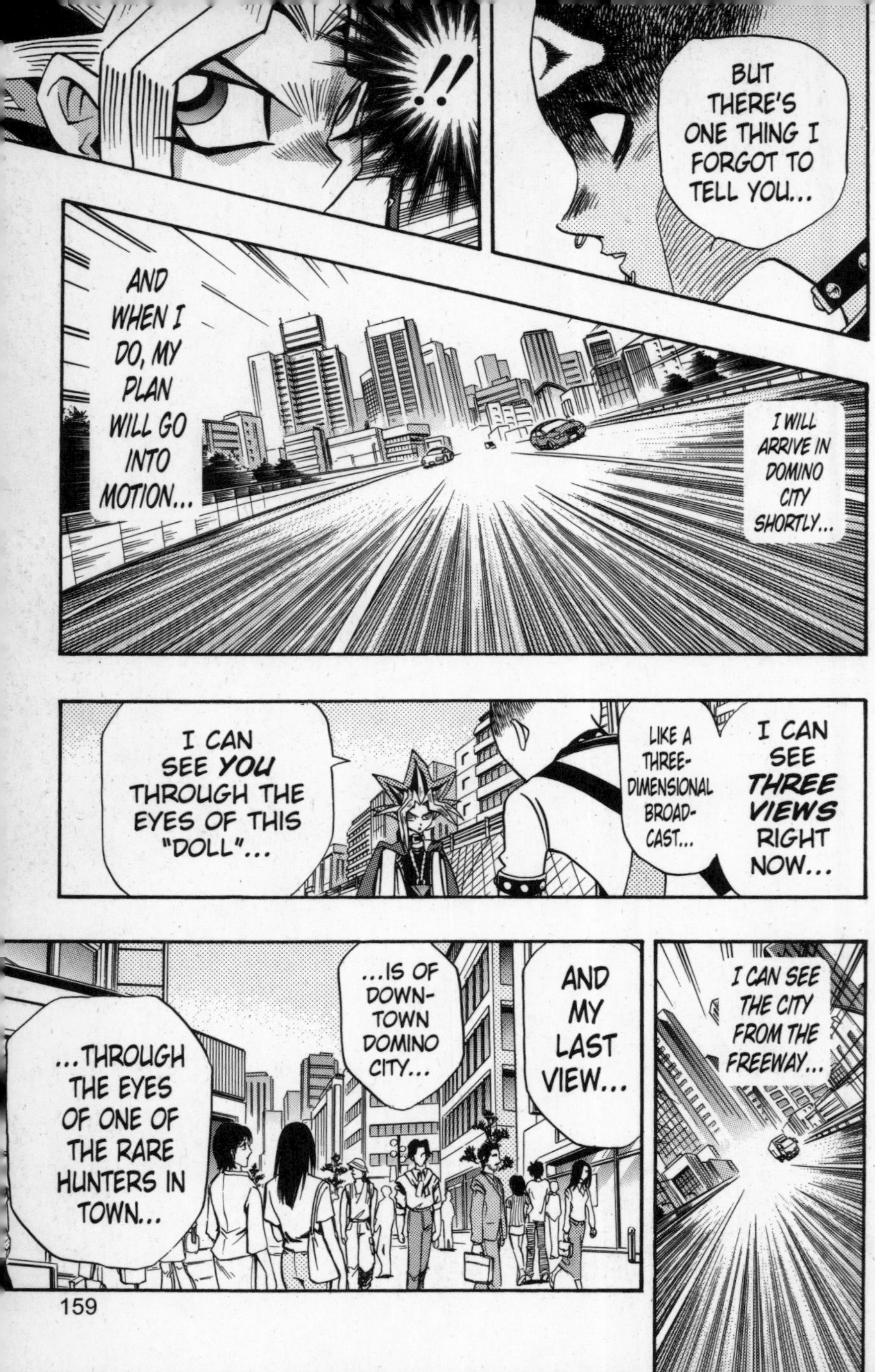
BUT THERE'S ONE THING I FORGOT TO TELL YOU...
!!
I WILL ARRIVE IN DOMINO CITY SHORTLY...
AND WHEN I DO, MY PLAN WILL GO INTO MOTION...
I CAN SEE THREE VIEWS RIGHT NOW...
LIKE A THREE-DIMENSIONAL BROAD-CAST...
I CAN SEE YOU THROUGH THE EYES OF THIS "DOLL"...
I CAN SEE THE CITY FROM THE FREEWAY...
AND MY LAST VIEW...
...IS OF DOWN-TOWN DOMINO CITY...
...THROUGH THE EYES OF ONE OF THE RARE HUNTERS IN TOWN...

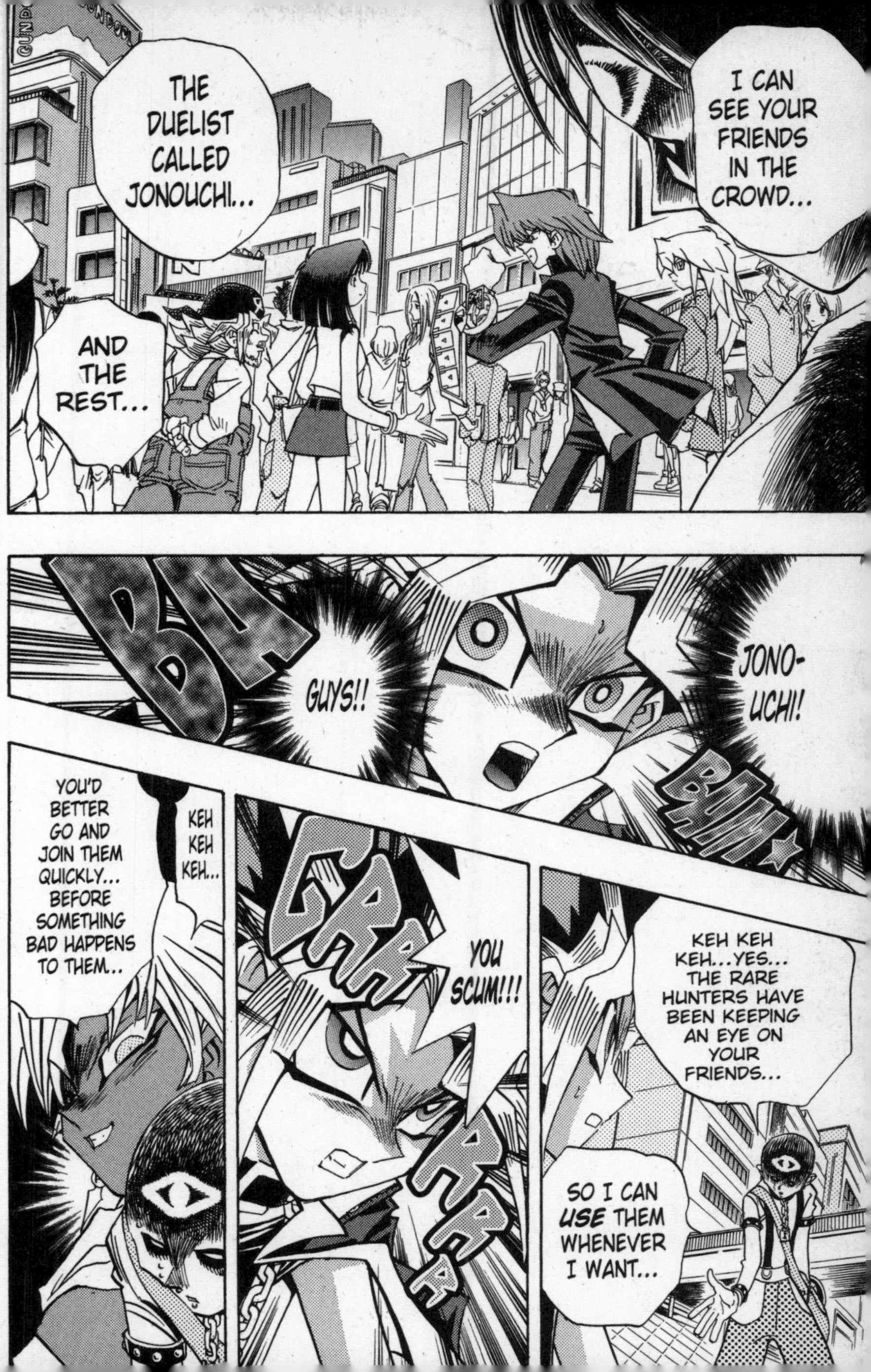
I CAN SEE YOUR FRIENDS IN THE CROWD...
THE DUELIST CALLED JONOUCHI...
AND THE REST...
JONO-UCHI!
GUYS!!
BAM★
KEH KEH KEH...YES... THE RARE HUNTERS HAVE BEEN KEEPING AN EYE ON YOUR FRIENDS...
SO I CAN *USE* THEM WHENEVER I WANT...
YOU SCUM!!!
KEH KEH KEH...
YOU'D BETTER GO AND JOIN THEM QUICKLY... BEFORE SOMETHING BAD HAPPENS TO THEM...

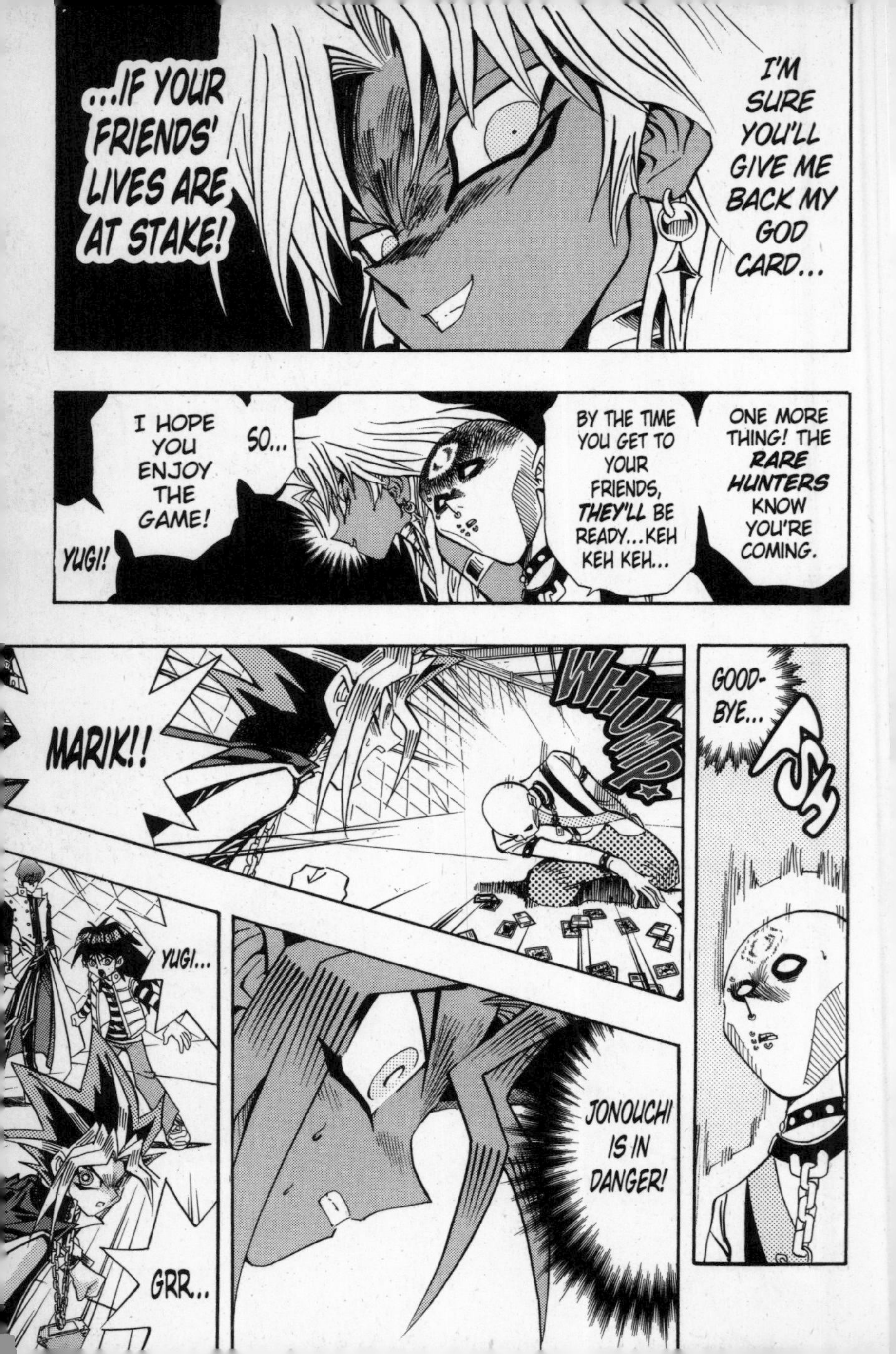
I'M SURE YOU'LL GIVE ME BACK MY GOD CARD...
...IF YOUR FRIENDS' LIVES ARE AT STAKE!
ONE MORE THING! THE **RARE HUNTERS** KNOW YOU'RE COMING.
BY THE TIME YOU GET TO YOUR FRIENDS, **THEY'LL** BE READY...KEH KEH KEH...
SO...
I HOPE YOU ENJOY THE GAME!
YUGI!
GOOD-BYE...
FSH
WHUMP
MARIK!!
JONOUCHI IS IN DANGER!
YUGI...
GRR...

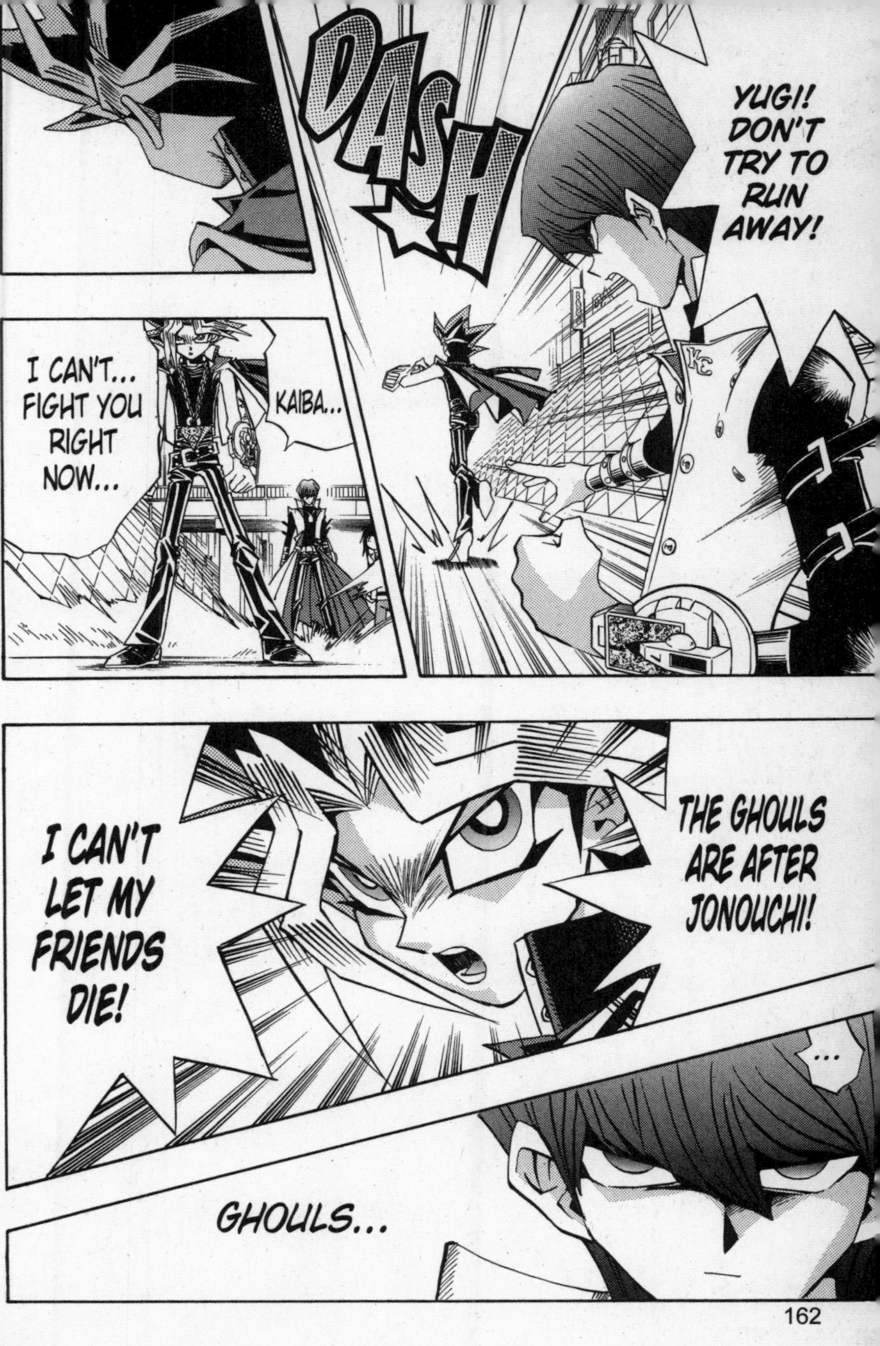
DASH
YUGI! DON'T TRY TO RUN AWAY!
I CAN'T... FIGHT YOU RIGHT NOW...
KAIBA...
THE GHOULS ARE AFTER JONOUCHI!
I CAN'T LET MY FRIENDS DIE!
...
GHOULS...

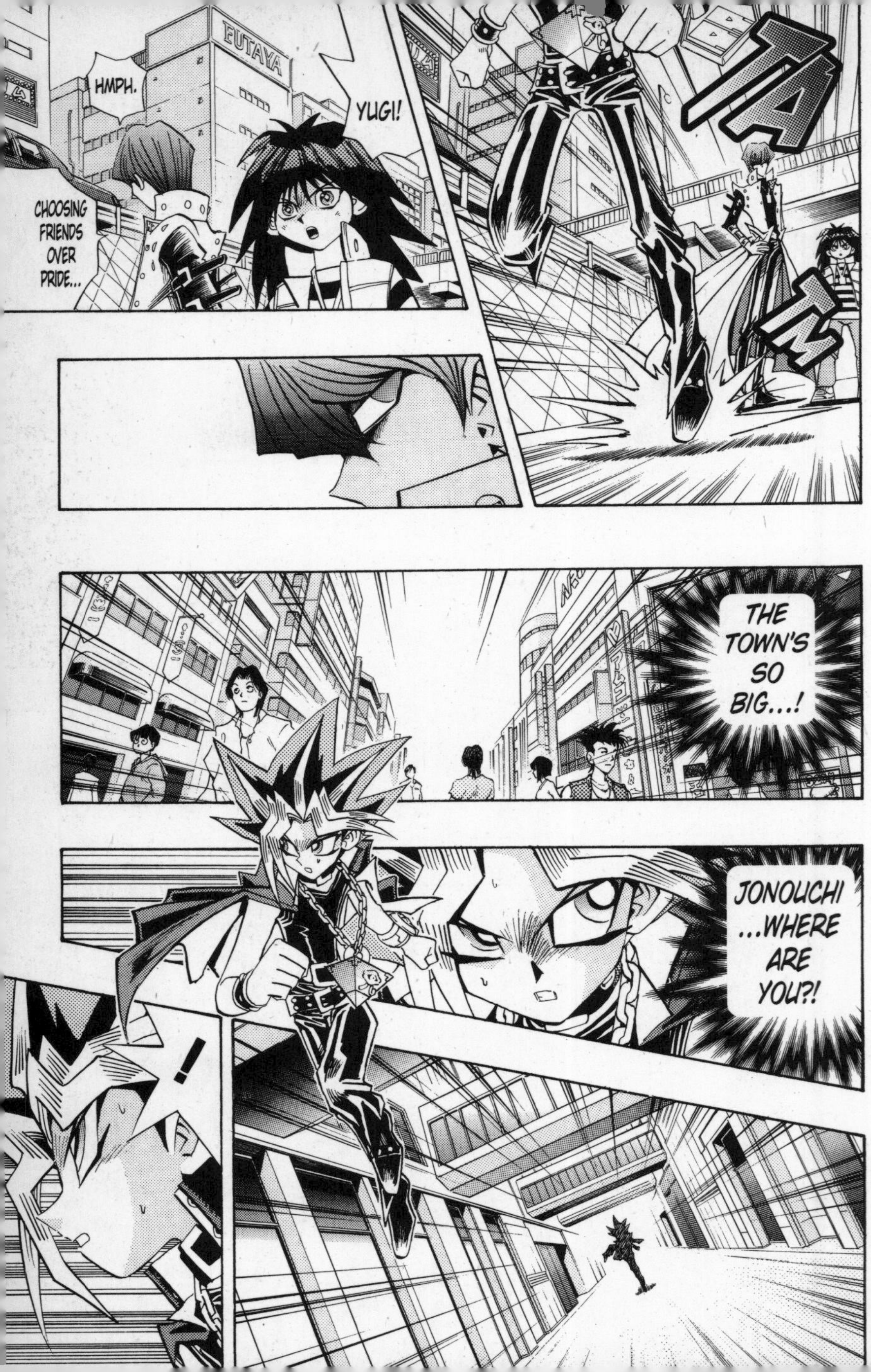
CHOOSING FRIENDS OVER PRIDE...
HMPH.
YUGI!
TA
TM
THE TOWN'S SO BIG...!
JONOUCHI ...WHERE ARE YOU?!
!

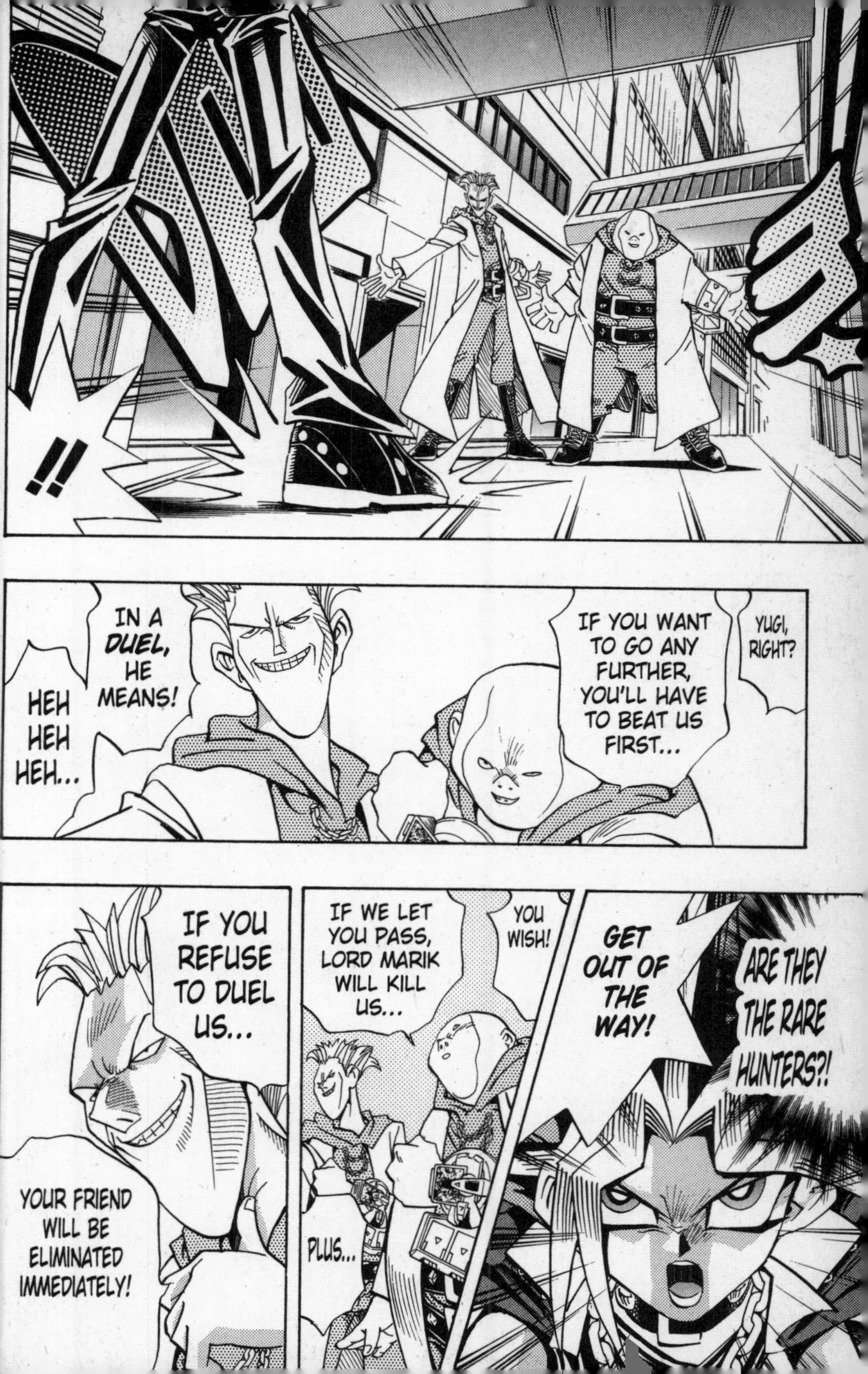
!!
YUGI, RIGHT?
IF YOU WANT TO GO ANY FURTHER, YOU'LL HAVE TO BEAT US FIRST...
IN A DUEL, HE MEANS!
HEH HEH HEH...
ARE THEY THE RARE HUNTERS?!
GET OUT OF THE WAY!
YOU WISH!
IF WE LET YOU PASS, LORD MARIK WILL KILL US...
PLUS...
IF YOU REFUSE TO DUEL US...
YOUR FRIEND WILL BE ELIMINATED IMMEDIATELY!

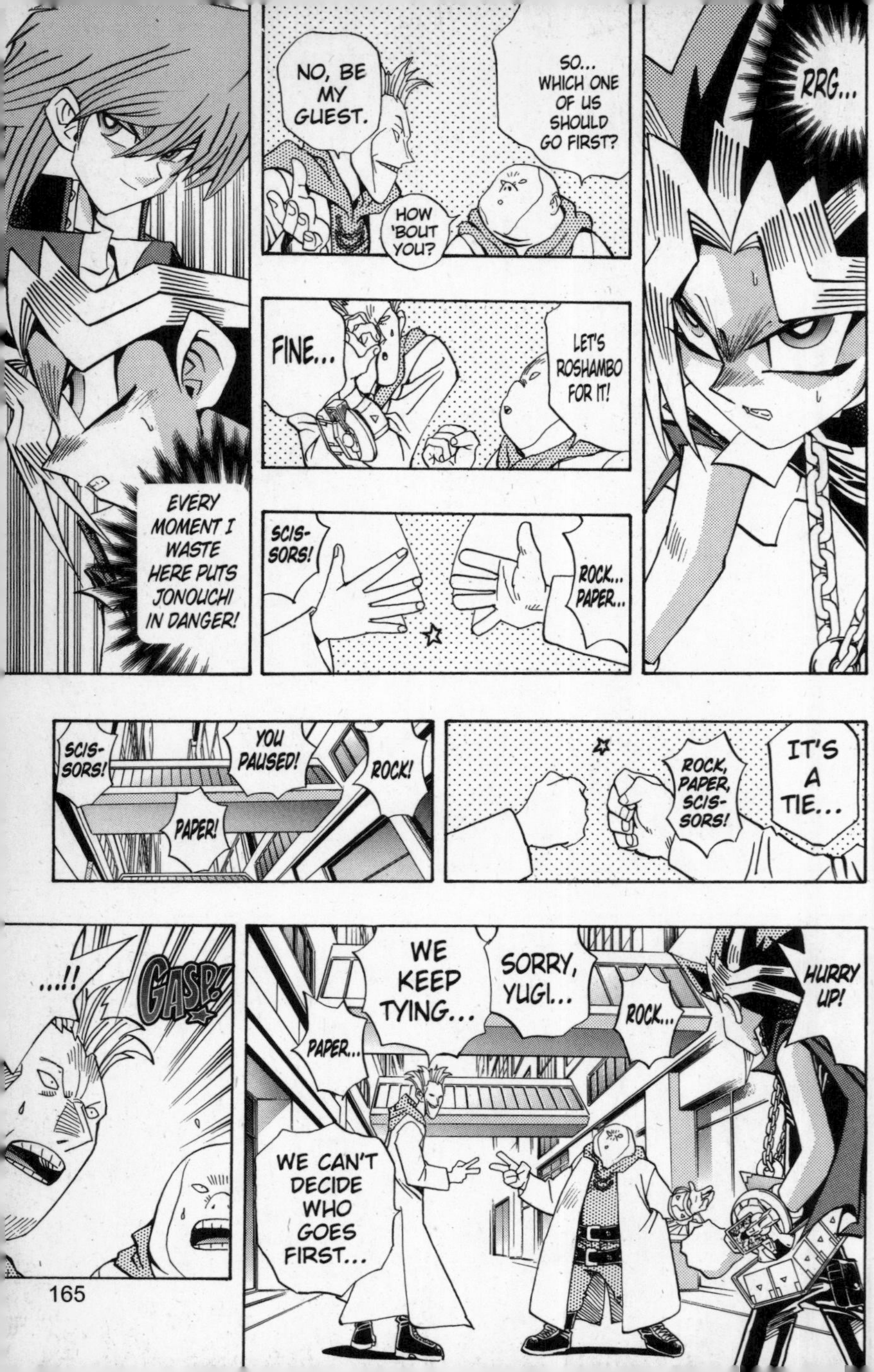
SO... WHICH ONE OF US SHOULD GO FIRST?
NO, BE MY GUEST.
HOW 'BOUT YOU?
RRG...
LET'S ROSHAMBO FOR IT!
FINE...
ROCK... PAPER...
SCIS-SORS!
EVERY MOMENT I WASTE HERE PUTS JONOUCHI IN DANGER!
IT'S A TIE...
ROCK, PAPER, SCIS-SORS!
ROCK!
YOU PAUSED!
SCIS-SORS!
PAPER!
HURRY UP!
ROCK...
SORRY, YUGI...
WE KEEP TYING...
PAPER...
WE CAN'T DECIDE WHO GOES FIRST...
GASP!
...!!

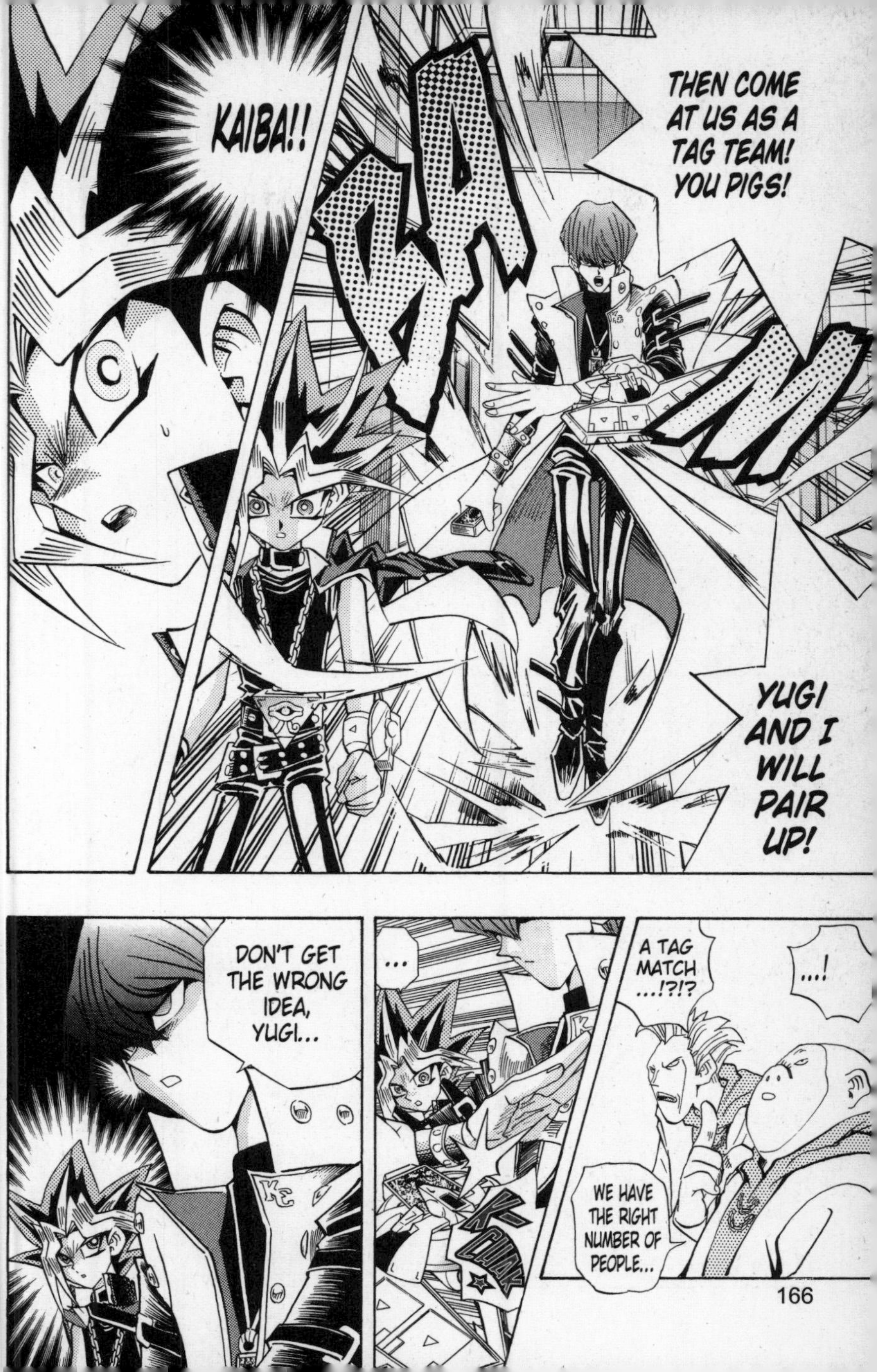
THEN COME AT US AS A TAG TEAM! YOU PIGS!
YUGI AND I WILL PAIR UP!
KAIBA!!
A TAG MATCH ...!?!?
...!
WE HAVE THE RIGHT NUMBER OF PEOPLE...
...
DON'T GET THE WRONG IDEA, YUGI...

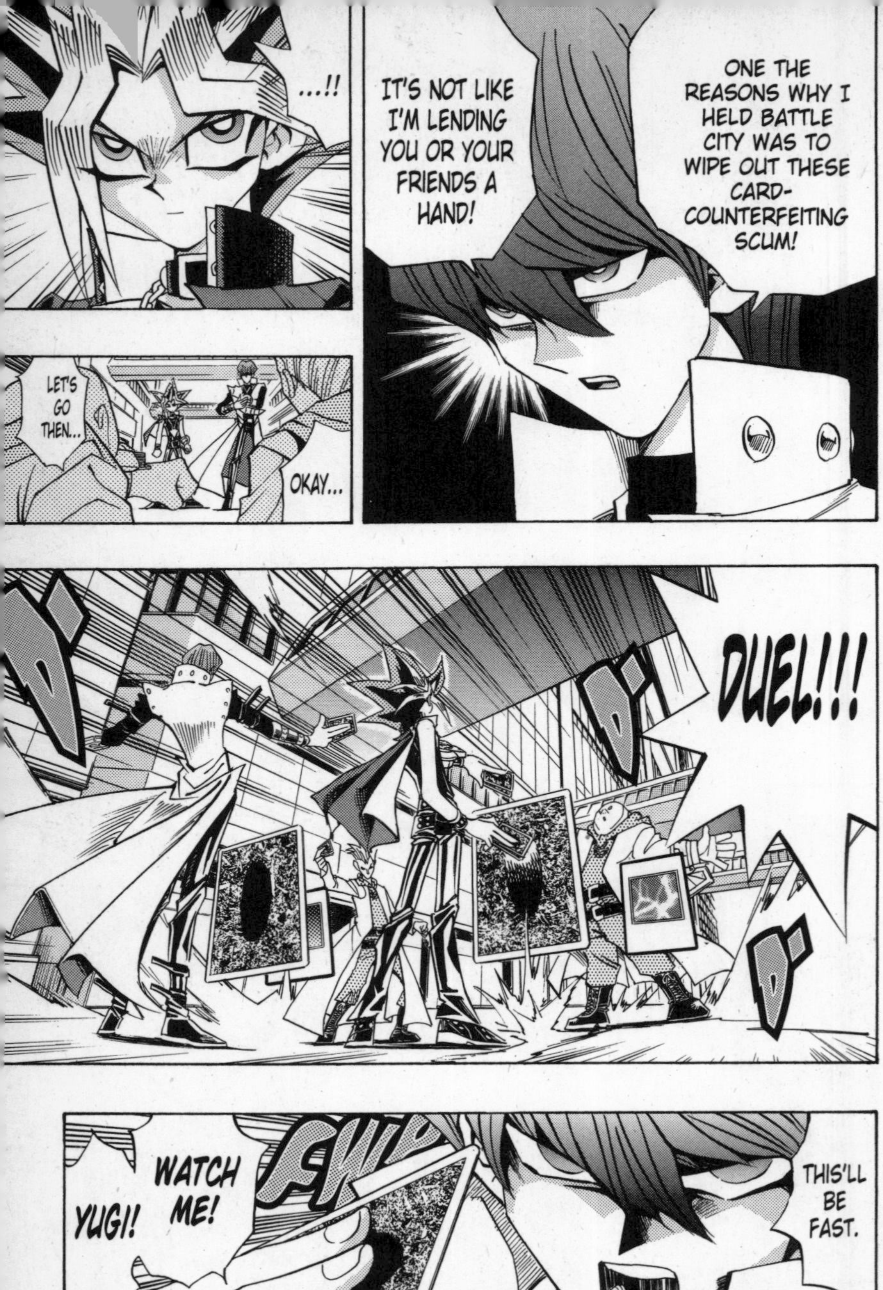
ONE THE REASONS WHY I HELD BATTLE CITY WAS TO WIPE OUT THESE CARD-COUNTERFEITING SCUM!
IT'S NOT LIKE I'M LENDING YOU OR YOUR FRIENDS A HAND!
...!!
LET'S GO THEN...
OKAY...
DUEL!!!
THIS'LL BE FAST.
WATCH ME!
YUGI!

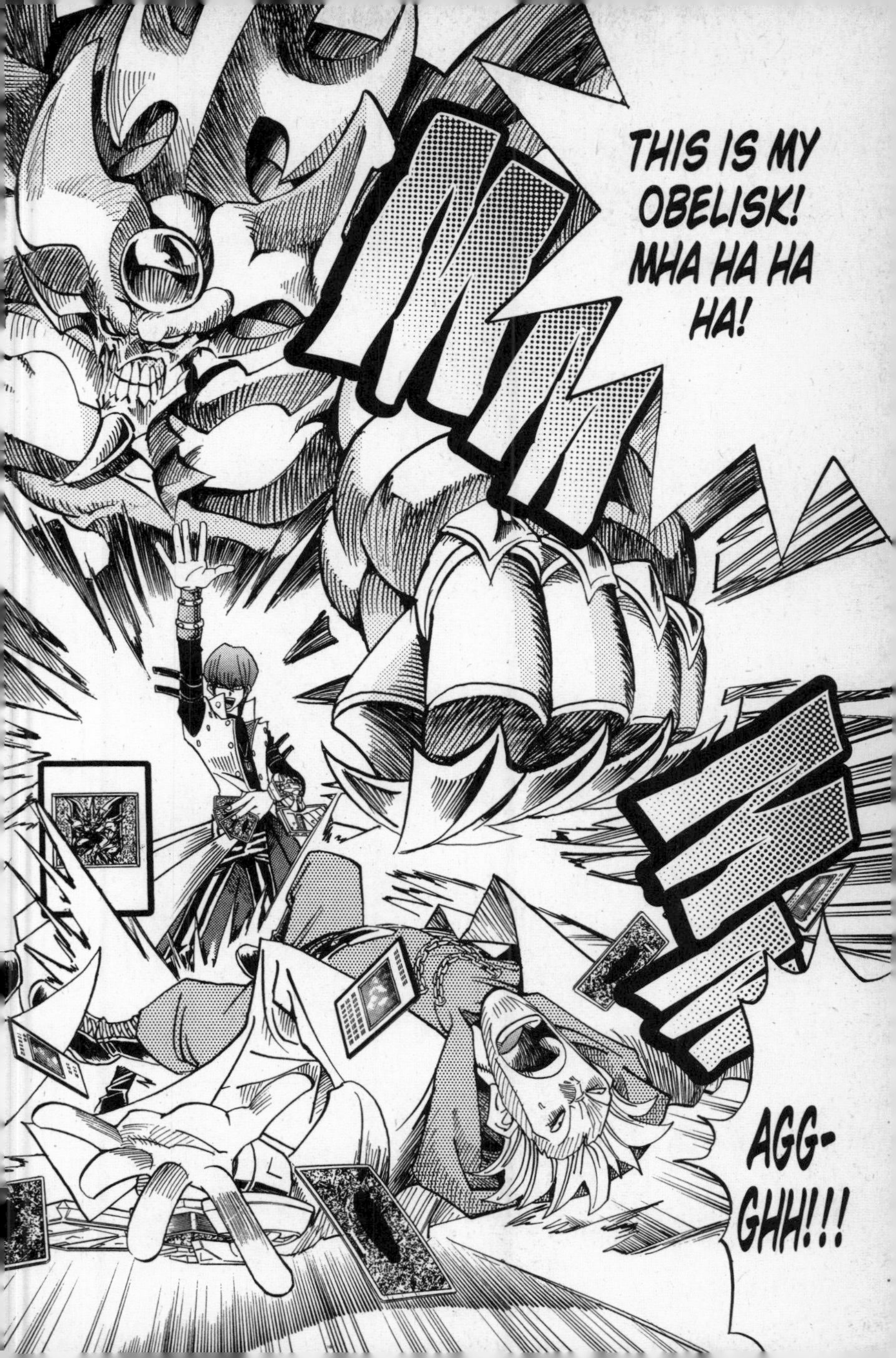
THIS IS MY OBELISK! MHA HA HA HA!
AGG-GHH!!!

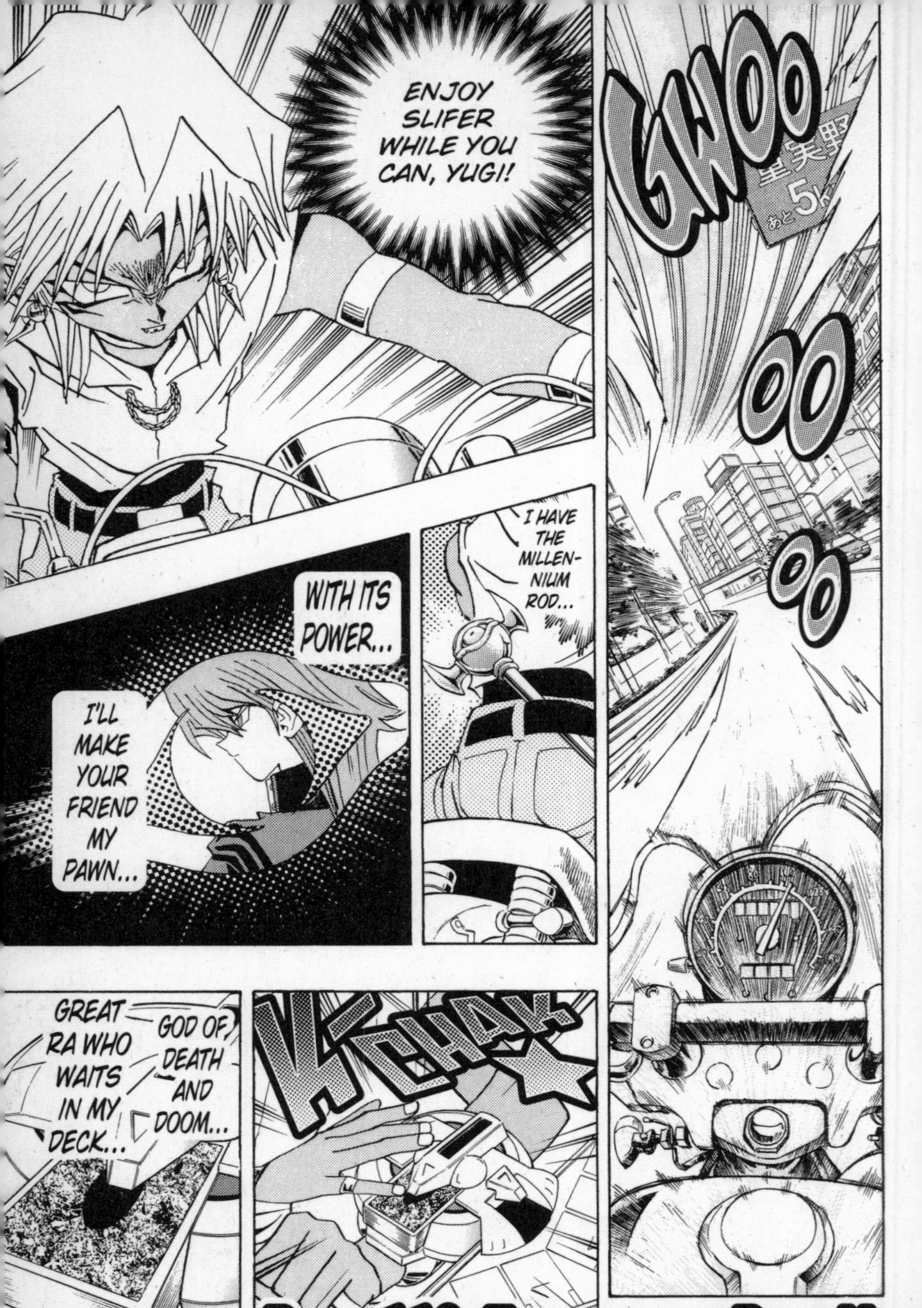
GWOOOOOO
ENJOY SLIFER WHILE YOU CAN, YUGI!
I HAVE THE MILLENNIUM ROD...
WITH ITS POWER...
I'LL MAKE YOUR FRIEND MY PAWN...
KCHAK
GREAT RA WHO WAITS IN MY DECK...
GOD OF DEATH AND DOOM...

DUEL 119: EVERYBODY DUEL!!

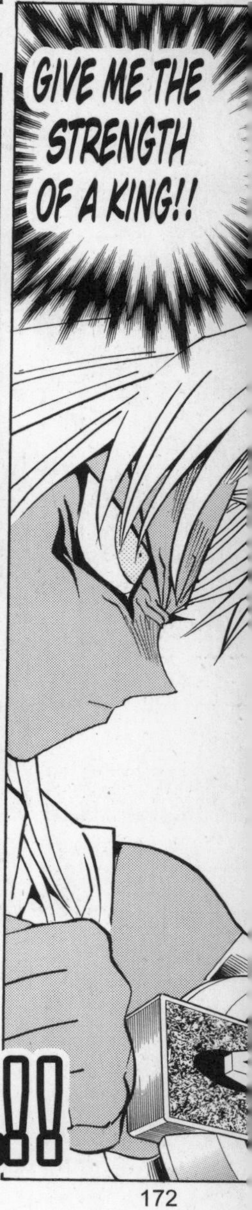
GIVE ME THE STRENGTH OF A KING!!

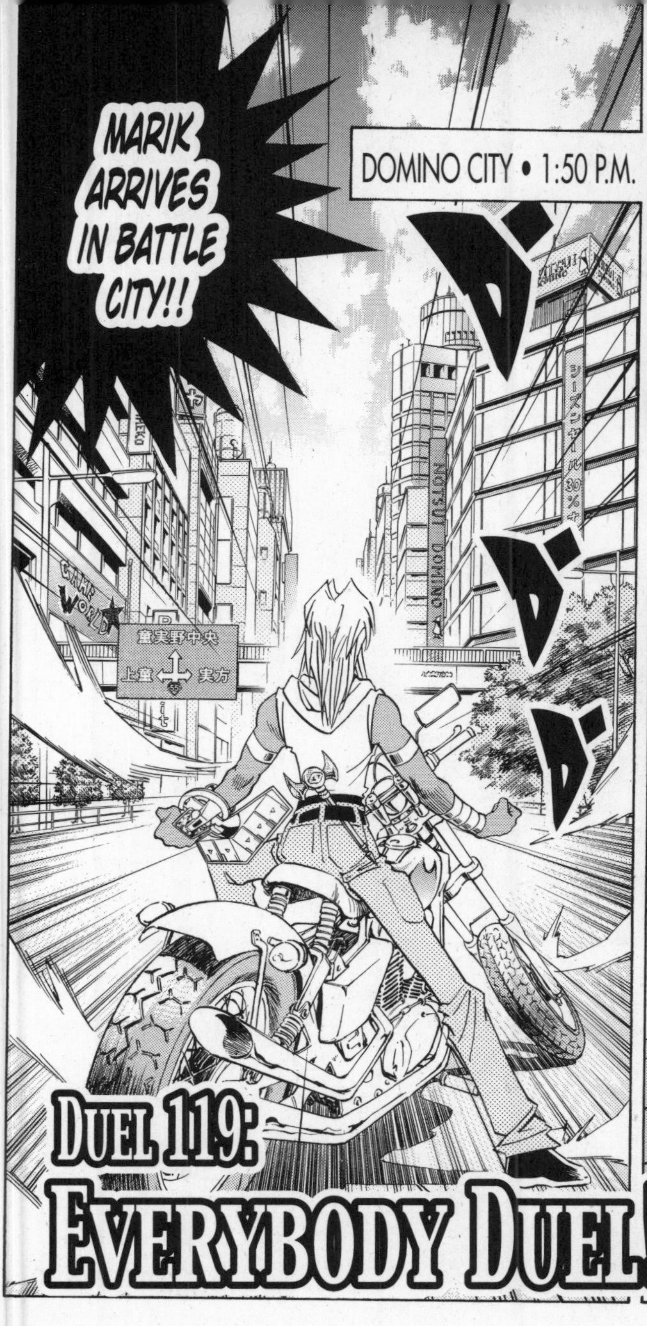
DOMINO CITY • 1:50 P.M.
MARIK ARRIVES IN BATTLE CITY!!
童実野中央
上童
実方

Duel 119: Everybody Duel!!

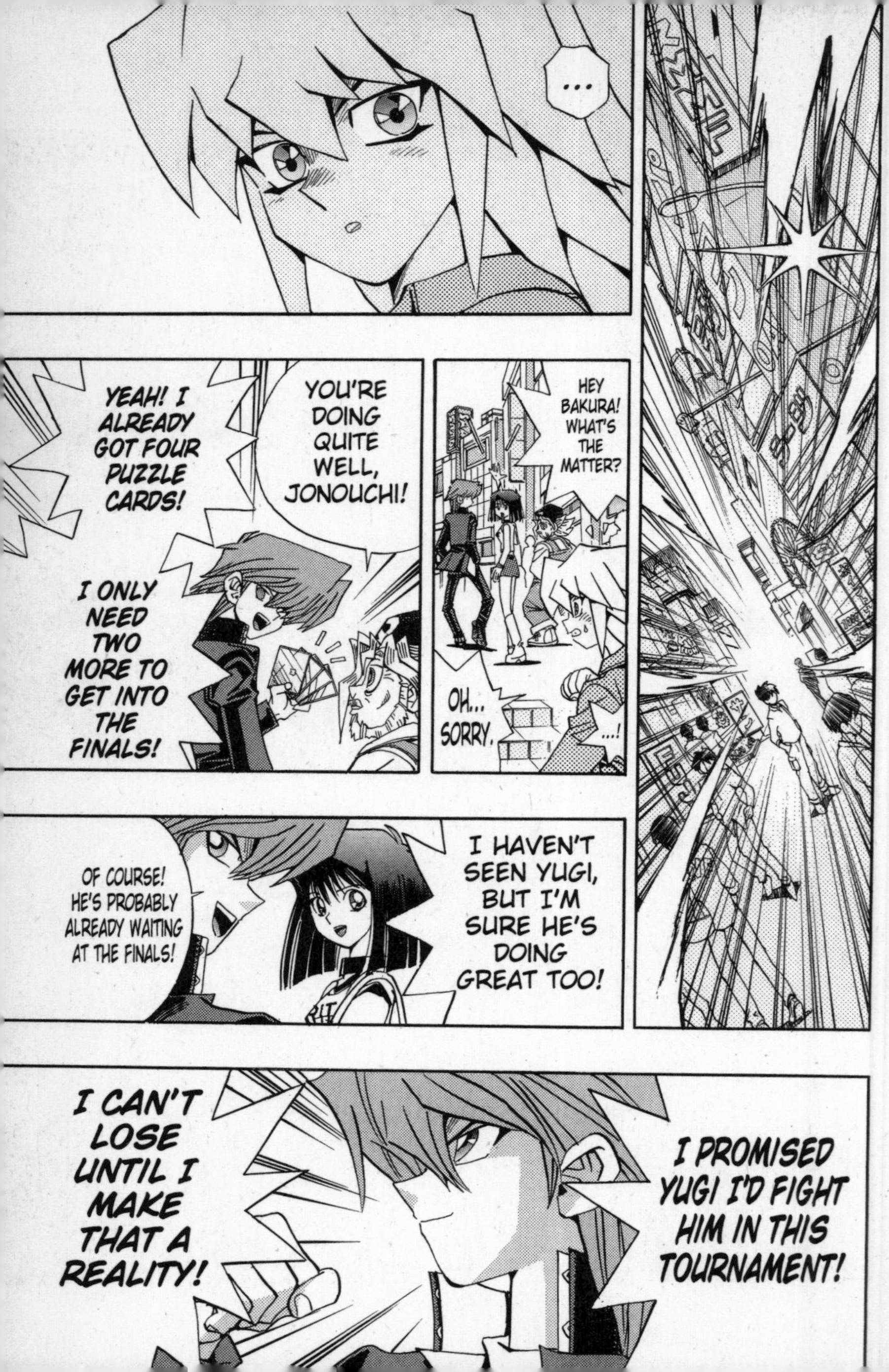
...
HEY BAKURA! WHAT'S THE MATTER?
...!
OH... SORRY.
YOU'RE DOING QUITE WELL, JONOUCHI!
YEAH! I ALREADY GOT FOUR PUZZLE CARDS!
I ONLY NEED TWO MORE TO GET INTO THE FINALS!
I HAVEN'T SEEN YUGI, BUT I'M SURE HE'S DOING GREAT TOO!
OF COURSE! HE'S PROBABLY ALREADY WAITING AT THE FINALS!
I PROMISED YUGI I'D FIGHT HIM IN THIS TOURNAMENT!
I CAN'T LOSE UNTIL I MAKE THAT A REALITY!

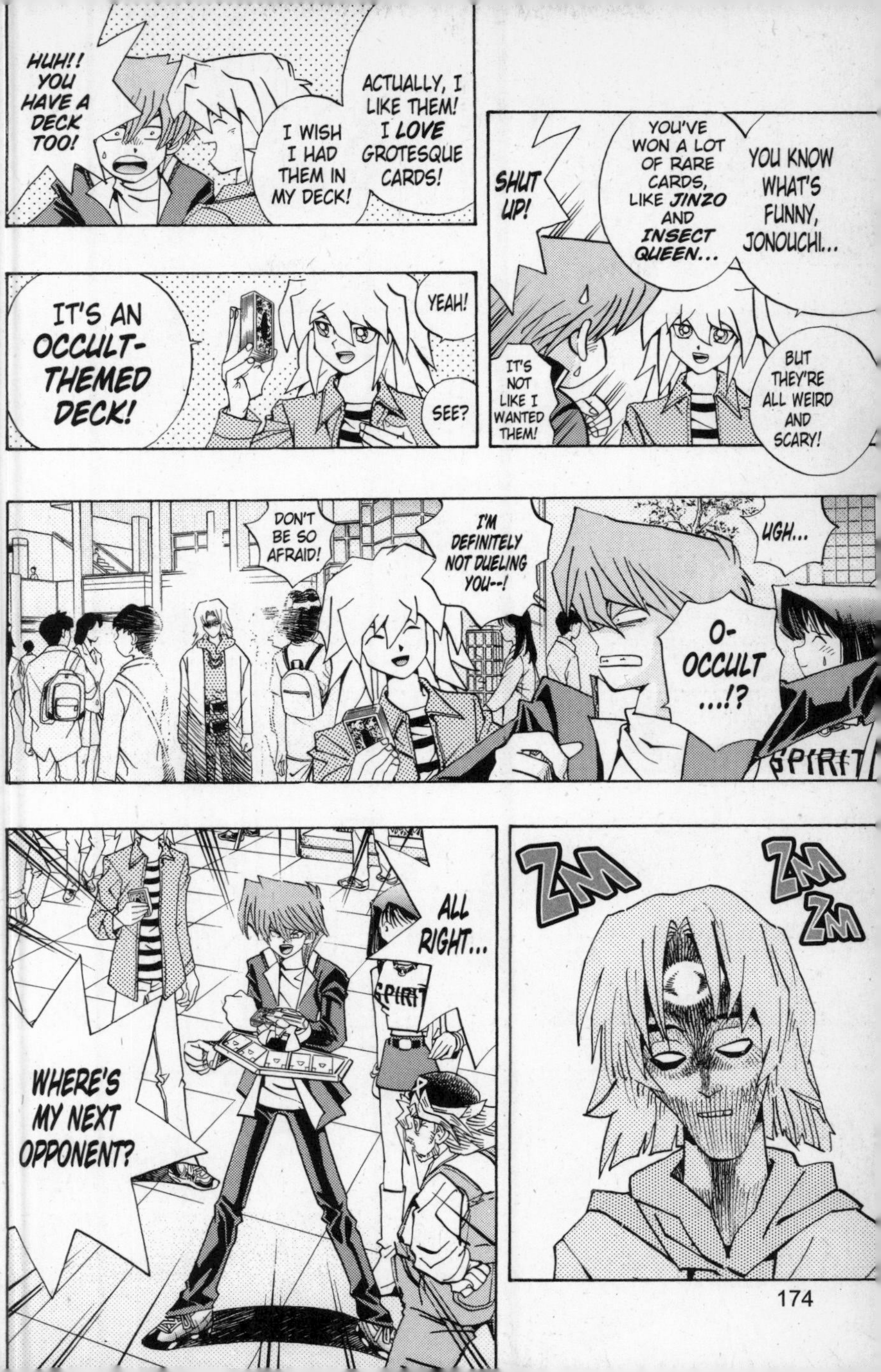

YOU KNOW WHAT'S FUNNY, JONOUCHI...
YOU'VE WON A LOT OF RARE CARDS, LIKE JINZO AND INSECT QUEEN...
SHUT UP!
BUT THEY'RE ALL WEIRD AND SCARY!
IT'S NOT LIKE I WANTED THEM!
ACTUALLY, I LIKE THEM! I LOVE GROTESQUE CARDS!
I WISH I HAD THEM IN MY DECK!
HUH!! YOU HAVE A DECK TOO!
YEAH!
SEE?
IT'S AN OCCULT-THEMED DECK!
UGH...
O-OCCULT ...!?
SPIRIT
I'M DEFINITELY NOT DUELING YOU--!
DON'T BE SO AFRAID!
ZM
ZM ZM
ALL RIGHT...
SPIRIT
WHERE'S MY NEXT OPPONENT?

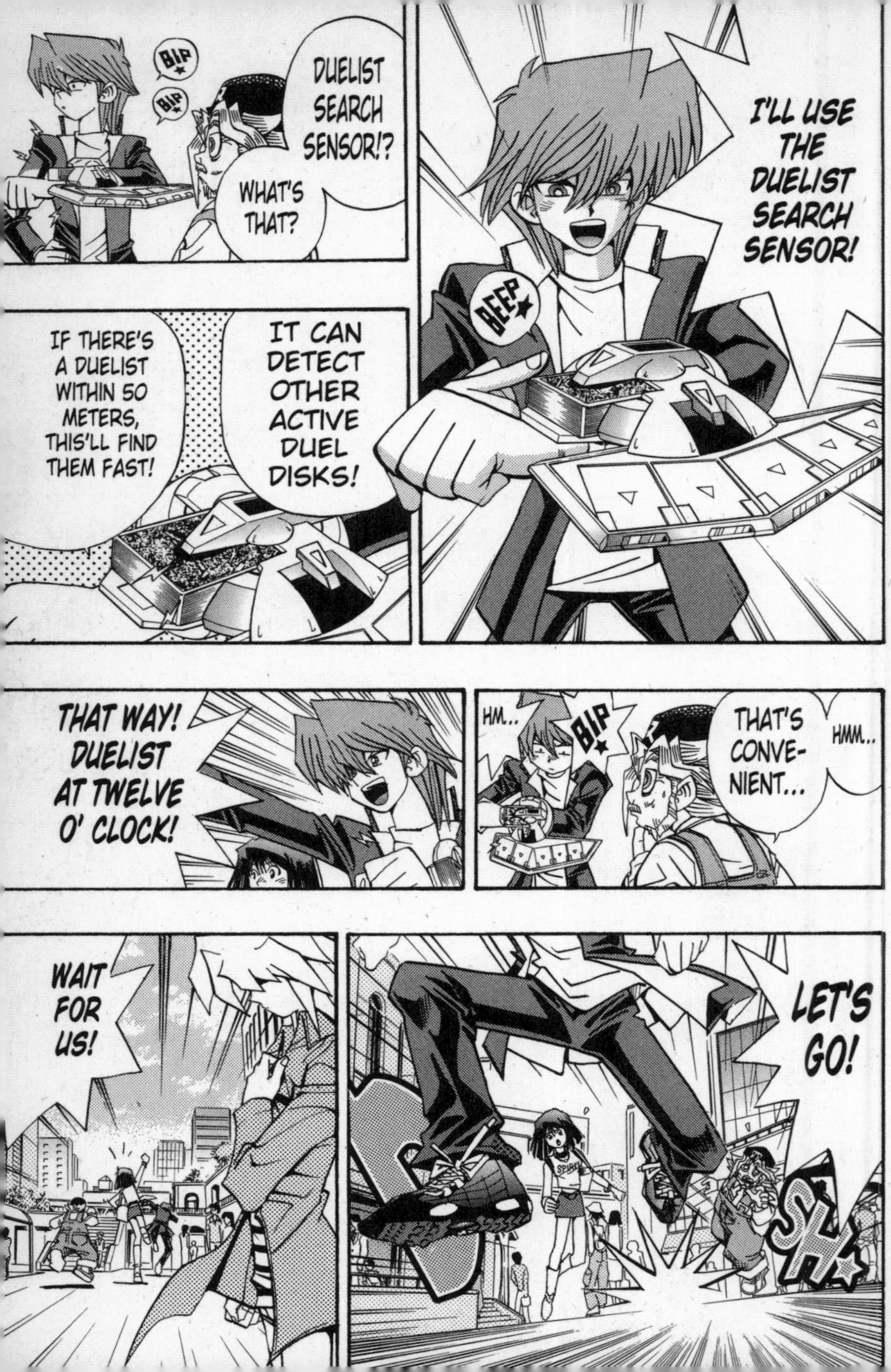
I'LL USE THE DUELIST SEARCH SENSOR!
BEEP
BIP
BIP
DUELIST SEARCH SENSOR!?
WHAT'S THAT?
IT CAN DETECT OTHER ACTIVE DUEL DISKS!
IF THERE'S A DUELIST WITHIN 50 METERS, THIS'LL FIND THEM FAST!
HMM...
THAT'S CONVE-NIENT...
BIP
HM...
THAT WAY! DUELIST AT TWELVE O' CLOCK!
LET'S GO!
WAIT FOR US!

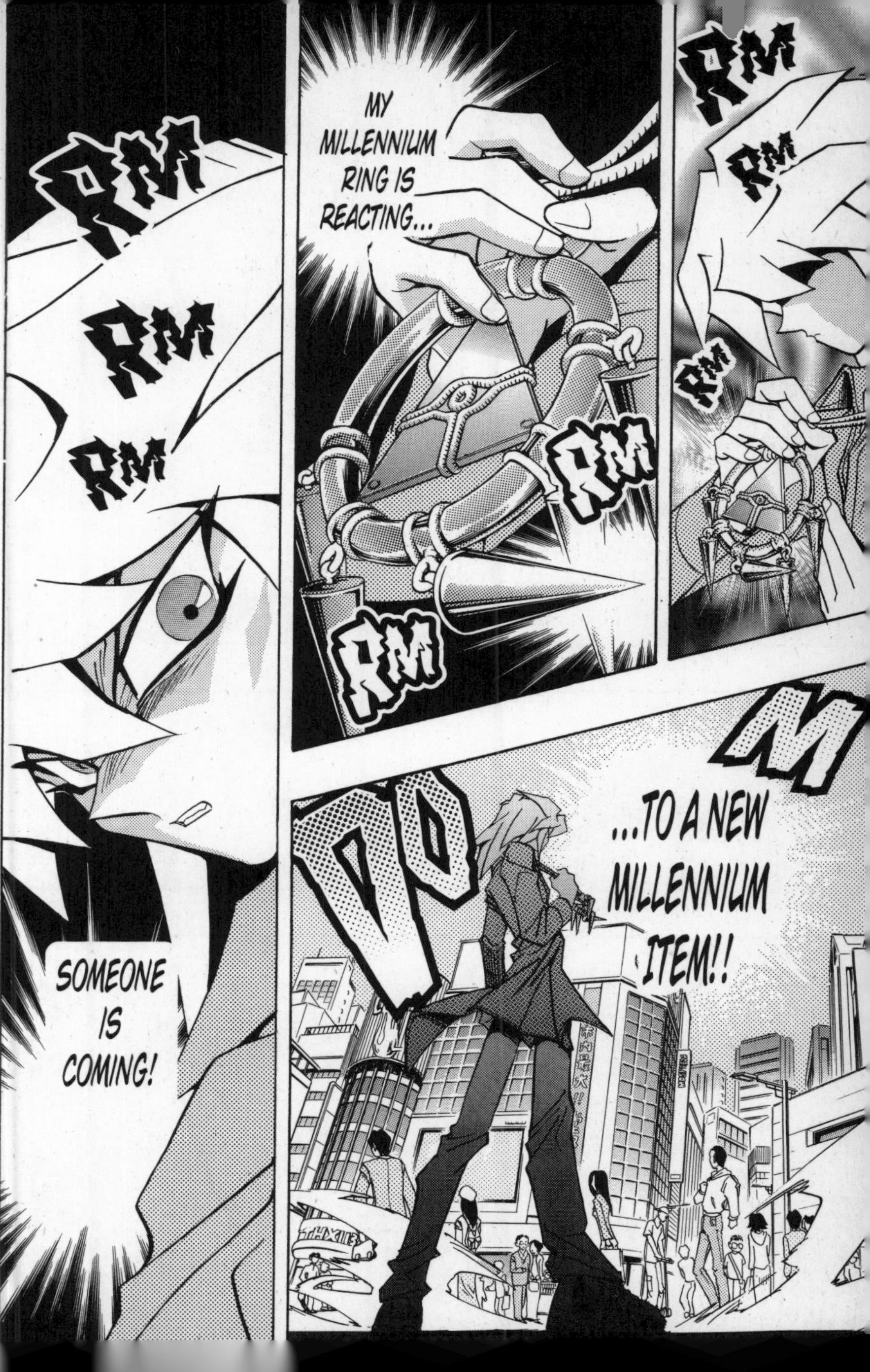

RM
RM
RM
MY MILLENNIUM RING IS REACTING...
RM
RM
M
ZO
...TO A NEW MILLENNIUM ITEM!!
RM
RM
RM
SOMEONE IS COMING!

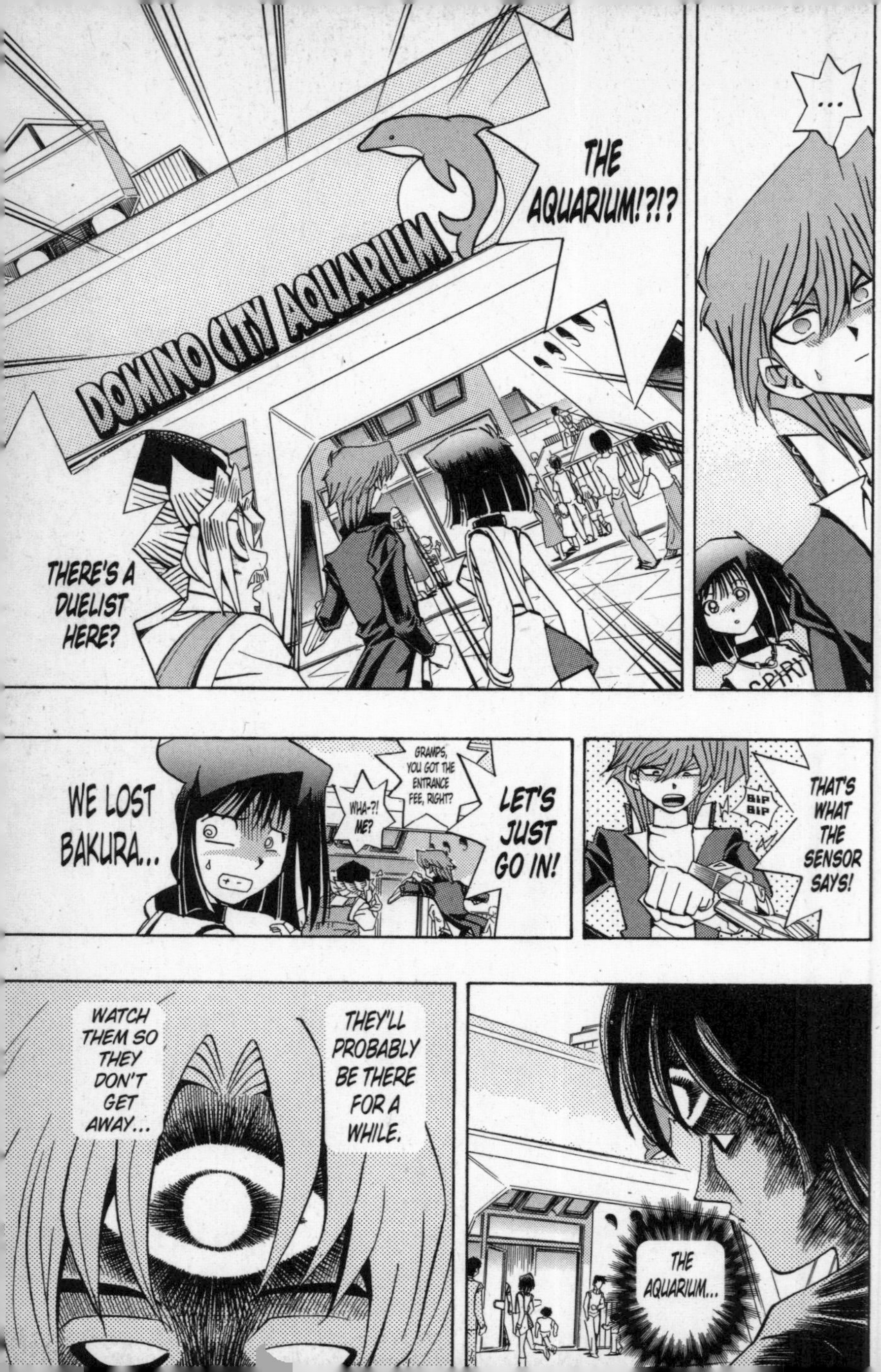
...
THE AQUARIUM!?!?
DOMINO CITY AQUARIUM
THERE'S A DUELIST HERE?
BIP BIP
THAT'S WHAT THE SENSOR SAYS!
LET'S JUST GO IN!
GRAMPS, YOU GOT THE ENTRANCE FEE, RIGHT?
WHA-?! ME?
WE LOST BAKURA...
THE AQUARIUM...
THEY'LL PROBABLY BE THERE FOR A WHILE.
WATCH THEM SO THEY DON'T GET AWAY...

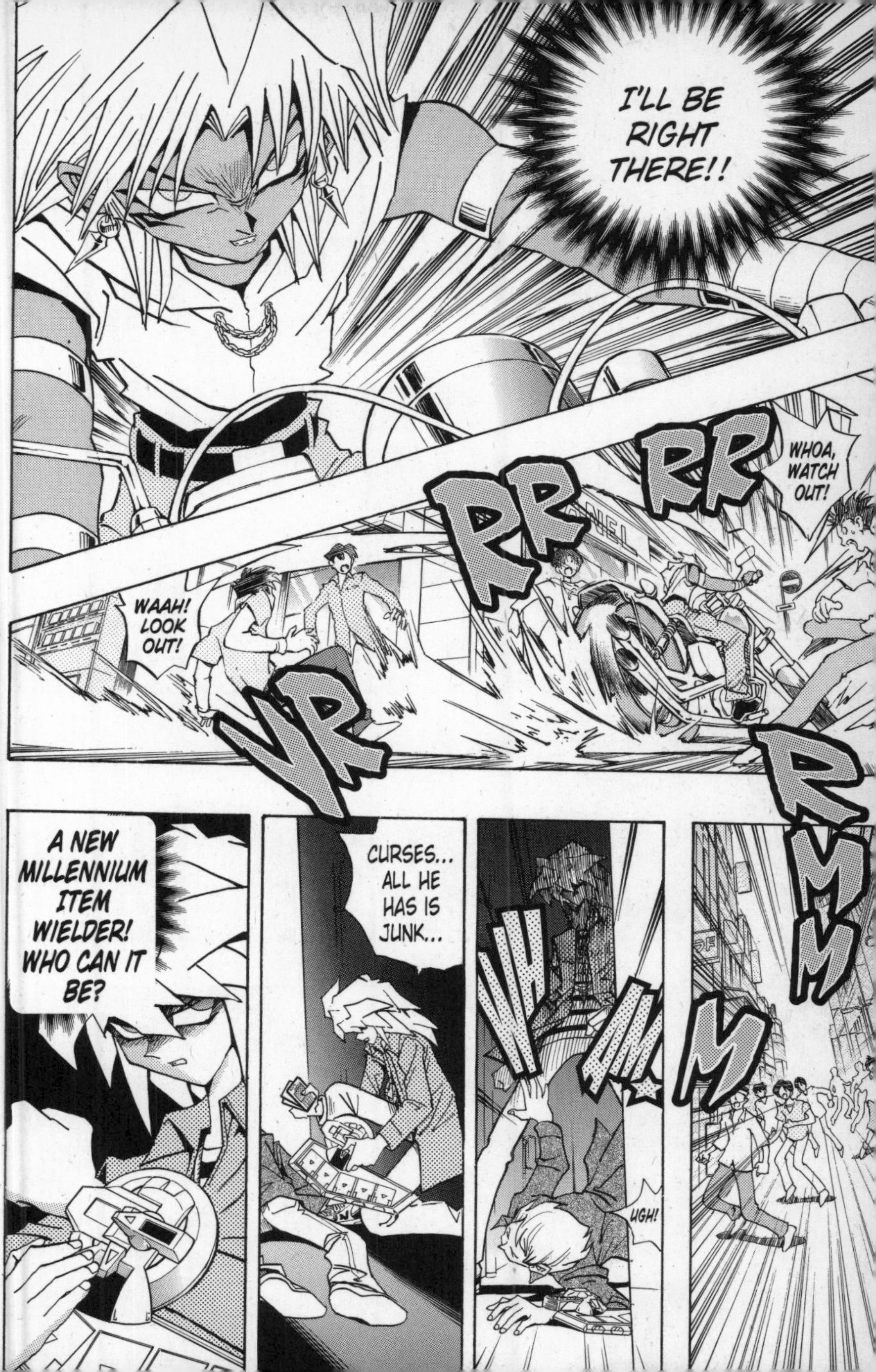

I'LL BE RIGHT THERE!!
WHOA, WATCH OUT!
RR RR
WAAH! LOOK OUT!
VR
R
M
M
M
WH
AM
M
UGH!
CURSES... ALL HE HAS IS JUNK...
A NEW MILLENNIUM ITEM WIELDER! WHO CAN IT BE?

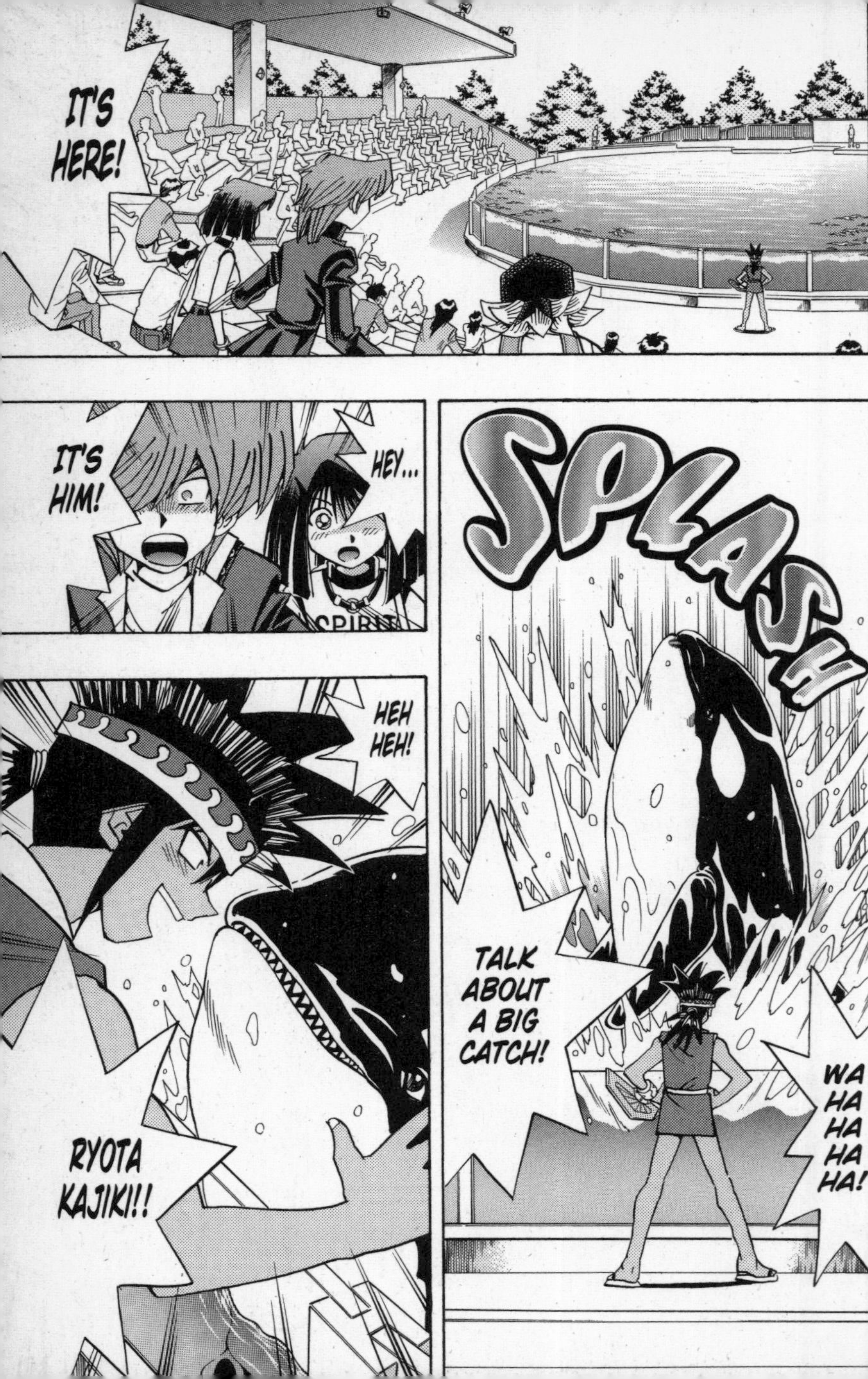
IT'S HERE!
SPLASH
TALK ABOUT A BIG CATCH!
WA HA HA HA HA!
HEY...
IT'S HIM!
HEH HEH!
RYOTA KAJIKI!!

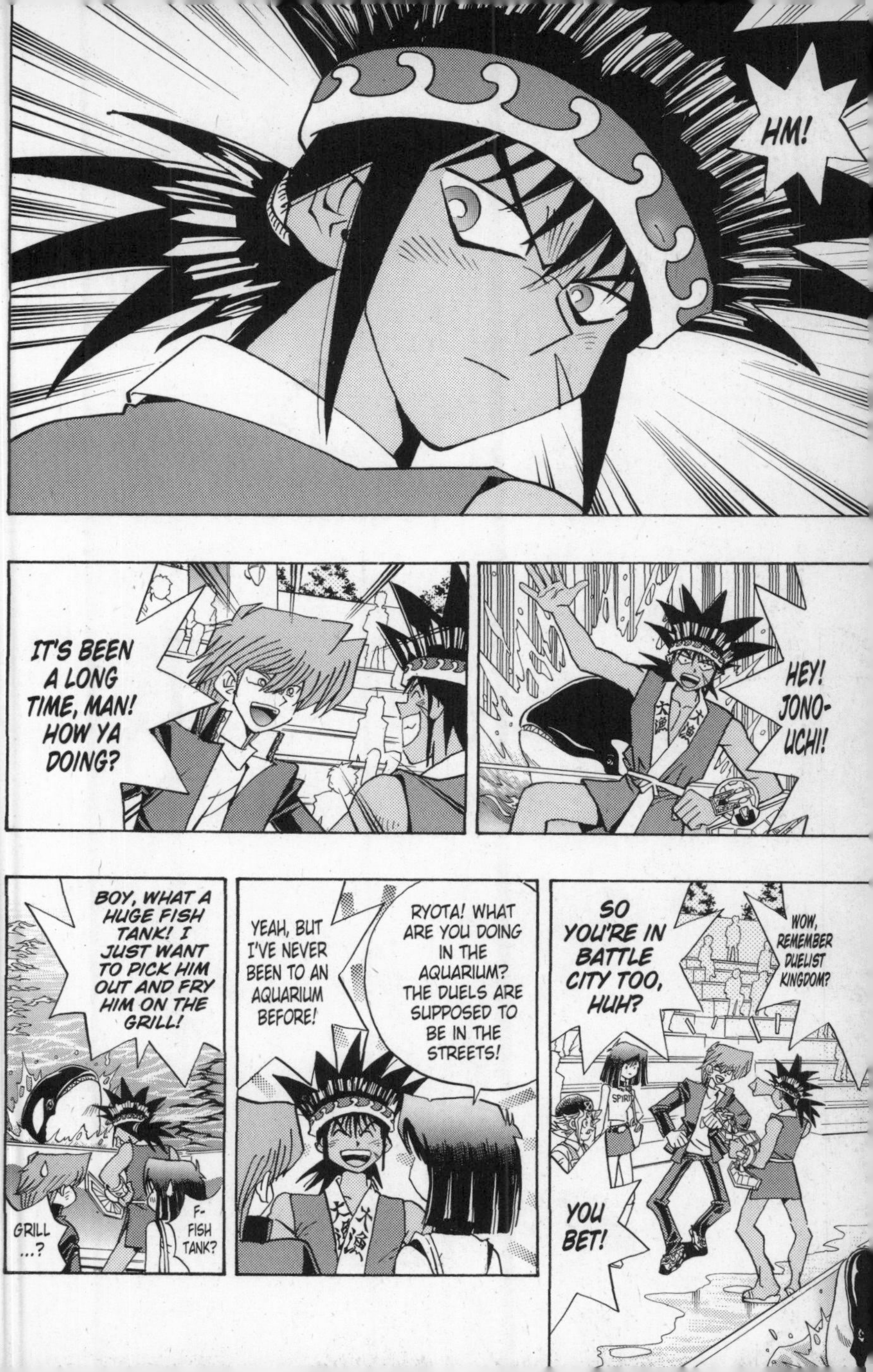
HM!
HEY! JONO-UCHI!
IT'S BEEN A LONG TIME, MAN! HOW YA DOING?
SO YOU'RE IN BATTLE CITY TOO, HUH?
WOW, REMEMBER DUELIST KINGDOM?
YOU BET!
RYOTA! WHAT ARE YOU DOING IN THE AQUARIUM? THE DUELS ARE SUPPOSED TO BE IN THE STREETS!
YEAH, BUT I'VE NEVER BEEN TO AN AQUARIUM BEFORE!
BOY, WHAT A HUGE FISH TANK! I JUST WANT TO PICK HIM OUT AND FRY HIM ON THE GRILL!
F-FISH TANK?
GRILL ...?

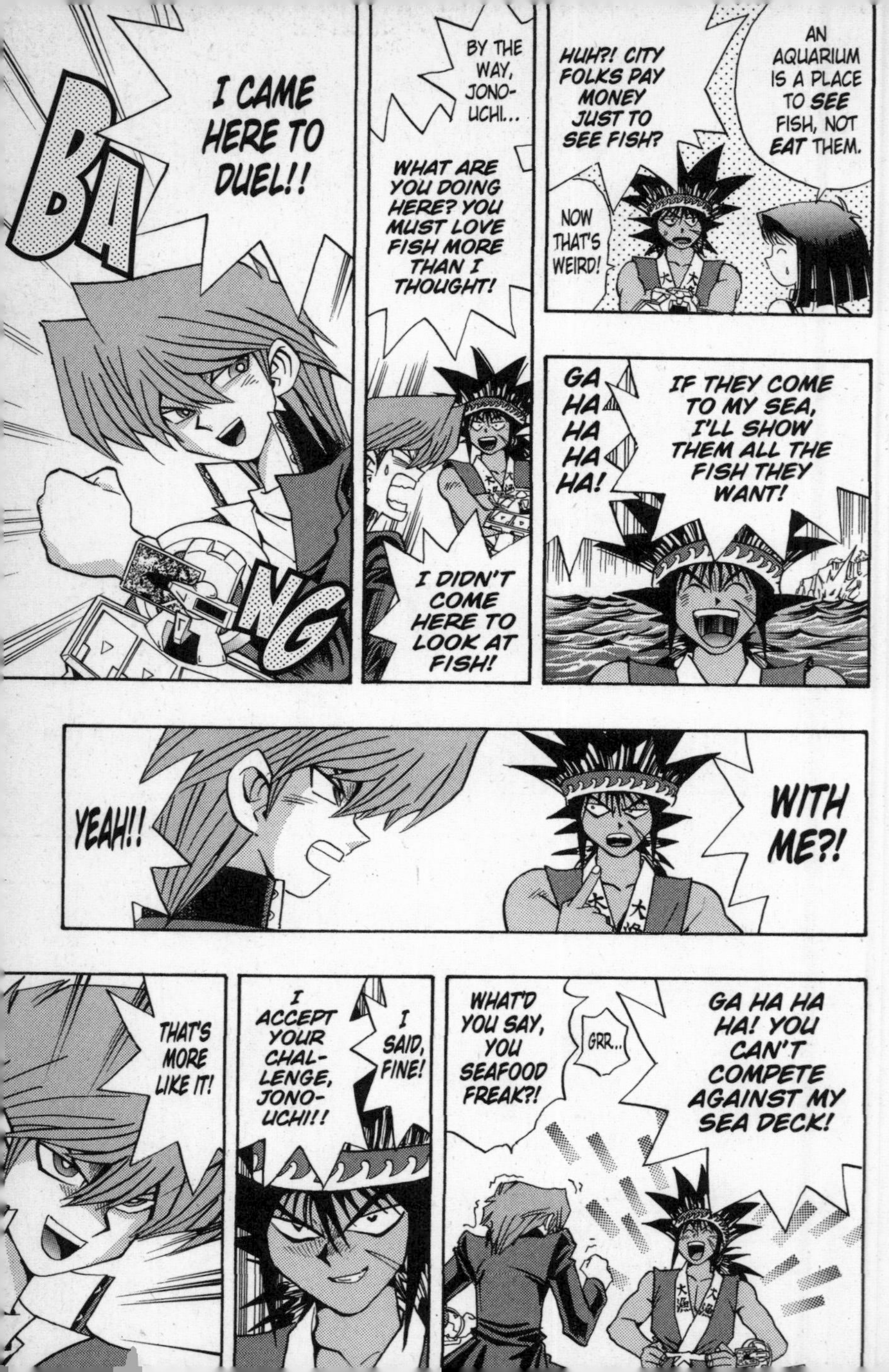
AN AQUARIUM IS A PLACE TO SEE FISH, NOT EAT THEM.
HUH?! CITY FOLKS PAY MONEY JUST TO SEE FISH?
NOW THAT'S WEIRD!
IF THEY COME TO MY SEA, I'LL SHOW THEM ALL THE FISH THEY WANT!
GA HA HA HA HA!
BY THE WAY, JONOUCHI...
WHAT ARE YOU DOING HERE? YOU MUST LOVE FISH MORE THAN I THOUGHT!
I DIDN'T COME HERE TO LOOK AT FISH!
I CAME HERE TO DUEL!!
BA
NG
WITH ME?!
YEAH!!
GA HA HA HA! YOU CAN'T COMPETE AGAINST MY SEA DECK!
WHAT'D YOU SAY, YOU SEAFOOD FREAK?!
GRR...
I SAID, FINE!
I ACCEPT YOUR CHALLENGE, JONOUCHI!!
THAT'S MORE LIKE IT!

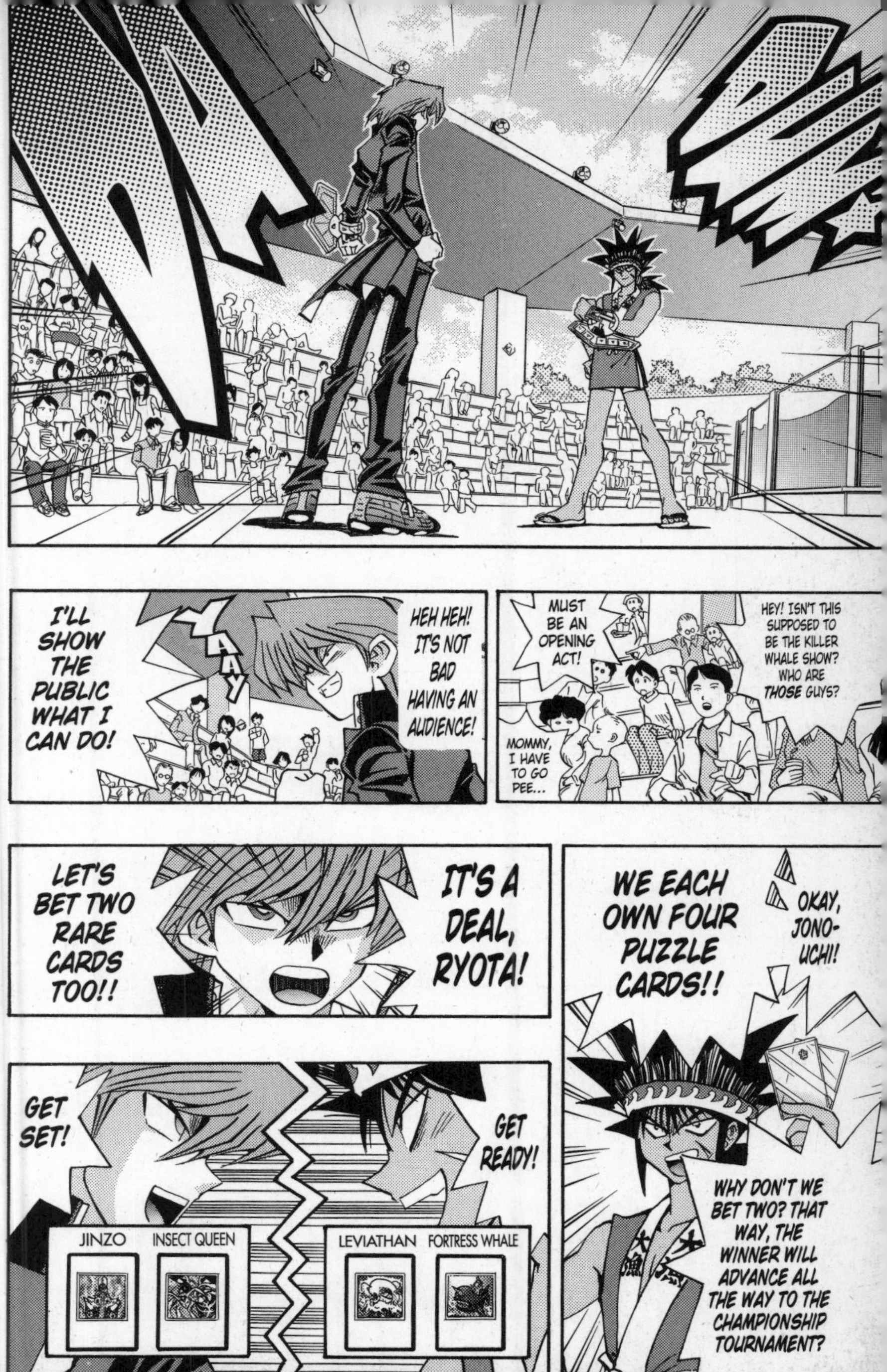
HEY! ISN'T THIS SUPPOSED TO BE THE KILLER WHALE SHOW? WHO ARE THOSE GUYS?
MUST BE AN OPENING ACT!
MOMMY, I HAVE TO GO PEE...
HEH HEH! IT'S NOT BAD HAVING AN AUDIENCE!
YAAY
I'LL SHOW THE PUBLIC WHAT I CAN DO!
OKAY, JONO-UCHI!
WE EACH OWN FOUR PUZZLE CARDS!!
WHY DON'T WE BET TWO? THAT WAY, THE WINNER WILL ADVANCE ALL THE WAY TO THE CHAMPIONSHIP TOURNAMENT?
IT'S A DEAL, RYOTA!
LET'S BET TWO RARE CARDS TOO!!
GET READY!
LEVIATHAN
FORTRESS WHALE
GET SET!
JINZO
INSECT QUEEN

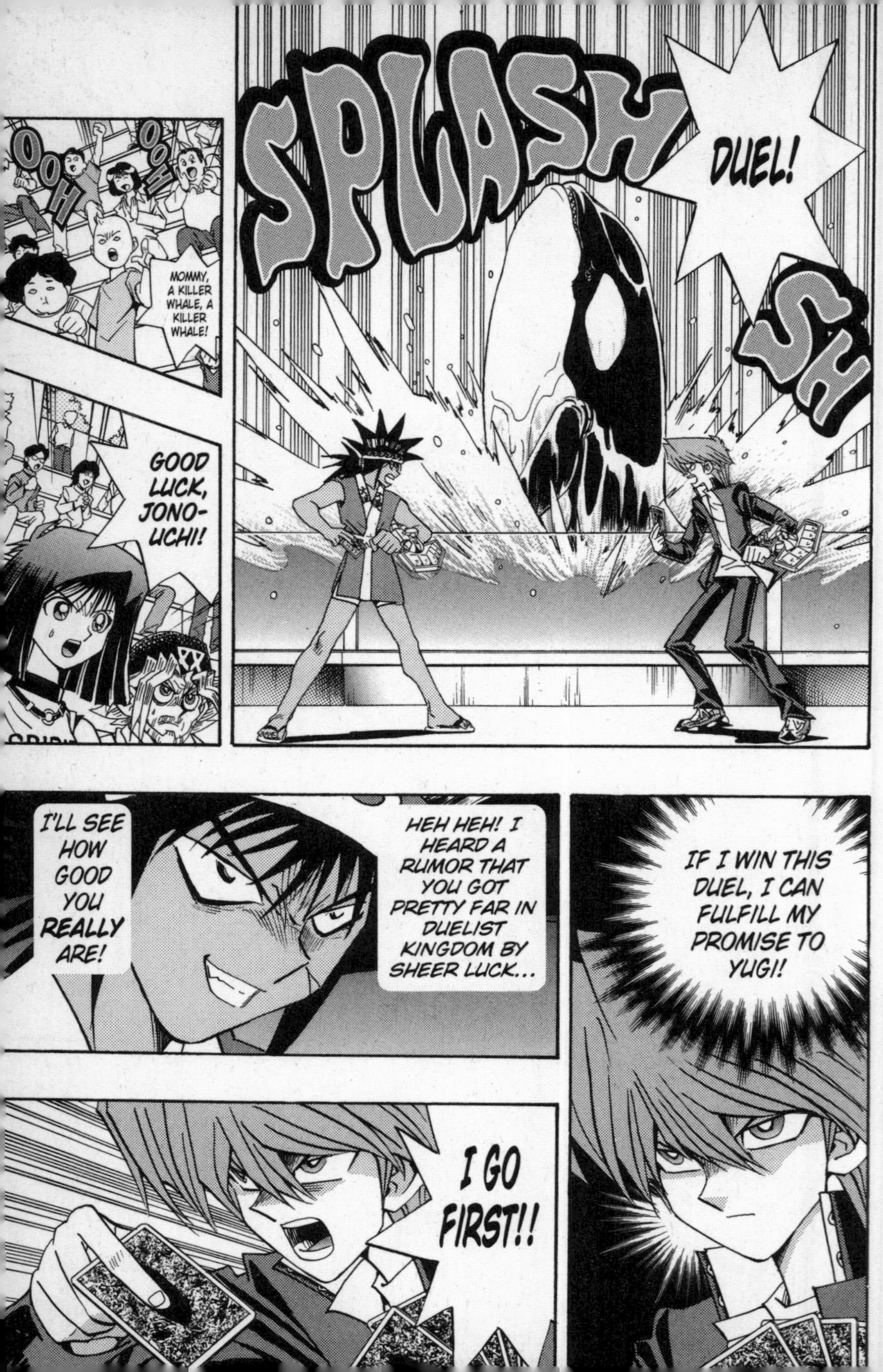
SPLASH
DUEL!
SH
OOH
OOH
MOMMY, A KILLER WHALE, A KILLER WHALE!
GOOD LUCK, JONO-UCHI!
IF I WIN THIS DUEL, I CAN FULFILL MY PROMISE TO YUGI!
HEH HEH! I HEARD A RUMOR THAT YOU GOT PRETTY FAR IN DUELIST KINGDOM BY SHEER LUCK...
I'LL SEE HOW GOOD YOU REALLY ARE!
I GO FIRST!!

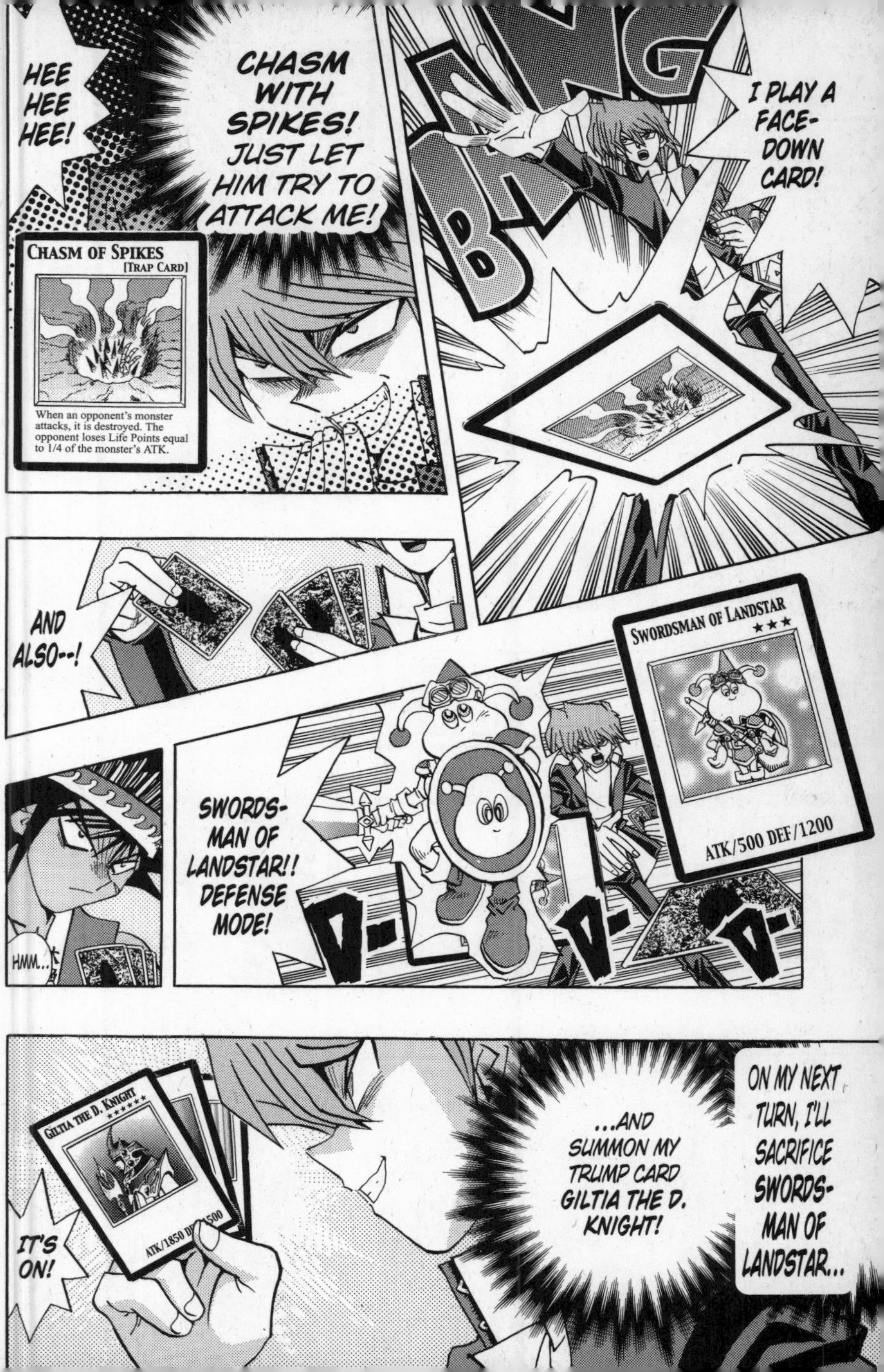
I PLAY A FACE-DOWN CARD!
CHASM WITH SPIKES! JUST LET HIM TRY TO ATTACK ME!
HEE HEE HEE!
CHASM OF SPIKES
[TRAP CARD]
When an opponent's monster attacks, it is destroyed. The opponent loses Life Points equal to 1/4 of the monster's ATK.
AND ALSO--!
SWORDSMAN OF LANDSTAR
ATK/500 DEF/1200
SWORDS-MAN OF LANDSTAR!! DEFENSE MODE!
HMM...
ON MY NEXT TURN, I'LL SACRIFICE SWORDS-MAN OF LANDSTAR...
...AND SUMMON MY TRUMP CARD GILTIA THE D. KNIGHT!
GILTIA THE D. KNIGHT
IT'S ON!

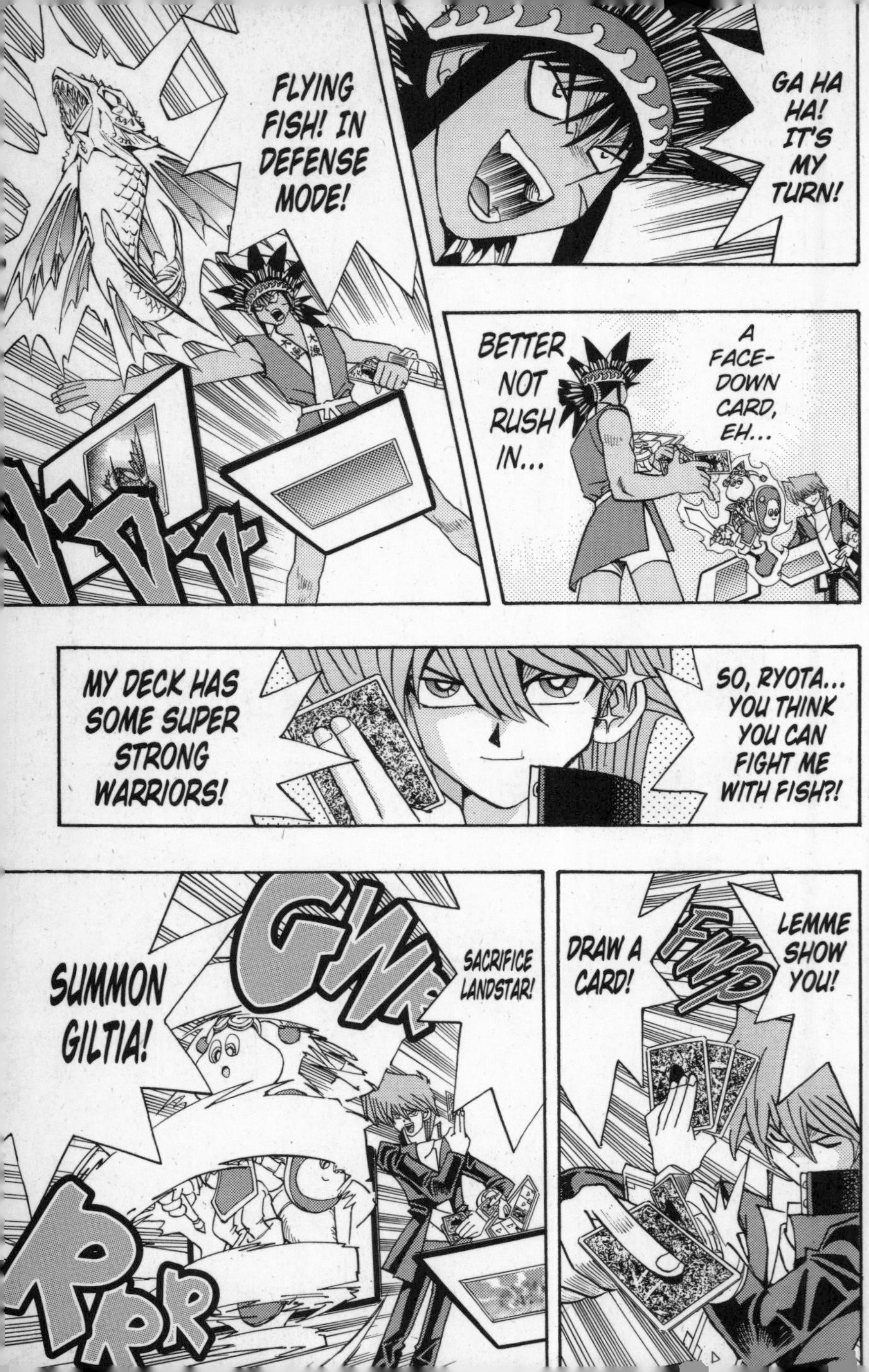
GA HA HA! IT'S MY TURN!
A FACE-DOWN CARD, EH...
BETTER NOT RUSH IN...
FLYING FISH! IN DEFENSE MODE!
SO, RYOTA... YOU THINK YOU CAN FIGHT ME WITH FISH?!
MY DECK HAS SOME SUPER STRONG WARRIORS!
LEMME SHOW YOU!
FWIP
DRAW A CARD!
SACRIFICE LANDSTAR!
SUMMON GILTIA!

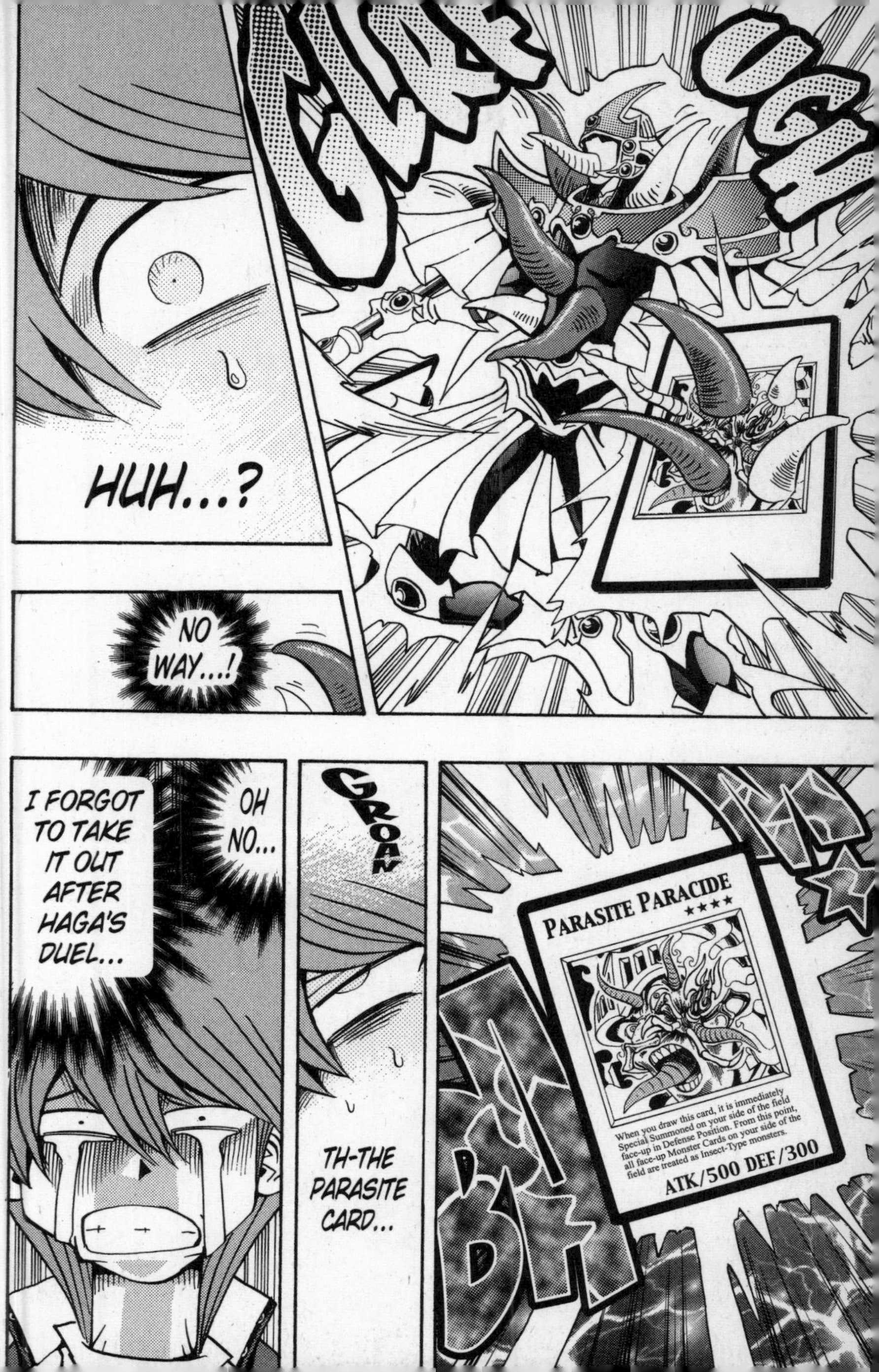
HUH...?
NO WAY...!
PARASITE PARACIDE
When you draw this card, it is immediately Special Summoned on your side of the field face-up in Defense Position. From this point, all face-up Monster Cards on your side of the field are treated as Insect-Type monsters.
ATK/500 DEF/300
GROAN
TH-THE PARASITE CARD...
OH NO...
I FORGOT TO TAKE IT OUT AFTER HAGA'S DUEL...

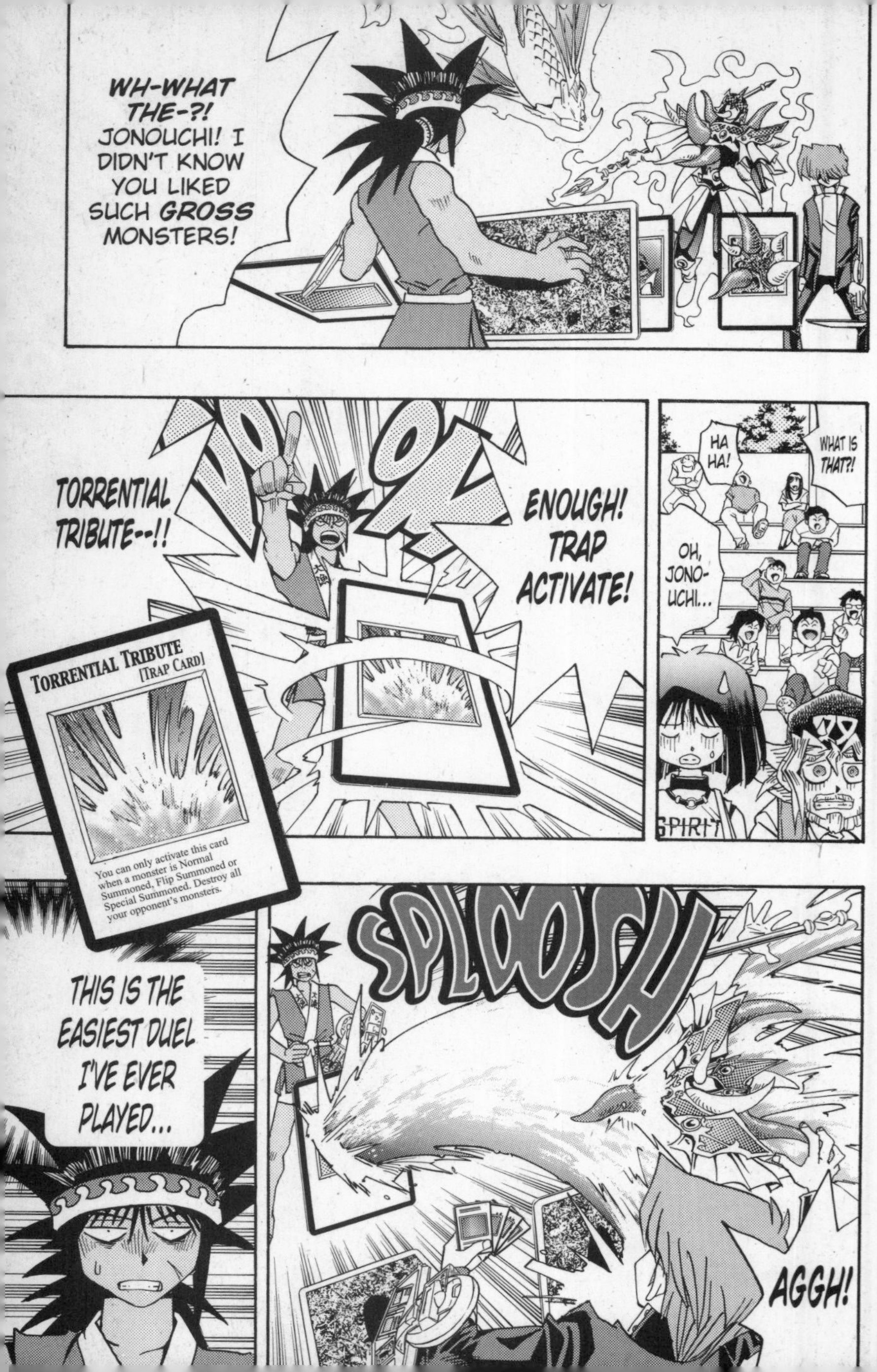
WH-WHAT THE-?! JONOUCHI! I DIDN'T KNOW YOU LIKED SUCH GROSS MONSTERS!
WHAT IS THAT?!
HA HA!
OH, JONO-UCHI...
SPIRIT
ENOUGH! TRAP ACTIVATE!
TORRENTIAL TRIBUTE--!!
TORRENTIAL TRIBUTE [TRAP CARD]
You can only activate this card when a monster is Normal Summoned, Flip Summoned or Special Summoned. Destroy all your opponent's monsters.
SPLOOSH
AGGH!
THIS IS THE EASIEST DUEL I'VE EVER PLAYED...

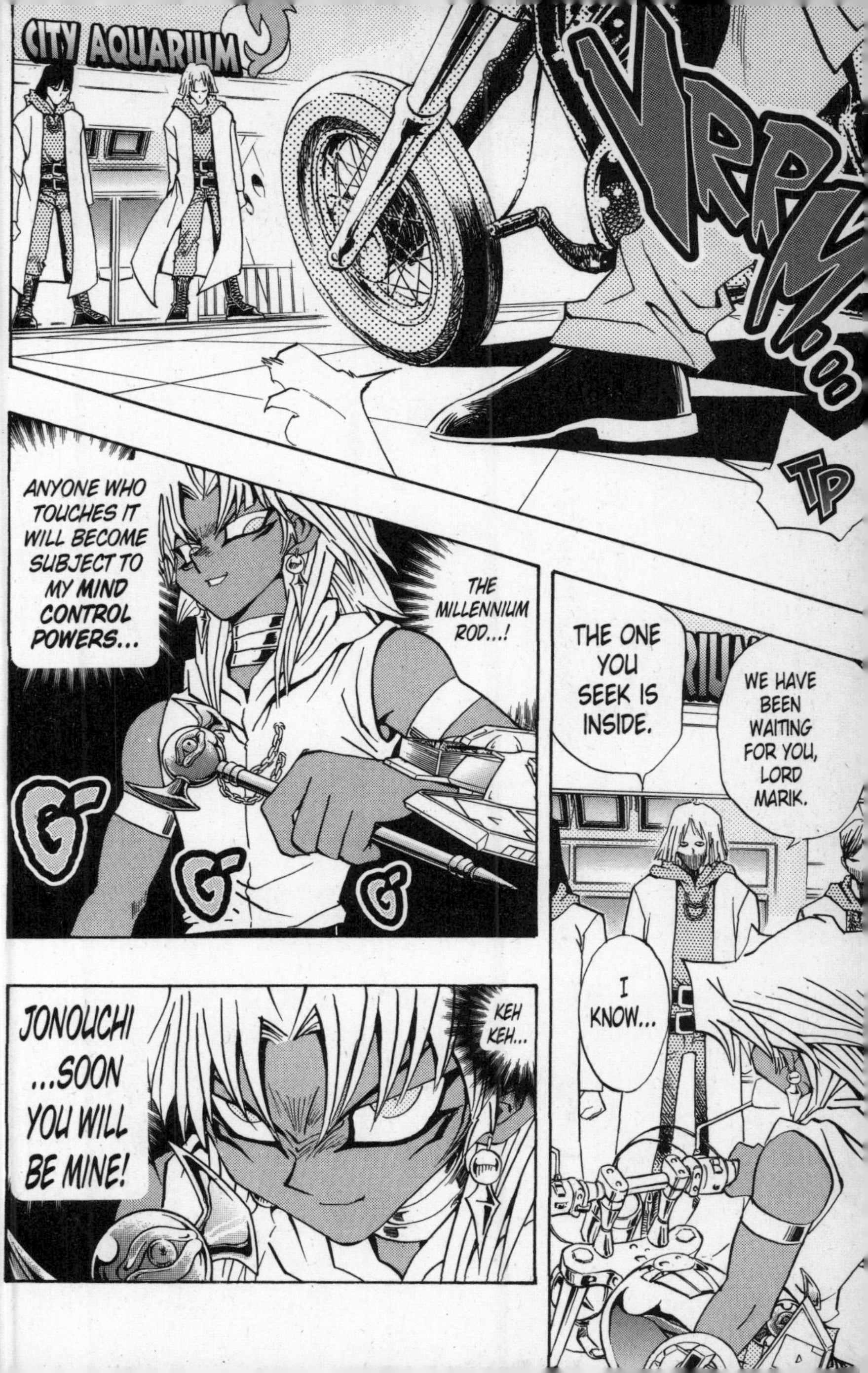
CITY AQUARIUM
VRRMM...
TP
WE HAVE BEEN WAITING FOR YOU, LORD MARIK.
THE ONE YOU SEEK IS INSIDE.
I KNOW...
THE MILLENNIUM ROD...!
ANYONE WHO TOUCHES IT WILL BECOME SUBJECT TO MY MIND CONTROL POWERS...
G
G
G
KEH KEH...
JONOUCHI ...SOON YOU WILL BE MINE!

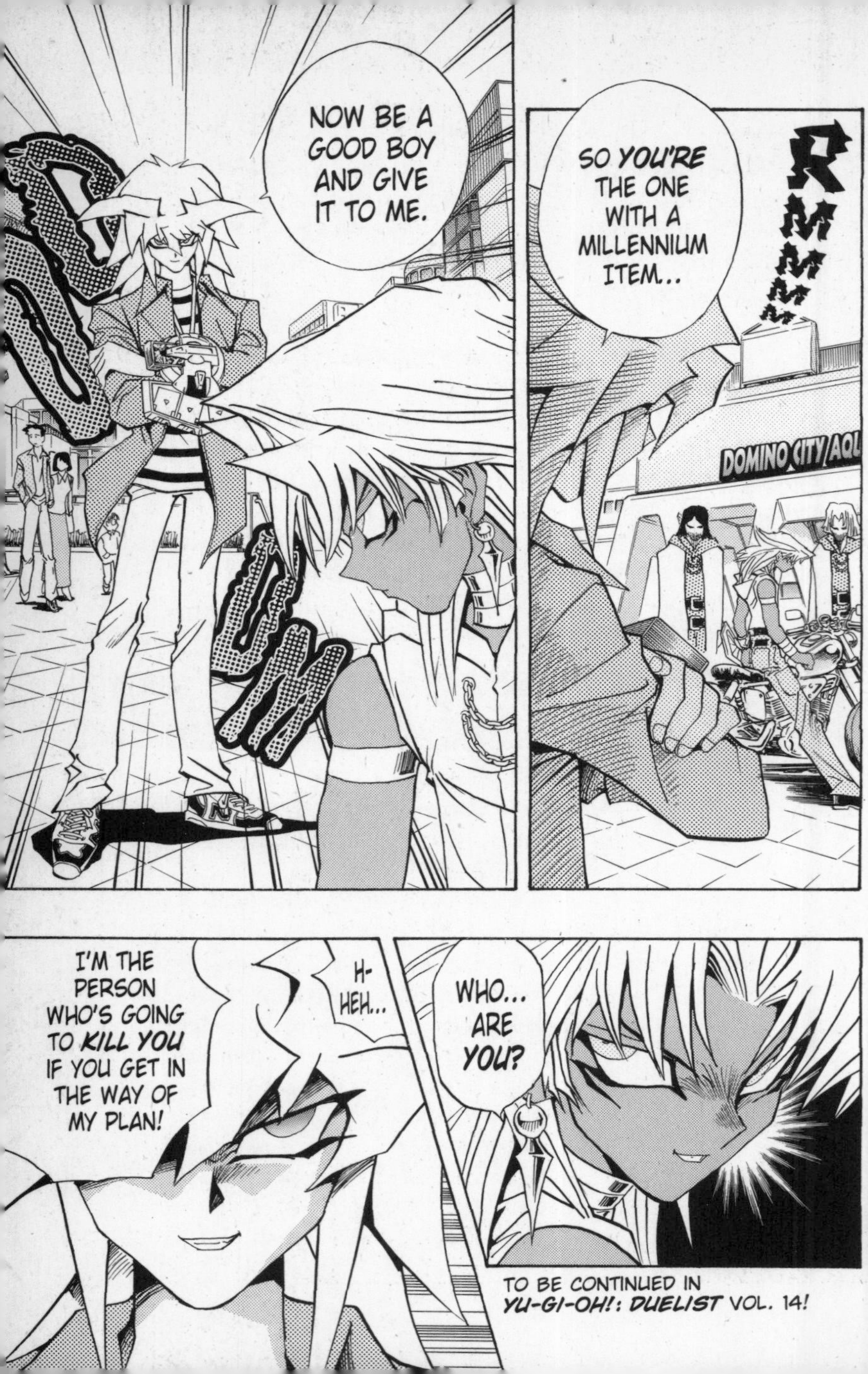
RMMMM
SO YOU'RE THE ONE WITH A MILLENNIUM ITEM...
DOMINO CITY AQU
NOW BE A GOOD BOY AND GIVE IT TO ME.
WHO... ARE YOU?
H-HEH...
I'M THE PERSON WHO'S GOING TO KILL YOU IF YOU GET IN THE WAY OF MY PLAN!

TO BE CONTINUED IN *YU-GI-OH!: DUELIST* VOL. 14!

MASTER OF THE CARDS

The "Duel Monsters" card game first appeared in volume two of the original **Yu-Gi-Oh!** graphic novel series, but it's in **Yu-Gi-Oh!: Duelist** (originally printed in Japan as volumes 8-31 of **Yu-Gi-Oh!**) that it gets really important. As many fans know, some of the card names are different between the English and Japanese versions. In case you play the game, or you're interested in playing, here's a rundown of some of the cards in this graphic novel. Some cards only appear in the **Yu-Gi-Oh!** video games, not in the actual collectible card game.

FIRST APPEARANCE IN THIS VOLUME	JAPANESE CARD NAME	ENGLISH CARD NAME
p.7	*Osiris no Tenkûryû* (Osiris the Heaven Dragon)	Slifer the Sky Dragon
p.8	*Black Magician*	Dark Magician
p.8	*Obelisk no Kyoshinhei* (Obelisk the Giant God Soldier)	The God of the Obelisk (NOTE: Called "Obelisk the Tormentor" in the English anime and card game.)
p.37	*Humanoid Slime*	Humanoid Slime

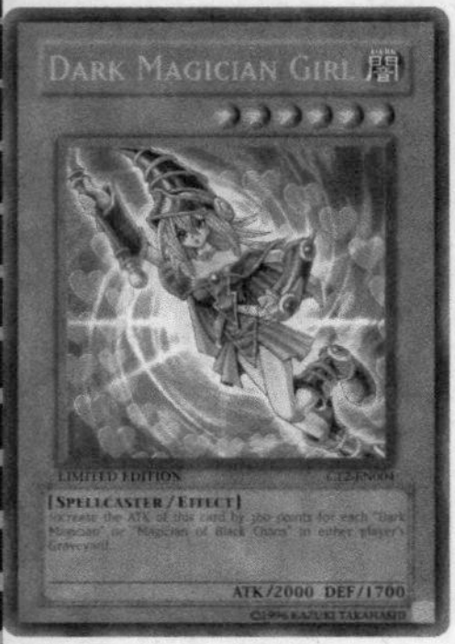

DARK MAGICIAN GIRL
LIMITED EDITION
[SPELLCASTER / EFFECT]
ATK/2000 DEF/1700

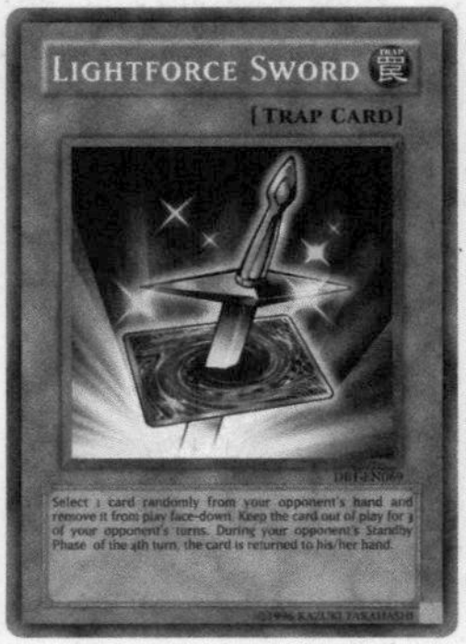

LIGHTFORCE SWORD
[TRAP CARD]

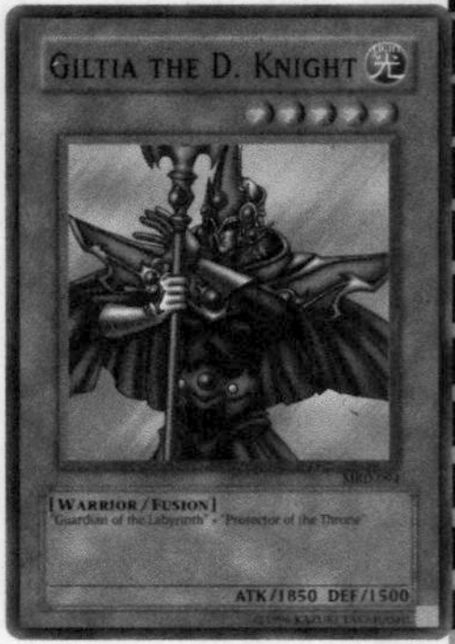

GILTIA THE D. KNIGHT
[WARRIOR / FUSION]
"Guardian of the Labyrinth" + "Protector of the Throne"
ATK/1850 DEF/1500

FIRST APPEARANCE IN THIS VOLUME	JAPANESE CARD NAME	ENGLISH CARD NAME
p.38	*Genjûô Gazelle* (Gazelle the Mythical Beast King)	Gazelle the King of Mythical Beasts
p.40	*Worm Drake*	Worm Drake
p.40	*Yûgô* (Fusion)	Polymerization
p.41	*Humanoid Drake*	Humanoid Worm Drake
p.42	*Sokkô* (Swift Attack)	Quick Attack (NOTE: Not a real game card)
p.44	*Yûgôkaijo* (Fusion Cancellation/Removal)	De-Fusion
p.52	*Buster Blader*	Buster Blader
p.52	*Magnet Warrior Beta*	Beta the Magnet Warrior
p.55	*Revival Slime*	Revival Jam

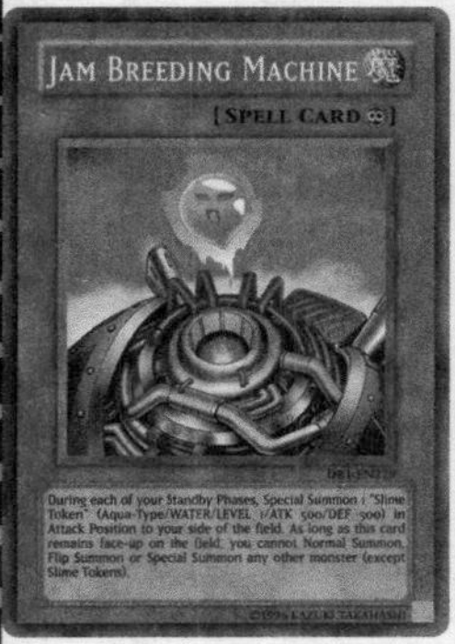
JAM BREEDING MACHINE
[SPELL CARD]
During each of your Standby Phases, Special Summon 1 "Slime Token" (Aqua-Type/WATER/LEVEL 1/ATK 500/DEF 500) in Attack Position to your side of the field. As long as this card remains face-up on the field, you cannot Normal Summon, Flip Summon or Special Summon any other monster (except Slime Tokens).
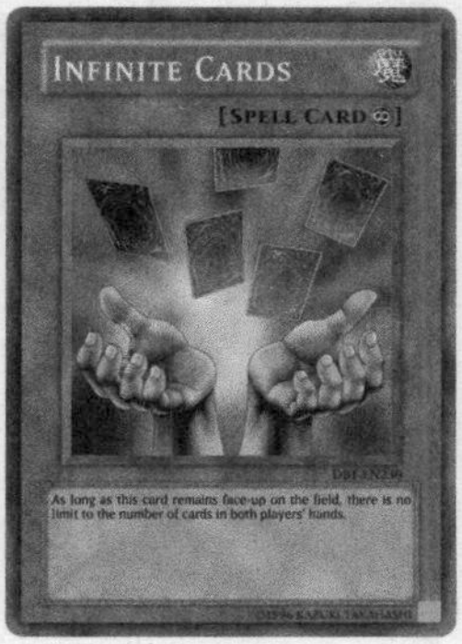
INFINITE CARDS
[SPELL CARD]
As long as this card remains face-up on the field, there is no limit to the number of cards in both players' hands.
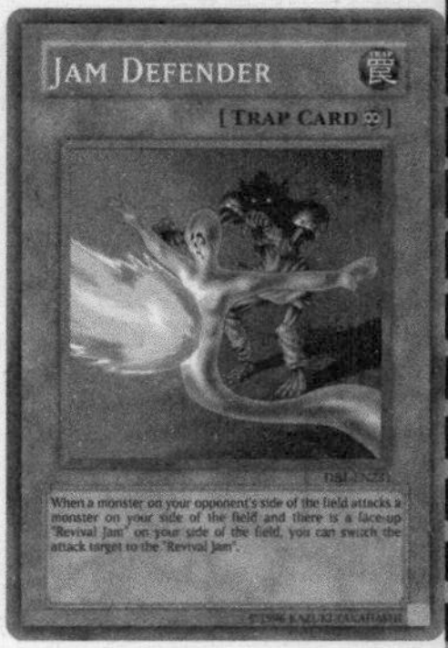
JAM DEFENDER
[TRAP CARD]
When a monster on your opponent's side of the field attacks a monster on your side of the field and there is a face-up "Revival Jam" on your side of the field, you can switch the attack target to the "Revival Jam".

FIRST APPEARANCE IN THIS VOLUME	JAPANESE CARD NAME	ENGLISH CARD NAME
p.55	*Slime Zôshokuro* (Slime Multiplication Reactor)	Jam Breeding Machine
p.63	*Akumu no Tetsuori* (Nightmare Steel Cage/Jail)	Nightmare Steel Cage (NOTE: Called "Nightmare's Steel Cage" in the English card game.)
p.73	*Mugen no Tefuda* (Infinite Cards)	Infinite Cards
p.73	*Seikan no Hôsatsu* (Treasured Card's Return to Life)	Card of Safe Return
p.73	*King* (NOTE: Card name is partially cut off)	Slime King (NOTE: Not a real game card)
p.76	*Kuribo*	Kuriboh

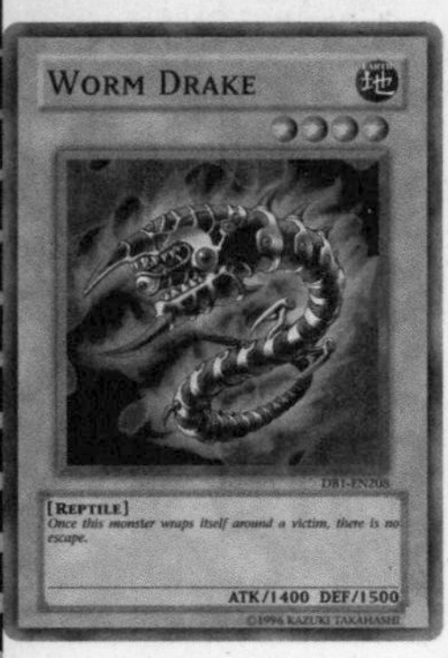
Worm Drake
[Reptile]
Once this monster wraps itself around a victim, there is no escape.
ATK/1400 DEF/1500

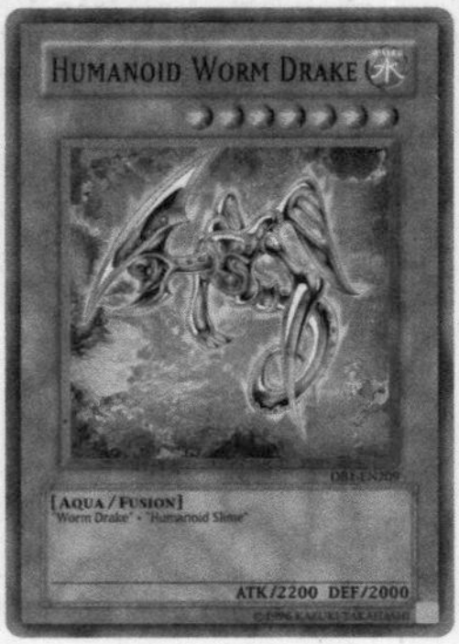
Humanoid Worm Drake
[Aqua / Fusion]
"Worm Drake" + "Humanoid Slime"
ATK/2200 DEF/2000

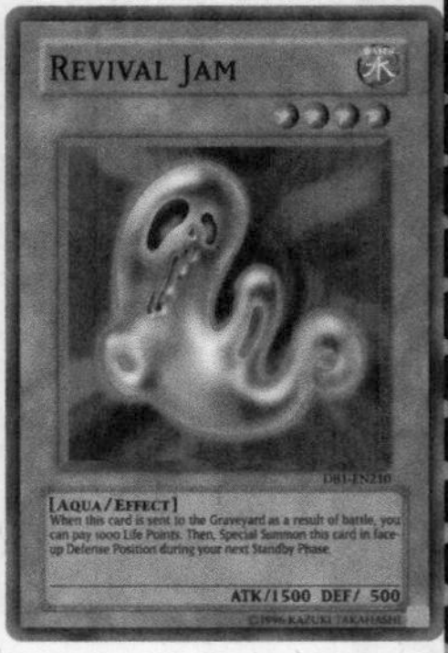
Revival Jam
[Aqua / Effect]
When this card is sent to the Graveyard as a result of battle, you can pay 1000 Life Points. Then, Special Summon this card in face-up Defense Position during your next Standby Phase.
ATK/1500 DEF/ 500

FIRST APPEARANCE IN THIS VOLUME	JAPANESE CARD NAME	ENGLISH CARD NAME
p.76	*Rokubôsei no Jubaku* (Binding Curse of the Hexagram)	Spellbinding Circle
p.76	*Hikari no Fûsatsuken* (Sealing Sword of Light)	Lightforce Sword
p.84	*Defend Slime*	Jam Defender
p.90	*Black Magician Girl*	Dark Magician Girl
p.91	*Magical Cylinder*	Magic Cylinder
p.95	*Magical Silk Hat*	Magical Hats
p.115	*Baphomet*	Baphomet (NOTE: Called "Berfomet" in the English anime and card game.)
p.115	*Big Shield Guardna*	Big Shield Guardna

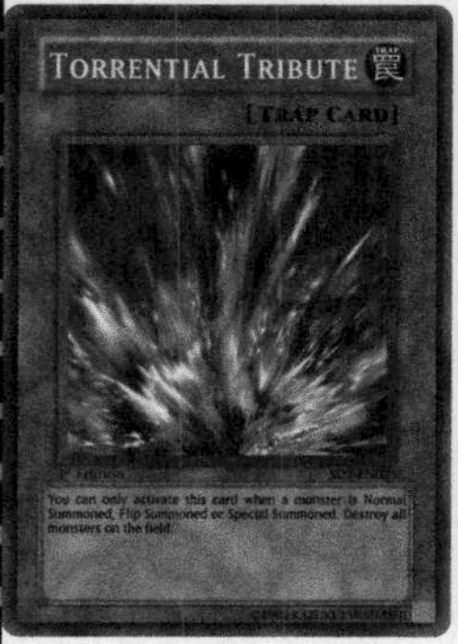
Torrential Tribute
[Trap Card]
You can only activate this card when a monster is Normal Summoned, Flip Summoned or Special Summoned. Destroy all monsters on the field.

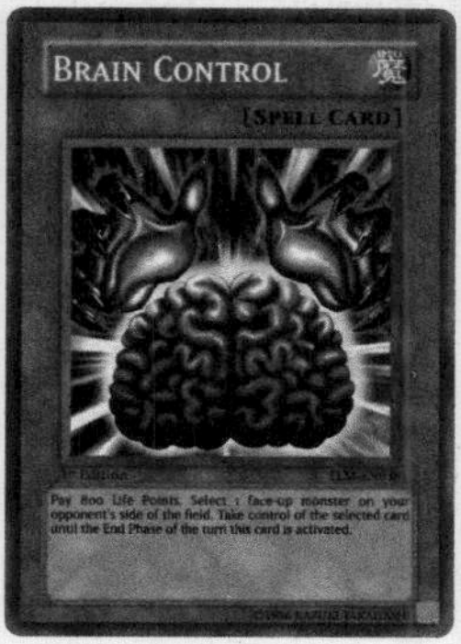
Brain Control
[Spell Card]
Pay 800 Life Points. Select 1 face-up monster on your opponent's side of the field. Take control of the selected card until the End Phase of the turn this card is activated.

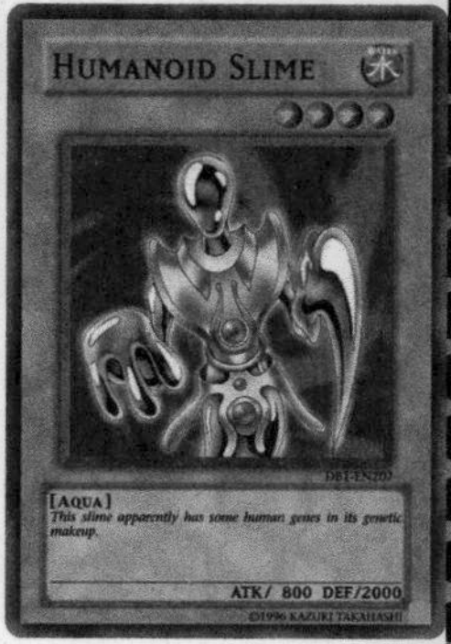
Humanoid Slime
[AQUA]
This slime apparently has some human genes in its genetic makeup.
ATK/ 800 DEF/2000

FIRST APPEARANCE IN THIS VOLUME	JAPANESE CARD NAME	ENGLISH CARD NAME
p.115	*Shisha Sosei* (Resurrection of the Dead)	Monster Reborn
p.141	*Sennô Brain Control* (Brainwashing/ Brain Control)	Brain Control
p.182	*Yôsai Kujira* (Fortress Whale)	Fortress Whale
p.182	*Leviathan*	Leviathan (NOTE: Not a real game card. Called "Kairyu-shin" (Sea Dragon God) in the video games.)
p.182	*Insect Queen*	Insect Queen
p.182	*Jinzô Ningen Psycho Shocker* (Android/Cyborg Psycho Shocker)	Jinzo

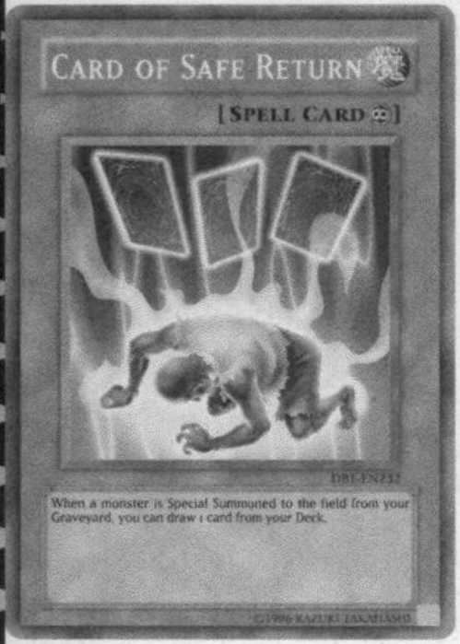
Card of Safe Return
[Spell Card]
When a monster is Special Summoned to the field from your Graveyard, you can draw 1 card from your Deck.
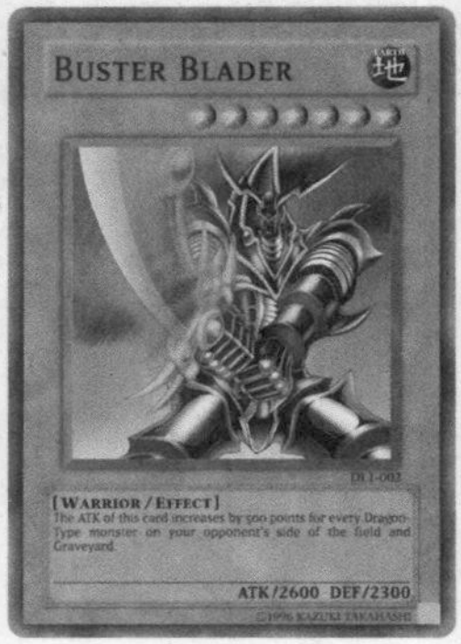
Buster Blader
地
[Warrior / Effect]
The ATK of this card increases by 500 points for every Dragon-Type monster on your opponent's side of the field and Graveyard.
ATK/2600 DEF/2300
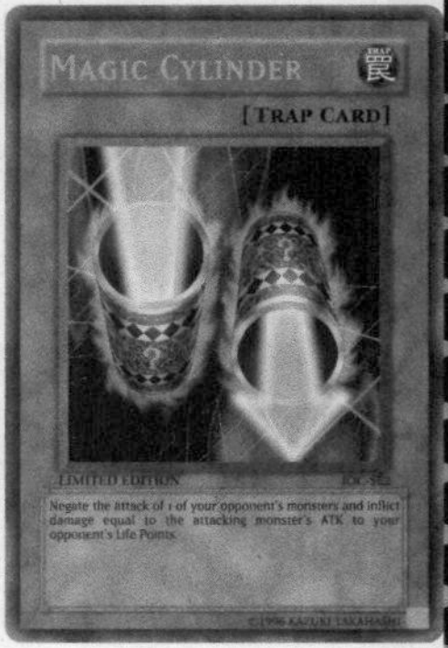
Magic Cylinder
罠
[Trap Card]
Limited Edition
Negate the attack of 1 of your opponent's monsters and inflict damage equal to the attacking monster's ATK to your opponent's Life Points.

FIRST APPEARANCE IN THIS VOLUME	JAPANESE CARD NAME	ENGLISH CARD NAME
p.184	*Otoshiana* (Pitfall)	Chasm with Spikes
p.184	*Landstar no Kenshi* (Landstar Swordsman)	Swordsman of Landstar
p.184	*Madô Kishi Giltia* (Magic Conducting/Guiding Knight Giltia)	Giltia the D. Knight
p.185	*Flying Fish*	Flying Fish
p.186	*Kiseichû Paracide* (Parasitic Insect Paracide)	Parasite Paracide
p.187	*Gekiryûsô* (Raging Torrent Burial)	Torrential Tribute

IN THE NEXT VOLUME...

Battle City goes off the deep end as Jonouchi fights Ryota Kajiki, the Duelist of the Sea! Meanwhile, Kaiba and Yugi must join forces for a tag-team duel on top of a skyscraper! Can the two archrivals work together to defeat the Rare Hunters, or will they fall to their deaths 13 floors below? And every moment that Kaiba and Yugi spend fighting, Marik gets closer to carrying out his insidious plans for Yugi's friends...

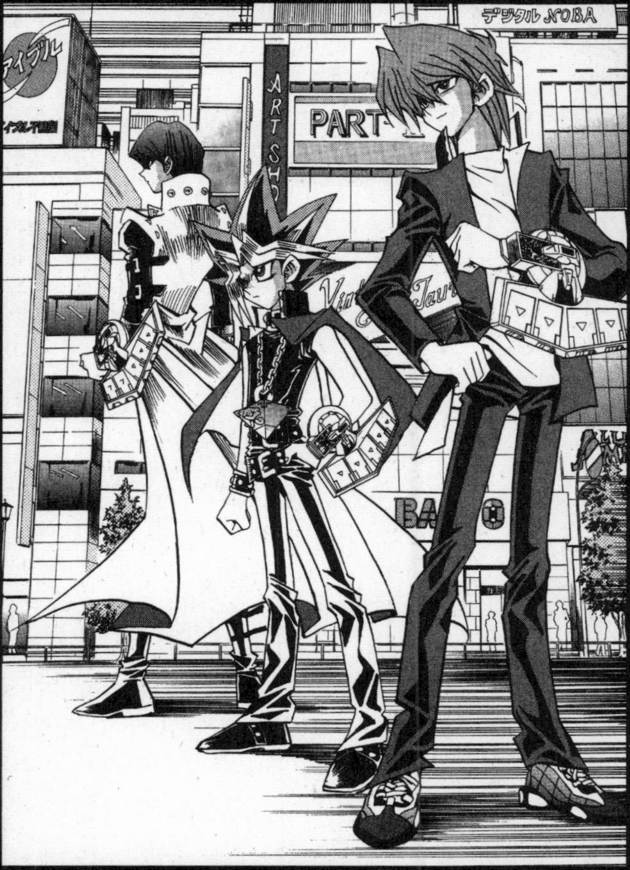
デジタル NOBA

AVAILABLE NOW!

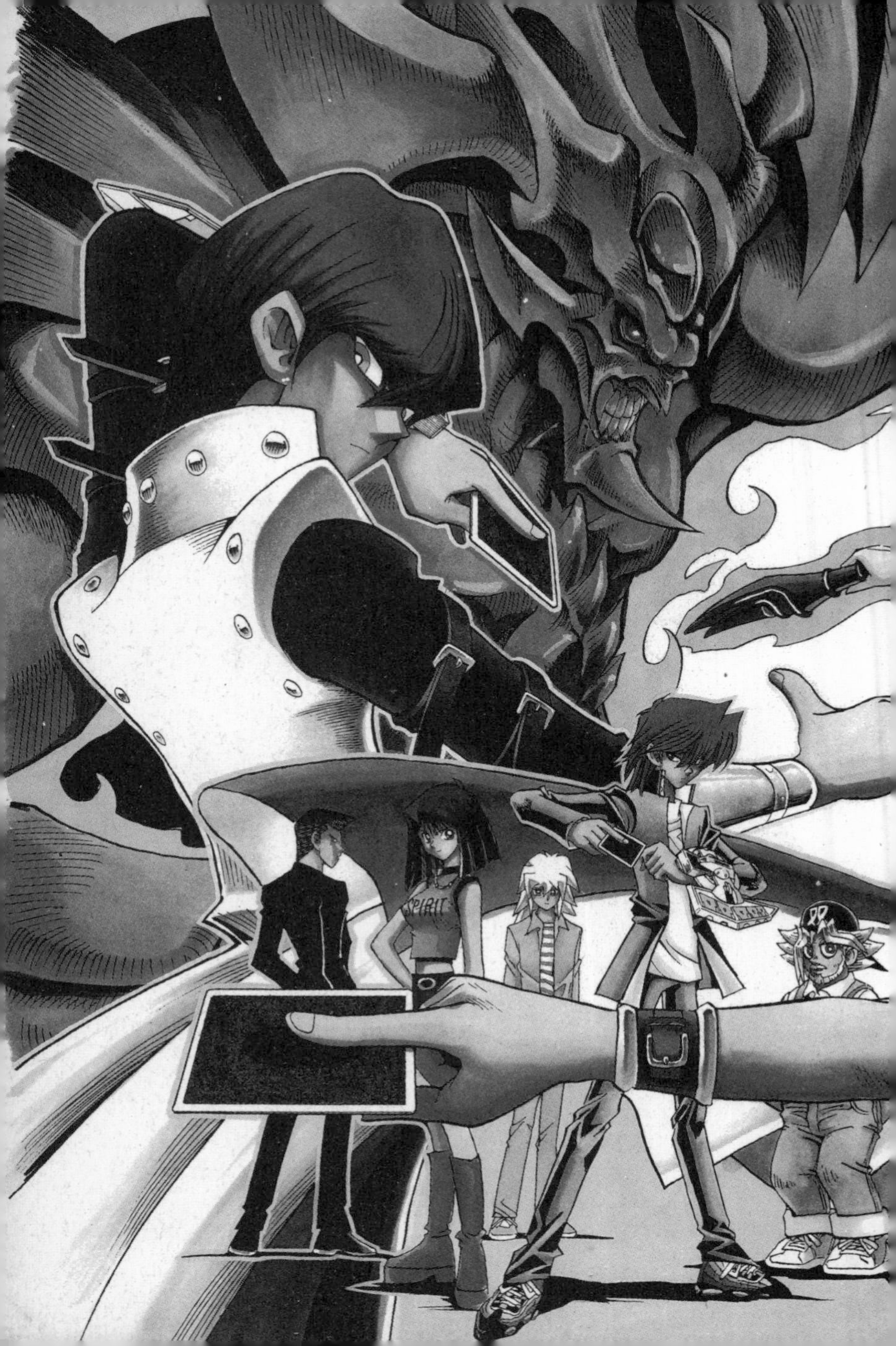
SPIRIT

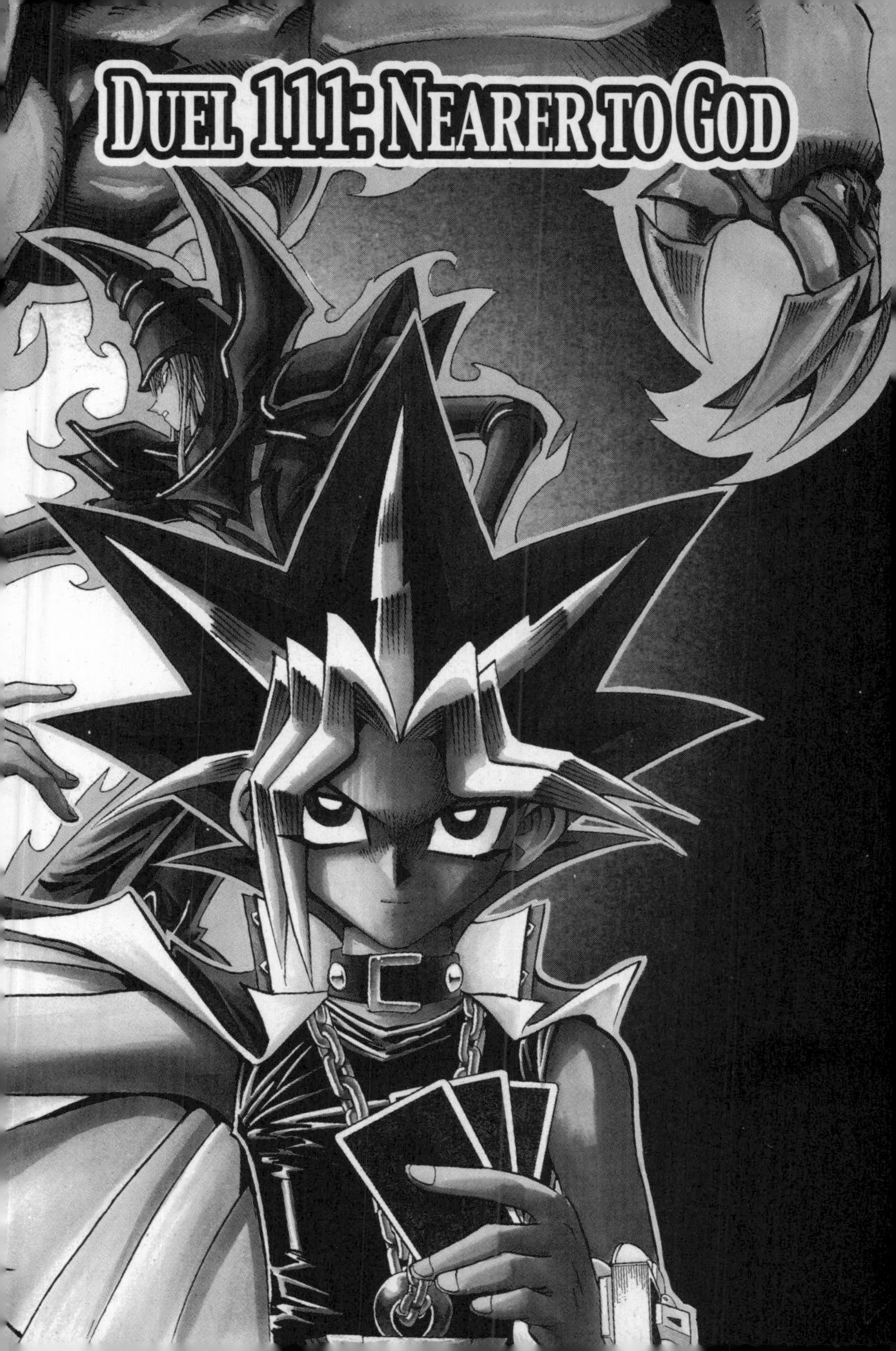
DUEL 111: NEARER TO GOD

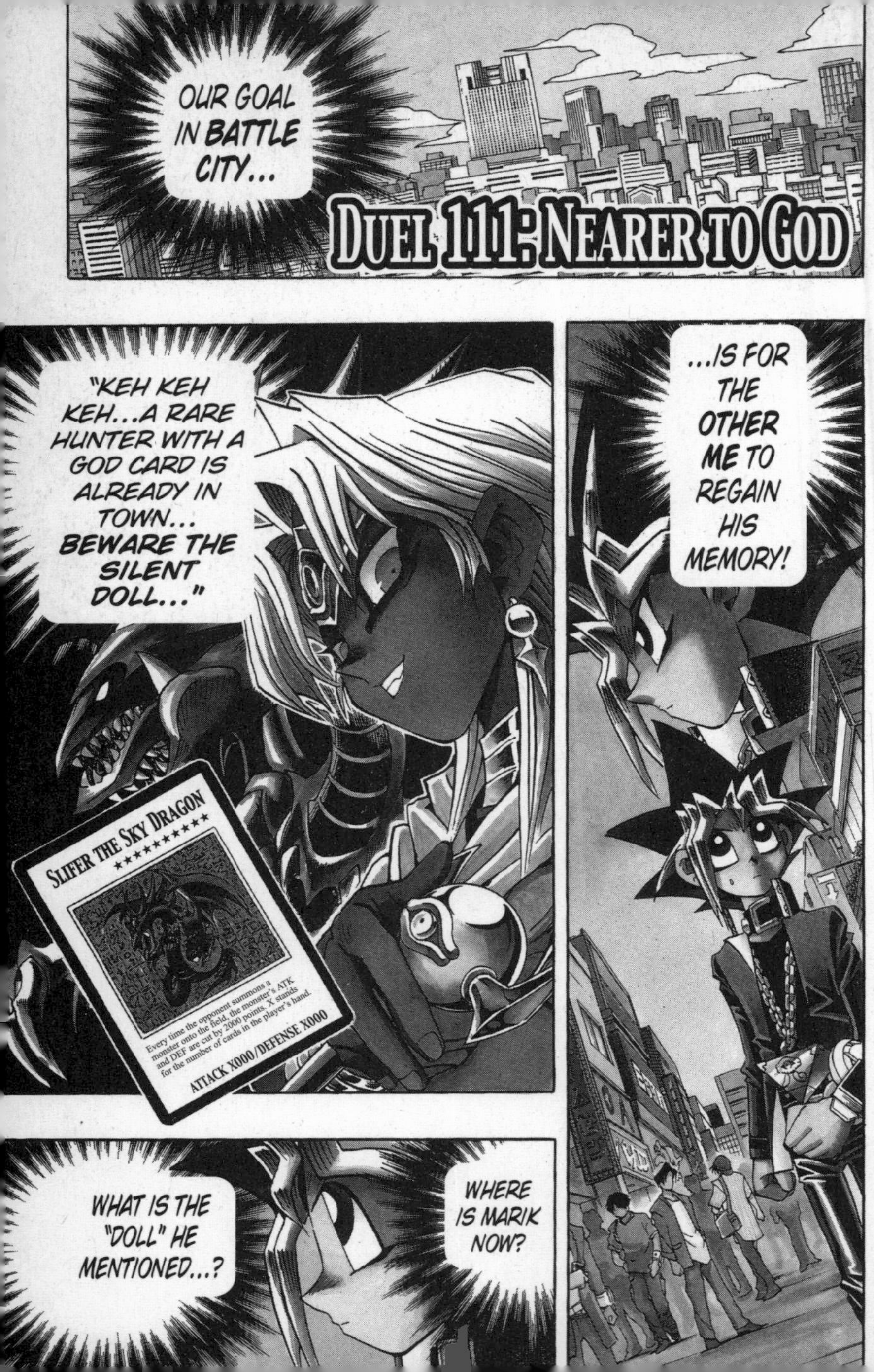
OUR GOAL IN BATTLE CITY...
DUEL 111: NEARER TO GOD
...IS FOR THE OTHER ME TO REGAIN HIS MEMORY!
"KEH KEH KEH...A RARE HUNTER WITH A GOD CARD IS ALREADY IN TOWN... BEWARE THE SILENT DOLL..."
SLIFER THE SKY DRAGON
Every time the opponent summons a monster onto the field, the monster's ATK and DEF are cut by 2000 points. X stands for the number of cards in the player's hand.
ATTACK X000/DEFENSE X000
WHERE IS MARIK NOW?
WHAT IS THE "DOLL" HE MENTIONED...?

Yu-Gi-Oh! DUELIST

Vol. 13

CONTENTS

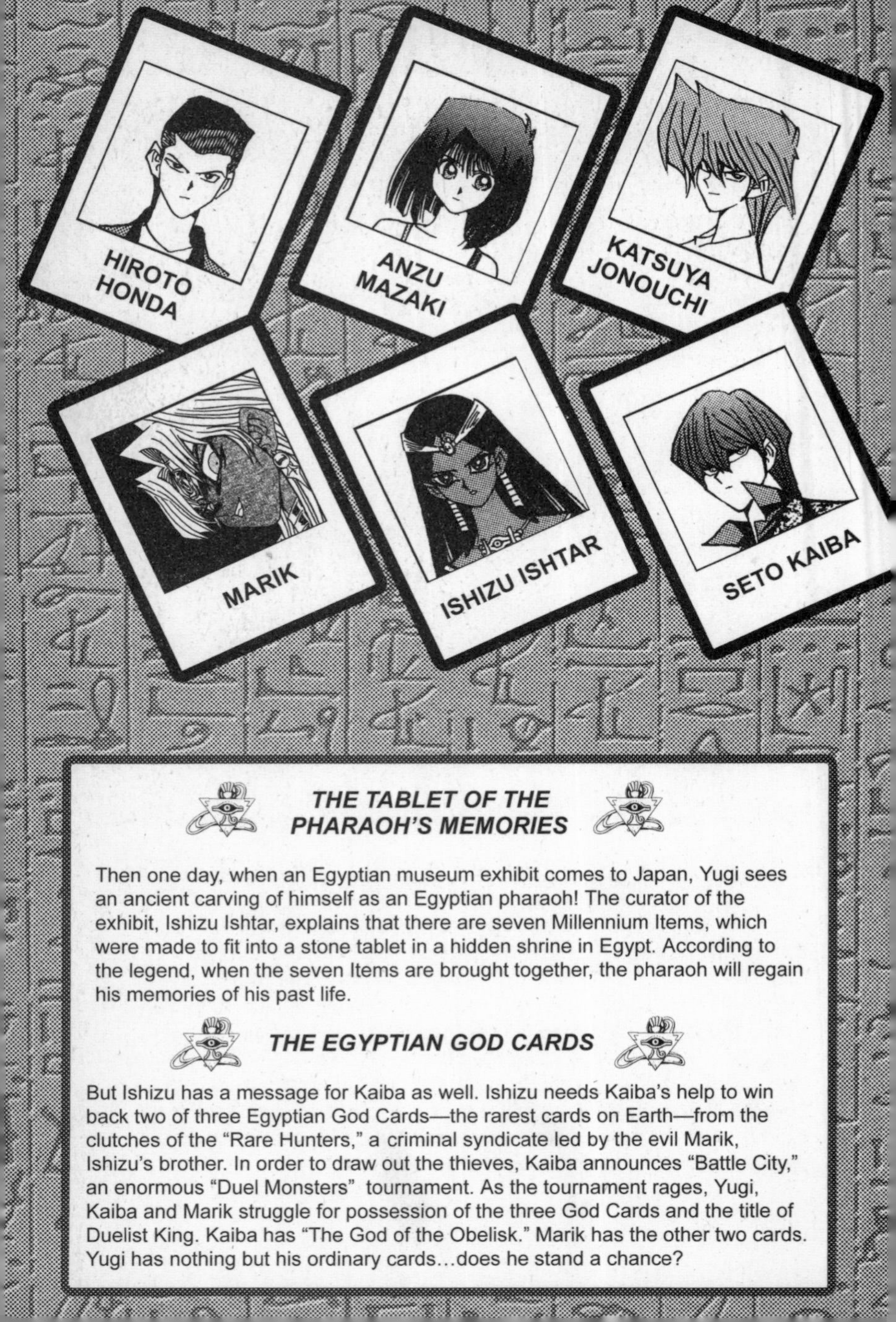
HIROTO HONDA
ANZU MAZAKI
KATSUYA JONOUCHI
MARIK
ISHIZU ISHTAR
SETO KAIBA

THE TABLET OF THE PHARAOH'S MEMORIES

Then one day, when an Egyptian museum exhibit comes to Japan, Yugi sees an ancient carving of himself as an Egyptian pharaoh! The curator of the exhibit, Ishizu Ishtar, explains that there are seven Millennium Items, which were made to fit into a stone tablet in a hidden shrine in Egypt. According to the legend, when the seven Items are brought together, the pharaoh will regain his memories of his past life.

THE EGYPTIAN GOD CARDS

But Ishizu has a message for Kaiba as well. Ishizu needs Kaiba's help to win back two of three Egyptian God Cards—the rarest cards on Earth—from the clutches of the "Rare Hunters," a criminal syndicate led by the evil Marik, Ishizu's brother. In order to draw out the thieves, Kaiba announces "Battle City," an enormous "Duel Monsters" tournament. As the tournament rages, Yugi, Kaiba and Marik struggle for possession of the three God Cards and the title of Duelist King. Kaiba has "The God of the Obelisk." Marik has the other two cards. Yugi has nothing but his ordinary cards...does he stand a chance?

THE STORY SO FAR...

**YUGI MUTOU/
YU-GI-OH**

When 10th grader Yugi solved the Millennium Puzzle, another spirit took up residence in his body...Yu-Gi-Oh, the King of Games, a dark avenger who challenges evildoers to "Shadow Games" of life and death!

YUGI FACES DEADLY ENEMIES!

Using his gaming skills, Yugi fights ruthless adversaries like Maximillion Pegasus, multimillionaire creator of the collectible card game "Duel Monsters," and Ryo Bakura, whose friendly personality turns evil when he is possessed by the spirit of the Millennium Ring. But Yugi's greatest rival is Seto Kaiba, the world's second-greatest gamer—and the ruthless teenage president of Kaiba Corporation. At first, Kaiba and Yugi are bitter enemies, but after fighting against a common adversary—Pegasus—they come to respect one another. But for all his powers, there is one thing Yu-Gi-Oh cannot do: remember who he is and where he came from.

SHONEN JUMP MANGA

Vol. 13

SLIFER THE SKY DRAGON

STORY AND ART BY
KAZUKI TAKAHASHI

YU-GI-OH!: DUELIST VOL. 13
The SHONEN JUMP Manga Edition

STORY AND ART BY 054069555
KAZUKI TAKAHASHI

Translation & English Adaptation/Joe Yamazaki
Touch-up Art & Lettering/Eric Erbes
Design/Andrea Rice
Editor/Jason Thompson

Editor in Chief, Books/Alvin Lu
Editor in Chief, Magazines/Marc Weidenbaum
VP, Publishing Licensing/Rika Inouye
VP, Sales & Product Marketing/Gonzalo Ferreyra
VP, Creative/Linda Espinosa
Publisher/Hyoe Narita

In the original Japanese edition, YU-GI-OH!, YU-GI-OH!: DUELIST and
YU-GI-OH!: MILLENNIUM WORLD are known collectively as YU-GI-OH!.
The English YU-GI-OH!: DUELIST was originally volumes 8-31
of the Japanese YU-GI-OH!.

Printed in the U.S.A.

Published by VIZ Media, LLC
P.O. Box 77010
San Francisco, CA 94107

SHONEN JUMP Manga Edition
10 9 8 7 6 5 4 3 2
First printing, January 2006
Second printing, October 2008

PARENTAL ADVISORY
YU-GI-OH!: DUELIST is rated T for Teen
and is recommended for ages 13 and
up. Contains fantasy violence.
ratings.viz.com

THE WORLD'S
MOST POPULAR MANGA

www.viz.com

www.shonenjump.com

高橋和希

VOLUME 20! IT'S BEEN FOUR WHOLE YEARS SINCE I
STARTED *YU-GI-OH!*. WHEN IT FIRST STARTED RUNNING
I THOUGHT "I'LL AIM FOR FIVE VOLUMES!" I NEVER
EXPECTED IT TO KEEP GOING THIS LONG. IT'S ALL
THANKS TO YOUR SUPPORT! I'VE ALREADY DECIDED ON
YU-GI-OH!'S LAST SCENE. THERE'S STILL A LONG WAY
TO GO BEFORE I REACH THE GOAL, BUT I HOPE TO
MAKE IT THERE SAFELY.
　　　　　　　　　-KAZUKI TAKAHASHI, 2000

Artist/author Kazuki Takahashi first tried to break into
the manga business in 1982, but success eluded him
until **Yu-Gi-Oh!** debuted in the Japanese **Weekly
Shonen Jump** magazine in 1996. **Yu-Gi-Oh!**'s themes
of friendship and fighting, together with Takahashi's
weird and wonderful art, soon became enormously
successful, spawning a real-world card game, video
games, and two anime series. A lifelong gamer,
Takahashi enjoys Shogi (Japanese chess), Mahjong,
card games, and tabletop RPGs, among other games.

Praise for Anne Perry's Charlotte and Thomas Pitt mysteries

BELGRAVE SQUARE

"So pulsates with the sights and sounds of Victorian London that the reader soon gets caught up in Anne Perry's picaresque story of life, love, and murder that involves both the upper and lower classes of that colorful era."

—*The Pittsburgh Press*

HIGHGATE RISE

"When it comes to the Victorian mystery, Anne Perry has proved that nobody does it better. Once again, her recreation of its manners and morality, fashions and foibles is masterful."

—*The San Diego Union-Tribune*

BETHLEHEM ROAD

"Perry once again demonstrates her true and lively passion. . . . Her finely drawn characters couldn't be more comfortable within the customs and sensibility of their historical period."

—*The New York Times Book Review*

SILENCE IN HANOVER CLOSE

"[A] complex, gripping and highly satisfying mystery . . . An adroit blend of thick London atmosphere and a convincing cast . . . A totally surprising yet wonderfully plausible finale."

—*Publishers Weekly*

Also by Anne Perry
Published by Fawcett Books:

Featuring Thomas and Charlotte Pitt

THE CATER STREET HANGMAN
CALLANDER SQUARE
PARAGON WALK
RESURRECTION ROW
BLUEGATE FIELDS
RUTLAND PLACE
DEATH IN THE DEVIL'S ACRE
CARDINGTON CRESCENT
SILENCE IN HANOVER CLOSE
BETHLEHEM ROAD
HIGHGATE RISE
BELGRAVE SQUARE

Published by Ivy Books:

Featuring Inspector William Monk

THE FACE OF A STRANGER
A DANGEROUS MOURNING
DEFEND AND BETRAY
A SUDDEN, FEARFUL DEATH

FARRIERS' LANE

Anne Perry

FAWCETT CREST • NEW YORK

A Fawcett Crest Book
Published by Ballantine Books
 Published in the United States by Ballantine Books, a division of Random House, Inc., New York, and simultaneously in Canada by Random House of Canada Limited, Toronto.

Library of Congress Catalog Card Number: 92-54390

ISBN 0-449-21961-5

Manufactured in the United States of America

First Hardcover Edition: April 1993
First Mass Market Edition: March 1994

For my mother

1

"Isn't he superb?" Caroline Ellison whispered to her daughter Charlotte. "He conveys so much feeling with the simplest word or a gesture!"

They were side by side in the red plush box in the theater in the semidarkness. It was late autumn and since there was no heating the air was cold. By the end of the first act the press of the crowd had warmed the stalls, but up here in the first tier of boxes it was different. The movement of applause and the stamping of feet then had helped, but now the drama was tense again, and the buzz of excitement shivery.

The stage was brilliant, the actors vivid figures against the romantic, plyboard scenery. One in particular commanded Caroline's attention: a man of just over average height, slender, with a sensitive, aquiline face full of humor and imagination, yet haunted with all the possibilities of tragedy. He was Joshua Fielding, principal actor of the company, and Charlotte was now quite certain he was the reason her mother had chosen this particular performance.

Apparently Caroline was waiting for a reply. Her face was quick and intelligent, but touched with an odd kind of vulnerability, as though Charlotte's answer might matter to her. She had been widowed a little while now. After the first grief had come a kind of euphoria, a sense of freedom as she realized how much she might do without restraint, since she was her own mistress. She read whatever she pleased, political, contentious, even scandalous. She joined societies and discussed all manner of subjects previously forbidden, and listened to lectures from reformers, travelers and scientists, many accompanied by photographs or slides.

But perhaps now a little of the pleasure of it was wearing thin and now and again a shadow of loneliness crossed her thoughts.

"Yes, indeed, Mama," Charlotte agreed sincerely. "He has a voice I could listen to for hours."

Caroline smiled and returned her attention to the stage, for the time being satisfied.

Charlotte looked sideways at her husband, but Pitt's eyes were on the occupants of a box some twenty yards away around the same tier of the balcony. One was a man in his early sixties with thinning hair, a broad brow, and at the present moment a fixed expression. He was staring at the stage. The other was a handsome, dark-haired woman, at least twelve or fourteen years younger. Her glittering jewelry caught the light as she fidgeted, turning her head, touching her hair and leaning slightly forward in her seat.

"Who are they?" Charlotte whispered.

"What?" Pitt was caught by surprise.

"Who are they?" she repeated quietly, looking past him to the other box.

"Oh—" He was a little uncomfortable. The visit to the theater was a gift from Caroline, and he did not wish to appear less than wholly involved in the play in spite of the fact it did not hold him. "A judge at the court of appeal," he whispered back. "Mr. Justice Stafford."

"Is she his wife?" Charlotte asked, seeking the reason for Pitt's interest.

He smiled very slightly. "I think so—why?"

Charlotte glanced towards the box again, only moderately discreetly.

"Then why are you looking at them?" she asked him, still in a hushed voice. "Who is that in the box just beyond them?"

"It looks like Mr. Justice Livesey."

"Isn't he young to be a judge? He's rather handsome, don't you think? Mrs. Stafford seems to think so too!"

Pitt turned a little in his seat. Caroline was too absorbed in the stage to notice. He followed Charlotte's gaze.

"Not the man with the black hair!" he said under his breath. "The one nearer. The young one is Adolphus Pryce. He is a Queen's Counsel. Livesey is the big man with white hair."

"Oh—well, why are you looking at them anyway?"

"I was just surprised he was so absorbed in the play," Pitt replied with a slight shrug. "It's rather romantic. I wouldn't have thought it of him. But his eyes haven't left the stage for ten minutes or more. In fact I haven't seen him blink!"

"Perhaps he's enamored of Tamar Macaulay?" Charlotte said with a little giggle.

"Who?" Pitt's face creased with confusion.

"The actress!" Charlotte was exasperated and for a moment her voice rose. "Really, Thomas! Do pay attention! She is the heroine!"

"Oh—of course. I forgot her name. I'm sorry," he apologized contritely. "Be quiet and watch the play."

They both faced the front and were silent for nearly a quarter of an hour until a small cry from the Staffords' box and a hasty, half-muffled activity drew their attention. Even Caroline was caused to look away from the stage.

"What is it?" she asked anxiously. "What has happened? Is someone ill?"

"Yes, it looks like it," Pitt replied, pushing his chair back as if to rise, and then changing his mind. "I think Judge Stafford seems to be unwell."

Indeed, Mrs. Stafford was on her feet, leaning over her husband in some agitation, attempting to loosen his collar and speaking to him in a low, urgent voice. However, he made no response except a spasmodic jerking of his limbs, not wildly, but as if he were in some distress. The same fixed, immobile expression remained on his face, as if he still could not bear to drag his attention from the stage and

3

the figures on it playing out their own predetermined drama.

"Should we help?" Charlotte whispered doubtfully.

"What could we do?" Pitt looked worried, his face puckered. "He probably needs a doctor." But even as he said it he pushed his chair farther back and rose to his feet. "I'd better see if she wishes someone to call for one. And they may need assistance to help him to a more private place, where he can lie down. Please excuse me to Caroline." And without waiting any longer he slipped out of the back of the box.

Once outside he hurried along the wide passageway, counting the doors until he came to the right one. There was no point in knocking; the woman had all she could cope with in trying to help her husband without coming to open a door which would not be locked anyway. In fact it was already ajar; he simply pushed it wide and went in.

Samuel Stafford was slumped in the chair, his face very flushed. Even from the doorway Pitt could hear his labored breathing. Juniper Stafford was at the far side of the box now, leaning against the rail, her hands up to her face, knuckles white. She seemed almost paralyzed with fear. Next to Stafford, half kneeling on the floor, was Mr. Justice Ignatius Livesey.

"Can I be of help?" Pitt asked quickly. "Have you sent for a doctor, or would you like me to?"

Livesey looked around, startled. Obviously he had not heard Pitt come in. He was a big man, broad-headed with a powerful face, with short nose and fleshy jaw. It was a face of conviction and courage, perhaps uncertain temper, belonging to a man of intense and sudden moods who commanded others with ease.

"Yes, send for a doctor," he agreed quickly after only a glance at Pitt to assure himself he was a gentleman, and not merely a curious intruder. "I am not a medical man, and I fear there is little I can do."

"Of course. I'll send my wife to be with Mrs. Stafford." Livesey's face showed acute surprise.

"You know him?"

4

"Only by repute, Mr. Livesey," Pitt said with the barest smile. The man in the chair was sliding farther down and his breathing was becoming slower. Without wasting any more time Pitt went out again, and passing his own box pushed the door open.

"Charlotte, it's serious," he said urgently. "I think the poor man may be dying. You'd better go and be with Mrs. Livesey."

Caroline looked around at him anxiously.

"Stay here, Mama-in-law," Pitt answered the unspoken question. "I'm going for a doctor, if there is one here."

Charlotte stood up and went outside with him, turning to the Staffords' box at a run, her skirts swinging. Pitt went the other way around towards the management offices. He found the right door, knocked sharply, then went in without waiting for an answer.

Inside a man with a magnificent mustache looked up angrily from the desk where he was studying some very indiscreet photographs.

"How dare you, sir!" he protested, half rising to his feet. "This is—"

"An emergency," Pitt said without bothering to smile. "One of your patrons, in box fourteen, is extremely ill. In fact I fear he may well be dying. Mr. Justice Stafford—"

"Oh my God!" The manager was aghast. "How appalling! What a scandal! People are so superstitious. I—"

"Never mind that," Pitt interrupted. "Is there a doctor in the theater? If not, you had better send for the nearest one as fast as you can. I am going back to see if I can do anything."

"Who are you, sir? Your name."

"Pitt—Inspector Thomas Pitt, Bow Street."

"Oh, sweet heaven! What a disaster!" The manager's face drained of all color.

"Don't be idiotic!" Pitt snapped. "It's not a crime! The poor man was taken ill, and I happened to be in a nearby box with my family. Even policemen come to the theater, on occasion. Now for goodness sake, man, go and find a doctor!"

The manager's mouth opened and closed without sound. Then suddenly he gathered up the photographs and pushed them into a drawer, slammed it closed, and was on Pitt's heels as he went out and along the corridor.

Back in box fourteen Samuel Stafford was now lying well towards the rear, out of the gaze of the inquisitive who might prefer the real drama to the one still following its course on the stage. The actors' discipline was sufficient to help them ignore any disturbance in the audience. Livesey had taken off his jacket and rolled it up under Stafford's head and he was kneeling beside him, peering at him with profound concern. Juniper Stafford sat on the other seat, leaning forward, her face intent on her husband's comatose form. His breath was even slower and the flush had gone from his skin. He looked white and clammy and he made no movement at all except for the faint rise and fall of his chest. His limbs were perfectly still. Charlotte knelt beside Juniper, her arm around her, holding one of her hands.

"The manager has sent for a doctor," Pitt said quietly, although he knew even as he said it that it would be of little use, and certainly too late.

Livesey felt for Stafford's pulse and then straightened up, biting his lip. He looked at Pitt. "Thank you," he said simply. His eyes expressed both the hopelessness of it and the warning not to speak in front of Juniper.

There was a very tentative rap on the door.

"Come in." Livesey looked at Pitt, then at the door. Surely it was too soon for a doctor, unless he had been not only in the theater, but in this tier of boxes as well.

The door opened, and Pitt recognized the smooth, dark face of Adolphus Pryce, Q.C. The man was embarrassed. His eyes went first to Juniper Stafford, hunched in her seat, clinging to Charlotte, then to the figure of Samuel Stafford on the floor. Even in the poor light reflected from the dim box lamps, and up from the brilliance of the stage across the auditorium, it was only too obvious he was in an extreme stage of illness.

"What happened?" Pryce asked very quietly. "Can—can I help? Is there—" He broke off. It was perfectly plain

6

there was nothing anyone could do without medical skill, and possibly not even then. "Mrs. Stafford?"

Juniper said nothing but stared at him with huge, desperate eyes.

"Yes," Charlotte said firmly. "If you would be so kind as to fetch a glass of cold water, and perhaps make sure that Mrs. Stafford's carriage has no difficulty in reaching the door, so that when it is time to go she does not have to wait."

"Of course! Yes, yes, naturally I shall." Pryce seemed to be immensely grateful for something positive to do. He looked for a moment more at Juniper, then turned on his heel and went out so rapidly that he brushed past a short man with gingerish hair in wild disarray and small, plump, very clean hands.

He came in and instinctively addressed Livesey as being the presiding authority in the matter.

"I am Dr. Lloyd. The manager said— Ah! Yes, I see." He stared down at Stafford on the floor, now scarcely breathing at all. "Oh, dear, oh dear me. Yes." He knelt down, peering at Stafford's face. "What is it? Do you know? Heart attack, I shouldn't wonder." He felt for a pulse, his face looking increasingly worried. "Mr. Justice Stafford, you say? I'm afraid I don't care for the look of him very much." He touched Stafford's pallid face with his hand. "Clammy," he pronounced, pushing out his lip. "Can you tell me what happened, sir?" This last was addressed to Livesey.

"The onset of the illness appeared quite rapid," Livesey replied, speaking in a clear voice, but very quietly. "I was sitting in the next box, and I saw him sink forward in his seat, so I came to see if I could be of assistance. At first I thought perhaps a stomach upset, or something of the sort, but I'm afraid now it does seem to be something a good deal more grave."

"He does not appear to have . . . vomited," the doctor remarked.

"No—no, indeed," Livesey agreed. "And of course it may in fact be his heart as you suggested, but he did not

7

complain of pain while he was conscious, and he seems to have been in something of a stupor since quite early on, almost drowsy, one might say."

"He was very flushed when I first came," Pitt offered.

"Oh? And who are you, sir?" Lloyd enquired, turning around and frowning at Pitt. "I apologize, I did not observe you before. I took this gentleman to be in charge."

"Thomas Pitt," Pitt replied. "Inspector, with the Bow Street station."

"Police? Good God!"

"Here in a private capacity," Pitt replied coolly. "I was with my wife and mother-in-law a few boxes away. I merely came to offer my assistance, or call a doctor, when I observed that Mr. Stafford was ill."

"Very commendable," Lloyd said with a sniff, wiping his hands on his trousers. "Don't want to call in the police over something like this—good heavens! It's tragic enough as it is. Perhaps someone would be good enough to look after Mrs.—er—Stafford? There is nothing whatever she can do here, poor creature!"

"Shouldn't I—I— Oh, Samuel!" Juniper caught her breath and pressed a handkerchief up to her mouth.

"I am sure you have already done all you could," Charlotte said gently, taking her by the arm. "Now it is up to the doctor. And if Mr. Stafford is not awake, he will not miss you. Come with me and let me find you a quiet place to sit until they can tell us something."

"Do you think so?" Juniper turned to Charlotte with desperate appeal.

"I have no doubt at all," Charlotte replied, glancing momentarily at Pitt, then back to Juniper. "Come with me. Perhaps Mr. Pryce will have found a glass of water and may even have located your carriage."

"Oh, I couldn't just go home!"

"Not yet, of course! But if that is what the doctor says, we do not want to have to wait in line, do we?"

"No—no, I suppose not. Yes, of course, you are right!" And with a little assistance Juniper rose to her feet. After thanking Livesey for his help, and with one more glance at the motionless form of her husband, she smothered a sob and allowed Charlotte to lead her outside.

Lloyd gave a deep sigh.

"Now we may get down to business, gentlemen. I gravely fear there is nothing I can do for Mr. Stafford. He is sinking very rapidly, and I have no medicine with me. Indeed I know of none which would help his condition." He frowned and regarded the now totally inert body of his patient. He touched Stafford's chest again, then the pulse in his neck, and lastly his wrist, shaking his head gently all the time.

Livesey stood beside Pitt, his back to the auditorium and the stage where presumably the players were unaware of the nature of the small, dark drama which was coming to a close in one of their boxes.

"In fact," Lloyd said after another few moments, "Mr. Justice Stafford has passed away." He rose to his feet awkwardly, brushing down his trousers to return them to their crease. He looked at Livesey. "Naturally his own physician will be informed, and his poor widow is already aware of the situation, poor woman. I am afraid I cannot pronounce the cause of death; I really have very little idea. There will have to be an autopsy. Very distressing, but it is the law."

"Have you no idea?" Pitt frowned. "Is it not an illness you are familiar with?"

"No sir, it is not!" Lloyd said rather testily. "It is not reasonable to expect any physician to diagnose a disease in a handful of minutes, with no history whatever, and a comatose patient—and all in the half-light of a theater box and a performance going on onstage. Really sir, you ask the impossible!"

"Not a heart attack, or an apoplexy?" Pitt did not apologize.

"No sir, not a heart attack, so far as I can see, and not an apoplexy. In fact if I did not know better, I would suspect he had taken some form of opiate, and accidentally prepared an overdose. Except, of course, men of his distinction do not take opium, and most certainly not a dose to produce this effect!"

"I doubt Mr. Justice Stafford smoked opium," Livesey said coldly.

"I did not suggest, sir, that he did!" Lloyd snapped. "In fact I went out of my way to explain to—to Mr.—Mr. Pitt here"—he jerked his head towards Pitt—"that I believed he did not. Apart from that, one could not smoke an amount sufficient to cause death in this manner. One would have to drink a solution of opium. Really—I do not know why we discuss the subject at all!" He lifted his shoulders in a violent shrug. "I do not know the cause of the poor man's demise. It will require an autopsy. Perhaps his own physician is aware of some condition which may explain it. For now, there is nothing more I can do, and I therefore beg you to excuse me that I may rejoin my family, who are endeavoring to have a rare evening out in each other's company with a little civilized entertainment."

He sniffed. "I am extremely sorry for your loss, and regret profoundly I could not prevent it, but it was too late—far too late. My card." He produced one like a conjurer and presented it to Livesey. "Good day, sir—Mr. Pitt!" And with that he stood to attention smartly, then bustled out and closed the door behind him, leaving Pitt and Livesey alone with the body of Samuel Stafford.

Livesey looked very grave, his skin pale, his body tired and yet tense, broad shoulders sagging a little, his head forward, the dim lights strong on his thick hair. Slowly he put his hand in his trouser pocket and pulled out a slim chased-silver hip flask. He held it out to Pitt.

"This is Stafford's," he said grimly, meeting Pitt's eyes. "I saw him drink from it just after the end of the interval. It is a hideous thought, but there may be something in it which caused his illness. Perhaps you should take it and have it examined—even if only to exclude it."

"Poison?" Pitt asked gravely. He looked down at Stafford. The more he considered the course of events he had observed, the less absurd did Livesey's words seem. "Yes," he admitted. "Yes, of course. You are quite right. It must at least be considered, even if only to prove it was not so. Thank you."

He took the flask and looked at it, turning it over in his hands. It was very slim, very expensive, chased in silver and engraved with Samuel Stafford's name and the date of its having been given to him, February 28, 1884; a recent gift, over five and a half years ago. It was a beautiful thing to be a vehicle of death. "I'll have it examined, of course," he went on. "In the meanwhile perhaps we had better find out what we can about Mr. Stafford's evening and precisely what happened."

"Of course," Livesey agreed. "And arrange for the body to be taken away discreetly. I shall have to explain to Mrs. Stafford why it cannot go to his home until it has been examined for the cause of death. How very distressing for her! The whole business is most grieving. Is there any lock to this door?"

Pitt turned around and looked at it.

"No, only an ordinary latch. I'll wait here until you can inform the management and have a constable sent. We cannot leave it open."

"No, naturally not. I'll go now." And without waiting any further Livesey went out and disappeared, leaving Pitt alone just as the curtain fell to a long and enthusiastic round of applause.

When Charlotte left the box with Juniper Stafford she met Adolphus Pryce almost immediately, returning with a goblet of water held out in front of him. He looked extremely agitated and his dark eyes gazed at Juniper with something that, were it not ridiculous to think it, Charlotte would have taken for fear.

"My dear—Mrs. Stafford," he said jerkily. "Is there anything at all I can do to be of service to you? Your coachman has been told and he will bring your carriage to the front the moment you wish it. How is Mr. Stafford?"

"I don't know," Juniper answered in a voice that caught in her throat. "He ... looked ... very ill! It was so—sudden!"

"I'm so sorry," Adolphus said again. "I had no idea he

11

was in poor health—none at all." He held out the goblet of water.

Juniper's eyes met his on a long, painful look. She took the goblet with both hands, the light catching on her rings. Her gorgeous dress now seemed ridiculously out of place. "No—of course not," she said hastily. "Neither—neither had I! That is what is so absurd." Her voice rose to a high, desperate pitch and broke off. She forced herself to drink a sip of the water.

Adolphus stared at her. Charlotte might not have been there at all for any awareness he showed of her. All his intense emotion was centered on Juniper, and yet he did not seem to know what else to say.

"The doctor will do all that can be done," Charlotte said. "It would be best if we were to find a quiet place where we can await the outcome, don't you think?"

"Yes—yes, of course," Adolphus agreed. Again he looked at Juniper. "If . . . if there is anything, Mrs. Stafford? At least, please let me know . . . how he is."

"Of course I will, Mr. Pryce. You are most kind." Juniper looked at him with a sort of desperation. Then clinging to Charlotte's arm she turned and walked away towards a small private room off the foyer where refreshments had been taken only an hour earlier. The manager stood in the doorway, wringing his hands and making inarticulate sounds of general anxiety.

It seemed an age to Charlotte that they sat there. Occasionally she took the goblet from Juniper, then handed it back, making small, meaningless remarks and trying to be of comfort without giving any foolish promises of a happy ending she believed could not possibly be.

Eventually Ignatius Livesey came. His face was very grave and Charlotte knew the instant she saw him that Stafford was dead. Indeed when Juniper looked up, the hope died out of her before she spoke. She took a deep breath, closed her eyes, the tears brimming over and running down her cheeks.

"I am extremely sorry," Livesey said quietly. "It pains me to have to tell you that he has gone. The only comfort

I can offer you is that it was quite peaceful and he will have felt no pain or distress except momentarily, and that was so short as to be forgotten in an instant." He filled the doorway, a figure of judicial calm, a stability in a dreadfully changing world. "He was a very fine man who served the law with great distinction for over forty years, and he will be remembered with honor and gratitude. England is a better place, and society wiser and more just, because of his life. That must be of great comfort to you, when this time of grief has lessened, and it will lessen with time. It is a legacy not every woman may boast, and you may justly be proud."

She stared at him. For a moment she tried to speak. It was painful to observe. Charlotte longed to help her.

"That is most generous of you," she said to Livesey, gripping Juniper's hand and holding it hard. "Thank you for coming on what must be a most difficult errand. Now perhaps if there is nothing more to do here, you would be kind enough to send a message so Mrs. Stafford's carriage may be brought. I imagine the doctor will take care of—of arrangements here?"

"Indeed," Livesey acknowledged. "But . . ." His face shadowed. "I regret the police may wish to ask a few questions, because it was so sudden."

Juniper found her voice; perhaps surprise was momentarily greater than grief.

"The police? Whatever for? Who— I mean, why are they here? How do they even know? Did you . . . ?"

"No—it is quite fortuitous," Livesey said quickly. "It is Mr. Pitt, who came to your assistance."

"What questions?" Juniper glanced at Charlotte, looking confused. "What is there to ask?"

"I imagine he will wish to know what Samuel ate or drank in the last few hours," Livesey replied gently. "Perhaps what he had done during the day. If it is possible for you to compose yourself sufficiently to give him answers, it will help."

Charlotte opened her mouth to say something, a protest of sorts, but no words came to her that were not futile. Stafford had died suddenly and without any cause that could be identified. It was unavoidable that there should be some formal investigation. Livesey was right; the sooner it could be settled, the sooner some sort of natural grief could begin, and then in time the start of healing.

The door opened and Pitt came in, closely followed by Adolphus Pryce.

Juniper looked up quickly, but at Pryce; then as if by an effort of will, away again.

"Mr. Pitt?" she said slowly. "I understand you are from the police. Mr. Livesey tells me you need to ask me some questions about . . . about Samuel's death." She took a deep breath. "I will tell you whatever I can, but I don't know anything that could help you. I had no idea he was ill. He never gave me the slightest indication . . ."

"I understand that, Mrs. Stafford." Pitt sat down without being asked, so that he was looking directly at her, instead of obliging her to stare up at him. "I am deeply sorry to have to trouble you at this most painful time, but if I were to leave it until later, you may by then have forgotten some small detail which would provide an answer." He looked at her closely. She was very pale and her hands were shaking, but she seemed composed, and still suffering too much shock to have given way to weeping or the anger that so often follows bereavement.

"Mrs. Stafford, what did your husband eat for dinner before he came to the theater?"

She thought for a moment. "Saddle of mutton, horseradish sauce, vegetables. Not a heavy meal, Mr. Pitt, and not an overindulgence."

"Did you have the same?"

"Yes—exactly. A great deal less, of course, but exactly the same."

"And to drink?"

She drew her brows down in puzzlement. "He took a little claret, but it was opened at the table and poured straight from the bottle. It was in excellent condition. I had half a glass myself. He did not take too much, I assure you! And he always drank very moderately."

14

"What else?"

"A chocolate pudding, and a fruit sorbet. But I had some also."

Pitt caught a movement out of the corner of his eye, and turned to see Livesey touching his hip pocket.

Pitt continued grimly. "Did your husband carry a hip flask, Mrs. Stafford?" he asked.

Her eyes widened. "Yes—yes, he did. A silver one. I gave it to him some four or five years ago. Why?"

"Did he fill it himself?"

"I imagine so. I really don't know. Why, Mr. Pitt? Do you . . . do you wish to see it?"

"I already have it, thank you. Do you know if he drank from it this evening?"

"I didn't see him, but it is most likely he did. He—he liked a small—" She stopped, her voice shaking and uncertain. She required a moment or two to regain her composure.

"Can you tell me what he did during the day, Mrs. Stafford, all that you know."

"What he did?" She looked doubtful. "Well, yes, if you wish. But I don't understand why—"

"It is possible that he was poisoned, Mrs. Stafford," Livesey said gravely, still standing near the door. "It is a most distressing thought, but I am afraid we must face it. Of course the medical examiner may find some disease of which we are unaware, but until that time we have to act in a way that takes account of all possibilities."

She blinked. "Poisoned? Who would poison Samuel?"

Pryce fidgeted from one foot to the other, staring at Juniper, but he did not interrupt.

"You can think of no one?" Pitt drew her attention back again. "Do you know if he was presently engaged in a case, Mrs. Stafford?"

"No—no, he was not." She seemed to find it easier to speak while her mind was concentrating on practical details and answers to specific questions. "That woman came to see him again. She has been pestering him for several months now. He seemed most upset by her, and after she left, he went out almost immediately."

"What woman, Mrs. Stafford?" Pitt said quickly.

"Miss Macaulay," she replied. "Tamar Macaulay."

"The actress?" He was startled. "Do you know what she wanted?"

"Oh yes, of course." Her eyebrows rose as if the question were unexpected. She had assumed Pitt would know. "About her brother."

"What to do with her brother, Mrs. Stafford?" Pitt asked patiently, reminding himself she was desperately newly bereaved, and should not be required to make sense as others might. "Who is her brother? Is he presently lodging an appeal?"

A flicker of hard, almost bitter humor lit her face for a moment.

"Hardly, Mr. Pitt. He was hanged five years ago. She wishes—wished Samuel to reopen the case. He was one of the judges of his appeal, which was denied. It was a very terrible murder. I think if the public could have hanged him more than once, they would have."

"The Godman case," Livesey put in behind Pitt. "The murder of Kingsley Blaine. I daresay you recall it?"

Pitt thought for a moment. A vague recollection came back to him, of horror and outrage, articles in the paper, one or two very ugly incidents in the street, Jews being mobbed. "In Farriers' Lane?" he said aloud.

"That's right," Juniper agreed. "Well, Tamar Macaulay was his sister. I don't know why they had different names, but actors aren't ordinary people anyway. You never know what is real with them, and what is not. And of course they are Jews."

Pitt shivered. There seemed a sudden coldness in the room, as if a breath of hate and unreason had come in through the open door, but Livesey had closed it. He looked at Charlotte and saw in her eyes a shadow of fear, as if she too had felt something new and dark.

"It was a very shocking case," Livesey said quietly, his voice grave and with an edge of anger in it. "I don't know

16

why the poor woman didn't leave it alone and let it die in everyone's memory, but some compulsion drives her to keep on raising it, trying to get it reopened." His face was dark with distaste, as if he would step back from the useless pain of it, did not duty prevent him. "She had some lunatic idea it would clear his name." He lifted his heavy shoulders a fraction. "Whereas, of course, the truth is the wretched man was as guilty as the devil, and it was proved beyond any doubt at all, reasonable or unreasonable. He had his day in court, and his appeal. I know the facts, Pitt, I sat on the appeal myself."

Pitt acknowledged the information with a nod, and turned back to Juniper.

"And Miss Macaulay came to see Mr. Stafford again today?"

"Yes—early in the afternoon. He was very disturbed by it." She took a deep breath and steadied herself, gripping Charlotte's hand. "He went out immediately after, saying he must see Mr. O'Neil, and Mr. Fielding."

"Joshua Fielding, the actor?" Pitt asked. For some reason he deliberately avoided Charlotte's eyes, Caroline's face in the theater painfully clear in his mind with all its tense excitement.

"Yes," Juniper agreed, nodding very slightly. "He was part of the company at the time—and of course he still is. You saw him tonight. He was a friend of Aaron Godman's, and I believe for a while a suspect—before they knew who it was, of course."

"I see. And who is O'Neil? Another member of the company?"

"Oh no! No, Mr. O'Neil was a friend of Kingsley Blaine, the murdered man. He was very respectable!"

"Why did Mr. Stafford wish to see him?"

She shook her head very slightly. "He was a suspect—in the very beginning. But of course that did not last long. I have no idea why Samuel wanted to see him. He didn't discuss it with me, I only knew because he was so distressed I asked him where he was going, and he just said to see Mr. O'Neil and Mr. Fielding."

17

Adolphus Pryce shifted uncomfortably, clearing his throat.

"Er—I—I know that to be true, Mr. Pitt. Mr. Stafford also came to see me today. He had already spoken to both Fielding and O'Neil."

Pitt looked at him with surprise. He had forgotten Pryce was there.

"Indeed? Did he discuss the matter with you, Mr. Pryce?"

"Well, yes—and no. In a manner of speaking." Pryce stared at him fixedly, as if he were with difficulty avoiding letting his eyes stray somewhere else. "He asked me some further questions about the Blaine/Godman case—that is how we referred to it, Blaine being the victim, and Godman the offender. I was the prosecuting counsel, you know. It was really a very clear case. Godman had motive; the means were to hand for anyone, and the opportunity. In fact he was observed by several people in the immediate vicinity, and did not deny it." A look of apology flickered across his face. "And of course he was a Jew."

Pitt felt a hardness inside him settle like a stone. He did not even try to keep the anger out of his eyes.

"What has that to do with it, Mr. Pryce? I can see no connection whatever!"

Pryce's delicate nostrils flared.

"He was crucified, Mr. Pitt," he said between his teeth. "I would have thought the connection was appallingly obvious!"

Pitt was stunned. "Crucified?" he blurted.

"To the stable door, in Farriers' Lane," Livesey put in from his position still close to the door. "Surely you remember the case. It was written about extensively in every newspaper in London. People spoke of little else."

A sharper recollection came back to Pitt. He had been working on another case himself at the time, and had no spare moments to read newspapers or listen to the recounting of events other than those of his own case, but this had rocked the entire city.

"Yes." He frowned, embarrassed to be so caught out. "I

18

do recall hearing of it, but I was in Barking on an investigation of my own. One can become very absorbed . . ." He smiled twistedly. "In fact I don't even know the details of the Whitechapel murders last year, I was so busy with a double murder in Highgate."

"I hardly think a Christian would have crucified anyone." Pryce was still determined to defend himself. "That is why being a Jew was relevant."

"Is O'Neil a Jew?" Pitt asked sarcastically.

"Of course not! But no one seriously suspected him for long," Pryce replied with an edge to his voice. "Fielding and Miss Macaulay were the other main suspects."

"It is all quite beside the point," Livesey interrupted with impatience. "Godman was guilty, and it is unfortunate his sister cannot accept the fact and leave the case to sink into oblivion, where it belongs." He shook his head and his lips tightened. "It can help no one at all to keep on raking it up. It will change nothing. She is a very foolish woman."

Pitt turned back to Juniper. "Do you know of anyone else Mr. Stafford saw today, or anywhere he went?"

"No." She shook her head. "No, that is all he spoke of. Then he came home. We had dinner a little earlier than usual—quite a light meal really." She swallowed with difficulty. "And then we came to the theater—here . . ."

Charlotte held her hand tightly, still sitting very close to her. She looked at Pitt.

"Is there really anything more you have to know tonight, Thomas? Would it not be possible for Mrs. Stafford to go home now and pursue whatever else there may be in the morning? She is exhausted."

"Yes, of course." Pitt stood up slowly. "I am extremely sorry to have had to speak of it at all, Mrs. Stafford, and I hope it may all prove to have been unnecessary." He held out his hand. "May I offer my deepest sympathy."

"Thank you." She took his hand, not merely to bid him good-bye, but with his assistance, to rise (somewhat heavily) to her feet.

"I'll come with you to your carriage," Charlotte offered.

Pryce came forward suddenly, holding out his arm, his face tight with emotion.

"Please—permit me! May I help you, Mrs. Stafford? You need someone to make sure you are not harassed or crowded on the way, and to support you. I should deem it an honor."

Her eyes were wide, almost feverish. She hesitated, as if to make some protest; then the practicality of it became apparent and she took a step towards him.

"You have been most kind, Mrs. Pitt," Pryce added, looking at Charlotte with sudden courtesy and a fragment of what was probably a characteristic charm. "But please allow me to be of some service, and yourself to remain with your husband."

"That is most generous of you," Charlotte accepted with relief. "I confess, I had completely forgotten about my mother, who is our hostess here. She may still be in our box, waiting for us."

"Then it is settled." Pryce offered Mrs. Stafford his arm. After a brief farewell, they went out together, she leaning upon him and he gently supporting her.

"Oh dear." Livesey pursed his lips. "A hard business, very hard. But I am sure you have handled it correctly, Mr. Pitt. And you, Mrs. Pitt, have been most considerate with your sympathy and kindness." He sighed. "However, I know there may be worse to come, if indeed his death was not natural. Let us pray that our fear is unnecessary."

"I don't think even God can change what is already done," Pitt said dryly. "What time did Mr. Stafford come to see you, sir?"

"Immediately before luncheon," Livesey replied. "I was to dine with a colleague, and was about to leave my chambers when Stafford came in. He stayed only a few moments—"

"Was he there in connection with the Blaine/Godman case?" Pitt interrupted.

A look of distaste crossed Livesey's broad face. "Not primarily, although he did mention it. It was regarding another matter, which is naturally confidential." He smiled very slightly. "But I can be of some assistance, Inspector. Just before leaving he took a small sip from his flask, and so did I. As you can see, I am in excellent health. So we know beyond question that the flask was untainted at that time."

Pitt looked at him in silence, digesting the information and its implications.

Livesey made a small gesture of amusement, a downward curling of his lips. "Corroborated, Inspector. My colleague, John Wentworth, an eminent Queen's Counsel, had arrived for our luncheon engagement. I am sure if you wish it he will confirm what I have said."

Pitt let out his breath quickly. "I did not doubt you, sir. I was considering the gravity of the conclusions which that obliges, should there prove to be poison in the flask."

"Indeed." Livesey's face darkened. "Exceedingly unpleasant, I fear, but perhaps unavoidable nonetheless. I do not envy you your task, sir."

At last Pitt also smiled. "Not mine, Mr. Livesey. I shall hand it over to my superiors tomorrow morning, if indeed it is a case at all. I was merely responding because I was here at the time. It would be irresponsible to ignore the opportunity to gather evidence, against eventuality."

"Commendable, and as you say, your duty." Livesey inclined his head. "And now if you will excuse me, I believe I can be of no further assistance. It has been a long and extremely unpleasant evening. I shall be relieved to find my carriage and take my leave. Good night to you."

"Good night, Mr. Livesey. Thank you for your help."

Charlotte returned to the box to find Caroline still there. Somehow after the reality of the tragedy its plush seats and cozy luxury, its view of the blank stage, seemed absurdly trivial. Caroline was facing the door, her expression one of anxiety. She rose to her feet as soon as Charlotte arrived.

"What has happened? How is he?"

"I am afraid he is dead," Charlotte replied, closing the door behind her. "He never regained his senses, which is perhaps a blessing. What is far worse is that the other

21

judge, Mr. Livesey, seems to think it may have been poison."

"Oh, dear heaven!" Caroline was aghast. "You mean, he took his . . ." Then realization struck her. "No—you don't, do you? You mean he was murdered!"

Charlotte sat down and took Caroline's hand to draw her down again too.

"Yes, it seems a strong possibility. And I am afraid there is worse, much worse . . ."

"What?" Caroline's eyes were wide. "What in heaven's name would be worse than that?"

"Tamar Macaulay visited him today, about a very dreadful case for which her brother was hanged, about five years ago."

"Hanged? Oh, Charlotte! How tragic. But whatever could Mr. Stafford have done about it?"

"Apparently she still believes he was innocent, in spite of all the evidence, and she wanted Stafford to reopen the case. Mrs. Stafford said Tamar had pestered him for a long time, and he was quite upset by it. After she left he went out very hastily and told Mrs. Stafford he was going to see the other principal suspects in the case."

"And you think one of them murdered him?" Caroline concluded with distress. "And that—that was what we saw: We saw him murdered?"

"Yes. But Mama, the other suspects were a man called O'Neil—and Joshua Fielding."

Caroline stared at her, her eyes hurt, her face full of confusion.

"Joshua Fielding," she repeated, blinking. "Suspected of murder? Who? Who was killed?"

"A man called Blaine. Apparently it was a very shocking case. He was crucified."

"What?" Caroline could not grasp what she had said. "You mean—no, you can't! It's . . ."

"Against a door," Charlotte went on. "They hanged Tamar's brother, but she has never believed him guilty. I'm sorry."

"But why Joshua Fielding? Why should he kill this man? What reason could he have?"

"I don't know. Mrs. Stafford just said that the judge went to see both Mr. Fielding and Mr. O'Neil after Tamar called on him today." She gave a harsh little laugh. "Or it must be yesterday, by now."

"What is Thomas doing?"

"Finding out all he can, so that when he hands it over to whoever will look into the case—if, of course, it is poison and there is a case—so that they have all they can to begin with."

"Yes. I see." She shivered. "I suppose it would be remiss not to act. I had no idea when you married a policeman of some of the extraordinary things we should find ourselves doing."

"Nor I," Charlotte said frankly. "But some of them have been wonderful, some terrifying, some tragic, and many most deepening of experience, and I hope of wisdom and understanding. I pity those women who have nothing to do but stitch embroidery, flirt, gossip and try to think of something to do which could be called charitable and yet not impair their reputations or get their fingers dirty!"

Caroline pulled a slight face, but did not voice the argument in her mind. She knew Charlotte well enough to appreciate the pointlessness of it, and a small part of her had a sneaking desire to dabble in such adventures herself, not that she would have admitted it.

A few moments later the door opened and Pitt stood in the entrance, his face grave. His eyes went first to Caroline.

"I'm sorry, Mama-in-law," he apologized. "But it seems as if it may be a case for the police, and since no one else is here now, I should go and see two of the actors. Stafford visited both of them earlier in the day. They may have some connection—or at least know something that explains what happened."

Charlotte rose to her feet quickly, absentmindedly straightening her skirt.

"We'll come with you. I don't want to wait here, do you, Mama?"

"No." Caroline stood up beside her. "No. I'd far rather come with you. We can wait somewhere where we shall not intrude."

Pitt stepped back and held the door open for them. Hastily they passed through, then walked along the corridor with him to the stage door, which apparently he had found. The manager was waiting for them, shifting from foot to foot, his face creased with anxiety.

"What has happened, Mr. Pitt?" he said as soon as Pitt was close enough he did not need to raise his voice. "I know the judge is dead, but why do you need to see Miss Macaulay and Mr. Fielding? What can they possibly do to help?" He put his hands in his pockets and then pulled them out again. "I don't understand, really I don't! I want to be of assistance, naturally—but this is beyond comprehension."

"Mr. Stafford visited with them earlier in the day," Pitt replied, his hand on the door to the stage.

"Visited with them?" The manager looked appalled. "Not here, Inspector! Certainly not here!"

"No," Pitt agreed as they walked in single file along the narrower passageway towards the room where Fielding and Tamar Macaulay had been asked to wait. "Miss Macaulay called upon the judge in his home. That at least we know."

"Do we! Do we?" the manager demanded. "I know nothing about it at all!" He stopped and flung open the door. "There you are! I wash my hands of the whole affair! Upon my soul, as if this wasn't bad enough! A judge dying in his box during the performance—and now the police! Anyone would think we were doing the Scottish play! Well go on, go on! You'd better do whatever it is you have to!"

"Thank you." Pitt accepted with only the slightest twist of irony. He held the door just long enough for Charlotte and Caroline to pass through, then closed it with a very slight bow, just as the manager came to it.

Inside the room was calm and comfortable. Half a dozen easy chairs were scattered about over a carpeted floor. There was a small stove in one corner and a kettle on it. The walls were almost covered with past playbills and posters. Some were lists of actors, others quite elaborate and beautiful evocations of glamour. Looking at them one could almost hear the music begin, see the lights dim. Pitt recognized the faces of Henry Irving, Sarah Bernhardt, Ellen Terry, Herbert Beerbohm Tree, the young Italian actress Eleanora Duse and Mrs. Patrick Campbell.

But the room was unimportant. The figures that dominated everyone's attention were standing side by side with a grace which was in all probability so practiced as now to be quite unconscious. Joshua Fielding was exactly as he had appeared through the lens of the opera glasses, except there was more humor in his face. Tiny lines around his mouth were less exaggerated than the gestures he had used to convey the same sense of wit and rueful amusement. He was perhaps less handsome. At a few yards' distance his nose was not quite straight, his eyes uneven, one brow different from the other. Yet the very imperfection of it was more immediate, and thus more lastingly attractive than the flawless stage appearance, which lacked a certain humanity.

Tamar Macaulay, on the other hand, was surprisingly different from her stage presence. Or perhaps neither Caroline nor Charlotte had looked at her so closely. She was smaller and leaner. The extreme femininity she had projected was part of her art, not a natural quality; and the intense vitality, almost lightness of character she played had been set aside with her costume. In repose she was motionless, all her strength inward. Yet her face was one of the most compelling Charlotte had ever seen. There was power of the mind in it and startling intelligence. She was extremely dark, her skin was sallow and her hair black, and yet she had the extraordinary gift of being able to portray anything from ugliness to dazzling beauty. She could never have been lush, warm or voluptuous; but in Charlotte's mind at least, she could have been anyone from Medusa, the Gorgon, to Helen of Troy, and been utterly convincing as either. With the power of personality behind her dark face, Charlotte could have looked at it and believed that men fought an eleven-year war and ruined an empire over her.

Pitt betrayed nothing so fanciful in his manner. He began with an apology.

"I am sorry to have had to ask you to remain," he said with a tight smile. "You must be tired at the end of so long a day. However, I daresay you have been informed that Mr. Justice Stafford died in his box during the performance this evening." He looked at Joshua, then at Tamar.

"I knew he was ill," Joshua replied, looking away from Caroline and at Pitt.

Pitt realized his omission. "I am sorry. May I present Mrs. Caroline Ellison, and my wife, Mrs. Pitt. I preferred not to leave them standing outside."

"Of course." Joshua bowed very slightly, first to Caroline, who blushed self-consciously, then to Charlotte. "I regret the circumstances of our meeting. I can offer you little comfort or refreshment."

"I knew he had been taken ill," Tamar said, returning them to the matter in hand. Her voice was low and of unusual timbre. "I did not know he had died." Her face pinched with sadness. "I am very sorry. I have no idea how we can be of help."

"You called upon him at his home earlier in the day?"

"Yes." She added nothing, no explanation. She had an extraordinary repose, even delivering such a bald reply.

"And I saw him later, in my lodgings," Joshua added. "He seemed perfectly well then. But is that really what you wished to ask?" He looked very relaxed, hands in his pockets. "Surely Mrs. Stafford is the one to tell you anything you need to know. Doesn't his own physician know his condition?"

Pitt corrected the misapprehension. "I am not a physician, Mr. Fielding. I am an inspector with the police."

Joshua's eyebrows rose and he straightened up, taking his hands out of his pockets. "With the police? I'm sorry—I thought he was taken ill. Was it an injury? Good heavens—in the theater?"

"No, it looks as if it may have been poison," Pitt said carefully.

26

"Poison?" Joshua was incredulous and Tamar stiffened. "How do you know?" Joshua asked.

"I don't," Pitt replied, looking from one to the other of them. "But the symptoms were alarmingly like those of opium poisoning. I should be irresponsible were I not to allow the possibility, and learn what I can, tonight, while memories are sharp and recent, before I hand the matter over to whoever will handle it when the medical report comes in."

"I see." Joshua bit his lip. "And you have come here because both Tamar and I saw him during the day, and you suspect us?" His face was tight, full of hurt. Almost unconsciously he put out his hand and touched Tamar's arm. It was a protective gesture, although she looked in some ways the stronger of the two. Her face was fiercer, less vulnerable than his.

Watching her, Charlotte thought of the little she had heard of the Godman case, and the appalling loss of her brother. She wondered what Aaron Godman had been like. If he resembled her, Charlotte could imagine how people might have feared him, and believed him at least capable of a passion that could have ended in murder!

"Among many others." Pitt did not prevaricate. "But it is also possible you may provide some observation which will simply guide us to the truth."

"You mean implicate someone else," Tamar said coolly. "We have been through a murder investigation before, Inspector Pitt. We cherish no illusions that it will be a pleasant affair, or that the police will rest before they have found evidence to satisfy a court of someone's guilt."

Charlotte was acutely aware of how exact was her use of words. The wound of her brother's conviction was far from healed.

"It is ours to present the evidence, Miss Macaulay," Pitt replied without anger or criticism in his face. "Not to decide on it—thank God. But I have never knowingly provided anything which I did not believe to be true. I am aware that you feel your brother was wronged, and that it

27

was in connection with that case that you visited Mr. Stafford today."

"Of course." Her amusement was genuine, if bitter. "I have no other reason for seeking his acquaintance. I am aware that actresses have a certain reputation. In my case it is not warranted. And I know no reason to suppose it was in Mr. Stafford's either." There was savage laughter in her eyes, a mockery of Stafford and of herself and all people suppressed of emotions. "He was a somewhat humorless man," she went on. "Lacking in imagination, and in the unlikely event he were to pursue a romance, I think he would be more discreet than to choose an actress with whom to do it!"

Charlotte looked at Pitt's face and saw the imagination take flight in him. Tamar was a woman a man might fall in love with, even passionately, but not a woman with whom he would have an affaire. She was the stuff of dreams, even of visions, not a pleasant pastime, a little laughter and sensuality away from the duties of marriage or the loneliness of a bachelor life. Charlotte could not imagine her as a comfortable woman, and she believed Pitt did not either.

"I do not leap to conclusions, Miss Macaulay." Pitt's voice cut across her thoughts. "Even when they seem on the firmest of ground."

A smile flashed across Tamar's face and vanished.

"And you, Mr. Fielding?" Pitt turned to Joshua. "Did Mr. Stafford come to see you about this case?"

"Yes, of course. I gathered from what he said that he was considering reopening it after all." He sighed heavily. "Now we have lost that chance. We have not managed to persuade anyone else to consider it at all."

"Did you see him alone, Mr. Fielding?"

"Yes. I imagine that there is no point in my telling you what happened, since there is no one to verify it." Joshua shrugged. "He simply asked me about the night Blaine was killed, and made me rehearse everything I know all over again. But he said he was off to see Devlin O'Neil— that was Blaine's friend, with whom he quarreled that evening—over money, I think."

"Did he have this with him?" Pitt pulled the silver flask out of his pocket and held it forward.

Joshua regarded it curiously. "Not that I saw, but then one doesn't usually carry such a thing where it is visible. Why? Is it poisoned?"

Tamar shrank a little into herself and looked at it with distaste.

"I don't know," Pitt replied, putting it away again. "Have you seen it before, Miss Macaulay?"

"No."

Pitt did not argue.

"Thank you. I expect whoever is in charge tomorrow will speak to you again. I'm sorry to have had to distress you this way."

Joshua shrugged gently, a smile crossing his face and disappearing.

Pitt bade them good-night and after the briefest exchange Charlotte, Pitt and Caroline took their leave. Outside the night was dark; the theater lights were dimmed now, only the ordinary street lamps like luminous pearls in a faint fog that was gathering in gauzy wraiths in the air. Carriage wheels hurried along the damp streets and hooves clattered sharply on the wet stone.

Had Stafford planned to reopen the case of murder for which Aaron Godman had been hanged? Was that why he had been killed? Tamar Macaulay wanted it reopened. Who wanted it kept closed—enough to murder?

Or was it something entirely different: a different person, a different fear—or hate?

Charlotte walked a little faster and linked her arm in Pitt's as he looked for a hansom to take them home.

2

MICAH DRUMMOND was in his office early in the morning. Since the case which had centered on Belgrave Square that summer, and produced so much horror and scandal, and for Drummond himself, knowledge that affected every part of his life, he was no longer happy with his own thoughts. Work was something of a relief, even though it offered reminders far too often of just what a tortuous web of obligations he had unknowingly entered when he accepted membership in the secret society of the Inner Circle.

Eleanor Byam was a different matter. The only way he could keep his mind from her was to sink it in the urgent and complicated problems of other people.

He was standing near the window in the thin autumn sunlight when Pitt knocked on the door.

"Come in," Drummond said hopefully. There was too little on his desk and what there was was stale. He had already read it and delegated it appropriately. Now all he could do was send for further reports every so often to keep him abreast of every new turn of events, which would be more interference than his officers deserved. "Come in!" he said again more sharply.

The door opened and Pitt stood in the entrance, his hair curling wildly, his jacket crooked and his cravat in imminent danger of coming undone completely. Drummond found him a remarkably reassuring sight, at once familiar and yet always on the brink of some surprise.

Drummond smiled. "Yes, Pitt?"

Pitt came in, closing the door behind him.

"I was at the theater last night." He put his hands in his pockets and stood in front of the desk, at anything but attention. In another man Drummond might have resented it, but he liked Pitt too much to wish to reaffirm their relative positions of authority.

"Oh yes." Drummond was surprised. It was not one of Pitt's regular habits.

"Invitation from my mother-in-law," Pitt elaborated. "Justice Samuel Stafford died in his box," he went on. "I saw him taken ill and went to offer any help I could." He pulled a silver hip flask out of his jacket pocket, a beautiful thing gleaming in the light.

Drummond looked at it, then at Pitt's face, waiting for the explanation.

Pitt put the flask on the green leather desk top.

"There's no medical report yet, of course, but it looked too much like opium poisoning to ignore the possibility. Justice Ignatius Livesey was there as well. He'd been in the next box and came to help too. Actually it was he who realized it might well be poison. He saw Stafford drink from the flask, so he took it from Stafford's pocket and gave it to me, for the medical examiner to look at."

"Samuel Stafford," Drummond said slowly. "He's an appeal court judge, isn't he." It was not a question, just an observation. "Poor man." He frowned. "Poison? Opium? Doesn't seem very likely."

Pitt lifted his shoulders and there was a rueful expression in his eyes.

"No, it doesn't, on the face of it," he agreed. "But I made a few enquiries into what he had done during the day, and some interesting things emerged. Do you remember the Blaine/Godman case, about five years ago?"

"Blaine/Godman?" Drummond came a little closer to the

31

desk. His face creased in thought, but apparently nothing came to his mind.

"A man crucified against a door, in Farriers' Lane," Pitt said.

"Oh!" Drummond winced. "Yes, of course I do. Fearful business, absolutely appalling! There was a terrible outcry. One of the most horrible cases I can remember." He looked at Pitt with a frown. "But what has Stafford's death in the theater last night got to do with Farriers' Lane? The man who did that was hanged at the time."

"Yes," Pitt said with anger and pity in his face. He hated hanging, whatever the offense. It only compounded one barbarity with another, and human judgment was far too often fallible, mistakes too easy, knowledge too little. "Stafford was one of the judges who denied Godman's appeal," he went on aloud. "His sister, the actress Tamar Macaulay, has been trying to reopen the case ever since then. She believes her brother was not guilty."

"Not unnatural," Drummond interrupted. "People find it very hard to accept that their relatives, even their friends, can be guilty of something so horrific. Surely she was on stage, wasn't she? She was hardly in a position to poison Justice Stafford's flask of—whatever it is—whiskey?"

"I've no idea!" Pitt picked it up and unscrewed the top, putting his nose to it delicately. "Yes—it's whiskey. Yes, she was on stage at the time he died. But she called on him earlier in the day, at his home." He screwed the top back on and set the flask on the desk again.

"Oh!" Drummond was surprised and concerned. The picture began to look darker. "But why would she kill Stafford? How could that possibly help her brother's cause? Or has she lost all sense of reason, and her wits as well?"

Pitt smiled. "I have no idea! I'm only telling you what happened last night, and handing over the flask to you, so you can give it to whoever is put in charge of the enquiry—if there is one."

"Mr. Samuel Stafford." Drummond smiled back, a charming expression that totally altered the gravity and somewhat ascetic cast of his face. "Justice of Her Majesty's

Court of Appeal. A most important person, indeed! A case worthy of your talents, Pitt! A delicate case, a most political one," he added. "It will require careful and tactful investigation, should it prove to be murder. I think you had better take care of it yourself—definitely. Yes—delegate whatever else you have on hand at the moment, and enquire into this." He picked up the flask from the desk and handed it back to Pitt, meeting his eyes with humor and challenge.

Pitt looked at him long and steadily, then reached out his hand and took the flask.

"Keep me informed," Drummond commanded. "If it is murder, we'd better deal with it pretty rapidly."

"We had better be right!" Pitt corrected fiercely. Then he smiled suddenly and widely, seeing Drummond's shadow of anxiety. "And diplomatic!" he added.

"Get out!" Drummond grinned, not because there was anything remotely amusing in the case, murder or not, but because quite unreasonably, he felt a lift of warmth inside himself, a reassertion that the odd, the eccentric, the unruly, the honest, that which would laugh and would pity, that which was essentially human, was infinitely more important than political expediency or social rules. Unbidden, Eleanor's face came to his mind, but with so much less pain than before, and none of the bleak hopelessness.

Pitt was surprised to have been given the case, although on reflection he should not have been. Drummond had been frank with him when Pitt had declined promotion because he did not want to sit behind a desk and tell other men how to do a job he was so eminently gifted for himself, and loved in spite of the relatively lower pay. An increase in salary would have meant so much. He would have taken it, for Charlotte's sake, and their children, and the difference it would have made to them, but it was Charlotte who had refused, knowing how much the work meant to him.

But from that time on Drummond had said he would give Pitt all the most delicate and political cases, a sort of lateral promotion, Drummond's way of rewarding him in spite of himself, and possibly also making the best use of his skills.

The medical examiner was a new man whom Pitt had not met before. When Pitt went into his laboratory he was standing behind a microscope at a huge marble-topped bench, an intense expression screwing up his face, bottles, retorts and vials all around him. He was huge, as tall as Pitt, and far heavier, but probably no more than thirty-five. His bright ginger hair stood out in a shock of tight little waves, and his beard looked like a fallen bird's nest.

"Got it!" he said with great enthusiasm. "Got it, by heaven! Come in and make yourself comfortable, whoever you are, and compose your soul in patience. I shall be with you in a moment." He spoke in a high voice with a soft Highland Scots accent, and never once did he take his eyes from his instrument.

It would have been churlish to be offended, and Pitt did as he was requested with good humor, taking the flask out of his pocket, ready to hand it over.

Several moments of silence passed by while Pitt stared around him at the chaotic wealth of jars, slides and bottles containing all manner of substances. Then the medical examiner looked up and smiled at Pitt.

"Yes?" he said cheerfully. "And what is it I can do for you, sir?"

"Inspector Pitt," Pitt introduced himself.

"Sutherland," the medical examiner responded. "I've heard of you. Should have recognized you—sorry. What is it? A murder?"

Pitt smiled. "For the moment, a flask. I'd like to know what is in it." He handed it over.

Sutherland took it and opened it up, holding it gingerly to his nose.

"Whiskey," he replied, looking at Pitt over the top of it. He sniffed again. "A very moderate malt—expensive, but still very moderate. I'll tell you what else, when I've had a look at it. What do you expect?"

"Perhaps opium?"

34

"Funny way to take it. Thought it was usually smoked. Not too difficult to get hold of."

"Don't think he took it intentionally," Pitt answered.

"Murder! Thought so. I'll let you know as soon as I do." He held up the flask and looked at it, reading the name engraved. "Samuel Stafford." His face sharpened. "Didn't he die last night? Heard the newsboys shouting something about it."

"Yes. Let me know as soon as you can."

"Most certainly. If it is opium, I'll know by tonight. If it's something else, or nothing, it'll take longer."

"The autopsy?" Pitt asked.

"It's the autopsy I'm talking about now," Sutherland replied quickly. "The whiskey'll only take a moment. Not complicated. Adulterate even a moderate whiskey and it's not hard to find."

"Good. I'll be back for it," Pitt said.

"If I'm not here, there is my home," Sutherland said vigorously. "I'll be there from about eight." And without adding anything further he resumed his study of the microscope. Pitt placed his card on the marble bench top, with the Bow Street station address printed on it, and set out to begin his investigation.

The first thing to determine was whether Stafford had intended to reopen the Blaine/Godman case or not. Surely if he had taken the time to go and see both Joshua Fielding and Devlin O'Neil, then he must at least have considered it. Would he have bothered to tell anyone other than Tamar herself if the matter must remain closed?

Or was Livesey right, and he intended only to prove once and for all that Godman was guilty and there could be no more question raised on the matter, or suggestions that somehow justice had miscarried? Constant doubts, however trivial or based in emotion, old loyalties and loves, still disturbed public confidence in justice and the administration of the law. When the law itself was not held in respect, then everyone suffered. It would be a natural and honorable thing for Stafford to do.

In seeking to establish Godman's guilt, and justify the law, even to Tamar herself, had he unwittingly stumbled on some irregularity? Had he frightened someone guilty of— what? Another crime? A private sin? A complicity of some nature?

The place to begin, regrettable as it was, had to be with the widow. Accordingly he strode along the pavement past elegant ladies on their way to see dressmakers and milliners, servants on errands, petty clerks and tradesmen about their business. It was a brisk, chilly morning and the streets were clattering with noise of horses' hooves, carriage wheels, shouts of drivers and costermongers, crossing sweepers, newsboys, running patterers singing the ballads of scandal and folk drama.

He hailed a hansom and gave the Staffords' home address in Bruton Street, off Berkeley Square, which he had obtained from the desk sergeant in Bow Street. He sat back as the cab bowled west along Long Acre, and began to contemplate the questions to which he must find answers.

It was an unpleasant thought that if the judge's death had nothing to do with the Blaine/Godman case, then since Stafford was not presently involved in any other plea, it might prove to be a personal matter, a private vengeance or fear, very probably to do with his family—his widow— perhaps money.

Tomorrow he would know more, at least if Sutherland found opium in the body and in the flask. But if Stafford had in fact died of some disease no one else had been aware of, if his private physician could offer some explanation, then he could happily forget the whole matter. But it was a hope that hovered beyond the edge of his mind, not a solution he expected.

The Staffords' house was easy to find. There were dark wreaths hung on the door and black crepes over the drawn curtains on the windows. A pale-faced maid in a hat and coat came up the areaway steps and set out along the footpath on some task, and a footman with a black armband carried a coal scuttle inside and closed the door. It was a house conspicuously in mourning.

Pitt alighted, paid the cabby, and went to the front door.

"Yes sir?" the answering parlormaid asked dubiously. She regarded Pitt with disfavor. He looked like a peddler at first glance, except that he carried nothing to sell. But there was a confidence in his manner, even an arrogance, which belied any attempt to ingratiate. She was flustered and overwhelmed with the drama of events. The housemaids were all in tears, the cook had fainted twice, the butler was more than a trifle maudlin, after a long time in his own pantry with the cellar keys, and Mr. Stafford's valet looked as if he had seen a ghost.

"I am sorry to disturb Mrs. Stafford at such a time," Pitt said with all the charm he could muster, which was considerable. "But I require to ask her a few questions about events last night, in order that everything may be settled as quickly and decently as possible. Will you please ask her if she will see me." He fished in his pocket and presented her with one of his cards, an indulgence which had rewarded him many times.

The maid took it, reading it for his occupation and not finding it. She put it on the silver tray used for such purposes and told him to wait while she delivered his enquiry.

He was not long in the dim hallway with its hastily placed crepes before the maid returned to conduct him to the room towards the back of the house where Juniper Stafford received him. It was expensively decorated in warm colors, with stenciled patterns around the doors lending an individual touch. A carved chaise longue had a woven rug draped on it in reds and plums, and no one had changed the bowl of late chrysanthemums on the polished table.

Juniper looked very tired this morning, and shocked, as if the realization of her husband's death was beginning to come to her, with all the changes in her life that it would mean. In the harsher daylight her skin looked papery and the tiny natural blemishes more pronounced, but she was still a handsome woman with excellent features and very fine dark eyes. Today she was dressed in unrelieved black, but the excellence of the cut, the perfect drape of the fabrics across the hips and the swath of the bustle made it a garment of fashion, and most becoming.

"Good morning, Mrs. Stafford," Pitt said formally. "I am truly sorry to disturb you again so soon, but there were questions I could not ask you last night."

"Of course," she said quickly. "I understand, Mr. Pitt. You do not need to explain to me. I have been a judge's wife long enough to appreciate the necessities of the law. Surely they have not done the . . ." She hesitated to use the word, it was so ugly.

"No, not yet." He saved her from having to say "autopsy." "I hope for it this evening. But in the meantime I should like to confirm for myself what Mr. Stafford's purpose was in going to see Mr. O'Neil and Mr. Fielding." He pulled a rueful face. "I am in some confusion as to whether he did intend to reopen the Blaine/Godman case, or simply to find further evidence to convince Miss Macaulay of the futility of her crusade."

"You are in charge of the matter, after all?" she asked, still standing, one hand resting on the back of the tapestried chair.

"I was given it this morning."

"I am glad. It would have been harder to face someone I did not know."

It was a delicate compliment and he accepted it as such, thanking her by expression rather than words.

She walked over towards the fire and the mantel shelf, above which was a particularly fine Dutch oil painting of cows in an autumn field, the sky warm with golden light behind them. She looked at it for a moment or two before turning to face him.

"What can I tell you, Mr. Pitt? He did not confide his intentions to me, but I assumed from what he did say that he had found some grounds on which to re-enquire into the case. If indeed he was . . . killed"—she swallowed, finding the word difficult—"then I have to assume it had some connection with that. It was a hideous case—bestial—blasphemous. There was terrible public outcry at the time."

She shivered and her lips tightened at the memory. "You must remember it. It was in all the newspapers, I am told."

"Who was Kingsley Blaine?" he asked. He could still recall the sense of horror he had felt when she had spoken of Farriers' Lane, but very little else came back to him, no details, no people behind the names.

"A fairly ordinary young man of good enough family," she replied, standing close to the mantel and staring beyond Pitt towards the window. The curtains were drawn closed now because of the mourning of the house. "Money, of course, but not of the aristocracy. He and his friend, Devlin O'Neil, went to the theater that night. Some say they had a difference of opinion, but it proved later to be of no importance. It was only money, a small debt or something. Nothing very large." She looked at the garnet ring on her finger and turned it slowly in the light.

"But Mr. O'Neil was suspected for a while?" Pitt asked.

"Only as a matter of course, I think," she replied.

"But Mr. Stafford went to see him yesterday?"

"Yes. I don't know why. Perhaps he thought he might know something. After all, he was there that evening."

"How did Aaron Godman come into the story?"

She let her hands fall and stared towards the window again, as if she could see through the curtains to the garden and the street beyond.

"He was an actor. He was playing in the theater that night. They say he was gifted." Her voice altered very slightly but it was an expression he could not gauge. "Blaine was having an affaire with Tamar Macaulay, and he stayed late backstage. As he was leaving someone handed him a note asking him to go and meet O'Neil at some gambling club. He never got there, because as he was passing through Farriers' Lane, on the way, he was murdered, and crucified to the door in the stable yard—with farrier's nails." She shuddered and swallowed as though there were an obstruction in her throat. "They said he was pierced in the side, as Our Lord was," she went on very quietly indeed. "One of the newspapers said that they had made a crown of old nails and placed it on his head."

"I recall it now," Pitt confessed. "But I had forgotten that particular horror."

She spoke very quietly, her voice subdued, full of fear, and close, with a drawing in of her body as if the emotion were still as sharp in her as it must have been five years ago.

"It was very ugly, Mr. Pitt. It was as if something had come out of a nightmare and taken living form. Everyone I know was just as appalled as we were." Unconsciously she included her husband. "Until Godman was hanged, we could think of little else. It intruded into everything like a darkness, as if it could come out of Farriers' Lane and that hideous yard, and slash and crucify us all!" She shuddered as though even this room were somehow not safe.

"It is finished, Mrs. Stafford," Pitt said gently. "There is no need to be concerned anymore, or to let it disturb you."

"Is it?" She swung around, facing him. Her dark eyes were wide, still full of fear, and her voice had a hard, frightened edge to it. "Do you think so? Isn't that why Samuel was killed?"

"I don't know," he confessed. "Mr. Livesey seems to think that Mr. Stafford was quite satisfied that the verdict was correct. He simply wanted to find further proof of it so even Tamar Macaulay would be convinced and let it rest. In the public good."

She stood very still, her body stiff under its black gown.

"Then who killed Samuel?" she said quietly. "And for heaven's sake, why? Nothing else makes any sense. And it was immediately after that woman came here, and he went to speak to O'Neil and Joshua Fielding about the evidence. Do you—do you think maybe one of them really killed Kingsley Blaine, and they are afraid Samuel knew something about it—and that he was going to prove it?"

"It is possible," he conceded. "Mrs. Stafford, can you think of anything he may have said which would help us to find out what he knew? Even what he intended, would help."

She was silent for several moments, her face heavy with concentration.

40

Pitt waited.

"He seemed to feel it was extremely urgent," she said finally, a deep line of anxiety between her brows. "He would not have gone to Devlin O'Neil again, someone so close to the murdered man's family, and a personal friend, unless he felt he had new information or evidence. I—I just know, from his manner, that he had learned something." She stared at him with fierce concentration. "It is only natural that he did not discuss it with me. It would have been improper. And of course I did not know the details anyway. All I knew was what was public knowledge. Everyone was talking about it. One could not bump into a friend or acquaintance anywhere, even at the opera or the dinner table, without it creeping into the conversation after a few moments. There was terrible anger everywhere, Mr. Pitt. It was not an ordinary crime."

"No." Pitt thought of the dark air of fear and prejudice which would blow from the bloodstained Farriers' Lane, even into the withdrawing rooms of London and the discreet, plush lined gentlemen's clubs with a clink of crystal and the aroma of cigar smoke.

"It wasn't, I assure you!" There was an urgency in her now, as if she thought he doubted her. "I have never known such a public fury over a crime—other than the Whitechapel murders, of course. And even so, there was an element of blasphemy in this which outraged people in quite a different way. Even gentle and pious people could not wait for him to be hanged."

"Except Tamar Macaulay," he observed.

She winced. "It is an abominable thought that she may have been right, is it not?"

"Indeed!" he said with a sudden surge of feeling. "In many ways far worse than the original crime."

She looked uncomprehending.

"The murder of Kingsley Blaine was the murder of one man," he explained with a bitter smile. "The murder, if you like, of Aaron Godman was the slow, judicial passion incurred by the fear and rage, and misjudgment, of a nation and what purports to be the justice system it practices. To

41

have criminals is a sad fact of humanity. To have laws which, when tested to their limit, exact an irretrievable punishment from an innocent person, in order to assuage our own fears, is a tragedy of a far greater order. We all consented to it; we are all tainted."

She looked very pale, her eyes hollow, skin tight on her throat.

"Mr. Pitt, that is—that is simply dreadful! Poor Samuel; if he feared that, no wonder he was so disturbed."

"He was disturbed?"

"Oh yes, he has been anxious about the case for some time." She looked down at the rich carpet. "Of course I was not sure to begin with whether it was simply that he was afraid Miss Macaulay was going to revive the subject in the public mind again and try to bring the law into disrepute. And of course that would have caused him great concern." She met Pitt's eyes. "He loved the law. He had given most of his life to it, and he held it in reverence above all things. It was like a religion to him."

He hesitated; the next thought that came to the edge of his mind was difficult to put to her without being offensive.

She was staring at him, waiting for his response, her eyes still haunted by fear.

"Mrs. Stafford," he began awkwardly, "I hardly know how to ask you, and I do not wish to be insulting, but—but is it possible he—he intended to protect the reputation of the law—in people's eyes . . ." He stopped.

"No, Mr. Pitt," she said quietly. "You did not know Samuel, or you would not need to ask. He was a man of total integrity. If he had further evidence that convinced him Aaron Godman might not have been guilty, he would have made it public, whatever the risk to the reputation of the law, or of any individual barrister or the original trial judge, or indeed to himself. But if he had such evidence, he would surely already have made it known. I think perhaps he had only a suspicion, and now he is—gone—we may never know what it was."

"Except by retracing his steps," Pitt replied. "And if it is necessary, then I shall do that."

"Thank you, Mr. Pitt." She forced herself to smile. "You have been most considerate, and I have every faith you will handle the whole matter in the best way possible."

"I will certainly try," he replied, conscious already that his findings might be far from what she could wish or foresee. It would not be easy to learn what Samuel Stafford had discovered so long after the event, and which had caused someone such terror they had again resorted to murder. He looked at her handsome face with its dark brows and well-proportioned bones, and saw the calmness in her eyes for the first time since he had seen her in her theater box watching the stage, before Stafford was taken ill. He felt guilty, because she placed a trust in him he doubted he would be able to honor.

He bade her good-bye with haste, because it embarrassed him, and after a brisk walk, took a hansom cab east again to the chambers of Adolphus Pryce, Q.C. They were in one of the larger Inns of Court, close by the Old Bailey, and the oak-paneled office was bustling with clerks and juniors with inky fingers and grave expressions. An elderly gentleman with white whiskers and a portentous air came up to him, peering at him over the top of his gold-rimmed pince-nez.

"And what may we do for you, sir?" he enquired. "Mr. er . . . ?"

"Pitt—Inspector Thomas Pitt, of the Bow Street station," Pitt supplied. "I am here in connection with the death last night of Mr. Justice Stafford."

"Terrible news." The clerk shook his head. "Very sudden indeed. We had not even heard the poor gentleman was ailing. Such a shock! And in the theater. Not the most salubrious place from which to depart this vale of tears, dear me, no. Still, what cannot be changed must be endured the best we can. Most unfortunate. But . . ." He coughed dryly. "In what way does that involve these chambers? Mr. Stafford was an appeal court judge, not a barrister. And we have no case presently before him, of that I am quite sure; it is my business to know."

Pitt changed his mind about his approach.

"But you have had in the past, sir?"

The clerk's white eyebrows rose. "But of course. We have tried cases before most of the justices of the bench, both in the Old Bailey and in appeal. So, I imagine, has every other reputable chambers in London."

"I have in mind the case of Aaron Godman."

Suddenly there was a hush as a dozen quill pens stopped moving and a junior with a ledger in his hands stood motionless.

"Aaron Godman?" The clerk repeated the name. "Aaron Godman! Oh dear, that is some time ago now, at least five years. But you are perfectly correct, of course. Our Mr. Pryce prosecuted that one, and secured a conviction. It went to appeal, I believe before Mr. Stafford, among others. There are usually five judges of appeal, but you will know that."

The junior with the ledger continued his journey and the pens began to move again, but there was a curious air of listening in the room although no one turned or looked at Pitt.

"Do you by any chance recall who they were?" he asked.

"Not by chance, sir, by memory," the clerk replied. "Mr. Stafford himself, Mr. Ignatius Livesey, Mr. Morley Sadler, Mr. Edgar Boothroyd and Mr. Granville Oswyn. Yes, that is correct. I believe Mr. Sadler has retired from the bench now, and I heard Mr. Boothroyd had moved to the Chancery division. Surely the case is no longer of any interest? As I recall, it was denied at appeal. There really were no grounds for opening up the matter again, none at all. Dear me, no. The trial was conducted with perfect propriety, and there was most certainly no new evidence."

"You are speaking of the appeal?"

"Of course. What else?"

"I had heard that Mr. Stafford was still interested in the matter, and had interviewed several of the principal witnesses again in the last few days."

Again the writing stopped and there was a prickly silence.

"Indeed? I had not heard that!" The clerk looked quite

taken aback. "I cannot imagine what that would mean. However, it did not concern these chambers, Mr.—er . . . Mr. Pitt, you say? Quite so—Mr. Pitt. We prosecuted the case, we did not defend. That, as I recall, was Mr. Barton James, of Finnegan, James and Mulhare, of Fetter Lane." He frowned. "Although it is most odd that Mr. Stafford should be enquiring in the matter. If indeed there is some new evidence come to light, I would have thought Mr. James should take it up—if it is of any importance?"

"Miss Macaulay, Godman's sister, appealed personally to Mr. Stafford," Pitt explained.

"Oh dear, yes indeed. A most tenacious young woman— most misguided." The clerk shook his head. "Unfortunate. An actress person, I believe. Most unfortunate. Well, sir, what is it that we may do for you?"

"May I see Mr. Pryce, if he is available? He was at the theater yesterday evening, and Mr. Stafford also called upon him earlier in the day. He may be able to give us some information which will throw further light upon Mr. Stafford's death."

"Indeed. He was a personal friend of Mr. and Mrs. Stafford; possibly Mr. Stafford confided some concern for his health. He has a client with him at the moment, but I do not believe he will be long. If you care to take a seat, sir, I will inform him that you are here." And with that he bowed very slightly, a stiff gesture, rather like a black crow that was about to peck and changed its mind. Pitt watched him walk away between the desks and files and high-backed stools where young men sat bent over books, scribbling industriously. Not one of them looked up as he passed.

It was over a quarter of an hour before the clerk returned to say that Mr. Pryce was free now, and conducted Pitt to his heavily ornate office, where carved oak chests and bookcases held a library of law books, and the mellow gleam of polished wood reflected the warmth of the fire. Two well-curtained windows looked out onto a small shaded courtyard. The single tree was already bright with autumn colors and the grass was sorely in need of clipping. Sunlight fell across a very formal desk, leather inlaid and

45

furnished with onyx and crystal inkwells, and a stand for pen, seals, knife, tapers and sand. A dossier, tied in ribbon, still sat on one polished corner of the wood.

Adolphus Pryce looked agitated. He was extremely fashionably dressed in black frock coat, pin-striped trousers and exquisitely cut waistcoat. He had a natural grace and a posture which made his clothes look even more expensive than they probably were.

"Good afternoon, Mr. Pitt," he said with an attempt at a smile, but it died on his lips almost before it was born. He looked as if he had slept little. "Withers tells me you have come about poor Stafford. I am not sure what else I can tell you, but of course I am more than happy to try. Please—be seated." He waved his hand towards the large green leather upholstered chair near Pitt.

Pitt accepted, leaning back and crossing his legs as if he intended to remain for some time. He saw the look of concern deepen in Pryce's face as he too sat down.

"Mr. Stafford came to see you yesterday," Pitt began, not sure how best to draw the information he wanted, indeed not sure if Pryce possessed it. "Can you tell me what that concerned? I realize you cannot break confidence with a client, but Mr. Stafford himself is dead, and the Godman case is in the public domain."

"Of course," Pryce leaned back a little and placed his fingertips together thoughtfully. "Actually he came entirely about the Godman case. Of course we exchanged a few pleasantries." His discomfort returned for a moment. "We—we have known each other for some time. But his reason for calling was his concern, indeed his intention to act, with regard to that case."

"To act? He told you so?"

"Yes—yes, indeed." Pryce stared at Pitt very fixedly. He was a man of considerable charm and poise, aristocratic features and sufficient individuality to remain unmistakable in the memory.

"To reopen the appeal?" Pitt pressed. "Upon what grounds?"

"Ah—that he did not say, at least not specifically."

"Why did he come to you, Mr. Pryce? What did he wish you to do?"

"Nothing. Oh, nothing at all." Pryce lifted his shoulders very slightly. "It was really something of a courtesy, since I had been the original prosecuting counsel. And I suppose he may have wondered if I had had any doubts myself."

"If he intended to reopen the appeal, Mr. Pryce, he must either have found some breach of correct conduct in the original trial or else some new evidence, surely? Or there would be no grounds for raising the matter yet again."

"Quite. Quite so. And I assure you the original trial was perfectly properly conducted. The judge was Mr. Thelonius Quade, a man of the utmost integrity, and more than sufficient skill to not make an error by mischance." He sighed. "It seems therefore an inevitable conclusion that Mr. Stafford had found some new evidence. He did intimate to me that it had to do with the medical testimony at the original trial, but he did not say what. He also implied that there was something else he felt was unresolved, but he did not elaborate."

"Medical evidence from the autopsy on Blaine?"

"I presume so." Pryce's eyebrows shot up. "But I suppose it is possible he meant some examination of Godman, although what that could have to do with it, I have no idea."

Pitt was surprised. "What medical evidence was there to do with Godman?"

"Oh—most disturbing. He was in a very poor shape when he came to trial. Several most unpleasant bruises and lacerations about the face and shoulders, and a serious limp."

"A fight?" Pitt was startled. No one had suggested self-defense; it had not even occurred to him. "Did Barton James not mention it during the trial?"

"Not at all. The defense put forward was that of not guilty—that it was not Godman but another person, or persons, unknown. There was not the slightest suggestion that Blaine and Godman fought and Blaine died as a result of it." His face tightened with revulsion. "And really, Mr. Pitt, it would be hard to countenance why Godman should have nailed the wretched man to the stable door. That is macabre—quite shocking! I think any jury in the land would find that indefensible, regardless of any provocation whatsoever!"

"Is that what you would have done, had you been defending him instead of prosecuting, Mr. Pryce?" Pitt asked. "Would you have claimed it was not your client at all, and kept silent about any struggle?"

Pryce chewed his top lip thoughtfully. "I find it hard to say, Mr. Pitt. I think on the whole I would have used self-defense; it would have had a better chance than not guilty. Godman was seen in the area very close to the time of the murder. He was identified by a flower seller, and he did not deny having been there; he simply said it was half an hour earlier than in fact it was. Others actually saw him coming out of the entrance of Farriers' Lane, what must have been moments after the murder, and with blood on his clothes."

"And yet Mr. Barton James chose to put forward a complete denial!" Pitt was astounded. It was incomprehensible. "Did Mr. Stafford wish to reopen the case on grounds of incompetence of the original defending counsel? Surely, one can hardly rectify the case now. The only people who could possibly tell us if there was a fight, and what happened, are Blaine and Godman, and they are both dead."

"Precisely," Pryce agreed ruefully. "I am afraid it is all speculation, and I can think of no way in which it will ever be anything more."

"And yet you say Mr. Stafford seemed to feel there was some purpose in pursuing it," Pitt pointed out. "By the way, why was Godman supposed to have killed Blaine? What motive had he?"

"Oh—sordid." Pryce wrinkled his brow very slightly. "He was a Jew, you know, as naturally was his sister. Blaine was having an affaire with her, or so it was alleged. He was unquestionably pursuing her with some vigor, and on that very night had given her a necklace of considerable value which his mother-in-law had owned." His face shadowed. "A very foolish thing to do, and in execrable taste. Well, Godman profoundly resented Blaine's attentions to his sister, being aware that of course he had no intention whatever of marrying her—quite apart from the fact that she was a Jewess, and an actress, Blaine himself was already married."

"And Godman felt so violently on his sister's behalf?" Pitt was surprised. Having met Tamar Macaulay, he found it hard to picture her as a romantic victim, in need of her brother's protection. But then love can make fools of even the most forthright people, and strength of character or purpose was no protection whatever; indeed sometimes the most powerful could be the most deeply hurt.

"Quite." Pryce nodded. "It was a matter of family honor, and religious and racial honor as well. Just as we would be appalled if one of our daughters were to become involved with a Jew, so it seems they are equally horrified if one of theirs becomes involved with a gentile." He tipped his chair a little farther back. "I suppose with a little imagination we might see their point of view. Anyway, that is why Godman killed Blaine—and he certainly would not be the first one to have knifed the seducer of his sister."

"No," Pitt agreed. "Not by a long, long way. But that was not used as a defense, was it?"

Pryce smiled. "I doubt society would have accepted Miss Macaulay's virtue as adequate cause to justify murder, Mr. Pitt. I regret that would have been laughed out of court."

"Is her reputation so stained?"

"Not at all. It is the reputation of actresses in general from which she would suffer. And I do not think a gentile jury would view with any kindness the excuse that he did not wish her to accept the favors of a gentile lover, as being tainting to her pure Jewish blood." He pulled a sour face. "If every man who had courted a beautiful Jewess were to be crucified, we should need more crosses than they had in Rome—and the existence of our forests would be in jeopardy!"

"Yes." Pitt pushed his hands into his pockets. "Altogether an extremely ugly case, and calling for no public sympathy at all. I am surprised that Miss Macaulay rose above the storm and still commands an audience in the theater."

Pryce shrugged. "I think she had a thin time of it for a while. But once Godman was hanged—and no one ever claimed she had had any part in it—then the public was satisfied, and chose to forgive her." He reached forward absently and his long fingers touched the smooth surface of the jasper inkstand. "And perversely, there were many who secretly admired her loyalty to her brother, even while at the very same moment they lusted to hang him from the highest gibbet in the land. Had she turned on him, they would have branded her a traitor." He let go of the stand. "It seemed she really did believe him innocent, and the public chose to believe her equally innocent of anything more than falling in love with a man who would never have married her."

"She lost her lover and her brother in one act," Pitt said grimly.

"It would seem so," Pryce agreed.

"But you said she accepted a valuable piece of jewelry from him—a family heirloom?"

"She says she wore it that evening, for supper, and then insisted he keep it."

"And did he keep it?" Pitt asked.

Pryce looked surprised. "I have no idea. It was not found on his body. Perhaps Miss Macaulay disposed of it, to lend truth to her story. To the best of my knowledge it has never been seen since." His face quickened with hope. "Perhaps Stafford had learned something about that. That would make far more sense than some purely medical evidence about Godman which can never be verified. Indeed, that is quite a viable idea."

"Who knew about the necklace?" Pitt asked, his mind racing over possibilities, new threads that Stafford might have followed till he came close to a truth as yet unguessed, and frightened someone into murder. "It cannot have been long from the time he gave it to her until Godman left the theater."

"No—it was not," Pryce agreed quickly. "It was testified

50

to by Miss Macaulay's dresser, Primrose Walker. She saw Blaine give it to her, and say that it had been in his family for years; in fact it had belonged to his mother-in-law. Miss Macaulay says that is why she gave it back to him, but unfortunately for her, there is no evidence to support that. Unless, of course, Stafford found something."

"Would he not have told you?"

"Not necessarily. I was prosecuting counsel, Mr. Pitt, not defense. He may well have intended to tell Barton James as soon as he was certain of his own facts. Indeed he did mention that he intended to call upon James in the very near future." He looked at Pitt with gravity, but there was a growing keenness in his face. "That would explain a great deal, which otherwise seems very odd." He stopped, as if he feared he might have said too much, and waited for Pitt's reply.

"Did the police not remark the absence of the necklace at the time?" Pitt questioned, still turning over the facts in his mind.

"No, not that I recall," Pryce said slowly. "At least they may have done so, but it did not appear in evidence in the trial. Miss Macaulay claimed that she returned it to Blaine, and I think they merely disbelieved her, assuming either that she kept it—it was quite valuable—or that she said that in order to help her brother's defense."

"Did it?"

Pryce shrugged ruefully. "Not in the slightest. As I said, she was not believed. Perhaps we owe her an apology." His face reflected regret, even a touch of pain. "I am afraid I implied that she was of dubious reputation in that regard, and that she would say anything to try to cast doubt on her brother's guilt. Not an unreasonable assumption in the circumstances, but perhaps not true, for all that." He winced. "It is a very ugly thought, Mr. Pitt, that one may have used one's skill to hang an innocent man. The argument that it is one's profession is not always satisfying."

Pitt felt an instinctive sympathy with him, and wounding memories of his own came sharply to mind. He liked

Pryce, and yet there was something that disturbed him, something very faint, too amorphous to name.

"I understand," he said aloud. "I face the same."

"Of course. Of course," Pryce agreed. "I wish I could tell you more, but that is all I know. I doubt Mr. Stafford knew any more, or he would surely have mentioned it." He stopped, a shadow in his eyes, for all the easy composure of his bearing. "I—eh—I'm sorry. He was a personal acquaintance."

"I appreciate your feelings." Pitt spoke because the situation seemed to require it. He did not often feel himself awkward or at a loss for words. He had faced others' bereavements so often that, although he had never ceased to care, he had learned what to say. There was something in Pryce that confused him, as, on reflection, there was in Juniper Stafford. Perhaps it was no more than a very natural eagerness to have the solution found as soon as possible, scandal avoided, ugly or stupid speculation, so that people might remember Stafford with honor and affection, and the hideous fact of murder could recede into something apart, a tragedy to be dealt with by the law.

"Thank you for your time, Mr. Pryce." Pitt rose to his feet. "You have been most generous, and given me much to consider. There were undoubtedly aspects of the Blaine/Godman case that Mr. Stafford would have been justified in pursuing, and evidence to suggest that was what he intended. If the medical examiner's report requires it, I shall follow them myself."

Pryce rose also, offering his hand.

"Not at all. Please let me know if I can be of any further service, if you need to know anything more about the original case."

"Of course. Thank you."

Pryce saw him to the door, opening it for him, and the dutiful clerk conducted him through the office to the street.

However, when Pitt went to see Mr. Justice Livesey in his chambers in the early afternoon, he met with a totally different response. Livesey received him graciously; indeed he seemed to have been expecting him. His rooms were very spacious, full of autumn sunlight reflecting on polished, inlaid furniture, a bureau of exquisite marquetry in tropical woods, wine-colored leather upholstered chairs, two vases of chrysanthemums. Two magnificent bronzes stood on a low bookcase and a marble mounted clock sat on the mantel.

"I am afraid that is absolute nonsense," Livesey said with a smile in answer to Pitt's first remarks on the case. He leaned back in his great chair and regarded Pitt tolerantly. "Stafford was an intelligent and deeply responsible man. He was learned in the law, and he understood his duty towards it. A judge, particularly a judge of appeal, has a uniquely important position, Mr. Pitt." His face was composed in an expression of quiet, profound confidence. "We are the last resort of the convicted to obtain mercy, or redress of a harsh or mistaken judgment. Similarly we are the final voice of the people in sealing a verdict forever. It is a monumental responsibility and we cannot afford error. Stafford was aware of that, as we all are."

He looked at Pitt with a growing smile touching his mouth. "I don't know why people say that without the law we would be no better than savages. We would be far worse. Savages have laws, Mr. Pitt—usually very strict laws. Even they understand that no society can function without them. Without law we have anarchy, we have the devil stalking the earth, picking us off one by one, the weak and strong alike." He pursed his lips. "We are all vulnerable at times. It is not only justice; in the end it is survival itself."

His steady eyes did not waver from Pitt's face. "Without law, who will protect the mother and child who are tomorrow's strength? Who will protect the geniuses of the mind, the inventor, the artist who enriches the world but has not the power of money or physical ability to defend himself? Who will protect the wise who are old, and might fall victim to the powerful and foolish? Indeed who will protect the strong from themselves?"

"I have served the law all my adult life, Mr. Livesey,"

53

Pitt replied, meeting his gaze. "You have no need to persuade me of its importance. Nor do I doubt Mr. Stafford's service to it."

"I am sorry," Livesey apologized. "I have not explained myself well. You are unfamiliar with the Godman case, which was unusually ugly. If you knew it as well as I, you would also be quite certain that it was dealt with justly and correctly at the time." He shifted his massive weight a little in his chair. "There was no flaw in the verdict, and Stafford knew that as well as the rest of us. He was disturbed because Tamar Macaulay would not let the matter drop." His face darkened. "A very foolish woman, unfortunately. Obsessed with the idea that her brother was not guilty, when it was plain to everyone else that he was. Indeed there was no other serious suspect."

"Not the friend . . ." Pitt had to stop to recollect his name. "O'Neil? Did he not quarrel with Blaine that evening?"

"Devlin O'Neil?" Livesey's eyes widened; they were an unusually clear blue for a man of his years. "Certainly they had a disagreement, but *quarrel* is too large a word for it. There was a difference over who had won or lost a trivial wager." He waved a heavy, powerful hand, dismissing it. "The sum involved was only a few pounds, which either of them could well afford. It was not an issue over which a man murders his friend."

"How do you know?" Pitt asked, equally pleasantly.

"I was one of the judges of appeal," Livesey said with a slight frown. "Naturally I studied the evidence of the trial very closely." Pitt's question perplexed him; the answer seemed so obvious.

Pitt smiled patiently. "I appreciate that, Mr. Livesey. I meant whose testimony do we have for it? O'Neil's?"

"Of course."

"Not proof of a great deal."

A shadow of darkness and surprise crossed Livesey's face. Obviously he had not considered it in that light.

"There was no cause to doubt him," he said with a trace of irritation. "The difference of opinion was observed by

54

others, and told to the police when they investigated the murder. O'Neil was asked to explain it, which he did—to everyone's satisfaction, except, apparently, yours."

"Or possibly Mr. Stafford's; he wished to see O'Neil again."

"That does not mean that he doubted him, Mr. Pitt." He lifted his broad shoulders a little. "As I have already said to you, Stafford had no intention whatever of reopening the Blaine/Godman case. There are no grounds to question any part of it. The conduct of the original trial was exemplary, and there is no new evidence whatever." He smiled, drumming his fingers on the leather desk top. "Stafford had no new evidence. He spoke to me yesterday himself. His intention was to prove Godman's guilt yet again, beyond even Tamar Macaulay's ability to question." He looked at Pitt fixedly. "It is for everyone's benefit, even Miss Macaulay herself, that she should at last accept the truth and allow herself to turn her attention to her own life, her career, or whatever she counts of value. For the rest of us, we should stop doubting the law and calling into question its efficacy or integrity."

"He told you this?" Pitt asked, uncertainty in his mind, weighing what Juniper Stafford had said, and Pryce. "As late as yesterday?"

"Not entirely yesterday," Livesey said patiently. "Over a period of time, and yesterday he did not change any part of it. He reaffirmed it, both by what he said and what he omitted to say. There was no change in his mind, and he certainly had discovered nothing new."

"I see." Pitt spoke only to acknowledge that he had heard. In truth, he did not see at all. Pryce had seemed so certain Stafford intended to reopen the case, and why should he have any interest in wishing Pitt to believe that, were it not true? Pryce had prosecuted, and seemed to feel a certain responsibility for the conviction. He would not want it overturned now.

And yet if Stafford had had no intention of reopening the case, why should anyone kill him?

Perhaps they had not, and it was some obscure disease

with poisonlike symptoms, and either he was unaware of it himself or he had chosen not to tell his wife, possibly not realizing how serious it was.

Livesey seemed to seize Pitt's thoughts. The judge's face was grave, all the impatience washed away as if it had been trivial, a momentary and shallow thing. Now he was returned to reality, which concerned him.

"If he was not reopening the case, why should anyone kill him?" Livesey said quietly. "A justified question, Mr. Pitt. He was not reopening the case, and even if he were, there is no one with anything to fear from it, except Tamar Macaulay herself, because it would have reawakened the public to her brother's disgrace and raised the whole matter in people's minds again. She cannot wish that, when there is no hope of exoneration." He smiled without humor or pleasure, only an awareness of the loss and wasted tears.

"I think the poor woman has been so steeped in her own crusade for these many years it has gained its own impetus, apart from any reality. She has lost sight of the truth of the case," he continued. "She is no longer thinking of evidence, only of her own desire to vindicate her brother. Love, even family love, can be very blind. We so easily see only what we wish to, and with the person absent, as happens with the dead, there is nothing to remind us of reality." His lips tightened. "The vision consumes. It has become like a religion with her, so important to her she cannot let go. She is a little intoxicated with it. It has taken the place of husband and child with her. It is really very tragic."

Pitt had seen such obsession before. It was not impossible to believe. But it did not answer the question of who had killed Stafford, if he had been killed.

"Do you think Stafford told her as much?" he asked, looking up at Livesey.

"And she killed him in rage because he had disappointed her?" Livesey bit his lip, frowning. "It strains the credulity, to be candid. She is obsessed, certainly, but I do not think she is so far unbalanced as to do that. It would have to be proved beyond question before I could accept it."

"Then what?" Pitt asked. "Mrs. Stafford said he was

presently involved in no other appeal. Revenge for some old matter?"

"On a judge of appeal?" Livesey shrugged. "Unlikely—in the extreme. I have heard convicted men make threats against witnesses, the police officer who arrested them, against prosecuting counsel or their own defense counsel, if they believed them inadequate—even against the trial judge, and once against the jury—but never against the judges of appeal! And there are at least five of us on any case. It seems farfetched, Mr. Pitt."

"Then who?"

Livesey's face darkened.

"I regret to say this, Mr. Pitt, but I have no alternative. It would seem there is little left but his personal life. Most murders are committed either in the course of a robbery or they are domestic, as I am sure you are already aware."

Pitt knew it.

"What reason would Mrs. Stafford have for wishing her husband dead?" he asked, watching Livesey's face.

Livesey raised his eyes from the desk and sighed heavily.

"I dislike intensely having to repeat this. It is shabby and an unworthy thing to say of a colleague or his family. But Mrs. Stafford's relationship with Mr. Adolphus Pryce is a great deal closer than it would at first appear."

"Improperly so?" For an instant Pitt was surprised, then small memories came back to his mind: a glance, a quick color in the face, an eagerness, an odd awkward moment, self-consciousness where there was no understandable cause.

"I regret to say it—but yes," Livesey confessed, his eyes on Pitt's face. "I had not thought it more than a rash affaire, a season's lust which would wear itself out as such passions often do. But perhaps it is deeper than that. I do not envy you, Mr. Pitt, but I fear you may be driven to investigating such a possibility."

It answered many questions, unpleasant as it was.

Livesey was watching him.

"I see you have thought of that also," he observed. "If Adolphus Pryce tried to convince you that Stafford was reopening the Blaine/Godman case, you may readily appreciate why. Naturally both he and Mrs. Stafford would prefer you to believe it was some guilty and fearful party to that case who had committed the crime of murdering her husband, rather than have you investigate either of them."

"Of course." Pitt felt unreasonably oppressed by it. It was foolish. He knew that what Livesey said was true. Now that he saw it, he knew he had been careless not to have noticed the small signs before. He stood up, pushing his chair back a little. "Thank you very much for sparing me time this afternoon, Mr. Livesey."

"Not at all." Livesey rose also. "It is a very grave matter, and I assure you I shall give you any assistance within my power. You have only to tell me what I can do."

And with that Pitt excused himself and left, walking slowly, heavy in thought. It was already late, the sun was low behind the rooftops and a slight mist gathered in the damp streets, smoke smearing gray across the pale color of the sky and the smell of it rank as people stoked their fires against the chill of the evening.

Perhaps the medical examiner would have the results of the autopsy. Or at least he might know if there was poison in the flask. This whole case might disappear, a hasty judgment, a fear not realized. He quickened his pace and strode out along the pavement towards the main thoroughfare and the chance of finding a hansom.

The light was still on in the medical examiner's office, and when Pitt knocked on the door he was commanded to enter.

Sutherland was in shirtsleeves, his hair standing on end where he had run his fingers through it. He had a pencil behind each ear, and another in his fingers, the end chewed to splinters. He jerked up from the papers he had been staring at, and regarded Pitt with ferocious interest.

"Opium," he said simply. "The flask was full of it. More than enough to kill four men, let alone one."

"Is that what killed Stafford?" Pitt asked.

"Yes, I'm afraid so. You were quite right, opium poisoning. Easily recognizable, if you know what you are looking for, and you told me. Nasty."

"Could it have been accidental, intended just as . . ."

"No," Sutherland said firmly. "One doesn't take opium in whiskey like that. It should be smoked. And anyone who took it regularly would know perfectly well that a dose that size would kill. No, Mr. Pitt, it was intended to be precisely what it was: lethal. You have a murder, unquestionably."

Pitt said nothing. It was what he had feared, and yet a small part of him had still kept hope that it might not be so. Now it was conclusive. Mr. Justice Samuel Stafford had been murdered—not apparently over the Blaine/Godman case. Was it Juniper Stafford and Adolphus Pryce? One of them—or both? As simple and as ugly as that?

"Thank you," he said aloud to Sutherland.

"I'll write it all out," Sutherland replied, screwing up his face, "and send it to the station."

"Thank you," Pitt repeated, and saw the look of rueful understanding in Sutherland's expression. "Good night."

"Good night." Sutherland picked up his pencil again and continued scribbling on the paper in front of him.

3

THE MORNING AFTER the theater Charlotte went out quite early, and during the rest of the day was fully occupied in domestic matters, since it was her maid Gracie's afternoon off. Therefore it was the following day, when Pitt already knew that Stafford had died of opium poisoning, that she began the long task of making a rich fruitcake, and had the opportunity to tell Gracie what had happened.

The first job with the cake was to prepare the fruit itself. The currants and sultanas had to be rubbed in flour to ease out the lumps. Charlotte was busy doing this in the center of the scrubbed kitchen table while Gracie took everything down from the dresser and washed the shelves and the plates and polished the saucepans. She had been with Charlotte for several years now, and was nearly seventeen, but in spite of all Charlotte's efforts, she was still almost as small and waiflike in appearance as when she had first come. However, her bearing had altered beyond recognition. She had a confidence greater than that of any other maid on the street, quite probably in half of Bloomsbury. She not only worked for a detective, the best in the whole metropolitan force, but she had actually assisted in a case herself. She had had adventures, and she did not accept a cheeky answer from any errand boy or tradesman, whoever they were.

Now she was perched on the dresser at risk to life and limb, a damp cloth in one hand and a china tureen in the other, her face set in concentration as she turned very slowly and set down the tureen before wiping the top shelf with first one side of the cloth, then the other, regarding the dirt with satisfaction, then doing it again.

Charlotte bent over the fruit, her fingers exploring the hard-packed knobs of currants and forcing them into separate pieces.

"Was it a wonderful drama, ma'am?" Gracie asked with interest, climbing backwards precariously.

"I don't know," Charlotte said with candor. "To tell you the truth I hardly noticed it. But the main actor was extremely attractive." She smiled as she said it, thinking of Caroline's vulnerability in the matter.

"Was 'e terrible 'andsome?" Gracie said curiously. "Was 'e dark and very dashing?"

"Not really dark." Charlotte pictured Joshua Fielding's highly individual, whimsical face. "Not really handsome, I suppose, in an ordinary way. But extremely appealing. I think because one felt he had such an ability to laugh without cruelty, and to be gentle. One imagined he might understand all sorts of things."

"Sounds very nice," Gracie approved. "I'd like to know someone like that. Was the heroine beautiful? What was she like? All golden 'air and big eyes?"

"No, not at all," Charlotte replied thoughtfully. "In fact she was about the darkest woman I have ever seen who was still English. But she could make you feel she was the most beautiful woman in the world when she wanted to. She really had a presence. Everyone else looked pallid and washed out beside her. She seemed to burn inside, as if other people were half alive—but not ostentatious, if you know what I mean?"

"No, ma'am," Gracie admitted. "Oss what?"

"Oh—outwardly showy."

"Oh." Gracie climbed down, her skirts and apron in a bunch, and went to the tap to wash her cloth. "I can't imagine a woman like that—but I'd like to. She sounds real ex-

61

citing." She wrung out the cloth with small, thin, very strong hands, and clambered back up onto the dresser. "Why was it you didn't enjoy the drama, then, ma'am?"

"Because there was a murder in the next box," Charlotte replied, tipping out more flour onto the sultanas.

Gracie stopped in midair, one hand on the top shelf, the other brandishing a sauceboat. She turned very slowly, her sharp little face alight with excitement.

"A murder? Really? Are you joshing me, ma'am?"

"Oh no," Charlotte said seriously. "Not at all. A very eminent judge was killed. Actually I exaggerated a little; it wasn't the next box, it was about four boxes away. He was poisoned."

Gracie screwed up her face, ever practical of mind. "How can you poison anyone in a theater? I mean on purpose—I ate some eels once wot made me sick—but nobody did it intentional, like."

"In his whiskey flask," Charlotte explained, kneading out the last lump from the sultanas and putting them all into the colander ready to wash them under the tap in order to remove the grit before she searched them for odd stalks.

"Oh dear—poor gentleman." Gracie resumed wiping the shelves. "Was it 'orrible?"

Charlotte took the colander to the sink.

"No, not really. He just sort of sank into a coma." Charlotte turned on the tap and flushed the water through the fruit. "I was sorrier for his wife, poor soul."

"She weren't the one wot done it?" Gracie asked dubiously.

"I don't know. He was a judge of the appeal court, and he had started to look into a case he dealt with several years ago—a very dreadful murder. The man who was hanged for it was the brother of the actress I told you about."

"Cor!" Gracie was now totally absorbed. She put the sauceboat back on the wrong shelf, without its dish. "Cor!" she said again, pushing her cloth into her apron pocket and standing quite still on the dresser, her head almost to the airing rail just below the ceiling. "Was it a case the master was on?"

"No—not then." Charlotte turned the tap off and took the fruit back to the kitchen table, tipped it out onto a soft cloth and patted it dry, then began to look for stalks. "But he will go into it all now, I expect."

"Why'd they kill the judge, then?" Gracie was suddenly puzzled. "If 'e were goin' ter look inter the case again, in't that what she'd want? Oh! O' course! You mean whoever really did the murder was scared as 'e'd find out it were them. Cor—it could be anybody, couldn't it? Were it very 'orrible?"

"Yes, very. Much too horrible to tell you about. You'll have bad dreams."

"Garn," Gracie said cheerfully. "Won't be worse 'n I already 'eard!"

"Possibly not," Charlotte agreed ruefully. "It was the Farriers' Lane murder."

"I never 'eard o' that." Gracie looked disappointed.

"You wouldn't," Charlotte agreed. "It was five years ago. You were only twelve then."

"That were before I could read," Gracie agreed with considerable pride. Reading was a real accomplishment, and placed her considerably above her contemporaries and previous social equals. Charlotte had taken time in which they should both have been employed in domestic chores in order to teach her, but the reward had been enormous, even if she was quite sure Gracie spent much of her reading time with penny dreadfuls.

"The master's goin' ter investigate it?" Gracie interrupted her thoughts. "Actresses and judges. 'E's gettin' ever so important, in't 'e?"

"Yes," Charlotte agreed with a smile. Gracie was so proud of Pitt her face shone when she mentioned his name. Charlotte had more than once overheard her speaking to tradesmen, telling them precisely who she worked for, whose house this was, and that they had better mind their p's and q's and provide only the very best!

Gracie began wiping the lower shelves of the dresser and

replacing the dishes and pans. Twice she stopped to hitch up her skirt. She was so small that skirts were always a bit too long for her, and she had not taken this one up sufficiently. Charlotte spread out the fruit on a baking tray and put it into the warm oven, which was well damped down to keep it from getting any hotter for the time being.

"Of course it may have been his wife," Charlotte said, referring back to the murder of Stafford. "Or her lover." She went to the pantry and took out the butter to wash away the salt, then wrap it in muslin and squeeze out any water or buttermilk.

Gracie hesitated for a moment, working out whether Charlotte meant the original murder in Farriers' Lane or the death two nights ago in the theater. She made the right choice.

"Oh." She was disappointed. It seemed too simple, not adequate to test Pitt's skills. It offered no adventure, and certainly nothing in which she herself could help. She swallowed. "I thought as you was a little worried, ma'am. I s'pose I got it wrong."

Charlotte felt a pang of guilt. She was touched by a considerable anxiety, just in case it had been something to do with Joshua Fielding. If it were the Blaine/Godman case, then he was implicated, and that would distress Caroline, the more so since she had actually met him.

"I shouldn't like it to be the actor," she explained. "My mother found him most pleasing, and when she met him . . ." She tailed off. How would she explain to the maid that her mother was enamored of a stage actor at least thirteen or fourteen years her junior? Of course it was only a superficial feeling, but still capable of causing hurt.

"Oh, I see," Gracie said cheerfully. She had heard how gentlemen felt about the Jersey Lily, and some of the music hall queens. "Like as she'd go to the stage door, if she was a man." She began to sieve the flour to remove the lumps. She would leave the grating of the orange peel and nutmeg to Charlotte. That required a certain amount of judgment. "Well, maybe it weren't 'im."

"I don't think it was the judge's wife," Charlotte said slowly.

"What are you going to do about it, ma'am?" Gracie said with no hesitation at all, no possibility in her mind that Charlotte would do nothing.

Charlotte thought for several minutes, her mind racing over the snatches she had pieced together in the theater, and the little Pitt had told her. Why did she not think it was Juniper? And was her judgment of any value? She had been wrong before, several times.

Gracie sieved the flour a second time.

"I suppose we should solve the murder in Farriers' Lane," Charlotte said expansively at last.

Gracie did not for an instant question her mistress's competence to do such a thing. Her loyalty was absolute.

"That's a good idea," she approved. "Then they couldn't say it were 'im. Wot 'appened?"

Charlotte summarized it concisely and not entirely accurately. "A young gentleman, who was married, was paying court to the actress Tamar Macaulay. After a performance someone followed him and murdered him in Farriers' Lane, and nailed him up to a door, like a crucifixion. They said it was her brother, because he thought the young gentleman was betraying her. They hanged him, but she has always believed he was innocent."

Gracie was too interested to look for any other job. She sieved the flour yet again, her eyes wide and never leaving Charlotte's face.

"'Oo does she think as did it?"

"I don't know," Charlotte admitted with surprise. "I don't know if anyone asked her."

"Does she think it was this—wot's 'is name?"

"Joshua Fielding? No—no, they are great friends."

"Then I'll wager 'e didn't," Gracie said firmly. "We got to show 'em as 'e's innocent, ma'am."

Charlotte heard the "we," and smiled inside herself, but said nothing aloud.

"A good idea. I'll have to think where to begin."

"Well, Mrs. Radley can't 'elp us this time," Gracie said thoughtfully. "Seein' as she's orf in the country."

It was true. Emily, Charlotte's sister and usual companion in such matters, was in the later stages of expecting her second child, and she and her husband, Jack, had taken a holiday in the west country away from the social bustle of London until after the birth. Charlotte received letters regularly and wrote back less often. Emily had so much more time, and was finding the hours heavy on her hands. She had more than ample means, inherited from her first husband, whereas Charlotte had extensive housework and the care of her own two children to keep her busy. Of course there was Gracie's help all the time, and a woman to do the heavy scrubbing three days a week, and the heavy linen was sent out; but Emily had a full staff of at least twenty servants, indoor and out.

"Well," Gracie went on cheerfully, "seein' as she can't, maybe your mam'd like to? Since she's smitten like, she'd care—wouldn't she?"

Charlotte tried to be tactful, not something at which she was naturally gifted.

"I don't think so. She doesn't approve, you know?"

"But if she likes 'im?" Gracie was puzzled.

"Will you pass me the fruit and open the damper in the oven?" Charlotte requested, beginning to mix her ingredients at last in the large yellow earthenware bowl.

Gracie obeyed, ignoring the oven cloth and using her apron as usual.

For a quarter of an hour they worked diligently till the cake was in tins and beginning to bake. Gracie put on the kettle and they were about to make tea when there was a ring at the front doorbell.

"If that's that greengrocer's boy come to the front again," Gracie said tartly, "I'll give 'im a flea in 'is ear 'e'll not forget in an 'urry!" And so saying she tightened her apron, patted her hair and then scampered along the corridor to answer the bell.

She was back in less than a minute.

"It's yer mam. I mean it's Mrs. Ellison."

And indeed Caroline was only a step behind her, dressed in a jacket of swirling green with fur at the collar, a beautifully swathed skirt, and a glorious hat dipped over her left brow and laden with feathers. Her cheeks were flushed, but there was anxiety in her eyes. She seemed oblivious of Charlotte's old blue stuff dress with sleeves rolled up, and a white apron hiding the front. She also ignored the kitchen, the sink full of bowls and spoons, and even the delicious smell of cooking coming from the oven.

"Mama!" Charlotte greeted her with pleasure and surprise. "You look wonderful! How are you? What brings you here at this hour?"

"Oh—" Charlotte waved a gloved hand airily. "Ah—well—" Then her face creased with concern and she abandoned the effort. "I wondered—" She stopped again.

Without being asked Gracie reached down the tea caddy and started to lay out the cups.

Charlotte waited. She knew from Caroline's search for words that it was nothing to do with Emily. Had there been a family illness or difficulty of any sort she would have looked troubled, but there would have been no inarticulacy in her manner.

"Are you all right, after the tragedy in the theater?" Caroline began again. This time she looked at Charlotte, but there was no concentration in her face. She seemed to be seeing beyond her, to something imagined.

"Yes, thank you," Charlotte replied warily. "Are you?"

"Of course! I mean—well—it was most distressing, naturally." Caroline at last sat down on one of the wooden chairs at the table. Gracie placed the steaming teapot and two cups on a tray and brought them over, with milk and sugar.

"Excuse me, ma'am," she said tactfully. "But if you please, I'd better be going to change the linen."

"Yes, of course," Charlotte agreed with gratitude. "That would be a very good idea."

As soon as Gracie had gone Caroline frowned again, staring at Charlotte with puckered brows as she poured the tea.

"Does Thomas know yet if . . ." she began tentatively, ". . . if the poor man was murdered?"

"Yes," Charlotte replied, having some inkling at last of what was disturbing her mother so much. "I am afraid he was. He was poisoned with opium in his flask, as Judge Livesey feared. I'm sorry you should have been involved in it, Mama, even so indirectly. But any number of perfectly respectable people were at the theater. There is no need to fear anyone will think ill of you."

"Oh, I'm not!" Caroline said with genuine surprise. "I was . . ." She looked down, a very faint blush in her cheeks. "I was concerned in case it should be either Mr. Fielding or Miss Macaulay who would be suspected. Do you—do you think Thomas believes they may be guilty?"

Charlotte was at a loss to answer. Of course it was not only possible but probable that Pitt would suspect both of them, and without question he would suspect Joshua Fielding, which was what she realized Caroline really had in mind. She remembered Fielding's wry, charming face and wondered what emotions lay behind it, and just how skilled an actor he might be. What might his words conceal about Aaron Godman, or the reason Mr. Justice Stafford had come to see him the day of his death?

Caroline was staring at her, her eyes intent, darkening with anxiety.

With a painful searching of memory Charlotte remembered how she had woven so many dreams in her youth, and made a mantle of them with which she had clothed her brother-in-law, Dominic Corde. It was so easy to imagine that a handsome face was filled with passion, sensitivity, dreams to match your own, and then invest the person with abilities he never possessed, or wished to—and in so doing to be blind to the real person.

Was Caroline doing the same to a stage actor she had watched wear other men's thoughts with such artistry that she had lost the distinction between the world of the mind and the world of reality?

"Yes. I'm afraid he will have to," she said aloud. "It can only be someone he saw that day who had the opportunity to put poison in the flask, and if he was indeed investigating the old murder, then that is an excellent reason why someone might wish him dead. How could Thomas ignore that?"

"I cannot believe that he did it!" Caroline said very quietly, a fierceness in her voice, an intense determination. "There is some other answer." She looked up quickly, all the indecision and awkwardness vanished from her. "What can we do to help? What could we find out? Whom do we know?"

Charlotte was startled. Did Caroline realize she had spoken as if she herself intended to become involved? Was it a slip of the tongue?

"We?" Charlotte could not help smiling.

Caroline bit her lip. "Well—you, I suppose. I have no idea how to—detect . . ."

Charlotte could not decide whether her mother was trying to excuse herself from taking any part or was seeking to be reassured that she could, in fact, be of use. She looked both vulnerable and determined. There was a vitality to her, a most odd mixture of fear and exhilaration.

"Do you know anyone?" Caroline persisted.

"No," Charlotte said quickly. "I never knew anyone; it is Emily who knows people. But we could attempt to make someone's acquaintance, I suppose."

"We must do something," Caroline said vehemently. "If the wrong person was hanged once—then left to themselves the police may do the wrong thing again. Oh! I'm so sorry! I did not mean to imply Thomas. Of course it will be different with Thomas in charge. But all the same . . ."

Charlotte smiled broadly and picked up her rapidly cooling cup of tea.

"That is all right, Mama. You had better not say anything further—you are only digging yourself deeper. Thomas is not infallible—he would be the first to say so." She sipped her tea. "And I would be the first to defend him to the death if anyone else said so. But I really know very little about this case, except what you know yourself. Apparently it was perfectly horrifying. Do you recall it? It was five years ago."

"Certainly not. Your father was alive, and I never read the newspapers."

"Oh. Well, I assume you did not know the Blaines, or anyone connected with them—and I am perfectly sure that when Papa was alive you did not know anyone on the stage."

Caroline blushed deeply and sipped her tea.

"I don't suppose Great-Aunt Vespasia did either," Charlotte said, trying to smother the laughter out of her expression. "At least not lately. Actors, I mean."

Caroline's eyebrows shot up, missing the humor entirely. "Do you think Lady Cumming-Gould would have known actors? Oh, I think that most unlikely. She is very well bred indeed."

"I know," Charlotte conceded, straight-faced with difficulty. "Well, enough not to need to care what other people thought. She would have known anyone she wished—discreetly, perhaps. But that doesn't help us. She is over eighty now. The actors she may have known are no use to us. They are probably dead. But she may just possibly have known someone who knew Kingsley Blaine—or knew of him. Perhaps I should ask her?"

"Oh, would you?" Caroline said eagerly. "Would you please?"

The prospect was very appealing. Charlotte had not seen Great-Aunt Vespasia for some time. She was not Charlotte's aunt at all, but Emily's by marriage to her first husband, but both Charlotte and Emily cared for her more than anyone else except most immediate family, and quite often more even than those.

"Yes," Charlotte said with decision. "I think that would be an excellent idea. I'll make arrangements to go tomorrow."

"Oh—do you think it can wait?" Caroline looked crestfallen. "Had you better not go today? It will surely not be easy. Had we not best begin as soon as possible?"

Charlotte looked down at her stuff dress, then at the oven.

"Gracie can take the cakes out," Caroline said quickly, at last showing awareness of the increasingly delicious aroma. "And she will be here when the children return from school, should you be held up. Or I will wait, if that would set your mind at rest. You can take my carriage, which is outside. That would be excellent. Now go upstairs and change into a suitable gown. Go on!"

Charlotte did not need a second tempting. If Caroline wished it so much, and was willing to remain here, then it would be churlish not to accede to her wishes.

"Certainly," she agreed, and without hesitation left the kitchen and went upstairs to find a suitable gown and inform Gracie of the change of plans.

"Oh," Gracie said with excitement lighting her face. "You are going to work on the case. Oh ma'am—I was 'opin' as you would!" She brushed her hands on the sides of her apron. "If'n there's anything I can do . . . ?"

"I shall surely tell you," Charlotte promised. "Regardless, I shall tell you all I discover, if I discover anything at all. For now I am going to call upon Lady Vespasia Cumming-Gould, to see if I can enlist her help." She knew Gracie admired Great-Aunt Vespasia intensely. Vespasia had been one of the leading beauties of her day, and had all the unconscious dignity and charm of total confidence, a biting wit, and an utter disregard for convention. Gracie had met her when she had called upon Charlotte and sat in the kitchen, fascinated by the impedimenta of washday, which she had never seen before. To Gracie she was a creature of magical dimensions.

"Oh ma'am, that's a wunnerful idea." Gracie applauded, her face shining. "I'm sure she'll 'elp, if anyone can."

It was an hour later that Charlotte arrived in Gadstone Park and was admitted by Vespasia's parlormaid, a girl Pitt had found in a workhouse in a previous case, and recommended to Vespasia. Then the girl had looked like a shadow; now the color had returned to her skin and her hair

71

was a shining coil on her head. She had learned Vespasia's preferences well enough to know that Charlotte was to be admitted at any time. She did not call on trivial social issues, only if there was some urgent adventure afoot, or some extremely interesting story to relate.

Vespasia herself was sitting in her private withdrawing room, not a reception room for visitors but a smaller, quietly furnished room full of light and boasting only three chairs, upholstered in cream brocade and with carved woodwork. A close-haired black-and-white dog lay on the floor in a patch of sun. She appeared to be something like a lurcher, a cross between whippet and general collie, with perhaps a touch of spaniel in the face. She was highly intelligent, but lean, built for running, and irregularly marked.

As soon as Charlotte came in she wagged her long tail and moved closer to Vespasia.

"Charlotte, my dear, how pleasant to see you," Vespasia said with delight. "Don't mind Willow, she doesn't bite. She's a complete fool. Martin's bitch got out and this is the result! Neither fish nor fowl, nor good red herring. And they were hoping to have a litter that would make good carriage dogs. They said the bitch is ruined, which of course is a lot of nonsense. But you can't convince people." She patted the little dog affectionately. "All this little creature does is stand in every puddle God made and jump about like a rabbit."

Charlotte bent and kissed Vespasia's cheek.

"Well, sit down," Vespasia ordered. "I assume since you have come unheralded and at a most unusual hour that you have something remarkable to say?" She looked hopeful. "What has happened? Nothing tragic, I see from your face."

"Oh." Charlotte felt abashed. "Well, it is—for those concerned . . ."

"A case?" Vespasia's clear, almost silver eyes were bright under her arched brows. "You are about to meddle, and you wish my assistance." There was a smile on her lips, but she was not unaware that no matter how bizarre or testing of the intelligence and the wits, a case meant also fear and loss to someone, and the far deeper tragedy of a life perverted and twisted out of all the happiness it might have had. Since chance had forced her acquaintance with Thomas Pitt, she had seen a darker side of life, a poverty and despair she had not perceived from her own glittering social circle, even in the political crusades for which she worked so hard. She had enlarged her own capacity for pity, and for anger.

None of this was necessary to explain between them. They had shared too much to need such words.

Charlotte sat down, and the little dog came over to her, sniffing gently and wagging her tail. She patted its soft head absently.

"Judge Stafford," she began. "At least it is half . . ."

"Half?" Vespasia was nonplussed. "You are half concerned with his death, poor man. The obituary said he had died suddenly in the theater. Watching a romance, a somewhat trivial work to be the last earthly engagement of so distinguished a luminary of the bench. Now that I come to think of it, the cause of his demise was conspicuously absent from the comments."

"It would be," Charlotte said dryly. "He drank liquid opium in his whiskey."

"Oh dear." Vespasia's highly intelligent face was filled with a curious mixture of emotions. "I assume it was not accidental, or self-inflicted?"

"It could not have been accidental," Charlotte replied. "Whatever sort of an accident would that be? But I admit no one has suggested suicide."

"They wouldn't," Vespasia said dryly. "Such people as Samuel Stafford are not supposed to commit suicide. It is a crime, my dear. We can scarcely try people for it, of course, but it is still a very serious offense on the statute books, and we all know a suicide is buried in unconsecrated ground and the punishment is delivered in the world to come—so it is believed." Suddenly her face was filled with a wild anger and pity. "I have even known unfortunate girls in despair dragged back from the brink of death and revived sufficiently to be hanged for it. God forgive us. Is there any reason to suppose Samuel Stafford might have done such a thing?"

Charlotte blinked and took a deep breath to smother the emotions inside her. "None at all," she replied. "And there seem to be several reasons why various people might have wished him dead."

"Indeed. Who? Is it something unbearably tedious, like money?"

"Not at all. His wife is said to be having an affaire, and either she or her lover may have wished him dead. They both had the opportunity to put something in his flask that day. But the matter which brings me to you is much darker."

Vespasia's eyes widened. "Is it? That seems quite dark enough to me. I thought you were going to ask me if I were acquainted with Mrs. Stafford. I am not."

"No—are you acquainted with anyone related to Kingsley Blaine?"

Vespasia thought for a moment, giving it her entire concentration.

"No, I am afraid the name Blaine means nothing," she said finally, her disappointment apparent.

"Godman?" Charlotte made a last attempt, although she really held no hope at all that Vespasia would have any acquaintance with Aaron Godman, except across the footlights.

Vespasia frowned, understanding coming very slowly.

"My dear Charlotte—you don't mean that abysmal affair in Farriers' Lane? What in heaven's name could that have to do with Mr. Justice Stafford's death in the theater two nights ago? That was all over in 'eighty-four."

"No, it wasn't," Charlotte said very quietly. "At least it may not have been. Mr. Stafford seems to have been looking into it again."

Vespasia frowned. "What do you mean, 'seems to have been'?"

"There is a difference of opinion," Charlotte explained. "What is indisputable is that the day he died he was visited by Tamar Macaulay, the sister of Godman, and after she left

he went and saw Adolphus Pryce, the barrister who prosecuted the case, Mr. Justice Livesey, who was another of the
judges who heard the appeal with him, and Devlin O'Neil
and Joshua Fielding, two of the original early suspects."

"Good heavens." Vespasia's face was intent, all amusement or doubt fled from it. "Then what question is there?"

"Whether he intended to reopen the case, or merely to
prove even more totally that the original verdict was correct."

"I see." Vespasia nodded. "Yes, I can quite understand
how that might raise a great many questions as to who
wished him to leave the matter, and if he would not, which
seems very plain, then to force the conclusion by killing
him."

Charlotte swallowed. "The matter is further complicated
because my mother has made the acquaintance of Mr.
Fielding, and is involved in his cause."

"Indeed." A very faint gleam flickered in Vespasia's
eyes, but she made no remark. "Then you wish to become
. . . involved?" She hesitated only momentarily before the
word. She sat up a little straighter. "I regret I do not know,
even on nodding terms, Mrs. Stafford or Mr. Justice
Livesey, or indeed Mr. Pryce. No doubt I should have little
difficulty in scraping an acquaintance with Mr. Fielding, but
it would now seem that that is redundant." She did not even
look at Charlotte as she said it, but her gentle amusement
was palpable, like a warmth between them. "But I do have
the acquaintance of the judge of the original trial." She hesitated minutely. "A Mr. Thelonius Quade."

"Oh, do you?" Charlotte was too pleased to have caught
the inflection in Vespasia's voice, and only realized its im-
port later. "Do you know him well enough to call upon
him? Could you raise the subject, or—or would it be . . .
indelicate?"

A shadow of a smile curled Vespasia's lips.

"I think it might be accomplished without indelicacy,"
she replied. "Do I conclude correctly that there is some
haste in the matter?"

"Oh yes," Charlotte agreed. "I think you do—thank you, Aunt Vespasia."

Vespasia smiled, this time with pure affection. "You are welcome, my dear."

One could not call upon a judge in the middle of the day and expect him to have time to indulge a purely social acquaintance. Accordingly Vespasia wrote a short note:

> My dear Thelonius,
>
> Forgive me for a somewhat abrupt, and perhaps questionably tasteful, request that you receive me this evening, but our friendship was never such that convention ruled, or polite excuses covered either thought or emotion. A matter has arisen concerning a very dear friend of mine, a young woman I regard as family, and I believe you may be able to help with recollections, in the public domain, but not in mine.
>
> Unless I hear that it is inconvenient to you, I shall call upon you in your rooms in Piccadilly at eight this evening.
>
> > Yours in friendship,
> > Vespasia

She sealed it and rang the bell for her footman. When he came she gave him the note with instructions to take it immediately to the chambers of Mr. Justice Thelonius Quade in the Inner Temple, and to await such reply as there might be.

He returned an hour later bearing a note which read:

> My dear Vespasia,
>
> What a delight to hear from you again, whatever the reason. I shall be in court all day, but have no engagements of any importance this evening, and shall be happy to see you, especially if you would care to dine, while you tell me of the concern for your friend.
>
> Be assured I shall do all in my power to help, and count it my privilege.

May I look forward to seeing you at eight o'clock?

> Always your friend,
> Thelonius

She folded it again and placed it in one of the pigeon-holes in her bureau. She would not yet keep it with the others of nearly twenty years ago. The space between them had been too great. Memories filled her mind, delicate, without sorrow now. She would accept the invitation to dine. It would be most pleasant to have time to speak of other things as well, to develop the conversation slowly, to enjoy his company, his wit, the complexities of his thoughts, the subtlety of his judgment. And there would be good humor, there had always been that—and honesty.

She dressed with care, not only for herself but also for him. It was a long time since she had worn anything to please anyone else. He had always liked pale colors, subtle tones. She put on ivory silk, smooth over the hip and with a very discreet bustle exquisitely swathed, and lace at the neck, and pearls, lots of pearls. He had always preferred their sheen to the brilliance of diamonds, which he thought hard, and ostentatious.

She alighted from her carriage at five minutes past eight, close enough to the appointed hour to be polite, and yet not so prompt as to be vulgar. The butler who answered the door was very elderly. His white hair shone in the light from the hallway and his shoulders were more than a trifle stooped. He looked at her for a moment before his features lit in a smile. "Good evening, Lady Cumming-Gould," he said with unconcealed pleasure, memories flooding back. "How very pleasant to see you. Mr. Quade is expecting you, if you will come this way. May I take your cape?"

It was twenty years since Thelonius Quade had been in love with her, and to be honest, she had also loved him far more than she had ever intended when she had begun their romance. He had been a brilliant barrister in his early forties, lean and slight with an ascetic dreamer's face full of beautiful bones, married to his career and the love of justice.

She had been sixty, still possessed of the great beauty which had made her famous, married to a man of whom she had been fond but never adored. He had been older than she, a chilly man who had little humor, and at that time he was retreating from life into a dour old age, seeking even more physical comfort and less involvement with other people, except a few like-minded friends, and a large number of acquaintances with whom he conducted an enormous correspondence about the dire state of the Empire, the ruin of society and the decline of religion.

Now as she found herself on the brink of seeing Thelonius Quade again, she was ridiculously nervous. It was too absurd! She was over eighty, an old woman; even Thelonius himself must be over sixty now! She had been perfectly composed when she suggested the idea to Charlotte, but as she followed the butler across the familiar hallway her heart was fluttering, and her hands were stiff, and she nearly missed her step between the parquet flooring and the Aubusson carpet of the withdrawing room.

"Lady Vespasia Cumming-Gould," the butler announced, opening the doors for her and stepping back.

Vespasia swallowed, lifted her head even higher, and went in.

Thelonius Quade was standing by the fireplace, facing her. He looked leaner than she had recalled, and perhaps taller. Even his face was gaunt, its sensitive lines thrown into sharper relief. The marks of age had given him a quality it would not be misplaced to call beauty, such was the power of his character that shone through.

He smiled as soon as he saw her, and came across the room slowly, holding out his hands a little, palms upwards.

Without thinking about it, she placed her hands in his, smiling back.

He moved no closer but stood searching her face, and finding in it what he had hoped.

"I suppose you must have changed," he said quietly. She had forgotten how good his voice was, how very clear. "But I cannot see it—and I do not wish to."

"I am twenty years older, Thelonius," she replied with a little shake of her head.

"Ah, but my dear, so am I," he said gently. "And that cancels it out. Come, let us move a little closer to the fire. The evening is chilly, and it would be hasty to begin dinner the moment you are through the door. We cannot possibly catch up twenty years in one short encounter, so do not let us pretend." He led her towards the warmth as he spoke. "Tell me instead what it is that concerns you so much. We do not need to play games of trivial conversation and skirt around what we mean. We never did. And unless you are totally different, you will not rest until we have dealt with the matter of importance."

"Am I so very . . . direct?" she said with a rueful smile.

"Yes," he replied without compromise. He searched her face carefully. She had not remembered his eyes were blue, or so perceptive. "You do not look deeply troubled. May I assume it is not a matter of distress?"

She lifted an elegant shoulder and the pearls on her bosom shone in the light.

"At the moment it is only interest, which may develop into concern. I am very fond of the young woman."

"You said in your note that you regarded her as family." He was standing next to the fireplace, facing her. She stood also; she had been sitting most of the day, and all the journey here, and she felt comfortable. In spite of her age, she was straight-backed and erect, and nearly as tall as he.

"She is the sister of a niece, by marriage."

"I detect a hesitation, Vespasia—an evasion?"

"You are too quick," she said dryly, but there was no irritation in her. On the contrary, it was vaguely comforting that he should still know her so well, and be willing to show it. "Yes, she is of very moderate family, and has chosen to appall them by marrying beneath herself, in fact a very great deal beneath herself—to a policeman."

His eyes widened, but he said nothing.

"Of whom I am also very fond!" she added defensively.

Still he forbore from commenting, still watching her.

"She—she frequently involves herself in his . . . cases."

Now she was finding it harder to explain so that it did not sound in the worst possible taste. "In a pursuit of truth," she said warily, searching his face and not knowing what she read in it. "She is an intelligent and individual young woman."

"And she is presently so . . . involved?" he enquired, the amusement so nearly in his voice.

"That will depend."

"Upon what?"

"Upon whether there is any way in which she can meet any of the participants in the affair in a manner which might be productive."

He looked confused.

"Really, Thelonius," she said quickly. "Detecting is not a matter of going 'round in a bowler hat asking impertinent questions and writing down what everyone says in a notebook! The best detecting is done by observing people when they are unaware that you have any interest in them, or knowledge of the matter deeper than their own—and of course by making the odd remark which will provoke a reaction in the guilty." She stopped, seeing him regard her with surprise and fast dawning amusement.

"Vespasia?"

"And why not?" she demanded.

"My dear! No reason on earth," he conceded. Then as the gong sounded, he took her by the arm and guided her through the archway to the dining room. The mahogany table was set for two, silver gleaming in the candlelight, tawny chrysanthemums smelling rich and earthy, white linen folded with monograms outward.

He pulled out her chair for her before the butler could reach it, then took his own seat. Tacitly the butler set about his duties.

"And what case is this friend of yours— Does she have a name?"

"Charlotte—Charlotte Pitt."

"Pitt?" His eyebrows rose and there was sharp interest in his face. "There is an inspector of considerable ability named Thomas Pitt. Is he by any chance the one towards whom you have developed this regard?"

"Yes, yes he is."

"An excellent man, so I have heard." He opened his napkin and spread it across his lap. "A man of integrity. What is this matter in which his wife is interested? Why is it you believe I may have any knowledge?"

The butler poured white wine for him. He sipped it, then offered it to Vespasia. She accepted.

"If it is in the public domain," he continued, "surely Inspector Pitt will know at least as much as I. And do I gather that he does not wish his wife to participate in the matter?"

"Really, Thelonius," she reproved him with amusement. "Do you imagine I would set Charlotte against her husband? Certainly not! No—the matter is some five years old, and your knowledge will be superior to almost anyone else's because you were involved yourself."

"In what?" He began his soup, a delicate cream of winter vegetables.

She took a deep breath. It was distasteful to intrude such an ugly affair into so pleasant an evening, but they had never restricted themselves to the purely pleasant. Their relationship had been deepened by the sharing of the tragic and the ugly as well as the beautiful.

"The Blaine/Godman murder—in Farriers' Lane in 'eighty-four," she said gravely. The lightness vanished. "It seems more than possible that the sudden death in the theater two nights ago of Mr. Justice Stafford is connected with his continued interest in the case."

His manner sharpened, his expression clouded with concern and he stopped, his spoon in the air.

"I did not know he had any continued interest. In what way?"

"Well, there is some difference of opinion on that," she answered, aware of the change in him, the undercurrent of old unhappiness. It darkened her mood also, but it was too late to retreat. His eyes were watching her with intensity, waiting.

"Mrs. Stafford and Mr. Pryce were present when Mr. Stafford died," she continued. "Both say that he was intending to reopen the case, although neither of them knew upon what grounds. Mr. Justice Livesey, on the other hand, who was also there, is quite sure that he was intending to prove once and for all that the verdict was true and in every way proper, so there would be no more speculation even by the hanged man's sister, who has been mounting a crusade to have his name cleared."

The soup dishes were removed and salmon mousse served.

"What is beyond argument," she resumed, "is that Mr. Stafford was reinterrogating many of the original participants. The day he died he saw Tamar Macaulay, Joshua Fielding, Devlin O'Neil and Adolphus Pryce, as well as Mr. Justice Livesey."

"Indeed," Thelonius said slowly, letting his fork rest on his plate, his salmon momentarily ignored. "But I assume he died before he could clarify the matter?"

"He did—and it seems . . ." She hated saying it. "It seems he died of poison. Opium, to be precise."

"Hence the interest of your Inspector Pitt," he said dryly.

"Exactly. But Charlotte's interest is more personal."

"Yes?" He picked up the fork again at last.

She found herself smiling. "I know of no delicate way of phrasing this, so I shall be direct."

"Remarkable!" he said with the gentlest of sarcasm. His face held only laughter, and she was reminded again how very much she had cared for him. He was one of the few men who was more than her intellectual equal, and who was not overawed by her beauty or her reputation. If only they had met when—but she had never indulged fruitless regrets, and would certainly not begin now.

"Charlotte's mother has conceived an affection for the actor Joshua Fielding," she said with a tight smile. "She is concerned he may be suspected, both of the Farriers' Lane murder and of poisoning Stafford."

He reached for his wineglass.

"I cannot see any likelihood of that," he said, still looking at her. "If that is what you wish to hear from me. I think Livesey is almost certainly correct, and Mrs. Stafford and Mr. Pryce are either mistaken in their interpretation of his remarks, or something uglier."

She did not need to ask him what that might be; the possibilities were apparent.

"And if it is Livesey who is incorrect?" she asked him.

Again the darkness came into his face. He hesitated several moments before answering her.

It was on the edge of her tongue to apologize for having raised the subject at all, but they had never skirted truth before. It would be a kind of denial to do it now, the closing of a door which she deeply wished to remain open.

"It was an extremely ugly case," he said slowly, his eyes searching her face. "One of the most distressing I have ever presided over. It is not just that the crime itself was horrifying, a man nailed against a stable door like a mockery of the crucifixion of Christ, it was the hatred it engendered in the ordinary man in the street." The ghost of a smile crossed his lips, a wry tolerance in it. "It is amazing how many people turn out to have religious susceptibilities when this sort of affront is given, people who customarily do not darken a church doorway from one year's end to another."

"It is easier," she replied frankly, "and often more emotionally satisfying to be mortally offended on behalf of your God than to serve Him by altering one's style and manner of life—and in a short space, it is certainly much more comfortable. One can feel righteous, very much one who belongs, while heaping vengeance on the heads of sinners. It costs a lot less than giving time or money to the poor."

He ate the last of his salmon and offered her more wine.

"You are becoming cynical, my dear."

"I was never anything else"—she accepted the wine—"where the self-proclaimed righteous were concerned. Was the case really so different from most?"

"Yes." He pushed his plate away and like a shadow the butler removed it. "There was a distinct alien culture which could be blamed," Thelonius continued grimly, his eyes sad and angry. "Godman was a Jew, and the resultant anti-

Semitic emotions were among the most unpleasant manifestations of human behavior that I have seen: anti-Semitic slogans daubed on walls, hysterical pamphlets scattered all over the place, even people hurling stones in the streets at those they took to be Jews—windows smashed in synagogues, one set fire to. The trial was conducted at such a pitch of emotion I feared it would escalate beyond my control." His face pinched as the memory became sharp in his mind. Vespasia could see in his eyes how much it hurt him.

Saddle of mutton was served in silence and they ignored it. The butler brought red wine.

"I am sorry, Thelonius," she said gently. "I would not willingly have reawakened such a time."

"It is not you, Vespasia." He sighed. "It seems it is circumstances. I don't know what Stafford could have found. Perhaps there really is new evidence." A wry expression crossed his face, half amusement, half regret. "It is not anything in the conduct of the original trial." His smile became more inward, more rueful and apologetic. "You know, for the first time in my life, I considered deliberately letting pass something incorrect, some point that would allow a diligent barrister to find grounds to call for a mistrial, or at least a change of venue. I was ashamed of myself even for the thought."

His eyes searched her face to read her reaction, afraid she would be shamed for him. But he saw only grave interest.

"And yet the hatred was so palpable in the air," he went on. "I was afraid the man could not receive a fair hearing in that court. I tried—believe me, Vespasia, I lay awake many nights during that time, turning it over and over in my mind, but I never found any specific word or act I could challenge." He looked down for a moment, then up again. "Pryce was excellent, he always is, and yet he never exceeded his duty. Barton James, for the defense, was adequate. He did not press hard—he seemed to believe his client was guilty, but I don't think one could have found an attorney in England who did not. It . . ." He seemed almost to hunch inside himself a little and Vespasia was keenly aware that the memory of it still caused him pain. But she did not interrupt.

"It was so . . . hasty," he continued, picking up his wine-glass and turning it by the stem in his fingers. The light shone brilliant through the red liquid. "Nothing was omitted, and yet increasingly I had the feeling that everyone wished Godman to be found guilty as rapidly as possible, and to be hanged. The public required a sacrifice for the outrage that had been committed, and it was like a hungry animal prowling just beyond the courtroom doors." He looked up at her suddenly. "Am I being melodramatic?"

"A trifle."

He smiled. "You were not there, or you would understand what I mean. There was a rawness in the air, a heat of emotion that is dangerous when one is trying to pursue justice. It frightened me."

"I have never heard you say such a thing before." She was startled. It was unlike the man she remembered, at once more vulnerable, and yet, in a curious fashion, also stronger.

He shook his head. "I have never felt it," he confessed. His voice dropped lower and was full of surprise and pain. "Vespasia, I seriously considered committing one injudicious act myself, so as to provide grounds in order that the whole thing could be tried again before the justices of appeal, without the hysteria, when emotions were cooler." He breathed in deeply and sighed. "I tortured myself wondering whether that was irresponsible, arrogant, dishonest. Or if I simply let it all proceed was I a coward who loved the pomp and the semblance of the law more than justice?"

With another man she might have leaped to deny it, but it would have made their conversation ordinary; it would have set a distance between them that she did not wish. It would be the polite thing to say, the obvious, but not the more deeply truthful. He was a man of profound integrity, but his soul was as capable of fear and confusion as any other, and that he should have slipped and given in to it was not impossible. To suggest it was would be to desert him, to leave him, in a particular way, desperately alone.

85

"Did you ever reach an answer you knew was true?" she asked him.

"I suppose it is all about ends and means," he said thoughtfully. "Yes—one truth is that you cannot separate them. There is no such thing as an end unaffected by the means used to obtain it." He was watching her face. "In effect I was asking myself if I would intentionally nullify a trial because there was a passion and a haste about it of which I personally did not approve. You understand, I did not think Aaron Godman was innocent, nor do I think so now. Nor did I think that any of the evidence offered was tainted or perjured. It was simply that I felt the police had acted more in emotion than in impartial duty."

He stopped for a moment or two, perhaps uncertain if he should continue. "I was perfectly certain Godman had been beaten while in custody," he said at last. "He was bruised and lacerated when he appeared in court, and the wounds were too fresh to have occurred before his arrest. There was an air of both outrage and urgency which had nothing to do with the seeking of truth, nor the proof of it. And yet Barton James did not refer to it. I could not prejudice his defense by raising the matter myself. I did not know the explanation of it, nor do I now. It is assumption on my part."

"Beaten by whom, Thelonius?"

"I don't know. The police, or his jailers I assume, but it is conceivable they were self-inflicted, I suppose."

"What about the appeal?" she asked.

He began to eat again. "It was raised on grounds of evidence not fully explained—something to do with the medical examination of the body. The doctor concerned, Humbert Yardley, had first stated that the wounds were deeper than could be accounted for by the farrier's nails that the prosecution stated were used, not only to nail him afterwards to the stable door, but actually to kill him—with a piercing wound to the side. Thank God he was dead when he was crucified!"

"You mean Godman might have used some other

weapon?" She was confused. "How does that affect the verdict? I don't understand."

"No other weapon was ever found either in Farriers' Lane or anywhere near it," he explained. "And the people who saw him come out of the lane with blood on his clothes were quite definite he had no weapon with him. And he had nothing of that nature on him when he was arrested, or in his lodgings."

"Could he not have disposed of it?"

"Of course—but not between the stable yard and the end of the alley where he was observed on the night of the murder. The alley lay between the sheer walls of buildings. There were no places to conceal anything at all. Nor was anything found in the yard itself."

"What did the judges of appeal say to this?"

"That Yardley was uncertain, and later under examination did not deny that a long farrier's nail might have caused the fatal injury."

"And that was all?" She was curious, troubled.

"So I believe," he answered. "They dealt with it quickly, and ruled that in every particular the trial verdict was correct, and should stand." He shivered. "Aaron Godman was hanged three and a half weeks later. Since then his sister has attempted to have the matter raised again, and failed. She wrote to members of Parliament, to the newspapers, published pamphlets, spoke at meetings and even from the stage. Always she failed, unless, of course, Mrs. Stafford is correct, and Samuel Stafford was intending to reopen the case before his death prevented him."

"There seems little reason," she said quietly. She looked up at him, meeting his steady, clear eyes. "Are you quite sure he was guilty, Thelonius?"

"I have always thought so," he replied. "I hated the manner in which the investigation was conducted. But the trial was correct, and I don't see that the judges of appeal could have found differently." His brow furrowed. "But if Stafford had learned something between then and his death, then possibly—I don't know . . ."

"And if not Aaron Godman, then who killed Blaine?" she asked.

"I don't know. Joshua Fielding? Devlin O'Neil? Or someone we know nothing about as yet? Perhaps we shall know more if we learn who killed Samuel Stafford, and why. It is an extremely ugly matter; every answer is tragic."

"There are seldom any answers to murder which are not. Thank you for having been so frank with me."

His body relaxed at last, his shoulders easing and the tension, the doubt, softening from his smile.

"Had you imagined I should prevaricate with you? I have not changed so very much as that!"

"You would not have told me anything I should better like to hear," she replied, and knew immediately that that was not true. There were other things, but they were indiscreet—foolish.

"Don't flatter me, Vespasia," he said dryly. "That is for acquaintances. Friends should tell the truth, or at worst keep silence."

"Oh, please! When was I ever capable of silence?"

He smiled suddenly and dazzlingly. "On a given subject, any time you chose. But tell me what you are presently engaged with—apart from your friend Mrs. Pitt. It would be impossible to relate all that you have done since we last spoke to each other with any candor."

So she told him of her crusades to reform the poor laws, the education acts, the housing acts, of the theater and the opera she had enjoyed, and some of the people she felt most deeply for—or against. The evening slipped by as present news was replaced by memories, laughter recalled, and sadness, and it was long after midnight when finally he saw her to her carriage steps, held her hands in his for a moment, and bade her farewell for what they both knew would not be long.

Micah Drummond could not free his mind from the Blaine/Godman case. Of course it was possible, very possible, that Samuel Stafford had been poisoned by his wife, or her lover, although there seemed to be no driving necessity for such a violent and dangerous act on their part. If they were discreet, and it appeared they had been, they could hope to continue seeing each other, on occasion, almost indefinitely. Divorce was out of the question; it was socially ruinous. Pryce could never marry a divorced woman and continue to practice the law as he did now. Society would be scandalized. Stafford was not only his friend, he was a most senior judge.

But an affaire was quite a different matter, as long as they did not flaunt it. Why should they do anything as ugly—and as dangerous—as killing him? There was no need. Juniper Stafford was well into her middle forties. She would hardly be hoping to marry Pryce and have children. The pleasure of domestic life together was something that had never been a possibility, unless they were prepared to forgo all social acceptance and reduce their standard of living to approaching penury by comparison with their present situations. And Pryce at least would never countenance that, on her behalf, even if he might on his own.

Was that enough to resort to murder?

He knew what it was like to love a woman so completely that she haunted all private moments; all pleasure was pervaded with thoughts of her, the desire to share; all loneliness and pain were reflections of being separated from her. But never in the blackest or most self-wounding times had he imagined any happiness lay in forcing the issue or resorting to physical or emotional violence.

If Juniper and Pryce had descended to an affaire, deceiving Stafford, Micah Drummond despised their weakness and their duplicity, but he also felt a compassion he could not deny.

He inclined to think Livesey had misunderstood Stafford's intentions about reopening the Blaine/Godman case, or else Stafford had intentionally misled him, for whatever reason. It had been an unusually ugly case. Emotions had been fever high, beyond the edge of hysteria. It would not surprise him to learn that some of that emotion had lasted this long, even though he could not think who would have killed Stafford, or what purpose they now hoped to serve.

Stafford had left no notes to indicate what evidence he was investigating, or what he believed to be the truth, who he suspected, even, of lying, far less of having killed Kingsley Blaine.

The only way to learn would be to investigate the case again themselves. Pitt would probably begin with the original witnesses and suspects. Drummond could start at the top, with the senior police officer in charge of the men who had conducted the investigation—a deputy commissioner, and senior to himself. Therefore he sent a brief note requesting an interview.

It was granted, and Drummond found himself in the ornate and overfurnished office of Deputy Commissioner Aubrey Winton at ten o'clock the following morning.

Winton was a man of average height, fair curling hair receding a little at the temples, and an expression of calm, satisfied confidence.

"Good morning, Drummond," he said civilly. "Come in—come in!" He held out his hand and shook Drummond's briefly, then returned to his seat behind the desk. He leaned back and swung around to face Drummond, indicating another chair. "Please, sit down. Cigar?" He waved his hand at a heavily scrolled silver box on the desk top. "What can I do for you?"

Drummond did not prevaricate; there was no time. They were colleagues, not friends.

"The Blaine/Godman case," he answered. "It seems it may be the cause of a further crime in my area."

Winton frowned. "That is most unlikely. It was all cleared up—five years ago." There was heavy disbelief in his voice. He was not going to accept anything so unpleasant without irrefutable proof. Already the atmosphere was cooler.

"Mr. Justice Stafford," Drummond explained, resenting the necessity, "was killed in the theater three nights ago. He had said he was reopening the case." He met Winton's eyes and saw them harden.

"Then I can only assume he found something improper

in the conduct of the trial," Winton said guardedly. "The evidence was conclusive."

"Was it?" Drummond asked with interest, as if the matter were still undecided. "I am not familiar with it. Perhaps you would acquaint me?"

Winton shifted his body but his face remained immobile, eyes on Drummond's face.

"If you insist, but I can see no purpose to it. The case was final, Drummond. There is nothing more to add. Stafford must have been pursuing something in the trial," he repeated.

"For example?" Drummond raised his eyebrows questioningly.

"I have no idea. I am not a lawyer."

"Nor I." With difficulty Drummond curbed his desire to be openly critical. "But Stafford was—and he heard the appeal. What could have arisen now that he did not have available to him then? He and the other judges of appeal must have had the whole trial before them at the time."

Winton's face pinched with anger and his fingers on the desk top were clenched. "What is it you want, Drummond? Are you implying that we did not investigate the case thoroughly? I suggest you refrain from making such offensive and ill-informed remarks on a case about which you know very little."

The swiftness and the belligerence of his response betrayed a sensitivity that took Drummond by surprise. Justification he had expected, but not such a leap to defend. Obviously Winton still felt a guilt, or at least a sense of accusation.

Drummond kept his temper with an effort. "I have the murder of a judge to investigate," he said in a hard, careful voice. "If you were in my position, and heard that he had been planning to reopen an old case, and was interviewing the chief witnesses again on the very day he was murdered, and they were among the few people who had the opportunity to have killed him, would you not look into the evidence of the case yourself?"

Winton took a deep breath and his face relaxed a little,

as though he realized his reaction had been excessive, exposing his own vulnerability.

"Yes—yes, I suppose I would, however pointless it proved to be. Well, what can I tell you?" He colored faintly. "The investigation was very thorough. It had to be. It was an appalling crime; the whole country was watching us, from the Home Secretary down."

Drummond did not make the polite assurances the remark invited. The very fact that Winton had defended himself so sharply indicated he doubted it.

Winton shifted his position again.

"The officer in charge was Charles Lambert, an excellent man, the best," he began. "Of course the public outcry was immense. The newspapers were headlining it in every issue, and the Home Secretary was calling us regularly, putting tremendous pressure on us to find the killer within a week at the outside. I don't know if you have ever handled such a case yourself." His eyes searched Drummond's face for understanding. "Have you experienced the pressure, the outcry, everyone angry, frightened, anxious to prove themselves? The Home Secretary actually came down here to the station himself, all frock coat, pinstripe trousers and white spats." His expression hardened at the recollection, and Drummond could imagine the scene: the Home Secretary irate, nervous, pacing the floor and giving impossible commands, not thinking how they might be obeyed, only of the pressure on him from the House of Commons and the public. If the murder were not solved and the man tried and hanged quickly, his own political reputation would be in danger. Home Secretaries had fallen before, and no man was secure if the outcry were sufficient. The Prime Minister would sacrifice him to the wolves of fear.

"We put every man on it we could," Winton continued, his voice sharp with memory. "And the best!" He grunted. "But in the event it turned out not to be particularly difficult. It was not a random lunatic; the motive was plain enough and he was not very clever. He was seen actually leaving Farriers' Lane at the time, with blood on his clothes."

"Seen leaving Farriers' Lane?" Drummond interrupted incredulously. If that were true, how could Tamar Macaulay possibly doubt his guilt? Surely even family love could not be so blind? "By whom?"

"A group of men lounging around," Winton replied.

Drummond caught some inflection in his voice, some lack of force which made him uncertain.

"Saw Godman—or saw someone?" he asked.

Winton looked fractionally less confident. "They did not identify him with any surety," he replied. "But the flower seller did. That was a couple of streets away, but she had no doubt whatever. There was no shadow there, and he actually stopped and spoke to her just after the clock had struck, joked with her, she said! So she not only saw his face and heard his voice, she also knew the time."

"Going away from Farriers' Lane or towards it?" Drummond asked.

"Away."

"So it was after the murder. And he stopped to talk to a flower seller? How extraordinary! Didn't she notice the blood on him? If it was visible to the layabouts in the street, it must have been very obvious to her."

Winton hesitated, anger flickering in his expressive eyes. "Well—no, she didn't see it. But that is easily explainable. When he came out of Farriers' Lane he was wearing an overcoat. He had disposed of it by the time he reached the flower seller. Which is natural! He could not afford to be seen in a coat covered with blood. And there must have been a hell of a lot of it from a murder like that."

"Why did he not leave it in Farriers' Lane, rather than come out still wearing it and risk being seen at all?" Drummond asked the obvious question.

"God knows!" Winton said savagely. "Perhaps it was being seen by the layabouts that made him aware of it. He may not even have noticed it himself until then. He was a man in an insane rage, demented enough to kill a man and crucify him, for God's sake! Don't expect logical thought from him."

"And yet he behaved like a perfectly normal man a couple of streets away, joking with a flower seller. Did you find the coat? There cannot have been much ground to look."

"No, we didn't!" Winton snapped. "But then that's hardly surprising, is it! A good winter coat doesn't lie around long, bloodstained or not, on a cold evening on the London streets. Wouldn't expect to find it, days after the event."

"Where did he go after the flower seller saw him?"

"Home. We got the cabby who took him. Picked him up in Soho Square and set him down in Pimlico. Not that it makes much difference. The murder was already committed by then."

There was little more for Drummond to say. He could sympathize with Winton and indeed with all the men who worked on the case. The pressures must have been constant and intense, newspapers screaming headlines of horror and outrage, the public in the street full of criticism and demand that the police do the job for which they were paid, grudgingly, and from taxes. And certainly the hardest to resist, the most powerful and most uncomfortable, would be from their own superiors, giving orders, demanding that solutions be found and proved within days, even hours.

And then there was the other pressure, which was between them in a silent understanding, not needing speech, certainly not explanation. Drummond was a member of the Inner Circle, that secret brotherhood dedicated to works of beneficence, discreet gifts to help charitable organizations, and the furtherance of the careers of individual members so that they should gain influence—and power. Membership was secret. Any given man might know a few by name, or by sign and word, but not all. Allegiance to the Circle was paramount; it overrode all other loves and loyalties, all other calls upon honor.

Drummond had no idea whether Aubrey Winton was a member of the Inner Circle or not, but he thought it extremely likely. And that pressure would be the greatest of all, because it would be hidden; there would be no appeal and no help.

His sympathy for Winton was sharpened. It was not an enviable position, then or now, except that it seemed he had done all that anyone could, and his behavior was beyond exception.

"I cannot think what Stafford was following," he said aloud. "Even had there been some irregularity in the trial—or in the appeal—it seems beyond question Aaron Godman was guilty. Nothing can be served by raking it up again. I begin to think the answer lies elsewhere."

Winton smiled for the first time.

"Not an appealing thought," he agreed. "I understand why you sought to find another answer, but I am afraid it doesn't lie with the Blaine/Godman case. Sorry."

"Indeed," Drummond said. "Thank you for your time." He rose to his feet. "I'll tell my man all you told me."

"Not at all. Very delicate," Winton said with understatement. "Sometimes our position is not easy."

Drummond smiled sourly and bade him good-day.

The afternoon was fine, with a brisk wind blowing away the clouds and allowing brilliant shafts of autumn sunlight into the streets. Trees along the pavement and in the squares and parks were shedding their last leaves and there was a sharpness in the air that made Drummond think of woodsmoke, ripening berries in the hedges, and gardeners turning the damp earth and lifting and breaking the clumps of perennial flowers ready to replant for the spring. In the past when his wife had been alive and his daughters young, before he sold the house and took a flat in Piccadilly, there would have been chrysanthemums blooming in the borders, great shaggy, tawny-headed things that smelled like loam and rain on leaves.

He ached to share such thoughts. As always lately, his mind turned to Eleanor Byam. He had seen her very little since the scandal. Many times he had wished to go to her, but then he had remembered how he and Pitt—no, that was untrue, it had been Pitt with Charlotte who had done it; but it was their investigation, their persistence and intelligence which had uncovered the truth, and that truth had ruined

Eleanor, made her a widow and an outcast where before her husband had been honored and she had been respected and liked.

Now she had sold their big house in Belgravia and retired to a small set of rooms in Marylebone, her income gone and her name only whispered in society, with awe and pity. There were no invitations, and precious few calls. Drummond was not responsible. No part of the crime or the tragedy which had overcome Sholto Byam had been his doing, and yet he felt the very sight of him must bring back to her only painful thoughts and comparisons.

Yet he found himself walking towards Milton Street, and unconsciously lengthening his stride.

It was late afternoon and the lamplighters were lifting their long poles to turn on the gas and bring the sudden glow of warmth along the darkening street when he came to Eleanor's rooms. If he stopped to think now his courage would fail him. He walked straight up to the door and pulled the bell. It was a very ordinary house, curtains drawn in grim respectability, small garden neat, bright with a few late daisies and golden leaves.

A middle-aged maid with a suspicious face opened the door.

"Yes sir?" The "sir" was an afterthought on seeing the quality of his coat and the silver head to his stick.

"Good evening," he said, lifting his hat a fraction. "I would like to see Mrs. Byam, if she is at home." He fished in his pocket and brought out a card. "My name is Drummond—Micah Drummond."

"Is she expecting yer, Mr. Drummond?"

"No. But"—he stretched the truth a little—"we are old friends and I was in the neighborhood. Will you please ask her if she will see me?"

"I'll take the message," she said less than generously. "But I can't do no more'n that. I work for Mrs. Stokes as owns the 'ouse, not for the ladies wot 'as the rooms." And without waiting for a reply she left Drummond on the step and went to discharge her errand.

Drummond looked around him, oppressed by the change

from the old circumstances. Such a short while ago, Eleanor had been mistress of a rich and spacious house in the best part of London, with a full staff of servants. Now she had a few rooms in someone else's building, and her door was answered by someone else's servant who it seemed owed her no allegiance, and precious little courtesy. What permanent staff she had he did not know. He had only seen one ladies' maid on his previous visit shortly after she had come.

The maid returned, her face pinched with disapproval.

"Mrs. Byam will see you, sir, if you come this way." And without waiting to see if he followed, she turned on her heel and marched along the passage towards the back of the house. She knocked sharply on a glass partition door.

It was opened by Eleanor herself. She looked very different from her days in Belgravia. Her hair was still dressed in the same manner, sweeping back from her forehead, jet-black with a peppering of gray which was broader now at the temples, almost a streak. Her face was still the same with olive skin and wide gray eyes. But there was a tiredness in it; the certainty and the composure had slipped away, leaving her vulnerable. She wore no jewelry at all, and her gown was very simple dark blue. It was well cut, but devoid of lace or embroidery. To Drummond she looked younger than before and, in spite of all that lay between them, more immediate, more warmly real.

"Good evening, Micah," she said, pulling the door wide. "How pleasant of you to call. Please come in. You look well." She turned to the maid, who was standing in the center of the hallway and was filled with curiosity. "Thank you, Myrtle, that will be all."

With a sniff Myrtle retreated.

Eleanor smiled as Drummond came in. "Not the most appealing creature," she said wryly, taking his hat and stick and setting them in the stand. "Please come into the sitting room." She led the way, offering him a seat in the small, modestly furnished parlor. He had never been farther than this, and guessed there was probably no more than a bedroom, maid's room, kitchen and possibly a bathroom or dressing room of some sort beyond.

She did not ask him why he had come, but he had to offer some sort of explanation. One did not simply arrive on people's doorsteps. And he could hardly tell her the truth—that he desired above all things merely to see her again, to be near her.

"I was—" He nearly said "passing." That was absurd, an insult she did not deserve. It would be idiotic to pretend the visit was chance. They both knew better than that. He should have thought what to say before he came this far. But then he would not have come at all had he stopped and weighed it. He tried again. "I have had a long and trying day." He smiled and saw the color creep up her cheeks. "I wanted to do something totally pleasing. I thought of chrysanthemums in the rain, and the smell of wet earth, and leaves and blue woodsmoke, and I knew of no one else I could share them with."

She looked away and blinked several times. It was a moment before he realized there were tears in her eyes. He had no idea whether he should apologize or be tactful and pretend not to have noticed. Or if he did that, would she find him unbearably cold? Or if he remarked it, would that be offensively intrusive? He was in an agony of indecision and felt his face burn.

"You could not have said anything kinder." Her voice was gentle and a little husky. She swallowed hard, and then again. "I am sorry your day was trying. Have you a difficult case? I suppose it is confidential?"

"No—not really, but it is most unpleasant."

"I'm sorry. I imagine most of them are."

He wanted to ask her about herself, how she felt, what she did with her days, if she was all right, if there was anything he could do for her. But it would unquestionably have been intrusive, and worse than that, it might seem as if it were based in pity, as if his entire visit were one of a sense of obligation and compassion, and she would hate that.

She was sitting looking at him, waiting, her face quick

with interest. Between them the low fire burned with just sufficient coal to keep it alight.

He found he was talking about himself, and that was not what he had wanted to do, apart from the ill manners of it. It was she he cared about, not himself, but he had to fill the silence and he was so afraid of appearing to condescend. He wanted to talk about music, or walking in the rain, the smell of wet leaves, the evening light across the sky, but then she would find him too pressing—too forward when she was so vulnerable.

So he told her about Judge Stafford, and what Aubrey Winton had told him of the Blaine/Godman case.

It was silent outside, and raining in the dark; the hall clock had struck eight, when he suddenly realized how long he had been there, and that it was past time he left. He had outstayed a social call. Now it had become difficult to return to politeness and excuse himself. The outside world intruded again.

He rose to his feet.

"I have kept you too long, because for a while I forgot my manners and simply enjoyed myself. Please forgive me."

She rose also, gracefully, but the shadows of reality returned to her face.

"There is nothing to forgive," she replied. It was the obvious thing to say, yet he felt she really meant it. For all the stilted words there was an ease of understanding between them. It was on the edge of his tongue to ask if he might call again, then he changed his mind. If she refused, and she might feel she should, then he had closed the door to himself. Better simply to come.

"Thank you for receiving me," he said with a smile. "Good night."

"Good night, Micah."

He hesitated only a moment, then picked up his hat and his stick and went out into the main hallway and back to the wet, lamplit street, the loneliness within him warmed and illuminated, and yet also sharper.

4

THERE WAS NOTHING Pitt could do on Sunday. There were no places of business open, and he was quite certain that none of the private persons he wished to speak to would be available and agreeable even to receiving him, let alone giving him the time and attention he would need in order to gain the information, or even the impressions, he desired.

So he had a thoroughly enjoyable day at home with Charlotte, Jemima and Daniel. It was the loveliest of autumn weather, utterly windless with hazy sunshine and a soft golden light, a sense of height in the sky that made it possible to forget all London around them and imagine that beyond the wall there were trees and harvest fields.

Pitt had little time to spend in his garden, but what there was was rare and precious, and he loved it fiercely. From the moment he laid down his knife and fork from breakfast, he went out and started to dig, dressed in old trousers and with his sleeves rolled up. He lifted the dark earth and turned it with intense satisfaction, breaking the clumps, parting the tangled roots of perennials now over, and dividing them into new plants for the spring. The Michaelmas daisies were blooming in blue-and-purple towers and the asters and chrysanthemums raised shaggy heads of cerise and lilac, gold, red, white and pink. The last roses were spare and precious. It was the final cutting of the grass, and the air was filled with the smell of it, and of earth mold, and sun on damp leaves.

Seven-year-old Jemima was dressed in last year's pinafore and was half squatting on the ground beside him, her face smeared with mud, deep in happy concentration, her fingers busy with untangling roots and getting out the weeds. A couple of yards away, Daniel, two years younger, was kneeling down listening to Charlotte trying to explain to him which leaves were chickweed and which flowers.

Pitt turned and looked over Jemima's head and caught Charlotte's eye. She smiled at him, hair across her brows, a smear of earth on her cheek, and he felt more totally happy than he could ever recall. There were some moments so precious the ache to hold on to them was a physical thing. He had to force himself to have faith that others as good would come, and the letting go must be easy, or they would be crushed in the very act of clinging.

By five o'clock the sun was slanting low; there were already deep shadows under the walls, and the dark earth was smooth and full of freshly planted clumps. They were all tired, filthy, and extraordinarily satisfied with everything.

Daniel fell asleep over tea, and Jemima's head sank lower and lower as Pitt read her a bedtime story afterwards. By half past six the house was quiet, the fire lit with Pitt dozing beside it, his feet propped up on the fender, and Charlotte was absentmindedly sewing buttons on a shirt. Monday morning seemed like another world.

But duty returned sharply enough with daylight, and nine o'clock found Pitt alighting from a hansom cab in Markham Square, Chelsea, with the intention of seeking the other witness Stafford had spoken to the day he had died, and whom Pitt had not yet met, Devlin O'Neil.

He had obtained the address from Stafford's chambers, and now paid the cabby and climbed the steps to the front door of a very substantial terraced house with wide porticoes and a brass doorknob in the shape of a griffon's head, and a fanlight above of stained glass. The house seemed to be at least three windows wide on either side of the door, and was four stories high. If Devlin O'Neil owned this establishment then he was indeed doing very well, and had no reason to have quarreled with his friend Kingsley Blaine over a few guineas' wager.

The door was opened by a smart maid in a dark dress and very crisp lace-trimmed cap and apron. She was cheerful and full of confidence.

"Yes sir?"

"Good morning. My name is Thomas Pitt." He handed her his card. "I apologize if I call inconveniently early, but I would very much like to see Mr. O'Neil before he leaves on the business of the day. The matter is connected with the death of an acquaintance of his, and is somewhat urgent."

"Oh dear! I'm sure as I don't know who's dead. You'd better come in, and I'll tell Mr. O'Neil as you're here." She opened the door wide for him, put the card on the silver card tray, and conducted him to the morning room. It was somber, fireless, but immaculately clean, and decorated in a highly conservative and traditional style. The furniture was large, mostly carved oak, and covered with every conceivable kind of picture and ornament, trophies of every visit, relative and family event for at least four decades. The chair backs were protected by embroidered antimacassars edged with very worn crochetwork. The high ceiling was coffered in deep squares, giving the room a classical appearance belied by the ornate brass light brackets. There were no flowers on the side table, but a stuffed weasel under a glass dome. It was a very common sort of domestic decoration, but looking into its bright, artificial eyes, Pitt found it both repulsive and sad. He had grown up on a large country estate, where his father had been gamekeeper, and he could so easily visualize the creature in the wild, savagely alive. This motionless and rather dusty relic of its being was horribly offensive.

The door opened while he was still looking at the weasel, and he turned around to see the maid's polite face.

"If you would like to come this way, sir, Mr. O'Neil will see you."

"Thank you." Pitt followed her back across the hallway and into a high-ceilinged square room looking onto an extremely neat garden where autumn flowers grew in paradelike rows.

The furniture inside the room was large and heavy, one sideboard reaching above eight feet high and decked with all manner of dishes, tureens and gravy boats. The curtains were swathed and looped in a wealth of fabric in wines and golds. Family photographs in silver frames covered the tops of other tables and bureaus, and there were several framed samplers on the walls.

Devlin O'Neil stood by the window and turned to face Pitt as soon as he heard the door. He was slender, perhaps a fraction over average height, and casually but most expensively dressed in a check jacket of fine wool, and a fresh Egyptian cotton shirt. The price of his boots would have fed a poor family for a week. He was dark haired and dark eyed, with a face full of humor and undisciplined imagination, although at the moment his expression was concerned.

"Pitt, is it? Gwyneth said you've called about someone's death. Is that so?"

"Yes, Mr. O'Neil," Pitt replied. "Mr. Justice Stafford. He died very suddenly in the theater last week. I daresay you are already aware of that."

"Ah—I cannot say that I am. I suppose I may have read it in the newspapers. Of course I'm very sorry, but I didn't know the man." He had a very slight accent, little more than a music in his voice which Pitt struggled to place.

"But you met with him the day he died," he pointed out.

O'Neil looked uncomfortable, but his dark eyes did not leave Pitt's face.

"Indeed I did, but he called on me over a matter of . . . I suppose you would call it business. I had never seen him before, and I never saw him again." He smiled fleetingly. "Not what you would call a friend, Mr. Pitt."

Pitt placed the accent. It was County Antrim.

"I apologize if I gave the wrong impression to your

maid." He smiled back. "I meant only that he was someone about whom you might have relevant information."

O'Neil's eyebrows shot up, high and arched. "He didn't discuss his health with me! And I have to say, he looked very well. Not a young man, of course, and I daresay a pound or two heavy, but none the worse for that."

"What did he discuss with you, Mr. O'Neil?"

O'Neil hesitated, then slowly his expression eased and the amusement in it was undisguised. He turned from the window and regarded Pitt curiously.

"I imagine you may know that already, Mr. Pitt, or you would not be here at all. It seems he was still interested in the death of poor Kingsley Blaine five years ago. I cannot think why, except that that unfortunate woman, Miss Macaulay, won't let go of it. And I daresay Mr. Stafford wanted to end the talk and the questions about it once and for all. Let the dead bury the dead, and all that—don't you agree?"

"Is that what he said?"

"Well, now, he didn't tell me in so many words, you understand." O'Neil walked across the room, his confidence apparent in the ease of his bearing. He sat sideways on the arm of one of the big chairs. He looked at Pitt with courteous interest. "He asked me about it all, of course. And I told him the same as I told the police, and the courts, at the time. There isn't anything else I can say." He waved at Pitt to sit in one of the chairs. "He was all very civil, very pleasant," he went on. "But he didn't say why he was asking. But then I don't suppose it's the way of gentlemen of his sort of position to confide in the likes of us, who are just the poor general public." He said it all with a smile, but Pitt could imagine he was disturbed by having the matter raised again, and not knowing for what reason. It can only have been painful. If Stafford was trying to lay the matter to rest, it would not have hurt him to have said so to O'Neil. On the other hand, if Stafford had been planning to reopen the case, he might well not wish to mention that.

"Do you mind telling me what he said to you, Mr. O'Neil?" Pitt sat down at last, specifically invited.

"Well, certainly I have no objection to your knowing, sir," O'Neil replied, watching Pitt's face closely in spite of his casual attitude. "But it would be a courtesy, you understand, if you were to tell me why. I would surely take it kindly."

"Of course." Pitt crossed his legs and smiled, looking directly at him. "Mr. Stafford was murdered that evening."

"Good God! You don't say so!" If O'Neil was not surprised he was a superlative actor.

"Very regrettable," Pitt answered. "At the theater."

"Indeed. And him a supreme court judge, and all. What kind of a blackguard would kill a judge, and him an old man too—or at least an old man from where you and I stand." O'Neil pulled a face. "Was it robbery, then?"

"No—he was poisoned."

"Poisoned!" There was a widening of surprise in his dark eyes. "Well, by all the saints—what an extraordinary thing to do. And why was he poisoned? Was it a case he was on, do you think?"

"I don't know, Mr. O'Neil. That is one of the reasons I would very much like to know what he said to you that afternoon."

O'Neil's stare did not waver in the slightest. His intelligent, volatile face was far more controlled than Pitt had first thought, and yet for all the natural charm, there was nothing ingenuous in it.

"Of course you would," he answered readily. "And so would I, were I in your position. I'll be happy to oblige you, Mr. Pitt." He shifted position very slightly. "He first asked me if I recalled the night Kingsley Blaine was murdered. All this was after the pleasantries had been exchanged, of course. To which I said that I most certainly did—as if I would be able to forget it, for all that I tried hard enough! Then he asked me to recount it all for him, which I did."

"Could you recount it for me, please, Mr. O'Neil?" Pitt interrupted.

"If you wish. Well, it was early autumn, but I daresay you know that. Kingsley and I had decided to go to the theater." He shrugged expressively, lifting his shoulders high and turning out his hands, palms upwards. "He was married, but I was fancy-free. For all that, he was very enamored of the actress Tamar Macaulay, and he intended to go backstage after the show and visit with her. He had a gift which he proposed to give her, and no doubt he foresaw that she would be suitably grateful for it."

"What was it?" Pitt interrupted again.

"A necklace. Do you not know that?" He looked surprised. "Of course you do! Yes, a very handsome piece. Belonged to his mother-in-law, rest her soul. And for sure he shouldn't have been giving it away to another woman. But then we all do foolish things at times. The poor devil's dead and answered for it now." He stopped for a moment, regarding Pitt with interest.

"Indeed." Pitt felt compelled at least to acknowledge that he had heard.

"But then he and I had something of a disagreement—nothing much, you understand, just a wager on the outcome of a fight." He grinned. "An exhibition of the noble art of pugilism, to you, Mr. Pitt. We disagreed as to who had won—and he refused to pay me, although according to the rules, the money was mine."

O'Neil pushed out his lower lip ruefully. "I left the theater early in something of a temper, and went to a house of pleasure." He smiled candidly, covering whatever embarrassment he might have felt. "Kingsley stayed with Tamar Macaulay, and left very late, so I gather. At least that was the testimony of the doorman. Kingsley, poor soul, was given a message, purporting to be from me, that he should meet me at a gambling club we both frequented in those days." He winced. "The way to it led through Farriers' Lane, and we all know what happened there."

"Was the message written or verbal?"

"Oh, verbal—all word of mouth."

"But you didn't see Mr. Blaine again?"

"Not alive, no, the poor soul."

"Was that all the judge asked you?"

"The judge?" O'Neil's dark eyes widened. "Oh—poor

Mr. Stafford, you mean? Yes, I think so. Frankly it seemed something of a waste of time to me. The case is closed. The verdict was given, and there was no real question about it. The police found the right fellow. Poor devil lost his head and ran amok." He pulled a slight face. "Not a Christian, you know. Different ideas of right and wrong, I daresay. They hanged him—no choice. Evidence was conclusive. That must have been what Mr. Stafford had in mind to do—prove it so even Miss Macaulay would have to admit it to herself and leave off pestering everyone."

That could so easily be the truth. Pitt had come because it was an obvious duty to retrace Stafford's steps. Someone that day had put liquid opium into his flask, or Livesey and his friend would have been poisoned when they drank from it earlier. But he had also hoped to learn something that would tell him whether Stafford intended to reopen the case or to close it forever. Perhaps that was a forlorn hope? O'Neil had been one of the original suspects. He would hardly wish the matter raised again.

Pitt looked at where O'Neil was lounging easily in the other large chair. If he was nervous he hid it better than anyone Pitt had ever seen. He looked casual, rueful, polite; a man dealing generously with a most unpleasant subject, yielding to an obligation socially demanded of him and which he understood without resentment.

"Did he ask you anything in any way new, Mr. O'Neil?" Pitt smiled bleakly, trying to keep an air as if he knew something he had not yet revealed.

O'Neil blinked. "No, not that I can think of. It all seemed to be old ground to me. Oh—he did ask if Kingsley carried a stick or a cane of any sort. But he didn't say why he wanted to know."

"And did Mr. Blaine carry a stick?"

"No." O'Neil pulled a face. "He was not the kind of man to enter into a fight with anyone. It was a personal murder, Mr. Pitt. If anyone is trying to say it was a struggle, a face-to-face fight of any sort, then they're just dreaming." All the light vanished out of his expression and he leaned forward. "It was brutal, swift and complete. I saw the body."

He was pale now. "I was the one who went to identify him. He had no family other than his wife and his father-in-law. It seemed the decent thing that I should do. There was no other mark on him, Mr. Pitt. Just the stab wound that killed him, in his side and up to the heart . . . and the—the nails in his hands and feet." He shook his head. "No—no, there was no way it was a battle involving two men both armed. He did not defend himself."

"Did Mr. Stafford not say why he asked?"

"No—no, he didn't. I asked him, but he evaded an answer."

Pitt could think of no reason why Stafford should make such an enquiry. Had it something to do with the medical evidence he had questioned? He must find Humbert Yardley and ask him.

"What was Kingsley Blaine like, Mr. O'Neil?" he resumed. "I don't have the advantage of knowing anything about him at all. Was he a large man?"

"Oh." O'Neil was taken aback. "Well—taller than I am, but loose limbed, if you know what I mean." He looked at Pitt questioningly. "Not an athlete, more of a . . . well, speak no ill of the dead—and he was a friend of mine—but more of a dreamer, you know?" He rose to his feet with some grace. "Would you like to see a photograph of him? We have a few in the house."

"Have you?" Pitt was surprised, although it was surely not unreasonable. The men had been friends.

"But of course," O'Neil said quickly. "After all, he lived here all his married life—which God bless him was only a couple of years."

Pitt was surprised. There had been nothing about this in the notes he had read.

"This was Kingsley Blaine's house?"

"Ah no." O'Neil was obviously amused at Pitt's confusion. "The house belongs to my father-in-law, Mr. Prosper Harrimore. And of course my grandmother-in-law, Mrs. Adah Harrimore, lives here too." He smiled again with total candor. "I married Kingsley's widow. You didn't know that?"

"No," Pitt admitted, rising to his feet also. "No, I didn't. Did Mr. Stafford speak to any of the rest of your . . . family?"

"No—no, not at all. He came later in the day, about four o'clock. I was home from a most agreeable late luncheon. He had sent a message 'round to my club. I preferred to meet him here rather than there." He went over to the door and opened it. "Didn't know what he wanted then, except that it was to do with Kingsley. It was not something I wished to discuss in public, or to remind my friends of, if I were fortunate enough that they had forgotten."

"And the other members of the family were not at home?" Pitt went through and into the hall.

O'Neil followed him. "No—my wife was out calling upon friends, my grandmother-in-law was taking a carriage ride, and my father-in-law was at his place of business. He has interests in a trading emporium in the City."

Pitt stood back for O'Neil to lead the way across the very fine hall, flagged in black and white with a magnificent stair rising to a wide gallery above. "I should be obliged to see a photograph," he said. He had no specific idea as to what he could learn from it, but he wanted to see Kingsley Blaine; he wanted at least an impression of the man who was at the heart of this tragedy which it seemed was still so dangerously alive five years after Blaine himself was dead and Aaron Godman hanged for his murder.

"Ah well, then," O'Neil said cheerfully, his good humor apparently returned. "I'll show you, with pleasure." And he opened the door and led Pitt into another larger and warmer room where a fire burned in the hearth, crackling noisily, flames leaping, and a young woman with fair brown hair and unusually high cheekbones sat on a padded stool, beside her a dark, curly-haired child of about two years old. Another child, whom Pitt judged to be about four, sat on the carpet in front of her, a thin, brightly colored book in her hands. She was quite different in appearance: Her hair was ash fair with only the slightest wave in it, and she had solemn blue eyes.

"Hello, my pretty," O'Neil said cheerfully, patting her head.

"Hello, Papa," she replied happily. "I'm reading a story to Mama and James."

"Are you indeed?" O'Neil said with admiration, not questioning her truthfulness. "What is it about, then?"

"A princess," the child answered without hesitation. "And a fairy prince."

"Oh, that's marvelous, sweetheart."

"Grandpapa gave me the book." She held it up with pride. "He said I could be a princess like that, if I'm good."

"And so you can, my love, so you can," O'Neil assured her. "Kathleen, my dear," he said to the woman, "this is Mr. Pitt, who has called on a matter of business. Mr. Pitt, may I present my wife."

"How do you do, Mrs. O'Neil," Pitt replied courteously. So this was Kathleen Blaine O'Neil. She was pretty, very womanly, and yet there was strength in the cast of her features, not masked by the soft chin and the gentle eyes.

"How do you do, Mr. Pitt," she said without any expression except a slight curiosity.

"Mr. Pitt is interested in photography," O'Neil said, keeping his back to Kathleen and facing Pitt. "There are one or two good pictures in here I wished to show him."

"Of course." Kathleen smiled at Pitt. "Please be welcome, Mr. Pitt. I hope they are of help to you. Do you take many photographs? I expect you have met some interesting people?"

Pitt hesitated only a moment. "Yes, Mrs. O'Neil, I have certainly met some very interesting people, with quite unique faces, both good and bad."

She continued to regard him without making any further remark.

"This is one that you might like," O'Neil said casually, and Pitt moved over beside him in front of a large, silver-framed photograph of a young woman, who was immediately recognizable as Kathleen O'Neil, in a very formal gown. Behind her was a man of apparently the same age, tall, still with the slenderness of youth, fair, wavy hair falling slightly over his left brow. It was a handsome face, good-humored, emotional, full of an easy, romantic sensuality. Pitt did not need to ask if it were Kingsley Blaine. He would ask O'Neil later, privately, if Blaine were the father of the elder child with the fair hair, but it would only be a formality; the answer was plain.

"Yes," he said thoughtfully. "An excellent picture. I am most obliged, Mr. O'Neil."

Kathleen was regarding him with interest.

"Is it helpful to you, Mr. Pitt? He was my first husband. He died about five years ago."

Pitt felt an abysmal hypocrite. Words raced through his mind. He should tell her he knew, but how without embarrassing O'Neil?

O'Neil came to his rescue.

"Mr. Pitt knows that, my dear," he said to his wife. "I explained to him."

"Oh. I see." But obviously she did not.

The conversation was rescued by the door opening and a man coming in. He looked first at O'Neil, then at Pitt, with a question sharp in his powerful, hatchet-nosed face. He was heavily built, barrel-chested, and he walked with a pronounced limp. Briefly he glanced at the children, and there was intense pride in his eyes for that moment before he turned back towards Pitt.

"Ah, a good morning to you, Papa-in-law," O'Neil said with a charming smile. "This is Mr. Pitt, a business acquaintance of mine."

"Indeed!" Harrimore looked at Pitt civilly enough, but with a carefully guarded expression. He had a remarkable face; at one moment it was almost intimidating with its strength, and yet when he moved, and the intelligence lit his eyes, it was also vulnerable. His mouth was twisted a little, but it was impossible to say whether with cruelty or his own pain. "Good of you to come to us at home, Mr. Pitt, and save us the trouble of traveling at this hour. Have you eaten, sir, or may we offer you some refreshment?"

"That is very kind of you, Mr. Harrimore, but I have eaten, thank you," Pitt replied. Kathleen might have accepted an interest in photography as his reason for being there, but he did not think Prosper Harrimore would be taken in so easily.

"Devlin was showing Mr. Pitt the photograph of Kingsley and me at our wedding," Kathleen said with a smile.

"Indeed?" Harrimore said, looking at Pitt narrowly.

"An excellent example of the art," Pitt offered, glancing at O'Neil.

"Indeed it is," O'Neil agreed, then turned to his wife. "Perhaps you had better take the children, my dear, and see to their morning walk, now the weather is so pleasant."

She rose obediently, recognizing an order when she heard it. She excused herself to Pitt and her father, and followed by the two small children, she went out into the hallway and closed the door.

"Mr. Pitt is here about the recent and sudden death of Judge Stafford," O'Neil said immediately, his face resuming its earlier gravity. "I saw the poor man the very day he died, so natural it is I should be asked."

"Tactful of you, Mr. Pitt," Harrimore said slowly, looking him up and down. "And why is it you are concerned with the matter, sir? You don't look like a policeman."

Pitt was not sure whether that was a compliment or a complaint.

"Sometimes an advantage," he replied quietly. "But I did not mislead Mr. O'Neil in the matter."

"No—no, I imagine not." Uncertain humor flickered in Harrimore's eyes. "And why do the police involve themselves with the death of Mr. Stafford?"

"Because I regret he did not die of any natural cause."

Harrimore's face tightened. "Not our concern, sir. We have had more than our share of murder in this house, as I am sure you will be aware. My late son-in-law met his death by violence. I would thank you not to rake up that matter and distress my family again. My daughter has already suffered profoundly and I will do all I can to protect them all from further distress." He looked at Pitt grimly and the tacit threat in him was unmistakable.

112

"That is why I refrained from mentioning the true cause of my visit in her presence, sir," Pitt answered quietly. "Mrs. O'Neil could know nothing of Mr. Stafford, since she was not at home when he called, so I judged tact to be the better part."

"At least that is something," Harrimore said grudgingly. "Although what Devlin could tell you I don't know."

"Very little," O'Neil said with feeling. "Only what Mr. Pitt already knows from others, Papa-in-law. But I suppose the poor man has a hard job to do."

Harrimore grunted.

The door opened again and a very elderly woman came in, heavy bosomed, narrow shouldered and broad hipped, but erect of carriage and with a fine head of hair. Her resemblance to Harrimore was so pronounced as to make introductions unnecessary, except for courtesy's sake.

"How do you do, Mrs. Harrimore," Pitt replied to her cool greeting.

Adah Harrimore regarded him with bright dark eyes, deep set like her son's, and acutely intelligent.

"Inspector," she said warily. "And what is it now? We have had no crime here. What do you want with us?"

"It's about Judge Stafford's death, poor man," O'Neil explained to her, patting a cushion in the chair to her side and plumping it up. "He died the other evening, at the theater, he did."

"For heaven's sake leave the thing alone!" she snapped, glaring at the chair. "I don't need to sit down yet. I am perfectly well! What if he did? Old men die all the time. I daresay he drank too much and took an apoplexy." She turned to Pitt and looked at him narrowly. "Why do you come here because a judge died at the theater? You had better have some excellent explanation for yourself, young man!"

"He did not die naturally, ma'am," Pitt replied, watching her face. "And he called here earlier that day, to see Mr. O'Neil. I wished to know his state of mind, and as much of what he said as Mr. O'Neil could recall."

"His state of mind was relevant to his death? Are you saying he took his own life?" she demanded.

"No. I regret to say he was killed."

Her nostrils flared very slightly as she let out her breath, and there was an almost imperceptible paling of the skin around her mouth.

"Was he. That is unfortunate, but it has nothing to do with this household, Mr. Pitt. He called here once, on some matter of enquiry, I am informed. We have not seen him either before or since. We regret his death, but other than that we can contribute nothing." She turned to O'Neil. "Devlin? I presume this man did not confide in you any concern for his safety?"

O'Neil looked at her with wide eyes. "No, Grandmama-in-law. He seemed to me perfectly composed and quite in command of the situation."

Her face was pale and there was a small muscle ticking in her right eyelid.

"Would it be impertinent of me to enquire what matter a judge came here to see you about? The family has no pleas before the court of appeal that I am aware of."

O'Neil hesitated only a moment, and he did not look at Pitt.

"Not at all, Grandmama-in-law," he said with an easy smile. "I did not mention it at the time, not to distress you, but the poor man was pestered by Tamar Macaulay to reopen the case of Kingsley's death, God rest him. He wanted to prove to her once and for all that it is closed. The verdict was correct, and she'll not change it, poor woman, by all her agitation. Let people forget and get on with their lives."

"I should think so," the old lady said vehemently. "The wretched creature must be demented to keep on raking it up. It is finished!" Her eyes were brilliant and hard. "Bad blood," she said bitterly. "You can't get away from it." She stared unwaveringly at O'Neil's face. "Kingsley's in his grave, and so is that damned Jew! Let us have some peace." Her face was hard, full of old hatred and a terrible grief.

"Quite so, Grandmama," O'Neil said gently. "Don't you

let it trouble you anymore. Now poor Mr. Stafford's in his grave too—or about to be. Let's hope that's enough even for Miss Macaulay."

Adah shivered and the look of loathing deepened in her eyes.

Prosper came to life suddenly as if until now he had been frozen and that instant obtained release.

"It is the end of it! Mr. Pitt, there is nothing we can do to help you," he said abruptly. "We wish you well, but whoever killed Mr. Stafford, you will have to seek for him elsewhere. No doubt he has personal enemies . . ." He left the rest unsaid, hanging in the air. He would not speak ill of the dead—it was vulgar—but the conclusions were implicit.

"Thank you for your courtesy in receiving me, ma'am." Pitt addressed Adah's rigid figure, and then Harrimore's. He accepted the inevitable. He would learn nothing more from O'Neil anyway. The answer that Stafford was only looking to establish the truth beyond question was too satisfactory, and too credible, for him to say anything different. And since apparently no one else had been at home, they could not be suspected, nor had they any motive. They were not involved in the murder of Kingsley Blaine; the original investigation had never considered them.

"Not at all," the old lady said stiffly, unbent only by the demands of civility. "Good day to you, Mr. Pitt."

Prosper glanced at his mother, then at Pitt, and smiled tightly, reaching for the bell to summon a maid who would show him to the door.

Outside in the quiet street Pitt turned it over in his mind. It looked more and more as if it were either Juniper Stafford or Adolphus Pryce who had put the opium in the flask. And indeed, futile and unnecessary as it was when looked at in the cold light of the mind, perhaps in the heat of passion they had imagined they could find some happiness with Stafford dead which would elude them as long as he lived. Obsession does not always see beyond the moment, and the hungers that consume and fill the mind until they are satisfied, whatever the cost.

Was that really what those two felt? It was something he would have to pursue, and the thought of it curled his lip with distaste. It was an intrusion he loathed. There were weaknesses in people no third party should know, and that kind of ill-balanced and devouring need for another person was one of them. It did not enlarge the one who felt it, it diminished, and in the end destroyed—as it seemed it had destroyed Juniper Stafford and her lover.

But before he began to search for evidence of that, he would clear the Blaine/Godman case from his mind altogether. He already knew quite a lot about it, but there might be other things, details known only to the police, which altered the picture. Also he wanted to form his own beliefs of the men who had conducted the original investigation, and the pressures they were under then, the area for mistakes, if possible their own impressions.

Consequently he walked slowly towards the main thoroughfare, hands in his pockets, thinking as he went. He did not like retracing other men's investigations, but he had no choice. Still he would try to do it as tactfully as possible, and he took a long time choosing the words with which he would begin.

He arrived at the Shaftesbury Avenue police station a little before noon.

"Yes sir?" the desk sergeant said politely, his face suitably blank.

"Inspector Pitt, from Bow Street," Pitt introduced himself. "I have a problem I think you might be able to help me with, if you'd oblige me with your time."

"Indeed, sir? I'm sure we'll do what we can. What problem might that be?"

"I've got a difficult case to which you might know some background. I'd appreciate speaking with the officer in charge of a case you handled about five years ago. A murder in Farriers' Lane."

The desk sergeant's face darkened. "That was all tidied

116

up at the time, Mr. Pitt. There in't nothing left over from that one. I was 'ere myself an' I know all about it."

"Yes, I know it was," Pitt agreed soothingly. "It is not a question of who was guilty of that, it is a matter arising out of the conclusion. I need to speak with the officer in charge then, if possible. He's still in the force?"

"O' course 'e is—been promoted since then. Did a fine job." The desk sergeant straightened his shoulders unconsciously and lifted his chin a fraction. "That's Chief Inspector Lambert. I daresay if 'e can 'elp you with your problem 'e'll be glad to. I'll certainly ask 'im for you, Inspector." And with that very firm putting of Pitt in his place, he retreated into the back regions of the office and returned several minutes later to tell Pitt that if he cared to wait for ten minutes or so, Mr. Lambert would see him.

Pitt accepted with a good grace, even though he itched to retaliate.

He kicked his heels for five minutes, then sat on the wooden bench and waited a further ten minutes, then stood again. Eventually a young constable appeared and conducted him to the small, untidy office where a roaring fire made the room claustrophobically hot after the cold outer office. Charles Lambert received him with a look of guarded civility. He was in his late forties, balding severely, but with good features and clear eyes.

"Good morning—Pitt, isn't it? Sit down." He waved towards the only other chair. "Sorry to keep you waiting. Very busy. Lot of nasty robberies. My sergeant says you need a spot of assistance. What can I do for you?"

"I'm working on the murder of Judge Samuel Stafford—"

Lambert's eyebrows rose. "Didn't know he was murdered! Thought he died in his box in the theater."

"He did. Of poison."

Lambert shook his head, pushing out his lower lip.

"My sergeant mentioned Farriers' Lane. What has Stafford's death to do with that?" His voice was guarded. "That was all over five years ago, and he wasn't the judge anyway. It was Quade—Thelonius Quade. Not that there

117

was any doubt about the verdict, or about the conduct of the trial."

"But there was an appeal," Pitt said as mildly as he could. He must remember all the time that he would get nothing if he angered Lambert and made him defensive. "No new evidence, I assume?"

"None. Just a desperate attempt to save the man from hanging. Understandable, I suppose, but futile."

Pitt took a deep breath. He was achieving nothing. Tact had its limitations.

"Stafford was enquiring into the case again. The day he died he interviewed most of the original suspects."

Lambert's face hardened and he sat up a little straighter.

"I don't know what for!" Already the note of defense was in his voice. "Unless the sister prevailed on him in some way." He shrugged in an open expression of his dismissal of the whole idea. "She's a handsome woman, and obsessed with the idea her brother was innocent. It's an ugly thing to suggest, I know." Again the edge was there in his tone, the guard against an expected attack. "But it happens. He wouldn't be the first man to lose his head over a beautiful and determined woman."

Pitt was irritated, but he tried to conceal it.

"No—of course not. And that may be all it was. But you will understand that if I am to say that, then I must have very good proof. The widow will not accept that easily—nor will his fellows on the bench." He forced a smile he did not feel. "It calls into question the virtue and good sense of all of them if we say he was simply a fool over a lovely face, and so far forgot his own mind and experience as to reopen a case for such a reason. I shall be in a very unenviable position if I say that and cannot prove it."

Lambert smiled back, relaxing a little as his mind moved from his own difficulties to Pitt's.

"You certainly will," he agreed with a feeling close to relish. "Their lordships will take very unkindly to that. You'll be looking for a job chasing pickpockets and card sharps in future."

"Precisely." Pitt shifted a little in his seat. The room was suffocating. "So can you tell me all you can recall of the Farriers' Lane murder, then I can tell my superiors he cannot have been following that for any sound reason at all." Mentally he apologized to Micah Drummond for the implicit slander.

"If you think it will help," Lambert replied. "It was all very straightforward, although we didn't expect it to be at the time."

"Ugly, I should think," Pitt murmured. "A lot of public outcry."

"Never known a case like it," Lambert agreed, moving back in his chair and making himself more comfortable. He understood what Pitt wanted now, and more importantly, why. "Except the Whitechapel murders—but of course they never caught the Ripper, poor devils. A few resignations over that."

"But you caught your man."

Lambert's eyes were sharp and clear hazel, meeting Pitt's with appreciation of all that was unsaid as well as the surface conversation between them.

"We did—and I got promoted. But it was all aboveboard." The edge came back into his voice. "The evidence was incontrovertible. I can't say we didn't have some luck, we did. But we also did a damnably good job! My men were excellent—disciplined, dedicated, and kept their tempers in difficult conditions. A lot of public hysteria. Lot of terror. Some very nasty incidents down the east end. Couple o' synagogues broken into, windows smashed, a pawnbroker near beaten to death. Posters all over the place and writing on walls. Some newspapers even called for all Jews to be run out of the city. Very ugly—but you can't blame them. It was one o' the worst murders in London." He was watching Pitt closely, studying his face, reading his expression.

Pitt tried to iron out his emotions and look impassive, and he was almost sure he failed.

"Yes?" he said politely. "I know the body of Kingsley Blaine was found in Farriers' Lane—by whom?"

Lambert recalled himself to the details with an effort.

119

"The blacksmith's boy early in the morning," he replied. "Gave the poor lad a turn he didn't get over as long as we knew him. Heard that after the trial he left London and went to the country. Sussex way."

"No one else passed through Farriers' Lane that night? Odd, wasn't it, if it was a usual passageway?" Pitt asked.

"Well, put it this way, if they did, either they didn't see Blaine nailed up to the stable door or they didn't report it. And I suppose either of those is quite likely. You'd be looking where you were going and in the dark not see him . . ."

"The stable wasn't in a direct path."

"No—no, it was over the far side of the yard."

"So whoever killed Blaine either lured him across the yard or was strong enough to carry him," Pitt reasoned.

"I suppose that follows," Lambert conceded. "But then he knew Godman; it wouldn't be hard to persuade him to come out of the alley into the yard . . ."

"Wouldn't it? I wouldn't go into a dark stable yard alone with a man whose sister I was seducing, would you?"

Lambert stared at him, his face growing pink with confusion and annoyance.

"I think you have leaped to a conclusion, Pitt, for which there are no grounds. Kingsley Blaine was a good-looking, well-spoken, rather naive young man who became enamored of a very skilled actress, not really all that beautiful, but . . . magnetic, a woman who knows how to manipulate men." There was both certainty and contempt in his voice. "If anyone was seduced, it was Blaine, not her. And Godman may have resented that like poison, but he knew it was true." He shook his head. "No, Pitt, Tamar Macaulay was not an innocent young girl seduced by a callous man. No one who knew the people concerned could have imagined that. I think it is quite easy to believe that Blaine would go to Godman, thinking himself quite safe."

Pitt thought for a moment, and kept his voice free from the skepticism he felt. "It may be that Tamar Macaulay was the leader in the affair, the seducer, if you wish—but do you suppose she allowed Blaine to realize that?"

"I have no idea." Lambert was contemptuous. "Does it matter?"

Pitt shifted position a little in the chair. He wished Lambert would open a window. The room was almost airless. "Well, it's not the truth of the relationship that matters, surely, but what Blaine thought it was," he pointed out. "If he imagined himself a hell of a fellow, having an affair with an actress, then he would have felt guilty, and wary—however ridiculous that was in fact."

"I doubt it," Lambert replied, his face hardening into resentment as he understood the point. "Godman was not a big man, either in height or build. Blaine was not heavy but he was tall. I don't think it would occur to him to have any physical fear."

Pitt shifted uncomfortably, instinctively pulling at his collar to ease it from choking him. "Well, if Blaine was a large man, and Godman quite slight, it is unlikely Godman could have carried Blaine once he was dead and lifted him up against the door while he nailed his hands and feet to it," he reasoned. "By the way, how did he manage that? Do you know?"

The color deepened in Lambert's face.

"No, I don't know, nor do I care, Inspector Pitt. The kind of rage he must have been in to do such a thing, maybe he found the strength after all. They say madmen have a superhuman power when the mania is on them."

"Maybe," Pitt said, heavy with doubt.

"What on earth could it matter now?" Lambert demanded harshly. "It was done. And he did it—that's beyond any question. Blaine, poor devil, was nailed up to the stable door." His face was pale, his voice charged with emotion. "I saw him myself." He shuddered. "Fixed there by farrier's nails through his hands and feet—arms wide like the figure of Christ, feet together, and blood all over the place. Godman was seen coming out of the alley with blood on him. He lifted the body up somehow, probably he nailed the hands one at a time."

"Have you ever tried to lift a dead body, Lambert?" Pitt asked very levelly.

"No—nor have I tried to crucify anyone—or ride a bicycle on a tightrope!" Lambert snapped. "But the fact that I can't do it doesn't mean it cannot be done. What are you trying to say, Pitt? That it wasn't Godman?"

"No. Just trying to understand what happened—and what it could have been that Judge Stafford was thinking when he questioned all the witnesses again. He was apparently concerned with the medical examiner's report. I wonder if it had to do with that."

"What makes you think it had anything to do with that? Did he say so?" Lambert demanded.

"He said very little. Wasn't the medical evidence the ground for the appeal?"

"Yes, but there was nothing in it. The appeal was denied."

"Perhaps that was what troubled Stafford," Pitt suggested.

"Then it is a legal point, not evidential," Lambert stated with absolute certainty. He leaned forward a little, again concentrating on Pitt's face, his expression hard, brows drawn together. "Look, Pitt, it was a very difficult case to investigate, not for the evidence—that was plain enough, and there were witnesses—but because of the atmosphere. My men were as horrified as the general public—more so. We saw the actual body, for God's sake. We saw what that monster did to him—poor devil."

Pitt felt an instant constriction. He had seen corpses, and felt the wrench of horror and pity, imagined the fear, the moment when death came, and the insanity of hatred that must have been there in the killer's face—or the terror they felt which drove them, and however briefly lost them their reason and something of their humanity.

Lambert must have seen the thought in his eyes.

"Can you blame them if they found it hard?" he said quickly.

"No," Pitt agreed. "No, of course I can't."

"And the deputy commissioner was onto us every day, sometimes several times a day, demanding we find whoever did it, and that we find proof of it." He shivered even in the hot room, and his face pinched into an expression of pain. "You don't know what it was like! He told us every day what the newspapers were saying, how there were anti-Jewish riots in the streets, slogans daubed on walls, people throwing stones and refuse at Jews, synagogue windows smashed. He went on about it as if we hadn't heard it for ourselves. He said we had to clear it up within forty-eight hours." His lips curled. "Of course he didn't tell us how! We did everything we could—and I'll swear to that, Pitt. And we did it right! We interviewed everyone in the area—the doorman who took the message from the boy—"

"What boy?" Pitt interrupted.

"Oh—Godman gave some street urchin the message to give to Blaine," Lambert explained. "By word of mouth—nothing written. At least he was clear and sane enough for that. Presumably Godman waited in the shadow at the far side of the street until he saw the theater lights go off and Blaine come out, then sent the urchin over to give the message right then. That way he'd be sure it reached him. Then Blaine turned and went north into Soho. We have the doorman's testimony of all that. And presumably Godman followed him, eventually cutting ahead of him and catching him in Farriers' Lane, where he killed him."

"Planned?" Pitt asked curiously. "Do you suppose he knew the farrier's nails were there? Or was that opportunism?"

"Doesn't matter," Lambert replied with a shrug. "The fact that he lured Blaine there with a message purporting to come from Devlin O'Neil shows that he intended no good. It's still a premeditated murder."

"Doorman's evidence?" Pitt asked.

"And the urchin."

"Go on."

"We also have the evidence of the layabouts who were hanging 'round the entrance of Farriers' Lane and saw Godman come out. When he passed under the street lamp they saw the blood on his coat. Of course at the time they simply thought he was a drunk, staggering 'round, and thought the blood was from some injury he had done himself, falling over, bloody nose, or whatever. They didn't care."

"He was staggering?" Pitt asked curiously.

"I suppose so. He was probably exhausted after his exertion, and more than a little mad."

"But he had composed himself so totally he could stop and make jokes by the time he reached the flower seller two streets away."

"Apparently," Lambert said irritably. "He was quite in control by then. The evidence was very specific. It was that really which hanged him." His voice was defensive again and he sat rigid in his chair. "He's a very good man, Paterson, the sergeant who found that."

"The flower seller?"

"Yes."

"May I speak with him?"

"Of course, if you wish, but he'll only tell you what I have."

"What about the coat with the blood on it?"

"He got rid of it somewhere between the end of Farriers' Lane and Soho Square, where he met the flower seller. We never found it, but that's hardly surprising. Any sort of coat wouldn't lie around in a London street for long. If no one kept it for themselves they'd sell it to the old clothes dealers for the price of a week's lodgings—or more."

Pitt knew that was true. A good gentleman's coat would fetch enough for a month in a penny gaff, and bread and soup besides. It could be the difference between life and death for someone. A little blood would be nothing at all.

"And the necklace?" he asked.

"The necklace?" Lambert was surprised. "For heaven's sake, man, no doubt she kept it. It was worth quite a lot, according to the dresser, who knew a diamond when she saw it. I suppose being an actress's dresser she saw quite a lot of the imitation *and* the real." There was an inflection in his voice, a shadow across his face that showed his contempt for artifice, professional or amateur. He made no distinction between illusion designed to entertain, or to convey a deeper truth, and the merely bogus intended to deceive.

"Did you look for it?" Pitt asked.

"Yes, of course. But she'd have a hundred places to hide it if she wished. It wasn't stolen; we could hardly institute a police search. She could simply have taken it to the nearest hock shop until the outcry died down."

"Has she ever been seen with it since?"

"I've no idea!" Lambert's voice rose in exasperation. "Blaine is dead and Godman's hanged. Who's to care?"

"Blaine's widow. Apparently it should have been hers."

"Well, I daresay she had larger losses to grieve over," Lambert snapped. "She was a very decent woman, poor creature."

Pitt kept his temper with difficulty, and only because it was in his own interest. A quarrel would achieve nothing, and in truth, he was finding Lambert difficult to like, even though not hard to sympathize with. It must have been a wretched, panicky, overwhelming time with public hysteria and superior officers crowding him, looking over his shoulders at every act, and demanding impossible results.

"What about the weapon?" Pitt asked.

Lambert's face tightened again. "Not conclusively. There were half a dozen long farrier's nails used to crucify him. The medical examiner concluded it was probably one of them."

"May I see Sergeant Paterson now?" Pitt asked. "I think you have told me all I need to know. I can't think of anything else you could have done, and I doubt anyone on the Stafford case will. The evidence against Godman seems conclusive so far. I don't know what Stafford could have been looking into. No one found the necklace or the coat. No one has changed their testimony. You haven't seen the flower seller again, or the urchin who gave the message to Blaine?"

"No, as you say, there's nothing." Lambert was mollified. "Sorry," he said, slightly apologetically. "I suppose I was rather uncivil." He forced a half smile. "It's a bad memory, and this Macaulay woman keeping on raising the issue and insisting we got the wrong man is pretty hard to take. If Stafford was trying to silence her once and for all, I wish to God he had succeeded!"

"Perhaps I can," Pitt said with an answering smile.

Lambert sighed, relaxing at last, his eyes lighting. "Then I wish you good luck. I'll get Paterson for you." And he rose to his feet and walked past Pitt, leaving him alone while he went out into the corridor and Pitt heard his footsteps receding.

Immediately Pitt rose to his feet and opened the window, gasping in the cold air with relief. He half closed it again after a moment and returned to his seat just as the door opened and a uniformed sergeant appeared, tunic immaculate, buttons gleaming. He was in his early thirties, of roughly average height and build, but his face was unusual. His nose was long and very aquiline, his mouth rather small, but the plainness of his features was redeemed by very good dark eyes and a fine head of hair waving back from a broad brow.

"Sergeant Paterson, sir," he announced himself, and stood upright, not quite at attention, but in an attitude of respect.

"Thank you for coming," Pitt said evenly. "Sit down." He waved his arm towards Lambert's chair.

"Thank you, sir," Paterson accepted. "Mr. Lambert said you wanted to speak to me about the Blaine/Godman case." His face shadowed, but there was nothing evasive in it.

"That's right," Pitt agreed. He did not owe the sergeant an explanation, but he gave it anyway. "A murder I am investigating seems to have some connection. Mr. Lambert has told me a great deal, but I would like to hear from you what you learned about Godman's movements that night."

Paterson's face reflected his emotions transparently. Even the memory of it brought back the anger and the revulsion he had felt then. His body was tense, his shoulders knotted and his voice changed as he began his answer.

"I was one of the first to get to the yard in Farriers' Lane. Blaine was quite a big man, and young." He stopped, his face tight with pity, and it was painfully apparent that he could recall every detail. He took a deep breath and continued, his eyes on Pitt's face, watching to see if he understood anything of the real horror of it. " 'E'd been dead for quite a while. It was a cold night, only a little above freezing, and 'e was stiff." His voice shook and he controlled it only with an effort. "I'd rather not describe 'im, sir, if you don't need to know."

"I don't," Pitt said quickly, sorry for the man.

Paterson swallowed. "Thank you, sir. Not that I 'aven't seen corpses before—too many of 'em. But this was different. This was a blasphemy." His voice thickened as he said the word and his body was rigid.

"Have you any ideas as to how a slight man like Godman could have got him up like that?" Pitt asked.

Paterson engaged his mind, leaving his emotions aside. His brow furrowed in concentration. "No sir. I wondered about that myself. But there was never any suggestion that anyone 'elped him. 'E was definitely alone, so far as we know. 'E came out of Farriers' Lane by 'imself. Not the sort of thing you do with anyone else. I reckon Godman must've known 'ow to lift people. Maybe it's part of his art as a actor. Like firemen."

"Possibly," Pitt agreed. "Go on. How did you trace his movements after he left Farriers' Lane?"

"Just patience, sir. Asking people all 'round, street peddlers, crossing sweepers, costers and the like. Found a flower seller who saw 'im very plain. She was under a streetlight in Soho Square, and 'e stopped and spoke to 'er. And there's no question it was 'im, 'e admitted it 'isself. 'E said it was quarter past midnight. She thought that was right at first, then when we questioned 'er closer, she agreed it was actually quarter to one, and she got it wrong the first time. Apparently 'e tried to tell 'er it was quarter past midnight. There's a clock just over there, above one of the 'ouses, and she 'eard it strike. It gives just one bell on each quarter, and two at 'alf past, not like most, which do three at the quarter before."

"Did it matter?" Pitt asked doubtfully. "You didn't know what time Blaine was killed, did you? Exactly? Surely the layabouts at the end of Farriers' Lane didn't know the time."

"No," Paterson agreed. "But we knew close, because we knew what time Blaine left the theater, which was after quarter past midnight. If Godman had been at the flower seller's then and 'eadin away from Farriers' Lane, he couldn't possibly 'ave delivered the message or killed Blaine in the stable yard, cos 'e took a cab straight after that, an' the cabby swore 'e took 'im right from Soho Square to 'is 'ouse in Pimlico, which is miles away. And at that time 'e got ter Soho Square an' the flower seller, 'e'd already got rid o' the coat. We never could shift the cabby on that. 'E'd picked up other fares straight after 'oo knew the time exact." Paterson's face creased with disgust, almost as if he had smelled something which made him feel sick. "It was a good attempt at an alibi, and if the flower seller'd believed what 'e said and 'e'd stuck to it, it might 'a worked."

"But she didn't?"

"No—she didn't actually look at the clock 'erself. It was behind 'er, she only 'eard it ring and accepted 'is word that it were quarter past and not quarter to one. And o' course there were the layabouts at the end o' Farriers' Lane."

"That sounds like good work, Sergeant," Pitt said sincerely.

Paterson flushed. "Thank you, sir. I was never on a case I cared about more."

"Did Godman ever admit it, when you arrested him, or later?"

"No, he never did," Paterson said bleakly. " 'E always claimed he was innocent. 'E looked astounded when we went for 'im."

"Did he struggle—put up a fight?"

Paterson avoided Pitt's eyes for the first time.

"Well—yes, 'e—er—'e cut up a bit rough. But we had the better of him."

"I imagine," Pitt said with a sudden discomfort. "Thank you, Sergeant. I can't think of anything more to ask you."

"Does that 'elp you with your case, sir?"

"I don't think so. But it clarifies it. At least I know all I can about the Blaine/Godman affair. I think maybe my case has nothing to do with it except coincidence. Thank you for being so frank."

"Thank you, sir." Paterson stood up and excused himself. Since there was nothing else to learn here, Pitt went to the desk sergeant at the front, thanked him for his civility, and went out into the windy street. It was just beginning to rain and a small boy in a lopsided cap was sweeping horse manure out of the road so two women in large hats could cross without soiling their boots.

Pitt saw Micah Drummond in the middle of the afternoon. It was raining hard, beating on the windows and streaming down in rivulets, making them so opaque it was impossible to see anything more than the dim blur of buildings beyond. Drummond sat behind the desk in his office and Pitt sat restlessly in the chair in front. The afternoon was darkening early and the gas hissed gently in the brackets on the wall.

"What have you learned about Stafford?" Drummond asked, tilting his chair back a trifle.

"Nothing," Pitt replied bluntly. "I've spoken to his widow, who not unnaturally says she thinks he was killed because he was going to reopen the Blaine/Godman case. And Adolphus Pryce says the same."

"I notice you say 'says she thinks,'" Drummond observed. "A very careful choice of words. You doubt her?"

Pitt pulled a face. "Their relationship with each other is a great deal more intimate than proper."

Drummond winced. "Surely not murder? There's no sense in it. They may be immoral, although you have no proof of that. But there is a great distance between falling in love with a married woman and murdering her husband. They are civilized people, Pitt."

"I know." Pitt did not argue as to whether civilized people did such things or they were confined to barbarians, whether by race or social class. It was not what Drummond meant, and he knew it. "I spent rather more time pursuing the details of the Blaine/Godman case," he said instead. "Trying to find out exactly what Stafford could have been intending to do."

"Oh dear." Drummond sounded weary. His face puckered with distaste. "Surely he was only trying to settle the matter once and for all. I looked into it myself. Godman was guilty, and you can't do any good by raking it up again. Unfortunately poor Stafford was killed before he could show Miss Macaulay how mistaken she was, which is a tragedy, not only for her but for the reputation of the law in England." He shifted in his chair a fraction and frowned at Pitt. "The woman is a little mad, which moves me to pity, but she is doing a considerable amount of damage. For heaven's sake, Pitt, don't, even inadvertently, give her the idea that there is the slightest chance that you will reopen the case."

"I am investigating the death of Samuel Stafford," Pitt said very directly, meeting Drummond's eyes. "I'll go wherever that takes me, nowhere else. But I spoke to O'Neil, and his family, who are not suspect, of course; and to Charles Lambert, who conducted the original investigation. As far as I can see there is nothing which Stafford could have taken any further." He shook his head a little. "Even if he found any of the missing physical evidence, which would be very unlikely after all these years, it still wouldn't prove anything different. It was a sordid tragedy at the time, and an ugly part of history now. I suppose I could go and see the other appeal judges, in case Stafford confided anything in them . . ."

"I wouldn't," Drummond said sharply. "Leave it alone, Pitt. There's nothing in it but old pain, and new doubt which is totally unjustified. You will call into question the professional integrity and skill of good men, who don't deserve that."

"I'll just see one or two of the other judges, in case—"

"No! I'm telling you, Pitt—leave it alone."

"Why?" Pitt said stubbornly. "Who wants us to leave it alone?"

Drummond's face tightened. "The Home Secretary," he

replied. "If it gets out you are looking into it again there'll be a lot of stupid speculation. People will assume there is some doubt about the conviction—which is not true—and there will be another public outcry." He leaned forward across the desk. "Feeling was very high indeed at the time. If it looks as though we are going to say we may have got the wrong man, or there could be some kind of a pardon, it will raise a storm of protest and a great deal of anti-Jewish feeling. And it's not fair to Tamar Macaulay. You'll give her hope which is completely unfounded. For heaven's sake, let the wretched man remain buried in whatever obscurity he can find—and his family learn to live in peace!"

Pitt said nothing.

"Pitt?" Drummond said urgently. "Listen to me, man!"

"I heard you, sir." Pitt smiled bleakly.

"I know you hear me. I want your word that you understand and will obey me."

"No, I'm not sure that I do understand," Pitt said slowly. "Why would the Home Secretary mind my looking into the case, if that's what Stafford was doing before he died? He must have had some reason—he wasn't a whimsical or irresponsible man. I want to know what that reason was."

Drummond's face darkened. "Well, I want you to find out who killed him. And that looks regrettably more and more like a personal matter. I have no idea who—or why—and you have no time to meddle in old cases when you should be out looking for some enmity that was deep enough to inspire murder. Perhaps he knew of some other crime, something he did not live to report to the authorities." Drummond's face brightened. "Maybe he learned of something, and as soon as he had proof he was going to tell us—but the criminal, whoever it was, realized he knew and killed him before he could speak to anyone?"

Pitt made a polite face which was acutely expressive of his total disbelief.

"Well, go out there and find out," Drummond said tartly.

Pitt stood up. He was not angry. He knew the pressures on Drummond, he knew the secret, iron-hard chain of the Inner Circle, and he both hated and feared it. He had felt its

131

power before, and he knew Drummond rued the day he had joined, when innocence blinded him to even the possibility that men of his own class and breed would seek and use such power.

"Yes sir," he said quietly, turning and going towards the door.

"Pitt?"

Pitt smiled, and ignored him.

5

"Is it the Inner Circle again?" Charlotte asked grimly, taking the pins out of her hair and running her fingers through it in relief at letting it down. She felt as if she had had half an ironmonger's shop in it keeping its heavy coils in place.

Pitt was standing behind her, debating whether to hang his jacket up or simply let it lie across the back of the chair.

"Probably," he replied. "Although I can't blame Lambert for not wanting the whole thing raked up again. It's a terrible feeling to have your cases reopened and questioned as to whether you were right—especially if the man was hanged. Worse if you are not absolutely sure you did all you could, and you doubt your own honesty at the time." He opted for laying the jacket on the chair. "It is so easy to make mistakes when everyone is crying out for a solution, and you are afraid for your own reputation, of being thought not good enough, not equal to the task." He sat on the edge of the bed and continued undressing. "And if your men are panicking because witnesses are lying, and frightened, and full of hate . . ."

"Are they like that over Judge Stafford?" Charlotte asked, swiveling around on her dressing table stool to look at him.

"No, I don't think so." He stood up, took his shirt off

and put it onto the chair as well, and his undervest on top of it. He poured warm water from the pitcher into the bowl and washed his hands, face and neck, and reached for his nightshirt and put it on, pulling it over his head, then trying to find the armholes. "It begins to look as if it may be personal, and nothing to do with the Farriers' Lane case at all," he added when he finally got his head through.

"You mean his wife?" Charlotte put her brush down, looked for a moment at the pile of clothes on the chair, and decided to leave them where they were and say nothing. It was not the occasion for fussing. "Juniper? Why would she kill him?"

"Because she was in love with Adolphus Pryce," he answered, climbing into bed. He was quite oblivious of the scattered things he had left around—at least she thought he was.

"Was she?" she said doubtfully. "Are you sure?"

"No—not yet. But I cannot think why Livesey should say so if it is not true. I'll have to enquire into it."

"That seems a bit extreme." She abandoned brushing her hair and rose to turn down the gas in the bracket on the far wall, then climbed into bed also. The clean sheets were cold, and she snuggled up to him comfortably. "I don't believe it."

"I didn't think you would." He put his arm around her. "But there doesn't seem to be anything in the Farriers' Lane murder worth looking into, certainly nothing to kill Stafford for."

"But you don't know what he found out," she protested.

"I know what I found out. Nothing at all. Godman was seen coming out of Farriers' Lane with blood on his coat, and identified by a flower seller in Soho Square, two streets away. He didn't even deny that, just the actual time, and that was proved to be a lie. Sorry, my love, but it looks incontestable that he did it. I know you would like him to be innocent, because of Tamar Macaulay, but it seems he can't be."

"Then why are the Inner Circle telling you to leave it alone?" she demanded. "If there's nothing to find out, why should they mind if you look?" She wriggled a little lower and knew Pitt was smiling in the darkness beside her. "In fact," she added, "they should be very glad if you prove they were right!"

He said nothing, but reached over with his arm and touched her hair gently.

"Except perhaps they aren't," she went on. "Are you going to leave it?"

"I am going to sleep," he said comfortably.

"But is the Farriers' Lane case really closed, Thomas?" she persisted.

"For tonight—yes!"

"But tomorrow?"

He pulled her closer, laughing, and she was obliged to leave the matter.

In the morning Pitt ate a hurried breakfast, having woken late, and then kissed Charlotte long and gently, and left at a run to take an omnibus to see the medical examiner again.

Charlotte set about the small chores of the day, beginning with a pile of ironing, while Gracie washed the breakfast dishes and then cleaned and blacked the grate in the parlor, laid the fire for the evening, swept the floor and dusted, and made the beds.

At eleven o'clock they both stopped for a cup of tea and a chance to gossip.

"Is the master still on the case o' the man wot was crucified in the stable yard?" Gracie asked with an elaborately casual air, stirring her tea in apparent concentration.

"I'm not really sure," Charlotte replied without any pretense at all. "You haven't any sugar!"

Gracie grinned and stopped stirring. "Won't 'e tell you nuffing?"

"Oh yes—but the more he looks into it, the less it seems as if Judge Stafford could have found out anything new about it. And if he didn't, then there isn't any reason why anybody from that case should have killed him."

"Then 'oo did? 'Is wife?" Gracie was transparently disappointed. Domestic murder was so much less interesting, especially if it were simply a matter of an affair, and the other party involved was known to them, and not really scandalous.

"I suppose so, or Mr. Pryce."

Gracie stared at her, ignoring her tea.

"What's wrong, ma'am? Don't you think that's 'oo did it?"

Charlotte smiled. "I don't know. I suppose they might. I just keep remembering how I felt when I watched her the evening her husband died. Maybe it's vanity to think I could not be so wrong in my judgment."

"Maybe it was 'er lover, an' she didn't know nuffing about it?" Gracie suggested, trying to be helpful.

"Maybe—but I rather liked him too." Charlotte sipped her tea and caught Gracie's eye over the top of the cup.

"'Oo is it as you don't like?" Gracie was ever practical.

"No one yet. But I've liked people who were guilty before."

"'Ave yer? Really?" Gracie's eyes were wide with interest and amazement.

"It depends why." Charlotte thought she ought to explain. She was about to elaborate, recalling some of Pitt's cases in which she had been involved, when the doorbell rang, and Gracie, in a flurry of surprise, put down her cup, stood up, straightened her skirts and scampered down the corridor to answer it.

She returned a moment later with Caroline, who was smartly dressed, but obviously she had dressed somewhat hurriedly, and without her usual attention to detail. After the greetings had been exchanged, and the answers that all were in good health, Caroline sat down at the kitchen table, accepted the tea Gracie gave her, and explained her reason for having come. She took a breath and plunged in.

"How is Thomas progressing with the murder of poor Mr. Stafford? Has he learned anything yet?"

"How devious and indirect you are, Mama," Charlotte said with amusement.

"What?"

"You used to criticize me for being too blunt," Charlotte replied cheerfully. "You said people did not like it, and that one should always approach things a little sideways, to give people a chance to avoid the subject if they wish."

"Nonsense!" Caroline expostulated, but there was a distinct pinkness in her cheeks. "Anyway, that was with strangers, and with gentlemen—and I am neither. And what I said was that it is indelicate to be too forthright—it is . . ."

"I know—I know." Charlotte waved her hand. "I am afraid he has discovered nothing new about the Farriers' Lane murder. He has no idea why Judge Stafford should have been looking into it again. It seems quite beyond question that Aaron Godman was guilty."

"Oh—oh dear. Poor Miss Macaulay." Caroline shook her head minutely, her face full of sorrow. "I think she really believed her brother was innocent. This will be very hard for her."

Charlotte put her hand on her mother's. "I only said he had found nothing new, so far. I don't think he will give up, unless it was Mrs. Stafford or Mr. Pryce, or both of them."

"And if it wasn't?"

"Then he will have to go back to the Farriers' Lane case—unless there is something else."

"What?" Caroline's face was creased with anxiety now and she leaned farther forward across the table, her tea forgotten. "What else?"

"I don't know—some other personal enmity. Something to do with money, perhaps, or another crime he knew about."

"Is there evidence of anything like that?"

"No—I don't think so. Not so far."

"It doesn't sound . . ." Caroline smiled bleakly. "It doesn't sound very likely, does it? He's bound to go back to the Farriers' Lane case. I would."

"Yes," Charlotte agreed. "It is what Mr. Stafford was doing the day he died. He must have had a reason. Even if all he intended was to prove forever that it was Aaron Godman, maybe someone else thought differently."

"That's illogical, my dear," Caroline pointed out ruefully.

"If Aaron Godman was guilty, then no one now would kill Mr. Stafford to prevent him from proving that. Miss Macaulay might grieve that she could no longer hope to clear her brother's name, but she would not kill Stafford because he believed him guilty. Apart from the fact that it would be ridiculous, everyone else believes him guilty. She cannot kill everyone. And why should she? It wasn't Stafford's fault." She bit her lip. "No, Charlotte, if Godman was guilty, there was no reason to kill Judge Stafford. But if someone else was, then there was every reason, if he knew that—or they thought he did."

"Someone like whom, Mama? Joshua Fielding? Is that what you are afraid of?"

"No! No." She shook her head fiercely, her face pink. "It could be anyone."

"Now who is being illogical?" Charlotte said gently. "The only people the judge saw that day were his wife, Mr. Pryce, Judge Livesey, Devlin O'Neil, Miss Macaulay, and Joshua Fielding. Mr. Pryce, Mrs. Stafford and Judge Livesey had nothing to do with Kingsley Blaine. They only came into the case when it came to trial, and Judge Livesey only when it went to appeal. They couldn't possibly be guilty of that crime."

Caroline looked very pale.

"Then we've got to do something! I don't believe it was Joshua, and we must prove it. Perhaps we can find out something before Thomas starts, while he is still investigating Mrs. Stafford and Mr. Pryce."

Charlotte felt a sudden, quick sympathy with her, but she could think of little that would be helpful. She knew the sense of fear that someone one liked could be implicated, hurt—even be guilty.

"I don't know what we could find out," she said hesitantly, watching Caroline's face and the anxiety in it, the awareness of her vulnerable situation. It was so easy to be foolish. "If Thomas has tried . . ." She shrugged. "I don't know where to begin. We don't know Mrs. Stafford— although of course I suppose I could call on her . . ." She knew her reluctance to do it was plain in her voice and in

138

her expression. "It's . . ." She struggled to find words that were not too abrupt. "She will know it is curiosity; she knows I am a policeman's wife. And if she is innocent, and grieving, whatever she feels for Mr. Pryce—and we don't know what her feelings are—it is only rumor—then it would be so offensive."

"But if innocent people were in jeopardy?" Caroline pressed, leaning forward across the table. "Surely that must be the most urgent thing, the most important."

"That is not yet the case, Mama, and it may never be."

"When it is, it will be too late," Caroline said with rising anxiety. "It isn't only charges and arrests, Charlotte—it is suspicion, and the ruin of reputations. That can be enough to destroy someone."

"I know."

"What did Lady Cumming-Gould say? You haven't told me."

"Actually I don't know. I haven't been to see her since then, and she did not send a note, so I assume she did not learn anything she thought of value." She smiled. "Perhaps the case really was decisive."

"Would you find out, please?"

"Of course," Charlotte said with relief. That would be easy to do.

"You can take my carriage again, if you like," Caroline offered, then blushed at her own forcefulness and the urgency with which she was pursuing the issue. "If that would help, of course," she added.

"Oh yes." Charlotte accepted with only the faintest smile. "That would help a great deal." She rose to her feet, the laughter in her eyes unmistakable now. "It is so much more elegant to roll up in a carriage than to walk from the omnibus stop."

Caroline opened her mouth to say something, then changed her mind.

Vespasia was out when Charlotte arrived at her house, but the parlormaid informed her she would be back in no more than half an hour, and if Charlotte cared to wait she could take tea in the withdrawing room. Lady Vespasia would be most disappointed to have missed her.

Charlotte accepted, and sat in Vespasia's elegant room sipping her tea and watching the flames leap in the fireplace. She had time to look around, which she had never had before, when it would have been obvious and seemed an intrusive curiosity. The room was stamped with Vespasia's character. There were tall, slender candlesticks on the mantel shelf, not at either end, as one might have expected, but both of them a little to the left of the center, asymmetrically. They were Georgian silver, very cool and simple. On the Sheraton table by the window there was an arrangement of flowers in a Royal Worcester gravy boat, three pink chrysanthemums low down in the center, and a lot of coppery beech leaves, and some dark purple red buds of which she did not know the name.

She lost interest in the tea and rose to her feet to look more closely at the few photographs which stood in plain frames on the top of the bureau. The one which drew her first was a sepia tint, oval faded away to nothing at the edges, a woman of about forty, slender necked, with high cheekbones and delicate, aquiline nose. Her wide eyes were heavy lidded under a perfect brow. It was a beautiful face, and yet for all its pride, and classic bones, there was individuality in it, and the romantic pose did not entirely mask either the passion or the strength.

It was several moments before Charlotte realized it was Vespasia herself. She had grown so accustomed to her as an old lady, she had forgotten that as a young woman she could be so different—and yet after a second look, so much the same.

The other pictures were of a girl of perhaps twenty, very pretty, but heavier boned, thicker of jaw and shorter nosed. The resemblance was there, and something of the charm, but not the mettle, not the fire of imagination. It must be Olivia, Vespasia's daughter, who had married Eustace March, and died after bearing him so many children. Charlotte had never known her, but she remembered Eustace vividly, with both anger and pity.

The third picture was of an elderly aristocratic man with a high-boned, gentle face and eyes that looked into a far distance, beyond the camera into some world of his own vision. There was sufficient resemblance to Vespasia for Charlotte to guess from the faintness, the fashion of the dress and the style of the photograph that it was Vespasia's father.

It was interesting that she should choose to keep in her favorite room a memory of her father, not her husband.

Charlotte was looking at the books in the carved bookcase when she heard a murmuring in the hall and footsteps across the parquet flooring. Quickly she turned around and moved towards the window, so that when the door opened and Vespasia came in, she was facing her, smiling.

Vespasia looked full of energy, as if she were about to go somewhere she anticipated with excitement, not as if she had just returned. Her skin glowed from the brisk wind, her back was straight and her shoulders squared, and she was dressed in the softest grape blue, a gentle color neither navy nor purple, nor yet silver. It was subtle, expensive and extremely flattering. There was almost no bustle, in the most up-to-the-moment fashion, and the cut was exquisite. No doubt she had left a sweeping brimmed hat in the hall.

"Good morning, Aunt Vespasia," Charlotte said with surprise and a very definite pleasure. She had never seen Vespasia in such health since before the death of Emily's first husband, Vespasia's nephew and the only reason they could count her as a relative. Today she seemed to have shed the years that grief had added to her and to be the vigorous woman she had been before. "You look most excellently well."

"There is considerable justice in that," Vespasia replied, but her satisfaction was obvious. "I *am* excellently well." She looked at Charlotte closely. "You look a trifle anxious, my dear. Are you still concerned about that miserable business in Farriers' Lane? For heaven's sake sit down! You look as if you were about to rush out of the door. You are not, are you?"

"No—no, of course not. I came to see you, and I have

nothing else to do immediately. Mama is at home, and will care for everything that may arise."

"Oh dear." Vespasia sat down gracefully, arranging her skirt with a flick of her hand. "Is she still enamored of the actor?"

Charlotte smiled ruefully and sat down opposite her. "Yes, I'm afraid so."

Vespasia's arched eyebrows rose. "Afraid? Does it matter so much? She is free to do as she pleases, is she not? If she has a little romance—why not?"

Charlotte drew in a deep breath, her mind full of all sorts of excellent reasons why not. But as she came to enumerate them, despite the intensity of her emotions about it, spoken aloud, they seemed silly and of no worth.

Vespasia's lips curled in amusement. "Just so," she agreed. "But you are concerned that this unfortunate man may be suspected of having some involvement with the death of Kingsley Blaine?"

"Yes—at least, no. Thomas seems to think there is nothing more to learn in that, and Stafford was simply trying to find enough evidence to persuade Tamar Macaulay to let the matter drop at last."

"But you don't?" Vespasia asked.

Charlotte raised her shoulders fractionally. "I don't know. I suppose it could have been the widow, but—I find it hard to accept. I was with her, holding her hand, when he died. I really cannot believe she clung onto me like that, watching him, and she had poisoned him herself. Apart from that, it would be so stupid—and so unnecessary!"

"The Farriers' Lane murder again," Vespasia said thoughtfully. "I did speak to Judge Quade about it. I have been remiss in not letting you know what I learned." Extraordinarily there was a faint touch of pinkness in her cheeks, and Charlotte noticed it with surprise. She had never seen Vespasia self-conscious before. She waited for an explanation, but none was offered. Instead Vespasia launched into recounting what her enquiry had elicited, very casually, and yet with a precise care for each word.

"Judge Quade found the case most distressing, not only

for the facts of the murder, but because the public emotion ran so high, and was so extremely ugly, that the whole matter was conducted in a fever and a haste in which it was not easy to ensure that the law was administered honorably, let alone that justice was done."

"Does he think it was not?" Charlotte asked quickly, both hope and fear rising inside her.

Vespasia's gray eyes were perfectly steady. "He thinks that justice was done," she replied gravely. "But not well done."

"You mean Aaron Godman was guilty?"

"I am afraid so. It was the atmosphere which troubled Thelonius, the fact that even Barton James, the counsel for the defense, seemed to believe his client guilty, and his handling of the trial was adequate, but no more. The whole city had worked itself into such a pitch of hatred that there was violence in the streets towards Jews who had nothing to do with it, simply because they were Jews. It would have been impossible to find an impartial jury."

"Then how could the trial be fair?" Charlotte protested.

"I daresay it could not."

"Then why did he allow it to proceed? Why did he not do something?"

For once there was no spark of humor or indulgence in Vespasia's eyes. She was quick to defend.

"What would you suggest he do?"

"I—I'm not sure." Then Charlotte realized the change in her tone, the subtle difference in her eyes. She could not bear to quarrel with her, and she remembered that Thelonius Quade was an old friend. Inadvertently she had questioned the honor of a man for whom Vespasia had regard. Perhaps it was a high regard? "I'm sorry," she said quickly. "I don't suppose there was anything he could do. The law is very binding, isn't it? He could hardly call a mistrial if nothing incorrect had been done."

Vespasia's face softened, her eyes bright.

"He considered doing something himself which would occasion the defense to do precisely that. Then he decided that would be dishonorable to his office, and a statement that he did not believe in the very law it is his calling to administer."

"Oh." Charlotte frowned, the extreme gravity of what Vespasia was saying impressing itself upon her. "If a judge had such thoughts, then it must have been very ugly indeed. How delicate of him to have weighed it so fairly, and cared enough to think of such a thing."

"He is an unusual man," Vespasia answered, looking down for a moment, and away from Charlotte.

Charlotte found herself smiling as she wondered what friendship there had been between Vespasia and Judge Quade. She had no idea how long ago it had begun. Had it been more than friendship, perhaps an affection? It was a nice thought and her smile grew broader.

She saw Vespasia's erect back and elegant head. She could imagine her voice saying, "And what is amusing you, pray?" But no words came. Instead there was only the warm color in Vespasia's cheeks.

"Thank you very much, Aunt Vespasia," Charlotte said gently. "I am grateful to you for having asked about it, even though it does seem there is really nothing more to learn."

"Yes, there is," Vespasia argued, gathering her attention again. "Not a great deal, and perhaps not indicative, but Judge Quade said he was quite certain that Aaron Godman had been beaten while in custody. When he appeared at his trial he was suffering bruises and lacerations which were too recent to have occurred at the time of the murder. And he was unharmed immediately prior to his arrest."

"Oh dear. How ugly. You think the jailers beat him while he was in prison?"

"Perhaps. Or the police when they arrested him," Vespasia replied, watching Charlotte's face with anxiety. "I am sorry, but it is not impossible."

"You mean he fought them?"

"No, my dear, I do not. The policeman concerned was totally unharmed."

"Oh." Charlotte took a deep breath. "But that doesn't

prove anything, does it? Except that, as you say, feelings were ugly, and very high. Aunt Vespasia . . ."

Vespasia waited.

"Do you think Mr. Quade is really saying, in a euphemistic sort of way, that he believes the police were so desperate to get a conviction, and satisfy the public's desire, that they would knowingly have charged the wrong man?"

"No," Vespasia said very definitely. "No. He was disturbed by the manner of the investigation, the haste of it and the emotion, and the indifference of the defense counsel, but he believed the evidence was true, and the verdict correct."

"Oh—I see." Charlotte sighed. "Then it seems that after all Judge Stafford was merely trying to prove once and for all that the matter was ended, and surely no one would have killed him for that. It must be his wife after all—or Mr. Pryce."

"I regret that it does seem so."

Charlotte looked at her. Was there a hesitation?

"Yes?"

"It is just conceivable that someone has something to hide of an ugliness so great that they feared Mr. Stafford's investigation, not knowing its nature, or even if they did know it." Her frown deepened. "And in case he was too thorough, they killed him. I admit it does not seem probable . . ."

"No," Charlotte replied, the lift in her voice belying the word. "But not impossible. Not really. I think we might pursue that, don't you? I mean . . ." She stopped. She had taken too much for granted. "Could we?" she asked tentatively.

"Oh, I don't see why not." Vespasia smiled with both amusement and pleasure. "I don't see why not, at all. I have no idea how . . ." Her fine eyebrows arched enquiringly.

"Nor do I," Charlotte admitted. "But I shall most certainly give the matter much thought."

"I wondered if you might," Vespasia murmured. "If I can be of any assistance, I shall be happy to."

"I wondered if you might," Charlotte said with a grin.

Charlotte was torn whether or not to tell Pitt of her visit to Great-Aunt Vespasia. If she did he would be bound to ask why she was so concerned in the matter. It would not take him long to deduce that it was because of Caroline's regard for Joshua Fielding, and his possible implication in both the murder of Kingsley Blaine and thus also of Judge Stafford. She could always try to convince him that it was because Caroline had been present in the theater and so was intricately involved in the emotion of the crime. But she knew Pitt would see beyond that very quickly, and he might think her foolish, an older woman, recently widowed and alone, falling victim to a fancy for a younger man, a glamorous man utterly out of her own class and experience, offering her a last glimpse of youth.

And put like that it was absurd, and not a little pathetic. Pitt would feel no unkindness, no criticism, but perhaps a gentle, wry sort of pity. She could not subject Caroline to that. She was surprised how protective she felt, how fierce to defend the extraordinary vulnerability.

So she told Pitt only that she had been to see Vespasia, and when he looked up quickly she kept her eyes down on her sewing.

"How is she?" Pitt asked, still watching her.

"Oh, in excellent health." She looked up with a quick smile. He would suspect if she simply stopped there. He knew her too well. "I have not seen her look in such spirits since poor George died. She is quite restored to herself again, with all the vigor she used to have when we first met her."

"Charlotte."

"Yes?" She raised wide, innocent eyes to him, holding her needle in the air.

"What else?" he demanded.

"About what? Aunt Vespasia looked in excellent health and spirit. I thought you would be pleased to know."

"I am, of course. I want to know what else it is you have discovered that is making you feel so pleased."

"Ah." She was delighted. She had deceived him perfectly. She smiled broadly, this time without guile. "She has looked up an old friend, and I think perhaps she is very fond of him indeed. Isn't that good?"

He sat up. "You mean a romance?"

"Well—hardly! She is over eighty!"

"What on earth does that matter?" His voice rose incredulously. "The heart doesn't stop caring!"

"Well, no—I suppose not." She turned the idea over with surprise, and then dawning pleasure. "No! Why not? Yes, I think perhaps it was a romance, at the time they first knew each other, and I suppose it could be again."

"Excellent." Pitt was smiling widely. "Who is he?"

"What?" She was caught out.

"Who is he?" he repeated, with suspicion.

"Oh . . ." She resumed her sewing, her eyes on the needle and linen. "A friend from some years ago. Thelonius—Thelonius Quade."

"Thelonius Quade." He repeated the name slowly. "Charlotte."

"Yes?" She kept her eyes studiously on the linen.

"You said Thelonius Quade?"

"I think so."

"Judge Thelonius Quade?"

She hesitated only a moment. "Yes . . ."

"Who just happens to have presided over the trial of Aaron Godman for the murder of Kingsley Blaine?"

There was no point whatever in lying. She tried evasion.

"I think their friendship had lapsed at that time."

He shook his head with a wry expression. "That is irrelevant! Why did she suddenly renew his acquaintance now?"

She said nothing.

"Because you asked her?" he went on.

"Well, I am interested," she pointed out. "I was there when the poor man died. I actually sat holding the hand of his widow!"

"And you don't think she killed him," he said with a harder edge to his voice. He was not angry—in fact there was a definite amusement in it—but she knew he would accept no argument.

"No, no, I really don't," she agreed, looking up at him at last. "But Judge Quade apparently was happy with the verdict, even if not with the conduct of the trial." She smiled at him, candid finally. "It does look as if poor Godman was guilty, even if they did not prove it in the best way. But Thomas, it is just possible, isn't it, that the fact that Judge Stafford was investigating the case again may have frightened someone so much, for some other reason, some other sin, that they killed him?" She waited anxiously, searching his face.

"Possible," he said gravely. "But not likely. What sin?"

"I don't know. You'll have to find out."

"Perhaps—but I'm going back to the murder of Stafford first, and some investigation into the evidence of Juniper Stafford or Adolphus Pryce having obtained opium. I need to know a great deal more about them."

"Yes, of course. But you won't forget the Blaine/Godman case, will you? I mean . . ." A sudden thought occurred to her. "Thomas! If there were some affair, some misconduct in the case, bribery, violence, another matter involved which concerns someone powerful, an affair which would ruin someone. Then that might be a reason to kill Judge Stafford before he found out—even if it did not change Godman's guilt. Couldn't it?"

"Yes," he said cautiously. "Yes, it's possible—just."

"Then you'll look into it?" she urged.

"After Juniper and Adolphus. Not before."

She smiled. "Oh good. Would you like a cup of cocoa before bedtime, Thomas?"

The following day Charlotte delegated Gracie to take care of matters at home and took an omnibus to Cater Street to visit Caroline. She arrived at a little after eleven o'clock and found her mother already gone out on an errand, and her grandmother sitting in the big, old withdrawing room by the fire, full of indignation.

"Well," she said, glaring up at Charlotte, her back rigidly

straight, her old hands clenched like claws across the top of her stick. "So you've come to visit me at last, have you? Realized your duty finally. A little late, girl!"

"Good morning, Grandmama," Charlotte said calmly. "How are you?"

"I'm ill," the old lady said witheringly. "Don't ask stupid questions, Charlotte. How could I be anything but ill, with your mother behaving like a perfect fool? She was never a particularly clever woman, but now she seems to have taken complete leave of her wits! Your father's death has unhinged her." She sniffed angrily. "I suppose it was to be expected. Some women cannot handle widowhood. No stamina—no sense of what is fitting. Never did have much. My poor Edward always had to take charge!"

At another time Charlotte might have ignored the insult. It was part of her grandmother's pattern of thought and she was accustomed to it, but at the moment she was feeling protective towards her mother.

"Oh fiddlesticks," she said briskly, sitting down on the chair opposite. "Mama always had a perfectly good sense of what was appropriate."

"Don't you fiddlesticks me!" Grandmama snapped. "No woman with the faintest idea of propriety would marry her daughter to a policeman, even if she were as plain as a horse and daft as a chicken." She waited for Charlotte to take offense, and when she did not, continued reluctantly. "And now she is making a fool of herself courting the friendship of persons on the stage. For heaven's sake, that's hardly any better! They may know how to speak the Queen's English, but their morals are in the gutter. Not one of them is any better than they should be. And half of them are Jews—I know that for a fact." She glared at Charlotte, daring her to argue.

"What has that got to do with it?" Charlotte asked, trying to look as if she were genuinely enquiring.

"What? What did you say?" The old lady was selectively deaf, and she was now choosing to make Charlotte repeat the remark in the hope it would cow her, or at worst leave time for her to think of a crushing answer.

"I asked you what that had to do with it," Charlotte repeated with a smile.

"What has to do with what?" Grandmama demanded angrily. "What are you talking about, girl? Sometimes you are full of the most arrant nonsense. Comes from mixing with the lower classes who have no education, don't know how to express themselves. I told you that would happen. I told your mother also—but does she ever listen to me? You are going to have to do something about her."

"There is nothing I can do, Grandmama," Charlotte said patiently. "I cannot make her listen to you if she does not wish to."

"Now listen to me, you stupid girl. Really, sometimes you would try the patience of a saint."

"I had not thought of you as a saint, Grandmama."

"Don't be impertinent!" The old lady flicked her stick sharply at Charlotte's legs, but she was just too far away for it to do anything more than catch her skirts with a thwack.

"Is she expected home soon?" Charlotte asked.

The old lady's faint eyebrows shot up almost to her gray hair.

"Do you imagine she tells me that?" Her voice was shrill with indignation. "She comes and goes all hours of the day—and night, for all I know! Dressed up like something out of a melodrama herself, stupid creature. In my day widows wore black—and knew their place. This is all totally indecent. Your father, poor man, hasn't been dead five years yet, and here is Caroline careering around London like a giddy twenty-year-old trying to make a marriage in her coming-out year, before it is too late."

"Did she say anything?"

"About what? She never tells me anything important. Wouldn't dare, I should think."

"About when she will be home." Charlotte kept her voice civil with difficulty.

"And if she had, what do you suppose that is worth, girl? Nothing! Nothing at all."

"What was it anyway?"

"Oh—that she had gone to the milliner, and would be

back in half an hour. Stuff and nonsense. She could be any-where."

"Thank you, Grandmama. You look very well." And indeed she did. She was bristling with energy, her skin was pink and her black, boot button eyes sharply alive. Nothing revived her like a quarrel.

"You need spectacles," the old lady said viciously. "I am in pain—all over. I am an old woman and need care, and a life without worry or distress."

"You would die of boredom without something to be offended by," Charlotte said with a candor she would not have dared a few years ago, certainly not when her father was alive.

The old lady snorted and glared at her. She only remembered to be deaf when it was too late.

"What? What did you say? Your enunciation is getting very slipshod, girl!"

Charlotte smiled, and a moment later heard her mother's steps in the hall outside. She rose to her feet, excused herself briefly, and leaving the old lady complaining about being excluded from everything, she arrived in the hallway just as her mother was halfway up the stairs.

"Mama!"

Caroline turned, her face alight with pleasure.

"Mama." Charlotte started up the stairs towards her. Caroline wore a very beautiful hat, its broad brim decorated with feathers and silk flowers. It was lush, extravagant, and totally feminine. Charlotte would have adored such a hat herself, but then she had nowhere to which she could wear it anyway.

"Yes?" Caroline said eagerly. "Have you heard something?"

"Not a great deal, I am afraid." She felt guilty for raising hopes ever so little, and an intense desire to protect such an openness to pain. "But at least it is a place to begin."

"There is something we can do?" Caroline turned on the step as if to come down already. "What have you heard? From whom—Thomas?"

"Aunt Vespasia, but it is not a great deal, really."

151

"Never mind! What can we do to help?"

"Learn more about them, the people involved, in case there is some other crime, or personal secret, as you suspected, which someone feared Judge Stafford might uncover."

"Oh, excellent," Caroline said quickly. "Where shall we begin?"

"Perhaps with Devlin O'Neil," Charlotte suggested.

"But what about Mrs. Stafford, and Mr. Pryce?" Caroline's face was pinched with concern, and a certain guilt because she was wishing them into such tragedy.

"We don't know them," Charlotte pointed out reasonably. "Let us begin where we can. At least Miss Macaulay or Mr. Fielding may help us there."

"Yes—yes, of course." Caroline looked Charlotte up and down. "You are dressed very becomingly. Are you ready to leave now?"

"If you think we may go without first obtaining an invitation?"

"Oh yes, I am sure Miss Macaulay would receive us if we go this morning. They rehearse in the afternoons, and that would be inconvenient."

"Do they?" Charlotte said with surprise and a touch of sarcasm. She had not realized Caroline was so well acquainted with the daily habits of actors and actresses. With difficulty she refrained from remarking on it.

Caroline looked away and began to make arrangements, calling to the footman to send for the carriage again, and informing the staff that she would be out for luncheon.

Several of the cast of the theater company rented a large house in Pimlico, sharing it among them. The manager, Mr. Inigo Passmore, was an elderly gentleman who had been a "star" in his day, but now preferred to take only character parts. His wife also had been an actress, but she seldom appeared on the stage these days, enjoying a place of honor and considerable power, directing the wardrobe, properties and, when it was required, music. They had the ground floor of the house, and thus the garden.

Joshua Fielding had the rooms at the front of the next floor, and a young actress of great promise, Clio Farber, the rooms at the back. The third floor was occupied by Tamar Macaulay and her daughter.

"I didn't know she had a child," Charlotte said in surprise as Caroline was remarking on the arrangements to her during their carriage ride from Cater Street to Pimlico. "I didn't know she was married. Is her husband in the theater?"

"Don't be naive," Caroline said crisply, staring straight ahead of her.

"I beg your pardon? Oh." Charlotte was embarrassed. "You mean she is not married? I'm sorry. I did not realize."

"It would be tactful not to mention it," Caroline said dryly.

"Of course. Who else lives there?"

"I don't know. A couple of ingenues in the attic."

"A couple of what?"

"Very young actresses who take the part of innocent girls."

"Oh."

They said no more until they arrived at Claverton Street in Pimlico, and alighted.

The door was opened to them by a girl of about sixteen, who was pretty in a fashion far more colorful than that of any parlormaid Charlotte had encountered before. Added to which she did not wear the usual dark stuff dress and white cap and apron, but a rather flattering dress of pink, and an apron that looked as if it had been put on hastily. There was no cap on her thick, dark hair.

"Oh, good morning, Mrs. Ellison," she said cheerfully. "You'll be to see Mr. Fielding, I daresay. Or is it Miss Macaulay? I think they're both at home." She held the door wide for them.

"Thank you, Miranda," Caroline said, going up the steps and into the hallway. Charlotte followed immediately behind her, startled by the familiarity with which the girl greeted Caroline.

"This is my daughter, Charlotte Pitt," Caroline introduced her. "Miranda Passmore. Mr. Passmore is the manager of the company."

"How do you do, Miranda," Charlotte replied, hastily collecting her wits and hoping it was the correct thing to say to someone in such an extraordinary position. Nowhere else had she met a haphazard parlormaid who was the daughter of a manager of anything at all.

Miranda smiled broadly. Perhaps she had met the situation many times before.

"How do you do, Mrs. Pitt. Please go on up. Just knock on the door when you get there."

Charlotte and Caroline obeyed, crossing the hall in which Charlotte at least would have liked to have remained for several minutes. Like the room in the theater where she had been too busy to look, it was entirely decorated with old theater posters, and she saw wonderful names that conjured images of limelight and drama, ringing voices and the thrill of passion and drama: George Conquest, Beerbohm Tree, Ellen Terry, Mrs. Patrick Campbell, a marvelous, towering figure of Sir Henry Irving as Hamlet, and another of Sarah Bernhardt in magnificently dramatic pose. There were others she had no time to see, and she followed Caroline reluctantly.

On the first landing were more posters, these for the Gilbert and Sullivan operas *Iolanthe* and *Patience* and *The Yeomen of the Guard*.

Caroline was uninterested; not only had she seen them before, but she was intent upon her mission, and drama behind the footlights held no magic for her in comparison. She hesitated only a moment on the first landing, and then continued on up the steps to the second. This was decorated only with one large poster of the dynamic and sensitive face of Sarah Bernhardt.

She knocked on the door, and after a few moments it was opened by Tamar Macaulay herself. Charlotte had expected her to look different in the harsher light of morning, and with no performance in the immediate future. But on the contrary she looked startlingly the same. Her hair was dead black, without the usual touches and lights of brown that even the darkest English hair so often possesses, and her eyes were deep and vivid with a flash of amusement in spite of the tension and the awareness of pain. She was dressed very plainly, but instead of being dull it merely emphasized the drama of her face.

"Good morning, Mrs. Ellison, Mrs. Pitt. How pleasant to see you."

"Good morning, Miss Macaulay," Caroline replied. "Forgive my coming without warning, and bringing my daughter with me, but I feel the matter is important, or may be, and there is little time to fritter away."

"Then you had better come in." Tamar stepped back to allow them to pass her and go into the large, open room. It was furnished as a sitting room, although perhaps it had originally been a bedroom when the house was occupied by a single family. There was an interesting mixture of styles. On one side stood an old Chinese silk screen which had once been of great beauty, now faded, its wooden frame scratched in places, but it still held an elegance that gave it charm and a comfortable grace. There was a Russian samovar on a side table, Venetian glass in the cabinet, a French ormolu clock on the mantel shelf above the fireplace, and a late Georgian mahogany table of total simplicity and cleanness of line which to Charlotte was the loveliest thing in the room. The colors were pale, creams and greens, and full of light.

Caroline was endeavoring to explain their errand.

Charlotte's eyes continued to wander around, looking for evidence of the child Caroline had mentioned. There was a casual untidiness, as of a place which is the center of the life in a house, a shawl laid down, an open book, a pile of playbills and a script on a side table, cushions in a heap, disordered. Then she saw the doll, fallen off the sofa and half hidden by the flowered frill. She felt a sudden and unreasonable sense of sadness, so sharp it caught her breath and her throat ached. A child without a father, a woman alone. Was it conceivable Tamar Macaulay had truly loved Kingsley Blaine? Or was that just a fancy, leaping ahead of fact? She had no reason to suppose he was the father. It could be anyone—even Joshua Fielding. Please heaven, not him. Caroline would find it intolerable.

"Of course," Tamar was saying. "Please sit down, Mrs. Pitt. Thank you for concerning yourself in the matter. We have struggled long enough with it alone, and now it looks as if it has become more dangerous, we may badly need help. It appears someone has been frightened, and reacted with violence—again." Her face was bleak.

Charlotte had not heard the conversation, but she guessed at its meaning. She accepted the invitation to sit.

"We were there when Judge Stafford died," she said with the shadow of a smile. "It is natural we should feel an involvement in finding the person who killed him, and being absolutely sure it is the right person, and not a miscarriage of justice."

The expression in Tamar's face was a mixture of irony, anger and pain, and a bitter humor. If there was still hope in it, it was beyond Charlotte's vision to see it. How had this woman kept courage all these years, after such a fearful bereavement? The death of someone you know is always hard, but public disgrace, the hatred, the slow torture of the person by the law is immeasurably worse. And then there was the knowledge that at a certain hour of a set day, they would come to take that person, still young, still in health, and break his neck on the end of a rope, deliberately, to satisfy a cheering crowd! How must he feel the night before? Does the darkness seem endless—or only too short? Could one dread daylight more?

Tamar was staring at her.

"Are you thinking of Aaron?" she said with total bluntness.

Charlotte was taken aback for a moment, then she realized how much easier it would be to speak frankly rather than skirt around such an agonizing subject, seeking a way to convey the meaning without actually using the words, and understand what someone meant beneath the layers of euphemisms.

"Yes." She allowed the shadow of a smile across her face.

"You allow the possibility there was an injustice?" Tamar asked.

"Of course," Charlotte agreed warmly. "I have known for a certainty of innocent men who would have been hanged but for chance. It could easily happen, and I am sure it has at times. I wish it were impossible, but it is not."

"That is a dangerous thought," Tamar said wryly. "People do not like it. They cannot live with the idea that we may be guilty of such a mistake. It is much better to convince yourself he was guilty and go to sleep."

"I did not have any part in it, Miss Macaulay," Charlotte pointed out. "I have no guilt in thinking he may have been innocent, only grief. The guilt will come if I do not do what I can now to find out the truth, both of the death of Kingsley Blaine and the death of Judge Stafford."

Tamar smiled openly for the first time. It was a gesture full of charm, lighting her face and changing its whole aspect.

"What an extraordinary creature you are. But then I suppose you would have to be, to have married a policeman."

Charlotte was surprised. She had not realized Tamar would have any appreciation of her affairs, or what they involved.

"Oh—Joshua told me," Tamar explained with amusement. "I gather your mother told him." She glanced around and saw that Caroline had left them. "I imagine that is where she has gone now. Possibly tact—or . . ." She lifted her slight shoulders expressively, but said nothing more.

Charlotte had a moment of discomfort, wondering if Caroline were making a fool of herself, being too bold, but there was no way in which she could retrieve it now without making her situation even worse. There was nothing she could profitably do but pursue the case.

"Do you know anything about the death of Kingsley Blaine that did not come out in court?" she asked bluntly. "Anything you told Judge Stafford which could have caused him to reopen the matter?"

Tamar shook her head. "Nothing that wasn't in the appeal. The medical evidence was shaky. Humbert Yardley,

157

the examiner, began by saying that the wound which killed Kingsley . . ." Her face tightened, the soft skin around her mouth almost white. She kept her voice level with an effort. ". . . Was caused by something longer than a farrier's nail. Then later he said it could have been an unusual nail."

"Was such a nail found?"

"No, but the police said he could have disposed of it anywhere—down the nearest drain. It was only the uncertainty on which we raised the appeal. We tried other things; the coat which no one found, the necklace. But they were explained away. They said the coat was picked up by a tramp, and that I kept the necklace."

"Didn't the flower seller also change her mind?" Charlotte asked.

"Yes—but only before the trial, not once they put her on the witness stand. God help her, she was only a simple person, and once it was fixed in her mind, she was too afraid of the police to argue."

"Miss Macaulay"—Charlotte looked at her gently, trying to convey in her face that she was asking only because she had to—"apart from love for your brother, why do you believe, in the face of so much, that he was innocent?"

"Because Aaron had no reason to kill Kingsley," Tamar replied, her eyes brilliant, wry, candid. "They said that Kingsley had seduced me and was playing with my affections, and Aaron killed him in revenge for me. But that was nonsense. Kingsley loved me, and was going to marry me." She said it quite quietly, as if it were a simple matter of fact and she did not care if Charlotte believed her or not.

Charlotte was shaken with total surprise, and yet her immediate reaction was not disbelief. Had Tamar been more emotional, more urgent to convince her, she might have doubted, but her simple statement, as of something long familiar to her, left her with no instinct to fight against it.

"But he was already married," she said, not to disprove it, but to seek explanation. "What was he going to do about that?"

Tamar bit her lip, for the first time shame in her face. "I did not know that then." She lowered her eyes. "To begin with I did not take him seriously." She shrugged. "One doesn't. Young men with time to spare and a roving eye come to the theater in hundreds. They only want a little entertainment, a little excitement, and then to go home to their wives as society expects of them. It was months before I could believe Kingsley was different. By then I had learned to love him, and it was too late to alter my feelings." She looked up quickly, her expression defensive. "Of course you will say I should have asked if he was married, and so I should. But I didn't want to know."

"What was he going to do about his wife?" Charlotte asked, refraining from making another judgment.

"I don't know." Tamar shook her head, but her eyes did not leave Charlotte's face. "I only learned after his death that he was married. If he meant to marry me, then I suppose he was going to leave her. Or perhaps he didn't mean to marry me, he only promised in order to keep me. But the point is, Aaron didn't know that either. He thought Kingsley was free, and would marry me."

"Are you sure?" Charlotte said softly. "Is it not possible he learned that Mr. Blaine was married, and that is why he killed him? That would be an excellent reason."

"It would be, if it were true. I saw Aaron just before he left the theater, and he didn't know then, any more than I did."

"Would he have told you—honestly?"

"Probably not, but he would not have spoken to Kingsley as he did. He was a good actor—but not good enough to deceive me like that. I knew him too well."

"You did not say that at the trial, did you?"

Tamar gave a bitter little laugh, more a choking on her own breath.

"No—Mr. James said no one would believe that Kingsley really intended to marry me, and it would only make me look ridiculous, and even more of a victim than if I pretended I were the seducer and were playing with him. That way I would seem less vulnerable, and Aaron have less cause to avenge me."

Charlotte could see the sense of it, and reluctantly she admitted it.

"I think had I been in his place, I might have done the same. It would not have helped to tell the truth."

Tamar pulled a face. "Thank you for that!"

"Did you tell Judge Stafford?"

"Yes. I have no idea whether he believed me or not. He had the kind of face and manner I could not read."

"Who else have you told?"

Tamar stood up and walked over towards the window, the sunlight harsh on her face, discovering every plane and line, and yet it made her more beautiful because of the honesty of her emotion.

"Everyone who mattered, who would listen. Barton James, the barrister for the defense, and before him Ebenezer Moorgate, Aaron's solicitor." She stared out of the window in front of her. "I even went to Adolphus Pryce. He said the same as Barton James. If I had said so at the trial, he would have made great capital out of it. I believed him. I saw the appeal judges as well—all of them. But none of them listened to me except Judge Stafford, poor man!"

"Why was he different?" Charlotte asked curiously. "Why was he prepared to look into the case again after five years?"

Tamar turned from the window and looked at her steadily. "I am not sure. I think he believed me about Kingsley, which no one else did. And he asked me several questions about the time Aaron left the theater, and the time Kingsley left, but he would not say why. Believe me, Mrs. Pitt, I have racked my brain to think why he was going to reopen it. If I knew that, I could take the evidence to Judge Oswyn. He seemed once or twice as if he might have listened, then his courage failed him."

"Courage?"

Tamar laughed and there was harshness deep and hard in it. "It would hardly be popular to say now that Aaron had been innocent. Think of it! The disgrace, the embarrassment, the people who were wrong—the things that cannot be undone. And worse than all that, the disrepute of the law." Regret overtook anger in her. "That is the worst thing about Stafford's death——he was a brave man, and an honest one. He died for it."

Charlotte looked at her passionate face and its blazing conviction. Was that what had moved Stafford: the power of her belief, rather than evidence? Or had he simply wanted to silence her once and for all, to save the shame she spoke of, the disrepute of the law?

"If it was not Aaron," she said aloud, "who was it?"

Tamar's face reflected laughter and pain at once.

"I don't know. I cannot believe it was Joshua, although he and I had been . . . close." She used the word delicately, allowing deeper meaning to be understood. "But it was over by then. It was really no more than propinquity and youth. The police suspected him out of jealousy, but I cannot believe that——not of him. I suppose the only other person would be Devlin O'Neil, but the quarrel would have to be far greater than the few guineas' wager they spoke of."

"He married Kathleen Blaine," Charlotte pointed out. "Perhaps he was in love with her then."

"Perhaps. It is not impossible."

"Did she have money?"

"How very practical of you!" Tamar's eyebrows rose. "Yes, I believe so, or at least very good expectations. I think she is an only child, and old Prosper Harrimore is wealthy——by our standards."

"Did Mr. O'Neil have money?"

"Good heavens, no, only enough to support a handsome style of life for a short while." She walked back to the sofa and sat down again facing Charlotte. "He rented his rooms and owed his tailor and his wine merchant——like most good-looking and idle young men."

"So he gained considerably by his friend's death?"

Tamar hesitated only a moment. "Yes——that is true, if ugly, and perhaps not relevant. But I don't know who else, unless it was a complete stranger——a robber . . ." She left it unfinished, knowing how unlikely that was.

"Who crucified his victims?" Charlotte said skeptically.

"No——that was obscene," Tamar admitted. "I don't know.

161

I don't know why O'Neil should do such a thing, except to try to put the blame on someone Jewish."

"Do you know Devlin O'Neil?"

"Not now. Why?"

"Well, the best way we might learn something more about it would be through him."

"He would hardly tell us something that incriminated him."

"Not intentionally, of course," Charlotte agreed. "But we can only learn the truth from those who know it."

There was a sudden lift in Tamar's face, a spark of hope in her dark eyes.

"You would be prepared to do that?"

"Of course," Charlotte said without giving it a minute's thought.

"Then we shall get Clio to take you. She still knows Kathleen, and it would not be difficult."

"Not we, I think," Charlotte corrected quickly. "It must be done as if by chance. They should not know I have any interest in the case."

"Oh—yes, of course. That was stupid of me. I'll introduce you to Clio. She is not in this morning, but next time—soon. She'll take you."

"Excellent! Explain to her what we need, and why, and I will do all I can."

When Charlotte began to discuss the case frankly with Tamar, Caroline realized that her presence was unnecessary, and very quietly she turned and walked over to the door, opened it and went out. She was down the stairs and in the hallway outside Joshua Fielding's room with her hand raised to knock before she realized how forward she was being, how indelicate and unlike everything she had been taught, and had tried to teach her own daughters. Had Charlotte behaved this way she would have been horrified, and told her so.

Self-consciousness overcame her and she stepped back again. It would look odd, foolish, but she would have to go back upstairs and hope no one would ask her for an explanation. She turned and was halfway across to the stairs upwards when Miranda Passmore came running up from the floor beneath.

"Hallo, Mrs. Ellison! Is Mr. Fielding not in? I thought he was, in fact I was sure. Here, let me knock again." And without waiting for an answer, and misunderstanding Caroline's gasp, she crossed the landing and rapped sharply on Joshua's door.

There was a moment of desperate silence. Caroline drew in her breath to protest.

The door swung open and Joshua Fielding stood in the entrance smiling, looking first at Caroline, then at Miranda.

"Oh Joshua, I thought you were there," Miranda said cheerfully. "Mrs. Ellison called to see you, but she could not make you hear." She smiled and ran on up the stairs and disappeared.

"I'm sorry I didn't hear you," Joshua apologized.

"Oh, you wouldn't," Caroline said quickly. "I didn't knock."

He looked puzzled.

"I—I came with my daughter, to see Miss Macaulay—about—about Judge Stafford's death. I thought . . ." She stopped, aware she was speaking too much, explaining where he had not asked.

"It is good of you to become involved in the matter." He smiled. There was both warmth and a certain shyness in it. "It must have been very distressing for you to have been there and seen the poor man die, and then learning it was murder. I am sorry it should have happened to you."

"I am also anxious that there should be no injustice done," she said quickly. She did not want him to think her feeble, simply concerned in the unpleasantness for herself, and unconcerned for others.

"I don't think you can help," he said, pulling a face. "Judge Stafford was going to reopen the case of Kingsley Blaine's death, but since he apparently left no notes on it, it looks as if it will remain closed—by default. Unless we can discover what he intended."

"That is what we must try to do," she said urgently. "Not

only to clear his name but also to protect you—and Miss Macaulay."

He smiled, but it was an expression full of self-mockery and pain.

"You think they will blame us for that death too?"

"It is not impossible," she said quietly, a sudden chill inside her as she realized the truth of what she said. "They will have no choice, if neither Stafford's widow nor her lover are guilty. It will be the natural thing to do."

"I don't think like a policeman," he said ruefully. "But please do not stand out here in the hallway. Would it be very improper for you to come inside? The house is full of people."

"Of course it would not," she said quickly, feeling the color burn up her face. "Nobody could possibly imagine—" She broke off. What she had been going to say would have been rude. She was trying too hard, because the thoughts racing in her mind were absurd. "That you would be other than courteous," she finished lamely, walking past him as he held the door open for her.

The room inside was highly individual, but the first glance startled her. She had previously met him only in the theater, or downstairs in the large sitting room of the Passmores, along with Tamar Macaulay. This room was quite markedly his. A huge portrait of the actor Edmund Keene, painted in sepia and black, decorated the far wall. It was dramatic in pose, and reached from the floor to above head height. It dominated the room with its presence, and made her realize far more powerfully than before how deeply he loved his art.

Along the narrow wall were shelves full of books. A small table was littered with papers which she thought were scripts of a play. Several easy chairs filled the open space, as if he frequently entertained many people, and she felt a sharp regret that she was not one of them, and could not be. A gulf of social status and experience divided them. Suddenly she felt horribly alone and outside all the laughter and the warmth.

"I wish I knew what to do about it." He resumed the first

164

conversation, pulling a chair a little straighter for her and holding it while she sat down. It was a gracious gesture, and yet it reminded her sharply that she was probably fifteen or sixteen years older than he, little short of a generation.

"We must fight back," she said briskly, battling her own misery with anger. "We must find the truth that they have not. It is there—they simply were content to accept the easiest answer. We will not."

He looked at her with dawning amazement—and admiration.

"Do you know how?"

"I have some idea," she said with far more certainty than she felt. She sounded like Charlotte, and it was appalling—and exciting. "We will begin by making the acquaintance of the people concerned. Who are they? I mean—who are all the people who might know the truth, or some part of it?"

"I suppose Tamar and myself," he replied, sitting down opposite her. "But we have talked about it so endlessly that I don't think there can be anything we have not considered."

"Well, if neither of you killed Mr. Blaine, and Aaron Godman did not, then there must be someone else involved," she said reasonably. Pitt's wry, intelligent face flashed into her mind, and she wondered if this was how he thought. "Who do you believe killed him?"

He thought for a moment, his chin resting on one hand. It might have seemed a theatrical pose in anyone else, and yet he looked totally natural. She was acutely conscious of his presence, of the sunlight from the window on the thick wave of his hair. He was too young for there to be any gray in the bright brown of it. Yet there were fine lines in the skin around his eyes; it was not a face without experience, or pain. There was none of the brashness or the untempered spirit of youth. Perhaps he was not so far short of forty.

But she was fifty-three. Merely naming it hurt.

"I suppose it has to be Devlin O'Neil," he said, looking up at her at last. "Unless it is someone we know nothing about. I don't suppose it is even imaginable that his wife knew he intended leaving her for Tamar, and employed someone to kill him." A bitter humor lit his eyes for an instant, and then changed to pity. "That is, of course, if he really did mean to leave her. I don't think he had much money of his own, and he would have given up a very comfortable life, and all social reputation. I've never told Tamar, but I think honestly it was unlikely he would have done such a thing. He probably told her he would because he really loved her, and couldn't bear to lose her, so he lied, hoping to keep it going as long as he could. But we'll never know."

She chose deliberately to ask the most painful question. It was there in her mind, and it would get all the blows dealt at one time.

"And would she have married him? Isn't she Jewish? What about her faith, marrying outside her own people?" She hated the words even as she heard herself saying them.

"Not desirable," he admitted, meeting her eyes very directly. "But we are not very strict. She would have done it."

"And her brother did not mind?" She pushed it to the sticking point.

"Aaron?" He lifted his shoulders very slightly. "He wasn't pleased. And of course Passmore wouldn't have been pleased either, if she had given up the stage and become a respectable matron—or perhaps respectable would have been impossible, since Blaine would have left his wife for her—but at least quietly domestic, raising a family. She is the best actress on the London stage at the moment—with the possible exception of Bernhardt."

"So he would have wished Blaine . . . elsewhere?"

He smiled broadly. "Certainly, had he known about it. But he didn't. He thought Blaine was just one more stage door johnnie. They were pretty discreet. And she did have other admirers, you know."

"Yes, of course. I suppose it is natural." Unconsciously she smoothed down her skirt.

"Very."

"Then it comes back to Devlin O'Neil," she said decisively. "We must make his acquaintance and learn all we can about him. If we cannot prove Aaron's innocence, then we must prove someone else's guilt."

His admiration was undisguised. "How wonderfully obvious! We have spent five years trying to show Aaron did not do it; we should have tried harder to show that someone else did. But we didn't have the necessary skills." He relaxed a little farther into the chair. "And of course O'Neil was not exactly well disposed towards us, nor ignorant of our interest."

"Of course not. But he does not know me, nor my daughter, who is quite practiced in these things."

"Is she? What a remarkable family you are. I shall never judge people so hastily again. You seem so utterly respectable. I apologize!" He laughed very lightly. "I supposed that you spent your mornings visiting dressmakers and milliners, writing beautiful letters to friends in the country, and ordering your households. And in the afternoons you would call upon acquaintances, or receive them, taking tea and cucumber sandwiches cut by your cook, and doing good works for the less fortunate, or stitching fine embroidery. I pictured your evenings at the very best social functions, or sitting by the fire reading improving books and holding suitable conversations—uplifting to the mind. I am truly sorry; I eat the bread of humility." The laughter was vivid in his face. "I was never so mistaken! Women are the most mystifying creatures, so often not at all what they seem. All the time you were out detecting fearful crimes and unearthing desperate secrets."

Caroline felt the color flooding up her cheeks, but she lied in her teeth.

"We should not succeed if we were open in the matter," she said with a catch in her voice and a fluttering in her stomach. "The art of detection lies in appearing quite harmless."

"Does it?" he said curiously. "We have been so singularly unsuccessful, perhaps that was one of our problems? We tried to appear too clever."

"Well, you were hopelessly handicapped by the fact that

167

everyone had to realize your interest in the affair," she pointed out. "Tell me, what was Aaron like? And what about Kingsley Blaine?"

For half an hour he told her of the two men, both of whom he had known and liked. He recounted anecdotes with gentleness and laughter, but all the time she was acutely aware that they were both dead, and their youth, their hopes and their weaknesses ended. He spoke softly, his voice holding the words with regret, as if they were more than mere memories. There was an emotion in him that made her wish both to laugh with him and to cry.

"You would have liked Aaron," he said with certainty. It was a compliment, and she found herself warming with pleasure. He said it not because Aaron Godman was so obviously charming a person, but because he had liked him himself, and he could not conceive of her being blind to the qualities which were so apparent to him. "He was one of the most generous people I ever knew. He was happy for other people's success." He pulled a little face. "That's one of the hardest things to do, but it came to him naturally. And he could be terribly funny." His face softened at the memory, then suddenly the sadness was so sharp it was close to tears. "I don't seem to have laughed the same way since he went."

"And Kingsley Blaine?" she said gently, longing to comfort him, and knowing it was impossible.

"Oh—he was a decent enough fellow. A dreamer, not much of a realist. He loved the theater, loved the imagination of it. He had no patience with the craft. But he was generous too. Never held a grudge. Forgave so easily." He bit his lip. "That's the worst part of it, the stupidest. They liked each other. They had so much in common it was easy." He looked at her, silently, full of apology for the emotion.

She smiled back at him and there was total ease between them, no need of explanation.

The sunlight filled the room in a brief blaze, and then clouded over.

It was past time for luncheon, and she had not even

thought of it, when Charlotte knocked on the door and reminded her of the present, and their role as visitors who must rise, bid farewell, and take their departure out into the busy, noisy street with all its urgent clatter.

"I suppose you have been out chasing after those theater people again!" Grandmama said as soon as Caroline was in the hallway. The old lady was standing in the entrance to the withdrawing room, having heard the carriage draw up. She was leaning heavily on her stick and her face was sour with curiosity and disapproval. "No good, any of them— immoral, dissolute and hopelessly vulgar!"

"Oh, I do wish sometimes you would hold your tongue," Caroline said abruptly, handing her cape to the maid. "You know nothing about it whatsoever. Go back to the withdrawing room and read a book. Have a crumpet. Write to a friend."

"My eyes are too weak to read. It is only two o'clock, and far too early to eat crumpets. And all my friends are dead," the old lady said viciously. "And my daughter-in-law is making a complete fool of herself, to my everlasting shame!"

"You have enough follies of your own to be ashamed about," Caroline replied briskly, for once not caring a jot what the old lady thought. "You don't need to concern yourself with mine!"

"Caroline!" The old lady glared after her as she swept across the hall and up the stairs. "Caroline! Come back here at once! Don't you dare speak to me like that! I don't know what's come over you!" She stood watching Caroline's straight back and erect head retreating up the stairs— and swore.

6

WHILE CHARLOTTE AND CAROLINE were concerned with the Blaine/Godman case, and the danger to Tamar Macaulay and Joshua Fielding, Pitt was sitting in the public omnibus returning his attention to the death of Judge Stafford, which was the core of his case. He did not know whether the Farriers' Lane murder was the original cause of it, or if the connection were accidental, mere chance that Stafford had been enquiring into it on the day of his death, and totally misleading. Surely if he had any evidence which would justify reexamining the case, he would have told others of it, the police, his colleagues—or at the very least, left notes.

The conductor pushed his way down between the seats and crowded passengers and took their money, swaying on his feet as the vehicle stopped and started. A fat man coughed into a red handkerchief and apologized to no one in particular.

Most murders were tragically simple, involving the passions of close relationships—love, jealousy, greed, fear—or the reactions of the thief caught in the act.

The best place to begin was with the crime itself, for the time being ignore motive. Someone had placed opium in Stafford's flask of whiskey after the time he and Livesey had both drunk from it in Livesey's chambers. Later he had visited Joshua Fielding, Tamar Macaulay, Devlin O'Neil and Adolphus Pryce, any of whom could have touched the flask before the evening, when he had gone to the theater, drunk from it, and then fallen into a coma and died. The only people with the opportunity were those he had visited and his wife, Juniper Stafford. To consider either the clerks in his office or the servants in his house seemed absurd. No one could suggest the slightest motive for such an act.

The omnibus was stationary again, behind a large brewer's dray. The traffic was creeping up an incline, horses straining and impatient. A carriage in front somewhere had broken a piece of harness. Footmen were scrambling about, cursing. A costermonger was shouting. Someone was ringing a bell and a carriage dog was barking hysterically. Everyone was cold and short of temper.

"It's getting worse every day," the man beside Pitt said angrily. "In another year or two nothing will move at all! London will be one vast jam of carts and carriages without room for a soul to take a step. Half this stuff should be taken away. Made illegal."

"And where would you put it?" the man opposite demanded, his face creased with anger. "They've as much right to travel as you!"

"On the railways," the first man retorted, straightening his tie with a tweak. "On the canals. What's wrong with the river? Look at that damned great load there." He jerked his hand towards the window where a wagon was passing by laden with boxes and bales twenty feet high. "Disgraceful. Send it up the river by barge."

"Maybe it's not going anywhere that's on the river," the second man suggested.

"Then it should be! Size of it!"

The omnibus moved forward with a jolt and resumed its slow progress, and the conversation was lost. Pitt returned his thoughts to the case. Motive he put aside for the moment. Opportunity was obvious. How about means? He had never had occasion to enquire into the availability of opium. Like any other officer, he knew there were opium dens in parts of London, where those addicted to the substance could obtain it and then lie in tiers of narrow cots and smoke themselves into their own brief, private oblivion. And of course he also knew a little about the opium wars with China which had occurred between 1839 and 1842, and then again between 1856 and 1860. They had been begun by the Chinese attempting to take action against British merchants dealing in the opium trade. It was a black page of British history, but Pitt did not know what bearing it had on the present availability of the drug to the ordinary public in London, except that apparently the opium traders, with the mighty naval power of the Empire behind them, had won the day.

Perhaps the best thing would be to try to purchase opium himself and see how he fared. He would put off going to see Judge Livesey until later. The omnibus had stopped again for traffic, and he rose to his feet, excused himself and picked his way with difficulty past the passengers seated along the benches on both sides of the aisle, trying not to step on feet. Amid grumbles about delay, noise, clumsiness, and people who did not know where they were going, he alighted, dodging a landau driven by an ill-tempered coachman. He leaped over a pile of steaming manure and an overflowing gutter, and strode along the pavement until he should see an apothecary's shop.

He found one within half a mile, but it was small and dark, and when he went inside the solitary young woman behind the counter, and the piles of jars and packets balanced on it, were of little help. She offered him alternative powders for toothache, the name of a dentist she recommended, or several other patent remedies for pain of one sort or another, but did not seem to know where he might obtain opium. She had a mixture adequate to give a crying baby, in order to lull it to sleep, which she thought might contain opium, but she was not sure since the ingredients were not listed on the bottle.

He thanked her and declined, then went out again to resume his search. He walked as briskly as he could through the swirls of people buying, selling, running errands and gossiping on the footpath and spilling onto the street, jostling the traffic, shouting at each other amid the clatter of hooves and wheels, the jingle of harness and whinnying of horses.

The second apothecary's shop he found was a much larger establishment, and when he went inside the counters were clear, the shelves behind stacked with a marvelous array of colored bottles filled with every manner of liquids, crystals, dried leaves and powders, all labeled with their chemical names in Latin. Another shelf was filled with packets, and occasionally along its length there were cupboards set in, their doors ostentatiously locked. The man superintending this alchemist's glory was small, bald headed, with spectacles halfway down his nose and a general expression of interest on his face.

"Yes sir, and what may I do for you?" he enquired as soon as Pitt was inside. "Is it for yourself, sir, or your family? You are a family man, yes?"

"Yes," Pitt agreed, smiling without knowing why, except that there was something about being seen to belong to a family which pleased him. But the admission rather altered what he had intended saying regarding opium.

"Thought so," the apothecary said with satisfaction. "Fancy I can judge a man pretty well by his appearance. Begging your pardon for the familiarity, sir, but it takes a good wife to turn a collar like that."

"Oh." Pitt had no idea anyone could tell his collar and cuffs had been taken off and turned so the worn bits were on the inside, thus prolonging the life of the garment. He put his hand up to it unconsciously, and realized his tie was crooked and thus Charlotte's neat stitching showed. He straightened it with a faint blush.

"Now, sir, what can I do for you?" the apothecary said cheerfully.

There was little point in anything but honesty now. The sharp-eyed little man would be insulted by deviousness, and probably be aware of a lie.

"I'm a police officer," Pitt explained, producing his identification.

"Indeed?" the apothecary said with interest. There was no shadow of anxiety in his open expression.

"I should like to know more about the availability of opium," Pitt replied. "Not to smoke, that I know already. I am looking into the liquid form. Do you have any information you could give me?"

"Good gracious, sir, of course I have." The apothecary looked surprised. "Easy to get as you like. Mothers use it to quieten a fractious baby. Poor souls need a little sleep, and give the child enough to keep it from crying half the night, keeping the whole house awake." He pointed to a row of bottles on one of the shelves behind him. "Godfrey's Cordial, sell a great deal of that. Made up of treacle, water, spices—and opium. Works very well, they say. And then there's also Steedman's powder. And Atkinson's Royal Infants' Preservative is very popular." He shook his head. "Don't know if it's the name, or the mixture, but people like it. Of course in East Anglia and the fen country you can buy opium in penny sticks or in pills from just about any little corner shop you like."

"Legally?" Pitt asked with surprise.

"Of course! Prescribed for all manner of ills." The apothecary ticked of his fingers. "Rheumatism, diabetes, consumption, syphilis, cholera, diarrhea, constipation or insomnia."

"And does it work?" Pitt asked incredulously.

"It kills pain," the apothecary replied sadly. "That's not a cure, but when a person is suffering, it's something. I don't approve of it, but I wouldn't deny a suffering person a little ease—especially if there's no cure for what's wrong with them. And God knows, there's enough of that. No one gets better from consumption or cholera—or syphilis for that matter, although it takes longer."

"And doesn't the opium kill?"

"Babes, yes, as like as not." The apothecary's face pinched and his eyes were weary. "Not the opium itself, you understand? They get so they're half asleep all the time, and they don't eat, poor little mites. Die of starvation."

Pitt felt suddenly sick. He thought of Jemima and Daniel, remembering them as tiny, desperately helpless creatures, so fiercely alive, and he found his throat tight and a pain inside him so he could not speak.

The apothecary was looking at him with sadness creasing his face.

"There's no use prosecuting them," he said quietly. "They don't know any different. Sickly, worked to their wits' end, and don't know what way to turn, most of them. Have a child just about every year, counting the ones that miscarry—no way to stop it except tell their husbands no—if they'll take no for an answer. And what man will? He has few enough pleasures, and he reckons that one's his by right." He shook his head. "Not enough food, not enough room, not enough anything, poor devils."

"I wasn't going to prosecute them," Pitt said, swallowing hard. "I am looking for someone who poisoned an adult man by putting opium in his whiskey."

"Some poor woman couldn't take any more?" the apothecary guessed, biting his lip and looking at Pitt as if he knew the answer already.

"No," Pitt said more loudly than he had intended. "A woman well past childbearing age, and a perfectly sober husband. She had a lover . . ."

"Oh—oh dear." The apothecary was taken aback. He shook his head slowly. "Oh dear. And you want to know if she could have obtained the opium with which he was poisoned? I am afraid so. Anyone could. It is not in the least difficult, nor is it necessary to register one's name for the purchase. You will be extremely fortunate to find anybody who recalls selling it to her—or to her lover, should he be the guilty party."

"Or anyone else, I suppose," Pitt said ruefully.

"Oh dear—the poor man had others who wished him ill?"

"It is possible. He was a man with much knowledge and authority." Since he had voiced his suspicions of the widow, and of her intimate affairs, he chose not to name Judge Stafford. If it were Juniper, it would be public knowledge soon enough, and if it were not, she had more than sufficient grief to bear as it was.

The apothecary shook his head sadly. "Dangerous stuff, opium. Once you begin with it, there's little stopping, and few that can manage to do without ever greater doses." A flicker of anger crossed his mild, intelligent features. "Misguided doctors gave it to their patients in the Civil War in America, thinking it would be less addicting than ether or chloroform, especially if given by the then new invention of hypodermic syringe, into the vein rather than the stomach. Of course, they were wrong. And now they have four hundred thousand poor devils slave to it." He sighed. "That's one war where we both won and lost, I think. Perhaps we lost the more."

"The American Civil War?" Pitt was confused.

"No sir, the opium war with China. Perhaps I did not make myself plain."

"No, you didn't," Pitt said agreeably. "But you are perfectly correct. Thank you for your assistance."

"Not at all. Sorry it is so little use to you. But I am afraid anyone with a few pence to spare could purchase sufficient sticks of opium to dissolve and put in the poor man's drink, and there would be no record of it, and nothing illegal in the mere buying of it anyway." He looked at Pitt discouragingly. "You could waste a year in going to every apothecary and corner shop within forty miles of London—or farther if the lady you suspect has the means and the opportunity to travel. As I said, opium is available with great ease all over East Anglia and the fen country, which is a mere hundred or hundred and fifty miles from London."

"Then I shall have to return to other means of learning the truth," Pitt conceded. "Thank you, and good day."

"Good day, sir, and good luck in your search."

It was not until mid-afternoon that Pitt obtained an appointment with Judge Ignatius Livesey and was shown into his chambers. It had turned colder outside and he was pleased to go into the warmth of the room with its well-stoked fire and rich carpets, the velvet curtains richly draped against the outside world, the ornate mantel speaking of solidarity, the leatherbound books, the bronze figures and Meissen china dishes adding touches of grace and luxury.

"Good afternoon, Pitt," Livesey said courteously. "How are you proceeding in the matter of poor Stafford's death?"

"Good afternoon, sir," Pitt replied. "Not very fruitfully so far. It seems opium is very readily obtainable by anyone with a few pence to spare. Indeed it is much purchased by the poorest people, I am informed, in order to ease their wakeful children, and treat a number of extremely diverse illnesses, sometimes even mutually contradictory ones."

"Is it indeed?" Livesey raised his eyebrows. "How very tragic. Public health is one of our greatest problems, coupled with ignorance and poverty. So endeavoring to trace the opium has profited you little?"

"Nothing," Pitt corrected.

"Please sit down, make yourself comfortable," Livesey invited. "It has turned cold outside, so my clerk informs me. It is a trifle early, but would you care for tea?"

"Yes, very much," Pitt accepted, sitting in the large leather-cushioned chair opposite Livesey, who was at his desk.

Livesey reached out and pressed a bell on the wall near him, and a moment later a clerk appeared, enquiring what he wished. Livesey requested tea for two, and then leaned back and regarded Pitt curiously.

"And what brings you to me again, Mr. Pitt? I appreciate the civility of your telling me of your progress, or lack of it. But I imagine that is not all you came for."

"I would like you to tell me all you can recall of the evening Judge Stafford died, sir," Pitt asked him. "From the time you met him in the theater."

"Of course, although I am not sure it will be helpful." Livesey sat back in his chair and rested his hands across his stomach, his heavy face calm. "I reached the theater about twenty minutes before the performance was due to begin. It was extremely crowded, naturally. These places usually are, if the play is any good at all, and this was a popular work, and performed by a fine cast." He smiled, an expression of indulgence and very slight contempt. "Of course there were the usual prostitutes of one degree or another, parading in the balconies and the gallery at the back, attired in a wonderful array of colors. Gorgeous, at a distance. And the men ogled them, and a good many did far more. But that is all quite customary, and no doubt you observed it yourself."

The clerk returned with a tray set with a silver swan-necked teapot, a silver cream jug and sugar bowl with tongs, and two china cups and plates and a basin and silver strainer. Two silver teaspoons had handles set with pearl shell. Livesey thanked him absently, and as soon as he left, closing the door silently behind him, Livesey poured tea for himself and Pitt.

"I observed one or two acquaintances," Livesey continued, looking at Pitt with mild amusement. "I believe I nodded to a couple of them, then proceeded to my box. Frequently I have guests, but on this occasion my wife was unable to come, and I had not invited anyone myself. I was alone. Which, I suppose, was one of the reasons I considered joining Stafford in the interval. As it was I merely passed some small pleasantry and left him to himself." He sipped his tea with absentminded pleasure. It was Earl Grey, delicate and expensive.

"Why was that, sir?" Pitt sat up a little straighter.

"He went to the smoking room," Livesey said, shaking his head a little and smiling. "A very public place, Mr. Pitt. The area where gentlemen may retire together to smoke, if they wish to, or to escape feminine company for a few minutes, and possibly to gossip with one another, or transact a little business, if they find it appropriate. There were a great many people there, some of whom I found tedious, and I did not wish to spoil my evening. I looked in, but did not remain."

"Did you notice if Mr. Pryce was there?"

Livesey's face darkened. "I follow your thoughts, Mr. Pitt. Most regrettable, but I fear now beyond the point where a man of any sense could avoid them. Yes, he was there, and he spoke with Stafford. That much I saw. But I cannot say that I observed any opportunity for him to have touched the flask." His steady eyes did not leave Pitt's face. "Personally, I did not see Stafford drink from it. I doubt he necessarily took it out during the interval at all. I think it more likely he drank from it quietly, in the darkness and the privacy of his own box. That is what I should do, rather than be seen to drink from my own flask in a public place, where refreshment could be purchased." He regarded Pitt with a sad smile, a comment on the weakness of a man not unlike himself, and for whom he felt a certain pity now. "Do you understand?"

"Yes," Pitt conceded, sipping his own tea also. It made excellent sense. He had never carried a flask—it was an utterly alien thought—but if he had done so, he would have drunk from it discreetly, in the privacy of a theater box, not in the public smoking room. "How was his manner?"

"Thoughtful," Livesey replied after a moment's consideration, as if reliving a memory. He frowned. "Somewhat preoccupied. I think Pryce would say the same, if he were in a temper to have noticed."

Pitt hesitated, considering whether to be obscure or direct: He settled for candor.

"You think he might have poisoned Stafford?"

Livesey drew in a sharp breath and let it out slowly. "I regret it, but it seems a distinct possibility," he replied, watching Pitt through half-closed eyes. "If it is beyond doubt that someone did." He drank a little from his tea again.

"Yes, it is beyond doubt—at least reasonable doubt," Pitt answered. "It is not a dose any man would take either to dull pain or treat any disease, nor for the mind to escape the trials and disappointments of reality. Nor would one take opium by accident." He took a little of his own tea, not quite sure if he really liked it. The thick curtains muffled the sounds of the street. He could hear the clock ticking on the bookcase.

"The only alternative is suicide," he went on. "Can you think of any reason whatever why Judge Stafford should take his own life—publicly, in his box in the theater, leaving no note and at such distress to his wife? It would be an extraordinary way to do such a thing—even supposing he wished to."

"Of course," Livesey agreed, pulling a small face. "I'm sorry. I was trying to avoid what is unavoidable. Of course he was killed. I am exceedingly grateful it is not my task to find out by whom, but I shall naturally do what I can to assist you."

He shifted his weight a trifle in his seat and regarded Pitt across folded hands. "No, Samuel Stafford's manner seemed to me to be unexceptional. He was courteous but detached. Which was his natural way." He pursed his lips. "I found nothing unusual in him, certainly no sense of strain or impending disaster. I cannot believe he feared death, or expected it, and least of all that he planned it."

"And you did not see him drink from the flask?"

"No. But as I have said, I did not remain in the smoking room."

"Mr. Livesey, have you any idea at all as to whether Mr. Stafford was aware of his wife's relationship with Mr. Pryce, or even suspected it?"

"Ah." Livesey's face darkened and his expression was heavy with sadness and distaste. "That is a much harder question. And it would be natural for you to ask me if knowledge of such a thing would make him despairing enough to take his life. I cannot answer the first question; knowledge is sometimes a very subtle thing, Mr. Pitt, not a matter of yes or no." He looked at Pitt carefully, as if weighing his perception. "There are many levels of awareness," he went on, his diction precise, his choice of words exact. "It is unquestionable that he knew his wife was distinctly cool towards him. That part of their relationship was mutual. He retained a regard for her, a respect that had become habit over the years, but he was not enamored of her anymore—if he ever was." He breathed in deeply. "He required that she behave with decorum and fulfill the role of a judge's wife that society expected of her—and to the best of my knowledge, this she did." The frown deepened in his

180

heavy face. The subject obviously was unpleasant to him, and he spoke with feeling. "But he did not require, and indeed did not wish, that she should involve him in profound emotions, or give him a constant companionship."

His eyes did not leave Pitt's face, and Pitt did not move. "Like many marriages which have been most suitable, and not unpleasant over the years, there was no sense of passion in it, no possessiveness of one another. Had she behaved indiscreetly he would have been angry with her. Had she openly flouted all the rules of society and become a scandal, he would have put her away, either by sending her to the country or, if she had proved utterly willful, as a last resort, and if she had justified such an extreme step, by divorcing her. That would have been an embarrassment which he would have sought to avoid."

He shrugged his heavy shoulders. "But that did not happen. Had he simply been aware that she was"—his lip curled—"giving her favors to another man, he would have looked the other way and affected not to be aware. Indeed, he may have endeavored to do so to such a degree that it touched no more than the periphery of his consciousness. It is not an uncommon arrangement, especially among those who have been married for some time, and grown"—he searched for a word that was not too indelicate—"a little used to one another."

"Then it is unlikely, in your judgment, sir, that he would have been thrown into despair by the discovery that his wife was having an affair with Mr. Pryce?" Pitt asked.

"It is inconceivable," Livesey replied with candor, his eyes wide.

"If he really was ... complacent in the matter," Pitt pressed, "why would Mrs. Stafford do something so extreme as to murder him?"

A weary and bitter humor flashed across Livesey's face and was gone. "Presumably her passion for Mr. Pryce is frantic," he answered, "and not satisfied by a mere affaire. With Stafford dead, she would be a widow of considerable means, and free to marry Pryce. I imagine in your work, Inspector, you have come across many relationships which began as infatuation, and have ended in sordidness and eventually crime? Unfortunately it is a tale that I have witnessed far more often than I care to, usually selfish, a little shabby, and deeply tragic. It afflicts all ages and classes, I regret to say."

Pitt could not argue. "Yes," he agreed reluctantly. "Yes, I have."

"Possibly Pryce was losing some of the heat of his desire," Livesey continued. "And she feared losing him to a younger woman. Who knows?" He lifted his shoulders a fraction. "The whole matter is dark, and totally tragic. Were poor Stafford not dead, I would have considered it so improbable I should have dismissed the possibility. But he is dead, and we must face the logical conclusions. I regret I cannot say anything more helpful—or less stark in its outcome."

"You have been most helpful, sir." Pitt rose to his feet. "I shall enquire into the nature of this sorry affair and learn all I can about it."

"I do not envy you." Livesey reached for the bell and rang it to summon the clerk. "You might begin with my wife, who is both observant and discreet. She was well acquainted with Juniper Stafford, but she will tell you the truth, without gossiping further to damage reputations unnecessarily."

"Thank you, sir," Pitt said with sincere gratitude. "That will be a most excellent place to begin."

He accepted Livesey's advice, and began after luncheon in the early afternoon, straightening his tie, pulling his jacket a little more to the square, and moving several small articles from one pocket to another to balance them and lessen the bulges, giving his boots a hasty brush on the backs of his trousers and running his fingers through his hair, the last of these efforts making things considerably worse than before. This time he took a hansom, not the public omnibus, and alighted in the highly fashionable Eaton Square and presented himself at the front door of number five. The bell was answered by a smart footman, who was tall and slender with excellent legs, well displayed by the silk stockings of his livery.

"Yes sir?" He had just the right touch of superciliousness that verged on the offensive without ever quite toppling over into it. He was employed in a very superior household, and would make certain that callers were aware of that.

"Good afternoon," Pitt said with a smile he did not feel, but it gave him the considerable satisfaction of unnerving the man. People did not smile at footmen. He smiled even more widely, showing his teeth. "My name is Thomas Pitt." He produced his card and placed it on the proffered silver tray. "Mr. Justice Livesey was kind enough to suggest that Mrs. Livesey might be able to provide me with some information which I require in the cause of justice. Would you be good enough to ask her if she will receive me, to that end?"

The footman's composure was severely shaken. Who on earth was this impertinent fellow who stood on the steps smiling from ear to ear with a confidence he had no right to? Possibly the judge really had sent him? He would like to have packed him off with some very well chosen words, but he dared not. Society was definitely declining and values going to the dogs.

"Yes sir," he said sourly. "I will certainly ask, but I cannot say what the answer will be."

"Of course not," Pitt agreed reasonably. "At least not until you do ask!"

The footman snorted, turned on his heel and disappeared, leaving Pitt on the step. There was a bootboy standing at the far side of the hall staring uncomfortably, to see that Pitt did not dart in and steal the ornaments or the sticks in the hall stand.

The footman reappeared after only a few moments, replaced the card tray on the hall table, and came to Pitt, regarding him with displeasure.

"Mrs. Livesey is at home and will see you, if you will follow me?" He held out his hand for Pitt's hat and coat.

"Thank you," Pitt accepted, passing them over. He was not especially surprised. Curiosity was frequently more powerful than social niceties, particularly with wives of a certain level in society, who had too little to occupy their time, and even less to fill their minds. Anything unexpected or new had a value purely for that reason.

The house was solid, old-fashioned and extremely comfortable. The room to which Pitt was shown was large, with windows along one side, and yet at first glance it did not seem large. The huge mantel dominated one wall and was flanked by bookcases to the ceiling. Dark upholstered armchairs were supplemented by very beautiful upright chairs with carved wooden backs like church windows. Everywhere there were ornaments, tapestries, potted plants, but the single most interesting feature was a transitional light fixture depended from the center of the ceiling. It was designed to function both with electricity and with gas, the arms for gas pointing upwards, the bulbs for electricity down. It was only the second one Pitt had ever seen.

Mariah Livesey herself was a handsome woman with thick gray-white hair with a heavy wave most becomingly swept back off her brow. Her features were well proportioned and agreeable. In fact looking at her Pitt thought she was quite probably better looking now than in her youth, when she might well have been comparatively ordinary. Years of comfort and security of status had given her an ease of manner, and expensive clothes of refined taste had given her distinction. She regarded him with barely concealed curiosity.

"Yes, Mr. Pitt? My footman tells me my husband advised you to come to me for some information. Is that correct?"

"Yes ma'am," Pitt replied, standing upright, but not in any way to attention. "I left his chambers very shortly before luncheon and he suggested I should begin my search with you. It is a most delicate matter, which clumsily handled would ruin a lady's reputation, perhaps quite unjustifiably. He said that you would be both candid and discreet."

Her eyes were bright with interest, and there was the faintest flush in her cheeks.

"Indeed? How generous of him. I shall endeavor to live

up to all that he has said of me. What is your enquiry, Mr. Pitt? I had not realized I knew anything of such a matter."

"I am investigating the death of Mr. Justice Stafford."

"Oh dear." Her face darkened. "A dreadful thing—quite dreadful. Please sit down, Mr. Pitt. We cannot discuss this in a few moments. Although I really cannot think that I would be of assistance to you. I know nothing about it at all."

"Not knowingly, I'm sure, or you would already have informed us," Pitt agreed, sitting in the large chair opposite her. "But you are acquainted with both Mr. and Mrs. Stafford, and you no doubt move in the same circles in society."

Her face showed complete surprise. "Surely you cannot be suggesting someone from their social acquaintance killed him? That is absurd! You must have misunderstood something my husband said, Mr. Pitt. That is the only possible explanation."

"I am afraid that is not possible." Pitt shook his head, smiling at her sadly. "He was quite plain. If you will permit me to ask you a few questions?"

"Of course." She looked puzzled.

"Mr. and Mrs. Stafford had been married for some considerable time?" he asked.

"Oh yes, at least twenty years, probably longer." Her voice lifted in surprise.

"How would you describe their relationship?"

Her confusion increased. "Oh—amiable, I should say. There was certainly never any animosity between them, so far as I am aware. If you are thinking of a quarrel, I have to tell you I find it very difficult to believe, if not impossible." She shook her head a little to emphasize the point.

"Why do you say that, Mrs. Livesey?" he pressed.

"Well . . ." She looked at him with some concentration. Her eyes were neither blue nor gray, but full of perception. He judged she was not a clever woman, but one with considerable judgment of others within her own social knowledge, and an excellent sense of what was fitting.

"Yes? I would greatly value your candor, ma'am."

She hesitated only a moment more, he thought weighing words rather than debating whether to answer him or not.

"It was not a relationship in which either party had sufficient depth of emotion to quarrel," she said at length. He thought from her expression she was measuring her words carefully. "It had long since declined to a more comfortable state," she went on, "where respect and usage had replaced any acute involvement in each other's day-to-day lives. Juniper always behaved discreetly, and fulfilled her social obligations. She is an excellent hostess, handsome to look at, well dressed, exceedingly well mannered." A slight flicker crossed her face and there was a momentary tightness in her mouth. It occurred to Pitt that she was focusing herself to say things which she believed only grudgingly.

"And to the best of my knowledge, Samuel Stafford was an honorable man, not given to any excesses either personal or financial," she continued, her expression relaxing a little. "She was always well provided for. If he—if he had any other . . . women in his life . . . he was so discreet about them I for one had no idea." She looked at Pitt, waiting for his comment.

"Indeed. That is what I had heard elsewhere," he agreed. "What about Mrs. Stafford's other relationships?"

"Oh—well—I suppose you mean Mr. Pryce?" She colored uncomfortably, though it was impossible to say whether it was embarrassment or guilt because she was mentioning it at all.

"Was there any other?" he enquired.

"No! No, of course not!" The color in her cheeks deepened.

"When did she first meet Mr. Pryce, do you know?"

She sighed and stared out of the window. "I think she had met him several years ago, but the acquaintance was slight, so far as I am aware. They have come to know each other far, far better in the last year and a half." She stopped abruptly, uncertain how much more to say. She was aware she had spoken unbecomingly vehemently, afraid she had betrayed something in herself, as indeed she had. She looked at Pitt with a furrow between her brows, waiting.

"In your opinion, Mrs. Livesey, what is Mrs. Stafford's feeling for Mr. Pryce?" he said gravely. "Please be honest with me. I shall not quote you to anyone; the information is simply so I may learn the truth. In the interest of justice, I have to know."

She bit her lip, considering for a moment before launching into her answer, her voice quick and hard. "She was infatuated with him. She did her best to be discreet, but to one who knows her as well as I do, it was quite apparent."

"In what ways?"

"Oh, the edge in her manner, her dress, the things in which she developed an interest." She laughed abruptly as if now she had begun she could not stem the tide of her feelings. "The things in which she lost all interest. The gossip she no longer cared to hear, the trivia which a year ago would have fascinated her, now she ignored. She began to behave as if she were far younger than in truth she was." The pinkness deepened in her cheeks. "When a woman is in love, Mr. Pitt, other women know it. The signs are not especially subtle, and they are also quite unmistakable."

Pitt felt uncomfortable without being certain why.

"And did Mr. Pryce, in your judgment, return this feeling?" He made a mental note to ask Charlotte if she thought she would notice such things about another woman.

"I cannot say quite why I believe so, but I do, quite definitely." The edge returned to her voice. "His courtesy towards her had a sharply personal quality. There was a look in his eyes which was unmistakable. All woman desire to see that look in a man's face some time in their lives." She smiled very slightly as she said it. "It is better than all the diamonds or the perfumes in the world, and headier than champagne to the mind. Yes, Mr. Pitt, Mr. Pryce came to return her feelings."

"Came to?" He searched her face and saw the emotion and the anger in it before she masked it. "Do I understand you to mean that her feeling preceded his?"

She did not evade his eyes. "If you mean did she pursue him, Mr. Pitt, yes, I regret to say it, but she did. One weekend in particular, we were all houseguests in the country. I could not fail to be aware of it."

"I see." He shifted his position on the large chair. "Mrs. Livesey, can you tell me what a man and a woman in such a position might be able to do about it, what their options would be? And the penalties for being indiscreet?"

"Of course. Their options, if they were to remain in society, are very slight," she said decisively. "Either they behave with entire moral correctness, and do not see each other except where it is unavoidable, and then only when there are suitable other persons present . . ." Her shoulders stiffened. "People are quick to malice, you know? You cannot defy all social conventions and remain unscathed." She was still watching Pitt, judging his understanding. "Or else they give in to their passions, but do it at the houses of mutual friends, on weekend house parties, and similar occasions, but with sufficient discretion that no one is forced to be aware of it."

"That is all?"

"All?" She frowned. "What else could there be?"

"What about marriage?"

"Juniper Stafford is already married, Mr. Pitt."

"Divorce?" he suggested.

"Unthinkable. Oh—" Her face looked suddenly bleak. "Are you imagining that either Juniper or Mr. Pryce may deliberately have poisoned Judge Stafford?"

"Do you not find it possible?"

She thought for several moments before replying very quietly. Now the preoccupation with society and all the small protocols and jealousies was gone.

"Yes—yes, it is possible. I . . ."

Pitt waited.

"I hate to say such a thing," she finished lamely. She looked acutely uncomfortable. "Juniper is not . . . wise, in her emotions."

"Do you believe Mr. Stafford was aware of the relationship?" Pitt asked.

Mrs. Livesey pushed out her lips. "Oh—oh, I doubt it. It is not the sort of thing men notice, unless they are predisposed towards jealousy. And he was decidedly not of such a nature. One can tell." Again she looked at him to see if he understood. "He did not watch her, or seem aware of whom she was with. There are differences in behavior that are not apparent to a man, unless he too is in love. Had they been newly married—perhaps . . ." She tailed off unhappily.

"Do you suppose other women of her acquaintance were more observant?"

"Undoubtedly," she replied with a rueful smile. "Adolphus Pryce is a most attractive man, and unmarried. He is the center of much attention. His smallest act will be remarked and analyzed. A considerable number of feminine eyes are upon him."

"Then Mrs. Stafford will not be popular," Pitt observed with a mixture of humor and pity.

"Hardly," she agreed vehemently, then was instantly self-conscious and rushed into explanation. "There are not sufficient eligible gentlemen to go around. For one woman to have two is a breach of all fairness."

Pitt looked at her broad figure and aging face and wondered what thoughts for Adolphus Pryce, or his like, had passed through her mind. How much did she resent the passions that Juniper had indulged in herself—and inspired in him?

"You did not say anything to Mr. Stafford which might have led him to realize his wife's regard for Mr. Pryce?" he asked aloud. "Even inadvertently, and in sympathy for his situation, perhaps?"

The anger lit her eyes, then was dimmed again as he explained himself.

"I did not," she said decisively. "I find it is best to refrain from any interference in other people's affairs. It never helps."

"No, I imagine not," he agreed.

He had probably learned all he could from her. The affaire had lasted between a year and two years, and was discreet, but not unknown, certainly to other women. There was every possibility some busy tongue had told Judge

Stafford, but if so he was not likely to have reacted violently or with great distress. Every new piece of information brought him back either to Juniper or Adolphus Pryce, or conceivably to both of them.

"Thank you, Mrs. Livesey," he said politely, forcing himself to smile. "You have been of great assistance to me. I hope you will keep the matter as discreet as you have so far. It would be an evil thing to malign Mrs. Stafford's reputation, or Mr. Pryce's, if it turns out they are quite innocent of any part in the judge's death. There are plenty of other possibilities; this is merely one it is unfortunately my duty to explore."

"Of course," she said hastily. "I quite understand, I assure you. I shall treat it with the utmost confidence."

He hoped she did, and was as wise as her husband believed, but as he rose and took his leave, Pitt was not entirely sure. There was an unhappiness in her which hungered for something beyond her reach. And he knew she had no love for Juniper Stafford. How much of her assessment of Samuel Stafford was actually her knowledge of her own husband?

The next person he sought was Judge Granville Oswyn, one of the other five appeal judges who had sat on the case of Aaron Godman. His opinion of that matter might help to clarify it further, and as a colleague of Samuel Stafford, he might have been aware of his personal relationships. Pitt needed to know if Stafford was aware of his wife's infatuation, and if he cared perhaps more than Livesey or Mrs. Livesey believed. Perhaps it was a futile search, but he must make it.

But when he arrived in Curzon Street at Judge Oswyn's house he was informed by the parlormaid who answered the door that the judge was traveling on business, and was not expected home until the following week, and Mrs. Oswyn was calling upon acquaintances. However, she was due to dine out this evening, so no doubt would be home before long, and if Mr. Pitt cared to wait, he might do so in the morning room.

Pitt did care to wait. He had nothing else to pursue of greater importance, and spent an agreeable forty-five minutes with a pot of tea in the comfortable morning room, until he was summoned again and conducted to the soft sepia-and-gold withdrawing room where Mrs. Oswyn eyed him with mild interest. She was a faded woman with fair brown hair, a plump figure, a face which had probably been pretty in her youth and was now lit by an amiability of character which had mellowed it until it held a gentleness which was remarkable.

"My maid tells me you are engaged in enquiring into the death of Mr. Justice Stafford?" she said with arched eyebrows raised. "I cannot think of any way in which I might assist you, but I am perfectly ready to try. Please be seated, Mr. Pitt. What is it you think I might tell you? I knew him, of course. My husband sat on the court of appeal with him on many occasions, so we were socially acquainted with both Mr. Stafford and his wife, poor creature."

He looked at her expression and thought he saw in it a pity which was more profound than the mere words which anyone might have said of a woman who was so recently widowed.

"You feel for her deeply?" he asked, meeting her eyes.

She waited some moments before replying, perhaps judging how much he already knew. She made up her mind.

"I do. Guilt is a most painful feeling, especially so when it is too late to make amends."

He was startled, not only at the thought, but at her extraordinary frankness.

"You think she was in some way responsible for his death?" He tried to retain his composure.

She looked amazed and a little abashed. "Good gracious, no! Most certainly not! I do beg your pardon if I allowed that impression. She was obsessed with Adolphus, and he was with her, but she was not in the slightest way responsible for Samuel's death. Whatever makes you think such a fearful thing?"

"Someone is responsible, Mrs. Oswyn."

"Of course," she agreed, folding her hands in her lap.

"One cannot pretend murder does not happen, much as one would like to. But it would not be poor Juniper who did such a frightful thing. No, no, not at all! She is guilty of having been unfaithful to him, of feeling an unlawful passion, a lust, if you will, and of indulging it instead of mastering it. That is guilt enough."

"Was Mr. Stafford aware of her indulgence?"

"Oh, I think he knew perfectly well there was something." She regarded him steadily. "After all, one cannot be completely blind, even though there are times when one would prefer to, for one's own comfort. But he chose not to look at it too closely. It would have done no good." She regarded Pitt steadily out of round, soft eyes. "He would not see what was better unseen; and when it was all over, it would have been so much easier to forgive and forget if he had never known the details. Very wise man, Samuel." She shook her head a little. "Now Juniper, poor woman, will never find that forgiveness, and when this dies—as I daresay it will, these passions usually do—then she will be left with nothing but the guilt. It is all very sad. I told her so—but when one is in love with such obsessive emotion, such a hunger, one does not listen."

Pitt was taken by surprise. There was a naïveté in her face, almost an innocence, and yet she spoke of violence and adultery as a child might speak of things whose names it had heard, but whose meaning it did not grasp. Her perception of character in spite of her innocence startled him, as did her ability to pity.

"Yes," he said slowly. "Yes, she will feel a grief which will be difficult to recover from, because there will be so much guilt in it. Unless—"

"No," she interrupted firmly. "I do not believe she killed him. Nor do I believe it was Mr. Pryce. He is a foolish man, infatuated, and he has lost his honor over a woman, which means he is weak. But he would not stoop so low as to murder his friend—even for that." She looked at Pitt gravely. "I will not believe it for a moment. He is foolish, as are many men, but she is considerably to blame. A woman may nearly always rebuff quite graciously and still make her disinterest plain. But she did the very opposite. They will both pay for it, mark my words."

Pitt did not contradict her. From what he had observed, he was inclined to think she might well be correct.

"Do you not think they will marry, Mrs. Oswyn, now that they are free to?"

"Possibly, Mr. Pitt, but they will not be happy. Poor Samuel's death has spoiled that for them, if it were ever possible. But you will have to look elsewhere for whoever killed him."

"Perhaps."

"Oh, you will," she said with absolute certainty. "I suppose you are already looking into that wretched affair in Farriers' Lane? Yes, naturally you are. I would not be surprised if it had something to do with that. Samuel could not let the matter rest, you know? He came here to speak to Granville more than once. Granville tried to persuade him to let the matter drop, that there was nothing else to learn, and certainly nothing good to accomplish. But Samuel would not be persuaded."

Pitt sat upright. "You mean Judge Stafford intended to reopen the case? Are you sure?"

"Well now." She unfolded her hands. "I didn't say I was sure, you understand? I simply knew that he discussed it with Granville, my husband, several times, and they argued over the matter. Samuel wished to pursue it, and Granville did not. I do not know if Granville managed in the end to persuade him of the futility of it, or if he still wished to continue."

"Judge Oswyn did not believe there was anything further to be learned? No miscarriage of justice?" Pitt pressed.

"Oh no, not at all," she denied with conviction. "Although he was not happy about the case. He always felt there was a certain haste, and a great deal of emotion which was extremely distasteful. But that did not alter the correctness of the verdict, and that was what he told Samuel."

"You don't know what reason Judge Stafford had for pursuing the case?" Pitt leaned forward, looking at her intently. "You don't know if he had discovered anything new, any evidence?"

"Dear me, no. My husband never discussed anything of that nature with me. It is not at all suitable, you know? Not at all." She shook her head, dismissing the idea out of hand. "No. I am afraid I have no idea what they said, only that it was to do with the case, and that it was most heated in tone."

Pitt was thrown back in confusion. He had dismissed the Farriers' Lane murder from his calculations, and now it seemed he was premature. Or was it simply that this woman was not in touch with reality, refusing to believe that people she knew and who were friends could be guilty of more than the regrettably common sins of adultery and deceit? He looked at her more closely, and met her gentle eyes, so knowing of her own immediate world and so sublimely ignorant of anything beyond it.

"Thank you very much, Mrs. Oswyn," he said with great courtesy. "You have been most helpful, and most generous with your time."

"Not at all, Mr. Pitt," she replied, smiling at him sweetly. "I hope you are successful in your quest. It must be very difficult."

"Sometimes." He rose to his feet, excused himself and bade her good-bye.

Pitt went to Micah Drummond's office to discuss the matter with him, but Drummond was out and not expected back until the next morning, so it was not until then that Pitt was able to see him. It was a chilly day with a heavy dampness in the air that drove through the wool jacket which had been sufficient the evening before, and he was glad to be in Drummond's warm office with the fire burning.

Drummond stood in front of it warming the backs of his legs. He had obviously not been in long himself. His thin face was grave and he looked at Pitt expectantly but with no lift of interest.

"Morning, Pitt," he said solemnly. "Any news?"

Pitt changed his mind, not about what he would say but rather how he would say it.

"No sir. I am pursuing Mrs. Stafford and Mr. Pryce to learn all I can about their relationship, but I still haven't found anything that would seem to be adequate motive to have killed Stafford."

"Love," Drummond said sharply. "You don't need to look any farther than that. Or if you wish to be more accurate, amorous obsession. For God's sake, Pitt, more crimes have been committed from lust than anything else except possibly money. What on earth is your problem with seeing that?"

"Society is full of similar affairs and obsessive lusts," Pitt replied, determined not to give ground. "Very few of them end in murder, and those that do are usually where someone has been deceived and found it out suddenly, and then killed the offenders in the heat of the emotion."

"Why do you keep on arguing the point?" Drummond screwed up his face, staring at Pitt. "Of course that is the cause of many of them. But it is also not unknown for two lovers to kill the husband or wife who stands in the way of their union. Why do you not believe that that is what happened here?" He moved around from the fire as he became too hot. He sat in one of the armchairs and waved at Pitt to sit in the other.

"It may have," Pitt said grudgingly. "But it seems so . . . hysterical. Stafford wasn't standing in their way. He was apparently close to complacent about the affair."

"He knew about it?" Drummond said sharply. "Are you sure?"

Pitt drew in his breath. He wanted to say "of course," but if he overstated his case he would only have to withdraw later, and then Drummond would wonder what else he had exaggerated. "Livesey's wife said he was uninterested, and Judge Oswyn's wife said she was sure Stafford knew, in essence, but he preferred not to know the details. As long as Juniper Stafford was discreet, and caused no public embarrassment, he was prepared to tolerate it. He was most certainly not passionately jealous. She was emphatic about that." He was about to add that Stafford had been close to sixty, then he realized that Drummond was probably over fifty himself, and the remark would be tactless.

"Yes?" Drummond asked, sensing that Pitt had withheld something.

"Nothing." Pitt shrugged. "Simply that apparently Stafford was not an emotional man. It was a civil relationship, amiable, but not close, and now somewhat staled by habit. Anyway, it was not Stafford who killed either his wife or her lover. Stafford was the victim. They had no need to kill him—he did not endanger their affaire."

"Perhaps they wanted to marry?" Drummond said with something of an edge to his voice. "Perhaps an affair was not enough for them? Maybe a stolen moment here and there was far too little for the emotion and the need they felt for each other? Would it be enough for you, Pitt, if you loved a woman intensely?"

Pitt tried to imagine himself in such a situation. He would hate the deceit, the knowledge through everything that any time together would always be bounded by partings, uncertainty, and the need to lie.

"No," he admitted. "I would always want more."

"And resent the husband?" Drummond went on.

"Yes." Pitt admitted that too.

"Then you can understand why a man as in love as Adolphus Pryce might eventually descend to murder." Drummond's face puckered with distaste. "It is an abysmal thing to have to uncover, and I am not surprised you are looking for some other answer, but you cannot evade the truth, or your duty towards it. It is not like you to try."

Pitt opened his mouth to deny it, then closed it again without speaking.

Drummond rose to his feet and went over towards the window. He looked down at the street, the drays clattering by, a coster shouting at a barrow boy who was stuck in his path. It was raining steadily.

"I understand your getting tired of it," he went on with his back to Pitt. "I do myself. I am not sure how much longer I shall continue. Perhaps it wants a sharper mind, a

man with more knowledge of crime—in a practical sense—
than I have. You've always mentioned that you prefer
detection in the street to commanding other men, but in serious cases you could do both . . ." He left it in the air, un-
defined.

Pitt stared at him, thoughts whirling in his mind, doubts
as to what Drummond meant, whether it was just idle complaint because it was a cold, dark day and the case de-
pressed him, or if he really were thinking of retiring to
some other pursuit, perhaps out of reach of the tentacles of
the Inner Circle and its oppressive, insatiable secret demands. Or if it were all really to do with Eleanor Byam.
After the scandal if Drummond were to marry her, he
would no longer be able to maintain the social position he
now held, and very probably not the professional position
either. Pitt felt powerful and conflicting emotions. He was
sorry for Drummond, and yet he was surprised how much
he found he wanted the post. His pulse was beating faster.
There was a new energy inside him.

"That's a judgment I could not make until I reached that
situation." Pitt chose his words very carefully. He must not
betray himself. "And that is not so today." He made an effort to keep his voice level. "I'll go back to the Stafford
case. Thank you for your advice." And before Drummond
could say any more, he excused himself and went out.

In spite of having agreed with Drummond about
Adolphus Pryce, Pitt still chose to go and see the other
judges in Aaron Godman's appeal and the Farriers' Lane
murder. Livesey he had seen already, Oswyn was out of
London for the time being, but it was not difficult to find
the address of Mr. Justice Edgar Boothroyd, even though he
had now retired from the bench.

It took Pitt all morning on the train and then an open dog
cart ride in the blustery wind before he finally arrived at the
quiet, rambling old house just outside Guildford. An aged
housekeeper showed him into a wood-paneled sitting room
which in better weather would have opened onto a terrace
and then a lawn. Now the wind was blowing dead leaves

across the unkempt grass, fading chrysanthemum heads hung shaggy in the flower beds, and starlings squabbled on the stone path, snatching up pieces of bread someone had left for them.

Judge Boothroyd sat in a large armchair by the window, his back to the light, and blinked uncertainly at Pitt. He was a lean man gone to paunchiness, his waistcoat creased over his stomach, his narrow shoulders hunched forward.

"Pitt, did you say?" he asked, clearing his throat almost before he had finished speaking. "Perfectly willing to oblige, of course, but I doubt there's anything I can do. Retired, you know. Didn't they tell you that? Nothing to do with the bench anymore. Don't know anything about it now. Just attend to the garden, and a spot of reading. Nothing much."

Pitt regarded him with a sense of unhappiness. The room had a stale feeling about it, as if in some way it had been abandoned. It was fairly tidy, but the order in it was sterile, placed by an unloving hand. There was a silver tray with three decanters on the table by the window, all of which were close to empty, and there were smudges on the salver as of a fumbling hand. The curtains were drawn back crookedly and one tie was missing. There was no sweetness in the air.

"It is not a current case, sir." Pitt added the title to give the man a respect he wanted to feel for him, and could not. "It goes back some five years."

Boothroyd did not look at him. "I've been retired about that long," he replied. "And my memory is not particularly clear anymore."

Pitt sat down without being invited. Closer to him, he could see Boothroyd's face more clearly. The eyes were watery, the features blurred not by age but by drink. He was a profoundly unhappy man, and the darkness inside him permeated the room.

"The Farriers' Lane case," Pitt said aloud. "You were one of the judges of appeal."

"Oh." Boothroyd sighed. "Yes—yes, but I cannot recall much of it now. Nasty case, but not—not much to argue about. Had to go through the motions, that's all." He sniffed. "I really don't have anything to say on the matter." He did not ask why Pitt wanted to know, and it was a curious omission.

"Do you remember the point on which the appeal was raised, sir?"

"No—no, I don't, not now. Sat on a lot of appeals, you know. Can't remember them all." Boothroyd peered at him, frowning. For the first time his attention was focused, and there was a crease of anxiety across his brow.

"It must have been one of your last cases." Pitt tried to bring back his recollection, but even as he said it, he knew he had little chance. Not only was Boothroyd's mind dimmed, fuddled by time and unhappiness and, Pitt suspected, drink, but he had the powerful impression that he did not want to remember. What had happened to the man? He must have been learned, his bearing commanding, his mind incisive once. He must have been able to weigh the evidence, the points of law, and make fine decisions. Now he looked as if all interest in life had gone, his self-respect, his dignity, his ability to reason impersonally. Yet Pitt doubted he was more than sixty-five at the most.

"Possibly," Boothroyd said, shaking his head. "Possibly it was. Still don't remember it. A medical point, I think, but I can't tell you more than that. Or it might have been something to do with a coat—or a bracelet or something. Don't know. Don't recall it."

"Did Judge Stafford come out to visit you lately, sir?"

"Stafford?" Boothroyd's face fell oddly slack, his eyes staring at Pitt, something close to fear in their shallow watery gaze. He swallowed. "Why do you ask?"

"I am afraid he was killed," Pitt replied, unexpectedly brutal. The words slipped out before he weighed them. "I'm sorry."

"Killed?" Boothroyd breathed in deeply. Something in his face eased out, a shadow left it, as if some fear had mercifully been removed. "Traffic accident, was it? Getting worse in town all the time. Saw some poor devil run over by a bolting carriage just last month. Dogs got into a fight, horse reared. Fearful mess. Lucky it was only one person killed."

"No, I am afraid not. He was murdered." Pitt watched Boothroyd's face. He saw him swallow convulsively and his mouth gape. He struggled for breath. Pitt felt a compassion that was inextricably touched with revulsion. He must at least try to probe Boothroyd's bemused memory, however little he believed in success. "Did he come out here to see you recently, sir? I am afraid I need to know."

"I—er—" Boothroyd stared at Pitt helplessly, seeking escape, and eventually realizing there was none. "Er—yes—yes, he did come out. Colleagues, you know. Very civil of him."

"Did he say anything about the Farriers' Lane case, sir?" Again he watched Boothroyd's face, the evasion and the misery in his eyes.

"Think he mentioned it. Natural. It was the last appeal we sat on together. Old memories, you know? No, I don't suppose you do. Too young." His eyes slid sideways. "Would you like a glass of whiskey?"

"No, thank you, sir."

"Don't mind if I do?" He stood up and lumbered over towards the three decanters on the table. He was not a heavy man, nothing like the weight of Livesey, and yet his movement was labored, as if he found difficulty with it. He poured himself a very generous portion from one of the decanters, filling the glass almost to the brim, and drank half of it still standing by the table before making his way back to his chair. Pitt could smell the aroma of the spirit as Boothroyd breathed out heavily.

"He mentioned it," he said again. "Can't recall what he said. Wasn't very important, far as I know. Who killed him? Robbery?" He looked hopeful again, eyes wide, brows raised.

"No, Mr. Boothroyd. He was poisoned. I am afraid I don't know by whom. I am still trying to find out. Did he say he planned to reopen the enquiry into the Farriers' Lane case? Find evidence Aaron Godman was not guilty after all?"

"Good God, no!" Boothroyd said explosively. "Absolute nonsense! Whoever told you that? Did someone say that? Who said that? It's nonsense!"

Perhaps it would have been more productive to have said yes, but Pitt's sense of embarrassment and pity prevented him.

"No sir, not to me," he said quietly. "I just thought it was possible."

"No," Boothroyd said again. "No—it was just a quick call, a matter of kindness. He was passing. Sorry I cannot help you, Mr. Pitt." He finished the rest of his whiskey in two gulps. "Sorry," he said again.

Pitt rose to his feet, thanked him, and escaped the dank room and its sour air, its confusion and unhappiness.

Mr. Justice Morley Sadler was as different a man as it was possible to imagine. He was smooth faced; remnants of fair hair straggled across his head, and fair whiskers only slightly touched with gray adorned the sides of his cheeks. His clothes were highly fashionable and excellently tailored so that they hung without a wrinkle and he seemed totally in command of himself and any situation he might face. He was smiling amiably when Pitt was shown in and he rose from his desk to greet him, shook his hand and offered him a broad, leather-padded chair.

"Good day, Mr. Pitt—Inspector Pitt, is it? Good day to you. How may I be of service?" He went back to the desk and sat in his own huge, high-backed chair. "I dislike rudeness, Inspector, but I have another appointment in about twenty minutes, which I am honor-bound to keep. Obligation, you understand. One must do one's best in all matters. Now, what is the subject upon which you wish my opinion?"

Pitt was forewarned he had little time. He came immediately to the point.

"Aaron Godman's appeal some five years ago, Mr. Sadler. Do you recall the case?"

Sadler's smooth face tightened. A tiny muscle flickered

in the corner of his eye. He stared at Pitt steadily, his smile fixed.

"Of course I remember it, Inspector. A most unpleasant case—but it was settled at the time. There is nothing more to add." He glanced at the gold face of the clock on the mantel, then back at Pitt. "What is it that concerns you now, so long after? Not that wretched Macaulay woman, is it? The grief turned her mind, I am afraid. She became obsessed." He pursed his lips. "It happens sometimes, especially to women. Their brains are not created to bear such strains. A somewhat lightly balanced creature in the first place, of a hysterical nature—an actress—what can you expect? It is very sad—but also something of a public nuisance."

"Indeed?" Pitt said noncommittally. He watched Sadler with growing interest. The man was obviously extremely successful; the furnishings of his chambers were opulent, from the coffered ceiling to the Aubusson carpet on the floor. The surfaces were highly polished, the upholstery new.

Sadler himself looked in good health and well satisfied with his position in life. And yet mention of the case caused him discomfort. Was it merely because of Tamar Macaulay's constant efforts to have it reexamined—with the obvious implication that the verdict was wrong, or at best questionable? It would be enough to try anyone's patience. Pitt would feel discomfited if someone cast such doubt on a case he had investigated to a conclusion so irretrievable.

"No," he said aloud, as Sadler was growing impatient. "No, it has nothing to do with Miss Macaulay. It is in connection with the death of Judge Samuel Stafford."

"Stafford?" Sadler blinked. "I don't follow you."

"Mr. Stafford was investigating the case again, and saw the principal witnesses the day he died."

"Coincidence," Sadler said, lifting both his hands from the desk top and waving them as if to dismiss the matter. "I assure you, Samuel Stafford was far too levelheaded a man to be rattled by a persistent woman. He knew as well as we all did that there was nothing to look into. Everything possible had been done by the police at the time. An extremely ugly case, but dealt with admirably by everyone concerned: police, the court at the original trial, and by appeal. Ask anyone with knowledge of the events, Mr. Pitt. They will all tell you the same." He smiled widely and glanced again at the clock. "Now if that is all, I have an appointment with the Lord Chancellor this evening, and I must prepare for it. I have the opportunity to do him some small service, and I am sure you would not wish me to be remiss in it."

Pitt remained seated. "Of course not," he said, but he did not make any move to leave. "Did Judge Stafford come to see you within the last week or two of his life?"

"I saw him, naturally! That occurs in the normal course of our duties, Inspector. I see a great many people, barristers, solicitors, other judges, diplomats, members of both the House of Lords and the House of Commons, members of the royal family, and of most of the great families of the nation, at some time or another." He smiled frankly, meeting Pitt's eyes.

"Did Mr. Stafford mention the case to you?" Pitt said doggedly.

"The Farriers' Lane case, you mean?" Sadler's pale eyebrows rose. "Not that I recall. There would be no reason to. The matter has been closed some five years or more. Why do you wish to know, Inspector, if I may ask?"

"I wondered upon what grounds he was considering reopening it?" Pitt replied, taking a gamble.

Sadler's face paled and his wide mouth hardened.

"That is quite untrue, Inspector. He was not. If he had been, I am sure he would have told me, considering my own part in the appeal. You have been misinformed—mischievously so, I have to say." He looked at Pitt steadily. "I assure you, he made no mention of the matter, none at all. Now, if you will excuse me, I am expecting my next appointment, a man of considerable distinction who wishes to refer to me a most delicate issue." He smiled widely, a fixed gesture. He rose to his feet and held out his hand.

"Good day to you, Inspector. I am sorry I cannot be of any assistance."

And Pitt found himself ushered out into the anteroom without protest, and unable to think of anything further to say.

7

For several days Pitt had continued trying to trace the love affair between Juniper Stafford and Adolphus Pryce without telling Charlotte more of it than a few brief details.

She thought on many occasions of the whole case, but her mind turned more towards the original murder in Farriers' Lane, and the question of whether it was conceivable that Aaron Godman had been innocent. And if he were, then who could have been guilty? Joshua Fielding?

What had been his relationship with Tamar Macaulay? Was he the father of her child? Or had it been Kingsley Blaine? If Joshua had still been in love with her, that would have been a motive. Perhaps he saw her feelings for Blaine and realized she was slipping away from him, and in a furor of jealousy murdered Blaine?

What had really happened in the theater dressing room that night? Kingsley Blaine had given Tamar a valuable necklace, a family piece which should have belonged to his wife. No one had seen it since. Had she given it back to Blaine? If she had, who had taken it from him?

Was that what Judge Stafford had investigated, and for which he had been killed? It was only a possibility. Pitt still seemed to be pursuing Juniper and Adolphus Pryce. But the fear sat like a chill weight in Charlotte's mind, because of Caroline.

And even if Joshua Fielding were totally innocent, that was hardly the problem solved. Caroline, who had always been so sensible, so obedient to all that society expected, so full of decorum, was behaving like a giddy girl! Charlotte bitterly resented Grandmama's remarks about her mother's being a fool, but they touched a nerve of real fear. Just how far was Caroline going? Was this simply a little romance, a concern for the welfare of someone she liked? Or could she be light-headed enough to feel something more?

And if she did, how would she cope with it? Would she realize its complete unsuitability, the fact that it would be ruinous to have anything but the briefest and most totally discreet romance—surely not an affaire? Not Caroline! She was fifty-three, and had grandchildren! She was Charlotte's mother! The very thought of it made Charlotte feel upset and curiously lonely.

If it looked like getting out of hand, should she send for Emily? Emily would know what to say, how to prevail upon Caroline's sense of proportion—even of survival.

But perhaps before taking such a radical step Charlotte should make absolutely sure what the situation was. She might be panicking quite unnecessarily. It was almost certainly nothing so absurd.

She would visit Caroline again and put the matter to her candidly. Caroline would understand her concern.

All this she thought lying awake in the darkness, and when morning came she saw Pitt off without even asking him where he was going, or what time he expected to be home. Not that they were questions he could answer, but it had been her habit to ask, simply as a demonstration that she cared.

Then she informed Gracie that she was going out on a matter of business to do with the murder in Farriers' Lane, with the implicit promise that when she came back she would tell her whatever she learned.

Gracie smiled happily and set about scrubbing the

kitchen floor with a vigor and enthusiasm quite out of proportion to her interest in the task.

Charlotte took the omnibus to Cater Street and arrived shortly after ten o'clock, not a suitable time for calling. She found Caroline busy sorting linen for the housemaid, and Grandmama still not emerged from her bedroom, where she was customarily served her breakfast on a tray.

"Good morning!" Caroline said with surprise and a slight frown of concern. She was dressed in plain brown stuff, with no trimmings but a cotton lace collar, and her hair wound loosely and with no fashionable curls or braids. She looked younger than usual, and prettier. Charlotte had not seen her so informally for several years, and she was taken aback by how comely she looked, how good her features and her skin. Without the additions of fashion, expensive clothes and elaborate hair she was more individual, softer, less like every other woman in society of middle years. Words rose to her lips to say so, then she thought perhaps it would be tactless.

"Good morning, Mama," she said cheerfully. "You look very well."

"I am." Caroline's brow creased. "What brings you here so early? Has Thomas learned something about the case?"

"I don't think so. If he has, he hasn't told me." Charlotte automatically took the other end of the bedsheet Caroline was examining and held it up, saw that it needed no mending, and helped her fold it again. "I came because I think it is time we learned more ourselves, don't you?"

"Indeed," Caroline agreed immediately, so immediately that Charlotte wondered if it were something she had been thinking about herself, or if it were simply another opportunity to take action, and probably to meet Joshua Fielding again.

"How much do we really know about the people involved?" she said, taking a pillowcase and trying to be tactful.

"You mean their actions on the night of the murder?" Caroline asked, not looking at Charlotte but at the pile of linen as yet unexamined.

"Well, that would do for a start," Charlotte said with less than enthusiasm. This was going to be difficult. "But we need to know a great deal more about their personalities than I do, at least. Perhaps you know more?"

"Yes—I should imagine so." Caroline explored the embroidery at the edge of the pillowcases, looking for places where it was weak and coming away from the fabric.

Charlotte hated herself for being so devious. "What about Tamar Macaulay? Do you know who is the father of her child?"

Caroline drew in a breath to expostulate, then let it out again slowly as the necessity for realism overtook her.

"Kingsley Blaine, I believe. She really did care for him, you know. It was not a quick romance, or a matter of seeking the presents he could give her."

"Did he give her many presents?"

"No—no, I don't think so."

"Isn't it possible someone else was in love with her also, and was sufficiently jealous of Kingsley Blaine that he might have killed him?"

Caroline looked up, her face pink, her eyes defensive. "You mean Joshua, don't you?"

"I mean anyone that could apply to," Charlotte said as levelly as she could. "Does that mean Joshua?"

"He was in love with her once," Caroline said with a gulp, looking at the linen again. She snapped a pillowcase sharply, and it slipped out of her fingers. "Drat!" she said angrily.

"Mama, don't you think we should find out a little more? After all, that's not surprising, is it? If people are attractive, and see each other a great deal, it is most probable they will have feelings for each other, at least for a while? Perhaps it passes, and then they may find the person who is right, not merely familiar. That doesn't mean that Joshua still felt anything for her afterwards except a friendly affection."

"Do you think so?" Caroline bent and picked up the pillowcase, keeping her eyes down. "Yes—yes, I suppose so. Of course you are right. We do need to know more. I shall lose my wits staying here wondering. But how can we do it without being appallingly intrusive?" She frowned, regarding Charlotte anxiously.

Grandmama appeared in the doorway, her stick hitting the lintel sharply. They were startled and stepped apart instantly. Neither of them had heard her footsteps.

"You are appallingly intrusive," she said to Caroline. "Which is socially unforgivable, as you must be aware! Goodness knows, I have told you so often enough. But immeasurably worse than that, you are giving the absurd impression that you are in love with this—this—actor!" She snorted. "It is not only ludicrous, it is disgusting! The man is half your age—and he is a Jew! You seem to have lost your wits. Good morning, Charlotte. What are you doing here? You didn't come to fold the laundry."

Caroline gulped, her breast rising and falling as she strove to control herself.

Charlotte opened her mouth to retort, and then thought it would be wiser to allow Caroline to defend herself; otherwise Grandmama would think she was unable to. Then when Charlotte was gone, Caroline would be even more vulnerable.

"You are the only person who thinks such a thing." Caroline stared at Grandmama, her cheeks flooded with hot color. "And that is because you have a cruel and quite mistaken mind."

"Indeed?" Grandmama said with exquisite sarcasm. "You are capering around in extravagant new clothes, to Pimlico, of all places. Nobody goes to Pimlico! Why should they?" She leaned heavily on her black stick, her face tight. "Simply because suddenly you have nothing better to do? I could most assuredly find you something. Yesterday's dinner was totally unplanned. I don't know what Cook was thinking of. Blancmange, at this time of the year? And artichokes! Ridiculous! And what, may I ask, could you possibly want in Pimlico?"

"There's nothing wrong with early artichokes," Caroline replied. "They are delicious."

"Artichokes?" Grandmama banged her stick on the floor.

"What have artichokes to do with anything? As I have just said, you are pursuing a man young enough to marry your daughter—and a Jew, to boot. Do you drink, Caroline?"

"No, I do not, Mama-in-law," Caroline replied, her face stiff and growing paler. "You appear to have forgotten, but I was in the theater when Judge Stafford died, and I was quite naturally interested in seeing that justice is done and there is no unnecessary pain caused to innocent persons."

"Balderdash!" Grandmama said fiercely. "You are besotted on that wretched poseur. On the stage. For heaven's sake, what next?"

Silently Charlotte folded the linen and slid it onto the shelf.

"You seem to have forgotten your own interest in the murder in Highgate," Caroline attacked the old lady. "You forced the acquaintance of Celeste and Angeline—"

"I did not!" Grandmama exploded with indignation, her voice quivering with offense. "I merely went to offer them my condolences. I had known them half my life."

"You went out of curiosity," Caroline replied with a harsh thread of amusement. "You hadn't seen or spoken to them in thirty years."

They both ignored Charlotte totally.

"They were hardly actresses cavorting about on the public stage." Grandmama took up the fight in earnest. "They were the maiden daughters of a bishop. One can hardly be more respectable than that. And I never chased after a man in my life. Let alone one half my age!"

Caroline lost her temper.

"That is your misfortune," she snapped, shoving the pile of pillowslips across the shelf. "Perhaps if you had ever met anyone as interesting, charming and totally full of wit and imagination as Joshua is, then you wouldn't be the bitter old woman you are now—with no pleasure left except making other people miserable. And I shall go to Pimlico as often as I choose." She smoothed down her skirts sharply and stood very straight. "In fact Charlotte and I are off there now—not to see Mr. Fielding, but to find out more about who killed Kingsley Blaine—and why!" And with that statement she swept past Grandmama, leaving both Charlotte and the old lady staring after her.

Grandmama swung around to Charlotte, glaring at her.

"I hold you to blame for this. If you hadn't married a policeman, and taken to meddling in disgusting matters which no decent woman would even have heard about—let alone concerned herself with—then your mother wouldn't be taking leave of her senses now and behaving like this."

"We cannot take you this time, Grandmama, no matter what you say." Charlotte smiled at her tightly, looking straight into her black eyes. "The subject is far too delicate. I am sorry."

"I don't know what you are talking about," the old lady snapped. "Why on earth should I wish to go to Pimlico?"

"For the same reason you went to see Celeste and Angeline, of course," Charlotte replied. "To indulge your curiosity."

For a moment the old lady was so angry she was robbed of words.

Charlotte smiled sweetly and turned around and went after her mother out across the landing and downstairs.

"Charlotte." The old lady's voice followed after her, sharp and plaintive. "Charlotte. How dare you speak to me like that! Come back here! Do you hear me? Charlotte!"

Charlotte ran down the last few steps and caught up with Caroline.

"Are we going to Pimlico?" she said quietly.

"Of course," Caroline replied, looking around for her cloak. "There's nowhere else we can begin."

"Are you sure that is wise? There is no point in going simply to ask the same questions again."

"Of course I'm sure," Caroline said urgently. "We can see Clio Farber at this time of day. Theater people rise late, compared with most, take a good luncheon, which they call dinner, and rehearse in the afternoon." Charlotte was about to say something, but Caroline hurried on. "She already understands the situation; she may have found a way in which we can meet this Devlin O'Neil. He is the only one we

211

know of who is a definite suspect. That is the right word, isn't it?"

"Yes—yes, it is." Charlotte reached for the cloak and held it while Caroline put it over her shoulders. She put her own coat back on again. "How do you know Miss Farber is aware of the situation?"

"Maddock!" Caroline called out. "Maddock! Will you please call the carriage for me? No—no, on second thought don't bother. I will take a hansom." She glanced up towards the landing where the grim figure of the old lady was staring down the stairs, her stick striking at the banisters.

"Caroline," she said loudly. "Caroline!"

"I am going out," Caroline replied, grasping Charlotte by the arm. "Come, Charlotte. We cannot waste time, or we shall miss them."

"You're going to run about after that actor again?" Grandmama called from halfway down the stairs. "That Jew!"

Caroline turned around in the front doorway. "No, Mama-in-law, I am going to see Miss Farber. Please don't make an exhibition of yourself by raising your voice in front of the servants. I shall be out for luncheon." And without waiting for anything further, she gripped Charlotte by the arm again and went outside, leaving Maddock to close the door behind her.

For ten minutes they walked briskly along the pavement, past acquaintances to whom Caroline nodded briefly with a word of greeting.

"Good morning, Mrs. Ellison." A large lady in green with a fur tippet stood squarely in the way, and it was impossible to continue without speaking. "How are you?" she demanded.

They were obliged to stop.

"In excellent health, thank you, Mrs. Parkin," Caroline replied. "And you?"

"All things considered, not badly, thank you." Mrs. Parkin stared at Charlotte enquiringly.

Caroline had no option but to outstare her.

"May I present my daughter, Mrs. Pitt. Mrs. Parkin."

"How do you do, Mrs. Parkin," Charlotte said obediently.

"How do you do, Mrs. Pitt." Mrs. Parkin smiled, her eyes going up and down Charlotte's rather plain coat and second-season boots. "I don't believe we have met before?" She made it a question.

Charlotte smiled back, brightly and just as blandly.

"I am sure we have not, Mrs. Parkin. I should have remembered."

"Oh." Mrs. Parkin was momentarily lost for words. The reply was not what she had planned. "How kind of you. Do you live in this area?"

Charlotte smiled even more brightly. "Not now, but of course I used to." Seeing the intent expression in Mrs. Parkin's face, and knowing the interrogation would continue, she carried the war into the enemy's camp. "Have you lived here long yourself, Mrs. Parkin?"

Mrs. Parkin was startled. She had considered herself in charge of the conversation, and all she had looked for were polite and truthful answers as befitted a socially junior woman. She regarded Charlotte's eagerly interested face with displeasure.

"Some five years, Mrs. Pitt."

"Indeed," Charlotte said quickly, before Mrs. Parkin could continue. "Most agreeable, don't you find? I know Mama does. I do hope you have a pleasant day. I think the weather is going to improve, don't you? Do you require a hansom?"

"I beg your pardon?" Mrs. Parkin said stiffly.

"Then you will forgive us if we take that one." Charlotte gestured vaguely. "We have an appointment some distance away. So very pleasant to have made your acquaintance, Mrs. Parkin." And with that she took Caroline's arm firmly and hurried along the pavement, leaving Mrs. Parkin standing staring after them with her mouth open and her breath drawn in to speak.

Caroline did not know whether to laugh or be horrified. She was torn between natural instinct and a lifetime of training. Instinct won and she giggled happily as they

213

walked with undignified haste towards a hansom cab waiting by the curb.

They alighted in Pimlico and were admitted to the Passmores' huge parlor. Joshua Fielding, Tamar Macaulay and several other people were sitting in large cane chairs, involved in animated conversation. Scripts lay about on table tops and several on the floor in piles. Miranda Passmore sat on a heap of cushions; this time the door had been opened by a youth with curly hair, bearing a strong resemblance to her.

As soon as Caroline and Charlotte came in, Joshua rose to his feet and welcomed them. Charlotte saw with remarkably mixed emotions the instant pleasure in his face and a gentleness in him unique in his glance towards Caroline. If it were possible he cared for her more than mere friendship, or a gratitude that she was so concerned for his welfare, then Caroline was not so wildly vulnerable, not open to such a humiliating rejection. That brought a rush of warmth to Charlotte and smoothed away some of her own fear.

And yet if he did have such feeling, it would only lead to disaster. At best a sad parting, because it was impossible—or at worst an affaire, with all the heartbreak when it ended, when he grew tired of her, or she came to her senses. And the ever-present risk of the most fearful scandal. Grandmama had no gentleness in her, no tenderness, but her fears were not ill founded. Society did not forgive. It was full of women like Mrs. Parkin with her prying questions and intrusive, knowing eyes. Those who broke the rules were never permitted to return. There would be no place for Caroline after that.

Joshua was speaking to Charlotte, and she had not heard a word he had said. He was standing in front of her smiling, with a shadow of anxiety in his eyes. He had a remarkably mobile and expressive face, full of possibilities for humor, passion, pain and wry, relentless self-knowledge. It would be terribly difficult not to like him, however much the thought of him with Caroline disturbed her.

"I'm so sorry," she apologized. "My mind was woolgathering."

"I doubt it," he said candidly. "I think you are concerned for this wretched affair, most generously on our behalf, and you are wondering what we can do next that would be of any use. Am I not right?"

She seized the chance. "Yes, indeed you are," she lied, meeting his eyes and forcing herself to smile back. "I think it is time we made the acquaintance of Mr. Devlin O'Neil, if Miss Farber is able to help us."

He turned and beckoned to a young woman in her early thirties, but casually dressed in something like an artist's smock. Her fair hair was wildly curly and she had not bothered to dress it except to pile it on her head and secure it with a couple of pins and a length of bright red fabric. It was quite beautiful, and flattered her wide-cheekboned face with blue eyes and broad, soft mouth. It was a face Charlotte liked immediately. As soon as the most perfunctory introductions were made, and acknowledgment of the others in the room, she turned to Clio.

"Has Mr. Fielding spoken to you of our concern?" *Concern* was such a tame word, but she could think of no better—at least until she knew more of the situation.

"Oh yes," Clio replied quickly. "And I am so glad you are going to do something! We none of us believed it was Aaron. We simply had no idea how to succeed in making anyone else accept that. Poor Tamar has struggled alone for all these years. It is wonderful to have someone really capable with her now."

Charlotte opened her mouth to say that she was not really so very capable, then changed her mind. It would be most unhelpful, even if true. It would discourage Tamar and make Clio Farber less likely to trust her.

"Well, we need all the help you can find," she said instead. "You see, it all depends on being able to observe people when they are unaware you have any interest in the matter at all."

"Oh yes, I see that," Clio agreed. "Tamar explained it quite clearly. I shall contrive a situation where you can meet Kathleen O'Neil in such a way it will all look most natural. I am good at that." Her face shadowed and she moved very slightly so that her back was towards the others in the room.

"I don't know if Joshua told you," she went on, "but I am . . . acquainted"—she hesitated delicately, but there was nothing sly in her, or intending innuendo—"with Judge Oswyn, who sat on the appeal." Her face shadowed. "With poor Judge Stafford."

"Did he know Judge Stafford?" Charlotte asked. "I mean personally?"

Clio's face was thoughtful, her answer quick, as if she had already considered the question and it troubled her. "Of course they were acquainted, but how much it was personal rather than simply professional I do not know. I feel it may have been. Granville, that is, Judge Oswyn, seemed to have some deep feeling about him. I rather think it was a kind of embarrassment. Or perhaps that is not quite right— maybe a sort of anger mixed with discomfort. But when I asked him why, he was evasive, which is most unlike him."

Charlotte was confused. She had assumed Clio's relation- ship with Judge Oswyn was casual and social, but from the candor with which she apparently spoke to him about the most indiscreet subjects, perhaps it was much more. Was she his mistress? It would be inexcusably clumsy to ask. How could she phrase her questions so as to elicit the in- formation and yet remain reasonably tactful?

"You think he would have discussed it differently had it not troubled him?" she said aloud.

"I am quite sure," Clio replied with a smile. "He is a very frank and gentle man. He likes to be open, to speak freely, to laugh about things, not unkindly, but to"—she shrugged slightly, an elegant and expressive gesture—"to be with friends. You know, friendship is rarer than one would care to think, especially for a man in his position."

"And he had not that friendship with Judge Stafford?"

"No—I think not. I formed the impression there was some matter between them which Judge Stafford kept pressing, and which Granville did not wish to discuss any- more."

"Aaron Godman?"

Clio frowned. "I am not certain. I know Granville was unhappy about it, and hated to speak of it. The trial was perfectly proper, of course, but he felt it had been poorly handled. It was a source of embarrassment to him."

"By Judge Quade?" Charlotte said with surprise.

Clio shook her head quickly. "Oh no—not at all. By the police, I think. I am really not sure. He would not discuss it with me. But then that is quite natural, since I knew Aaron, and cared for him very much. He was a very sweet man."

"Was he? No one has said very much about him, personally, only about the case. Tell me about him," Charlotte asked.

Clio lowered her voice even more, so Tamar, a few feet away, could not hear her.

"He was two years younger than Tamar—twenty-eight—when he died five years ago." Her face had a curious expression of sweetness mixed with pain. "He was slight, like her, but not really so dark, and of course a lot taller. In fact he was not so unlike Joshua. They used that, sometimes, on stage. He had a lovely sense of humor. He loved to play the most terrible villains and provoke the audience to scream." She smiled as she said it, then her eyes quite suddenly filled with tears and she sniffed hard and turned her head away for a moment.

"I'm sorry," Charlotte said quietly. "Please don't go on if it is painful. It was thoughtless of me to ask. It is Devlin O'Neil we have to know about."

Clio sniffed again. "That is really too bad of me," she said fiercely. "I thought I had better control of myself. Please forgive me. Yes, of course. I shall arrange for you to meet Kathleen O'Neil." She fished for a handkerchief. "I know just how I shall do it. She is very fond of romantic music, and there is a soiree the day after tomorrow, at Lady Blenkinsop's house in Eaton Square. I know the pianist well, and he will invite us. Can you come?"

Charlotte considered asking if Clio were sure it would be socially acceptable, and then decided she really did not care if it were or not.

"Certainly," she said firmly. "I shall enjoy it. Tell me who I am supposed to be. I cannot be myself, or they will tell me nothing. In fact they will probably ask me to leave."

"Of course," Clio agreed cheerfully. "You had better be a cousin visiting from—from Bath!"

"But I don't know Bath," Charlotte argued. "I would look ridiculous if I fell into conversation with someone who knew it well. Let it be Brighton; at least I have been there."

"By all means." Clio smiled and stuffed her handkerchief away. "Then it is arranged? If you come here first, we can travel together. I shall say you are up visiting because you are interested in the stage. Can you sing?"

"No. Not at all!"

"Well, you can certainly act! At least your mother says so. She has recounted some of your adventures to Joshua, just two or three days ago, and he told us. We were all very entertained—oh, and impressed, of course."

"Oh dear." Charlotte was taken aback. She knew Caroline disapproved of her involvement in Pitt's cases. How much she had changed, at least on the surface, if she was now regaling her new friends with accounts of them. How much she was denying her previous self in order to please. That was a most uncomfortable thought, and she pushed it away. There was no time for it now.

"I think it is quite thrilling," Clio went on enthusiastically. "More dramatic than anything we do—because it is real. Remember not to dress too fashionably, won't you? You are supposed to be a provincial cousin."

"Oh, certainly," Charlotte said with a perfectly straight face. What did Clio Farber imagine policemen earned, that their wives might dress in the current vogue?

In the event, without Emily to borrow from, and not daring to approach Vespasia for anything less than a reception or a ball, Charlotte asked Caroline if she might try something of hers from last season, or even the one before. Her request was granted with alacrity, and considerable disappointment that it was really not advisable for her to go also. But it would risk being conspicuous for three of them to turn up to such a function, and Kathleen O'Neil would not find it the chance encounter it was intended to seem.

But she did not refuse the offer of Caroline's carriage to pick her up at home in Bloomsbury.

She left a note for Pitt on the kitchen table.

Dearest Thomas,

I have been invited to a soiree with a friend of Mama's and I am going because I am a little anxious about her lately. She is becoming very fond of people I do not know at all, and this will give me an excellent opportunity to make their acquaintance rather better. I shall not be late, it is only an hour or two of music.

Your dinner is in the oven, mutton stew with potatoes and plenty of onion.

I love you,
Charlotte

She went first to Pimlico to collect Clio Farber. They arrived at Eaton Square, alighting in a swirl of nervous laughter, and climbed the wide steps up to a most imposing doorway flanked by liveried footmen who enquired for their names.

Clio took charge, informing them that she was a friend of the soloist who was to perform for their guests' enjoyment, and was accompanied by her cousin. The footman hesitated for a moment, glanced across at his colleague, then inclined his head graciously and allowed them in.

The hallway was most impressive, flagged in black-and-white marble like a chessboard. There was a large statue of a youth after the Greek style in an alcove near the foot of the stairs, which swept up in an arc to the landing and the balustrade which bordered a gallery along half its length.

It was already filled with people all most elegantly dressed, the women in gowns glitteringly embroidered, lots of bare shoulders gleaming in the light from the chandeliers.

"You didn't tell me it was going to be so formal," Charlotte whispered to Clio. Already she was feeling not only like a provincial cousin but a very poor one, positively from the woods. She had thought Caroline's gown quite becoming when she put it on at home, but now it was not only two seasons out of date, it seemed very unimaginative and pedestrian. The deep brandy shade was far too conservative. She must look fifty in it.

"To tell you the truth, I didn't know it was going to be," Clio whispered back. "Reggie said it was just a score or so of friends. They must have enlarged it since then. Still, that will make it easier to run into Kathleen without being so obvious. Come on. This is an adventure."

Charlotte had rather more experience of adventures, and knew they could very easily become unpleasant if taken too casually. Nevertheless she followed Clio into the huge withdrawing room where sixty or so seats were arranged artistically in groups so people might hold intelligent and uplifting conversations with each other between the musical items.

For several minutes Charlotte and Clio moved around the edge of the throng of people, trying to appear as if they were looking for someone. Clio introduced Charlotte to her friend Reggie, who was standing gracefully in the region of the piano, ready to play when the signal should be given and the hostess introduced him.

They were conversing amiably and perhaps from nervousness. They told of one or two amusing recollections. Charlotte burst into laughter, and Clio put both her hands up to her face to stifle a giggle. Several people glanced at them with severe disapproval. One aristocratic young woman stared over her fan, flicking it noisily.

"Who are those persons?" she asked her neighbor in a penetrating voice. "I don't believe I know the person in the pink gown. Do you?"

"Certainly not," the neighbor replied with a sniff. "Whatever made you suppose I might know her? Really, Mildred. I don't know anyone who dresses like that."

"Oh, you mean the brown? Yes, extraordinary, isn't it. I swear Jane Digby-Jones had something like that—two years ago."

Charlotte was aching to retaliate. She looked at Clio and saw the tide of color up her cheeks.

"Who is the lady with the loud voice?" she asked, smiling at the pianist, her own voice carrying at least the distance between them. "The one with the crystal necklace." She knew perfectly well it was diamonds, and heard the gasp of outrage with satisfaction.

"A Miss Cartwright, I think," the pianist replied, trying to keep his face straight. "Or maybe it is Wheelright?"

"Waggoner," Clio corrected with a smile.

"Something like that," Reggie agreed. "To do with transport of some sort. Why?"

"Why?" Charlotte was confused.

"Why do you ask? Would you care to know her dressmaker?"

"No!" It was a squeak. "I mean, no, thank you," she amended. "Really—we must . . ."

"Of course. The matter is in hand," Clio agreed. "I'm so sorry." She linked her arm in Charlotte's and together they walked past Miss Waggoner with dazzling smiles. They continued on through the crowd until Clio stopped next to a young woman with fair hair swept up stylishly and a most individual face, high cheekbones and brown eyes.

"Good evening, Kathleen," Clio said, affecting great surprise. "How very nice to see you again. You look so very well. May I introduce my dear friend Charlotte? Actually she is a sort of cousin, come up to stay with us for a while. I was sure this would be the most excellent evening for her, and now doubly so for the chance of meeting with you. It seems such a long time. How are you?"

Kathleen O'Neil had little alternative but to accept the introduction so ingenuously required, but she showed no disinclination.

"How do you do." She could not add Charlotte's name because Clio had not supplied it, presumably a deliberate omission to avoid lying. "I am delighted to make your acquaintance. I hope you are enjoying your stay. Have you come far?"

"Oh, not very," Charlotte said, swallowing her guilt and

dismissing it. "I am sure I shall have a most interesting and enjoyable time. It is kind of you. I imagine you are used to an evening like this, but it is quite a treat for me."

"Indeed?" Kathleen was saved from having to find anything else to say by the arrival of a man Charlotte knew immediately must be Devlin O'Neil. He was very dark, with the cast of features filled with humor and a certain fey imagination which she had seen only in Irishmen. He was not strictly handsome, there was something uncertain in his face, possibly a weakness but more probably only ambivalence. But he was confident and full of charm. He responded warmly to Clio's greeting and the introduction to Charlotte.

"How delightful to see you again." He smiled at Clio. "It has been far too long. We have met the stuffiest people lately." He put his arm around his wife proprietorially and stood close to her. "Forgive me, my dear?" He pulled a very slight face and glanced around them. Indeed, his comment was easy to understand. The company was unusually proper, even for such an event.

Charlotte plunged in. She must at least attempt some detecting. She was not here to be entertained merely by social observation to no purpose.

"Are you here more by duty than inclination, Mr. O'Neil?" she said sweetly.

He smiled back at her. "Entirely by duty, ma'am. To accompany my father-in-law and his mama. She is fond of amateur musical evenings—at least she is fond of being seen by those who frequent them. And of catching up with events."

"But of course," Charlotte agreed quickly. "There is nothing so interesting as gossip if you know the people spoken of and have someone to whom you can repeat it who will appreciate all its nuances to the full."

"My goodness, you have no fear in speaking your mind," he said with a sharp light of amusement in his eyes.

Two young women passed by them, glancing at O'Neil over their fans and swishing skirts with ostentatious grace.

"Do you not find it so, Mrs. O'Neil?" Charlotte turned to Kathleen.

Kathleen smiled, but it was the guarded gesture of one who had been wounded by precisely such thoughtless acts. "I confess it interests me only occasionally. I find people can be most malicious at times."

Charlotte wondered if quite suddenly in the midst of all the inconsequential chatter she had heard a word of true emotion. She was reminded sharply that here was a woman whose husband had been murdered, after having an affair with someone else. It said a great deal for Kathleen O'Neil that she could continue a friendship with Clio Farber, a woman so close to the cause of such misery: not only another actress, but a friend and colleague of Tamar Macaulay herself. Charlotte felt a surge of admiration for her, and a dislike for her own role of one seeking to place the guilt on the shoulders of her second husband. The duplicity alone was offensive, and the fun she had felt for a moment fled out of it.

"Of course," she said with instant sobriety. "When it is hurtful it is quite a different matter. I suppose a great deal of it is. A lot of people are ill informed, and their remarks better not made. I was thinking only of trivia, and perhaps I spoke too lightly anyway." She accepted a glass of lemonade from a passing footman, as did the others.

"Oh no, it is I who should apologize," Kathleen said, blushing a little. "I did not mean to be so contrary. It is only that I am acquainted with people who have been hurt by unthinking repetition of matters which were not fully true, or were of a deeply private nature. And of course those are the things gossips delight in most."

Around the room there was a murmur of expectation, and then a lessening of sound. Apparently something was about to begin. Instinctively they turned towards the piano, where a large lady with a gown winking with beads at the bosom was attempting to command attention.

"Ladies and gentlemen," she began. There was a murmur of polite applause. The evening's entertainment had commenced. Charlotte smiled at Kathleen and deliberately took

223

a seat beside her, aware of Clio's eyes on her, and then her head turning away as she engaged Devlin O'Neil in whispered conversation.

The pianist began to play, without flourish or more than a single glance at his audience. He seemed to be rapt in his music and to be conjuring it out of his instrument solely for his own enjoyment. Or perhaps *enjoyment* was the wrong word. Watching him, Charlotte felt as if it were a necessity for him, more of a sustenance to his soul than the dainty sandwiches and pastries were to the bodies of his assembled listeners. She was not highly educated in music, but she did not need an experienced critic to tell her that this young man was excellent, far beyond the ability of his fashionable audience to appreciate.

When he finished his final piece before the interval there was a courteous applause. He rose, took a very slight bow—no more than was necessary to acknowledge their presence—and left, walking with long strides under the archway into the room beyond.

The silence filled with chatter again, and pretty maids in white caps and lace-trimmed aprons came around with trays of sweetmeats, and liveried footmen came with chilled champagne. Charlotte did not care in the slightest for either, but she accepted automatically because it was easier than the constant refusal. She was too full of the glory of the music to wish to make a comment which could not possibly do it justice.

"Very good, don't you think?" Devlin O'Neil said, almost at her elbow. She had not heard him approach. He was smiling again. She judged it an expression which came to him very readily, out of a great good nature and an expectancy of being liked, rather than any particular pleasure.

"Brilliant," she replied, hoping she did not sound gushing.

Before he could reply to her, they were joined by a large thick-chested man with the appearance of unusual strength. His face was remarkable, with a great hatchet nose and small, very bright, intelligent eyes. On his arm, clinging to him for actual physical support, as well as a certain air of possession, was a woman a generation older. A facial resemblance about the eyes and brow made it instantly apparent she must be his mother.

"Oh, Grandmama-in-law," Devlin O'Neil said, his smile broadening. "Did you enjoy the music? May I present to you . . ." He hesitated, realizing for the first time that he did not know Charlotte's full name. He overcame the inconvenience by glancing at Clio and introducing her first. It was so smooth that if Adah Harrimore noticed, she gave no sign of it.

"How do you do, Miss Farber." She inclined her head graciously, but there was no interest in her face. "How do you do, Miss Pitt," she added, when Clio had supplied the missing name. Charlotte did not bother to correct the title (something she would normally have leaped to do), but any possible connection with Thomas was to be avoided.

"How do you do, Mrs. Harrimore," she replied, regarding the old lady curiously. She had a remarkable countenance, powerful, and yet with a knowledge of fear, a guardedness about it that was at the same time belied by its boldness. There was iron will in it, and yet also anxiety, a looking for reassurance to her son. It was full of contradictions.

"I did enjoy the music." Charlotte summoned her thoughts to the present. "Did you not think the pianist was excellent?"

"Very gifted," Adah conceded with the slightest pucker between her brows. "Many of them are, in that field."

Charlotte was lost. "I beg your pardon. Many of whom, Mrs. Harrimore?"

"Jews, of course," Adah replied, her frown increasing as she looked at Charlotte more closely, surveying her strong face and rich, deep coloring, her hair like polished chestnut. "Not that I suppose that has anything to do with it," she added inconsequentially.

Charlotte knew at least a smattering of history in the matter.

"It might have. Did we not in the past deny them most other occupations apart from medicine and the arts?"

"I don't know what you mean—deny them!" Adah said sharply. "Would you have Jews into everything? It's hard enough they are in all the finances of the nation, and I daresay the whole Empire, without being everywhere else as well. We know what they do in Europe."

Devlin O'Neil smiled briefly, first at Adah, then at his father-in-law. He stood very close to his wife. "It's as bad as the Irish, isn't it?" he said cheerfully. "Let them in to build the railways, and now they're all over the place. One is even obliged now and then to meet them socially. And into politics too, I'll wager."

"That is not at all the same thing," Prosper Harrimore said, without even the faintest flicker of answering humor in his face. "The Irish are just like us, my dear boy. As you know perfectly well."

"Oh indeed," O'Neil agreed, putting his arm around Kathleen. "For some they even are us. Was not the great Iron Duke himself an Irishman?"

"Anglo-Irish," Prosper corrected, this time the shadow of a smile on his narrow lips. "Like you. Not the same thing, Devlin."

"Well, he certainly wasn't a Jew," Adah said decisively. "He was good blood, the best. One of the greatest leaders we ever had. We might all be speaking French now without him." She shivered. "And eating obscenities out of the garden, and heaven only knows what else, with morals straight from Paris. And what goes on there is not fit to mention."

Charlotte did not know what possessed her to say it, except perhaps a desire to break the careful veneer of good manners and reach some deeper emotion.

"Of course Mr. Disraeli was a Jew," she said distinctly into the silence. "And he was one of the best prime ministers we ever had. Without him we would forever be having to sail all the way 'round the bottom of Africa to get to India or China, not to mention getting our tea coming back. Or opium."

"I beg your pardon!" Adah's eyebrows shot up and even Devlin O'Neil looked startled.

"Oh." Charlotte recollected herself quickly. "I was thinking of various medicines for the relief of pain, and the treatment of certain illnesses, which I believe we fought China very effectively in order to obtain—in trade . . ."

Kathleen looked polite but confused.

"Perhaps if we hadn't gone meddling in foreign places," Adah said tartly, "then we would not have acquired their diseases either! A person is better off in the country in which God placed him in the first instance. Half the trouble in the world comes out of people being where they do not belong."

"I believe Her Majesty was devoted to him," Charlotte added inconsequentially.

"To whom?" Kathleen was totally lost.

"Mr. Disraeli, my dear," O'Neil explained. "I think Miss Pitt is teasing us."

"I never doubted they were clever." Adah fixed Charlotte with a bright, brittle glance. "But that does not mean we wish to have them in our homes." She gave a convulsive little shudder, very tiny, but of a revulsion so intense as to be akin to fear.

Kathleen looked at Charlotte with apology in her eyes.

"I am sorry, Miss Pitt. I am sure Grandmama did not mean that as distastefully as it may have seemed. All sorts of people are most welcome in our house, if they are friends—and I hope you will consider yourself a friend."

"I should like to very much," Charlotte said quickly, grasping the chance. "It is most generous of you to ask, especially in view of my remarks, which were in less than the best of judgment, I admit. I tend to speak from the heart, and not from the head. I so enjoyed the pianist I rushed to his defense where I am sure it was quite unnecessary."

Kathleen smiled. "I do understand," she said softly, so her grandmother would not hear. "He momentarily transformed me onto a higher plane, and made me think of all manner of noble things. That is not entirely the composer's art, it is his also. He gave voice to the dreams."

"How well you put it. I shall most certainly continue your acquaintance, if I may," Charlotte said, with sincerity as well as the desire to know more of Kingsley Blaine, and what manner of man he had been. Had he truly intended to leave this seemingly warm and impulsive woman for Tamar Macaulay, and knowing the cost that would be to him? Or had he simply been weak, and in indulging his physical passions placed himself in a situation where he could not bring himself to leave either of them? How extraordinary that two such women should have loved him so deeply. He must have had a unique charm. It was growing increasingly important that she find a way to see him as objectively as possible, through the eyes of someone not so blinded by love. Perhaps if she visited the home of Kathleen O'Neil she might have a further opportunity to speak with Prosper Harrimore. His face was shrewd, guarded. Kingsley Blaine had been the father of his grandchild, but she imagined a man such as he was would not be easily hoodwinked by charm. His eyes on Devlin O'Neil suggested an ability to stand back, an affection not without judgment. He might be the key to a less emotional view, a perception that would see danger and weakness as well.

The pianist returned and the second half of the evening's entertainment commenced, and for its duration Charlotte forgot all about Kingsley Blaine, his family, or the death of Samuel Stafford. The passionate, lyrical, universal voice of human experience took over and she allowed herself to be swept up by it and carried wherever it took her.

Afterwards the O'Neils and the Harrimores had become engaged in conversation with other acquaintances. Prosper was deep in discussion with a man who had the portentous air of a merchant banker, and Adah was listening with acute attention to a thin, elderly woman who was holding forth at some length and would brook no interruption. Once Charlotte caught Kathleen's eye and smiled, receiving a flash of humor and understanding in return, but other than that solitary instance, Charlotte and Clio left without further encountering them.

Micah Drummond stood in his office staring out of the window down at the street where two men were haggling over something. It was latched against the blustery evening, and the rain beginning to splash now and then against the pane, so he could not hear their voices. It all seemed far away, divorced from any reality that mattered, and of less and less importance to him. He was forced to admit, the death of Samuel Stafford was rapidly becoming the same.

He should care. Stafford had been a good man, conscientious, honorable, diligent. And even if he had not, no decent person could condone murder. His brain told him he should be outraged, and in some distant part of his mind he was furious at the arrogance of it, the destruction of a life, and the pain. But on the surface where his concentration was, all he could care about intensely was Eleanor Byam. Everything he did had value to him only as it had reference to her. He could not remove from his mind the picture of her face in all its moods, the light and shadow as she laughed, and, when the sadness returned, the memory of pain, and her loneliness now that all the world she had known had disappeared and shrunk into the lodging house in Marylebone and the few tradesmen with whom she had dealings.

He ached to be able to give her more, and yet he was perfectly sure that what he felt was not pity; indeed he found the word offensive applied to her. She had far too much courage, too much dignity for him to dare such an intimate and intrusive feeling.

And yet he was aware with an ache of pain how her life had changed.

But the most powerful emotion in him was still the longing to be with her, to share his thoughts, his ideas, the experience of the things he loved. He imagined walking across a wide field with her by his side, the smell of the dawn wind off the sea, and the clouds piled and shredded in veils of light. The loveliness of it would fill him till he could scarcely contain it, and he would turn to her, and know she saw it with the same bursting heart that he did. And in that sharing all loneliness would vanish.

It flickered through his thoughts that if Adolphus Pryce felt this same consuming emotion for Juniper Stafford, and over years, perhaps it had driven from him all sense of proportion, and ultimately of morality. But it did not remain with him long, nor form itself into coherent ideas.

Instead of being with Eleanor, he was here, in Bow Street, waiting for reports on a murder he knew he would not solve. If it was solved at all, it would be by Pitt. It would be Pitt's anger at waste and injustice, and Pitt's insight, helped no doubt by Charlotte's curiosity, which would find the answer, whether Drummond was there or not.

The job had completely lost its savor for Drummond, and he realized gloomily that he was in danger of making some stupid, unnecessary error, which would spoil his reputation and close his career with shame instead of honor.

He turned from the window and strode across to the hat stand, where he picked up his hat and cane, took his coat from the peg and went out into the corridor.

"Poulteney, I'm going out. Put the reports on my desk when they come. I'll see them in the morning. If Inspector Pitt comes back, tell him I'll see him tomorrow."

"Yes sir. Will you be coming back tonight, sir?"

But Drummond was already striding away and he did not register the question.

Outside he walked the short length of Bow Street and around the corner into Drury Lane, where he caught a hansom. He gave the driver Eleanor's address, and sat back trying to compose his mind and prepare what he was going to say. He changed the words a dozen times between Oxford Street and Baker Street, but when he got out at Milton Street and paid the driver it all sounded so much less than he meant. He even considered calling another cab and going away again. But if he did, the situation would not improve. He would be no more than delaying what was for him inevitable. He must ask her, and there was nothing to be altered or gained by delaying.

The same surly maid answered the door, and when he informed her he wished to see Mrs. Byam, she conducted him with ill grace through the hallway and back to Eleanor's private door.

"Thank you," he said briefly, and waited while she glared at him, then turned on her heel and went.

With suddenly beating heart and dry lips he raised the knocker and let it fall.

It was several moments before he heard her steps at the far side and the handle turn, and then it swung open. It was Eleanor herself; presumably her one maid was otherwise occupied. She looked surprised to see him. For an instant there was pure pleasure in her face, then within seconds it clouded with anxiety, almost a foreboding as she met his eyes. Perhaps she saw his emotions there, as naked as he felt, and it was not acceptable to her. Instantly he was embarrassed. He had said nothing at all yet, and already he had begun badly.

"Good afternoon, Mr. Drummond," she began, then blushed at the clumsy formality of it. Surely neither of them needed to pretend quite so much? A little social grace to hide behind was good, but too much and it ceased to be a shield and became a mask.

"How kind of you to call," she said in a rush. "Please come in. It's turning a little cold, don't you think? Is it too late to offer you tea?"

"No—thank you," he accepted, and followed her in. "I mean, no, it is not too late. I should very much like a cup of tea." The small room was exactly as he had remembered it, cramped, narrow windowed, shabby carpets worn in the center, mismatched furniture, only made special by her few small possessions kept from the house in Belgravia: a painting of the western isles, a small bronze figure of a horse, a few embroidered cushions.

She rang the bell and when her one maid appeared requested tea with a courtesy few women used towards servants. He could not remember whether it was her usual manner or something new since her wildly reduced circumstances. Either way, its graciousness warmed him ridiculously, and its necessity touched him to new sadness.

Eleanor stood by the mantel shelf, looking down at the fire, unlit. It was too early in the season to burn a fire all day, for one who had to be careful of the coal.

231

"I hope you are not concerned for me?" she said quietly. "It is not necessary, I assure you. My means are sufficient. And I really have no desire now to mix in society." She looked at him suddenly, her eyes very serious.

"I did not come out of any anxiety for you," he replied, meeting her gaze.

She blushed, the color rising up her cheeks in a dark tide.

Again he felt exposed. He knew his emotions were in his face, and he had no idea how to hide them.

"How is your case progressing?" she asked quickly. "Are you doing any better?"

She had changed the subject that was unspoken between them, and yet as obvious as if everything had been heard in words. He resented it, and yet he was also grateful.

"No, I think we really know no more than last time I was here," he replied ruefully. "Pitt is determined it is not the wife or her lover, but I think he is wrong. There really is no evidence either way."

"Why do you think it is them?" she asked, sitting down at last, and permitting him to do so as well.

"Tragic as it is, it is still the most likely," he answered. "The only other alternative seems to be to do with the Farriers' Lane case. And that was closed five years ago. Eleanor . . ."

She looked up, waiting, her breath indrawn as if she too were about to speak.

"Eleanor, I really don't care about the case—or any other case especially. It has become less and less important to me lately . . ."

"I'm sorry—but I expect you will get over it. We all experience a touch of ennui occasionally. Familiar things become tedious for a while. Maybe you need a break from London? Have you thought of going away for a few days? Even a week or two, perhaps?"

All sorts of answers came to his mind. He could not leave Bow Street until this case was resolved. The murder of a judge was too important. It would look as if he did not care, even though there was nothing he could do that Pitt would not do better. He did not wish to inflict his restlessness on his daughters, who would expect him to join their family life. A fortnight with either of his sons-in-law would be far from restful, and he hated being in someone's house when he had neither a true guest's status nor a resident's independence. He would be bored and lonely staying in a hotel, and long walks in the autumn solitude of the hills would leave his problem untouched.

Instead he spoke the simple truth.

"My feeling has nothing to do with London, or the death of Judge Stafford. It has simply sharpened my knowledge of what I must do."

There was a flicker of fear in her face, which might have meant anything. With a cold hollow in his stomach he plowed on, dreading her response, and yet determined now not to shirk the issue. He was capable of more pain than he had believed, but he was not a coward.

She was waiting, accepting now that she could not dissuade him.

"I must acknowledge that my happiness lies with you." He could feel the blood hot in his cheeks. "And ask you if you will do me the honor of becoming my wife."

Almost before he had finished the denial was in her face, the misery in her eyes.

"It would be an honor, Micah. But you must know I cannot."

"Why not?" He heard his voice and hated himself for his lack of dignity, his childishness, as if arguing could make a difference. Why was he vain enough to have imagined that her gratitude, her innate kindness was anything akin to love?

"You know the answer to that." Her voice was low and full of pain. Her face had the baffled look of one who has been struck unexpectedly.

"You do not care for me." He forced the words out, preferring to say them himself so he would not hear them on her lips.

She looked down at the floor.

"Yes, I do," she said very quietly, less than a smile touching her mouth, merely a softness. "I care for you very

233

much—far too much to allow you to marry a woman who is socially such an outcast that alliance with her would ruin you."

He drew in his breath to argue.

She heard him, and looked up quickly.

"Yes, it would. The scandal surrounding Sholto will never be forgotten. I am inextricably tied to it, and I always will be. I was his wife. There will always be people who remember that."

"I don't—" he began.

"Hush, my dear," she interrupted him. "It is very noble of you to say that you do not care about society, but you have to. How could you hold the position you do, commanding the investigation into delicate cases where political discretion is needed, and immense tact, scandals that involve our greatest families, if your own wife had been so closely tied to the very worst of them?" Her eyes were intense. "I know very little of the police, but I can see that much. I am sensible of your honor, that you would not withdraw an offer once made, no matter what your greater wisdom might tell you, but please—we have been friends. Let us at least keep honesty between us. It would ruin you, and I cannot let that happen."

Again he wanted to speak, to argue, but he knew she was right. He could never continue in his position if he were married to Eleanor Byam. Some scandals were forgotten, but that one would not be—not in ten years, not in twenty. The absurdity was that if he were to keep her as his mistress there would be whispers, a little laughter, perhaps a good deal of envy. She was a beautiful woman, but their affair would be largely ignored. Whereas if he did what was immeasurably more honorable, and married her, he would be distrusted and eventually shunned.

"I know," he said very quietly. He wanted to touch her. He wished to so intensely it was a physical effort not to, but he knew it would be wrong, clumsy, and somehow indelicate. "But I count your company a greater happiness than any social or professional position."

She looked away quickly, for the first time her composure breaking. The tears filled her eyes. She stood up and walked over to the mantel shelf.

"You are very generous, and I admire you immensely for it. But it does not alter anything. I cannot let you do such a thing." She turned around and forced herself to smile at him, the tears standing out in her eyes. "What kind of love would I have for you if I were to take my own well-being at such a price to you? It would be no happiness."

He could think of no argument. What she said was perfectly true. Everything worldly he could offer her would be reduced by her very acceptance. And he would never have married her if by doing so he would have ruined her.

Very slowly he rose to his feet, a little stiffly, even though it had been only a short time.

"I'm sorry," she whispered, her voice husky.

For a moment he thought of going to her and taking her in his arms. But it would be intrusive, unfair, and it would change nothing. He had no idea what to say. To take leave formally now, as if he had only called for tea, would be ridiculous. He met her gaze, and knew that his face betrayed all his emotions. For a moment he stood still, then he turned and went out, passing the ladies' maid in the hallway. The tea tray was sitting on the table. She was a discreet woman, and had understood more than he gave her credit for. She opened the door for him, then hesitated a moment.

"I hope you will call again, sir."

He looked at her and saw in her set, tense expression that the words were not idle, not simply a very customary way of bidding farewell.

"Oh yes," he said very firmly. "I shall certainly call again."

Pitt had also found little satisfaction in the day. He had spent some considerable time further pursuing the relationship of Juniper Stafford and Adolphus Pryce, learning what he could about how it had deepened from a social acquaintance brought about by Pryce's professional contact with Judge Stafford. It had been extremely difficult to do without at any time suggesting to those who did not know that it was now an immoral liaison and could have led to murder. The people he spoke to were agog for gossip and innuendo. Had they not been, they would have been of little use in his quest for facts, but their very sensitivity meant he had to be the more careful. As a result the picture he had gained was unclear, full of shadows and implications of passion, but without substance.

He came home tired and dispirited, feeling that he was pursuing something whose reality he would never know beyond doubt, and certainly never prove.

Charlotte had an excellent dinner ready: rich mutton stewed with potatoes and sweet white turnip, and flavored with rosemary. He ate slowly and with more satisfaction than he had felt all day. He had finished and was sitting in the parlor by the fire with his feet on the fender, sinking slowly farther and farther down in his chair, before he realized that she was preoccupied and looked now and then a little worried.

"What is it?" he asked reluctantly, wishing it would be nothing, some domestic triviality he would not have to bother with.

She bit her lip and turned from the work box where she had been sorting threads.

"The relationship between Mama and Joshua Fielding."

"Is she going to be very upset if he is implicated in the Farriers' Lane murder?" he asked. He liked his mother-in-law, although he was more than a little in awe of her, and he certainly would not wish her to be hurt. However, being disappointed now and then was part of caring, and the only way to avoid it was to care about no one, which was a kind of death. "I don't see why he should be," he went on. "Everything I have found out indicates it was Aaron Godman, just as the original trial decided."

She pulled a face. "I almost wish he *were* involved."

"You aren't making sense." He was confused.

Her face screwed up even farther, and she closed her eyes. "Thomas, I think she is really in love with him. I know that's absurd—but—but I think it's true."

"It *is* absurd," he said, eager to dismiss it. He slid lower in the chair till his ankles were on the fender and his feet so close to the fire the soles of his slippers were hot. "She is a very respectable society widow, Charlotte. He is an actor, a Jew, and twenty years younger than she. You are exaggerating out of all proportion. She is probably bored, as Emily is half the time, and looking for something to become involved in. This is more colorful, and more dramatic, than tea parties and fashion. She will forget it once she has seen him cleared."

"Do you think so?" Charlotte looked hopeful, her eyes wide and very dark.

Her expression, far from cheering him, suddenly made him consider the matter properly. He recalled Caroline's face as she had looked at Joshua Fielding, the heightened color, the altered tone in her voice, the frequency with which she mentioned his name. And Charlotte was much more sensitive to such delicate changes than he was. Women understood other women in a way a man never could.

"You don't, do you?" Charlotte challenged, almost as if she read his thoughts.

He hesitated, on the edge of denying it, then the honesty between them won.

"I don't know—perhaps not. It seems absurd, but then I suppose love very often is. I thought I was absurd falling in love with you."

Suddenly her face was radiant, as if the sun had illuminated it.

"Oh, you were," she said happily. "Quite ridiculous. So was I."

And for a while Caroline was forgotten, and her pain or her foolishness put aside.

However, to Mrs. Ellison senior, it was the most urgent matter in the world, and excluded everything else: the weekly edition of the *London Illustrated News*, the latest escapades of the Prince of Wales and his various lady friends, the opinions of the Queen, such as were known or

237

guessed, the sins of the government, the vagaries of the weather, the general inadequacies of the domestic servants, the decline of good manners and morals, even her own various illnesses and their symptoms. Nothing was as important, or as potentially disastrous, as Caroline's infatuation with this wretched actor person. An actor. Of all the absurdities. How grossly unsuitable. In fact *unsuitable* was far too mild a word for it—it was unacceptable—that is what it was. And as for his age . . . He was twenty years her junior—or fifteen at least, in a good light. And that was more than bad taste: it was disgusting.

She must tell her so. It was her duty as her erstwhile mother-in-law.

"Thank heaven poor Edward is dead and in his grave," she said purposefully, as soon as Caroline arrived at the dinner table. The dining room table once had Caroline, Edward, their three daughters and their son-in-law, Dominic Corde, around it, as well as Grandmama. It was now set merely for the two of them, and they were marooned at either end of it, staring down the long oaken expanse at one another. They each required a cruets set; it was too far to pass them.

"I beg your pardon?" Caroline forced her attention to this extraordinary remark.

"I said, thank heaven Edward is dead and in his grave," the old lady repeated loudly. "Are you losing your hearing, Caroline? It can happen as one gets older, you know. I have noticed your sight is not as good as it used to be. You squint at things nowadays. It is unbecoming. It causes wrinkles where one does not wish them. Not, I suppose, that there is anywhere one does. But it cannot be helped at our age."

"I am not your age," Caroline said tartly. "I am nowhere near it."

"Rudeness will not help," Grandmama said with a sickly smile. The conversation was well in her command. "You are moving towards it. Nothing stays the hand of time, my dear. The young often imagine it will somehow be different for them, but it never is, believe me."

"I don't know what you are talking about," Caroline said tersely, putting salt into her soup, and discovering it did not require it. "I am not young, nor am I your age. You are my mother-in-law, and Edward was several years older than I."

"An excellent arrangement," Grandmama said, nodding her head. "A man should be a little older than his wife. It makes for responsibility and domestic accord."

"What absolute balderdash." Caroline peppered the soup and found it did not need that either. "If a man is irresponsible, marrying a younger woman will do nothing to cure him. In fact more probably the opposite. If she has no sense either, then they will both be in debt."

Grandmama disregarded that. "If a man is a little older than his wife," she said, sipping her soup noisily, "then she will obey him the more easily, and there will be peace and happiness in the home. An older wife may be headstrong." She sipped her soup again. "And on the other hand, she may be so foolish as to allow him to lead, when he has no maturity and no judgment—and certainly no authority. Altogether it will be a disaster, and end in ruin."

"What complete tarradiddle." Caroline pushed her soup away and rang the bell for the butler to remove it. "A woman with any sense at all will go entirely her own way, and allow her husband to think it is his. That way they will both be happy, and the best judgment will prevail." The butler appeared. "Maddock, please serve the next course. I have changed my mind about the soup. Tell Cook it was excellent, if you have to tell her anything at all."

"Yes ma'am. Will you be taking fish?"

"Yes, please, but only a very small portion."

"Very good, ma'am." He looked enquiringly at the old lady. "And for you, ma'am?"

"Of course. There is nothing wrong with me."

"Yes ma'am." And he withdrew.

"You should eat properly," Grandmama said to Caroline before the door was closed. "There is no point thinking of your figure. Elderly women who get scrawny are most unattractive. Necks like turkeys. I've seen better things dead on Cook's bench in the kitchen."

"Much better," Caroline snapped. "At least their mouths are shut!"

Grandmama was furious. That remark was totally uncalled for, and unforeseen.

"You never had what one would call delicate manners," she said viciously. "But you are getting worse. I should be embarrassed to take you into company that mattered."

Maddock came in and served the fish, then withdrew again.

"I cannot recall your taking me anywhere at all," Caroline replied. "And you haven't known anyone that mattered for years."

"That is the lot of widows," the old lady said with sudden triumph. "And if you had any dignity or common sense, or idea of your place, neither would you." She attacked her fish with relish. "And you certainly would not be gallivanting around goodness only knows where, chasing after a man half your age, with an occupation not fit to mention. All decent people who aren't laughing at your expense are busy feeling pity for you, and for me, because my daughter-in-law is making a complete spectacle of herself." She sniffed loudly and speared her fish with a fork. "He'll use you like a common bawd, you know. And then laugh about it to his disreputable friends. You'll be the subject of saloon bar jibes—and . . ."

She got no further. Caroline rose from the table and glared at her.

"You are a miserable, selfish old woman with a venomous tongue and a thoroughly dirty mind. I have done nothing, and shall do nothing, to make me the talk of anyone at all, except those like you who have no lives of their own and nothing to talk about but other people's. You may finish your dinner on your own. I do not wish to dine with you!" And she swept out of the door just as Maddock came in, leaving Grandmama openmouthed and for once taken completely by surprise.

However, when she reached her bedroom Caroline found her eyes pricking with tears and her throat aching so unbearably it was a relief to lock the door and curl up in a heap on the bed and let go of the sobs that were welling up inside her.

It was all true. She was behaving like a fool. She was in love as she had never been before, with a man fifteen years younger than herself, who was socially impossible. That he was impossible for her was so unimportant it did not matter a jot. What hurt like a physical wound was that she would be just as impossible for him.

It was three more days before Caroline screwed up her courage and called upon Charlotte so that they might between them endeavor to close the matter of Kingsley Blaine's death. Whatever transpired between herself and Joshua Fielding, however hopeless and absurd it was, he was still in danger of being involved once more in suspicion, and all the misery and loss that that would bring.

"We could call on Kathleen O'Neil," Charlotte suggested, looking at Caroline, her face full of concern.

"Excellent." Caroline turned away, concealing her gaze in case Charlotte saw too clearly her vulnerability, and the fact that for all the sense of her reasoning, she could not keep either the emotion or the tiny pinpoint of hope away from herself. "We really do need to know a great deal more about Mr. Blaine if we are ever to learn who killed him. And why," she went on resolutely, "Tamar Macaulay seems so certain it was not her brother. Joshua believes that too—and I do not think it is simply affection which makes him feel so."

"Good," Charlotte said with a gentleness not usual in her, in such a pedestrian matter as an afternoon call. "We'll go today. I must change, of course, and we'll take luncheon here, if you like."

"Yes—yes," Caroline agreed. "And we will think what we shall say."

"If you like, although I always find plans are of little use, because the other people never say what you intended."

Mid-afternoon found Charlotte and Caroline alighting from Caroline's carriage at Prosper Harrimore's house in Markham Square. They presented Caroline's card at the door so that Mrs. O'Neil might be informed that they had called upon her, if she would receive them. Then they held a sudden and extremely hasty debate as to how they should account for Caroline's name being Ellison, while Charlotte's was Pitt. They concluded the only safe answer would be a widowhood and a second marriage, if they were forced to say anything at all.

A very few moments later the maid returned to say that indeed Mrs. O'Neil would be delighted to receive them, and was in the withdrawing room, where if they would care to, they might join her.

Kathleen O'Neil was not alone, but she welcomed them courteously, and with obvious pleasure, introducing them to the two Misses Fothergill who were also calling. Conversation recommenced and was so trivial that neither Charlotte nor Caroline paid it more than the bare minimum of attention necessary not to make a crass remark. Charlotte noticed that even Kathleen was growing a little glassy eyed.

They were rescued by the arrival of Adah Harrimore, dressed in deep plum-colored wool and looking very dignified. Her rather dour presence seemed to awe the Misses Fothergill, and after a short interval they took their leave. Then Adah herself received a visit from an elderly clergyman, whom she preferred to entertain in private, so she excused herself and repaired to the morning room with him.

"Oh, thank heavens," Kathleen said with heartfelt relief. "They are very well meaning, but they are so terribly boring!"

"I am afraid some of the kindest people can be very hard work to entertain," Caroline said with wide eyes. "After my husband died there were so many people, not unlike the Misses Fothergill, who called on me, intending to take me out of my grief—and I suppose in a fashion they did—at least for as long as they were there." She smiled at Kathleen, and felt a terrible guilt at her duplicity.

"I'm so sorry," Kathleen said quickly. "Was your loss recent?"

"Oh no. It is several years now, and it was not especially sudden." Caroline made a mental apology to Edward, but

242

felt less guilt towards him than to Kathleen. In later years they had been reasonably comfortable, but much of the trust had gone. There had been tolerance, and some gradual understanding, but not the closeness she dreamed of. She could not even remember knowing the laughter and the tenderness she knew Charlotte and Pitt shared.

"But I am sure you must have felt it deeply, all the same." Kathleen was looking at her with sympathy in her eyes. "I lost my first husband in the worst possible circumstances, and I always felt that people like the Misses Fothergill still have it in their minds when they call here. I think that is why they are so stilted. They cannot yet think quite what to say to me. I suppose one can hardly blame them."

Caroline wanted to pursue the subject, but it was too blatant, and she found herself stuck for words. Apparently Charlotte felt no such qualms.

"Since you are so obviously happy with Mr. O'Neil, I am surprised they still think of your first husband." She lifted her voice at the end to make it half a question.

Kathleen looked down.

"If you knew the circumstances you might understand," she said very quietly, almost under her breath. "You see, Kingsley was murdered. There was a great scandal at the time, and a big court case when they caught the man who killed him. And then even though he was convicted, he appealed." She twisted her hands in her lap. "Of course they denied it, and he was hanged soon afterwards. There was a great deal of feeling; people seemed to care so very much." A faint surprise crossed her face, as though even with hindsight she still found it incomprehensible. "People who knew nothing about us wrote letters to the *Times*. Members of Parliament spoke about it in the House of Commons, demanding that the conviction stand, and such barbarity be punished to the utmost, for all our sakes. It was terribly distressing. There seemed never a second we could escape from it."

"It must have been dreadful," Charlotte agreed. "I can barely imagine such a thing." She glanced at Caroline briefly, hoping she understood the apology she intended for what she was about to say. "Although my own eldest sister was murdered, several years ago now, so I do have the deepest sympathy with you."

Kathleen looked startled, and then immediately profoundly sympathetic. She regarded Charlotte anxiously. "Does that sound heartless? But you cannot grieve at fever pitch all the time. You get so tired, so incredibly weary. You need to be able to think of something else for a space, just to remind yourself that there is still a normal life separate from your loss." She smiled self-consciously, then instantly was grave again. "You see, all London seemed to be obsessed with our tragedy and the horror of it. They talked about it day and night."

"However, the court case was over quickly," Charlotte hastened on. "And there was no appeal. The poor creature was quite mad." She frowned. "Why on earth did this man appeal? Surely there can have been no purpose but to prolong everyone's agony?"

"He always maintained he was not guilty." Kathleen bit her lip. "Right to the gallows steps, so I heard." She looked down at her hands clenched in her lap. "I sometimes have nightmares that that was true, and he died just as wrongfully as poor Kingsley—and in a way, even more terribly, because it was cold-blooded, if we can say such a thing of so public a rage." She looked up at Charlotte. "I'm sorry. This is quite an appalling thing to be discussing with people one barely knows who have called for tea. I am ashamed of myself, but you were so quick to understand—and I do appreciate that."

"Please don't apologize," Charlotte said quickly. "I would far rather discuss reality. I assure you I am not in the least interested in the weather, I know very little of society, and I care even less. And I cannot afford to be fashionable."

On any other occasion Caroline would have kicked Charlotte under her skirt for such indiscreet candor, but this time she cared far too much about the real issue behind their presence.

244

Kathleen smiled ruefully. "You really are the most refreshing person to speak with, Miss Pitt. I am so grateful you came."

Charlotte felt a stab of guilt, then thought of Aaron Godman, and it was immediately overridden.

"I should not let it trouble you," she said gently. "Some people will protest, even when they are most certainly responsible for what happened. Why was he supposed to have done such a thing? Robbery? Or did they know each other?"

"They knew each other," Kathleen said very quietly indeed. "Kingsley, my husband, was having an affaire with the man's sister, and she believed he would marry her—which of course was nonsense. But she was misled, as women so often are, when they are in love." A sad reflective smile touched her lips, utterly without bitterness. "We all have our dreams, and some are so precious it is not easy to let them go."

"How dreadful for you." Charlotte meant it wholeheartedly. The thought of Pitt even entertaining desires for another woman was acutely painful. How she would bear it if she learned he was actually having an affaire she had no idea. "I am so terribly sorry!"

Caroline was silent, allowing Charlotte to lead the conversation.

Kathleen heard the anguish in Charlotte's voice and shook her head a tiny fraction, dismissing the grief.

"Oh, Kingsley was very charming, and amusing, and generous," she said gently. "And I never saw him in an ill temper, but I always knew he was weak. He liked to please, which can be a fault as well as a virtue. I imagine he loved her also, and never found the courage to hurt her by telling her the truth." She looked at Charlotte with wide, dark eyes. Then, as if reading her thoughts: "You see, he had very little money of his own. We lived quite well because Kingsley did small jobs for Papa, in his business. He was so charming he was excellent at entertaining people and cementing a bargain. But if he had left me, society would have ostracized him completely, and Papa would have made

245

quite certain that any chance he might have had would be ruined."

Her eyes softened. "Papa can be such a gentle man, I cannot imagine anyone more patient or concerned than he is with my children, and he is always affectionate with me, and with Grandmama. But he can be very different when he detects cruelty or dishonesty in people. He hates evil with a passion—and he would have regarded Kingsley leaving me to be quite evil. And for all his ease and pleasantness, Kingsley knew that."

"And it could not have been a chance robbery?" Charlotte tried to put concern in her tone, as though she did not already know possibly more of the facts than Kathleen herself.

"I doubt it." Kathleen winced. "It was far too dreadful and pointless a thing to have done simply to rob someone. And it did—it did seem to have been someone Jewish. I think that is why Grandmama now feels so strongly about them. She was very fond of Kingsley."

"Oh dear—you must have suffered greatly." Charlotte meant it. "I should not trouble yourself anymore with doubts about"—she caught herself just in time from mentioning his name—"the man who was hanged. After all, if it was not he, then who could it have been?"

"I don't know." Kathleen shrugged very slightly. "I wondered if it was the other actor—did I say that the man they hanged was an actor? No. Well, he was. You see, it was an actress Kingsley was having an affaire with." For all her frankness, she still avoided saying "in love."

Charlotte swallowed. "The other actor?"

"Yes—Joshua Fielding. He is Jewish also—and he was in love with Kingsley's actress."

"You think he was jealous?" Charlotte asked, her throat tight, painfully aware of Caroline sitting rigid a few feet away, her hands clenched hard in her elegant gloves.

"Or that he knew Kingsley would never marry her," Kathleen replied. "And he hated him for hurting, albeit without really intending to. Kingsley had a terrible quarrel with him only a couple of days before he was killed."

246

"With—Joshua Fielding?" Caroline interrupted for the first time. Her face was white and her voice husky.

Kathleen turned to her, as if only now fully aware of her presence.

"Yes. He came home most upset and with his clothes ruffled and dirty. I think it must have been very fierce."

"He told you this?" Caroline tried to keep the fact at bay.

"Yes—you had to know him," Kathleen explained, totally misunderstanding Caroline's distress. "He did not tell the truth if it was painful, but neither would he deliberately lie. I knew something was very wrong, and of course I asked him. He said he had had a violent quarrel with Joshua Fielding. But when I asked him the subject, he said I would not wish to know, and kissed me, and went to change from his soiled clothes before retiring." She shook her head. "Of course when his relationship with—with his mistress came out in the trial, I realized what the quarrel must have been."

"Yes," Charlotte said quickly, aching for Caroline, knowing the pain as if it were a tangible thing. Her stomach was clenched, and a little sick. "Yes, I see." She scrambled for something else to say. She wished they could leave, but it would be pointedly rude, and make a return impossible. And they needed to return. She was convinced there was far more they could learn about Kingsley Blaine which might lead to his murderer, even if it was what they most dreaded to hear. To stop now would be worse than if they had never begun.

"Even so." She tried to put a lift into her voice, but her throat was so tight it sounded more like a squeak. "Even so, I still think you should not feel any remorse. It was none of it your fault. He was fairly tried."

"But I did not tell anyone about the quarrel," Kathleen said, looking from Caroline to Charlotte and back again, her face pale. "No one asked me, and I did not offer it. Do you think it might have made a difference?"

"No," Charlotte lied. "None at all. Now I really don't wish to distress you anymore. The last thing I want is for

247

you to think of my visit as a time of anxiety and the raking up of old wounds."

She was lying, and yet it was certainly true she did not wish to hurt Kathleen, even less now that she knew her better. But Joshua Fielding's wry, gentle face filled her mind as she tried to imagine it contorted with the hatred that would stab a man to death and then crucify his corpse. It was impossible. And yet he was an actor. It was his art and his living to convey passions he did not feel, and hide those he did.

And more powerful than her own doubt or unhappiness over it was a biting misery for Caroline. The wound would be so deep, so out of proportion to the brief time she had known him. But emotion has little to do with time, and love nothing at all.

Kathleen was talking again, but she did not hear her words. The rest of the visit was spent in more pleasant conversation. Charlotte was forced to drag her mind from her thoughts and concentrate. Caroline could only sit and stare, making the odd remark when civility made it absolutely necessary.

When they took their leave it was full of smiles and thanks, and they went out into the blustery wind with skirts whipping around their ankles and a bleak unhappiness inside, as if the sun had disappeared.

8

P*ITT RETURNED AGAIN* to Juniper Stafford. All he
had learned about her, and her relationship with Adolphus
Pryce, still left him uncertain whether he suspected her or
not. Perhaps his reluctance was purely emotional, because
he had been there as she watched her husband die. He had
not believed her guilty then; all his thought had been of
pity for her. He had never doubted her grief. He had heard
no false note in it.

Was it vanity that made it so hard for him to change his
mind, or was there a sound instinct, some observation a little below conscious level, which told him her grief was
real? Or was it that he wanted Aaron Godman to have been
innocent? That was an ugly thought. It would bring tragedy
to everyone involved except Tamar Macaulay, the real and
believable tragedy of dishonor.

He stood outside the Staffords' house, raised the door
knocker and let it fall. There were still black crepes on the
windows, the curtains half drawn. There was a desolate air
about it, a weariness.

The door opened and a footman with a black armband
looked at him enquiringly.

"I am sorry to disturb Mrs. Stafford," Pitt said with more
authority than he felt. "But there are some further questions

I need to discuss with her regarding the judge's death." He produced his card. "Will you ask her if she will see me?"

"Yes sir," the footman said with obedience devoid of feeling.

Five minutes later Pitt was in the chilly morning room when Juniper Stafford came in. She was wearing black, but it was beautifully cut, fashionable and gleaming. She wore jet jewelry discreetly set with seed pearls at her ears and throat, and there was a glow to her skin, a faint flush. Her eyes were soft and alive. He was surprised, and instantly he knew the truth of Livesey's statement that she was in love.

"Good morning, Mr. Pitt," she said with a slight smile, stopping just inside the door. "Have you made any progress?"

"Good morning, Mrs. Stafford," he replied soberly. "I regret it is very slight. Indeed, the more I learn of the matter, the less does it point to any solution."

She came farther into the room and he was aware of a subtle perfume about her, elusive, less sweet than lavender. She moved with a rustle of silk like a breath in leaves, and yet her gown looked like barathea. If she grieved for Samuel Stafford, it was an emotion overpowered by that other emotion which so elated her and made the blood run more swiftly and high in her cheeks. Even so, that did not necessarily mean any guilt in her husband's death.

"I don't know what else I can tell you to help." She was looking at him very directly. "I know almost nothing of his cases, only what the general public can read. He did not discuss them." She smiled, her eyes puzzled. "Judges don't, you know. It is not an ethical thing to do. And I doubt any man would discuss such things with his wife."

"I know that, ma'am," he conceded. "But women are very observant. They understand a lot that is not said, especially about feelings."

She shrugged very slightly in acknowledgment. "Please sit down, Mr. Pitt."

She sat first, gracefully, a little sideways on one of the large chairs, her skirts falling naturally in a sweeping arc around her. The art of being totally feminine came to her so easily she attended to such details without conscious thought.

Pitt sat opposite her.

"I should be most grateful if you would tell me everything you can remember about the day your husband died," he requested.

"Again?"

"If you please. Perhaps with hindsight you may see something new, or I may understand the relevance of something I did not grasp the first time."

"If you think it will be helpful." She looked resigned. If there were anxiety in her he could not see it, and he searched her smooth face for anything beyond sadness and confusion at the memory.

Detail by detail she retold him exactly what she had said the first time: their rising; breakfasting; Stafford's spending some time in his study with various letters; Tamar Macaulay's visit; the raised voices, not in anger but in vehemence of feeling; then her departure; and very shortly afterwards, Stafford's departure also, saying he wished to interview again the people concerned in the Farriers' Lane murder. Juniper had not seen him after that until he returned in the evening, deep in thought, preoccupied and speaking only briefly, telling her nothing at all.

They had dined together, eating the same food from the same serving dishes, then changed into formal dress and left for the theater.

During the interval Stafford had excused himself and gone to the smoking room, and returned to his box only just in time for the curtain going up again. What had happened after that, Pitt was as aware of as she.

"Surely it must be someone involved in the Farriers' Lane case, Mr. Pitt?" she said with a frown. "It is repugnant to accuse anyone, but in this case it seems unavoidable. Poor Samuel discovered something, I have no idea what, and when they realized that, they—they murdered him. What other possibility is there?"

"Everything I have been able to learn indicates the verdict in that case was perfectly correct," he replied. "The conduct of the case may have been hurried, and there undoubtedly seems to have been far too much ugly emotion, but the outcome remains unaltered."

For the first time there was a spark of anxiety in her dark eyes. "Then there must be some fact which Samuel discovered, something deeply hidden. After all," she argued, "it took him many years to find it. Even the court of appeal failed to, so it cannot be easy. It is hardly surprising you have not learned it in so short a time."

"If he had been sure of it, Mrs. Stafford, would he not have told someone?" he asked, meeting her gaze. "He had more than adequate opportunity. He saw Judge Livesey alone that day, and yet said nothing about it."

Again there was that faint flush on her cheeks, the merest pinkening of the skin.

"He spoke to Mr. Pryce about it."

"That is what Mr. Pryce says," Pitt agreed.

She took a deep breath, hesitated at the edge of saying something, and then changed her mind. She looked down at her hands in her lap, then up at Pitt again.

"Perhaps Judge Livesey is lying." Her voice was husky and the color was now deep in her skin.

"Why should he do that?" Pitt asked levelly.

"Because his reputation would be in jeopardy if the appeal were wrong after all." Now her words were hasty, falling over each other as if her tongue would not obey her. "It was a very infamous case. He gained immensely in stature for his handling of it, the dignity and sureness of his dispatch. People felt safer because of his presence on the bench. Forgive me, Inspector, but you do not understand what it means for a judge of appeal to go back on his considered verdict. He would be admitting he was wrong, that he did not discover all the facts of the case; or worse, that his assessment of them was incorrect, and unwittingly connived at a terrible injustice. I doubt there would be any official censure, but that is hardly what matters. It is the public shame, the loss of all confidence in him which would be so appalling. His judgments would never stand in the same way again; even his past cases would not have the weight they used to."

"But surely that would apply to Judge Stafford equally, if the verdict were overturned for a reason they could have known at the time?" Pitt reasoned. "And if it were something they could not have known, then they were in no way at fault."

She was about to argue, certainty in her face and patience to explain to him. Then confusion overtook it. "Well, I—I suppose so. But why should Mr. Pryce lie about it? He was prosecuting counsel. It was his duty to obtain a conviction if he could. He is in no way to blame if the defense was inadequate or the judgment faulty."

He watched her closely. "There is always the possibility it had nothing to do with the Farriers' Lane case, Mrs. Stafford."

She blinked, the shadow of fear plain in her eyes now.

"Then he would have even less reason to lie," she argued.

"Unless the motive were personal." He hated doing this. It was like an animal toying with its prey. For all the gravity of the crime, he felt no satisfaction in the end of the chase. He could not feel the anger that would have made it easy. "I am aware, Mrs. Stafford, that Mr. Pryce is deeply in love with you." He saw the color fade from her skin, leaving it pallid, and the alarm in her eyes. Were there no guilt, no fear for him—or perhaps for herself—then such a remark would have made her blush. "I am afraid his motive is all too clear," he finished.

"Oh no!" she cried out almost involuntarily, her body tightening, her hands clenched in her lap. "I mean—I . . ." She bit her lip. "It would be foolish now to deny that Mr. Pryce and I have . . ." She stared at Pitt fiercely, trying to measure how much he knew, what he was merely guessing. "That we have an affection for each other. But it . . ."

He waited for her to deny that it had been an affaire. He watched the struggle in her face, the fear mounting, the attempt to weigh what he would believe, and then the defeat.

"I confess, I wished that I were free to marry Mr. Pryce,

and he had given me reason to suppose he felt the same." She gulped at the air. "But he is an honorable man. He would never have resorted to such—such wickedness as to have . . . killed my husband." Her voice rose in desperation. "Believe me, Mr. Pitt, we loved each other, accepted that it was impossible it could ever be anything more than a few snatched moments—which you may disapprove of." She shook her head fiercely. "Most people may, but it is not a crime like murder—it is a misfortune which afflicts many of us. I am not the only woman in London who found her true love with a man not her husband!"

"Of course not, Mrs. Stafford. But neither would you be the only woman in the center of a crime of passion, were it so."

She leaned forward urgently, demanding his attention.

"It is not so! Adolphus—Mr. Pryce—is not . . . he would never . . ."

"Be so overcome by his passions as to resort to violence to be with the woman he loved," he finished for her. "How can you be sure of that?"

"I know him." She looked away. "That sounds absurd, doesn't it? I realize before you say so."

"Not absurd," Pitt said quickly. "Just very usual. We all of us believe those we care for are innocent. And most of us believe we know people well." He smiled, knowing he spoke for himself as well as for her. "I suppose half of falling in love is a feeling that we understand, perhaps uniquely. That is a great deal of what that closeness is, the idea that we have found something noble, and perceived it as no one else does."

"The words seem to come to you easily." She looked down at the hands clenched in her lap. "But all the explanation does not make it untrue. I am sure Adolphus did not murder my husband. You will not shake me from that."

"And I imagine he is equally sure you did not," Pitt replied.

This time she jerked her head up to stare at him as if he had struck her.

"What? What did you say? You—oh, dear God—did you say all this to him? Did you make him think I . . ."

"That you were guilty?" he finished for her. "Or that you had blamed him?"

Her face was white, her eyes brilliant with a sudden and hectic fear. Was it for Pryce or for herself?

"Surely you are not concerned he would think such a thing of you?" he went on.

"Of course not," she snapped. And in that instant they both knew it was a lie. She was terrified Pryce would think it was she; the humiliation and the horror were hideously obvious.

She swung around, away from him, concealing her face. "Have you been to Mr. Pryce?" she said again, barely controlling her voice.

"Not yet," he replied. "But I shall have to."

"And you will try to put it in his mind that I murdered my husband, in a desire to be free so that I might marry him." Her voice was shaking. "That is monstrous! How dare you be so—to portray me as—so—insatiable . . ." She stopped, tears of anger and fear in her eyes. She started again. "He would think . . ."

"That you may have?" he finished for her. "Surely not, if he knows you as you apparently know him."

"No." With great difficulty she was regaining mastery of herself again, at least of her voice. "I was going to say he would think that I was very immodest, taking too much for granted. It is for a man to speak of marriage, Mr. Pitt, not a woman!" Now her cheeks were white, with two spots of color high on the bones.

"Are you saying that Mr. Pryce never spoke to you of marriage?" he asked.

She gulped. "How could he? I am already married—at least I was. Of course he didn't!" She sat very straight, and again he knew she was lying. They must have talked of marriage often. How could they not? Her chin came up a little higher. "You will not maneuver me into blaming him, Mr. Pitt."

"You are very sure, Mrs. Stafford," he said thoughtfully.

"I admire your confidence. And yet it leaves me with a profoundly ugly thought."

She stared at him, waiting.

"If it was one of you, and you are so certain it was not Mr. Pryce . . ." He did not need to finish.

Her breath caught in her throat. She tried to laugh, and choked.

When she had recovered, she was unable to say the words of denial. "You are mistaken, Mr. Pitt," she said instead. "It was not one of us. I swear it was not me. Certainly I wished at times I were free, but wished, that is all. I would never have hurt Samuel!"

Pitt did not speak. He looked at her face, the fine beads of sweat on her lip, no more than a gleam, the pallor of her skin, almost bloodless.

"I—I felt so sure. No, I still cannot believe that Adolphus would . . ."

"His emotion was not strong enough?" he said gently. "Was it not, are you really sure of that, Mrs. Stafford?"

He watched the expressions chase each other across her face: fear, pride, denial, exultancy, and fear again.

She looked down, avoiding his probing gaze.

She could not bear to deny his passion; it was a denial of the love itself. "Perhaps not," she said falteringly. "I could not bear to think I was guilty of provoking such a . . ." Her head came up sharply, her dark eyes bright and bold. "I had no knowledge of it. You must believe me! I still only half credit it. You will have to prove it to me beyond any doubt whatsoever or I will still say you are mistaken. Only I know, before God, it was not I."

There was no pleasure in victory. He rose to his feet.

"Thank you, Mrs. Stafford. Your candor has been a great help to me."

"Mr. Pitt . . ." Then again she found no words. What she wanted to say was pointless. To deny Pryce's guilt was too late. She had already committed herself and there was no retreat. "The footman will show you out," she finished lamely. "Good day."

"Good day, Mrs. Stafford."

His interview with Adolphus Pryce was conducted in Pryce's office, and began comfortably enough with Pitt sitting in the large easy chair which was provided for clients. Pryce himself stood by the window with his back to the bookcase, a slender figure of innate grace.

"I don't know what else to add, Inspector," he said with a slight shrug. "Of course I know opium is sold in all sorts of general shops, so one supposes it may be purchased fairly easily. I have never used it myself, so it is only a deduction on my part. But surely that applies to anyone? To the unfortunate members of Aaron Godman's circle as much as to me, or anyone else Judge Stafford met that day?"

"Indeed," Pitt agreed. "I asked only as a formality. I never imagined it would produce anything of value."

Pryce smiled and moved a little away from the window, swinging his chair around behind his desk and sitting down in it, his legs elegantly crossed.

"So what can I tell you, Inspector? All I know of the Farriers' Lane case is a matter of public record. I believed at the time it was Aaron Godman, and I have not learned what it is that made Judge Stafford doubt it. He said nothing specific to me."

"Do you not find that surprising, Mr. Pryce?" Pitt asked as ingenuously as he could. "Considering your own part in the case."

"Not if he was still only suspicious," Pryce said, his voice cultured and reasonable. If he felt any anxiety he was masking it. Pitt could have sworn the subject was causing him no personal concern, only the professional interest that was his duty. "I would expect him to wait until he had irrefutable evidence before reopening such a notorious case," Pryce went on, "and calling into question a verdict already reached by the original court, and later by five justices of appeal." He leaned a little farther backwards in his chair. "Perhaps you are not aware of just how deep the feeling was at the time. It was profoundly ugly. A lot of reputations were at stake, possibly even the reputation of English justice itself. No, I am quite sure Mr. Stafford would have to have been very certain indeed of his evidence before he would have mentioned it to anyone at all. Even in the utmost confidence."

Pitt looked at him as closely as he could without appearing to stare. Juniper had been filled with fears. Pryce seemed completely confident. Was it simply greater self-mastery, or had he a good conscience, and no slightest thought that it might have been she who had poisoned Stafford?

Deliberately Pitt tried to break the calm.

"I take your point, Mr. Pryce. But of course I have to consider the alternative as well. Very possibly it had nothing to do with the Farriers' Lane case, but was a personal matter."

"I suppose that is possible," Pryce said carefully, but the tone of his voice had altered very slightly. He did not ask in what way. He was not as easy to rattle as Juniper.

"I regret the necessity for being so blunt, Mr. Pryce," Pitt continued. "But I am aware of your relationship with Mrs. Stafford. For many men that would be a motive."

Pryce breathed in and out slowly before replying. He uncrossed his ankles.

"I daresay, but not for me. Is that what you came here to ask?"

"Among other things," Pitt conceded with a slight shrug. "Are you telling me that you were not tempted? You must have wished Judge Stafford . . . gone? Or have I misjudged the depth of your feeling for Mrs. Stafford?"

"No." Pryce picked up a stick of sealing wax and played with it absently, his eyes avoiding Pitt's. "No, of course not. But no depth of feeling excuses murder."

"What does it excuse?" Pitt asked, still courteously, even though his words were harsh.

"I am not sure that I understand you," Pryce said guardedly, but his confidence was gone. His fingers were fiddling nervously with the sealing wax and he was breathing more rapidly.

Pitt waited, refusing to help or to dismiss the subject.

"Love." Pryce moved a little in his chair. "It explains a great deal, of course, but it excuses nothing, nothing of any moment. Of course it doesn't."

"I agree, Mr. Pryce." Pitt kept his eyes on Pryce's face. "Not deceit, seduction, the betrayal of a friend, adultery—"

"For God's sake!" Pryce snapped the wax. His face was white. He sat back, rigid, struggled for something to say, and then was suddenly limp. "That's—that's true," he admitted quietly, his voice a little hoarse. "And you will never know how I regret it. I have been excessively foolish, lost all sense of judgment and allowed myself to be led—" He stopped, looking up swiftly and meeting Pitt's eyes. "But it is still not murder."

Again Pitt said nothing, but looked unwaveringly back at Pryce.

Pryce took a long, slow breath, his face almost white, but a little of his composure regained. The effort had been tremendous.

"Of course I appreciate you have to consider the possibility. Logic demands it. But I assure you, I had no part in his death. None whatever. I . . ." He bit his lip. "I don't know how I can prove that, but it is the truth."

Pitt smiled. "I had not expected you to confess to it, Mr. Pryce—any more than Mrs. Stafford."

Pryce's face was suddenly tight again, and his body stiff in his chair.

"You have said the same to Mrs. Stafford? That's . . ." Then he stopped, as if new thoughts crowded his mind.

"Naturally," Pitt replied calmly. "I have been led to believe that her feeling for you is very deep. She must often have wished for her freedom."

"Wishing is not . . ." Pryce's fists clenched. He took a deep breath. "Of course. It would be ungallant of me to say I did not hope so—and untrue. We both wished she were free, but that is a far cry from committing murder to make it so. She will have told you the same." He stopped, waiting for Pitt's reply.

"She denied it," Pitt agreed. "And denied, of course, that you would have had anything to do with it either."

Pryce turned away, laughing very slightly, a husky, nervous sound.

"This is ridiculous, Inspector. I admit—Mrs. Stafford and I have a relationship that—that—was improper—but not"—this time he did not look at Pitt—"not a mere dalliance, not just . . ." He stopped and then started again. "It is a very deep emotion. It is some people's tragedy that they fall truly in love with someone when it is impossible they can marry. That is what has happened to us." His words were very formal, and Pitt had no idea whether he believed them without shadow, or if he were saying what he hoped was true.

"I am quite sure," Pitt said, aware he was turning the knife. "Otherwise you would hardly have risked your reputation and your honor by having an affaire."

Pryce lifted his eyes sharply and glared at him.

"There are some circles in society where such a thing is ignored," Pitt continued relentlessly, "if it is discreet enough, but I doubt the law is one of them. Surely judges' wives, like Caesar's, should be above suspicion?"

Pryce stood up and walked over to the window, his back to Pitt. For several seconds he did not reply, then when he spoke his voice was thick.

"Judges' wives are human, Inspector. Were your acquaintance with the gentry deeper than a passing ability to quote the odd thought or two from Shakespeare, you would not need me to tell you that. We may have slightly different codes of behavior from one social class to another, but our emotions are the same."

"What are you trying to tell me, Mr. Pryce? That your passion for Mrs. Stafford drove you to put opium into Samuel Stafford's flask?"

Pryce swung around. "No! No—I did not kill him! I did not harm him in any way at all—or contribute to it. I—I have no knowledge of it—before, or since."

Pitt kept his face a mask of disbelief.

Pryce swallowed hard, as if choking. "I am guilty of adultery, but not of murder."

"I find it hard to believe that you have no knowledge as to who is," Pitt replied, although that was not true.

"I—I— What are you waiting for me to say?" Pryce was gasping between words as if he had to force himself to speak. "That Juniper—Mrs. Stafford—killed him? You'll wait forever. I'll not say it."

But he had said it, and the irony of it was in his eyes. The thought had been in his mind, and found its way to his lips.

Pitt rose to his feet. "Thank you, Mr. Pryce. You have been most candid. I appreciate it."

Pryce's face reflected self-disgust.

"You mean I have allowed you to see that I am both shallow in my defense of Mrs. Stafford and that I am afraid for her? I still do not believe she had any part in her husband's death, and I will defend her to the limit of my ability."

"If she did, Mr. Pryce, then the limit of your ability will be very rapidly reached," Pitt answered, going to the door. "Thank you for your time."

"Pitt!"

Pitt turned, his face questioning.

Pryce swallowed hard and licked his lips. "She is a very emotional woman, but I really don't—I don't . . ." He stopped, honesty preventing him from making a plea for her after what he had already confessed.

"Good day," Pitt said quietly, and went out into the cold corridor.

"No sir, I doubt it," he said later in the day to Micah Drummond.

Drummond stood in front of the fire in his office, his feet spread a little, his hands behind his back. He regarded Pitt with a frown.

"Why not? Why not now, more than before?"

Pitt was sitting far back in the best chair, his legs sprawled comfortably.

"Because when I saw her, to begin with she defended him," he replied. "She was sure he could not possibly have done it. I don't think she had really considered him. Her emotions would not permit it. Then when I told her the unlikelihood of Aaron Godman being innocent, and there being any motive for anyone in the Farriers' Lane case wanting to kill the judge, she could no longer avoid the inevitable thought that it was either herself or Pryce." He looked at Drummond. "Her immediate fear was that it was Pryce. I saw it in her face the moment she first thought it."

Drummond looked down at the carpet thoughtfully.

"Is she not clever enough to lead you to think precisely that?"

"I don't believe even Tamar Macaulay could act well enough to look as she did," Pitt said honestly. "Acting is broad gestures, movements of the hands and body, tones of voice, inflections; not even the most brilliant can make the blood drain from the face."

"Then perhaps it *was* Pryce?" Drummond said, almost hopefully. "Maybe he grew impatient waiting. An affaire was not enough for him, he wanted marriage." He shrugged. "Or he grew nervous of a continued illicit relationship. She might have been growing indiscreet, or pressing him for more attentions?"

"So he resorted to murder?" Pitt said with a touch of sarcasm. "Pryce does not seem like a hysterical man to me. Unwise in his passions, ungoverned, selfish, allowing an obsession with a woman to destroy his moral judgment, certainly; but not to the degree where he would throw everything away and gain nothing. He knows the law better than to imagine he could succeed."

"Why not?" Drummond interrupted. "Is it such a long step from adultery and the betrayal of a man who trusted him, who was his friend, to killing that man?"

"Yes, I think it is," Pitt argued, leaning forward. "But quite apart from that, Pryce is a barrister. Adultery is a sin, but it is not a crime. Society may shun you for a while if you are too blatant about it. They hang you for murder. Pryce has seen that happen too often to ignore it."

Drummond dug his hands deep into his pockets and said nothing. His mind was not engaged in it as Pitt's was, and

Pitt knew it. He had come because it was his duty, and he needed Drummond's authority to pursue the Farriers' Lane case.

"Added to that," he went on, "when I went to him and pressed the point that he was the most obvious person to suspect, he became frightened and directed me towards her."

For the first time Drummond's expression betrayed a deep emotion. His lips curled in disgust and his eyes were full of pain.

"What a tragic spectacle," he said very quietly. "Two people who were in love, trying to deflect suspicion from themselves by each placing it on the other. It proves their supposed love was no deeper than infatuation, come quickly and dying as soon as self-interest raises its head. You have proved it was appetite, lust." He stared at the fire. "You have not proved it was not strong enough to provoke murder. Self-preservation is answer enough. Many a criminal will betray his accomplices to save himself."

"That is not what I said," Pitt retorted a trifle more sharply. He was finding it difficult that Drummond's mind lacked its usual accuracy. "Pryce began by being quite sure it would not have been Mrs. Stafford, then suddenly he realized it could have been. He was afraid for himself, certainly, but for the first time he was afraid for her—not that she would be blamed wrongly, but that she might actually have done it."

"Are you sure?" Drummond drew his brows down. "You seem to be saying that in fact neither of them did it. Is that what you mean?"

"Yes, it is." Pitt controlled his impatience with difficulty. "They are guilty of self-indulgence, of mistaking obsession for love and deceiving themselves it excused everything, when it excuses nothing. Ungoverned hunger is understandable, but there is nothing noble in it. It is selfish and ultimately destructive." He leaned farther forward, staring at Drummond. "Neither of them truly cared for the well-being of the other, or they would never have allowed passion to dictate behavior." He looked at Drummond's face. "I sound pompous, don't I?" he admitted. "But the justification makes me so angry! If they had ever been honest they wouldn't have destroyed so much, and in the end been left with nothing."

Drummond stared into the distance.

"I'm sorry." Pitt straightened up. "I have to go back to Farriers' Lane."

"What?" Drummond looked up at him sharply.

"If it isn't Juniper Stafford or Pryce, then I have to go back to Farriers' Lane," Pitt repeated. "It was someone he saw that day, because the flask was all right when Livesey and his luncheon companion drank from it. Which leaves only those involved in the case."

"But we've been over that," Drummond argued. "Everything we've looked at still leads to Godman being guilty, and if he was, why should anyone kill Stafford because he wanted to open up the case again? And there is no proof that he did want to. Livesey said he didn't."

"Livesey said he had no knowledge that he did," Pitt corrected. "I accept Livesey believes the case is closed, but that does not mean Stafford found nothing that day. He may well have wished to keep it to himself until he had proof."

"Of what?" Drummond demanded exasperatedly. "That someone other than Godman killed Blaine? Who, for heaven's sake? Fielding? There's no evidence. There wasn't at the time and can you think of what anyone, let alone Stafford, could find now?"

"I don't know," Pitt admitted. "But I want to reinvestigate the entire case. I have to, if I am going to find out who killed Stafford."

Drummond sighed. "Then I suppose you had better do it."

"With your authority? Lambert won't like it."

"Of course he won't. Would you?"

"No. But once I had wondered whether I was wrong in the first place, I would have to know."

"Would you?" Drummond said wryly. He moved away from the fire towards his desk. "Yes, of course with my authority, but you'll still have to be diplomatic if you hope to achieve anything. It is not only Lambert who will not like it! You are treading on a lot of toes. The assistant commissioner has been onto me to get the murder of Stafford solved as quickly as possible, and to do it without raking up the Farriers' Lane case and causing a lot of public unease and questioning of the original verdict. There are enough people trying to cause unrest as it is. We mustn't give them the ammunition to undermine the law any further. The Whitechapel murders did the police a lot of harm, you know."

"Yes, I know," Pitt agreed quietly. He was very well aware of the resignations that matter had caused, and the questions in the Houses of Parliament, the public resentment of a police force paid for from taxes. There were still many people, some of considerable influence, who believed that a police force was a bad idea and would willingly have gone back to sheriffs and the Bow Street runners.

"And the Home Secretary has been down as well," Drummond went on, looking at Pitt and chewing his lip. "He doesn't want a lot of scandal."

Pitt thought of the Inner Circle, but he said nothing. Drummond was as helpless as he was to fight against that. They might guess who belonged; they would not know unless favors were called for, and then it was too late.

"For God's sake be careful, Pitt," Drummond said urgently. "Be sure you are right!"

"Yes sir," Pitt agreed obediently, rising to his feet. "Thank you."

Pitt found Lambert early in the morning, still looking a little sleepy and far from pleased to see him.

"I can't tell you anything more," he said before Pitt asked.

"I assumed if you knew anything you would have said so at the time," Pitt replied. He hoped he sounded casual, not condescending, but the thought flickered through his mind to wonder if Lambert were of the Inner Circle as well. But regardless, he hated checking another man's work as if he expected to find an error of such magnitude, but he felt no alternative. He looked at Lambert's rumpled, angry face. In his place he would have resented it, but as he had told Drummond, he would also have wanted to know. The uncertainty would have been worse, the lying awake at night turning it over and over in his mind till every mistake possible seemed real and guilt marred everything, confidence waned, all other decisions seemed flawed.

He looked at Lambert again, sitting uncomfortably in his chair. "Don't you need to know?" he said frankly.

"I do know." Lambert avoided his eyes. "The evidence was conclusive. I have enough present-day cases without investigating past ones that are closed." He looked up, guilt and anger in his face. "We were a trifle hasty in the way we handled it, I give you that. I wouldn't say every decision is the one I would make if I had it to do again, with more time for judgments, and nobody hounding me day and night for an arrest. But then I daresay you'd conduct a few of your cases differently if you had a second chance. Beginning with the Highgate case."

"I would," Pitt said quietly, remembering the second death with a sick unhappiness. "But I still intend to go over the Farriers' Lane case. I don't want to do it without you, but I will if you force me." He met Lambert's unhappy eyes. "If you are certain you were essentially correct, all I can do is prove that." He leaned forward. "For heaven's sake, man, I'm not trying to find fault with your procedure! All I want is to make sure of the facts. I know what it is like to work under pressure with the newspapers demanding an arrest in every issue, people shouting at you in the streets, the assistant commissioner breathing heavily and sending for reports every day, and the Home Secretary facing questions in the House of Commons."

"Not like this case, you don't," Lambert said bitterly, but he looked slightly mollified.

"May I see the files and ask Paterson to help me find the witnesses again?" Pitt asked.

"You can speak to Paterson, but I can't spare him to go 'round with you. He'll tell you what he remembers. You'll get the names from the files, and where they are now you'll just have to find out. Not that it will do you any good," he added, rising to his feet. "You'll never find the layabouts who saw him come out of the lane. They're probably half of them dead by now. The doorman'll just say the same, and the urchin, who is the only one who really saw him, is totally unreliable, even if you can get hold of him. Still, the flower seller's all right, and I'll get Paterson for you."

"Thank you," Pitt accepted.

Lambert went to the door and pulled it open. He called for a sergeant and told him to fetch the files on the Farriers' Lane case, then he came back into the room, looking at Pitt with a frown.

"If you find anything—I'd like you to tell me."

"Of course."

The sergeant came in before any further speech was necessary, and Pitt thanked him and took the files away to read in the small room Lambert had provided.

He had read Joshua Fielding's statement, and Tamar Macaulay's, and was halfway through the theater doorman's when Sergeant Paterson came in. He looked anxious but there was no anger yet in him, no sense of having been offended.

"You want to see me, sir?"

"Yes, please." Pitt indicated the chair opposite him and Paterson sat on it reluctantly, his face still full of questioning.

"Tell me again everything you remember of the Farriers' Lane case," Pitt asked him. "Begin with the first you heard of it."

Paterson sighed very slightly and began.

"I was on duty early. A constable sent a message that the blacksmith's boy in the Farriers' Lane smithy had found a dreadful corpse in his yard, so I was sent straight 'round to see what was what." His eyes were on Pitt's face. "Sometimes we get reports like that, and it turns out to be a drunk, or someone died natural. I went straightaway, and found P.C. Madsen standing at the entrance to Farriers' Lane, white as a sheet and looking fit to be buried hisself."

His voice was a tight monotone, as if he had said this

several times before and still hated it just as much. "It was barely daylight even then, and he took me back through the alley to the stable yard by the smithy, and as soon as I got into the yard and turned 'round, there it was." He faltered and then continued. "Nailed up to the stable door like, beggin' yer pardon, sir, like Christ as you see in crucifixes, with great nails through 'is 'ands an' feet—and through 'is wrists. I suppose that was to 'old the weight of 'im.'" Paterson's own face was white and there was a beading of sweat on his lip. "I'll never forget that as long as I live. It was the most awful thing I ever saw. I still don't know 'ow anybody could do that to another 'uman being."

"According to the medical examiner, he was already dead when they did that," Pitt said gently.

Two light pink spots burned on Paterson's cheeks. "Are you saying that makes it any better?" he said thickly. "It's still blasphemy!"

Pitt thought about all the arguments that it was not blasphemy to a Jew, and knew they would mean nothing to this angry young man, still outraged five years after by the violence of act and of mind that he had seen. So much hatred had wounded him unforgettably.

"I know," he agreed. "But at least there was less pain. He may actually have died quite quickly—which is some comfort to those who loved him."

"Maybe." Paterson's face was tight, his body stiff. "I don't see as it makes no difference to what kind of a monster'd do something like that. If you're trying to say that excuses anything, I think you're wrong." He shuddered as memory brought back all the anger and fear. "If we could've 'anged 'im twice, I would 'ave."

Pitt did not comment. "How do you think Godman, or whoever it was, managed to nail him up like that?" he asked instead. "A dead body is extremely awkward to carry, let alone prop up and hold while you nail it by the hands—or wrists."

"I've no idea." Paterson screwed up his face, looking at Pitt with a mixture of puzzlement and disgust. "I often thought about that and wondered myself. I even asked 'im,

268

when we 'ad 'im. But 'e just said it weren't 'im." His lips curled with contempt. "Maybe madmen do 'ave the strength o' ten, like they say. Fact is, 'e did it. Unless you're sayin' there was someone else 'elped 'im? Is that what you're looking for—an accomplice?"

"I don't know," Pitt replied. "Tell me, what happened then? Kingsley Blaine was quite a big man, wasn't he?"

"Yes, near six foot, I should think. Taller'n me. I couldn't 'ave lifted 'im, dead weight, and 'eld 'im up."

"I see. What did you do next?"

Paterson was still tense, his face white and strained.

"I sent the P.C. to get Mr. Lambert. I knew it were too big for me to deal with on my own. Waiting for 'im to come back was the longest 'alf hour o' my life."

Pitt did not doubt it. His imagination pictured the young man standing in the slowly broadening daylight on the gleaming cobbles, his breath pale in the chill air, the cold forge unlit by the terrified boy, and the ghastly corpse of Kingsley Blaine still crucified to the door, the wounds in his hands wet and red.

Paterson must have been seeing it in his mind's eye again. His face was sickly and his mouth pulled askew with the effort of his self-control.

"Go on," Pitt prompted. "Mr. Lambert came, and then the medical examiner, I imagine?"

"Yes sir."

"Had the farrier's boy touched anything?"

Paterson's face would have been comical in any other circumstance. Now it merely added the urgently ludicrous and human to the tragic.

"God no, sir! Poor little devil was out of 'is mind wi' fear. Fit for Bedlam, 'e was. He wouldn't 'ave touched that corpse if 'is life 'ad rested on it."

Pitt smiled. "No, I imagine not. Who took him down?"

Paterson swallowed. He looked so white Pitt was afraid he was going to be sick.

"I did, sir, with the medical examiner. The nails was put in so 'ard it took a crowbar to get 'em out. We borrowed it from the forge. The smithy 'isself were in by then.

269

Looked terrible ill, 'e did, when 'e saw what 'ad appened. 'E sold up and went back to the village wot 'e came from." He shivered. "Never bin a forge since then. Brickyard now, for all it's still called Farriers' Lane. Maybe in a few years it'll be Brick Lane."

Pitt hated to bring him back to the subject he would so obviously rather forget, but he had no choice.

"What did the medical examiner tell you then, before he looked at him properly? You must have asked him."

"Yes sir. 'E said the man, we didn't know 'is name then, that was before we—we looked in 'is pockets. I know I should 'a done that straightaway, but I couldn't bring meself to." He looked at once defiant and savagely apologetic. Pitt could imagine the tumult of emotions inside him. " 'E said as 'e'd been killed before 'e were nailed up," Paterson went on. "As 'is 'ands 'adn't bled much, nor 'is feet. It was the wound in 'is side wot killed 'im."

"Did he say what he thought caused that?" Pitt interrupted.

"Well, yes, 'e made a guess," Paterson said reluctantly. "But after 'e said as 'is guess were wrong."

"Never mind, what was his guess then? What did he say?"

" 'E said 'e thought it were probably a knife o' some sort, a very long thin one, like a dagger, the Italian ones wi' them narrow blades." Paterson shook his head. "But afterwards, when 'e'd 'ad a proper look, 'e said it was more probably one o' them farrier's long nails, like 'e were nailed to the door with."

"Did he say what time he had died?"

"Midnight or around. 'E'd been dead quite a while. Even though it were cold, 'e could be sure it weren't in the last two or three hours. It were about 'alf past six by then. 'E said it must 'a bin before two in the morning." Paterson's face tightened with impatience. "But we know what time, sir, because o' the evidence o' the theater doorman, and the men 'anging around the end o' Farriers' Lane what saw Godman come out after 'e'd done it."

"You didn't know that then," Pitt pointed out.

"No."

"What did you learn from the corpse?"

" 'E were a gentleman," Paterson began, his whole body rigid as he recalled the picture to his mind. "That were plain from 'is clothes, 'is 'ands—'e'd never done any 'ard work. 'Is clothes were expensive, and 'e'd been at some sort o' party because 'e were all dressed up, black tailcoat, frilled shirt, gold studs, silk scarf, all that. And an opera cloak." He shivered again. "First thing we did was start looking for people who'd been around the area all night. Found some beggars and drunks who'd been sleeping on the street at the south end o' Farriers' Lane and started askin' them." He relaxed a fraction as he moved from the corpse to the circumstances. "They'd been up 'alf the night 'round a bit of a fire in the roadway, chestnut brazier, or something, drinking like as not. They said they'd seen this gent go into Farriers' Lane about 'alf past midnight, tall gent with a top 'at, fair 'air, as much as they could see of it, but it fell over 'is face a bit. No one followed 'im in. I asked 'em that in partic'lar, and they were quite sure. So 'ooever did that to 'im were waiting there for 'im." Paterson shuddered convulsively.

"Go on," Pitt prompted him. He could see it in his mind's eye, as he knew Paterson could. He did not want him dwelling on it again or the emotion would cripple his thought. "How did they describe the man they saw coming out of Farriers' Lane? I assume there was only one?"

"Oh yes!" Paterson said fiercely. "There weren't another for an hour or more. God knows 'ow 'e felt when 'e 'eard what 'e'd passed! This one were kind o' furtive, they said."

"Did they?" Pitt asked, amazement lifting his voice. "That sounds like an unusual word for such men to use."

"Well"—Paterson colored very slightly—"what they said actually was that he looked scared, like 'e'd rather not be seen. He came to the end o' the alley, out o' the shadows, stood still for a moment to see who was passing, then put 'is shoulders back and walked fairly quickly along the footpath, not looking to right nor left."

"And where were they standing?"

" 'Round a brazier, 'alf in the gutter."

"Yes, but which side of the street? Did Godman actually pass them?"

"Oh—no. Opposite side, but close to Farriers' Lane entrance. They saw 'im clear enough," Paterson insisted.

"Opposite side of the street, after midnight, a group of layabouts and drunks! Is there a lamp near the end of the lane?"

Paterson's expression tightened. "About twenty yards. 'E passed under it. Right under it!"

"How did they describe him?" Pitt went on. "Tall, short, thin, large? What did they say? How was he dressed?"

"Well . . ." Paterson pulled a face. "They said he seemed fairly large, but 'e was dressed in an 'eavy overcoat, dark, but it could have been undone and that would 'ave made 'im look a bit bigger. They weren't that close, and they didn't pay particular attention. Why should they?"

"What about the blood? Your report mentions blood, and there must have been a lot. You can't commit a murder like that without blood all over the place."

Paterson winced and looked at Pitt with loathing. "They said they saw the dark stain, but they reckoned as 'e'd bin in a fight, or got a bloody nose."

"So there was really no description," Pitt pressed.

"No," Paterson admitted grudgingly. "Not close, but good enough. It weren't like there was more 'n one man come out o' the lane all the time they were there. And there's a light in that yard. No innocent man'd 'ave come out 'o that place an' jus' walked away!"

"No," Pitt conceded. "That has to be true. What did you do after that?"

"The medical examiner told us who 'e was," Paterson continued. " 'E found 'is name on some things in 'is pockets, and there was the stub of a theater ticket too, for that night. So we knew where 'e'd been until an hour or so before 'e was killed. Naturally we went there."

"Who did you see?"

"Well, the only ones who could tell us much were Miss

Macaulay's dresser, a Miss Primrose Walker, and the doorman, don't remember 'is name now . . ."

"Alfred Wimbush," Pitt supplied. "What did they say?"

"The doorman said as Mr. Blaine came to the theater pretty regular, like, and always visited backstage with Miss Macaulay afterwards," Paterson recounted. "Quite often 'e'd stop for a bite o' supper. She didn't say nothing, but it were pretty obvious as they were fond o' each other, putting it at its best." There was a very slight sneer in his voice and Pitt ignored it with difficulty. "She was very badly shook by it," Paterson said more gently. "Took it 'ard. She said Mr. Blaine 'ad been there that evening, an' 'ad stayed late with 'er. Later she admitted 'e'd given 'er a very 'andsome necklace which 'e said 'ad been in 'is wife's family fer years. An' Miss Macaulay 'ad said she'd wear it for supper, but then 'e 'ad to take it back, as keeping it weren't right. Least that's what Miss Walker said, but it don't look as if he did take it back, cos it weren't on 'im when we found 'im."

"So Kingsley Blaine stayed late with Miss Macaulay, and left when?"

"About midnight, or a minute or two after, say five past," Paterson replied. "Wimbush told us that. 'E saw Mr. Blaine go out and closed the door after 'im. He said Blaine was scarcely out onto the footpath when a young lad came running across the street from the far side and latched on to 'im, telling 'im a message, something about meeting someone at a club to patch things up. Blaine seemed to understand it, said yes 'e would, turned 'is collar up and went off towards Farriers' Lane—or in that direction, up north towards So'o."

"Did the doorman see who gave the boy the message?" Pitt asked.

Paterson shrugged very slightly. "A figure, not much more. Said 'e thought it were someone fairly large, but then 'e changed 'is mind and weren't sure whether it was because 'e were standing in the shadow. Certainly the doorman didn't see 'is face."

"So as far as he knew, it could have been Aaron Godman, or almost anyone else?" Pitt said.

"Anyone of more or less average height," Paterson agreed. "But then if it was Godman, he would be careful not to be seen, wouldn't 'e?" He raised his eyebrows. "Because 'e would know the doorman would recognize 'im, and remember."

"That's true. You found the boy. What did he say?"

Paterson looked less certain. "Like I said, 'e weren't a very good witness. Just a street urchin, begging, stealing, surviving 'ow 'e could. 'Ated the police, like all 'is kind." He sniffed and shifted a little in the seat. " 'E said the man what gave 'im the message was old, then young. Said 'e were big, then ordinary. Frankly, sir, I don't think 'e knew. All 'e cared about was the sixpence the fellow gave 'im. 'E did say 'e 'ad a Jewish nose, and seemed very excited. But then 'e would be. 'E were planning to murder a man."

"Was he always uncertain, or did he change his mind?" Pitt asked, watching Paterson's face.

Paterson hesitated. "Well ... 'e changed 'is mind, but honestly, I don't think 'e ever knew. 'E were un'elpful right from the start. That sort is. Don't know the truth from lies 'alf the time."

"Did he identify Aaron Godman?"

"No, not definite. Said 'e couldn't be sure. But then 'elpin' the police don't come natural to them."

"What put you onto Godman? Why not O'Neil, or Fielding?"

"Oh, we considered them, right enough." Paterson's voice had a hard edge to it now and his face was full of anger. "And I admit it often crossed my mind that Mr. Fielding might 'a known more than 'e ever said. But it was proved fair and square that it was Godman as did it."

"Wasn't there a quarrel between Blaine and O'Neil?"

"Yes, and according to some gentlemen we found who overheard it, it was pretty bad at the time, but the sort of 'eated quarrel young gentlemen 'ave when they're a bit the worse for champagne and think their honor's been questioned." He looked at Pitt irritably, as if Pitt were raising the issue beyond reason. "It was all over a wager, and only a few pounds at stake. Which might seem a lot to you an' me, but to the likes o' them it weren't much. Nobody but a madman would murder 'is friend over a few pounds." His lips pulled crooked with the memory, and once again rage and horror overtook his momentary annoyance with Pitt. "Beggin' your pardon, sir, but you didn't see that body. A man would 'ave to be insane with 'ate to do that to anyone. That weren't caused by no quick temper over a wager—'ooever did that 'ad 'ated long and deep before it came to that night."

Pitt did not argue. The fierceness in Paterson's voice and the sick memory in his eyes stifled it before it came to his tongue.

"O'Neil is married to Blaine's widow, you know," he said instead.

"I know that," Paterson said between his teeth. "And don't think I 'aven't wondered since if 'e 'ad that in 'is mind before Blaine was dead," he went on sharply. " 'E may 'ave. That don't mean to say 'e killed Blaine. No sir, Godman did that." His face set hard and there was a flicker of loathing in his blue eyes. "Blaine were playing fast and loose with 'is sister. Got 'er with child, and promised to marry 'er, which 'e never intended to," he said bitterly. "And when Godman found that out 'e lost 'is 'ead. You know Jews don't like us touching their women any more'n we like it when they touch ours. They think we're not as good as they are—sort o' lesser, if you like. They're the chosen race o' God, and we're not."

His body stiffened and he shook himself a little. "They think Christ was a blasphemer, and they crucified 'im. I guess some of 'em anyway still 'ate us. An' Godman was one of 'em. And when 'e found out what 'ad 'appened to 'is sister 'e just went mad." He shivered and let out his breath sharply, staring at Pitt.

Pitt could feel the emotion in the room, the air still charged with it. Suddenly he perceived, as he had not before, what it had been like in the original investigation, the horror that had soaked everything, the fear of violence and madness, and then the anger. It reached out and touched him now like a sick coldness. He had been trying to understand with his mind. He should have used his imagination, his instinct.

"Why are you so sure it was Godman?" he asked as calmly as he could, but he heard his own voice shake. "Apart from the motive."

" 'E were seen," Paterson answered immediately, his shoulders square, his chin up. "Positively. No shadows, no doubt. 'E stopped to buy flowers, the arrogant bastard! Sort of a celebration o' what 'e'd done!" His voice was thick with fury. " 'E stood right under the light. Anyway, the woman knew 'im. Seen 'is face on a poster and recognized 'im straightaway. In So'o Square, less than half a mile from Farriers' Lane, and a few minutes after it 'appened. 'E lied. Said it were thirty minutes earlier."

"I see. Yes, you found the flower seller, didn't you? Good piece of work."

"Thank you, sir."

"What was O'Neil doing at the time of the murder?"

"Gambling at a club about a mile and a half away."

"Witnesses?"

Paterson lifted one shoulder. "More or less. 'E could 'ave stepped out, but 'e'd 'ave been seen when 'e got back. There must 'ave been blood all over the place after a killing like that." Again his face mirrored his horror and the outrage he still felt even now.

"And Fielding?"

"Went 'ome. No proof, o' course." Paterson shrugged. "But no reason to suspect 'im, since Godman was definitely alone. The men at the end o' Farriers' Lane swore to that. Fielding may've known about it, or guessed afterwards, but 'e definitely weren't there at the time."

"Thank you. That's all very clear."

"Is that all, sir?"

"I think so."

Paterson stood up.

"Ah—just one more thing," Pitt added quickly.

"Yes sir?"

"When Godman came to court he was badly bruised, as if someone had beaten him. Who was that?"

Paterson flushed a hot, dull red. "I—er—well, 'e weren't an easy prisoner."

Pitt raised his eyebrows very high. "He resisted?"

Paterson stammered and then fell silent.

"Yes?" Pitt asked again.

Paterson's face set hard. "If you'd seen what 'e did to Blaine, sir, you wouldn't ask, cos you'd feel the same."

"I see. Thank you, Paterson. That's all."

"Yes sir." Paterson stood to attention sharply, then turned on his heel and went out.

Over the next two days Pitt patiently followed Paterson's footsteps. He found Primrose Walker, Tamar Macaulay's dresser, very easily. She was still in the company, and still working at the same task. She repeated what she had said originally, that Kingsley Blaine had visited Miss Macaulay frequently, and on that night he had given her a gift of an expensive necklace. She described it quite closely: a diamond scroll set with turquoise. She said Miss Macaulay had accepted it reluctantly, and only to wear that evening, then to return it. Had Miss Walker seen her return it? No, of course not. She did not attend the champagne supper. She could add nothing more.

It was only a formality that Pitt had asked her. It was a foregone conclusion in his mind that she would repeat what she had said before, and it would support Tamar Macaulay, and thus Aaron Godman. The only thing that slightly surprised Pitt was that when speaking of Kingsley Blaine her face had softened and it was obvious her memory of him was gentle. Even now there was no dislike in her, no sense that he had betrayed her mistress.

And Wimbush, the theater doorman, also repeated his original evidence. He was a small, lugubrious man with a long nose.

"No, I didn't see 'im proper," he replied when Pitt asked him about the man on the far side of the street who had sent the boy over with the message. "Jus' looked like a big geezer in the shadow o' the wall opposite."

"Can you remember anything about him?" Pitt pressed. "Close your eyes and imagine it again. Go through your mind, exactly as it happened. You were standing at the doorway, making sure everyone left so you could lock up. Kingsley Blaine came out. Was he the last?"

"Oh, yes sir."

"What about Miss Macaulay?"

"She come out a few minutes before," Wimbush replied. "Mr. Blaine went back for 'is gloves wot 'e left on the table. I got Miss Macaulay an 'ansom and she was gone before Mr. Blaine came back. I said good-night to 'im, an' 'e were about ter go and look for a cab 'isself, when this skinny little lad, about eleven or twelve years old, come scarperin' across the street an' pulled at 'is sleeve. I were about to tell 'im ter clear orf, when 'e said as 'e'd got a message from a Mr. O'Neil, and to say as 'e were sorry about the quarrel they'd 'ad, and Mr. Blaine were right after all. An' would Mr. Blaine meet 'im at Dauro's Club right away and they'd make it up." He shrugged his thin shoulders. "So Mr. Blaine said yes 'o course 'e would, thanked the lad an' gave 'im a couple o' pence, then 'e set orf along the path towards Farriers' Lane, poor devil. And that's the last I ever saw of 'im alive."

"And the man who sent the message? Did he look like Mr. O'Neil to you?"

Wimbush pulled a face. "Can't say as 'e did. I can't say as it looked like Mr. Godman neither. It were just a shape in the shadow, big like, with an 'eavy coat on. But I'll tell you this—either it were a toff or someone got up to look like one."

"So everyone assumed it was someone who knew Mr. Blaine," Pitt said as civilly as he could. He should not have been disappointed, but he was.

"Yer asked me what I remembered," Wimbush said with injured sensibility. "I told yer, 'e were a toff. Top 'at, silk scarf. I remember seein' the light on it—all white 'round 'is neck."

"Did Mr. Godman have a top hat and a silk scarf?"

"Not unless 'e were goin' somewhere special." Wimbush's lips curled in a smile heavy with contempt. " 'E were 'ere to work. Even gents don't go to work in top 'ats and silk scarves."

"And that night?" Pitt said, trying to keep the urgency out of his voice. Lambert would already have asked this, even if Paterson had not.

"No 'e didn't," the doorman replied. "But then you'll just say as 'e got one out o' the dressers' room or summink. That's what they said before. Although why 'e should do that no one bothered wi' askin'! Just make 'im more like to be noticed, I'd say. Them rozzers don't think like ordinary folks." He cleared his throat as if he were about to spit, then glanced at Pitt's face and changed his mind.

"Did you see Mr. Godman leave that night?"

"No, I didn't. Wish I 'ad. Leastways I spec' I saw 'im, but I didn't take any special notice."

"I see. Thank you." He must remember to ask if Godman had had a scarf on when he was arrested.

He spoke to Tamar Macaulay again, but she repeated what she had said before, and he found himself embarrassed for the cruelty of having to remind her of an act which had robbed her at once of both her brother and the man she loved. Her dark face was unreadable as she stood in the dust of the stage wings, the bare boards drafty, the huge canvas backdrops hanging on their pulleys over their heads, the limelight dead. He could see her only in the yellow glare of a gas bracket on the passageway towards the dressing rooms. Some theaters were already lit with electricity, but this was not one of them.

He looked across at the strength in her, the hollows of her eyes, the perfect balance of nose, cheek and jaw which gave her face its power. Her tenderness, her laughter, would be worth waiting for, worth earning. How had Kingsley Blaine ever imagined he could play with such a woman and then expect to walk away freely? He must have been a fool, a daydreaming, irresponsible and complete fool. She would be capable of a passion fierce enough to crucify. Did she defend her brother so intensely, and at such cost to herself, because she believed Blaine had deserved it? And would she have done it herself, had she the physical strength? Was it guilt which drove her now?

"Miss Macaulay," he said aloud, breaking the eerie half silence of their island of unreality. All around them the theater was alive with sounds of preparation. "If it was not Mr. Godman killed Kingsley Blaine, who was it?"

She turned and faced him with a sudden flash of humor. In the half-light it was exaggerated, and oddly without malice.

"I don't know. I suppose Devlin O'Neil."

"Over the quarrel about a wager?" Pitt allowed his disbelief to show.

"Over Kathleen Harrimore," she corrected. "Perhaps the passion sprang from his feeling for her, and the knowledge that Kingsley was betraying her with me." A shadow of remorse passed over her face and unmistakable pain. "And it may have crossed his mind that Kathleen stood to inherit Prosper Harrimore's estate, which is very considerable. And of course to have an excellent and assured living in the meantime." She turned around to meet his eyes. "You think it is vicious of me to accuse him? I don't think that it is—you asked me who else. I don't believe it was Aaron. I never will."

Pitt did not argue. There was nothing else to say. He thanked her and took his leave to seek the urchin who was the one person who had seen the murderer's face, albeit in the shadows, and had heard his voice.

But although he searched every avenue he could think of, through police records, the general knowledge of the constables in Lambert's station, his own contacts in the streets and the fringes of the semicriminal underworld, he had no success. There were whispers, false trails, information that turned out to be untrue, or too late. Joe Slater apparently did not wish to be found.

It was on the third day, gray and cold with a knife-edge wind out of the east, before Pitt at last found him in Seven

Dials, next to a stall selling secondhand boots. He was gangling, thin and fair-haired, his face wary and full of suspicion.

"I don't remember," he said flatly, his eyes narrow. "I said all I know when yer asked me afore! Now leave me alone! Yer 'anged the poor sod! Wot else d'yer want? I dunno nuffink more!"

And that was all Pitt could get from him. He refused to discuss it again. He was angry, bitterness deep in his face.

Pitt was going up the steps into the police station when he met Lambert coming down, his face white, his eyes hollow with shock. He stopped abruptly, almost bumping into Pitt.

"Paterson's dead," he said thickly, stumbling over his tongue. "Hanged! Someone hanged him! Judge Livesey just found him!"

9

P_{ITT} FOLLOWED LAMBERT into the hansom and sat
cold and shocked beside him while they struggled through
the traffic across the Battersea Bridge towards Sleaford
Street and the house where Paterson had lodgings.

"Why?" Lambert said more to himself than to Pitt. He
was hunched up, his collar high around his neck, half hiding his face, as though there were a bitter wind inside the
cab. "Why? It makes no sense! Why kill poor Paterson?
Why now?"

Pitt did not reply. The answer he thought of was that Paterson had learned, or remembered, some evidence which
changed the verdict of the Farriers' Lane case. Of course it
was possible it was something else, another case, or even
something personal, but that was on the edge of his mind,
so faint it barely touched his thoughts.

The cab halted abruptly and the sound of shouting intruded, dislocating thought and making speech impossible.

Lambert shifted restlessly. The delay scraped his nerves
raw. He leaned forward and demanded to know what it was
that held them up, but no one heard him.

The cab swiveled around. A horse squealed. They jerked
forward again.

Lambert swore.

Now they were moving at a steady trot.

"Why Paterson?" Lambert demanded again. "Why not me? I was in charge of the case. Paterson only did what he was told, poor devil." His voice was harsh and his face twisted with an anger he could not control, and a deep tearing pain. He stared in front of him and clenched his fists. "Why now, Pitt? Why after all these years? The case is closed!"

"I don't think it is," Pitt replied grimly. "At least for Judge Stafford there was something still to be resolved."

"Godman was guilty," Lambert said between his teeth. "He was! Everything pointed to him. He was seen, by the urchin he gave the message to, by the men at the entrance to Farriers' Lane, and by the flower seller. He had motive, better than anyone else. And he was a Jew. Only a Jew would have done that! It was Godman. The original trial proved it, and the appeal judges upheld it—all of them!"

Pitt did not reply. There was nothing he could say which would answer Lambert's real question, or ease the travail inside him.

They arrived at Sleaford Street. Lambert threw open the door, almost falling onto the footpath, and leaving Pitt to pay the driver. Pitt caught up with him at the steps. The front door was already half open and there was a white-faced woman standing in the passageway, her hair screwed back in an untidy knot, her sleeves rolled up.

"Wot's 'appened?" she answered. "Are you the p'lice? The gennelman upstairs sent out Jackie to fetch the p'lice, but 'e wouldn't say wot's wrong." She grabbed Lambert's sleeve as he brushed past her. " 'Ere! 'As 'e bin robbed? It ain't none o' us! We never robbed nobody! This is a decent 'ouse!"

"Where is he?" Lambert shook her off. "Which room? Upstairs?"

Now she was really frightened. "Wot's 'appened?" she wailed, her voice rising. Somewhere behind her a child began to cry.

"Nobody's been robbed," Pitt said quietly, although he was beginning to feel a little sick himself. It was only a few days ago, such a short time, that he had sat in the office talking to Paterson. "Where is the man who sent for the police?"

"Upstairs." She jerked her head. "Number four, on the first landing. Wot's 'appened, mister?"

"We don't know yet." Pitt went after Lambert, who was already striding up the stairs two at a time. At the top he swung around, glanced at the doors, then banged irritably on number four and immediately tried the handle. It opened under his pressure and with Pitt at his heels he burst in.

It was a large, old room, like thousands of other bachelor lodgings, with dull wallpaper, heavy furniture, all a little worn but immaculately clean. There was little of character. It was all chosen for utility and a veneer of comfort, but no personal taste of the man who had lived here.

Ignatius Livesey was sitting in the best armchair. He was very pale, his eyes dark and a little hollow with shock, and when he rose to his feet he was not quite as in control as he had thought. His limbs trembled for a moment and he had to reach twice to grip the chair so he could steady himself.

"I am glad you have come, gentlemen." His voice was hoarse. "I am ashamed to say that being alone here has not been an experience I have found easy. He is in the bedroom, where I found him." He took a deep breath. "Beyond ascertaining that he is dead—a fact of which there is little doubt—I have touched nothing."

Lambert looked at him for only an instant, then walked past and opened the bedroom door. He stopped with an involuntary gasp.

Pitt strode over. Paterson was hanging from the hook which should have supported the small, ugly chandelier now lying skewed sideways on the floor. He was held by a rope, an ordinary piece of hemp about twelve or fourteen feet long, such as any carter would use, except there was a running noose in one end. His body was stiff; his face, when Pitt moved around to see, was purplish, eyes protruding, tongue thick between his open lips.

Lambert stood motionless, swaying a little as if he might faint.

Pitt took him by the arm, having to pull hard to force him from the spot.

"Come," he ordered sharply. "You can't do anything for him. Mr. Livesey!"

Livesey suddenly realized he could help and started forward, taking Lambert's other arm and guiding him to the chair.

"Sit down," he said grimly. "Get your breath. Nasty shock for you, when you knew the poor man. Sorry I don't carry brandy, and I doubt Paterson would have had any."

Lambert shook his head and opened his mouth as if to reply, but no words came.

Pitt left them and went back into the bedroom. All the same questions that had teemed in Lambert's mind were in his now, but before he addressed any of them, he must see what facts he could observe.

He touched Paterson's hand. The body swung very slightly. The flesh was cold, the arm rigid. He had been dead several hours. He was dressed in plain dark uniform trousers and tunic, which was torn, his sergeant's insignia ripped off. He still wore his boots. It was nearly midday now. Presumably it was what he had worn when he came home from the last duty of the day before. If he had slept here, risen in the morning and dressed ready to go out, the body would still have some warmth left, and be limp. He must have died sometime late yesterday evening, or during the night. It would almost certainly be the evening. Why should he be wearing his street clothes all night?

The hook was in the middle of the ceiling, about ten or eleven feet high, where one would expect to find a chandelier. There was no furniture near enough to it for him to have climbed on. It had taken a strong man to lift Paterson up and then let him fall from that height. He must have used the rope as a pulley over the hook. There was no conceivable way Paterson could have done it himself, even supposing he had some cause to, or believed he had.

Pitt glanced around, simply as a matter of course, to see

285

if there were any letter, although he knew it had to be murder. Physically, suicide was impossible.

There was nothing. It was a plain, tidy, characterless bedroom. A bed with a wooden headboard occupied the far end. A sash window looked out over a narrow alley with a few sheds and what appeared to be a stable.

There was a wardrobe to the right, and some four or five feet from it a chest of drawers. There were three chairs, one padded, the other two hard seated and straight backed. All of them were upright and against the wall. Had Paterson used them to stand on they would have been under the chandelier, and probably fallen over.

He went over to the chairs and examined them one by one. He could see no mark on any of them. But then if the man had taken off his shoes, there would be none.

He heard Livesey's footsteps at the door and looked around.

"Have you learned anything?" Livesey said very quietly.

"Not a great deal," Pitt replied, straightening up and glancing around the room again. Its impersonalness hurt him, as if Paterson had lived and died leaving no mark. And yet had he seen books, photographs, letters, handmade articles chosen with meaning and care, perhaps it would have hurt more. Except that there was a sense of futility, a loneliness as if someone had slipped away unnoticed, his loss seen only when it was too late. He could not have been more than thirty-two or thirty-three. He had barely begun. And now there was nothing.

Lambert's question rang in his head. Why? Who could have done this, and why now?

"I think he was dead a long time before I got here," Livesey said quietly. "I wish to God I had come when I got his note last night! I could have saved him."

"He sent you a letter?" Pitt said in amazement, then immediately felt ridiculous. He should have asked Livesey what he was doing here. Appeal court justices did not normally visit police constables in their lodging houses. "Sorry," he apologized. "I was going to ask you why you were here."

"He sent me a note yesterday." Livesey's voice was still husky, as if his mouth were dry. "He said he had learned something which troubled him deeply, and he wanted to tell me about it." He fished in his pocket and pulled out a folded piece of paper. He passed it over to Pitt.

Pitt read in scribbled writing which even in its haste and emotion showed the form of its copperplate letters.

My lord,
Forgive me writing you like this, but I have learned something terrible which I have to tell you, or I cannot rest with myself a night longer. I know you are a very busy man, but this is more important than anything, I swear it. I dare tell no one else.
Please answer me when I can speak to you about it,
Your humble servant,
D. Paterson, P.C.

"And you don't know what it was that troubled him so much, or why he wouldn't simply tell Inspector Lambert?" Pitt asked.

"No, I'm afraid I don't," Livesey replied, lowering his voice still further so Lambert would not hear him in the next room. "But the suggestion implicit is not a pleasant one. I must say, poor Lambert does look very shaken. I assume it is some case Paterson is presently engaged in, and which was a great deal more serious than he at first supposed." He winced, his heavy face looking tired and shocked. "I fear it may involve some possible misbehavior or corruption. I refuse to speculate further and possibly do someone a profound injustice."

"Why did he choose you, Mr. Livesey?" Pitt asked, endeavoring to make his tone so courteous as to rob the words of any rudeness. "Did he know you?"

"By repute, I suppose," Livesey replied with profound unhappiness. "Certainly to the best of my knowledge I had never met him. Of course I knew his name, because I read his evidence at the trial of Aaron Godman. Similarly, he may have known that I sat on the appeal. But not personally, no. We had never met."

Pitt was still puzzled.

"That does not really answer the question."

"I agree," Livesey said, shaking his head. "It is extraordinary. I can only suppose that the poor young man discovered, or thought he had discovered, something which he dared not take to his own superiors, and he chose someone whose name he knew, with the position, and the integrity, to help him. I feel appallingly guilty that I did not come last night, when I could have saved his life."

There was no comment Pitt could make that would be helpful. He could not deny it. To do so would be condescending, and neither of them would believe it. Livesey did not deserve that. Instead he walked over to the body, still hanging from its rope, regarded the noose, then pulled one of the chairs over to see if it would give him enough height to lift the body down at last and lay it where it could rest decently until the medical examiner came and took it away.

That was something Lambert could do, send for the appropriate people. Presumably Livesey had not done so. He turned to look at him.

"Do you—do you need a little help?" Livesey said, swallowing and stepping forward. "I . . ." He cleared his throat. "What would you like me to do?"

"I was going to ask you if you had called the medical examiner," Pitt answered.

"No—no, I just sent the boy for the police. I thought . . ."

"Lambert can do that," Pitt said quickly. "I can't untie the rope, his weight will have pulled it tight. I'll need a knife."

"Er . . ." Livesey was beginning to look ill, as if his years had caught up with him. "I'll go and see if the landlady has one. You'll need to preserve the rope, I imagine. Evidence."

"Thank you. Ask Lambert to send for the medical examiner, will you?"

"Yes. Yes, of course." And as if escaping the room and

288

its fearful burden, Livesey turned on his heel and went out of the door. A moment later Pitt heard his steps heavy in the passage outside, and then on the stairs.

Pitt went back and stood in the room until Livesey returned with the knife.

Livesey was too shaken to touch the corpse. His face was pale and there was sweat on his brow and lip and his hands were clumsy, as if he could no longer coordinate them. Pitt held the body up as far as he could to ease the weight. Livesey cut the rope, taking several seconds to saw it through, then Pitt felt the full weight of Paterson suddenly collapse on him.

Livesey swore, his voice choking, and together they laid the body on the floor.

"There's nothing else to do here," Pitt said quietly, moved by pity for Livesey, and anxiety in case he could not bear the horror any longer. "Come. We'll wait for the medical examiner in the next room."

Two hours later Pitt had questioned the landlady, now alternately shrieking with outrage and mute with fear, and then the other tenants, and learned nothing from any of them. The medical examiner had been and gone, taking the body with him in his mortuary van, the horse stamping and blowing as it caught the smell of fear from passersby. Livesey, still pink-faced and now suddenly cold, had excused himself. Pitt and Lambert stood on the landing outside the door, the keys in the lock.

Lambert shook his head.

"I don't understand," he said yet again. "What on earth could he have wanted to tell Livesey? Why not us? If not me, then you?" He took the keys out of the door and gave them to Pitt. In single file they went down the stairs.

The landlady was still standing in the hall, her face haggard and eyes blazing.

"Murder!" she said furiously. "In my very own 'ouse! I always said I never should 'ave 'ad police as lodgers! Never again! I'll take my oath on that, never again!"

Lambert swung around on her, his face white, his eyes blazing.

"A young policeman is murdered in your house, and you've got the impertinence to blame him! Perhaps if he'd never come here then he'd be alive today. What sort of a house do you keep anyway?"

" 'Ow dare you?" she shrieked, her cheeks scarlet with outrage. "Why you—"

"Come on." Pitt took Lambert by the arm and half pulled him out, still turned towards the woman, wanting to fight. The rage and the grief in him needed to lash out at someone, lay blame where he could see and hear.

"Come on," Pitt repeated urgently. "We've got a lot to do!"

Reluctantly Lambert went with him. Outside the sky was overcast and it had begun to rain. Passersby were huddled into themselves, collars up, faces averted from the driving cold.

"What?" Lambert demanded between his teeth. "Who murdered poor Paterson? We haven't even found out who killed Judge Stafford! We don't know why! Do you know, Pitt?" He dodged off the pavement into the running gutter, then back on again. "Have you even got an idea? And don't tell me Godman wasn't guilty—that doesn't make any sense. If he wasn't, why would anybody rake it all up now? They've got away with it. It was the perfect murder. Godman is hanged and the case is closed."

"What else was Paterson working on?" Pitt asked, matching his pace to Lambert's as they walked along Battersea Park Road to a place where they could find a hansom back to the station.

"An arson case. A couple of robberies," Lambert answered. "Nothing much. Nothing anyone would kill him over. Garotte him in a dark alley, maybe; or stick a knife into him if he went to make an arrest. But not go to his house and string him up on a rope. It's insane. It's that damn Macaulay woman. She's out on a rampage of revenge." He stopped in his stride, turning to face Pitt, his eyes brilliant and wretched. "She's insane! She's coming after the people she holds to blame for her brother's hanging!"

"She's not doing it alone," Pitt said, trying to keep calm. "No woman by herself strung up Paterson. He's a big man and was in good health."

"All right then," Lambert snapped. "She had help. She's a clever woman, beautiful, and has got that sort of personality. Some poor devil fell in love with her, and she's got 'im so obsessed he helped her do that." He was talking too fast and Pitt could hear the hysteria rising in his voice. "Or maybe 'e did it for her," he went on. "Go and find him, Pitt. Prove it! Paterson was a good man. Far too good to die for the likes of her! You do that! Prove it!" And he snatched himself away from Pitt's outstretched hand and strode along the wet pavement towards the Battersea Bridge, and the carriages and cabs clattering back and forth along it.

Pitt began the long and tedious job of investigating the murder of Constable Paterson. The medical examiner's report said that death had been caused by strangulation brought about by hanging, exactly as it had appeared. He had died some time the previous evening; his guess was that it had been earlier rather than later.

As a matter of course Pitt checked where Judge Livesey had been at that time, and was not surprised to learn that he had attended a dinner given by several of his colleagues and had been observed by at least a score of people for all of the relevant time. Not that Pitt had for a moment thought he might have been guilty; it was simply a matter of routine to check.

His mind was far more taken up with wondering what Paterson could possibly have learned that he wished so desperately to communicate with the judge. Did it concern the Farriers' Lane case, as they had instinctively supposed, or was it something quite different?

He left Lambert to pursue the physical evidence: the witnesses who might have seen someone going into the lodging house; where the rope had come from; any signs of an intruder, a footprint, a scrap of cloth; anything at all that indicated a struggle.

He himself went searching for meaning, motive for such an apparently senseless act. If it lay in a case Paterson had been working on currently, or in some part of his personal life, then it was Lambert who would have the background to find it. But if it lay in the Farriers' Lane case, then it was only in pursuing that that the answer could be learned.

Had Paterson tried to contact anyone other than Judge Livesey? Might he have tried one of the other judges also? It was too late for Stafford, he was already dead. Sadler had retreated from all responsibility and would have given no answer. Boothroyd was too involved in his conspicuous philanthropy, his seeking for friends and influence, to have taken any part in such a wildly unpopular cause as reopening the Farriers' Lane case.

That left Judge Oswyn, or perhaps the other lawyers in the case. Aaron Godman's solicitor, and his barrister who had pleaded for him at the trial. Surely they would have been the natural people with whom to begin, if indeed there were anything new, anything that pointed to a different verdict, or an accomplice.

Why Livesey? Did he imagine him to have some integrity or power others did not?

Pitt began by seeking an appointment with Judge Granville Oswyn in his chambers, and was pleasantly surprised to be granted it almost immediately.

The room was large, sprawling and untidy, full of books, some in cases, some in piles covering tables and heaped on stools. There were several big plush armchairs, none matching anything, but all forming a comfortable whole. Old theater playbills decorated one of the walls, political cartoons by Rowlandson another. Oswyn was a man of interesting and catholic tastes. A beautiful bronze of a hunting dog stood on the bookcase, and there was a jasper-and-rock crystal paperweight on the desk.

Oswyn himself was a large, genial man in clothes that fitted him ill. He had the sort of face that seemed somehow familiar, even though Pitt knew perfectly well they had never met. A smile illuminated his features as though he were genuinely pleased to see Pitt.

"My dear fellow, come in, come in." He rose from his seat behind the desk and waved at the best chair. "Do sit down. Be comfortable. What can I do for you? I have no idea, but do tell me." He sat in his chair again, still smiling.

There was no point whatever in being devious, and no advantage to surprise.

"I am investigating the death of Judge Stafford," Pitt began.

Oswyn's face darkened. "Very nasty affair," he said with a frown. "Very nasty indeed. Can't think why. Honorable man. Hadn't thought he had an enemy in the world. Seems I was wrong." He leaned back and crossed his legs carefully. "What can I tell you that you don't already know?"

Pitt sat back a little.

"He was reinvestigating the Farriers' Lane case, you know?"

Oswyn's face lost its geniality, and a flicker of anxiety crossed his eyes.

"No, I didn't know. Are you sure you are not mistaken? There really was nothing else to pursue. We went through it very thoroughly at the appeal." He looked at Pitt with concern crossing his face, leaning back and resting his elbows on the arms of his chair, making a steeple out of his fingers. "He was far more likely just trying to satisfy that poor Macaulay woman. She would not let it drop, you know. Very sad. Devoted to her brother, and simply would not believe it. But there was no basis for doubt, you know. None at all. Everything was correct at the time."

"What were the grounds for the appeal, sir?" Pitt asked, as if he had had no idea.

"Oh—medical. A formality really. Had to have something."

"And did you treat it like that—as a formality?"

Oswyn's face was aghast and he dropped his hands instantly. "Good heavens, no! Of course not. A man's life was at stake, and even more, the whole principle of British justice. Must not only be done, but be seen to be done, and to the satisfaction of everyone. Or else justice ceases to be upheld, and then it works for no one. Oh, we examined the case in minute detail. There was no flaw in it, none at all." He screwed up his eyes, looking at Pitt anxiously.

"Did Judge Stafford mention it to you lately?" Pitt felt his way, seeking for the question which would probe between the certainties of the obvious answers.

Oswyn hesitated only minutely, a moment of indecision, but it was there, and Pitt saw it. Oswyn smiled, understanding the expression in Pitt's eyes, knowing he had seen.

"Well, yes, he did say something." He shrugged. "But it was—not serious, if you know what I mean."

"No," Pitt said unhelpfully. "How could such a matter not be serious?"

But Oswyn had had time to think now. His answer came with assurance. "It was a nuisance. The poor Macaulay woman was still troubling him, trying to find someone to believe her and reopen the matter. And Stafford, poor devil, was the man she was directing her efforts towards." He shrugged and smiled, attempting to look at ease. "He merely mentioned that. It was an embarrassment. Surely you can understand that, Inspector?" He laughed very slightly, but there was no nervousness in it, and no humor.

"In case there had been an omission, or an error?" Pitt asked.

"No!" Oswyn leaned forward, banging his hand down on the surface of the desk. His face was a little pink, his eyes earnest. "There was no . . ." He shook his head. "There was no error. The matter was very simple." He stared at Pitt earnestly. "The appeal was raised on the grounds of the medical evidence. Yardley said originally that he thought the wound that killed Blaine had been caused by some sort of dagger. Then on examination he admitted that it could have been a particularly long farrier's nail."

"Farriers' nails only come in certain lengths," Pitt argued. "They have to go into horses' hooves. There's a limit to how long they can be, even though they are clipped off."

"Yes, of course." Oswyn waved the thought away impatiently. "All right, then an ordinary nail. The man is a surgeon, not a blacksmith. Perhaps it was just a loose piece of metal 'round the yard. The point is, it did not have to have been a dagger."

"Were there any nails like that, or longer pieces of metal 'round the yard?" Pitt asked. "Surely a bloodstained piece would have been easy enough to find."

Oswyn looked startled. "I have no idea. For heaven's sake, man, we sat on the appeal. That was weeks after the trial, which itself was weeks after the crime. Every man and his father could have been through the yard by then, and probably had."

"So whatever the weapon was, it was never found?"

"I suppose not. Perhaps it was one of the nails he used to hang him up by." With an effort he lowered his voice. "But whatever it was, Inspector, it is far too late now to shed any light on it. Poor Stafford could hardly have been investigating that, could he?" He had scored a point of logic and he knew it.

"Nevertheless," Pitt argued. "If Yardley changed his mind, then there was an element of uncertainty in the evidence. It seems to have been considered sufficient to take it to appeal."

"A desperate measure." Oswyn screwed up his face, his broad, mobile mouth rueful. "A man will try anything to avoid the rope, and who is to blame him?"

"Do you remember P.C. Paterson?" Pitt changed the subject abruptly.

"P.C. Paterson?" Oswyn repeated the name thoughtfully. "I don't think so. Why?"

"He was the constable who carried out a great deal of the investigation."

"Oh yes. Wasn't he the one who found the final proof? The flower seller who saw Godman in Soho Square just after the crime. Good piece of work. Hero of the moment, Paterson. Why?"

"He was murdered on Tuesday night."

Oswyn's surprise and his sorrow both looked acutely real.

"Oh dear—I'm so sorry! What a damned shame. Very

295

promising young officer." He shook his head. "Dangerous trade, policing. But then of course you know that."

"It was not in the course of duty, sir. He was murdered in his own home. Hanged, to be precise."

"Good God!" Oswyn was totally stunned. The blood fled from his skin, leaving it pasty white, and all the sense of well-being and geniality that had been so much a part of him vanished. "How dreadful—how— Who was it?"

"We have no idea so far."

"No idea! But surely—" He stopped abruptly, confused and profoundly unhappy. "You cannot think it had anything to do with Kingsley Blaine! I mean . . ." Instinctively his hand went up to his throat and he pulled at his collar, loosening it a fraction. "Why, for God's sake?"

"That is what I am trying to determine, sir." Pitt watched him closely. "I had questioned Paterson in some detail regarding his original investigation of the case. I am wondering if something I said prompted him to an act, a word to someone which may have resulted in his murder."

Oswyn passed a hand over his brow, temporarily hiding his face from Pitt. "Are you trying to say that Godman was not guilty, and someone else is, and that person is now murdering anyone who appears likely to reopen the case? That makes little sense, Inspector. Have you been attacked?"

"No," Pitt admitted. "But then I am still as confused as I was at the beginning. I have discovered no evidence at all to suggest Godman was not guilty. In fact the more I learn, the more certain it seems he was."

Oswyn breathed in deeply and shook himself a little as if suddenly immensely relieved. "Indeed." He swallowed hard. "Indeed. A tragic and extremely ugly case, but settled at the time." He bit his lip. "I have been a servant of the law all my life, Inspector. I should—er—I should hate to think we could have made such a mistake. It would— jeopardize much that I believe to be of immeasurable value to the British people. Indeed, it is a model for the world." He sounded oddly pompous, as if he did not entirely mean it. "A great deal of the law of the United States of America is based upon our common law. I suppose you were aware of that—yes, of course you were. The law is above us all, more important than any individual."

"Surely the law can only be measured by how it deals with the individual, Mr. Oswyn?"

"Oh. I think that is too—too sweeping a statement, too simplistic, if you will forgive my saying so? There are profound issues at stake—" He stopped suddenly, his face pink. "But that does not help you in your quest to find out who murdered Mr. Stafford, or this unfortunate constable. How can I possibly help you?"

"I am not sure that you can," Pitt conceded. "The last thing he did before he was killed was send a letter to Judge Livesey saying that he had learned something terrible and wished to tell him as soon as possible. Unfortunately—" He stopped. The color had fled again from Oswyn's face and he looked ill.

"He—er . . ." Oswyn stammered. "He—he wrote to Livesey? What—what was it he had learned? Did he say? Do you know?"

Pitt was about to say no, then changed his mind.

"The letter was to Judge Livesey. It was he who found him, when he went the following day."

"But what was in the letter?" Oswyn said urgently, leaning forward across the desk towards Pitt. "Livesey must have—"

"That is why I have come to see you, sir," Pitt said, speaking the truth, and knowing a lie would be understood. "The Farriers' Lane case—"

"I don't know! I thought Godman was guilty. I still do." There was a beading of sweat on his lip now. "I cannot say differently. I know nothing, and speculation would be totally irresponsible." His voice was rising a little and threaded with anxiety again. "A man in my position cannot start making wild suggestions about miscarriages of justice. I have responsibilities—I can think . . ." He took a deep breath and let it go. "I owe—debts of obligation to the law I have served. I have duties. Of course if you have evidence, that would be different." He stared at Pitt, his eyes wide and troubled, demanding an answer.

"No. No evidence yet."

"Ah." Oswyn let out his breath in a long sigh. "Then when I can help you, please come back and let me know."

It was a polite dismissal and Pitt accepted it. He could learn nothing more from Oswyn anyway. There were no facts, only a profusion of impressions.

"Thank you, sir." He rose to his feet. "Yes, certainly I will. As soon as I have found out exactly what that letter meant."

"Yes—yes, of course."

It was the next morning before Pitt could make arrangements to see Ebenezer Moorgate, the solicitor who had handled Aaron Godman's case. He preferred to meet Pitt not in his chambers, which he shared with several others, but in a public house some mile and a half away. It was a small place, crowded with petty clerks, small tradesmen and idlers. Ale was slopped in the sawdust on the floor, and the smell of boiled vegetables mixed with that of stale beer, dirt, and too many people.

Moorgate looked out of place in his smart suit with its clean white shirt and stiff wing collar, and his well-barbered face. He had an ale mug in his hand, but he had not touched it.

"You are late, Inspector Pitt," he said as soon as Pitt pushed his way through the throng and joined him at a small table in the corner. "Although I fail to see the purpose of this meeting. The case you refer to was over a long time ago. We appealed—and lost. It can only cause more grief, quite uselessly, to open it up again."

"Unfortunately it is not an old case anymore, Mr. Moorgate. Two more people are dead."

"I don't know what you mean," Moorgate said guardedly, his fingers clasping his mug more tightly. "It cannot have anything to do with the case. That's nonsense, if you'll forgive my saying so."

"Judge Stafford, and now Constable Paterson."

"Paterson?" Moorgate's eyes widened. "I didn't know about that. Poor fellow. But it is coincidence. Tragic, but chance. Has to be."

"He wrote to Judge Livesey just before he was murdered, saying he had something urgent to tell him—urgent and dreadful."

Moorgate swallowed. "You did not say he had been murdered."

At the next table a man turned around, his face full of curiosity. Beyond him another man stopped talking and stared.

Moorgate licked his lips. "What are you suggesting, Pitt? That someone from the Farriers' Lane case is murdering people? Why? Revenge for Godman? That's preposterous." His voice rose a pitch higher and he was speaking more rapidly, unaware of the stir he was causing. "From what you say, it seems to me that Paterson may have discovered who murdered Stafford! Or thought he did. Obvious, don't you agree? Could have been the Macaulay woman. Loss of her brother, all the scandal and such an appalling end, turned her mind." He was staring at Pitt fixedly. "Known lesser things than that to drive a woman mad. Poison is a woman's method, more often than not. Would have thought you could prove it." He looked angry and faintly accusing.

"Possibly," Pitt agreed. "Although since Stafford appeared to be considering reopening the case, I cannot see her motive. He was the one person she would most wish to remain alive."

"Nonsense!" Moorgate dismissed it with a flick of his free hand. "Absolute nonsense, my dear fellow," he repeated. "There is nothing to reopen it for. I am very familiar with it, you know. I was the instructing solicitor at the time. If ever I saw a hopeless case, that was it. Did all we could, of course. One has to. But there was never any chance!" He shook his head sharply. "Wretched fellow was guilty as the devil."

Suddenly he remembered his ale and took a sip of it, looking around at the considerable number of people now staring at him. "Miss Macaulay could not accept it. Quite often takes the family like that. Natural, I suppose. But Stafford probably told her so that day, and I daresay in her disappointment and frustration she killed him. She would view it as a kind of betrayal. Very intense woman, you know, very emotional. I suppose actresses are like that—lightly balanced. No fit occupation for a woman—but then no gentlewoman would take it up, so there you are."

"She didn't kill Paterson," Pitt said with an unreasoning distaste that surprised him.

"Are you sure?" Moorgate did not bother to conceal his skepticism.

"Quite sure," Pitt said sharply. "He was hanged from the ceiling, in his own lodgings. No woman on earth could have accomplished that. It must have been a powerful man to do it. Just as it took a powerful man to lift Kingsley Blaine up and hold him while he nailed his wrists to the stable door."

Moorgate winced and put down his ale mug as if it had turned suddenly sour and undrinkable. Now every man within twenty feet of them was silent and staring.

"Let me understand you, Inspector. Just what are you suggesting?" Moorgate said with considerable anger and a pink color rising up his cheeks.

"The facts suggest, Mr. Moorgate, not I," Pitt replied calmly.

"They suggest a personal quarrel to me." Moorgate swallowed. "Had he a love affair of some sort? Perhaps a jealous husband is involved."

"Who hanged him?" Pitt raised his eyebrows. "Is that your usual experience, Mr. Moorgate?"

"I have no 'usual experience,'" Moorgate said coldly. "I am a solicitor, not a barrister. And please keep your voice down. You are making a spectacle of us! Murders are rare in my practice. And I have very little idea of what jealous husbands or lovers do when they find they are betrayed."

"Something hot-blooded or physically violent," Pitt replied with a twisted smile, aware of the crowd around them. It was not his voice which had aroused their interest. "Shoot if they have a gun," he went on. "Stab if a knife is available, which is not hard to find. If a spontaneous fight breaks out, then they strike, or even throttle. To go to a man's home taking a length of hemp, and then remove the chandelier, presumably either before he arrives, or while you have him unconscious, or bound, then string him up by the neck and hang him till he is dead—"

"For God's sake, man!" Moorgate exploded furiously. "Have you no decency at all?"

"Calls for a great degree of premeditation and cold-blooded planning," Pitt finished relentlessly.

"Then it was some other motive," Moorgate snapped. "Regardless, it was nothing to do with any case of mine, and I cannot help you." He put his ale down at last, slopping on the table to his intense annoyance. "I should advise you to look very closely into the wretched man's personal life, if I were you. Perhaps he owed money. Usurers can be violent if they are cheated. I really have no notion, but it is your task, not mine, to discover the truth. Now, if there is nothing further, I must return to my chambers. I shall shortly have clients awaiting me." And without concerning himself with whether Pitt had any further questions or not, he rose to his feet, knocking the table and slopping the ale mug still further. He inclined his head stiffly, and took his leave.

Barton James, the barrister for the defense, was a very different man, taller, leaner, of a more distinguished and assured appearance. He received Pitt in his chambers and enquired courteously for his health, then invited him to be seated.

"What can I do for you, Mr. Pitt?" he said with interest. "Does it concern the death of poor Samuel Stafford?"

"Indirectly, yes." Pitt had decided to be more circumspect this time, at least to begin with.

"Indeed?" James raised his eyebrows. "In what way can I assist? I knew him, of course, but only very slightly. He was an appeal judge; it is some time since he sat at trial. I have not pleaded before him for fifteen or sixteen years."

"But you took one of your most celebrated cases to appeal before him."

"Several," James agreed. "That does not constitute a relationship. I am not aware of knowing anything at all which has relevance to his death. But by all means, ask me what you wish." He sat back, smiling agreeably. His manner was assured, his voice excellent. Pitt could imagine him commanding a courtroom, holding a jury with the power of his personality. How hard had he pleaded for Aaron Godman? What passion or conviction had he used on his behalf?

With an effort he brought his mind back to the present, and the slow building up to the questions that mattered.

"Thank you, Mr. James. You see, it is not only the murder of Mr. Stafford I am investigating, but there seems to be another murder linked to it." He saw James's eyes widen. "That of Constable Paterson."

"Paterson? Is that the young officer who was on the Farriers' Lane case?" James asked, a tiny muscle flicking on his brow.

"Yes."

"Oh dear. Are you quite sure it is connected? Policework can be very dangerous, as I am sure you do not need me to tell you. Might it not be a coincidence? The Farriers' Lane case was closed some five years ago. Oh, I know Miss Macaulay keeps trying to arouse interest in it again, but I am afraid she is in a hopeless cause. It is only her devotion to her brother which drives her. She has no hope of success."

"You are quite certain he was guilty?"

James shifted minutely in his seat. "Oh indeed, quite certain. I am afraid there was no doubt."

"Did you think so at the time?"

"I beg your pardon?"

"Did you think so at the time?" Pitt repeated, watching James's face, the long patrician nose, the mouth on the verge of humor, the careful eyes.

James pushed out his lower lip in a rueful expression.

"I would like to have thought him innocent, of course,

but I confess, as the case proceeded it became more and more difficult."

"You believed the verdict a true one?"

"I did. So would you, had you been there, Mr. Pitt."

"But you lodged an appeal."

"Naturally. It was what Godman wished, and his family. It is natural to try every possible step, however slight the chance of success, when a man is to be hanged. I warned them of the unlikelihood of its being granted. I held out no false hopes, but nevertheless, of course I did my best. As you know, it was refused."

"The grounds were insufficient?"

James shrugged. "The medical examiner, Humbert Yardley—a very reliable man, no doubt you know him?—did seem to change his mind about the weapon. It is not like him to do that. Possibly with the horror of the whole affair—it was a spectacularly gruesome crime, as you must know—he may temporarily have lost his customary cool-headedness." He leaned back in his chair again, his face a trifle puckered. "It was an outrage in a very extraordinary sense, you know. The man was not only murdered, but crucified. The newspapers made banner headlines. All sorts of very deep and violent emotions were roused. In some quarters there were anti-Jewish riots. Pawnshops were broken into and vandalized. Men who were known to be Jewish were attacked in the streets. It was all extremely ugly."

He smiled with bitter humor. "I was even subjected to considerable abuse myself for defending him. I had the expensive and embarrassing experience of being pelted with rotten fruit and eggs when passing through Covent Garden. Thank God it wasn't Billingsgate!"

Pitt hid a smile. He had walked by the fish market on a warm day. "Did you ever think him innocent, Mr. James?"

"I assumed him innocent, Mr. Pitt. That is my duty. Not the same thing. But my own thoughts are irrelevant." He looked at Pitt gravely. "I did the best for him I could. And I do not believe any barrister in the land would have obtained an acquittal. The evidence was overwhelming. He was actually seen not half a mile from the spot, at the relevant time, and quite clearly, by someone who knew him by sight. Then there was the evidence of the street urchin who delivered the message for him which brought Blaine through Farriers' Lane, and of the idlers who saw him leave the lane, covered with blood."

"Did the urchin identify him?" Pitt said quickly. "I thought he was uncertain."

James pushed out his lips thoughtfully. "Yes—I suppose stretching a point, he was. And if you stretch the point even further, so were the idlers. And quite literally, they may have exaggerated the blood. It is hard to know what a man sees at the time, and what his imagination paints in afterwards, with the knowledge of hindsight." He shook his head, smiling again. "But the flower seller knew him by sight, and had no doubt at all. He actually stopped and spoke to her, which shows either an extraordinary cool head or an arrogance that amounts to the insane."

"And you have no doubt as to his guilt," Pitt pressed.

James frowned. "You speak as if you do. Have you discovered something not available to us at the time?"

It was an interesting choice of words. He had taken care to guard against the implication that he could have been remiss. Discreetly, by implication rather than openly, he was defending himself.

"No," Pitt replied cautiously. "Not that I am certain of. But it seems an unavoidable conclusion that Paterson may have reconsidered his investigation, after I questioned him about it, and in doing so discovered something, or realized a different interpretation for it. His letter to Livesey spoke—"

"Letter to Livesey?" James was startled and suddenly alarmed, his body stiff, his voice tight. "Judge Ignatius Livesey?"

"Yes—did I not mention it?" Pitt affected a blindness he did not feel. "I apologize. Yes, before Paterson was murdered—incidentally, he was hanged, with a noose, from the chandelier hook in the middle of the ceiling of his room." James's face was pinched with disgust and increasing distress. "Before he was murdered," Pitt went on, "he wrote a letter to Judge Livesey, saying that he had discovered something appalling and must tell him as soon as possible. It was poor Livesey who found him, the morning after. Unfortunately he could not get there that evening."

James remained silent for several moments, his face grave. Eventually he came to some decision.

"You did not tell me that. It puts a very different and very ugly complexion upon things." He shook his head slightly. "I am afraid I can think of nothing whatever that might be of use to you, indeed, nothing even remotely relevant."

"Neither Paterson nor Judge Stafford communicated with you in the matter?"

"Paterson certainly did not. I have not spoken to him since the trial." He shifted very slightly in his chair. "Stafford did call on me, some weeks ago. Miss Macaulay had been writing to him, as she did to numerous people, attempting to generate interest in the case. She still hopes to clear Godman's name, which of course is quite impossible, but she will not accept that." His voice was growing more rapid. "She had progressed beyond reason on the subject. But I did not take any of it seriously. I was already aware of her . . . obsession. It was to be expected she might harass Stafford. I am surprised he took any notice, but she is a most . . . eloquent woman, and has a type of appeal which is difficult for some men to resist."

"What did Judge Stafford wish you to do, Mr. James? Forgive me for asking, but he cannot tell me, and it may help to learn who killed him."

"Much the same as you are asking, Inspector. And I regret I can help neither of you. I know nothing I did not know, and say, at the time."

"Is that all? Are you certain?"

"Well." James was still uncomfortable, but he did not evade the question. "He asked about Moorgate, the instructing solicitor, his reputation and so on." He looked embarrassed. "Poor Moorgate has declined more than a little since then. I have no idea why. But he is still perfectly adequate, and at that time he was an excellent professional man."

"But like you, he believed Godman guilty," Pitt added.

James's face darkened. "On the evidence in hand—still uncontested—there was no other reasonable conclusion to draw, Mr. Pitt. And you yourself have not produced anything yet to refute it. I have no idea who murdered Stafford, or Paterson; and I agree it does suggest itself that their connection with the Farriers' Lane case has some part in it. But I have no idea what. Have you?"

It was a challenge.

"No," Pitt said quietly. "Not yet." He pushed his chair a fraction backwards. "But I intend to. Paterson was only thirty-two. I mean to know who hanged him by the neck—and why." He rose to his feet.

James rose also, still courteous. He held out his hand.

"I wish you good fortune, Mr. Pitt. I look forward to hearing of your success. Good day to you."

"Just one other thing." Pitt hesitated. "Godman was severely beaten while he was in custody. Do you know how that happened?"

A spasm of acute distaste passed over James's features.

"He said that one of the police beat him," he replied. "I have no proof whatsoever, but I believed him."

"I see."

"Do you." It was a challenge, and there was definite anger in it. "I did not mention it at the time because I could not prove it, and it would only have alienated the jury even further that he seemed to be maligning the forces of order, and thus indirectly the public in general. Besides which, it was irrelevant to the fact." There were two spots of pink in James's cheeks. "It would not have altered the verdict."

"I know that," Pitt said honestly. "I just wanted to know, for myself. It explains a little of Paterson's attitude."

"It was Paterson?" James demanded.

"I think so."

"How very ugly. I presume you have automatically thought of revenge?"

"Not Tamar Macaulay. Not the way Paterson was killed. It had to have been a man of considerable strength."

"With Fielding's help? No? Well, it is a possibility you

must consider. Thank you for your candor, Inspector Pitt. Good day to you."

"Good day, Mr. James."

Pitt reported to Micah Drummond, not because he expected any comment from him, and certainly not any specific help, but because his duty required it.

"Whatever you think appropriate," Drummond said absently, staring at the rain lashing against the window. "Is Lambert being difficult?"

"No," Pitt replied honestly. "The poor devil was extremely shaken by Paterson's death."

"It is a dreadful thing to have a junior killed," Drummond said with tight lips. "That is an experience you have not yet faced, Pitt. If you do, you will have more sympathy for Lambert, I promise you." He kept his face to the streaming glass. "You will feel just the same grief, self-doubt, even guilt. You will reexamine everything you said or did to find some fault in your orders, some oversight, anything that you could have done differently, and avoided it. You will lie awake and agonize, feel sick about it, even wonder if you are fit to have command."

"I don't have command," Pitt said with a thin smile, not because he cared about it but because he could hear the weariness in Drummond's voice, and the knowledge of Lambert's pain.

"What did the medical examiner say?" Drummond asked. "Hanging, just as it seemed?"

"Yes," Pitt replied carefully. "That's all, just hanging. That is what killed him."

Drummond turned around at last, frowning. "What do you mean, just hanging? That's enough to kill anyone. What more did you expect?"

"Poison, strangling, a blow to the head . . ."

"Whatever for, for heaven's sake? You hardly need to poison a man and then hang him."

"Would you stand still while someone put a noose around your neck, threw it over the chandelier hook and hauled you up by it?" Pitt asked.

307

Several expressions flashed across Drummond's face: comprehension, anger, impatience with himself, and then curiosity.

"Binding on his wrists?" he asked. "Ankles?"

"No—nothing. It requires some explanation, doesn't it?"

Drummond's frown deepened. "Where are you going next? You had better do something. I've had the assistant commissioner down here again. Nobody wants this thing dragged on any longer."

"You mean they don't want the Farriers' Lane case opened up any further," Pitt said bitterly.

Drummond's face tightened. "Of course not. It's extremely sensitive."

"I'll follow Paterson's last few days, from the time I spoke to him until he died," Pitt answered the urgent question.

"Let me know what you find."

"Yes sir, of course."

Lambert was little use. As Drummond had expected, he was still deeply shocked at the death in such a manner of one of his own men. He had questioned everyone in the lodging house, everyone in the street, all the men who had worked with Paterson or known him personally. He was no nearer finding who killed him.

But he did report to Pitt the record of Paterson's police duties for the last week of his life, and after tedious piecing together of testimony, times, places, Pitt realized there were considerable gaps in the account of his days when no one knew where he had been.

Pitt guessed he had gone to retrace his entire original investigation of the Farriers' Lane murder.

He began his own pursuit of Paterson by going back to the theater doorman. It was curiously dead at this time of the day; no color, only the gray daylight, no laughter and the shiver of expectancy before a performance, no actors or musicians entertaining the crowds, just women with mops sitting on the steps with the dregs of a cup of tea, reading the leaves.

Pitt found Wimbush in his small room just inside the stage door entrance.

"Yes sir. Mr. Paterson came back again." Wimbush screwed up his eyes in thought. "That'd be about six days ago, or maybe five."

"What did he say to you?"

"All about the murder o' Mr. Blaine, sir. Jus' like you did. An' I told 'im just the same as I told you."

"What did he say?"

"Nothin'. 'E just thanked me, and then went orf."

"Where to, do you know?"

"No sir, 'e din't say."

But Pitt did not need the doorman to tell him. He spoke to Tamar Macaulay's dresser, who told him the same. Paterson had seen her, and asked all the old questions. She had given him the same replies.

Pitt left the theater and turned north, towards Farriers' Lane. It was late afternoon on a cold, gray day with the pavements gleaming wet from the rain and the wind chasing rubbish along the gutters.

He passed beggars, street traders, peddlers and those with nothing to do but stand around huddled against the cold, looking for a place to shelter for the night, doorways to sleep in. A brazier with a one-armed man selling roasted chestnuts was a welcome glow in the gloom, and a small island of warmth. There were a dozen men standing around it.

It reminded Pitt of the men who had been idling near Farriers' Lane on the night Kingsley Blaine was murdered. He knew their names. They were there on the original records he had read in the beginning. He had read it again, to remind himself.

There was little chance of finding any of them now. They could have moved to other areas, found a better way of life, or a worse one. They could be ill, or dead, or in prison. Mortality was high, and five years a long time.

Had Paterson bothered to look for them? Or for the urchin, Joe Slater?

Surely he would have gone to the flower seller first? If she was still there.

And yet as he was within a few hundred yards, Pitt found himself drawn to Farriers' Lane.

He quickened his pace, striding over the wet cobbles with urgency, as though he might miss something if he hesitated. He turned the last corner and saw ahead of him, far on the left side, the narrow opening of Farriers' Lane, a black slit in the wall. He slowed his step. He wanted to see it, and at the same time it repelled him. His stomach clenched, his feet were numb.

He stopped opposite it. As Paterson had said, the street lamp was about twenty yards away. The wind was whining in the eaves of the roofs above him and rattling an old newspaper along the road. The half-light was dimming and the gas in the lamps had already been lit. Still Farriers' Lane was a dark gulf, impenetrable.

He stood roughly where the idlers had been that night and stared across the street. He could have seen a figure quite clearly, the darkness of a man walking would have been unmistakable. But unless he had stopped and faced him, under the light, he could not have seen his face.

He stepped out across the street and with faster beating pulse and a catch in his throat, went into Farriers' Lane.

It was narrow, smooth underfoot, but he could see almost nothing ahead of him except the outline of the last wall before the stable yard. There must be a light there; its glow was unmistakable even from the first yard or two. He imagined Kingsley Blaine having come this way as a shortcut to the club where he expected to meet Devlin O'Neil. Had he even thought of anyone as he stepped out of the uncertain light of the street into the shadows of the lane? Had the attack come as a complete surprise?

Pitt's footsteps rang on the stones, urgent, sharp with fear. The mist caught in his throat and his breath was uneven. He could see the lamp on the wall now illuminating the yard ahead of him. It had been a smithy. Now it was a brickyard. He walked out into it, slowly, trying to imagine what it had been like that night. What had Kingsley Blaine

310

seen? Who had been waiting there for him? Aaron Godman, the slender, mercurial actor dressed for the theater, a white silk scarf gleaming in the stable lamp, a long pointed nail in his hand? Or a dagger which no one had ever found? Surely that hardly mattered? It would be easy enough to lose such a thing, wouldn't it? Of course the police had searched and found nothing. All it needed was a drain.

Or had it been someone else? Joshua Fielding? Even Tamar herself—helping, urging him on.

That was a hideous thought and without knowing why he thrust it away from him.

He stood still, staring around him. That must be the old stable over to the left. Half a dozen boxes. One door was different from the others, newer.

He felt a little sick, the sweat cold on his body.

He turned and went back into the darkness of the alley, almost at a run. He burst out into the street again breathlessly, his heart beating in his throat, then stopped abruptly and stood for a minute. Then he walked on back towards Soho Square where the flower seller had her position.

He was traveling so rapidly now he bumped into people as he passed, his feet clattering on the pavement, his breath rasping.

The flower seller was there, a short, fat woman wrapped in a rust brown shawl. Automatically she pushed forward a bunch of mixed flowers and went into her singsong patter.

"Fresh flowers, mister? Buy a posy o' fresh flowers fer yer lady, sir? Picked today. Look, still fresh. Smell the country air in 'em, sir."

Pitt fished in his pocket and took out a threepenny piece. "Yes, please."

She did not ask if he wanted change, she simply clasped the coin and gave him two bunches of flowers, her face lighting up with relief. It was getting colder with the darkness and it seemed she had had a poor day.

"Been here long?" Pitt asked.

"Since six this morning, sir," she replied with a frown.

A couple passed by on the way to a party, her long skirts wet from the pavement, his silk hat gleaming.

"I mean have you had this place for many years?" Pitt asked the flower seller.

"Oh. Yeah, 'bout fourteen." Her eyes narrowed. "Why?"

"Then it was you who saw Aaron Godman after the Farriers' Lane murder?"

Somewhere over the far side of the square a horse squealed and a coachman swore.

"Beggin' yer pardon, sir, but what's that ter you?" she asked, squinting narrowly at him.

"Did you already know Mr. Godman?"

"I seen 'is picsher."

"What was he wearing that night, do you remember?"

"Coat, o' course, that time o' night. What else would 'e be wearin'?"

"Top hat? White silk scarf?"

"Go on wi' yer! 'E were an actor, not a toff—poor devil."

"You sound sorry for him."

"Wot if I were? That bastard Blaine did 'is sister up proper, poor bitch. 'Anged the poor soul anyway."

"Was he wearing a white scarf?"

"I already told yer, 'e were dressed for workin'!"

"No scarf. Are you sure?"

"Yeah! 'Ow many times do I 'ave ter tell yer? No scarf!"

"Have you seen Constable Paterson lately?"

"An' if I 'ave?"

Pitt reached into his pocket and produced a sixpence. "I'll have some more flowers."

Wordlessly she took the sixpence and handed him four bunches. He had to put them half in his left-hand pocket to hold them all. A couple of gentlemen in evening dress passed him, top hats gleaming, and looked at him with amusement.

"Have you seen Paterson in the last few days?" he said again.

"Yeah. 'E came 'ere day afore yesterday," she replied. "Asked me all the same questions again, 'e did. An' I answered 'em the same. Then the clock struck." She jerked her head backwards towards the building behind her. "An' 'e asked me about that."

"What about it? Wasn't that the clock that told you he was here at a quarter to one?"

"That's what Mr. Paterson said to me. 'E were positive it were. Couldn't shake 'im. In the end I could see as it must 'ave bin. But first off I said as it were quarter past midnight, as that's wot I thought it were! Yer see . . ." She squinted at him, making sure he was giving her his full attention. "Yer see, it's a funny kind o' clock, that. It don't ring once fer the quarter past, twice fer the 'alf, an' then three times for the quarter to, like most, but only once at the quarter to as well. 'E said it must 'a bin quarter past, cos of 'ow much I'd sold. But I first thought it were quarter to one, cos w'en that clock's bin cleaned, like it 'as now, it rings funny. Makes a kind o' whirring sound on the quarter to. Didn't do it that night." She opened her eyes very wide and suddenly frightened. "That means it were a quarter past midnight, don't it?"

"Yes . . ." Pitt said very slowly, a strange almost choking feeling welling up inside him, excitement, horror and amazement at once. "Yes, it does mean that, if you are sure. Quite sure? Did you see him take the hansom?"

"Yeah—from that corner there." She pointed.

"You sure?"

" 'Course I'm sure! I told Mr. Paterson that an' 'e looked sick. I thought 'e were goin' ter pass right out in front o' me. Poor bastard looked fit to drop dead 'isself."

"Yes." Pitt took out the rest of the change from his pocket and offered it to her, about two shillings and nine-pence halfpenny.

She stared at it incredulously, then put out her hand and grabbed it, pushing it deep into her pocket, holding her hand there.

"Yes, he would," Pitt said quietly. "If Aaron Godman bought flowers from you at quarter past midnight, and took a hansom cab straight home to Pimlico, then he could not

313

have been the one who murdered Kingsley Blaine in Farriers' Lane at half past."

"No," she said, shaking her head fractionally. "Come ter that, I don't suppose 'e could, poor little swine! Still, 'e's 'anged now—can't bring 'im back. God rest 'im."

10

PITT ARRIVED HOME a little before eleven o'clock, wet through from the steady rain, his face white, hair plastered over his brow. He took off his outer clothes in the hall and hung them on the hook, but the weight of the water in them pulled them off, and they lay in a sodden heap on the linoleum. He ignored them and went down the corridor towards the kitchen and the warmth of the stove where he could take off his soaking boots and thaw out his feet.

Charlotte met him at the kitchen door, her face startled and her hair loose around her shoulders. She had obviously been asleep in the rocking chair waiting for him.

"Thomas? Oh, you're wet through! What on earth have you been doing? Come in! Come—" Then she saw his face, the expression in his eyes. "What is it? What's happened? Is—is somebody else dead?"

"In a way." He slumped down in the chair beside the stove and began to unlace his boots.

She knelt in front of him and started on the other one.

"What do you mean, 'in a way'?"

"Aaron Godman. He didn't kill Blaine," he replied.

She stopped, her fingers curled around the wet laces, staring up at him.

"Who did?"

"I don't know, but it wasn't him. The flower seller was

wrong about the time, and Paterson discovered it the day he died. Maybe he knew who it was, and that was why he was killed."

"How can she have been wrong about the time? Didn't they question her properly?"

He told her about the clock, and the malfunction when it was cleaned. She finished undoing his boots, took them off and put them close to the stove to dry out, then his socks, and rubbed his frozen feet with a warm towel. He wriggled his toes in exquisite relief, explaining how Paterson had misunderstood, how he had pressed until his conviction that Godman was guilty had overridden the woman and she had given in.

"Poor Paterson," she said quietly. "He must have felt dreadful. I suppose it was his guilt over that which made him reckless for his own safety. He must have wanted desperately to put things right." She went to the kettle which was singing quietly on the back of the stove, and pulled it forward onto the hot plate to bring it right to the boil, reaching with the other hand for the teapot and the caddy.

"Why did he write to Judge Livesey and not to you, or to his own inspector?" she asked.

"I don't know." He continued rubbing his cold feet, rolling up his trousers to keep the wet fabric from his legs. "I suppose he thought Livesey had the power to reopen the case. I certainly hadn't, without some absolutely conclusive evidence, and even then I could only take it to the courts. Livesey could do it much more directly. And he was involved with the original appeal; in fact he was in charge of it. It was he who presented the judgment."

Charlotte poured the scalding water onto the tea and closed the lid of the pot. "I suppose he couldn't be . . . at fault, could he?"

"He had nothing to do with the original case," he replied. "He certainly couldn't have killed Blaine—and he couldn't have killed Paterson. He was at a dinner all evening until well into the small hours of the morning. By which time Paterson was dead. We can prove all that by the medical evidence, and also by the landlady's testimony of the time the outer doors were locked."

She brought the teapot to the kitchen table, and cups, milk from the pantry, and a large slice of brown bread, butter and pickle. She poured the tea, gave him his, and sat down opposite him as he began to eat hungrily.

"I suppose it must have been whoever killed Blaine," she said thoughtfully. "Paterson must have told them he knew, which means that he had worked it all out. I wonder how." She frowned. "I don't see how knowing it couldn't have been Godman tells him who it was."

"Nor do I," Pitt said with his mouth full. "Believe me, I've racked my mind over and over to think of what he could have seen or deduced which told him the answer—and I cannot think of it." He sighed. "I wish to heaven he'd told someone! It was only in retracing his steps I even discovered that he'd found out Godman wasn't guilty."

She held her mug of tea in both hands.

"Who have you told?" she asked very quietly.

"Drummond—only Drummond," he replied, watching her face. "It isn't something anyone wants to know. It means they were all wrong—the police, the lawyers, the original trial and jury, the appeal—everyone. Even the hangman executed an innocent man. I imagine he'll see that in his nightmares for a while." He shivered and hunched his shoulders as though it were cold in the kitchen, in spite of the stove. "And the newspapers, the public—everyone, except Joshua Fielding and Tamar Macaulay."

"What did Mr. Drummond say?"

"Not much. He knows as well as I do what the reaction is going to be."

"What will it be? They cannot deny it—can they?"

"I don't know." He set his mug down wearily. "There'll be a lot of anger, probably a lot of blame, everyone saying someone else should have known, should have been more competent, should have done something differently." He smiled with a bitter humor. "I think Adolphus Pryce is about the only one who will come out of it without blame of some sort. He was supposed to prosecute, and he did.

317

But Moorgate, Godman's solicitor, is going to feel guilty for not having believed his client, whatever he does about it now; and Barton James for not having pressed the flower seller harder—but then he believed Godman was guilty, so he wouldn't have seen any point. But he still had an innocent client, and let him be hanged."

He picked up the mug again but it was nearly empty. "And Thelonius Quade, who tried the first case, will be bound to wonder if he could have or should have directed something differently and found the truth. Lambert will feel guilty for having charged the wrong man—and just as bad, let the right one go, not only free but unsuspected, to kill again."

"And the appeal court judges," Charlotte added, reaching for his mug and refilling it. "They denied the appeal and confirmed the wrong verdict. They are not going to retreat easily." She passed him back the mug. "When will you tell Tamar Macaulay?"

"I don't know. I haven't even thought about that yet." He passed his hand over his eyes, rubbing them and shaking his head. "Tomorrow, maybe. Maybe later. I would really rather have a better idea of who it was before I tell her. I'm not sure enough what she'll do."

"Anyway"—she smiled bleakly—"not tonight. In the morning it will look different, maybe clearer."

He finished his tea. "I doubt it." He stood up. "But for the moment I don't care. Let us go to bed, before I get too tired to climb the stairs."

"Could it be Joshua Fielding?" Charlotte said over the breakfast table, her face pale with anxiety, watching Pitt as he spread his toast with marmalade. "Thomas, if it is, what am I going to do about Mama?"

Reluctantly he forced his mind to that problem. He did not want to face it. He had enough to occupy his mental and emotional energy with Paterson's death and the fact that Godman was innocent, but he heard the fear in her voice and he knew it was well founded.

"To begin with, don't tell her that Godman is innocent,"

he said slowly, thinking as he spoke. "If it is Fielding, she is much safer if he has no reason to think he is suspected."

"But if it is?" she said urgently, panic rising inside her. "If he murdered Blaine, and Judge Stafford, and Paterson—Thomas, he's—he's absolutely ruthless. He'll murder Mama, if he thinks he needs to, to be safe!"

"Which is exactly why you don't tell her Godman is innocent!" he replied decisively. "Charlotte! Listen to me—there is no point whatever in telling her Fielding might be guilty. She is in love with him."

"Oh, rubbish!" she said hotly, feeling a strange choking inside her, a sense of loneliness, almost of betrayal, as though she had been abandoned. It was absurd, and yet there was an ache in her throat at the thought of Caroline really in love, as she was in love with Pitt—emotionally, intimately. She took a deep breath and tried to compose herself. "That's nonsense, Thomas. She is attracted to him, certainly. He is interesting, a kind of person we don't even meet in the normal way of things. And she was concerned that justice should be done."

His voice cut across her. "Charlotte! I haven't time to argue with you. Your mother is in love with Joshua Fielding. I know you have been trying hard not to accept that, but you will have to. It is a fact, however you dislike it."

"No, it isn't!" She thrust it away from her. "Of course it isn't. Thomas, Mama is well over fifty!" She could feel the choking in her throat again, and a revulsion against the pictures that were forming in her imagination. Thomas should understand that. "It is friendship, that is all!" Her voice was growing higher and louder. She knew it was unfair, but she resented Emily being away in the west country and avoiding all this. She should have been here to help. This was a crisis.

Pitt was staring at her, irritation in his eyes.

"Charlotte, there is no time for self-indulgence! People don't stop falling in love because they are fifty—or sixty—or any other age!"

"Of course they do."

"When are you going to stop loving me? When you are fifty?"

"That's different," she protested, her voice thick.

"No, it isn't. Sometimes we grow a little more careful in what we do, because we have learned some of the dangers, but we go on feeling the same. Why shouldn't your mother fall in love? When you are fifty Jemima will think you as old and fixed as the framework of the world, because that is what you are to her—the framework of all she knows and that gives her safety and identity. But you will be the same woman inside as you are now, and just as capable of passions of all sorts: indignation, anger, laughter, outrage, making a fool of yourself, and of loving."

Charlotte blinked fiercely. It was stupid to feel so close to tears, and yet she could not help it.

Pitt put his hand over hers. Her fingers were stiff. She pulled away.

"What am I going to do about her?" she asked abruptly, sniffing hard. "If he killed Kingsley Blaine, not to mention Judge Stafford, and now poor Paterson, then he's about as dangerous as a man could be! He wouldn't think twice about killing her if he thought she was a threat to him." She sniffed again. "And if he didn't, how can I stop her behaving like a fool? People can, when they fall in love. I should have tried to discourage her sooner. I should have warned her—told her his faults. And she can't possibly marry him, even if he's totally innocent." She shook her head fiercely. "Even if he were to ask her—which of course he won't."

"If he asks her to marry him, you are going to do nothing," Pitt replied with a hard edge to his voice that took her by total surprise, leaving her staring at him in amazement.

"Nothing!" she protested. "But Thomas—"

"Nothing," he repeated. "Charlotte, I will tell her what we know of the case, in a few days, when I have weighed the evidence further. Then she will make her own decisions as to what to do."

"But, Thomas—"

"No!" His hand was warm and hard over hers. "I know what you are going to say, but it would do no good. My

320

dear, when did anyone in love listen to the good advice of their families? When you point out that he may be dangerous, guilty, unsuitable, unworthy, anything else you think of, the more she will be inclined to be loyal to him, even against her own better judgment."

"You make her sound so foolish." She pulled away, but he would not let her go.

"Not foolish, just in love."

She glared at him, tears prickling in her eyes. "Then you have got to find out whether he killed Kingsley Blaine or not. And if it wasn't he, then who was it?"

"I don't know. I suppose Devlin O'Neil."

She pushed her chair back, scraping the legs on the floor, and stood up. "Then I am going to find out more about them." She drew in her breath quickly. "And don't you dare tell me I mayn't. I shall be very discreet. No one will have the slightest idea why I am interested, or that I have the least suspicion of anything even immoral, let alone criminal." And before he could argue she swept out and raced up the stairs to start sorting through her gowns to see what she should wear to visit Caroline, Clio Farber, Kathleen O'Neil, or anyone else who might prove helpful in solving the Farriers' Lane case.

Actually she did not succeed in arranging anything until the day after, and that was with great difficulty, and the assistance of Clio Farber. It was something of a contrivance. Clio invited Kathleen O'Neil to meet her at the British Museum, a place Adah Harrimore much enjoyed visiting. It gave her the opportunity to walk around slowly (her health was still excellent), to gossip and stare at other people, while at the same time feeling that she was improving her mind, without obligation to any hostess, or the need for invitation, or a return of hospitality. One could wear what one pleased, come at any hour, and leave when one had had sufficient. It was the perfect answer to all the intricate rules and restrictions of social hierarchy and etiquette.

Clio informed Charlotte of this arrangement, and accidentally Charlotte bumped into them at the Egyptian exhibit at exactly quarter to three, with a show of surprise and pleasure. She had considered asking Caroline to come, and then rejected it, because she was not sure enough of her own ability not to betray her knowledge that Aaron Godman was innocent, and her consequent fear that Joshua was guilty. Devlin O'Neil was another matter altogether. She liked Kathleen and would grieve if he proved to be guilty, but her art of concealment was perfectly able to match that eventuality.

"How charming to see you," she said with just the right degree of surprise. "Good day, Mrs. Harrimore. I hope you are well?"

Adah Harrimore was dressed in dark brown with a sable trim and a hat which had been extremely elegant a couple of seasons ago and had since been altered to mask its year of vogue.

"I dislike the winter, but I am quite well, thank you," she replied with an air of graciousness. "And you, Miss Pitt?"

"Very well, thank you. I do agree with you, the cold can be most disagreeable. But you know, I don't think I should care for the heat such as they have in Egypt either." She looked with intensity at the artifacts on display in the case in front of them: copper instruments, shards of pottery and beautiful turquoise and lapis beads. A small glass jar caught her attention in particular. "It makes one wonder about the lives of the people who fashioned and wore these, doesn't it?" she went on enthusiastically. "Do you suppose they were so very different from us, or if actually their feelings were much the same?"

"Quite different," Adah said decisively. "They were Egyptian—we are English."

"That will affect our habits, and the clothes we wear, our houses, what we eat. But do you think it changes the way we feel, and what we value?" Charlotte asked as politely as she could. It was a quite genuine question, but the fierce and instant response from Adah had startled her, and she saw something in the old woman's face which disturbed her. It was not merely an opinion which would not be moved, it was a flicker of fear, as though there were some-

322

thing dangerous in the alien quality of those people from another land, and so long dead.

Adah looked at the artifacts, and then at Charlotte.

"If you forgive my saying so, Miss Pitt, you are very young, and consequently naive. I daresay you have had little experience of peoples of other races. Even if they are born here in England, and grow up amongst us, they still have an element which is different. Blood will tell. You may teach a child as much as you wish; in the end his heritage will come through."

They were passed by two ladies in the height of fashion who inclined their heads graciously and continued walking.

Adah smiled stiffly. "How can you expect those who are born elsewhere," she continued to Charlotte, "and grow up among totally different beliefs, to have anything in common with us but the most superficial manners? No, my dear Miss Pitt, I do not think they feel as we do about anything at all—at least anything of sensitivity or moral value. Why should they?"

Charlotte opened her mouth to reply, then realized she had no answer which would not sound either trite or rude.

"They worshiped fearful gods, with heads like animals." Adah warmed to her subject. "And they tried to preserve the corpses of their dead! For goodness sake! We may find them most interesting to learn of, edifying to know the past, I am sure, and uplifting to realize how superior is our own culture. But to imagine we have anything in common with them is sheer folly."

Charlotte scrambled for some dim recollection out of her schoolbooks.

"Was there not a pharaoh who believed in one god?" she enquired.

Adah's eyebrows rose. "I have no idea. But he was not our God—that is beyond question. Pharaoh tried to kill Moses, and all his people! That was unarguably wicked. No one who believed in the real God would do such a thing."

"People sometimes do terrible things to their enemies, especially when they are afraid."

A shadow passed over Adah's face, something in her

eyes that for a moment froze. Then with a supreme effort it was conquered, and vanished.

"That is perfectly true, of course. But it is in moments of panic that our deeper natures are exposed, and you will find that foreigners will behave differently from us, because at heart they are different. That is not to say that some of them do not create most beautiful things, and know much that we may benefit from seeing."

A governess in plain brown stood at the next exhibit, her twelve-year-old charge giggling at a bust of a long-dead queen.

"I find that particularly true of the Greeks," Adah continued, her voice raised. "Some of their architecture is quite marvelous. Of course they were a people of most exquisite self-discipline, and sense of proportion. My grandson-in-law, Mr. O'Neil, whom you met, has been to Athens. He said that the Parthenon is beyond description. He finds the Greeks most uplifting. He admires the work of Lord Byron, which I admit I find somewhat questionable. I greatly prefer our own Lord Tennyson. You know where you are with Lord Tennyson."

Charlotte gave up without further struggle. To continue to argue would lose her far more than she could possibly gain. And the look in Adah's eyes still haunted her mind.

"That must have been a wonderful experience," she said dutifully. "Are there good Greek exhibits here?"

"Most certainly. Let us go and see some of the urns and vases. This way, I think!" And with a sweeping gesture Adah led the way out of the Egyptian hall and into the next chamber.

Charlotte passed Clio and Kathleen on the steps. She smiled, then hurried after Adah, catching up with her just as they entered the room where the Greek artifacts were displayed.

"How very fortunate of Mr. O'Neil to have been able to go to Greece," she said conversationally. "Was it recently?"

"About seven years ago," Adah replied.

"Did Mrs. O'Neil go with him?" Charlotte kept her voice

politely interested, although she knew Kathleen had been married to Kingsley Blaine then.

"No," Adah said flatly. "That was before their marriage. But no doubt they will go again some time in the future. I take it you have not been to Greece, Miss Pitt?"

"No, I am afraid not. That is why it is so fortunate to be able to come to the museum and see such lovely things here. Have you been, Mrs. Harrimore?"

"No. No, I never traveled. My husband did not care to." A look of bleak unhappiness crossed her face, a tightness of the skin and of the muscles beneath as if a pain uglier than mere grief had been reopened.

"It does not suit everyone," Charlotte said quietly, answering the words because the feeling was too private to acknowledge, and too subtle to understand. "Some people become quite ill, especially at sea."

"So I believe," Adah said through thin lips.

"And it can be very costly," Charlotte went on, walking in step with her. "If the family is large. One does not always wish to leave younger children behind for long periods of time, and yet one also does not feel advised to take them where the climate may not be healthy, the food will certainly not be what they are accustomed to, and one has no idea what medical help may be available. There are many reasons for such a decision."

Adah stared at a large marble figure of a woman clothed in fine drapes, her body solid, massive, and yet the very lines of the stone giving it all such a simple and fluid grace one felt a draft might move the suggested fabric. It was chipped, the face disfigured, and yet it still had a grave loveliness.

"We were not a large family." Adah spoke to the statue, not to Charlotte. "There is only Prosper, no more."

They stood close in front of the statue. Clio and Kathleen had followed them and were admiring some exhibit at the far end of the room, and out of earshot. Adah seemed to have forgotten them, and there was no one else except two elderly gentlemen, one apparently lecturing the other on the artistic merits of a vase. Her emotions consumed her, as if she had found a place of complete privacy where she could relax her inner vigilance for a few moments before taking up the burden again. She looked tired, and oddly naked.

Charlotte wished she could touch her, extend some comfort less crass than words, but it would have been intrusive and impertinent on so short an acquaintance—and considering their respective ages. And always at the edge of her mind was Aaron Godman. Funny how she had given him a face, although she had never met him, nor seen a likeness.

"What a shame. Mr. Harrimore is a man of such character . . ."

"You do not understand." Adah stared at the stone figure ahead of her a moment longer, then moved on to a fine black and terra-cotta vase with figures around it in a scene of debauchery Charlotte was quite sure the older woman did not see, in spite of her fixed eyes. Her expression would never have retained that intense, painful immobility if she had. "You are very naive, Miss Pitt, and no doubt your remarks are well meant . . ."

Such damnation in the turn of a phrase. But Charlotte quashed her instinctive rebellion and continued.

"I—I don't think I see—"

"Of course you don't," Adah agreed. "You have never had to, and with God's grace you never will. He is flawed, Miss Pitt."

Charlotte was confused. It was an extraordinary thing for a woman to say of her son, and yet, looking at Adah's face, there was no doubt she meant it passionately. It was not a passing remark, but something which troubled her so much it remained in the forefront of her mind.

Charlotte fumbled for something to say in reply.

"Are we not all flawed in one way or another, Mrs. Harrimore?"

"Of course we are none of us perfect." Adah moved on from the vase to a set of shards which composed pieces of dishes of an earlier period, again without seeing them as anything but a faint blur. "That is trite, and perfectly obvious. Prosper has a clubfoot. I cannot believe you failed to notice it."

"Oh—yes, I see what you mean."

"What did you imagine I meant? Never mind! Never mind. It is not serious, not a crippling thing, not fatal. But other children—once the well is poisoned . . ." Suddenly she recollected where they were and pulled her shoulders back sharply as if coming to attention. "I should not have spoken of myself. It is hardly the uplifting and educational experience you were seeking. Talk of my husband"—again the bitterness crossed her face—"is not edifying for you. Let us go and see some of the Chinese exhibits. A very clever people, not even European, let alone English, but I believe most civilized, after their own fashion, and a great many years ago. Heaven only knows what they are now, of course! We were at war with them over something or other when I was a girl. We won—naturally."

"Would those have been the opium wars?" Charlotte struggled to recall her fairly recent history. "In the eighteen-fifties?"

"Quite possibly that was the name of them," Adah conceded. "Certainly it was just after the war in the Crimea, and then the awful mutiny in India. We seemed to be always at war with someone in those days. Of course our dear Queen had only been on the throne for twenty years. Now it is quite different. Everyone knows who we are, and they have more sense than to start wars with us."

Such monumental assurance was unanswerable, and Charlotte was happy enough to see Clio and Kathleen O'Neil in the distance, and attracted their attention with a smile.

Some thirty minutes later they left the exhibits and retired to take afternoon tea and converse about various subjects such as fashion, one's health, the weather, the Princess of Wales, the books one had read, all harmless and quite suitable for such an occasion.

"How is your dear Mama?" Kathleen enquired courteously, looking at Charlotte over the cucumber sandwiches. "I do hope she will be able to join us, perhaps for an evening at the opera, or the theater?"

"I am sure she would love to," Charlotte said with more

honesty than they knew. "I shall tell her that you mentioned it. It is most kind of you to ask. She has taken something of an interest in the theater lately. My Papa died some few years ago, and since then she has not gone out to such places as much as she used. She is just beginning to enjoy it again."

"Very natural," Adah agreed, nodding her head. "One has to mourn for a certain period. It is expected. But after that, one must continue one's life."

"I know she has become fast friends with Joshua," Clio said quickly, smiling. "Indeed, it is really quite romantic."

"Romantic?" Adah said stiffly. Then she swiveled around to Charlotte, her eyebrows raised.

"Well . . ." Charlotte hesitated, then she took a decision she was afraid she might desperately regret. "Yes—yes, it is. I have—I am not quite sure how I feel. Perhaps the word is *apprehensive*."

Clio continued to eat and reached for a tiny cream cake.

Kathleen glanced at Adah, then at Charlotte, and changed the subject.

When they rose to leave, Adah grasped Charlotte by the arm and drew her aside, her face tense, her eyes full of pain.

"My dear Miss Pitt, I do not know how to put this to you without seeming intrusive in what is your most private affair, but I cannot stand by and say nothing. Your mother is in a most vulnerable situation, bereaved of her husband, alone in the world, and quite naturally wishing to move into society again. But really—an actor!"

Charlotte agreed with her intensely, and at the same time instinctively rushed to defend Caroline. "He is very agreeable," she said with a gulp. "And a pillar of his profession."

"That is immaterial!" Adah's voice was fierce, her grasp on Charlotte's arm painful. "He is a Jew! You cannot possibly allow your mother to have—to have anything but—how can I say this with the remotest delicacy? For love of heaven, my dear, you cannot allow her to have relations with him!"

Charlotte felt herself blushing hotly. The idea was repel-

328

lent to her, not because of anything to do with Joshua Fielding, but because she could not imagine her mother in such a situation. It was profoundly ... distressing, offensive.

"I can see you had not thought of it," Adah went on, misreading her reaction entirely, thinking only of the word *Jew*. "Of course not. You are innocent. But my dear, it is not impossible—and then your mother would be ruined! Of course it is not as if she were still of childbearing age, so it would not contaminate her, but all the same."

"Contaminate?" Charlotte was confused.

"Naturally." Adah's face was twisted with pain, pity, memory of something too ugly for her to speak of. "Having"—she hesitated on the word—"union—with a Jew—will leave a person ... different. It is not something one can explain to a maiden lady of any sensibility at all. But you must believe me!"

Charlotte was speechless.

Adah mistook her silence for doubt.

"It is perfectly true," she said urgently. "I swear it. God forgive me, I should know!" Her voice was raw with shame and misery. "My husband, like many men, satisfied his appetites beyond the walls of his own home, only he did it with a Jewess. I was with child at the time. That is why poor Prosper is deformed." She caught her breath on the word as though the act of forcing it through her lips was a further wound to her. "And why I never had another child."

Suddenly Charlotte saw the barren years, the shame, the sense of betrayal, of being unclean, which had lasted even until now. She felt a pity so intense she longed to reach out and put some kind of balm on the wound. And yet she was also revolted. It was alien to all her beliefs to imagine that there was a kind of human being who was so different that union with them was unclean, not because of immorality or disease, but simply by the nature of their race.

She did not know what to say, but Adah's passionate face demanded some reply.

"Oh." She felt idiotically inadequate. "I am sure—I am

329

sure my mother is unaware of that." It was the only thing she could think of to say, and at least that much was true.

"Then if you have any care for her at all, you must tell her," Adah urged intensely. "Never mind her age in life," she went on. "It is the beginning of downfall. Who knows what may be next? Now we must join the others, or they will wonder what is amiss. Come!"

The day after the trip to the museum, Charlotte accompanied Caroline, at Caroline's invitation, to visit Joshua Fielding and Tamar Macaulay at the theater, after rehearsal and before the evening performance. Charlotte felt acutely uncomfortable. It was one of the least enjoyable times she had ever spent in her mother's company. She longed to be able to tell her that Pitt knew Aaron Godman had been innocent, but she had promised Pitt she would not, and she knew his reasons for demanding such a thing were excellent. But still she felt deceitful, and she doubted Caroline would understand, even when she knew the full truth.

She was also horribly afraid that perhaps Joshua Fielding was the one who had murdered and crucified Kingsley Blaine, and then poisoned Judge Stafford because he was going to reopen the case—and now killed Constable Paterson because he also knew the truth.

And if he were not guilty, but it was Devlin O'Neil, or someone else, then what if Caroline did have an affair with him? How could Charlotte possibly govern her emotions about that? She could not be happy for it. And all the reasoning in the world, and Pitt's arguments, which were so sensible, still did not alter the way she felt.

So she accompanied Caroline, who looked less smart than was her custom a few months ago, and definitely younger. She was not in the height of fashion at all, rather more in the romantic vision of the pre-Raphaelites, her gown with a design of flowers and leaves, her hair more loosely dressed, and no hat at all.

They were welcomed at the theater door and permitted in as if they were old friends, which in itself disturbed Charlotte. The rehearsal was just coming to an end. It was a comedy, although there were highly dramatic elements. Even as an amateur with very little experience of the theater, Charlotte could see the skill in the timing of a line, the precise inflection of a voice, the gesture of a hand, the line of the body. It fascinated her to see how much greater was the skill of Tamar Macaulay than that of any of the others on the stage; and how much more her eye was drawn to Joshua than to the other men. It was not that he concerned her personally, or that Caroline never took her eyes from him, it was that he had a magnetism which would have compelled anyone.

When the final line was delivered, almost before Mr. Passmore gave them leave to go, Tamar turned and came towards Charlotte, her vivid face tense, her eyes searching. Charlotte was taken by surprise. She had not even thought Tamar aware of her presence; her concentration had seemed total. She did not bother with any formality.

"Charlotte! How good to see you. I had feared you had abandoned us. I would hardly blame you." She took Charlotte by the arm and guided her away from the wings where they had been waiting and along a bare-board passage. "We have been trying for five years, and achieved nothing. It was most unfair of me to place my hopes upon you, and in a matter of weeks. I am most sincerely sorry, and the inexcusable thing is that I shall certainly go on doing it. I cannot help it." She took a deep breath, facing Charlotte, her black eyes burning. "I still do not believe Aaron was guilty. I don't believe he could have killed Kingsley, and I am quite sure he would not have done that to him afterwards." A brief, ironic smile crossed her lips and there was a catch in her voice. "And he cannot have poisoned Judge Stafford."

"Or hanged Constable Paterson," Charlotte added impulsively.

Tamar blinked. "Hanged Constable Paterson?" she said confusedly. "Why was he hanged? Was it he who killed Judge Stafford? But why? And how can he be hanged so soon? I didn't even read of a trial."

"He was not executed," Charlotte explained. "He was

331

murdered. We don't know why, or by whom, but it seems most probable that it had to do with the Farriers' Lane case, although of course it is not certain."

Tamar reached past her and opened the door to the small, cramped dressing room. It was filled with costumes on a rail in one corner, a hamper with petticoats spilling out in another, a table with a mirror, jars of greasepaint and powder, and three stands with wigs. But as she was the leading actress, it was at least private.

"Tell me," she demanded, leading the way in, pushing a chair around for Charlotte and then leaning backward to close the door again.

"Constable Paterson was the—" Charlotte began.

"I know who he was," Tamar interrupted. "What happened to him?"

"He was murdered," Charlotte said simply. "Someone came in the late evening and hanged him from the chandelier fitting in his own bedroom."

"You mean attacked him?" Tamar was incredulous. "Did he not fight to defend himself?"

"It seems not." Charlotte shook her head. "Perhaps it was someone he knew, and he did not expect to be harmed, and the person contrived to get behind him and garotte him."

"I suppose it could have happened like that," Tamar agreed, coming away from the door into the room. It had an odd smell, unfamiliar, at once musty and exciting. "It is the only thing which seems to make sense," Tamar went on. "But who, and why? At the time of the trial I certainly hated the man." Her face wrinkled with the pain of memory. "He hated Aaron so much. He was not dispassionate, he was full of rage, his voice shook when he was in the witness box. I remember him very clearly. And I believe it was he who beat Aaron, although Aaron would never say—at least not to me. But I think that was to protect me." She stopped, for a moment having to struggle to keep any control at all. She turned away, fumbling for a handkerchief, bumping against one of the wig stands. Suddenly all the fear and the terror were back again, as if Aaron Godman were still alive, still suffering . . .

Charlotte could hardly bear to keep silent. It was only the knowledge of Caroline a few yards away, with Joshua Fielding, which held her from telling Tamar now that Aaron was innocent, and at last Pitt could prove it.

Nothing anyone could say would heal the past, words would be stupid and only betray a complete failure to understand. The only balm was to speak of something else.

"Don't give up hope," she said quietly to Tamar's stiff, shaking back. "We are very close to the end now. I cannot yet tell you, but I am not simply speaking to comfort you. It really is close—I give you my word!"

Tamar stood absolutely still, then very slowly she turned around to face Charlotte. For several moments she did not speak but searched Charlotte's face, trying to judge both her sincerity and her actual knowledge.

"Would it be pointless to ask you how you know?" she said almost under her breath. "Why you can say that?"

"Yes," Charlotte replied. "If I could tell you I would have. But please believe me—it is true."

Tamar took a deep breath and then swallowed hard. "Aaron will be cleared?"

"Please, don't ask me to say any more now—and if you wish it to happen, say nothing to anyone—not even to Mr. Fielding. He may inadvertently say or do something which will ruin everything. I believe that Aaron did not do it—but I have no idea who did."

Tamar smiled with a sad, ironic humor, sitting a little sideways on the clothes hamper.

"What you mean is you think it may have been Joshua," she answered.

"Is that impossible?" Charlotte said very quietly.

Tamar sat a little farther back.

"I would like to say that of course it is, but I assume you are asking not for emotions but for reason. No, it is not impossible. He said he did not know whether Kingsley would have married me or not, and would not have interfered anyway; and that he went home straight from the theater that night. But there is no way he can prove it." She lifted her chin a little. "I don't believe it was him, but I don't imagine that will weigh heavily with you."

"I cannot allow it to," Charlotte replied, knowing that was less than the truth. Part of her wished it to be Joshua. It would remove any threat from Caroline. It would end the uncertainty, the odd mixture of loss and anger, tenderness and jealousy. Jealousy! At least she had recognized the feeling, and the very pain of naming it was partially healing.

"No, of course not." Tamar squared her shoulders and smiled. She stood up again, the wicker of the hamper squeaking. "Shall we take some tea? I am sure you must be cold, and quite ready to sit comfortably and talk of something more cheerful . . ." She hesitated at the door.

"Yes?" Charlotte waited.

"If I can help, you will tell me?" Tamar asked anxiously.

"Of course."

Caroline was still standing on the edge of the stage when Joshua Fielding turned and smiled at her. He must have known she was there, even though his attention had apparently been on the other actors. She felt a sudden warmth, as if the sun had come out from the clouds. She wanted to move forward to him, but reticence held her back.

He waited a few moments, speaking to Clio, then an older actress, congratulating her with a touch on the arm. Mr. Passmore addressed them all, except Tamar, who had disappeared, giving last-minute instructions for the evening's performance, encouragement, criticism, praise, prophecy of a magnificent success, carefully guarded by superstitious formulae against the bad luck of overconfidence. Amulets were touched, hands went to pockets for lucky pieces to reassure for the umpteenth time that they were still there. When he had finished he turned away, a large figure in a frock coat and flowing tie, and Joshua came over to Caroline.

But instead of greeting her with words of welcome and enquiry as ordinary courtesy dictated, he simply met her eyes, the questions understood between them. It was a familiarity which warmed her far more than she expected, and left her wishing for words, and finding none of them satisfactory.

"Was that Charlotte I saw with you?" Joshua asked quietly.

"Yes—yes, she wished to come."

He took her by the arm and guided her away from the stage wings towards the audience seats, out of earshot of the others, and into the half shadow.

"Is she still pursuing Kingsley's death?" he asked very quietly, his voice filled with anxiety.

"Of course," she replied, meeting his eyes. "We can hardly give up."

"I don't think she needs to anymore." He spoke as if he were feeling his way through complicated thoughts. "Since Judge Stafford's death the police are involved. It is no longer as if it could be forgotten or marked as closed. Poor Aaron cannot be blamed for this. Please, Caroline, persuade her to leave it to those whose profession it is."

"But they have not been very successful so far," she reasoned. She felt a stab of guilt towards Pitt, but her fear for Joshua far outweighed it. "They have not succeeded yet. It does not appear they suspect either Mrs. Stafford or Mr. Pryce, in fact the very contrary. They are persuaded they are innocent."

"Are you sure?"

"Certainly I am sure. Thomas would not lie to me."

He smiled, a mixture of affection and amusement. "Are you sure, my dear? Might he not tell you something less than the truth, in the knowledge that you have formed a friendship for Tamar"—he colored very faintly—"and for me, which might incline you to be biased in the matter?"

She felt the heat burn in her cheeks. "He might well tell me less than the truth, but he would not fabricate something gratuitously," she replied. "I have come to know him quite well over the years. He was certainly not my choice of a husband for my daughter, it is true, but I have learned that there are occasions when a man who is socially unsuitable may make one far happier than any man one's friends or one's family may have chosen—" She stopped, realizing she had spoken her thoughts too frankly. They were capable of interpretation for herself, as well as for Charlotte.

He made as if to respond, then changed his mind, cleared his throat and began again, but she did not miss the momentary flash of laughter in his eyes.

"All the same, I think it would be well for Charlotte to leave the matter," he said gravely. "It may become dangerous. If it was not Aaron, then it was someone else, someone who obviously does not hesitate to kill again, and again, if he feels endangered. I have no idea whether Charlotte will come close enough to him for that, but she may, even without knowing it. She and Clio have become friendly with Kathleen O'Neil. I can only imagine it is to pursue Devlin. If he realizes that, or only fears it . . ." He left the rest unsaid.

Caroline was torn. Was Charlotte really in danger? More than she had been in every other case in which she had helped? Who would suspect a woman, an ordinary wife and mother? "Of being overly inquisitive, perhaps," she said aloud. "Of being vulgar in her curiosity. Of trying to intrude where she has no—no right of background or breeding." How disloyal she sounded. "But that is not dangerous, merely undignified and possibly absurd."

"Judge Stafford is dead, and so, I read, is Constable Paterson," he pointed out.

"But they were officers of the law," she argued vehemently. "And you say she and Miss Farber are pursuing Devlin O'Neil. But the police are far more likely to pursue you. Have you no fear for yourself?"

"Caroline!" He took both her hands in his, gently but holding her too hard for her to withdraw. "Caroline! Of course I have. But what kind of friend would you consider me if I placed my own fear of being suspected ahead of Charlotte's danger from whoever really killed Kingsley— and the others? Please, tell her she must leave the matter altogether. I am too afraid that it may really have been Devlin O'Neil. I cannot think of anyone else it could be—except

336

some madman. But if it was that, there would surely have been others the same, and there have not been."

"And what about you?" she said urgently, still in her own mind clinging to the hope that Charlotte might solve it, as she had other crimes in the past. "The police were wrong once, and there was nobody who could save Aaron."

"I know that, my dear, but it does not alter the situation." His voice was very gentle, his hands over hers warm, but his hold was hard and there was no wavering in his eyes. "I know the police suspect me. I will at least have a trial, and a chance to appeal. Whoever is killing people will not give Charlotte as much."

"No," she said quietly. "No, I suppose not. I will tell her."

He smiled, letting go of her hands but at the same time taking her arm. "Shall we go somewhere pleasant and take afternoon tea? We can forget the world and its dangers and suspicions, tonight's performance, and simply think how much we enjoy talking. There are so many other things." He started to move and pull her gently with him. "I have just read a fascinating book about a journey of the imagination. Quite impossible to turn into a play, of course, but I am still enormously enriched to have read it. Provoked all kinds of thoughts—and questions. I shall tell you about it, if I may? I want to know what you think."

Caroline gave in to the sheer pleasure of it. Why not? She wished this sweet intimacy could last forever, but she was realist enough to know that of course Grandmama was right; it was a dream, a delusion, and waking would be much the colder afterwards. But it was not afterwards yet, and she would give all her heart to it while she could.

"Of course," she agreed with a smile. "Please tell me."

"You 'aven't said anyfink about the murder for days, ma'am," Gracie said to Charlotte the next morning as they were working in the kitchen. Gracie was cleaning the knives with Oakey's Wellington knife polish, made of emery and black lead; and Charlotte cleaned the spoons and forks with a homemade mixture of hartshorn powder, water and alcohol.

"That is because I haven't learned anything further," she explained, pulling a face. "We know it wasn't Aaron Godman, but we are no nearer knowing who it really was."

"Don't we know nuffink at all?" Gracie said, squinting around the knife she was holding up.

"Yes, of course we know some things," Charlotte replied, polishing industriously. "It was someone who knew his name and that he was at the theater, and deliberately sent him to a place where he would pass through Farriers' Lane to get there. And to do what was done to him, they must have hated him very much indeed." She reached for a fresh cloth to raise a shine. "Apart from the obscenity of it, it would be dangerous to remain there any longer than necessary after having killed him. The rage must have outweighed the sense of self-preservation."

"You're tellin' me," Gracie said with feeling. "If I'd just murdered someone I wouldn't 'ang around to nail 'im up to a door—which can't 'a' bin easy!" She tipped more polish out of the tin into a saucer. "I'd 'ave been out o' there as fast as me legs 'd carry me! Afore anyone else came an' found me there!"

"So it was someone so overcome with hatred they would rather take the risk, or else they didn't even think of it," Charlotte concluded.

"Or else . . ." Gracie rubbed the knife blade furiously. It was already shining. "Or else it were someone wot 'ad another reason for doin' it—like to put the blame on someone else. Which since poor Godman was 'anged fer it, worked very well."

"But how did crucifying him put the blame on Aaron Godman?" Charlotte asked, passing the buffing cloth to Gracie.

"Well, it made everyone think it were someone as were Jewish," Gracie reasoned.

"But a Christian person wouldn't do that, surely?"

"Maybe 'e would! Maybe that's exactly what 'e would do, if 'e 'ated Jews and wanted 'em blamed."

"Why would anyone hate Jews that much?" But already Charlotte's mind was racing over the Harrimores, Adah's beliefs, Devlin O'Neil's knowledge that Kingsley Blaine was in love with Tamar Macaulay, a Jewess. Perhaps in some twisted way he had hated not only Blaine but all the theater people, and when he killed Blaine he had suddenly thought of a way to implicate someone else in the crime.

"You don't think so, do you, ma'am?" Gracie said, watching her face carefully. "You still fink as it were Mr. Fielding, 'im wot Mrs. Ellison likes."

"I don't know, Gracie. I suppose it could be Mr. O'Neil. Part of me wishes it were. Mama is going to be terribly hurt if it is Mr. Fielding. And yet if it isn't . . ." She sighed, and refrained from saying what was in her mind.

"You shouldn't ought to worry so much, ma'am," Gracie said, her little face puckering up with anxiety, the knives momentarily ignored. "Mrs. Ellison'll do what she wants ter, and there in't nothing you nor the master can say as'll change it. But I do understand as yer gotter know 'oo done the murder in Farriers' Lane. An' I keep on thinking about it, like." She stopped even pretending to work and put her cloth down, staring at Charlotte with total concentration. "That lad wot took the message across the street to Mr. Blaine at the door. If the master could speak to 'im proper, away from all them other rozzers, maybe 'e'd be able ter say summink more as ter wot the man were like." Her face was sharp with hope. "The rozzers before, the ones wot did the case in the beginning, they told 'im as it were Mr. Godman. Well, bein' as 'e were just a lad on the street, 'e wouldn't want ter argue wiv 'em, would 'e? But bein' as you know it weren't Mr. Godman, maybe 'e'd say summink 'elpful?"

"Mr. Pitt found him," Charlotte said with a bleak smile. "He wouldn't say anything that was helpful at all, I'm afraid. But it was a good idea."

"Oh." Gracie renewed her polishing, but her face was deep in thought, and she said little more for the rest of the morning, except to look very carefully at Charlotte just before they began peeling the vegetables for dinner.

"You goin' ter the theater termorrow wif them 'Arrimores?"

"Yes."

"Well, you be careful, ma'am! If it were that Mr. O'Neil as done it, then 'e's a very wicked man, an' 'e don't care nuffink for nobody 'cept 'isself. Don't you go askin' questions."

"I shall be very careful," Charlotte promised. But there was a sinking feeling in the bottom of her stomach and a catch in her throat, as if she were close to something that would prove to be very dreadful.

Charlotte felt guilty that Pitt was not included in the evening visit to the theater because it was such a vivid, exciting event quite apart from any information that might be gleaned from the Harrimores or the O'Neils. But had Pitt come it would almost certainly have put an end to any discussion at all, now, and in the future.

So with an effort of will she followed Caroline up the wide stairs behind Kathleen O'Neil on Devlin's arm, and Adah Harrimore leaning heavily on Prosper, who, although he limped in an ungainly fashion, seemed to feel no pain in his foot. Presumably the limp's cause was the deformity with which he was born, and not a degenerative disease.

The entire foyer was filled with people. The chandeliers blazed so one could barely look at them, shedding cascades of light. Jewels sparkled in elaborate coiffures and at arms, throats and wrists, and on hands. Feathers waved as heads turned. Pale shoulders gleamed amid bowers of silk, taffeta, voile and velvet of every shade, the pallor of lilies, the warmth of peach and rose, the flaring vibrancy of scarlet, magenta and blue, and behind them all the stark black and white of dinner suits.

Everywhere was the rustle and whisper of fabric, the murmur of voices, every few moments a burst of laughter.

Charlotte turned once on the stairs to look behind her and remember it all, the quickening of the pulse, the overflowing life, the expectancy as if a thousand people all knew that something thrilling was about to happen.

340

Then Caroline pulled at her arm and obediently she went on up and around the wide balcony towards the Harrimores' box, where she and Caroline were offered center seats, as guests, between Adah on their left and Kathleen on their right. The two men sat on the outside a little to the rear. It was some fifteen or twenty minutes before the performance was due to begin. Watching others arrive was a great deal of the pleasure of such an event, and of course being seen oneself.

A very handsome woman walked up the aisle beneath them, dressed in shades of fuchsia and palest pink, her black hair piled luxuriantly, her step graceful, but nonetheless a slight swagger. She looked from right to left, smiling a little.

"Who is she?" Charlotte asked quietly.

"I don't know," Caroline replied. "She is certainly most striking."

Kathleen gave a very tiny laugh, and stifled it immediately.

"No one," Adah answered crisply. "She is no one."

Charlotte was puzzled.

Adah turned to face her, her expression a mixture of amusement and distaste.

"Such persons may pass in front of you, my dear, but you do not see them. To a lady, they are invisible."

"Oh—oh, I see. She is . . ."

"Precisely." Adah waved her arm very slightly towards one of the boxes farther around the tier of the balcony. "On the other hand, or perhaps not. That is Mrs. Langtry—the Jersey Lily."

Charlotte did not bother to hide her smile. "Has anyone ever seen Mr. Langtry? I've never even heard him mentioned."

"I have," Adah answered dryly. "But I shall not repeat what was said—poor man."

She obviously meant it, so Charlotte did not ask. Instead she looked farther around the tier of boxes for other people of interest. It did not take her long to observe that at least half those she watched were turned towards one particular box over on the far side where there was a considerable amount of coming and going, of both men and women. The men especially were dressed in the height of fashion, although what fashion was harder to say. Their hair was far longer than customary, they were clean-shaven, and large, floppy ties overflowed their collars. However, there was an elegance about them, almost a languor, which was quite distinctive.

"Who are they?" Charlotte asked, her interest piqued. "Are they critics?"

"I doubt it," Devlin replied with a smile. "Actors come frequently very well dressed, but a little more conventionally than that. They are almost certainly members of the aesthete set, very self-consciously artistic of soul, even if not necessarily of output. I am afraid Mr. Gilbert guyed them terribly in his opera *Patience*. You should see it; it is extremely entertaining, and the music is delightful."

"I shall, quite definitely." She smiled back at him cordially, then suddenly remembered what she was here for. She froze, still looking at him. For a moment the situation struck her with all its farcical quality. They were dressed in their very best clothes, he in black dinner suit with gold cuff links, and onyx and mother of pearl studs, she in a gown borrowed from Caroline and retrimmed to be more up to date, but a shade of dark wine which suited her marvelously, and she knew it, deep at the bosom and with only a tiny bustle. They were here as guests of Prosper Harrimore, waiting for the curtain to go up on the stage where the people who had brought them together by virtue of a notorious tragedy were going to play out a comedy of manners, all saying words no one meant, on stage or off it. And all the time she was trying to determine whether he was the person who had murdered and crucified Kingsley Blaine and allowed Aaron Godman to be hanged for it.

Devlin O'Neil was looking at her curiously.

She forced her eyes away, turning her head to look back at the great sweep of the auditorium, the boxes tier on tier, plush lined, filled now with expectant people, the pallor of their faces turned towards the stage. Their own dramas were played out, or temporarily forgotten. Lillie Langtry sat well forward, not only to see, but to be seen. Even the aesthetes were for once oblivious of each other and had their faces towards the curtain, their own wit set aside.

What an extraordinary convention that a few hours of precise and formal unreality should hold them spellbound, together and yet unreasonably separate, all held by the power of the imagination woven by a few men and women in borrowed costumes speaking borrowed words.

The murmur of voices died and the silence quivered with indrawn breath, and the faint rustle of fabric and creak of whalebone. The curtain went up. There was a sigh like a wind stirring leaves. The lights picked out Tamar Macaulay standing alone in the center of the stage. She did not move, and yet she was a figure of such arresting power that every eye was fixed upon her. Even Lillie Langtry ignored her admirers and stared ahead. Tamar had not the Jersey Lily's beauty, nor her fame, but she had a depth of emotion that surpassed both, and for this space of time, the audience was hers.

Joshua Fielding came onto the stage. Beside Charlotte, Caroline stiffened, held her breath and leaned a little forward. The drama began.

Charlotte watched the stage as well, but more often she turned to look at the people in her own box. Kathleen O'Neil sat graciously, a slight smile on her lips, her eyes on the figures on the lit stage below her. Charlotte searched her expression when she looked at Joshua and saw nothing in the smooth cheeks, the slanted eyes, no suspicion, no curiosity. If she wondered about Aaron Godman's guilt, about Joshua's part in the tragedy, those thoughts did not seem to occupy her now.

Then Tamar was back on the stage, the lights brilliant on her face as she spoke her lines, her voice ringing with emotion.

A flicker crossed Kathleen's brow. Her mouth narrowed and her tongue touched her lips. She would have been less than human had she not wondered what this woman was like, what fire burned in her, that Kathleen's own husband had risked so much to stay with her. But even staring as openly as she dared, Charlotte could see no hatred in Kathleen's eyes, no violence of feeling, only a sad curiosity, and behind her Prosper's hand on her chair tightened, the knuckles white. Perhaps he relived her pain more than she did herself.

Kathleen turned, not seeing Charlotte, and smiled at Devlin O'Neil, standing behind Adah. He smiled back, a warm, gentle look, and her lips curled upwards as she moved her head back to watch the stage.

How long had Devlin O'Neil been in love with her? Long before Kingsley Blaine's death? It was a very ugly thought, and Charlotte resented its necessity. She liked them both. One tragedy was more than enough.

She looked again at Devlin's arm on Adah's chair. His hand was fine, well manicured, the cloth of his jacket excellent gabardine, his shirt with its gold links was made of silk. What had it been before his marriage to Kathleen?

Charlotte looked away, her eyes going to Adah, seeing her face set in hard lines of some emotion that troubled her deeply. It was not new, there was no urgency in it, only an old pain she had borne a long time. It had already cut deep into her; it was a matter of enduring it.

What was it? Disappointment? No, it was too sharp. It was not fear. It was harder than grief.

Charlotte turned to Prosper where he stood beyond Caroline, his hand still over Kathleen's chair. His heavy face with its deep-set eyes and hatchet nose was fixed on the stage, oblivious of his family and guests. Was it the drama which held him, or Tamar Macaulay, who had stolen his daughter's husband?

Everyone else was totally unaware of Charlotte or the O'Neils, or Adah or Prosper Harrimore. Only Joshua Fielding turned and moved in the spotlight.

Charlotte looked at Adah again, and then she knew what the emotion was that tore at her: guilt.

Why?

Was it still because Prosper had a clubfoot and she felt responsible? That ridiculous idea that her husband had defiled himself with a Jewess, and then contaminated her, causing her unborn child's deformity?

Adah looked around and caught Charlotte staring. Her eyes widened.

Charlotte gulped and felt her face flush.

"I am so grateful to you for inviting us." She forced the words out of her mouth and felt an abject hypocrite. "It is a marvelous drama. What that woman is suffering for her child. I find it most moving—" She stopped. The words stuck on her tongue.

"I am pleased you are enjoying it," Adah said with an effort. "Yes, it is very powerful."

They sat in silence for several more minutes, perhaps almost a quarter of an hour. Then the action of the stage came to a climax with the entrance of the child in the play. Charlotte had not expected a real child and she was startled when he appeared, slender, fair-haired, with a wistful, innocent face. He reminded her intensely of someone else she had seen, but she could not think who. He was nothing like her own children, he was fairer, softer of feature.

Then she heard Kathleen O'Neil gasp and saw her hand fly to her lips as if to stifle a further cry, and behind her Prosper Harrimore's hand clench so tight on the chair back, his nails drew a thin trickle of blood down his wrist.

The child was startlingly like Kathleen's daughter, only this was a boy, or dressed to look like one. They must have been within a few months of the same age. And the child stood in front of Tamar Macaulay, his mother in the drama, and surely in life as well?

Kingsley Blaine's child—by a Jewess—a beautiful child, perfect in face and limb. Tamar must have carried him when Kathleen was carrying her daughter.

With a sudden sick realization Charlotte understood Adah's guilt, and the fear she had seen in her before—and what emotion it was which drew blood in Prosper Harrimore's clenched hands.

It was not Aaron Godman who had killed Kingsley Blaine, nor was it Joshua Fielding in jealousy, nor Devlin O'Neil to win Kathleen. It was Prosper Harrimore, hating and fearing that which was different and which he thought responsible for his own imperfection, his deformity. And then history had repeated itself with his daughter betrayed by her husband with a Jewess; and while she was carrying his child—another child to be born deformed, imperfect.

There was no proof, no way to be sure except in her own intense conviction. But she had no doubt. It was there in Adah's face, and it was in his as he stared at the child on the stage.

11

"HARRIMORE?" Drummond said incredulously. "That doesn't make any sense, Pitt! For heaven's sake, why?" He stood in front of the bookcase in his office. The fire was burning strongly, its warmth spreading through the room. "He may have discovered that Blaine was deceiving his daughter, but no sane man murders over something like that! He could have stopped him easily enough, if he had just confronted him with it! After all, Blaine was dependent on him for his livelihood." He looked at Pitt sharply. "And don't tell me he confronted Blaine in the smithy's yard in Farriers' Lane and they fought over it. That's rubbish. He could have faced him with it quite comfortably in his own home. The man lived in his house. He didn't need to rig up an elaborate charade to get Blaine to Farriers' Lane in the middle of the night. And you'll have to do better than tell me Prosper Harrimore is insane. He's a thoroughly well thought of member of the business community, at least as respectable as anyone in trade can be."

Pitt smiled very slightly. "You've answered all the arguments I haven't made," he replied.

"What?" Drummond frowned. He was sharper tempered and slower of perception than usual. Pitt knew his heart was no longer in the pursuit.

347

"I said that you have answered all the reasons I did not give," he repeated.

"Oh. So what reason do you believe Harrimore had for murdering his son-in-law? How did you come to the conclusion anyway? You haven't told me that."

Pitt bit his lip and felt abashed.

"That is less easy. Actually Charlotte came to the conclusion." He looked at Drummond quickly, but did not see the impatience he expected. He drew breath and plunged on. "She had cultivated the acquaintance of Adah Harrimore, Prosper's mother, and spent some time in conversation with her. We knew she had very deep feelings against Jews, but I assumed it dated from her belief that a Jew murdered her granddaughter's husband in a particularly brutal and offensive way." He pushed his hands deeper into his pockets, a comfort he would not have felt possible in front of any other superior.

"A great many people felt the same who didn't even know him. But it seems her anti-Jewish feeling dates from long before that; in fact it has been there probably from childhood. She believes Jews are unclean, that they are responsible for the crucifixion of Christ."

"They are," Drummond exclaimed, his eyes troubled.

"Of course they are," Pitt retorted exasperatedly. "Almost everyone in the entire story, good, bad and indifferent, including Christ Himself, was Jewish! So were Mary, and Mary Magdalene, and the apostles. All the Old Testament prophets as well."

"I suppose so." Drummond frowned as if the thought were new to him. "But what has that to do with Adah Harrimore, and still less to do with Prosper?"

"She subscribes to the view, held by several people," Pitt explained with embarrassment, "especially prize stock breeders—I came across this when I was growing up in the country—if a good bitch gets out and gets with pup to a mongrel—"

"Pitt! For God's sake, man," Drummond exploded. "What the devil are you talking about?"

"That the bitch is ruined," Pitt finished. "All her litters after that will be contaminated."

"I suppose you know what you are talking about."

"Yes. Adah Harrimore believed that a woman who had sexual congress with a Jew was contaminated ever after. Any further children would be damaged."

"Why should that explain Prosper Harrimore murdering Kingsley Blaine?" Drummond said impatiently.

"Because Adah's husband betrayed her with a Jewess while she was carrying Prosper—and he was born with a deformed leg and foot," Pitt said wearily. "She believes it was a direct result of the connection with Jews. She taught Prosper that. He blames his deformity on his father's acts. When he saw that Kingsley Blaine was about to betray his daughter—also with child—in exactly the same way, he took violent, passionate steps to prevent it, before his grandchild was deformed, and his daughter defiled for all future children."

"Good God!" Drummond shook his head a little. "I didn't know that. Is there any truth in it? Can breeding stock be—be spoiled like that?"

"No," Pitt said furiously. "It's vicious and superstitious rubbish. But there are ignorant people who believe it, and the Harrimores are among them. Old Adah actually said so to Charlotte."

Drummond was abashed that he had credited it, even for a moment. There was a pink flush up his cheeks.

"She admitted it?" he said with surprise.

"She admitted that Jews were unclean, in her estimation," Pitt answered. "And that was the cause of Prosper's deformity."

Drummond sighed. "But you have no proof, have you?"

"No. Not yet."

"Well, you'd better see if you can get it. I think I'll refrain from telling anyone about Aaron Godman until we have something conclusive."

"I'll do what I can. I'll go back to the theater doorman and see if he can remember anything more clearly." He

349

walked over to the door and was about to open it when Drummond spoke again.

"Pitt."

Pitt turned. "Yes sir?"

"When the case is closed I am going to resign. I have already told the assistant commissioner. I am recommending you to take my place. Before you argue, it will not be entirely a desk job. You can govern for yourself a great deal of what you do." He smiled very slightly, but there was affection in it, and respect. "You won't have anyone to rely on as I have on you. You will need to do a lot of the investigation of more serious cases yourself, particularly the politically sensitive ones. Don't refuse without thinking about it very carefully."

Pitt swallowed hard. He should not have been surprised, but he was. He had thought Drummond's mood would pass, but now he realized it had to do with Eleanor Byam, and was final.

"Thank you, sir," he said quietly. "I shall miss you deeply."

"Thank you, Pitt." Drummond looked embarrassed, and pleased, and vulnerable. "I daresay I shall see you from time to time. I . . ." He stopped, uncertain how to continue.

Pitt smiled. "Yes sir." He met Drummond's eyes and knew that Drummond understood, and it was better unsaid. "I'll go and see the doorman."

Micah Drummond felt immensely relieved, almost light-headed, now that he had not only made the decision but also committed himself to it. He had told Pitt. There was no honorable way he could go back on it. It would not matter financially. He would have less money, of course, because he would lose his police salary. To Pitt it would be a vast improvement, but to Drummond the salary had always been pleasant but in no way necessary. He had inherited considerable means and come into the position as a gentleman— not promoted from the ranks, but appointed because of his military experience, his administrative ability, and precisely because he was a gentleman, reliable, commanding men easily, and one of the same class and nature as those who chose him.

Pitt would be an entirely different matter, but he knew from previous delicate conversations that there were those in power in the Home Office who would approve his appointment.

There would also be those who would disapprove, who would resent and distrust a man who was of working-class origins, no matter how well he spoke. He could never be one of them; that was something to which you had to be born. But it was time that men in charge of the solving of major crimes were professionals, not distinguished amateurs, no matter how respected or agreeable.

Within fifteen minutes of Pitt leaving the office, Drummond collected his hat, coat and stick, and left also. By mid-afternoon it was accomplished. He had tendered his resignation, one month from that date, and it had been accepted with reluctance. And as had been implied to him earlier, he had been assured that Thomas Pitt would be appointed his successor. That had not come without a struggle, and a great deal more devious politicking than he had ever practiced before. But now he strode down Whitehall in the bitter wind with a spring in his step and his head high. He entered Parliament Street and hailed a cab, his voice ringing out in the sharp air almost like a challenge.

The cabby stopped. "Yes sir?"

He gave the man Eleanor Byam's address and climbed in. He sat back with his heart beating. He was putting it to the test. If he asked her now there would be no answer but acceptance, or that she did not regard him in that way. There were no excuses left that it would cost him his position either professionally or socially. He turned it over and over in his mind as the cab rattled eastward through the traffic and he was hardly aware of his passage. He thought over every argument she might use, and how he would counter it, all the assurances he would give. All the while a small, sane part of his mind was telling him the words made no difference. Either she wished to accept him, in which case the arguments were unnecessary, or she did not, and then they were pointless. You cannot reason someone into loving.

Still the surface of his brain occupied itself with words. Perhaps it was a kind of anesthetic until he should arrive and the die was cast. Words were easier than feelings, less painful, in so many ways less real.

" 'Ere you are, sir!" The cabby's voice intruded and with a start he brought his attention back to the present and scrambled out.

"Thank you." He paid the man generously, almost as a superstitious offering to fortune. And before he would have time to think, and doubt himself, he knocked on the door.

As before, it was opened by the surly maid.

"Oh—it's you," she said with a twist of her lip. "Well, you'd better come in, although what Mrs. Bridges'll say I don't know. This is a respectable 'ouse, and she don't like her lodgers to 'ave callers in a reg'lar way. Least not as you'd say was followers, like."

Drummond blushed. "Maids have followers," he said tartly. "Ladies have acquaintances, or if seeking their hands in marriage, then suitors. If you wish to retain your position, I would remember the difference, and keep a civil tongue in your head!"

"Oh! Well, I—"

But she got no further. He brushed past her and went quickly down the bare corridor towards the back, and Eleanor's rooms. Once there he knocked more loudly than he had intended, and after the briefest moment heard footsteps on the other side. The door swung open and the maid saw him and her face flooded with pleasure, even relief.

"Oh sir, I'm so glad as you've come. I was so afraid you might not be back."

"I promised you I would," he said quietly, liking the woman enormously for her loyalty. "Is Mrs. Byam in?"

"Oh, yes sir. She don't often go nowhere. In't really nowhere to go."

"Will you ask her if she will see me?"

She smiled, and kept up the fiction. "O' course, sir. If you'll wait 'ere." There was no morning room or library,

352

only a tiny anteroom, less than a hall, but he stood as she had requested while she disappeared, and came back only a moment later, her face full of hope.

"Yes sir, if you'll come this way." She took his hat, coat and stick and hung them up, then she led him again into the small sitting room full of Eleanor's things. He did not even hear her leave.

Eleanor was standing by the window and he knew immediately she had not remained seated because she felt at a disadvantage. In some subtle way she was afraid of him.

Instead of anger he felt sympathy. He was afraid too, of the hurt she could do him if she refused.

"How nice to see you, Micah," she said with a smile. "You look very well, in spite of the weather. Is the case progressing at last?"

"Yes," he said with slight surprise. "Yes, it is. Pitt knows who did it, and why."

Her dark eyebrows rose. "You mean it was not Aaron Godman?"

"No—no, it wasn't."

"Oh, the poor man." Her voice dropped and her face was bleak with the pain she imagined. "How dreadful." She looked out of the window at the wet walls of the next building. "I always thought hanging was barbaric. This makes it doubly so. How must his family feel?"

"They don't know yet. We cannot prove who it was." Drummond wanted to go over to her, but it was too soon. With an effort of will he remained where he was. "I am quite sure Pitt is right, or at least, I should say, Charlotte. It was she who came upon the answer. But there is no proof and, as yet, no evidence that would convince a jury."

"But Godman is innocent?"

"Oh yes. The proof of that is quite good enough."

She looked at him quickly. "What are you going to do?"

This time he smiled. "Very little. Pitt will do it."

"I don't understand. I know Pitt will do the actual questioning of people. I can recall enough to know that. But surely the decisions are yours?" A flicker of self-mocking humor passed across her face, and a host of memories.

"That depends when the solution comes, although I expect it will not take long from now. He is angry enough, and sad enough, to give it a passionate attention."

"I still do not understand. You seem to be meaning something far more than you are saying." There was a question in her voice and anxiety in her eyes. "Do you wish me to know, or . . . ?" She left it unfinished.

"Yes, of course I do. I'm sorry." It was ridiculous to be playing games with her, or with himself. He should have the courage to put it to the test. He breathed in deeply and let it out again. "I have given the commissioner my resignation, effective one month from now. And I have recommended Pitt to succeed me. I think he will do it better than anyone else. He will make mistakes, but he will also be more likely than any of the others to achieve something positive."

She looked startled. "You have resigned! But why? I know you have lost a certain interest, but surely it will come back. You cannot just give up."

"Yes, I can, when there are other things which are of more importance to me."

She stood still, looking at him very gravely, the question in her eyes.

Now was the time. There was no point in trying to be indirect or to surprise her. "Eleanor, you already know that I love you, and that I wish to marry you. When I asked you before, you pointed out that it would cost me my career, and you said that that was the reason you refused. Now it no longer stands in the way. Marrying you could not harm me, it would only bring me the greatest possible happiness. You cannot refuse me now, unless it would not bring the same happiness to you—" He stopped, realizing he had said all he meant, so it would be clumsy to press too hard, to repeat.

She stood still, her face a little flushed, her eyes very solemn but a very slight smile about her mouth. For several seconds they both stood motionless. Then she held out her hand towards him, palm down, as if to take hold of his. It was an offer, and with a surge of joy he knew it. He was smiling, his heart beating in his throat. He wanted to sing, shout, but to have made a noise at all would have spoiled it. He strode forward and took her hand, pulling her very gently closer to him. Countless times he had longed to do this, imagined it, and now she was here. He could feel the warmth of her body through the fabric of her dress, smell her hair and her skin, more urgent and exciting than all the perfumes of lavender or roses.

Gently he kissed her, then more powerfully, then at last with total passion, and she answered him with a completeness he could not have dreamed.

Gracie also had made a decision. She was going to help solve this case, and she knew how; not exactly—that would have to wait until she learned a little more—but certainly she knew how she would begin, and what she intended to accomplish. She would find this wretched boy from the streets who refused to tell Pitt about the man who had given him the message for Kingsley Blaine at the theater door. From what the mistress had said, Aaron Godman, poor soul, had looked very little indeed like Mr. Prosper Harrimore. For a start, Harrimore had been twice his age, and twice his height! The boy could not be such a fool as not to have noticed such a thing, if he put his mind to thinking about it, and remembering.

It would take a little time, a day or two at least, and it would not be easy to make an excuse that would be believed. But she had been a good liar in the past and no doubt could be again, in the right cause. She had already learned the boy's name from Pitt, and thus how to find him.

"Please, ma'am," she said with downcast eyes, "me mam's in a spot o' difficulty. May I 'ave a day orf ter go an 'elp 'er? I'll try an' be back as soon as I can; if I can sort everythin' terday, can I go termorrer? I'll get up at five an' do all the fires and the kitchen floor afore I go. An' I'll be back in the evenin' ter do the veges and the dishes after dinner, an' the beds an' things. Please, ma'am?"

The only thing that struck guilt into her heart was the look of concern on Charlotte's face, and the readiness with which she gave her permission. But it was a good cause. Now please heaven she could find this miserable boy and shake some sense into him!

She hurried out before any more questions could be asked, and set to her present chores with a will.

The following morning she was as good as her promise. She rose at five, stumbling in the dark and shivering with cold. She crept down the stairs to riddle the ashes in the kitchen fire, clean it out, black the grate, lay it and light it and fetch up the coal; then the parlor fireplace, black it and lay it. Next she filled the pail with water and scrubbed the kitchen table, then the floor, and by seven she had swept the parlor and passage as well and left everything ready for breakfast.

By quarter past seven, just before daylight, she let herself out of the front door before Charlotte came down to put on the kettle. Once she was out in the street, the gray dawn still lit by the yellow of the lamps, she hurried towards the main thoroughfare and the omnibus stop where she could begin her journey to Seven Dials.

She was not completely sure what she intended to do, but she had been with Charlotte more than once when she had gone detecting. It was a matter of asking the right questions of the people who knew the answers, and most important, of asking them in the right way. Which was why she was better suited to this particular task than either Charlotte herself or even Pitt. She would meet Joe Slater as an equal, and she was convinced she would understand him better. She would know if he were lying, and possibly even why.

It was a windless day, but bitterly cold. The pavements were slippery with it, and the chill ate into the bones through thin shawls and stuff dresses. Her old boots were little protection from the icy stones.

When the omnibus stopped she alighted with several others and looked around her. It was only a hundred yards to the place Pitt had mentioned, and she walked smartly. It was a narrow street and all along the left side were barrows and stalls selling small goods, mostly of fabric and leather.

She knew very few of them were new; nearly all were re-made from old fabric, the good parts cut out and used again. The same was true of the shoes. The leather was unpicked, recut and restitched.

Now she must begin to look for Joe Slater. Slowly, as if searching for a bargain, she moved along the lines of rickety barrows and benches made of planks of wood, or even goods set out over the stones of the curb. She did not feel the guilt that Pitt did when seeing the pinched faces, hollow, anxious eyes, thin bodies shivering in threadbare clothes. She had tasted poverty too thoroughly herself. Its familiar smells and sounds settled over her, making her wish she could turn and go back to the omnibus and leave it all behind. There was a warm kitchen at home in Bloomsbury, and hot tea at eleven o'clock, sitting with her feet by the stove, and the odor of clean wood and flour and laundry.

The first half dozen sellers were middle-aged, or women, and she kept on going, eyes averted so she did not get drawn into haggling. When she finally found a youth she looked at him carefully before speaking.

"Yer want summink, or yer just 'ere ter stare?" he demanded irritably. "Do I know yer?"

Gracie shrugged and half smiled at him. "I dunno—do yer? Wot's yer name?"

"Sid. Wot's yours?"

"D'yer know Joe Slater?"

"Why?"

"Cos I wanter buy summink orf 'im, o' course," she snapped.

"I got plenty that's good. Want a new pair o' boots? I got boots abaht your size," he said hopefully.

Gracie looked at the array of boots in front of him. She would have liked a new pair. But what would Charlotte say if she wore ones like these, remade from old leather, other people's castoffs? Maybe she wouldn't notice. Who looked at boots under a long skirt? And all Gracie's skirts were on the long side because she was so small.

"Mebbe . . ." she said thoughtfully. " 'Ow much?"

He held up a light brown pair. "One and fivepence ha'penny, fer you."

"One and twopence three farthings," she said immediately. She would not have dreamed of paying the first price asked.

"One and fourpence farthing," he replied.

"One and tuppence three farthings, or forget about it," she said. They were very nicely shaped boots, and a good color. There was only one piece of leather on them that looked really scuffed. She made as if to turn away.

"All right! One and threepence," he offered. "You can go a farthing."

She fished in her large pocket and brought out her purse. She counted out two sixpences and a threepenny piece but kept them in her hand.

"Where can I find Joe Slater?"

"In't them boots good enough for yer?"

"W'ere is 'e?" Her fingers closed over the money.

"Leather aprons, 'bout ten stalls down." He held out his hand for the money.

She gave it to him, thanked him and took her boots.

She found Joe Slater approximately where Sid had told her. She regarded him discreetly for several minutes, judging what she would say to him, how to begin. He was a lean, scrawny youth with fair hair and careful gray eyes. She liked his face. Of course it was a swift judgment, and she was very prepared to change it if it proved necessary, but so far there was a quality in his features which pleased her.

She made up her mind. She lifted her chin, straightened her back and walked over to him, her eyes bright and very direct.

"You Joe Slater?" she asked cheerfully, her voice conveying her own certainty that he was.

" 'Oo are you?" he said with mild suspicion. One had to be careful.

"I'm Gracie 'Awkins," she replied with total candor. "I want ter talk to yer."

"I'm 'ere ter sell, not talk ter bits o' girls," he said. But there was no abruptness in his voice, and his expression was not unpleasant.

"I in't stoppin' yer sellin'," she pointed out. Now came the lie, at least the first one. "I works for a lady in the theeayter wot yer could 'elp, if yer cared to."

"Wot's in it fer me?"

"I dunno! Nuffink fer me, that's certain. But I reckon as fer you it could be summink good. She in't poor, and she in't mean."

"So why me? Wot does she want me ter do for 'er?" He screwed up his face in considerable doubt. "You 'avin' me on?"

"I got better things ter do wif me time than come traipsin' down 'ere lookin' fer someone I never 'eard of afore, just ter 'ave yer on!" She laughed sharply and with derision. "It 'as ter be you, cos yer the only one wot knows."

"Knows wot?" In spite of himself he was interested.

"The face of a man wot killed someone. Murdered 'im pretty 'orrible, an' got the wrong man 'anged fer it."

His expression pinched and a closed, angry look came into his eyes.

"Yer mean 'im wot was murdered in Farriers' Lane, don't yer? Well, I already told the rozzers all I know an' I in't sayin' no more ter no one. The rozzers send yer 'ere after me? Gawd, won' them bastards never leave me alone?" Now there was real bitterness in him and his body was stiff, his hands clenched tight.

"Oh yeah?" she said sarcastically, angry with herself for having spoiled the mood, and with him. "I'm part o' the rozzers, I am. I only look like this w'en I'm out on a case. Really I'm six foot 'igh and strong as an ox. A real rozzer, I just left me uniform at 'ome terday."

"Oh, very smart tongue," he sneered. "So you in't a rozzer. Why d'yer want ter know about 'im, eh? It's all over, and in't nuffink ter me now. The bleedin' rozzers 'ave 'ounded me like a rat ever since then. First they tried ter tell me I saw a man as I didn't. They near broke me arms." He hunched his shoulders experimentally to see if it still

359

pained. " 'Urt fer munfs after, they did. Then w'en the trial came up they 'ounded me again. I argued wif 'em an' they told me as they'd put me in the Coldbath Fields fer thievin'." He scowled. "D'yer know 'ow many folks dies in there o' gaol fever? Fousands! Put me on the treadmill, one of them cockchafers—w'ere yer can't breathe fer suffocation, and if yer don't keep on walking them steps yer fall over, an' the 'ole thing 'urts yer privates terrible. I in't tellin' nobody nuffink about that night, not fer you nor yer lady in the thee-ayter. Now go away and bother someone else. Garn!" He flapped his hand, dismissing her, and glared out of narrow, angry eyes.

For a moment she was stumped. She did not argue; she knew enough of the police from the wrong side of the law to believe what he said. She had had uncles and a brother who had been hounded, and a distant cousin who had been sent to prison. She had seen him when he had come out, slow-witted, wasted by gaol fever, his joints aching, his walk shambling and uncertain from the agony of the cockchafer.

"Garn," he said again, more sharply. "I can't tell yer nuffink!"

She stepped back a bit, disconcerted, but not defeated, not yet.

A customer came and haggled for several minutes before finally buying an apron, then another one came, argued, and bought nothing. For over an hour Gracie stood and watched, getting colder and colder, her hands becoming stiff holding the new boots.

Joe left and went to a barrow on the next street to get himself an eel pie. Gracie followed him, and bought herself one as well. It was hot and tasted delicious.

"There in't no use yer followin' me," Joe said when he saw her. "I in't tellin yer nuffink! Nor I certainly in't goin' ter no rozzers." He sighed, licking the juice off his lips. "Listen, yer stupid lump! The rozzers swear they got the right geezer. They 'ad 'im arrested and tried! The toffs were 'appy wif it! They argued 'round an' 'round, like they always do. They said 'e were guilty, they'd done right ter nab 'im, and they 'anged the poor swine." He took another bite of his pie and went on with his mouth full. "If yer think they're goin' ter say now as they was wrong, on the word o' some nobody orf the street, then yer daft enough fer Bedlam, an that's a fact." He swallowed. "Yer mistress is dreamin' an she'll only 'urt 'erself, an' you too, if you've got no more sense than to listen to 'er."

"It weren't 'im wot done it," Gracie began.

" 'Oo cares?" he cut across her angrily. "Listen, you idjut! It don't matter 'oo done it. Wot matters now is 'oo's made ter look bad cos they 'anged the wrong bloke. They in't goin' ter say as they did that—no matter wot." He jerked his hand in the air with his pie in it. "Think abaht it, if yer've got anyfink in yer 'ead at all besides sawdust. Which o' them toffs is goin' ter say as they 'anged the wrong bloke? None o' them—and yer can lay money on that."

"They won't 'ave no choice," she said fiercely, biting into her own pie. "The p'lice already knows as it weren't the man they 'anged. They've got proof. An' they know 'oo it were—they just can't get proof o' that neither."

"I don't believe yer."

"I don't tell lies," Gracie said furiously, filled with indignation because this was not a lie but the absolute truth. "An' yer got no right to say as I do. Yer just 'aven't got the guts ter stand up to 'em and say wot yer know." She tried to fill her expression with utmost contempt, but having her mouth half full got in her way.

"Yer damn' right I in't," he agreed. "An' fer why? Because it won't do no good. Now you go back ter yer mistress and tell 'er ter ferget it. Garn!"

"I in't goin' nowhere till yer come an' look at this geezer wot really done it." She took another huge bite of her pie. "An' then yer say as if it were 'im wot spoke to yer outside the thee-ayter. An' we should find them geezers wot was 'anging 'round the end o' Farriers' Lane that night, an' find out wot they really saw, not wot the rozzers told 'em they saw."

"Wotcher mean 'we'?" His voice rose to a squeak. "I in't

goin' anywhere. I 'ad more'n enough o' the rozzers w'en the murder 'appened—I don't need ter go lookin' fer 'em now."

"O' course you as well," Gracie said exasperatedly, swallowing the bite of pie. "In't no point me goin' by meself. I weren't there. I din't see 'im."

"Well, I in't goin'."

"Please."

"No."

"The geezer wot really done it is still out there," she protested.

"Don't matter ter me. Now go away an' leave me alone, won't yer?"

"No. I in't goin' ter leave yer till yer come wif me an' 'ave a real look at this geezer, an' say if 'e were the one or not."

"Yer can't foller me 'round!"

"I can."

"Look." He was exasperated. "I can't do nuffink fer yer. An' I go places as it in't right for yer to come. Nah go away!"

"I in't goin' till yer comes an' 'as a look at this geezer."

"Well, yer goin' ter wait a long time." And with that he turned his back and began talking to a potential customer, making a considerable show of ignoring Gracie.

Gracie followed him back to his stall, and then stood clasping her coat closer around her and waited, watching. It was cold and her feet were so chilled she had lost feeling in them. But she was certainly not going to give up, if she had to follow him until he went to bed.

Late in the afternoon Joe tidied his stall and locked his few goods away for the night, then left. Gracie came to attention and followed after him. Twice he turned around, caught sight of her, and glared, at the same time waving his hand to shoo her away. She made a face back at him and continued to follow.

He went into a public house and pushed his way to the counter, and she went in after him, wriggling and following through people to find a place beside him, luxuriating in the warmth after the biting cold outside.

"Go away," Joe said furiously, glaring at her.

Half a dozen people turned to look at him, then at Gracie.

"Not till yer come an' look at the bloke wot did it," she replied stubbornly, sniffing as the sudden warmth made her nose run.

"Don't yer never give up?" he whispered. "I told yer— they won't believe me, whatever I say. I'd be wastin' me time. Don't yer 'ave no wits at all?"

She did not bother to argue her intelligence.

"You just come an' look at this bloke. If it were 'im, they'll believe yer."

"Yeah? Why's that then?" Skepticism was deep in his thin face.

She was not going to tell him Pitt knew Harrimore was guilty. He might not understand the necessity for proof. Nor could she easily explain how she knew such a thing.

"I can't explain everything to yer." She sniffed again.

"Yer don't know."

"Yes, I do so. An' I'm still goin' ter foller yer till yer 'ave a real look at 'im. The rozzers won't bovver yer, if that's wot yer scared of."

"Don't yer talk down ter me like that, yer miserable little article," he said furiously. "Yer'd be scared too, if'n yer 'ad two wits to rub tergether. You any idea wot them rozzers can do, if they takes a real nasty to yer? And they do, if yer says as their evidence in't no good. Ask me—I know!"

"You don't 'ave ter tell the rozzers, not ter begin wif," she said triumphantly. "Jus' come and look at 'im, and tell me." He turned away and she pulled at his sleeve. "An' I swear I'll leave yer alone. If'n yer don't, I'll come wif yer everyw'ere."

"No rozzers?" he said warily.

"I swear it."

"Then I'll meet yer 'ere at six, and we'll go an' look at 'im. Now leave me alone to 'ave a pint in peace."

"I'll wait outside for yer." She sniffed again.

"Gawd, woman. I said I'll come."

"Yeah—and mebbe I believe yer, an' mebbe I don't."

"Go on outside then. And stop sniffing!"

As a show of goodwill Gracie withdrew reluctantly out into the biting cold again. She waited patiently in the dark and the slow drizzle, watching carefully in case he should try to slip out past her.

But half an hour later she saw his thin form and pale face with a surge of relief as if he had been a long-standing friend. She darted forward, nearly slipping on the slick stones and finding her feet were totally numb. She was cold to the bone.

"Yer ready now, then?" she said eagerly.

He looked at her sideways with disgust, and she knew with a funny little sinking inside her that he had hoped she had given up and gone. She grunted with determination, and a full intention of showing how she did not care. This was entirely a matter of business. Who cared what he thought of her?

Wordlessly they walked side by side along the narrow footpath, freezing paving stones gleaming under the lamps as they passed from one pool of light to another. Dim halos of rain ringed each one, and beside them in the street wheels splashed and hissed on the wet road. Carriages loomed out of the darkness and disappeared into it again.

"Can't yer keep up?" Joe demanded, then immediately gripped her hand and held it hard, keeping her close to him as they passed groups of people, some huddled around braziers of hot chestnuts or other food, others pressing into the half shelter of doorways.

"We gotter get an omnibus," Gracie said breathlessly. "It's up west. 'E's a toff."

"W'ere west?" he demanded.

"Chelsea—Markham Square."

"Then we'll go on the train," he replied.

"Wot train?"

"The underground train. Ter Sloane Square. In't yer never bin on the underground train?"

"I never 'eard of it." Then she realized how ignorant that

made her sound. "Me mistress goes by 'ansom, or in someone's carriage," she added. "We don't 'ave no need o' trains unless we're goin' away."

"In't you grand," he said sarcastically. "Well, if yer got money fer an 'ansom I'll be very 'appy ter ride wif yer."

"Don' be daft." She dismissed the suggestion with equal scorn. "So we'll go in the train. 'Ow much?"

"Depends 'ow far we go—but not much. Penny or so," he replied. "Now save yer breath an' keep up wif me."

She trotted along beside him for what seemed like miles, carrying her new boots under her arm, but it was probably not much more than a mile and a half. Then they went down flights of steps into a cavernous railway station where the trains ran like moles through tunnels, roaring and clanking in a manner which would have terrified her if she had had time to think about it, and not been far too excited, and too determined to match Joe for wits, courage and any other quality he cared to think of.

She did not like the sensation of sitting in a carriage as it hurtled through a tunnel, and had to concentrate very hard on thinking of something else, or she might have shrieked as she was bumped from side to side, knowing how far she was from daylight and fresh air. She looked sideways at Joe once or twice, and found he was looking at her, so she turned away again quickly. But her heart was thumping with pleasure, and the fear did not matter so much.

At last they came out at Sloane Square station and set out to walk again, this time according to Gracie's instructions, until in a fine, cold rain they came to Markham Square and stopped under the trees at the far side of Prosper Harrimore's house.

"All right, then," Joe said with exaggerated patience. "Now wot? Wot if 'e don't come out again ternight? W'y should 'e? Only fools and them as 'as no 'omes comes out an' stands in the rain."

Gracie had already thought of that. "So we gotta get 'im out, ain't we?"

"Oh yeah? An' 'ow yer goin' ter do that?"

"I'm goin' ter knock on the door."

"An' o' course 'e's goin' ter answer it 'isself—'is footmen 'ave all got the night off," he said wearily. "Yer the daftest woman I ever met, an' that's sayin' a lot w'ere I come from."

"Yeah, well I don't come from w'ere you come from," she said quickly, although it was probably not true. "You jus' watch 'im." And with that she marched across the street, boots under her arm, and up the steps of the Harrimore house and knocked on the door.

She did not really know much about the houses of the well-to-do, only the little bits she had overheard from Charlotte, and what she had gathered from her newfound art of reading. However, she had fully expected the door to be opened by a footman, so she was not taken by surprise when it was.

"Yes, miss?" he said, eyeing her with disgust. He was about to suggest she go to the servants' entrance, thinking her a relative of one of the maids, although even they should not have received callers at this hour. When she spoke, her words came out in a rush, her heart beating so it nearly choked her.

"Please, sir, I got a message for Mr. 'Arrimore, personal like, an' I darsen't give it ter no one else."

"Mr. Harrimore does not take messages from the likes of you," the footman said stiffly. "If you give it to me, I'll tell him."

"That in't no good," she said quickly, shifting the boots around to hold them more firmly. "I were told special, no one but Mr. 'Arrimore 'isself. I'll wait 'ere, an' you go an' tell 'im as it's ter do wif a lad 'e met outside a thee-ayter, five year ago, an' give a message ter. You tell 'im that, an' 'e'll come ter see me."

"Nonsense! Be off with you, girl."

She remained where she was.

"You go an' tell 'im that—then I'll go."

"You go now!" He waved his hand briskly. "Or I'll send for the police. Come 'ere botherin' decent folk with your tales and messages!" He made as if to close the door.

"You don't want the police 'ere," she said with desperation. "That family's 'ad enough o' police an' tragedy. You jus' go an' give 'im that message. It ain't yer place ter decide for 'im 'oo 'e sees an' 'oo 'e don't. Or do yer think yer 'is keeper?"

It may have been her argument, or it may have been only the force of her personality and the determined look in her small, fierce face, but the footman decided against debating any further on the step, closed the door firmly and took the message inside.

Gracie waited, swallowing on a dry mouth, body shaking with cold and with tension. She held the boots in her arm; her hands were too cold to feel. Only once did she turn around to make sure Joe was still there on the opposite side of the street, well in the shadows, but peering towards Harrimore's door.

It was several moments before at last it opened and a very large man stood staring at Gracie. He seemed to tower over her and to fill the entire doorway. His hatchet nose and sweeping brow were highly unusual, his deep-set eyes angry and full of surprise.

"Who are you?" he demanded. "I've never seen you before, and I don't know what you are talking about a thee-ayter. Who put you up to this?"

Gracie backed away a step, thoroughly frightened.

He frowned, and came farther out of the doorway towards her.

She backed again and slipped on the wet marble, slithering backwards onto the pavement, and the only reason she did not fall flat on her back was that Joe had crept across the street and was there to catch her.

Harrimore stood transfixed, his face blank with dawning horror.

"Sorry, mister," Joe said, staring up at Harrimore, his eyes devouring his features, his own face white. He gulped, his voice cracking. "She's a bit touched, like," he blurted. "She can't 'elp it. I'll take 'er 'ome. Good night, mister." And before Harrimore could stop him he grabbed Gracie's arm and dragged her away, plunging off the curb, running

367

across the street and into the shadow of the alley on the far side. He stopped and swung her around, still holding her hand.

"That's 'im," he said between gasps. "That's the geezer wot give me the message fer Mr. Blaine that night. Geez! 'E must 'a' bin the one wot killed 'im, and nailed 'im up like a cross. Gawd Almighty, wot are we goin' ter do?"

"Tell the p'lice!" Her heart was racing, bumping inside her so hard she could scarcely get the words out. She had succeeded! She had detected a murderer!

"Don' be daft," Joe said furiously. "They didn't believe me before, they in't goin' ter now, five years after, w'en they already 'anged the other poor sod."

"There's a new rozzer on it now, cos o' Judge Stafford bein' poisoned," she argued, clinging onto the boots. " 'E'll believe yer, cos 'e already knows it weren't Godman wot done it."

"Yeah? An' 'ow do you know that?"

"Cos I do." She was not yet ready to admit to lying about who she worked for.

Suddenly he stiffened, his body rigid, shaking, and she could feel his terror like a charge of electricity. She swung around and saw the huge shadow of Prosper Harrimore outlined against the yellow haze of the street lamps. She could feel the breath strangle in her throat and her knees so weak she nearly crumpled where she stood.

With a cry Joe yanked her around so hard it wrenched her shoulder, and she almost dropped the boots. He started to run, half dragging her after him, the heavy, uneven steps of Prosper following close.

They ran down the alley to the far end, swinging around the corner into the lighted footpath again, Gracie clasping her long skirts to keep from tripping, then across the empty street and into the opposite alley, ducked into a dark areaway and crouched down beside the steps like two frightened animals, hearts thumping, blood pounding, faces and hands ice cold.

They dared not move at all, certainly not raise their

heads to look, but they heard Prosper's heavy, bumping tread pass along the pavement above them, then stop.

Joe put his hand over Gracie's, holding her so hard had she not been numb with cold it would have hurt.

Slowly Prosper's footsteps moved on, stopped again, then receded a little way into the distance.

Wordlessly Joe climbed to his feet, pulling her after him, and went back up the steps, looking from right to left all the time. Prosper was standing about a hundred yards away, turning slowly.

"Come on," Joe whispered, and set off running along the pavement in the other direction.

But Prosper had heard them and swung around. He could run surprisingly swiftly for a man with such a limp.

They passed the next alley, but went down the one after, dodging rubbish bins, tripping over an old barrow and scrambling up again, out into the street beyond, and then back into a mews, past stables where a single light cast a yellow pool. Startled horses whinnied and snorted.

Gracie and Joe scrambled over a gate, Gracie tripping on the top, banging her legs and getting tied up in her long, wet skirts. Joe half dragged her through a garden, tripping over plants and borders, fighting their way through bushes, branches snapping back in their faces, only just avoiding thick, prickly holly. Gracie still clung to her boots. They ran over a gravel drive which sounded like an avalanche of rocks to their pounding hearts.

Joe stopped suddenly, holding Gracie close to him, but their own breathing was too loud for them to know whether they could hear Prosper's footsteps behind them or not.

"People," Gracie gasped. "If we could find a street wif people we'd be safe. 'E wouldn't dare do nuffink to us in front o' people."

"Yeah 'e would," Joe said bitterly. " 'E'd yell 'Thief!' an' tell everyone we'd nicked 'is watch or summink, an' they'd 'elp 'im."

She knew immediately that was true.

"C'mon," he said urgently. "We gotta go east. If we get inter our own patch 'e'll never find us." And he set off again, this time walking rapidly with Gracie, breathless, running every now and then to keep up, still clutching her boots under her arm and her skirt bunched up to keep from falling over it. By the time they were back in the street, they realized they had left Prosper behind.

"Bloomsbury," she said when she could catch her breath. "We gotter get ter Bloomsbury, then we'll be safe."

"Why?"

"That's w'ere me master lives. 'E'll fix it," she gasped.

"Yer said before as it were yer mistress."

"So it is—but the master's the one ter take care o' Mr. 'Arrimore. C'mon. Don't argue wif me. We gotter get an omnibus ter Bloomsbury!"

"Yer got money?" he demanded, stopping and glaring backwards over his shoulder.

"Course I 'ave. An' I can't run no further."

"Never mind, yer won't 'ave ter," he said softly. "Yer not bad, fer a girl. C'mon. We'll get an omnibus at the next place fer stoppin' one."

She gave him a huge smile, overwhelmed with relief.

Without warning he leaned forward and kissed her. His lips were cold, but he was very gentle and after a moment the warmth came through with a sweetness that ran inside her like singing and fire, and she kissed him back, dropping the boots on the pavement.

Then suddenly he drew away, blushing furiously, and stalked off, leaving her to pick up the boots and run behind him. She caught up at the corner of the thoroughfare where the omnibuses ran past.

Half an hour later they stood in Charlotte's kitchen, shivering cold, wet through, scratched, dirty, clothes torn, but safe.

Joe was appalled when he recognized Pitt and realized he was right in the camp of the enemy, but it was too late to retreat, and the blessed warmth removed the last of his instinctive horror.

"Where in the name of heaven have you been?" Charlotte demanded furiously, her voice thick with fear and relief. "I was worried sick about you!"

Pitt put his hand on her shoulder and the pressure of it silenced her.

"What happened, Gracie?" he asked levelly, standing in front of her. "What have you been doing?"

Gracie took a deep breath and looked directly at him. She was overwhelmingly relieved to be safe, she was in awe of Pitt, she knew she would have to face Charlotte some time, and she was also proud of herself.

"Joe and me went to see Mr. 'Arrimore, as killed poor Mr. Blaine, sir. And Joe took a real good look at 'im, an' 'e knows it were 'im that night, sir, and 'e'll swear to it in court."

Joe opened his mouth to argue, then regarded Gracie's determined little figure and thought better of it.

Pitt looked at him enquiringly. "Is that true? Was it Mr. Harrimore you saw that night?"

"Yes sir, it were," Joe answered dutifully.

"Are you sure?"

"Oh, yessir. An' 'e knew it too. It were plain in 'is face, an' 'e followed us. Came after us more'n a couple o' miles, 'e did. Reckon as if 'e'd caught us we'd 'a' bin nailed ter some stable door too." He shuddered at the thought, as if a bitter cold had struck him even in the warm kitchen.

Charlotte opened her mouth to say something, but instead told Gracie to take off her wet boots and put them in front of the grate. Then she went to put the kettle to the front of the stove and got some bread and butter and jam.

"And you will swear to it now?" Pitt pressed.

Joe glanced at Gracie. "Yeah—if I 'ave ter."

"Good." Pitt turned to Gracie. "You have been very clever, and very brave," he said solemnly.

She flushed with pleasure, her frozen feet tingling.

"You have done an excellent piece of detective work," he added.

She stood if possible even straighter, staring up at him.

"And you have also lied to Mrs. Pitt as to where you were going and why, put your life in danger, not to mention Joe's life, and very possibly given yourself pneumonia. And if you ever do it again I shall discipline you to within an inch of your life. Do you understand me, Gracie?"

But he had not said the one thing she really feared—that she would be dismissed. He had very carefully not said that.

"Yes sir," she said with an attempt at meekness which failed utterly. "Thank you, sir. An' I won't do it again, sir."

He grunted doubtfully.

The kettle started to whistle and Charlotte made the tea and brought it to the kitchen table along with the bread and jam.

Joe ate almost before it was on his plate, and Gracie sat holding her steaming mug in her cold fingers, its warmth aching through her as life came back to her hands. She smiled across at Joe, and he smiled back for a moment before looking away.

"I had better find some dry clothes for you." Charlotte looked dubiously at Joe. "Although I don't know where from. And you will go to your bed," she said to Gracie. "I'll tell you when you can get up again."

"Yes ma'am."

Pitt sat on the edge of the table.

"Will you go an' arrest 'im, sir?" Gracie asked.

"Of course."

"In the morning?"

"No," Pitt replied with distaste, hunching his shoulders and standing down off the table. "Now, before he takes alarm and runs off."

"You're not going alone!" Charlotte's voice was sharp with fear.

"No, of course not," he assured her. "But don't wait up for me." He kissed her quickly, bade good-night to Gracie and Joe, and went out of the kitchen door and along the hallway to collect his coat, hat and scarf.

It was the best part of an hour before Pitt and two constables took a hansom to Markham Square. It was late, bitterly cold, with a steady drizzle soaking everything, glistening on the footpaths and making hazy swirls of rain around the street lamps. Wet leaves clogged the gutters on the more gracious avenues and only a stray carriage disturbed the silence. Curtains were drawn and light escaped in a few thin cracks.

Pitt lifted the heavy knocker on the door. One constable stood by the areaway steps, just in case Harrimore should choose to come out that way and attempt to escape. The other was posted at the mews entrance.

After a considerable time a footman opened the door and regarded Pitt's looming shape suspiciously.

"Yes sir?"

"Good evening. My name is Pitt, from the metropolitan police. I require to speak to Mr. Prosper Harrimore."

"I'm sorry sir, but Mr. 'Arrimore has retired for the night. You'll 'ave to come back in the morning." He made as if to close the door again.

Pitt stepped forward, to the man's alarm.

"That won't do."

"It'll 'ave to do, sir! I told you, Mr. 'Arrimore 'as retired!"

"I have two constables with me," Pitt said grimly. "Don't oblige me to make a scene in the street."

The door swung wide and the footman retreated, his face pale. Pitt followed him into the hall, beckoning to the constable by the area steps to follow him.

"You had better waken Mr. Harrimore and ask him to come downstairs," he said quietly. "Constable, go with him."

"Yes sir." The constable obliged reluctantly and the footman, looking acutely unhappy, went up the broad wooden staircase.

Pitt waited at the bottom. Once or twice his eyes wandered around the walls looking at paintings, finely carved doorways, an elegant dado, but every few moments he looked back at the stair again. He saw the sticks in the hall stand and went over to them, examining them one by one. The third was beautifully balanced, with a silver top. It was a moment or two before he realized it was also a sword. Very slowly, feeling a little sick, he pulled it out. The blade was long and very fine, its steel gleaming in the light. It was clean all but for a tiny brown mark around the band where the blade met the hilt. The blood would have run down the shaft when he put it down to crucify Blaine.

He was facing the dining room door when he heard the sound above him and looked up sharply. Devlin O'Neil stood with his hand on the newel post at the top of the stairs. He was wearing a dressing robe and looked anxious.

"What brings you here at this time of night, Inspector? Don't say there's been another murder."

"No, Mr. O'Neil. I think you had better be prepared to look after your wife, and your grandmother-in-law."

"Has something happened to Prosper?" He started down rapidly. "The butler told me he went out some time ago, and I didn't hear him return. What was it? A street accident? How badly is he hurt?" He missed his step a little on the last stair and stumbled into Pitt, only catching himself by snatching at the newel at the bottom.

"I'm sorry, Mr. O'Neil," Pitt went on, and some sense of real tragedy in his voice must have struck O'Neil. His face lost every vestige of color and he stared at Pitt without speaking. "I am afraid I have come to arrest Mr. Harrimore," Pitt went on. "For the murder of Kingsley Blaine, five years ago, in Farriers' Lane."

"Oh God!" O'Neil slid as if his legs had buckled beneath him, and sat in a heap on the bottom stair, his head in his hands. "That's—that's—" Perhaps he had been going to say "impossible," but some recollection or instinct stopped him, and the words died in his throat.

"I think you had better have the footman fetch you a stiff brandy, and then be prepared to look after Mrs. Harrimore and your wife," Pitt said gently. "They are going to need you."

"Yes." O'Neil swallowed and coughed. "Yes—I'll do that. Would you be kind enough to—no, I'll do it myself." And rather awkwardly he climbed to his feet again and stumbled across the hall to pull the bell rope.

He had just let it go when Prosper appeared at the top of the stairs, followed right on his heels by the constable. He

374

looked bewildered, as though walking in his sleep. He came down slowly, holding on to the rail for support.

"Mr. Harrimore . . ." Pitt began. He looked at Harrimore's face. It was curiously dead; only his eyes were frantic, full of darkness and pain. "Mr. Harrimore," Pitt repeated quietly. He hated this even more than first telling the bereaved. "I am arresting you for the murder of Kingsley Blaine, five years ago, in Farriers' Lane, and of Judge Samuel Stafford, and of Police Constable Derek Paterson in his home. I would advise you to come without resisting, sir. It will distress your family more than is necessary, and it will be hard enough for them as it is."

Prosper stared at him as if he had not heard, or not understood.

Adah was coming down the stairs, clinging to the banister, her face ashen, her long gray hair over her shoulders in a thin braid, a shawl hanging open to show the thick fabric of her nightgown.

At last Devlin O'Neil came to life. He moved from where he had been standing by the bell rope and came towards the stairs.

"You shouldn't be here, Grandmama-in-law," he said gently. "Go back up to bed. I'll come and tell you what's happened. You go back and keep warm now."

Adah waved her hand at him absently, as if to shoo him away. Her eyes were on Pitt.

"Are you taking him?" she asked, her voice cracking.

"Yes ma'am. I have no alternative."

"It's my fault," she said simply. "He did it, but it's my fault, my guilt before God."

Devlin O'Neil made as if to grasp at her, but she brushed him off, still staring at Pitt.

"Is it?" Pitt stared back at her tormented face. He did not need to know, but he knew she was going to tell him, and that the compulsion was beyond her to stop. Half a century of guilt and agony had to find release.

"I knew he was defiled before he was born," she said. "You see my husband lay with a Jewess, and then with me while I was carrying him. I knew what would happen. I tried to get rid of him." She shook her head. "I tried everything I knew—but I failed. He was born anyway—but deformed, twisted, like you see. I didn't know he killed Kingsley, but I feared it. It was history all over again, do you see?" She stared at him, searching his face to be certain he understood.

"Yes," Pitt said very quietly, sick with the misery of it. "I see." He imagined Adah as a young woman, betrayed, bitter, believing without question the superstition she had been taught, hating the child inside her and terrified of the contamination she truly believed in, alone in some bathroom trying desperately to abort the baby in her womb.

He touched her arm, holding her. "There is nothing you can do now. Go back to bed. It's over."

She turned and looked at Prosper and for a moment their eyes met. Neither of them spoke. Then like a very old woman she did as Pitt had bidden her, and climbed back up the stairs, her feet leaden, her back bowed. Never once did she look behind her.

"I did not kill Judge Stafford," Prosper said, staring at Pitt. "I swear by God, I did not. Nor did I kill Paterson. And I can prove it."

It was a moment before Pitt fully comprehended what he had said, and that he meant it.

"But you killed Kingsley Blaine."

"Yes—God help me. He deserved it!" His face came to life at last, his mouth twisted with anger and pain. "He was betraying my daughter with that Jewess. And doing to my grandchildren what my father did to me." Suddenly the hatred vanished, leaving him wide-eyed. "But I did not kill Stafford! I never saw him within weeks of the day he died. And I didn't kill Paterson. I was at a friend's house all evening, and there are twenty men and women who will swear to that."

Pitt's mind was whirling. If Prosper had not killed Stafford, or Paterson, then who had—and why? For heaven's sake—why?

Wordlessly he took Prosper by the arm and the constable fell in beside him on the right, and they walked to the front door past Devlin O'Neil, still stunned, his robe slack, oblivious of the cold. The constable opened the front door, and the three of them stepped outside back into the rain, Pitt carrying the sword stick.

12

Caroline was ecstatic. It was all over, and Joshua was freed from any suspicion whatever. He was guilty of nothing, and it had been proved. The anxiety was ended, even the smallest fear niggling at the back of the mind. The relief was overwhelming. She wanted to laugh aloud, to cry, to run and shout.

She looked at Charlotte's face and saw the shadows in her eyes, the conflicting emotions tearing at her.

"What?" she said quickly, her mind confused. "What else? There is something you haven't told me. What is it?"

"What are you going to do now?" Charlotte asked. They were standing in the withdrawing room in Cater Street. It was early morning and the fire was still only just burning up and there was little heat in it.

"I'm going to tell Joshua, of course," Caroline replied, still puzzled. "And Tamar, naturally."

"I didn't mean right this minute . . ."

"Then what?"

"I—I mean about Joshua. There is no need to worry about him now." She stopped, uncertain how to continue.

"I have no idea," Caroline answered very quietly. "That depends upon him. I shall enjoy each day, and let the one after take care of itself. And Charlotte, my dear . . ."

"Yes?"

"That is all I am prepared to say on the subject, either to you or to Grandmama."

"Oh."

"And now I am going to order the carriage and go and tell Joshua and Tamar the news. You may come if you wish."

"Yes—yes, I will tell Tamar. I would like to do that."

"Of course. I think you should."

It was too early to find anyone at the theater, so Charlotte and Caroline went to the house in Pimlico. They were let in by a surprised Miranda Passmore, but as soon as she saw their faces she knew the news was good. She threw open the door and ushered them in, taking Caroline by the arm and calling loudly for her father.

"Is Miss Macaulay in her rooms?" Charlotte asked, caught up in the happiness of the moment in spite of her own reservations about Caroline and Joshua.

"Yes, I'm sure. She wouldn't have gone out this early. You want to tell her yourself? You should. It is all over, isn't it?" Miranda swung around to face them. "I didn't even ask you, but I can see you've discovered something wonderful. He was innocent, wasn't he?" Her words tumbled over each other. "Can you prove it at last? You can—can't you?"

Charlotte found herself smiling, unable to deny such pleasure.

"Yes—and better than that, last night they arrested the man who really did it."

"Oh, that's marvelous!" Miranda did a little twirl around on the spot out of sheer joy, then clasped Charlotte in a spontaneous hug. "That's wonderful! You are brilliant! You'd have liked Aaron, he was a bit like you—impulsive and full of ideas. Come, you must tell Joshua too." This last was to Caroline. "He'll be in his rooms as well, probably having breakfast. Come on up."

Charlotte left Caroline outside Joshua's door. She did not need to hear Caroline's voice lifted in excitement and happiness, the relief in him, the thoughts and memories of a dead friend, the sense of victory, and the sorrow that all of it was so dreadfully, disastrously late.

She went on up behind Miranda to Tamar's rooms and knocked on the door.

Tamar opened it after a moment, looked first to Miranda's shining face, then at Charlotte.

"It's over," Charlotte said quietly. "They arrested Prosper Harrimore last night, and he did not even deny it. All the world will know Aaron was innocent."

Tamar stood motionless, simply staring at Charlotte, searching her face to make absolutely sure she could not be mistaken, then as she believed it the tears spilled over and ran down her cheeks. She lifted her hands, and then let them fall.

Charlotte forgot everything about decent restraint, good manners and all rules of etiquette and threw her arms around her, holding her tightly and finding her own eyes stinging. Caroline was forgotten. If she too was in Joshua's arms and they laughed or cried or clung to each other, it did not matter, at least for now.

Pitt felt far from happy. To have solved the murder in Farriers' Lane reversed an old and bitter injustice, but it could not help Aaron Godman now. Nothing could undo his suffering or retrieve his loss. It was a small balm to the living, but any redress of wrong was worth fighting for, even when it would cause the guilt and the questions that this would, including the ruin of several reputations.

But he had expected it also to solve the murders of Samuel Stafford and Constable Paterson. And it had not. Apart from the fact that he believed Harrimore, it took him only an hour to ascertain that it was physically quite impossible for him to have committed either crime. His time was fully and unequivocally accounted for.

So who had killed Stafford, and why?

Was it conceivable that it was not anyone they had so far suspected? No one in the theater had any motive that he could imagine. If Stafford had indeed been considering re-opening the Farriers' Lane case, then it was supremely in their interest that he should remain alive. None of them was guilty. That was now undisputed.

He was forced to think again of Juniper and Adolphus Pryce. But they had each feared it was the other.

Who did that leave?

No one.

He could think of no alternative but to go back once more and retrace Stafford's actions all that last day, speak again to anyone who had seen him, cross-check every piece of evidence and see if he could draw anything new from it.

He set out for the police station where he had gone to tell Drummond that he had ascertained that Harrimore could not be guilty of Stafford's death or Paterson's. The day was crisp and cold. A weak sun shone fitfully through the drifting clouds of smoke from countless chimneys, and the paving stones were slippery with ice. Fresh horse manure in the street steamed gently in the freezing air.

He did not expect to learn anything from those involved with the case of Kingsley Blaine. It seemed after all as if Stafford's death had no connection with it except that of coincidence. O'Neil would have more tragedy than any man could deal with today, and Pitt would certainly not intrude on him unless it were a matter of crisis. And neither had he any wish to see Joshua Fielding or Tamar Macaulay. They would be celebrating the end of five years' nightmare. Nothing would bring back the dead, but at last the shame was gone. And although it had had nothing to do with Pitt at all—far from it, he had been the one to resolve it—still he felt implicated because he represented the law to them. He was a member of the police who had unwittingly wronged them so irretrievably.

He paced along the footpath deep in thought, narrowly avoiding bumping into people. The clatter of wheels and hooves, the cries of coachmen, costers and crossing sweepers passed over him in a sea of sound he ignored. When the early afternoon newspapers carried word of Harrimore's arrest all London would know of it. His mind was filled with the furor it would cause. He even wondered if he should go and tell Lambert himself. But how could he phrase it? Simply to announce it would sound like self-praise, and criticism that Lambert had been tragically wrong. To express sorrow or sympathy would be unforgivably condescending. Lambert would be bound to think he had come in order to savor his victory.

No. Let him read it in the newspapers and nurse his defeat alone. Perhaps privacy was the best he could offer.

That was something Paterson would be spared, poor devil. He would not have to face the public embarrassment. Although what was that, compared with the private guilt?

And what about the officers of the courts? Thelonius Quade had doubted all the time, so much so that he had even considered in some way invalidating the proceedings so a mistrial would be called. But in the end his trust in the law had prevailed. How much would he blame himself for that?

And the appeal judges. Was some suspicion of haste, of emotion governing judgment, what had driven Mr. Justice Boothroyd to retirement and drink? Or might it have happened anyway? Did he see something, perceive a lie, a doubt in the transcript of the original trial, and not have the courage to say so? It would take a brave man, in the climate of the time, to tell the law and the public that it had convicted the wrong man, the case was not over at all. There was no closing the file and putting it in the past, no saying that, yes, it was a tragedy, but it was resolved, could be forgotten, with honor.

Forgetting would be sought in vain, and there was no honor for anyone.

The first person Pitt resorted to again was Juniper Stafford. He found her still in black, but this time it was plain, even dull. It was still an expensive cloth and well cut, but it was fashionable rather than possessing any character and it no longer rustled when she moved; nor was her perfume more than the pleasing scent of cleanliness. She looked truly bereaved in every sense. In seeing her face he was intensely aware of loss, even of failure. It was not Samuel Stafford she mourned, and perhaps not even Adolphus Pryce. He felt it was something in herself, a belief, a dream which had died, and the self-knowledge which had taken its place was a bitter fruit.

"Good morning, Inspector Pitt," she said without interest. "Do you have some news? My maid tells me the afternoon newspapers say that you have arrested another man for the murder of Kingsley Blaine. I assume he murdered Samuel also, and for some reason they have not mentioned it. It seems an odd omission." She stood in the center of the morning room. The fire cast a glow on her cheeks, but it could not put life into her eyes, or mobility in her expression.

"The omission was necessary, Mrs. Stafford," he replied. She had assumed Harrimore guilty, as indeed he had himself, but Juniper did not even ask why. Did she suppose Stafford had threatened him with discovery, or did she no longer particularly care? "Prosper Harrimore did not kill the judge," he said aloud.

She frowned very slightly. "I don't understand. That's ridiculous. If he didn't, then who did? And why?" The first very faint flicker of humor lit her eyes, totally without fear. "You cannot have returned because you imagine it was I—or Mr. Pryce. You have very effectively proved that it was not, by helping us to blame each other." She turned a little away from him. "I will not say you made it happen, that would be to give you too much credit—or blame. Had we been stronger, had we the love we imagined we had, you could not have done such a thing." She brushed her hand over her skirt, removing a fleck of thread. "So why have you come?"

He was sorry for her, in spite of the contempt he had felt before. Disillusion is one of the bitterest of all griefs.

"Because I am driven back to the beginning again," he replied candidly. "All the information I thought I had is of little use. The judge's death appears, after all, to have had nothing to do with the Farriers' Lane case. Or if it does, it is a connection I haven't seen, and still cannot see now. There is nothing for me to do but go back to the physical details and reexamine each one to see if I have missed something, or misinterpreted it."

383

"How tedious," she said without feeling. "I can repeat everything I told you before, if you believe it may be helpful." And without waiting for him to reply, in a monotone she recited the events of the last day of Stafford's life, from seeing him at breakfast through Tamar Macaulay's visit, his agitation, to his leaving to go and interview Joshua Fielding and Devlin O'Neil again. She told him of Stafford's return, his preoccupation, which was not particularly unusual, the dinner they had shared.

"And he was perfectly well then?" he interrupted. "He was not sleepy, unusually inattentive? He ate well, without complaint of pain or discomfort?"

"Yes, he ate excellently. And we were served from the same dishes. There was nothing he took which I did not. More, of course, but just the same dishes. He cannot have been poisoned in this house, Mr. Pitt."

"No, I had already concluded that, Mrs. Stafford. Besides, we found the traces of opium in his flask. I wondered if he could have taken anything from it already, before the meal, that's all. I am checking everything . . ."

"I can see you are totally lost," she agreed with a flicker of a smile.

He could not entirely blame her, although her amusement stung. It was he who had shed light on a truth that maimed her so much. Without him she might never have seen her love for Pryce as anything less than a great passion. She would have to have been a woman of great generosity not to have hated him for it.

"May I speak with the valet, please?" he asked.

"Of course. He is still here, although I shall have to dismiss him presently. I have no need for his services." She reached for the bell rope embroidered in silk, and pulled it to summon a servant.

But the valet could tell him nothing useful. He had not seen the flask that evening, nor did he think that the judge had drunk from it. It was not his habit to use the flask when in his own home where he could send for a drink from the decanter merely by ringing a bell. Nor could any of the other servants add anything to what they had already said. He could feel their unspoken contempt that after this time, and all the questions, he was reduced to going over old facts he had known all along, and still he found no pattern from which he could deduce an answer. He was disgusted himself, and discouraged and angry.

The next person he saw was Judge Livesey, but he had to wait until the middle of the afternoon and find him in his chambers between other engagements. Livesey looked surprised to see him, but not disconcerted.

"Good afternoon, Inspector. What may I do for you on this occasion? I hope you have no further disasters to report." He said it with a smile, but there was no ease in his face, and certainly no humor. He looked tired; the purplish smudges under his eyes and the creases in his face from his nose to the corners of his lips were deeper, his mouth set in harder lines. Pitt remembered how harsh the news of Harrimore's arrest would be to him. The Godman appeal had been one of the achievements of his career. The dignity and assurance with which he had conducted it had earned him considerable praise both from the general public and, which would be sweeter, from his peers. Now, when it was too late, he was proved tragically wrong.

"No," Pitt said quietly. "No, there is nothing new, thank God. I am still back with the first crime for which I was called in. I am no further forward in learning who killed Mr. Stafford than I was at the beginning."

"Frustrating for you," Livesey remarked, almost without expression. "I have no idea how I can help you. I know nothing more than I did then."

"No sir, I had not held any hope that you did. But perhaps there are questions I omitted to ask which I might put to you now?"

"Of course." Livesey sat down heavily in the chair close to the fire, which must have been lit long before he returned from court. He indicated the other chair opposite, not so much in an invitation as a request that Pitt should cease to stand over him. "Please ask what you must. I will try to be of service to you." He sounded tired and as if the courtesy cost him a considerable effort.

"Thank you, sir." Pitt reclined less than comfortably. He did not bother to go over Stafford's visit to Livesey earlier that day, and the proof that the flask was uncontaminated when Stafford left. They had already exhausted that. He started with their meeting at the theater.

"You first saw him in the foyer, you said?"

"That is correct, but I did not speak to him then. There was a considerable crush of people, and a great deal of noise, as I daresay you recall?"

"Yes, indeed." Pitt remembered vividly the air of excitement and expectation, the raised voices, the constant, jostling movement. Conversation would have been difficult. "Where did you go from there?"

Livesey thought for a moment. "I started off up the stairs towards my box, then in the gallery I saw someone I knew and was about to stop for a word when he was accosted by a woman I find exceedingly tedious, so I changed my mind and went back down again for about five minutes, by which time they were gone. I went up to my box then, and sat down alone from that time until the curtain went up." He shrugged his heavy shoulders very slightly. "Of course I saw several other people I knew, taking their seats, but I spoke to none of them. One cannot, without making a spectacle of oneself." He searched Pitt's face curiously. "Is this really of any service to you, Inspector?"

"Not so far," Pitt admitted. "But it may be. Anyway, I know nowhere else to look."

"It will be regrettable if you are obliged to leave the matter unresolved," Livesey said with a curious, bitter twist to his mouth. "Not, I imagine, what you wish."

"I have not reached that stage yet."

There was nothing so crude as disbelief in Livesey's voice, or in the very gentle arching of his eyebrows. "Well, I shall certainly relate all that I remember of that evening, if you feel it may assist. You were in the box on the far side of him, one or two spaces away, as I recall. No doubt you saw all that I did."

"I don't mean anything of what happened in the box," Pitt said quickly, then as he saw Livesey's expression, realized his error. "No, that is foolish," he corrected himself before Livesey could do so. "I do not know what is relevant. If you saw anything at all, please tell me."

Livesey shrugged, and this time there was definitely humor in his face—dry, entirely intellectual, but very real.

"Of course. Naturally I did not spend the majority of the evening looking sideways at Mr. Stafford's box, but I glanced that way on several occasions. He was sitting towards the back to begin with, a little behind Mrs. Stafford. I formed the opinion that he had come largely on her account. He did not seem to have his attention entirely upon the stage, but to be concerned with his own thoughts. Not surprisingly. I have taken my wife to many events for her pleasure, not my own."

"Did he appear ill?"

"No, merely thinking. At least that is how it seemed to me. With the wisdom of hindsight I appreciate that he may have felt unwell." Livesey was watching Pitt now, and his blue eyes were amused. "Are you trying to ask me if I saw him drink from his flask? I don't believe so, but I cannot swear. He did reach for something from his pocket, but I was not paying sufficient attention to see what it was. I am sorry."

"It is not of importance. He did drink from it at some time, that is beyond question," Pitt said flatly.

"Indeed, tragically, that is true." Livesey frowned. "Tell me, Pitt, what is it you hope to learn? If I knew I might be better able to answer you. I confess, I don't see what you believe there is that could help. We know the poison was in the flask, and that he died of it. What assistance would it be if someone had seen him actually drink? Surely it is inescapable that it did happen?"

"Yes, of course it is," Pitt conceded. "I admit, I don't know. I am simply fishing for anything I can find."

"Well, I cannot think of anything further to add. I saw him drift into what I took at the time to be a sleep. It was not remarkable. He would certainly not be the first man to sleep in the theater!" Again the flash of humor crossed his face. "It was only when I saw Mrs. Stafford's agitation that I realized he was ill. Then, of course, I rose and went out of my own box and into theirs, to see if I could offer any assistance. The rest you know yourself."

"Not quite. There is the interval. Did you leave your box?"

"Yes. I went to find a little refreshment, and to stand. One gets stiff sitting for so long."

"Did you see Stafford leave his box?"

"No. I'm sorry."

"Did you go to the gentlemen's smoking room?"

"Very briefly. I looked in, and then left again immediately. To tell the truth there were one or two people there I preferred not to see. They insist on speaking of legal matters, and I wanted to enjoy an evening away from such things."

"And you didn't see Stafford until you returned to your box?"

"No. I'm sorry." Livesey rose to his feet, pushing himself up from the arms of his chair. "I am afraid there is nothing else I can tell you, Inspector. Nor could I usefully suggest anywhere further for you to look, except into poor Stafford's domestic life."

"Thank you for sparing me your time." Pitt stood up also. "You have been very patient."

"I am sorry I could be of no help." Livesey held out his hand and Pitt shook it. It was an unusual courtesy from a judge to a policeman, and he appreciated it.

After luncheon he went to the offices of Adolphus Pryce and was obliged to wait nearly half an hour before Pryce was free to see him. The office was the same, comfortable, elegant, and individual. Pryce himself was just as graceful, but there was a tiredness in his face and his gestures looked habitual, devoid of the inner energy they had had before. He too was disappointed in himself: his dreams had been shown to be shallow, his emotions dishonest, and it hurt him where there was no evasion, and as yet no healing.

"Yes, Pitt? What can I do for you?" he said politely. "Do sit down." He indicated the chair opposite. "I really feel I have already told you everything I know, but if there is something more, please ask me." He smiled bleakly. "I should congratulate you for solving the Farriers' Lane case. That was an excellent piece of work. You have certainly put the rest of us to shame. Poor Godman was innocent. That is a fact I shall not live with easily."

"Nor, I imagine, will many others," Pitt said grimly. "But you have nothing to reproach yourself for. Your duty was to prosecute him. You were the only one in the court who was an enemy in plain guise, and he knew you for one. The others were either on his side or supposed to be impartial."

"You are too hard on them, Pitt. Everyone believed him guilty. The evidence was overwhelming."

"Why?" Pitt asked, his eyes meeting Pryce's with challenge.

Pryce blinked. "I don't understand you. What do you mean, 'why'?"

"Why was it overwhelming? What came first, the evidence or the belief? I begin to think perhaps it was the belief."

Pryce sat down wearily. "Perhaps it was. We were all horrified, and a little frightened. You know the public is a savage animal when you disturb its deeper beliefs and awaken its fears. There is no purpose whatever in trying to reason with it, explain what you can do, and what you cannot, tell them how difficult it is. All they want is results. They do not care how you obtain them, they don't want to know the details or the cost. But you are a policeman, you must know that. I don't imagine they have left you uncriticized or harried over poor Stafford."

"No," Pitt said ruefully. "Although there hasn't been a public outcry. It was a quieter crime. It lacked the horror. I suppose people feel that a judge is somehow different from themselves, and so the fear is a step removed, not personal. There is no unreasoning monster out there in the

389

shadows crucifying people. Though certainly the Home Secretary has been down to chivvy us once or twice."

Pryce crossed his legs and a faint flicker of amusement touched his mouth.

"You sound bitter, Pitt. What can I help you with? I really have no idea who killed Stafford, or why."

"Neither have I," Pitt said sourly. "I am reduced to going over the facts again—and again. Did you see him during the interval that evening?"

Pryce looked vaguely surprised, as if he had been expecting some difficult question.

"Yes. He was in the smoking room, talking to various people. I don't think I can remember who. I spoke to him myself, but only briefly. Something of no meaning at all— the weather, or the latest cricket disaster, I think. I didn't see him drink from the flask, if that is what you are hoping."

"Did he have a glass in his hand?"

Pryce's eyes widened. "Come to think of it, yes, he did. Doesn't make a lot of sense, does it? Why does a man drink from a flask if he has a glass of whiskey in his hand?"

"A second one, I suppose," Pitt said thoughtfully. "He did drink from the flask, because he drank the poison. It was in the flask when we tested it. That is about the only fact which is incontrovertible."

"Well, there must be a limited number of people who could have put it there, by the mere physical facts," Pryce said logically. "One can reduce their number, surely? Disregard motive, for the time being. It has to be someone who had access to the flask after he left Livesey, because both Livesey and his companion were seen to drink from it then, and they are both in perfect health. And yet it was in the flask when Stafford drank from it later, presumably in the theater. It could be someone in the interval, I suppose."

"Who else was in the smoking room?"

"A couple of hundred people."

"They didn't all speak to Stafford. Can you recall the

names of anyone who might have been close enough to him to have spoken to him, or seen what happened?"

Pryce sat silent for a moment or two, looking bleakly at Pitt.

"I remember the Honorable Gerald Thompson," he said at last. "He has a voice that would break glass, and never stops talking. He was close to Stafford, and facing him. And Molesworth was there, from Chancery. Do you know him? No, I don't suppose you do. Big man, bald, with a white beard."

"Is that all you remember?" Pitt asked.

"There was a tremendous crush in there," Pryce protested. "Everyone elbowing their way through, trying not to spill drinks, vying for attention, all talking at once. And there was a bit of a commotion going on because Oscar Wilde was there, and at least a dozen people wanted to speak to him. I can't think why. He was close to Stafford." Pryce's face lit with malicious amusement. "You could always go and ask him."

"Is he likely to have noticed anything?"

Pryce's eyebrows shot up. "I have no idea. I should doubt it. Too busy being amusing."

"Thank you." Pitt rose to his feet. At least Pryce had given him something to pursue, although he had no plan beyond that, nothing else to seek, no one to question.

"Not at all," Pryce replied. "I imagine I will see you again. What I've given you will be of little use. Even if someone did see him drink from the flask, it won't tell you anything, unless they saw someone else put something into it—and that seems a little like hoping someone will tell you the Derby winner before the day."

Pitt took his leave without further comment. They had said it all.

Outside it was bitterly cold with a wind off the river which cut through the wool of his coat, into his flesh. He walked rapidly along the footpath, head down, woollen muffler tight, collar up over his ears, until he came to the main thoroughfare where he could hail a cab back to Bow Street. Before he could ask those gentlemen what they

391

could remember of the smoking room in the theater on a night now several weeks ago, he must find out where they lived.

The Honorable Gerald Thompson fitted Pryce's description unpleasantly well. He did indeed have a voice which was unusual in tone, a little high and extraordinarily penetrating, and a braying laugh Pitt heard before he saw him.

He received Pitt in the hallway of his club in Pall Mall, preferring not to be seen in the company of a questionable character in one of the main rooms. This way he could pretend, if anyone asked him, that Pitt was merely on some errand and it was not a personal call at all.

"Thank heaven you had the wit to come in your own clothes," he said dryly. "Well, what can I do for you? Don't be long about it, there's a good fellow."

Pitt swallowed the rejoinder he would have used were he free to, and came straight to the point. "I believe you were in the smoking room at the theater the night Judge Stafford died, sir?"

"As were several hundred other people," Thompson agreed.

"Indeed. Did you see the judge, sir?"

"I believe so. But I have no idea who slipped poison into his flask. If I had, I should have told you so long before now. My moral duty."

"Of course. Do you remember if the judge had a drink in his hand when you saw him?"

The Honorable Gerald screwed up his face for several moments, then suddenly opened his eyes wide. "Rather think he had, but he finished it while I was watching him. Saw him raise his hand to attract the waiter for another."

"Did you see the waiter bring it to him?"

"No, come to think of it, the fellow didn't appear at all. Fearful melee in those places, you know. Fortunate to get anything at all. Suppose that was why he took a sip from his own flask, poor devil. Not that I saw him do it. Can't help you."

"Thank you, sir." Pitt asked him a few more questions

about others who might have observed something, and learned nothing of profit. He thanked the Honorable Gerald and took his leave.

The learned Mr. Molesworth was even less help. He had seen Stafford certainly, but standing, trying to attract the waiter's attention and failing. He had not observed him drinking from his own flask, or talking to anyone in particular. He was brisk, businesslike and obviously in a hurry.

Mr. Oscar Fingal O'Flahertie Wills Wilde was as different as it was possible to be. Pitt took some time to find him, but eventually he was successful in catching him at his desk in his own rooms. He received Pitt with interest and a remarkable courtesy, rising to greet him, waving his hand and inviting him to be seated. The room was filled with books and papers, and it was apparent that Pitt had interrupted his working.

"I am sorry to intrude, sir," Pitt apologized sincerely. "I am at my wits' end, or I should not have imposed."

"It is when one is at one's wits' end that one lets go and finds a courage and imagination in despair not possible in the more comfortable emotions," Wilde replied immediately. "Over what do you feel such a passion, Mr. Pitt? And what may I do, beyond offer you my pity, which you have gratis, for all it may mean to you."

"I am investigating the murder of Mr. Justice Stafford."

"Oh dear." Wilde screwed up his face. "What execrable taste. What an uncivilized thing to do—murder a man in his box at the theater! How can we poor playwrights compete with such a thing? I am a critic, Mr. Pitt, but even my bitterest and most damaging remarks have not gone so far. I may write that a work is poor, but I shall offer my remarks and leave the playgoer to make his own decision. This was pure sabotage—and quite inexcusable."

Pitt had prepared himself to be surprised; nevertheless, he was still disconcerted by Wilde's attitude. It was apparently callous, and yet looking at the long face with its slightly drooping eyes and large mouth he saw no cruelty in it, and innocence rather than indifference.

393

"I believe you were in the smoking room during the first interval?" he said aloud.

"Certainly. A most agreeable place, full of posings and attitudes, everyone trying to appear what they wished to be, rather than what they were. Do you like observing people, Inspector?"

"It is very often my job," Pitt replied with a slight smile.

"And mine," Wilde agreed quickly. "For utterly different reasons, of course. What did I observe that may be of interest to you? I didn't see anyone slip poison into the poor devil's flask." His eyes widened. "You see—I read the newspapers, not just the criticisms, although art is even better organized than life. Crime so seldom has any humor, don't you find? Real crime, that is. I loathe the squalid. If one has to do something distasteful, one should at least do it with flair."

"But you did see the judge?"

"I did," Wilde agreed, his eyes never leaving Pitt's face. He seemed to find him both interesting and agreeable. In spite of his pose, Pitt could not help liking the man.

"Did you see him drink from his flask?"

"You know, this is absurd—I didn't—but I did see him hand it to someone else, a Mr. Richard Gibson. I only know the judge from his obituary photograph in the newspapers, but Gibson I have met. Stafford took the flask out of his pocket and passed it to this acquaintance, who thanked him and took a good-sized gulp from it before handing it back." He raised his eyebrows and looked at Pitt curiously. "I assume that means that someone poisoned it after that? I don't envy you. I did not know opium would kill anyone so rapidly. But I assure you that is what happened." He leaned back a fraction, concentrating on his inner vision. "I can see it quite clearly in my mind. Stafford gave the flask to this man, who drank from it and handed it back. Stafford didn't drink from it himself. He was smoking, a large cigar. The bell rang for the second act, and Stafford took the cigar out of his mouth, pulled a face as if he disliked it, then knocked the burning end off and put it in his jacket pocket." He frowned.

"You mean in his cigar case," Pitt corrected.

"No, I don't," Wilde said. "I mean in his pocket, as I said. Filthy habit. But he didn't drink, of that I am positive. And Gibson is still alive and flourishing. I saw him only the other day. What a curious circumstance. How do you explain it?"

Pitt was thinking the same thing, ideas half formed whirling in his head.

"You are quite sure?" he asked.

"Of course." Wilde's eyebrows rose. "What would be the purpose in inventing such a thing? It is only interesting if it is true."

Pitt stood up.

Wilde looked up at him, his face alive with interest. "You have thought of something! I can see it in your eyes. What is it? I have provided you with the vital clue! All is revealed—you know the heart of the murderer—and less interesting but more to the point, you know his face."

"I may." Pitt smiled in spite of himself. "Certainly I have an idea as to the weapon—"

"Opium in the whiskey flask."

"Perhaps not. Thank you, Mr. Wilde. You have been of the utmost help. Now if you will excuse me, I have something extremely unpleasant to do."

"Shall I now have to scan the newspapers to learn what it is?" Wilde asked plaintively.

"Yes—I'm sorry. Good day, sir."

"Interesting, frustrating, interrupted, in patches most stimulating," Wilde answered. "*Good* is far too tame and pedestrian a word. Have you no imagination, man?"

Pitt smiled back at him from the doorway. "It is otherwise occupied."

Wilde waved him out with total agreeability and resumed his work.

Pitt took a hansom straight to Stafford's house and asked to see Juniper.

"I expected you back, Mr. Pitt," she said tartly. "I confess to that—but not so soon. I appreciate that you are confounded, but I have done everything I can. I really cannot help you any further."

"Yes, you can, Mrs. Stafford," he said quickly. "May I see Mr. Stafford's valet again? I must know what has happened to Mr. Stafford's clothes."

Her face pinched. "Of course you may see the valet if you wish. My husband's clothes are still here. I have not had the heart to dispose of them yet. It will have to be done, of course, but it is a duty I have not steeled myself for." She reached for the bell, still looking at him. "May I ask what you hope to learn from them?"

"I would prefer not to say until I am certain," he answered. "If I might speak to the valet first . . ."

"If you wish." There was very little interest in her face or her voice. All the vitality which had been so vivid in her before was drained away, killed. She wanted an end to it, but the details were of no importance anymore.

When the butler answered her summons she ordered him to take Pitt upstairs to the master's dressing room and have the valet wait upon him there.

When the valet arrived, a little out of breath, he regarded Pitt with perplexity. He was a very stout man with black hair and a homely face, and he did not conceal his surprise at seeing Pitt again.

"Yes sir. What can I do for you?"

"Judge Stafford's suit the night he died. Where is it now?" Pitt asked.

The man was genuinely shocked.

"That was Mr. Stafford's best suit, sir! 'Ad it made for 'im just a few months back. Best quality wool barathea."

"Yes, I'm sure, but where is it?"

" 'E was buried in it, sir. What you'd expect?"

Pitt swore in weariness and exasperation.

The valet stared at him. He was too well trained for anything a man did to shake his composure, unless of course it was another servant, which was entirely a different matter.

"And his cigar case, where is that?" Pitt demanded.

"In 'is dresser, sir, as it ought. I took all 'is things out of 'is pockets, natural."

"May I see the cigar case?"

The valet's eyebrows rose. "Yes sir. O' course you may." He kept his voice civil, but his belief was plain that Pitt was eccentric at the very least. He went to the dresser and opened the top drawer. He took out a silver cigar case and passed it across.

Pitt opened it with shaking fingers. It was empty. It was foolish, but he was bitterly disappointed.

"What did you take out of this?" he said in a low, tight voice.

"Nothing, sir." The man was aggrieved.

"Not the best cigars—to smoke yourself?" Pitt pressed, although if he had, it would disprove his theory. "Not a butt?"

"No sir. There weren't nothing in it! I swear by God it was just like it is now. Empty."

"The judge smoked half a cigar at the theater that night, and put the other half back in his pocket. What happened to it?"

"Oh, that." Relief flooded the man's face. "I threw it out, sir. Couldn't bury the poor man with a cigar butt in his pocket. Messy thing, it was."

"Messy? Coming to pieces?" Pitt asked.

"Yes sir."

"And that suit is still on Mr. Stafford?"

"Yes sir." The valet stared at him with growing alarm.

"Thank you. That's all." And without waiting any further he went downstairs, bade the footman in the hall thank Mrs. Stafford, and took his leave.

"You what?" Drummond demanded incredulously, his face dark.

"I want to exhume the body of Samuel Stafford," Pitt repeated as calmly as he could, but still his voice shook. "I have to."

"For the love of God—why? You know what he died of!" Drummond was appalled. He leaned across his desk,

397

staring at Pitt in consternation. "Whatever purpose can it serve, apart from distressing everyone?" he demanded. "We've got enough public anger and blame over this already. Don't make it immeasurably worse, Pitt."

"It's the only chance I have of solving it."

"Chance?" Drummond's voice rose in exasperation. "Chance is not sufficient. You must be sure, if I am going to ask the Home Office for permission to dig him up. Explain to me exactly what you will achieve."

Still standing in front of the desk like a schoolboy, Pitt explained.

"On the cigar?" Drummond said with slowly widening eyes. "As well as in the flask? But why? That's absurd."

"Not as well as, sir," Pitt said patiently. "Instead of. That would explain why the whiskey in the flask didn't have any effect on the other man who drank it."

"Aren't you forgetting we found opium in the flask?" Drummond asked with only a slight edge of sarcasm. He was too worried to give it full rein. "And all this on the word of Oscar Wilde, of all people? I know you're desperate, Pitt, but I think this is taking it too far. It isn't sense. I don't think I could get you an exhumation order on the evidence, even if I wanted to."

"But if the opium was on the cigar butt, not the flask, it changes everything," Pitt argued desperately. "Then there is only one conclusion."

"It was in the flask, Pitt! The medical examiner found it there. That is a fact. And anyway, the cigar butt was thrown out, you told me that."

"I know, but if it was in his pocket for several hours, and crumbling, as the valet said, there may be enough there for traces of opium to be found."

Doubt clouded Drummond's eyes.

"It's the only explanation we've got," Pitt said again. "There's nothing else to pursue. Are you prepared to close the case unsolved? Someone killed Judge Stafford . . ."

Drummond took a deep breath. "And poor Paterson," he added very softly. "I feel very badly about that. I don't know whether the Home Office will grant it, but I'll try. You'd better be right."

Pitt said nothing, except to thank him. He had no certainty to reassure either of them.

Until Micah Drummond should tell him whether he had succeeded or not, there was nothing further for Pitt to do regarding the exhumation. But one thing was quite clear in his mind. The solution to Paterson's death would not be answered by finding opium in Stafford's pocket. That was still as big a mystery as it had been the very first morning when they found the body. Only one thing was beyond question. Harrimore had not killed him.

Without forming a conscious decision, Pitt found himself outside on the pavement in Bow Street looking for a hansom. When he stopped one, he gave the address of Paterson's lodgings in Battersea, and sat uncomfortably as the vehicle lurched forward and clattered along the street.

When they arrived he climbed out, paid the driver and went to the door. It was opened by the same pale, grim woman as before. Her face darkened as soon as she recognized Pitt, and she made as if to close it.

He put his foot against the lintel. "I want to see Constable Paterson's rooms again, if you please," he asked.

"They ain't Constable Paterson's rooms," she said coldly. "They're mine, an' I let 'em to a Mr. 'Obbs. I can't go openin' 'em up an' disturbin' 'im, for any ol' p'lice as comes 'ere."

"Why would you want to stop me from finding out who murdered Paterson?" he asked with a hard edge to his voice. "It would be most unpleasant for you if I were obliged to have police watching the house day and night, and question all your lodgers again. I'm surprised you don't think it altogether a better thing to let me come in and look at one room."

"Or'right," she snapped. "Bleedin' rozzers. I s'pose there in't nuffin' I can do ter stop yer. Bastard!"

He ignored her and went up the stairs to the door of what had been Paterson's rooms, and were now presumably those of Mr. Hobbs. He knocked loudly.

There were several seconds of silence, then a scuffling of shoes on the far side, and the door opened about six inches. A face appeared a foot or so below him, pale, surrounded by gray whiskers. Anxious blue eyes looked up.

"Mr. Hobbs?" Pitt asked.

"Y-Yes, y-yes, that's me. What can I do for you, sir?"

"I am Inspector Pitt of the metropolitan police . . ."

"Oh—oh dear!" Hobbs was filled with alarm. "I assure you, I know of no crime, sir, none at all! I am sure I regret, but I can offer you no assistance whatever."

"On the contrary, Mr. Hobbs, you can allow me inside to look at your rooms, which as you are no doubt aware were the scene of a tragedy."

"Oh, no sir, you are mistaken," Hobbs said in considerable agitation. "That was next door, I assure you! Yes, yes, next door."

"No, Mr. Hobbs, it was here."

"Oh! But you must be mistaken. The landlady assured me . . ."

"Possibly. But I was among those who found the body. I remember quite clearly." He felt sorry for the man's distress. "It seems you have been lied to, possibly in order to secure your tenancy. But they are very agreeable rooms. I wouldn't let it dissuade you."

"But really—murder, sir. This is dreadful!" Hobbs moved from one foot to the other.

"May I come in?"

"Well—yes, I suppose so, if you must. I am a law-abiding man, sir. I have no right to stop you."

"Yes, you have, until I obtain a warrant, but I shall certainly do so, if you make it necessary."

"No! No, not at all. Please." And he opened the door so far back it knocked against the stop and shuddered forward again.

Pitt went in, remembering sharply and with a peculiar jolt of sadness his first time here, Livesey sitting in the chair looking sick, and the body of young Paterson still hanging by its rope in the bedroom.

"Thank you, Mr. Hobbs. If you don't mind, it is the bedroom I wish to see."

"The bedroom. Oh, my sainted aunt! The bedroom!" Hobbs's hand flew to his face. "Oh dear—you don't mean—not in the bedroom? The poor soul! I shall have to have the bed moved. I can't sleep there now."

"Why not? It is no different from last night," Pitt said with less sympathy than he might have felt were there not so many other problems boiling in his mind.

"Oh, my dear sir—you jest at my expense." Hobbs followed him anxiously to the bedroom door. "Or you are totally without sensitivity."

Pitt had no time to be concerned about him. He knew he was being abrupt, but his mind was turning over every possibility, new ideas forming painfully. He looked at the room. It had not changed from his first visit except that of course the dreadful corpse of Paterson was no longer there, and the chandelier had been hung up again. Other than that it appeared totally untouched.

"What are you looking for?" Hobbs demanded from the doorway. "What is it? What do you think is here?"

Pitt stood motionless in the center of the floor, then began to turn very slowly, looking first at the bed, then the window.

"I'm not sure," he replied absently. "I won't know unless I see it—perhaps . . ."

Hobbs let out a gasp and fell silent.

Pitt turned towards the chest of drawers. It looked vaguely out of place, and yet he was sure it had been precisely there the first time.

"Have you moved that?" He looked around at Hobbs.

"The chest?" Hobbs was startled. "No sir. Most definitely not. I have moved nothing at all. Why should I?"

Pitt walked over to it. The picture on the wall was too close to it. But the picture had not been moved. He lifted it to make sure. There was no mark on the paper behind it, no pinhole. He ran his fingers over it to make doubly sure.

"What are you looking for, sir?" Hobbs said angrily, alarm making his voice rise in both pitch and volume.

Pitt bent down and looked very carefully at the floorboards, and at last he saw it, a very slight indentation about six inches from the front foot of the chest of drawers. There was a second indentation six inches from the back foot. That was where it had been accustomed to stand! It had been moved. And when he took off the cloth and looked at the polished surface there were scratch marks such as if someone had stood on it wearing boots, and slipped a little, losing his footing. He felt a little sick.

"You are sure you haven't moved this?" He swung around to stare at Hobbs.

"I've told you, sir, I have not moved it," Hobbs said furiously. "It is exactly where it was when I came here. Do you wish me to take my oath upon it? I will."

Pitt rose to his feet. "No, thank you, I don't think it will be necessary, but if it is, I shall call upon you to do so."

"Why? What does it mean?" Hobbs was pale with agitation and mounting fear.

"It means, I think, that Constable Paterson moved this piece of furniture out of its place in order to climb up and take down the chandelier, then place his noose over the hook, and jump," Pitt answered him.

"You mean his—murderer!" Hobbs gasped.

"No, Mr. Hobbs," Pitt corrected. "I mean Paterson himself, when he realized what he had done to Aaron Godman; when he realized how he had allowed his horror and his rage at the time to blind him not only to the truth but to both honor and justice. He not only reached the wrong conclusion, he reached it by dishonest means. He did not listen to the flower seller; he made up his mind what had happened and coerced her into believing it. He was so sure he was right he forced the issue—and he was wrong."

"Stop it," Hobbs said in anguish. "I don't want to hear it. It is quite terrible! I know what you are talking about—that murder in Farriers' Lane. I remember when they hanged Godman. If what you are saying is true, then what hope is there for any of us? It can't be! Godman was tried and found guilty, the judges all said so. You must be wrong." He was wringing his hands in consternation. "They haven't convicted Harrimore yet—and they won't. You'll see. British justice is the best in the world. I know that, even if you don't."

"I don't know whether it is or not," Pitt said evenly. "It doesn't really matter."

"How can you say that?" Hobbs was beside himself, his face white but for two hectic spots of color high in his cheeks. "That is monstrous. What matters on earth, if that doesn't?"

"It doesn't matter whether other people's justice is better or worse," Pitt explained with an effort at patience. "It matters that in this case we were wrong. You may find it painful. So will many others. That won't change it. The only choice we have now is whether we will lie about it still and try to conceal it, condoning the act, becoming party to Godman's death, or if we will uncover it and make damnably sure it doesn't happen again—at least not easily. Which would you rather, Mr. Hobbs?"

"I—I, er . . ." Hobbs fell silent, staring at Pitt as if he had changed shape in front of him into something hideous. But he had neither spirit nor conviction to argue. Something in him knew Pitt was right.

Pitt said nothing more. He tipped his hat very slightly and went out past Hobbs, thanking him, and left.

"I haven't got your exhumation order yet," Drummond said quickly as soon as Pitt came into the office. "I'm still trying."

Pitt threw himself down in the chair by the fire without waiting to be asked.

"Paterson committed suicide," he said.

"You told me he couldn't have," Drummond replied. "And anyway, why on earth should he?"

"Wouldn't it cross your mind, if you realized you had manufactured evidence that had hanged an innocent man?" Pitt demanded. He sank farther into the chair. "Paterson wasn't a bad man. The Farriers' Lane murder sickened him.

He let his emotions govern his behavior. He was outraged, and frightened. He needed to find whoever was guilty, not just for the law but for himself, because he could not live with the idea that whoever it was was beyond the law to catch."

"Not a weakness I fail to understand," Drummond said quietly, standing looking down at Pitt. "I think a few of us suffer from that. It frightens me to think that such crimes can happen at all. We need to believe we can find the killers and prove their guilt. We need to believe in our own superiority, because the alternative is too dreadful." He pushed his hands deep into his pockets. "Poor Paterson."

Pitt said nothing. His mind was darkened by pity for him, imagining what he must have thought that last day of his life as he stood in his bedroom, bitterly alone, facing the ultimate failure. It was a knowledge he could never have denied, but he took a perverse satisfaction in turning the knife in himself, simply because it was truth, it was not escape, and he was sickened by escape. "He tore off his own stripes," he said aloud. "It was a mark of dishonor, his own way of confessing."

Drummond was silent for a long time.

"I still don't see how you can be right," he said at last, breaking into Pitt's thoughts. "You said there was no way Paterson could have done it himself. There was nothing near for him to have climbed on. What are you saying happened?"

"That it was tidied up in order to look like murder," Pitt replied quietly.

"For heaven's sake, why? And by whom?"

"By Livesey, of course, when he found him, before he called us."

"Livesey!" Drummond's voice was high with disbelief. "Why? Why should he care if poor Paterson was condemned as a suicide? He may have pitied the man, but he is an appeal court judge. He wouldn't tamper with evidence."

Pitt rose to his feet. "Nothing to do with pity. That was

before we knew Godman was innocent. Tell me when you have that exhumation order."

"I don't even know if I can get it. Pitt! Where are you going?"

"Home," Pitt said from the doorway. "There's nothing more I can do now. I'd like to go home to something clean and innocent before I dig up Stafford. I shall go and tell my children some fairy story before they go to bed, something about good and evil, where it all ends happily."

The exhumation order was granted late in the evening, but Micah Drummond kept it till the early morning, and collected Pitt at seven o'clock in the drizzling darkness before dawn. The streets were wet, lamplight gleaming on the pavements and the splash and hiss of wheels in the water mingled with the clatter of hooves and slam of doors.

There was nothing to say. They sat together huddled up in greatcoats in the back of the cab and journeyed through the streets to the graveyard where they got out still in silence. Side by side they walked through the squelching mud over to the little group of men in rough clothes leaning on their spades. There was already a deep hole in the cold earth, bull's-eye lanterns glowing like angry flares, showing the dark soil where it was turned. Pitt could smell the wet earth and feel the rain running down the back of his neck. Two lengths of rope were in place.

" 'Allo, Guv," one of the men said to Drummond. "You want that there coffin lifted now?"

"Yes, please," Drummond replied.

Pitt stood beside him, chilled through, the wind in his face. The lamp was held high, light gleaming on the wet handles of the spades.

Slowly the men hauled on the ropes and the coffin rose into sight, handles shining where they had been wiped by a rough hand. One man leaned forward and brushed the loose earth off the top, smearing it in the rain. With difficulty they pulled it sideways out of the hole and set it on the ground. One of the men slipped in the mud and sent a shower of pebbles rattling down into the hole. Someone swore and crossed himself.

"Open it," Drummond ordered.

The man took a screwdriver out of his coat pocket and obeyed. One of the others held the lantern higher. It took him several moments before finally he had all the screws removed and he could lift the lid. He looked away as he did it, his face pale. One of the others shuddered and said a few words of prayer.

"Thank you." Pitt stepped forward. He had requested this. He must be the one to look.

The body was not as decayed as he had expected, probably because it was winter and the ground was cold. Still he would not look at the gray face more than once. With considerable difficulty he eased the limp body up and was immensely relieved when one of the men came forward and helped him. Very carefully he undid the jacket and slipped it off first one arm, then the other, then pulled it from underneath, laying the body back carefully. He looked at the jacket. As the valet had said, it was good cloth. Very gently he put his fingers into the pockets one by one. He was acutely conscious of the nasty smell and a sweetness that was unpleasant. He was glad of the freezing rain on his face. In the first pocket there was nothing except a clean handkerchief. What an odd thing to be put there. It was a thought which he found curiously pitiful, as if someone had done it for him as if he could need it.

Pitt took a deep breath and tried the next pocket. His fingers met tobacco fragments and a slight stickiness. He took his hand out and smelled it. There was only a faint odor of tobacco. He looked up at Drummond.

"Anything?" Drummond asked.

"I think so. If this is opium then we have the answer. I'll take it to the medical examiner." He turned to the diggers. "Thank you. You can close it again and put it back."

"That all, Guv? Yer jus' want 'is coat?"

"Yes, thank you, just his coat."

"Jeez!"

Drummond and Pitt turned away and Pitt folded the coat

to carry it carefully. The dawn was graying very slightly in the east, dull and heavy in the overcast. They walked slowly, picking their way back down the sodden path to the waiting cab, where the horse was stamping in the roadway and snorting white breath as the smell of the grave frightened it.

"I'm coming with you," Drummond said as soon as they were inside. "I want to know what the medical examiner says."

Pitt smiled grimly.

"Opium," the medical examiner stated, looking up at Pitt through his eyebrows. "Paste of opium."

"Strong enough to kill a man if he put a cigar end with that on it into his mouth?" Pitt asked.

"That concentration, yes. Not immediately, but after thirty minutes or so, could be."

"Thank you."

"But there was opium in the whiskey," the medical examiner said hastily.

"I know," Pitt agreed. "But someone else was seen to drink from the flask in the theater, and came to no harm."

"Impossible. The concentration in that flask was enough to kill anyone!"

"Pitt?" Drummond demanded. Both men were looking at him now.

"The opium that killed Stafford was on the cigar. The opium in the flask was put there after he was dead," Pitt explained.

"After . . ." Drummond was very still, his face pale. "You mean, to confuse us. But that means . . ."

"Precisely," Pitt replied.

"Why? For God's sake, why?" Drummond was confused and distressed.

"One of the oldest of reasons," Pitt answered. "To keep the public image, the honor and the status he had earned over the years. To be proved wrong now would be a blow he could not take. He is a proud man."

"But murder," Drummond protested.

"I daresay it began simply as coercion, a tacit conspiracy among them all." Pitt drove his hands into his pockets and hunched his shoulders. "They must have realized only very slowly that there was a possibility they had overlooked something, been too hasty to accept an answer because they needed one so badly. The public were clamoring. The Home Office would not wait. Everywhere they turned there was hysteria, pressure, fear. They clung together, bolstering each other up, and privately each took his own way of escaping from it, into retirement, the bottle, building allies against the day they might need them, salving conscience with good work—all except Stafford. His conscience nagged him until he found the courage to go back and look again. And it cost him his life."

Drummond looked tired and sad, but he said nothing.

"They killed Godman," Pitt said quietly. "I daresay they believed it was right at the time, a service to the law—and the people. But in the end he ruined them all, one way or another. Now if you will excuse me, I have a duty to carry out."

"Yes—yes, of course. Pitt!"

"Yes sir?"

"I have no regrets over leaving the police force—but I might have had, were it not you taking my place."

Pitt smiled, raised his hand as if to salute, then let it fall.

He entered Judge Livesey's chambers without knocking and saw Livesey sitting behind his desk.

"Morning, Pitt," Livesey said wearily. "I didn't hear you knock." Then he saw Pitt's face and he frowned, slowly, the color dying from his cheeks. "What is it?" His voice was husky, forming the words with difficulty.

"I have just exhumed Samuel Stafford's body."

"What for, for God's sake?"

"His dinner jacket. The opium on the unsmoked portion of his cigar . . ."

The last of the blood drained from Livesey's face. His eyes met Pitt's and he knew the end, as a man recognizes death when he sees it.

"He betrayed the law," he said very quietly, so quietly Pitt barely heard him, although the words fell like stones.

"No," Pitt argued with passionate belief. "It was you who betrayed the law."

Livesey rose from his chair like a man asleep.

"Allow me the dignity of walking out of here without manacles," he said.

"I had no intention of manacling you," Pitt answered him.

"Thank you."

"I have no wish to take anything from you. You have already robbed yourself of everything of worth."

Livesey stopped and looked at him out of dead eyes. He perceived what Pitt meant, and understood despair.

The newest Detective Thomas and
Charlotte Pitt mystery

THE HYDE PARK
HEADSMAN

by

Anne Perry

is now available in hardcover
in bookstores everywhere.

At dawn's half light, a romantic couple about to
take a boat ride in Hyde Park discovers a decap-
itated man in one of the boats. This explosive
case is Thomas Pitt's first since his promotion to
superintendent of Bow Street Station, and he is
going to need all the help his intrepid wife Charlotte can give him to wrap up this case.

A Fawcett Columbine book.

Read on for the opening pages of
THE HYDE PARK HEADSMAN . . .

1

"*Oh George.*" Millicent let out her breath in a sigh of happiness. "Isn't it beautiful? I've never been out in the park at this time of the morning before. The dawn is so romantic, don't you think? It's the beginning of everything!"

George said nothing, but tiptoed a little more rapidly over the wet grass.

"Look at the light on the water." Millicent went on ecstatically. "It's just like a great silver plate."

"Funny shape for a plate," George muttered, regarding the long, narrow snake of the Serpentine with less enthusiasm than she.

"It will be like fairyland out there." Mildred had no respect for the practical at a time like this. She had crept out through the park to sail on the dawn-lit water alone with George. What place had the literal at such a point? She picked up her skirts to keep them from getting soaked in the dew; this much was merely common sense, which was a totally different thing. No one wanted the wet, heavy fabric flapping around their ankles.

"There's someone already out," George said with disgust. And in the broadening light it was quite plain that there was indeed one of the small boats about three yards from

413

the shore, but the figure in it was curiously bent over, as if looking for something in the bottom of the boat by his feet.

Millicent could hardly contain her disappointment. Where was the romance if someone else was present, someone not part of the idyll? One could pretend Hyde Park, in the middle of London, were a wood in some European archdukedom and George a prince, or at least a knight, but some other mundane-minded oarsman would definitely spoil it; apart from the fact that she should not be here, unchaperoned, and a witness was not welcome.

"Maybe he'll go away," she said hopefully.

"He's not moving," George replied with annoyance. He raised his voice. "Excuse me, sir. Are you quite well?" He frowned. "I can't see the fellow's face at all," he added to Millicent. "Wait here. I shall see if he will be a gentleman and move a little away." And he strode down towards the bank regardless of getting his shoes soaked, hesitated on the verge, then stumbled to his knees and slid with a violent splash into the water.

"Oh!" Millicent was horrified, painfully embarrassed for him, and having difficulty stifling her intense desire to giggle. "Oh, George!" She ran down the grass to where he was thrashing around in the shallows making a fearful noise and stirring up mud without seeming to regain his feet. Extraordinarily, the man in the boat took no notice whatsoever.

Then in the fast strengthening light, Millicent saw why. She had assumed he was bent forward, as had George. It was not so. His head was absent. There was nothing above his shoulders but the blood-soaked stump of his neck.

Millicent crumpled into total oblivion and fell headlong onto the grass.

"Yes sir," the constable said smartly. "Captain the Honorable Oakley Winthrop, R.N. Found 'eadless in one o' them little rowboats on the Serpentine. This mornin' about dawn. Two young lovers off for a romantic trip." He invested the word *romantic* with infinite scorn. "Poor souls fainted clean away—got no stomach for the likes o' that."

"Not unnatural," Superintendent Thomas Pitt said reasonably. "I should find it a very worrying thought if they had."

The constable quite obviously did not understand him.

"Yes sir," he said with bland obedience. "The local bobby were called, when the gentleman pulled 'isself together and got out o' the water. I gather as 'e fell in wi' the shock o' the event, like." His lips twitched very slightly but his voice was carefully ironed of even the suspicion of humor. "Constable Withers, that was 'im what was called, 'is bein' on duty in the park, like. 'E took one look at the corpse an' knew as e'd got a real nasty one, so 'e sent for 'is sergeant, an' they looked a bit closer, like." He drew in his breath, waiting for Pitt to say something.

"Yes?" Pitt prompted.

"That's when they found 'oo the dead man were," the constable continued. " 'Im being an important naval man, and an 'Honorable,' like, they thought as it should be someone o' your rank to 'andle it—sir." He looked at Pitt with satisfaction.

Pitt was newly promoted to superintendent. He had fought it long because he knew his real skill, which was very considerable, lay in working with people, both with the denizens of the semiunderworld, the poor or the truly criminal, and with the inhabitants of the servants' quarters, the front parlors, and the withdrawing rooms of the gentry.

Then in the late autumn of last year, 1889, his superior, Micah Drummond, had retired from office in order to marry the woman he had loved ever since the appalling scandal that had ruined her husband and finally taken his life. He had recommended Pitt to fill his place on the grounds that although Pitt was not a gentleman, as Drummond most certainly was, he had the experience of actual police work, at which he was undoubtedly gifted, and had proved himself able to solve even the most delicate cases involving the politically or socially powerful.

And after the fiasco of the Whitechapel murders, still unsolved and perhaps destined to remain so, and the fierce unpopularity of the police, the public lack of faith in them, it was time for a bold change.

415

So now in the spring of 1890, the dawn of a new decade, Pitt was in charge of the Bow Street station, with special responsibility for sensitive cases which threatened to become explosive if not handled with both tact and extreme dispatch. Hence P.C. Grover was standing in front of him in the beautiful office which he had inherited from Micah Drummond, telling him of the decapitation of Captain the Honorable Oakley Winthrop, knowing that Pitt would be obliged to handle the case.

"What else do you know about it?" Pitt asked, looking up at Grover and leaning back in his chair, although at times like this he still felt it to be Drummond's chair.

"Sir?" Grover raised his eyebrows.

"What did the medical officer say?" Pitt prompted.

"Died of 'avin' 'is 'ead cut orf," Grover replied, lifting his chin a little.

Pitt considered telling him not to be insolent, but he was still feeling his way with the men in his command. He had not worked with them closely before, always having had one sergeant with him at most, more often no one at all. He was regarded more as a rival than a colleague.

They had obeyed Micah Drummond because he was from a distinguished family with private means and had a career in the army behind him, and thus was of a class doubly used to command. Pitt was totally different, a gamekeeper's son who spoke well only because he had been educated, by grace, with the son of the estate. He had neither the manner nor the appearance of one born to lead. He was tall, but he frequently stood awkwardly. His hair was untidy, even on his best days. On his worst it looked as if he had been blown in by a gale. He dressed with abandon, and kept in his pockets a marvelous assortment of articles which he thought might one day prove handy.

The Bow Street men were slow to get used to him, and he was finding leadership alien to his nature. He was used to disregarding the rules, and being tolerated because he succeeded. Command placed quite different obligations on him and required a stiffer and less eccentric example to be

416

set. Suddenly he was responsible for other men's orders, their successes and failures, even their physical safety.

Pitt fixed Grover with a cold eye. "Time of death, Constable," he said levelly. "That would be more instructive to know. And was he killed in the boat or brought there afterwards?"

Grover's face fell. "Oh, I don't think we know that, sir. Not yet. Bit of a risky thing to do, though, chop a man's 'ead orf right there in the park. Could 'ave bin seen by anyone out for a walk."

"And how many people were out for a walk at that hour, Grover?"

Grover shifted his feet.

"Oh, well, don't seem as if there were nobody but them two as found 'im. But your murderer couldn't 'ave counted on that, could 'e." It was a statement rather than a question. "Could've been anyone out for a morning ride," he went on reasonably. "Or even someone comin' home late from a party, or a night out, takin' the air . . ."

"That is if it was done in daylight," Pitt pointed out. "Perhaps it was done long before that. Have you found anyone else who was in the park yet?"

"No sir, not yet. We came to report it to you, Mr. Pitt, as soon as we realized as it were someone important." It was his ultimate justification, and he knew it was sufficient.

"Right," Pitt agreed. "By the way, did you find the head?"

"Yes sir, it was right there in the boat beside 'im, like," Grover replied, blinking.

"I see. Thank you. Send Mr. Tellman up, will you."

"Yes, sir." Grover stood to attention momentarily. "Thank you, sir." And he turned on his heel and went out, closing the door softly behind him.

It was less than three minutes before Tellman knocked, and Pitt told him to enter. He was a lean man with a narrow aquiline face, hollow cheeks and a tight sarcastic mouth. He had come up through the ranks with hard work and ruthless application. Six months ago he had been Pitt's equal, now he was his junior, and resented it bitterly. He stood to attention in front of the large leather-inlaid desk, and Pitt sitting in the easy chair behind it.

"Yes, sir," he said coldly.

Pitt refused to acknowledge he had heard the tone in Tellman's voice. He looked across at him with innocent eyes. "There's been a murder in Hyde Park," he said calmly. "A man by the name of Oakley Winthrop, Captain the Honorable, R.N. Found a little after dawn in one of the pleasure boats on the Serpentine. Beheaded."

"Unpleasant," Tellman said laconically. "Important, was he, this Winthrop?"

"I don't know," Pitt said honestly. "But his parents are titled, so we can assume he was, at least in some people's eyes."

Tellman pulled a face. He despised those he considered passengers in society. Privilege stirred in him a raw, bitter anger that stretched far back into his childhood memories of hunger, cold, and endless weariness and anxiety, a father beaten by circumstances till he had no pride left, a mother who worked till she was too tired to talk to her children or laugh with them.

"I suppose we will all be trudging holes in our boots so we can get the beggar who did it," he said sourly. "Sounds like a madman to me. I mean, why would anyone do anything so—" He stopped, uncertain what word he wanted. "Was his head there? You didn't say."

"Yes it was. There was no attempt to hide his identity."

Tellman pulled a face. "Like I said, a madman. What the hell was a naval captain doing in a pleasure boat on the Serpentine anyway?" A smile lit his face quite suddenly, showing a totally different side to his nature. "Bit of a comedown, isn't it? Fellow like that'd be more used to a battleship." He cleared his throat. "Wonder if he was there with a woman. Someone else's wife, maybe?"

"Possibly," Pitt agreed. "But keep such speculation to yourself for the time being. First of all find out all the physical facts you can." He saw Tellman wince at being told something he considered so obvious. He disregarded the man's expression and continued. "Get all the material details. I want to know when he was killed, what with, whether it took one blow or several, whether he was struck from the front or the back, left hand or right, and if he was conscious at the time or not . . ."

Tellman raised his eyebrows.

"And how will they know that, sir?" he inquired.

"They've got the head," Pitt replied. "They'll know if he was struck first—and they've got the body, they can find out if he was drugged or poisoned."

"Won't know if he was asleep," Tellman pointed out sententiously.

Pitt ignored him. "Tell me what he was wearing," he went on. "And the state of his shoes. Did he walk across the grass to the boat, or was he carried? And you certainly ought to be able to work out whether his head was chopped off there in the boat or somewhere else." He looked up at Tellman. "And then you can drag the Serpentine to see if you can find the weapon!"

Tellman's face darkened. "Yes, sir. Will that be all, sir?"

"No—but it's a start."

"Anyone in particular you want me to take on this job, sir? Being as it's so delicate?"

"Yes," Pitt said with satisfaction. "Take le Grange." Le Grange was a smooth-tongued, rather glib young man whose sycophantic manner irritated Tellman even more than it did Pitt. "He'll handle the possible witnesses very well."

Tellman's expression was vile, but he said nothing. He stiffened to attention for an instant, then turned on his heel and went out.

Pitt leaned back in his chair and thought deeply. It was the first major case he had been in charge of since taking over from Micah Drummond. Of course there had been other crimes, even serious ones, but none within the scope for which he was particularly appointed: those which threatened scandal or tragedy of more than purely private proportions.

He had not heard the name Winthrop before, but then he

did not move in society, nor was he familiar with the leading figures in the armed services. Members of Parliament he knew more closely, but Winthrop was not of that body, and if his father ever took his seat in the House of Lords, it had not so far been to sufficient effect for it to have reached public awareness.

Surely Micah Drummond would have reference books for such an occasion? Even he could not have stored in his memory all the pertinent facts of every important man or woman in London.

Pitt swiveled around in the chair and stared at the immaculate bookshelves. He was already familiar with many of the titles. It had been one of the first things he had done on moving in. There it was—*Who's Who*. He pulled it out with both hands and opened it on the desk. Captain the Honourable Oakley Winthrop was not present. However, Lord Marlborough Winthrop was written up at some length, more for his heritage than his achievements, but nonetheless the book gave a very fair picture of a proud, wealthy, rather humorless man of middle age whose interests were tediously predictable. He had had a host of respectable minor offices and was related to a wide variety of the great families in the land, some quite distantly, but nevertheless each connection was duly noted. Some forty years ago he had married one Evelyn Hurst, third daughter of an admiral, later ennobled.

Pitt closed the book with a feeling of foreboding. Lord and Lady Winthrop were not likely to be placated easily if answers were slow in coming, or displeasing in their nature. It was probably unfair, but already he had a picture of them in his mind.

Was Tellman right—was a madman loose in the park? Or had Oakley Winthrop in some way brought it upon himself by courting another man's wife, welshing on his debts, or cheating? Or was he privy to some dangerous secret? These were questions that would have to be asked with subtlety and extreme tact.

In the meantime he would like to have gone to the park

and sought the material evidence himself, but it was Tellman's job, and it would be time wasting as well as impolitic to oversee him in its pursuance.

Look for the novels of
ANNE PERRY
in a bookstore near you.
Published by Fawcett Books.

"I believe you were in the smoking room during the first interview," he said aloud.

Freyjugötu 36